I0124320

RETURN —TO— HARVEST

A Novel of Hope about
Recovering from PTSD

BANKS HUDSON, LMFT

Illustrations by Walter Johnson

Copyright © 2014 Banks Hudson, LMFT
All rights reserved.

ISBN: 0615932495
ISBN 13: 9780615932491
Library of Congress Control Number: 2013922192
Banks Hudson, Nicholasville, KY

The information contained in this book is intended to provide helpful insight into the nature of PTSD and a model for treatment and healing of this dis-ease of the mind and body. It is not intended to serve as a substitute or replacement for medical and psychological treatment and advice. Any use of the ideas presented in this book is at the discretion of the reader. The author and publisher specifically disclaim any and all liability arising directly or indirectly from the use or application of any information contained in this book. Professionals in the medical and psychological field should be consulted regarding treatment, advice, and questions concerning the information presented in this book.

DEDICATION

This book is dedicated to all combat veterans. Some were wounded in body, mind, and/or spirit and some lost their lives. Most of us at home went about our lives with little understanding of the trauma, hell, and sacrifices experienced and endured by these soldiers. It is also dedicated to the families who suffered untold emotional pain and loss and whose lives will never be the same again.

ACKNOWLEDGMENTS

I am grateful to all those researchers, authors, and clinicians who over the years have advanced the understanding and treatment of PTSD and related subjects designed to promote health and healing in this journey of life. I highly recommend the book, *The Post-Traumatic Stress Disorder Sourcebook*, Second Addition, by Glenn R. Schiraldi, Ph. D. This comprehensive work contains invaluable information and resources which I believe answers almost every question one could ask about PTSD.

I am especially grateful to all my clients over the years who taught and inspired me with their determination and courage to embrace the healing process. They make this book possible.

One of my cats, Charcoal, sat on my lap through most of the writing of this book. I firmly believe that her purring, energy, and spirit contributed to helping me with creativity and my ability to complete the book. She died two weeks after I finished the book.

I am thankful to Larry Vaughn, a colleague and friend, who was an invaluable source of feedback and support.

Thanks to my brother-in-law, Walter Johnson, who spent untold hours reviewing the book and helped with format and grammar. At times, when I bogged down in the task, his encouragement and support were invaluable. He is also the artist responsible for the drawings which I believe give additional life and energy to the story.

Thanks to my sister, Anne Johnson for her encouragement. She read and re-read the book and made helpful comments and suggestions. Thanks to my daughter, Asiah Welty, for her love, encouragement and insights into the nature of emotional pain and addiction. And to my son, Banks Hudson IV, I am thankful for his love, support and the sharing of his life's journey and valuable lessons learned.

And finally to my loving wife, Patricia, who daily encouraged me to stay focused and attentive to the process. As a survivor of sexual, physical, and emotional trauma, her invaluable insights into the nature of trauma were extremely helpful.

"...you have to understand that when we come to Afghanistan, part of us never leaves. Part of me will always be here, among the mountains, among the suffering that I've seen. Most of us learn to live without that part of ourselves. Some of us don't. And the truth is, the gap between us soldiers and those who have never been to war, those who have not seen and so cannot understand is unbridgeable. For some of us, the loneliness - the inability to explain - goes on and on. The Army does what it can, but in the space inside us where the war never ends, everything it does will never be enough. I've lost five soldiers I knew personally to suicide in the past 18 months. I don't say any of this lightly, but there are some torments that all the health care and all the support in the world will not ease. If this war has taught me anything, it has most certainly taught me that."

Sergeant Alexandra Grey, Bagram Airfield, Afghanistan
August 6, 2012
As it appeared in *Time Magazine*

CONTENTS

CONTENTS

INTRODUCTION

This is is the story of two combat veterans, Corporal Jett Hollander and Sergeant Ace Frost. They grew up together, trained as Army Rangers, and spent two tours in Iraq. They returned from the war suffering from Post-Traumatic Stress Disorder (PTSD).

Some soldiers return from combat and seem to adjust without too much intrusion from their experience in the war. Others return with various symptoms of PTSD. Even though Jett and Ace returned with some of the same PTSD symptoms, they also had unique and different symptoms.

In the first section of the novel, you get to know Jett and Ace. You are with them through the last long range patrol of their second tour in Iraq. You follow their experience of coming home to Harvest, North Carolina and the daily challenges they face to unsuccessfully maintain some sense of sanity.

The second section of the book introduces you to Doc, a psychologist hired by the National Institute of Mental Health to design a treatment approach to help combat veterans find a path out of the darkness of PTSD into the light of hope. He selects ten soldiers, including Jett and Ace, who are suffering from PTSD and who to varying degrees have lost hope for any chance of healing.

Most of the soldiers in the group are resistant and reluctant to be a part of this experience, but they are desperate to find some relief from the flashbacks, nightmares, panic attacks, and other intrusive aspects of their PTSD. You walk with them through their hopelessness, rage, despair, and tears. They experience hope and possibility not always through what Doc teaches, but through the close bond they form. They stand together to cry and laugh and relive their trauma to find hope in the midst of utter hopelessness from a source they never expected.

The material for this novel is taken from my forty years experience in working with clients who suffer from PTSD, panic disorder, obsessive compulsive disorder, phobias, acute stress, and anxiety. It is inspired by many of these clients who discovered, embraced, and believed in the potential of the human spirit within them and were determined and committed to doing whatever it took to access that potential and find the resources for hope and new beginnings.

There are degrees of severity with PTSD. See Appendix A for a listing of some of the symptoms. If you are suffering from this disorder, please get help from professionals trained in the treatment of PTSD. A list of resources is listed in Appendix B.

If you are suffering from any impairment as a result of PTSD, this novel is in no way intended to be a substitute for seeking and obtaining appropriate medical and psychological treatment. This novel is intended and designed to demonstrate that there is hope for the combat veteran and anyone else suffering from this disorder. It serves only informational and educational purposes. The resources in Appendix B give a wide range of resources to assist in obtaining professional help.

Banks Hudson

1

THE LAST PATROL

It was late afternoon in the desert and the heat was sucking the oxygen out of the air. Ace and I were on our second tour in Iraq and had one month to go before being shipped home. Assigned to an Army Ranger battalion, we were preparing for a reconnaissance mission that departed the airfield at 2200 hours. A small oscillating fan kept the air moving but sweat beads on our forehead occasionally dripped and splat on our equipment and on the floor.

Ace said, "Hey, go down the list of equipment. I think I've gotten everything, but I'm not sure."

We have been friends since the first grade and are as different as night and day. Even though it was true, people told us we looked like brothers. We had black hair with dark complexions, but Ace was six feet two inches and weighed about 220 and I was six-feet and weighed about 190.

I had a ritual I went through before a mission to insure I had every needed piece of equipment. He had no ritual and there was no organization to his preparation. I knew he wouldn't forget his power bars or two Camelbak water containers. I said, "I'm sure glad you got me to take care of your lazy unorganized ass."

He smiled, "Jett Hollander, I've saved your organized ass more times than I can count. Come on. Read down the list."

I started reading, "Night vision goggles, fixed blade knife, infrared chemical lights, Gerber tool, two tourniquets, assault gloves, extra batteries, M67 hand grenades, M79 grenade launcher with grenades, three magazines, bolt cutters, and last but not least, your H&K 416 assault rifle."

The LT ("ell tee" short for lieutenant) poked his head in our tent and said, "Sgt. Frost, the squad leaders will meet in my tent at 1830. Cpl. Hollander, I want you at the meeting too." He looked at Ace. "Also we'll need an extra radio tonight." He was gone.

Ace said, "If we're gonna make that meeting, we better get some chow."

We parachuted in from 10,000 feet and landed about three miles from the suspected site. We split into two patrols of six, Bravo 1 and Bravo 2 and set off on our reconnaissance. Ace and I were in Bravo 1.

We had five hours to complete our mission and return to the landing zone. We were to remain there under cover the following day and the next night travel four miles on foot to a designated point where we would be picked up by a helicopter.

There was a light breeze which helped some, but the heat of the day lingered in the shadows like some kind of dark force working against us. The sand still held the heat. Despite there being no moon and a light haze in the sky, the visibility was pretty good.

Scrub brush and scattered boulders provided us with decent cover, making it possible to move forward with less chance of being detected. We were experienced in this terrain and were accustomed to the various shadows that seemed to appear and disappear in a moments notice. Except for the heat, the conditions were favorable.

We moved in single file. Tim (Holton) had been designated as the "point," the first in line, in our patrol. He was followed by Migs (Rivera), Ace and then me. The LT and Conklin pulled up the rear.

The "Intel" on this site was sketchy. Apparently the satellites had picked up suspicious movement, but the data was about four days old. We didn't know what to expect, which was true ninety percent of the time on all our missions, but were prepared for the worst.

We knew if it was a training site, they would have perimeter posts with guards and possible IEDs (Improvised Explosive Device). Our orders were to avoid any contact with the enemy. We were to gather as much information as we could and then get the hell out.

As we approached to within fifty meters of the perimeter, Tim stepped on an IED. There are no words to express what it feels like to be close to the force of the explosion. The deafening noise and the blinding flash. I seemed to lose consciousness for a few moments and when I opened my eyes, I could see that Ace was wounded. I low crawled to him and saw that his legs were bleeding. His left leg was the worst. More flesh was exposed and there was more blood.

"How bad are you hurt?"

He grimaced, "I don't think it's too bad. What about you?"

"What about me?" I said.

"You have a gash under your left eye."

"I'm okay. I'm going to check on Tim and Migs. I'll be right back." I continued to low crawl. It was hard to see. I made out a form lying on the ground. Migs had multiple shrapnel wounds over his upper body. A boulder about belly high had protected his lower body.

The LT crawled over and assessed his injuries. "Here's my bandage pack; you know what to do."

His radio was turned down low, but we heard over and over, "Bravo 1, Bravo 1, Come in. Come in." As soon as he instructed me about the bandages, he clicked his radio, "Bravo 2-1. IED. Here Now!!"

"Roger, ETA five."

He said, "Try to stop the bleeding. I'm goin' forward to check."

Migs slowly opened his eyes and a little above a whisper said, "I know Tim is dead. Is anyone else hurt?"

"Just a few scratches," I lied.

"I'm not ready to die Holly. Do your stuff!"

I said, "You ain't dying on my watch Migs. I got you covered."

There was no gurgling in his throat so maybe there wasn't any serious internal damage, but there was so much blood. His head had several deep lacerations, but the bleeding only slowly oozed. There was a bad leak somewhere. I got his pack off and started cutting off his shirt and sleeves. I found the culprit. It was right above his left armpit. A piece of shrapnel was lodged and had torn a hole in his flesh. As I pulled the material from the wound, blood squirted in my face. I quickly applied pressure between the wound and his heart and the blood stopped flowing and started oozing again.

The LT crawled back. I briefed him on Migs.

He said, "Just keep that pressure right where you have it." He started wrapping Mig's head with bandage and kept on talking. "Migs, we're gonna get you fixed up. You're gonna be fine." He turned to me, "Its quiet out in front. I don't trust that, but there's not much we can do now. A chopper will be here in about an hour. I'm going to check on Ace and Conklin. Doc will be here in a couple minutes."

Every patrol has a Ranger with special training in tending to war-wounds, consequently we always call them, "Doc." Morris was our Doc and he was with Bravo 2. The LT didn't mention Tim and I knew why. We had seen too many soldiers step on IEDs. There wasn't much left.

All I could think about was Tim's family. Time stood still and I could see the Army soldiers in dress uniform knocking on the door of their house with the news that their son, husband, brother, father…was dead. One more time, the thought burst into my mind, "This fucking war is insane!"

Then reality hit; we were facing a fight for our lives. How long would it take those bastards to be on top of us? Then behind me I heard someone running. It was Doc. I quickly briefed him on what I found.

"Keep the pressure right where you have it." He started doing his job. There was movement behind us; men from Bravo 2. Hanks appeared with four men behind him, all crouching down.

"The LT thinks the site might be abandoned since we haven't had any kind of response. Foley and I will take a closer look while Fredericks and Pulley cover us from up where the IED exploded. Holly, the LT wants you back with Ace and Conklin. Donut (Baker) can stay here and help Doc."

Doc instructed, "I'll need Holly to keep that pressure on for a few more minutes."

Hanks and company disappeared.

As Doc worked on Migs, Donut asked, "Where are those assholes? They should be on us by now."

Migs whispered, "Doc, how bad is it and don't fucking sugar coat it? Tell me the truth."

Doc replied, "You have some bad lacerations and have lost some blood, but Holly's got our main problem covered. We need to get you outta here. A choppers on the way."

"OK," he replied and closed his eyes.

Doc was feeling around the area where my hand pressed, trying to find exactly where we needed to apply the pressure. He said, "Donut give me your three fingers and I'm going to guide them to the place where I want you to apply the pressure. Holly, I will slide them partially under your hand and don't let up until I tell you." We nodded. It was a smooth transition as Doc continued to work on Migs.

I asked, "Do you need me anymore?"

"No go ahead."

The LT was working on Conklin who had a bad gash on the right side of his head. I went right to Ace. The LT asked, "How's Migs?"

I answered, "Doc says as long as we can keep pressure on that artery, he should be okay. But that chopper can't get here fast enough."

The LT said, "I know. Because of the distance, an hour was the best they could do. They're also sending along a medevac chopper with a real doc."

Ace was leaning against a rock. I asked, "Are you okay?" He winced with pain and said a little above a whisper, "Tim is dead, right?"

"Yeah, no miracles tonight. How're you doin'?"

"I've lost a bunch of blood from my left leg, but the LT got the bleeding slowed down." There was a pool of blood starting to soak into the sand and I wondered just how much blood he had lost.

"Jett, you need to go back out there and keep an eye out for those assholes. If they come, I'm goina take a few of those 'mother fuckers' with me."

The LT said, "Calm down Ace. We've got the situation under control."

I said, "Let me get you some water."

"Stop trying to be...." And his voice trailed off.

"Ace, stay awake!" I shook him gently. "Ace, wake up!"

I reached for my Camelbak and poured some water on my sweat towel and gently slapped his face. "Ace, wake up!"

He groaned a little and said, "Where am I?"

I wiped his face with the towel. "You're with me and I'm taking care of you."

A little above a whisper he said, "And that's suppose to make me feel better? You don't know shit about first aid."

He started to fade again. "Ace, talk to me," and I slapped his face again.

Doc came back and looked at Conklin and asked the LT if he needed any help. "No, check on Ace."

I told Doc, "I can't get him to come to."

He slapped Ace quite a bit harder than I had and he groaned a little and opened his eyes. "Try to get him to drink some water." I gave Ace some water and he choked some, but was able to get down a few swallows. Doc cleaned the wounds, put on antiseptic, wrapped them and gave him a shot.

He turned to me and said, “Let me look at that place on the side of your face.”

“It’s nothin’, don’t waste your time!”

He said, “It’s close to your eye. I’m not taking any chances.” He didn’t wait for me to respond. He cleaned it and applied antiseptic and said, “I’m going back to check on Migs.”

Then I heard some mumbling out in front of us and Hanks appeared. I saw he was crouched down, but not crawling. Hanks said to the LT in a lowered voice, “The camp looks deserted. They must have left a few days earlier. There’re signs they haven’t been gone long and we don’t know if they still might be close by. The others will stay out in front to keep an eye out. How’re you two guys doin’?”

“Conklin and Ace replied, “Good.” The Ranger spirit: “If I’m alive, I’m good.”

The LT made Conklin move over and lean against the same rock as Ace. “Holly you stay here with Ace and Conklin.”

He turned to Hanks. “I’ll keep watch on the rear. Take your men and spread out in a 180 arc in front of us. It’s 0230. Meet me back here at 0315. You know what to do.”

Hanks turned to leave and the LT said, “I think they left this place ‘cause they knew we were coming. I’m betting at a minimum there are some snipers close by.”

Hanks agreed, “Yep, me too.”

Hanks was gone and the LT said to us, “At 0300, I’m to radio the choppers and let them know if the area appears secure.” He looked at me. “I’m going to leave the radio with you. I’ll be back by 0300.” He was gone. I was able to get Ace and Conklin to take a few more swallows of water. I was worried about Ace because he was slipping in and out of consciousness. I assumed it was due to blood loss.

Time passed at a snails pace. Doc checked on us once, saying that he and Donut were taking turns applying pressure and that Migs was holding on. He checked over Conklin and Ace. They both seemed to be a little better and were drinking more water. My head was throbbing and I felt like I was going to puke.

He turned to me and said, "Let me check that gash on your face again."

I didn't resist even though under these circumstances, I thought it was a waste of his time.

He said, "I don't like how it looks. It's deeper than I originally thought and closer to your eye than I realized."

He cleaned it and rubbed on more antiseptic ointment. "You need to have that looked at by a specialist as soon as we get back to base."

"Okay Doc, thanks."

The LT also checked on us once and Conklin said to him, "When you were talking about calling the chopper, I remember you said you would let them know if the area 'appears' secure. I had to smile. Some of those chopper pilots and crews are crazy; like a bunch of cowboys."

"Yeah," said the LT. "They've saved our asses in a number of situations where the area not only didn't 'appear' secure, it was down-right hot with activity."

I smiled remembering my own stories of similar helicopter rescues.

The LT came back and radioed the choppers that everything was still quiet here and they gave their ETA as 0325. Hanks returned at 0315 and he instructed him to prepare an LZ (landing zone) for the choppers. We would use the Chem lights to guide the choppers to the LZ. The perimeter would stay in place till all the wounded were safely on the medevac and then one-by-one the guys on the perimeter would load up. Everyone knew that we had not been able to secure the area. We were still vulnerable and we would be ready and we would not be surprised.

They came right on schedule with the medevac landing first. The other chopper hovered about a hundred meters to cover the medevac. The medics were out on the ground in a flash. They had a stretcher for Migs and a body bag for all the parts of Tim's body they could find.

While all this was going on, a medic ran over to us with a stretcher. The medic asked Conklin if he could walk. He said he could so I helped him over to the chopper. When I came back, he had Ace on the stretcher.

The LT appeared and said to me, "Help him get Ace on the chopper and I want you to stay with the medevac." I nodded.

About that time we all heard shots. Hanks over the radio, "Move to 3 o'clock, sniper fire 100 meters out. Within seconds, we were returning fire. The medevac needed a couple more minutes to complete loading. We got Ace on and the remaining medics ran toward us with what was left of Tim's body. The MD with a few medics was working on Migs. I didn't like the expression on his face. We lifted off.

The covering chopper fired some missiles and we saw several explosions near the area from where the shots were fired. There was no more sniper fire. The chopper dropped down and we saw our guys piling on and then it lifted off and we were on our way back to base.

When we landed, they rushed Migs into the hospital. Ace and Conklin went to treatment areas next to each other. I was allowed to stay with Ace. Donut came in a few minutes later and sat with Conklin. About five minutes later, the LT, followed by everyone else, came in and checked on us. Then they headed for the OR waiting area to wait for Migs to get out of surgery.

A few minutes later the battalion commander, company commander, and the S-2 (intelligence officer) came in to check on us. After a short stay, they also went to the OR waiting area. The medics were busy working on Ace and Conklin. One took a look at my face and said it should be fine, but I was going to have a one inch scar.

They put in a few stitches and the MD told me that he didn't think my eye sight would be affected.

Two hours later the LT came in and told us that Migs didn't make it. He said the preliminary report was that he must have had some heart problems because his heart gave out during surgery and they couldn't bring him back. Ordinarily, a normal heart would have been able to withstand the trauma of the applied pressure and the injury. He said I had done a good job and if his heart had been normal, I would have saved his life. He gave me a military hug and left. Ace had not heard a thing; he was out.

I looked down and realized I had Migs' blood on much of my uniform, on my neck, and some dried remnants on my hands. Some of that belonged to Ace and some was my blood.

I washed my hands and went outside and found a secluded spot. For the first time in three years, I cried. I didn't know if I could take another month of this endless insanity.

Several days after that, my gash became infected and the Army decided because I only had four weeks left they would ship me out with Ace to a hospital in Germany. The guys came to the ward in the hospital to give us a farewell party. After what we had been through together, it was bittersweet. We had a moment of silence for Tim and Migs and the other friends we lost.

After four weeks treatment at the base hospital, Conklin was returned to the unit with light duty for a couple of months. He had about eight months left on his tour.

As our plane lifted off, I looked out the window at the war torn villages and desert below. We'd seen and done horrible, unspeakable things during our two years in this god forsaken place. We had seen and been involved either directly or indirectly in the killing of men, women, and children and in blowing up their villages and towns. We watched our friends suffer untold agony and sometimes die in our arms. Others lost limbs and their eyesight. These memories would surely be with us and haunt us as we tried to put our lives back together.

Our bodies were going home, but there was a part of our minds that would never leave this place. Back home no one could understand the hell we'd been through. More veterans were committing suicide and we had been warned about PTSD. It seemed certain we were leaving one war zone where most of the time we could identify our enemy only to enter another war zone at home where the enemy would reside somewhere in the deep recesses of our mind.

2

WALTER REED ARMY MEDICAL CENTER

Ace and I arrived at Walter Reed Army Medical Center in Washington, D.C. on an Army bus from Andrews Air Force Base. His left leg was almost good as new, but his right leg needed more time to heal. The MD said he might always have a limp. He was on crutches, but was able to put some weight on the leg. They wanted to watch him and start him on his physical therapy before discharging him.

The gash on my face was nearly healed. The infection was gone and there appeared to be no damage to my left eye. I had the scar and didn't care. When I arrived at Walter Reed, I was discharged from the Army.

I stayed with Ace a few days. On the day I was leaving, he said, "I don't want you to go."

I responded, "Yeah, I feel like I'm deserting you."

"Well it's true you're deserting me and leaving me here to fend for myself. Who's gonna have my back? Oh, that reminds me. Before you leave, go to the Post Exchange (PX) and get me a box of Milky Ways."

"Don't order me around Sgt. Frost. I do have your back. I already got you two boxes."

He said, "OK, hand 'em over. I'll talk to you in a week or two."

I gave him the boxes and we smiled at each other. Neither of us needed to say anything and the silence was comfortable. He laid the boxes on the bed and got out of the wheel chair and faced me. We did our ritual greeting that we had done for years. We locked forearms, made a fist to the heart, touched knuckles, and a finger to the sky. And then our embrace and we held it for awhile. Some people may have thought we were gay. We didn't give a shit if anyone saw us or what they thought. We'd been to hell and back together. There was a bond between us that words would never describe.

We had been blood brothers since we were ten years old. In Ranger School, everyone was paired with another person who remained your Ranger Buddy throughout the training. You did everything together - well, almost everything. During our survival training in the freezing cold in the high country of northern Georgia, we spent the night wrapped in a poncho with nothing on but our boxers. The idea is to learn that body heat helps you survive.

I smiled and he said, "What are you smiling about?"

"You remember the poncho experience in northern Georgia."

He replied, "Yeah. What about it?"

"Remember that course in psychology where one expert wrote that all human beings have latent homosexual tendencies?"

He answered, "No, I don't remember that. I must have been asleep."

"Well, I remember being afraid that I would get a hard on."

He laughed, "I wasn't afraid I would get a hard on, I was afraid you would."

We laughed. It got quiet again. Tears started running down my cheeks. I didn't cry much, but I had never seen Ace cry.

I asked, "Why don't you ever cry?"

He answered, "Because I'm not a sissy like you Bro."

"Who's calling who a sissy; you were scared shitless a little while ago when that nurse came in to give you a shot."

He said, "That's not the same. You know how I hate needles."

We smiled and embraced again. He told me some months later that I would have been proud of him because after I left, he found a deserted corner on the ward and cried like a baby.

I said, "See if you can talk the MD into letting you out of here in a week or so."

"I will, but I'm not getting my hopes up."

I continued, "I'll come and get you when you're discharged."

"I know Mom and Dad will wanna pick me up, but they'll understand. I need you to help me get ready for goin' home."

"Yeah," I said, "Who's deserting who? Who's gonna help me prepare for my home coming tomorrow?"

"I'll be there in spirit Bro."

I said, "Now that makes me feel real good."

"Well then, stay here with me."

"I can't disappoint Mom. She has my welcome home party planned for tomorrow afternoon."

He commented, "That's the only good reason I can think of that I'm staying here. The only welcome home party I would dread more than yours is my own. At least I get to miss yours and hope to god I can talk Mom outta having one for me."

I said, "After I've had a week or so at home, I'm coming back for a couple of days to visit. I can stay in the WR guest-house at Forest Hills."

"That'll help break up my stay. That means a lot Bro."

I said, "Great, then that's settled. What time will your mom and dad and Jeffery (his younger brother) get here tomorrow?"

"They're driving half-way after Dad gets off work this afternoon, so I think they'll get here around noon."

I asked, "It's been about a year since you've seen them. How will it be?"

"OK I guess. Mom will make over me and Jeff will have a thousand questions. I'm not looking forward to it."

He continued, "Jett, what's wrong with me? That doesn't feel right."

"I know. I feel the same way and you know how much I love my family. We've got some shit to work on. You know how much I love my dog Spot and my cat Journee and I even feel uncomfortable thinking about seeing them."

I went on, "In my last letter from April, (Ace's former girlfriend) she was looking forward to seeing us. I think she still loves you."

The three of us had been close since third or fourth grade and spent lots of time together. She and Ace were a couple throughout high school and broke-up somewhere near the end of our junior year in college. She and I remained close and she wrote to both of us from time to time while we were in the service. I always answered her letters, but Ace didn't.

He said, "I don't think that's true and even if she did, there's been too much shit between us. Last I heard she had a boyfriend." After a pause he asked, "Are you gonna leave or are you gonna hang around here 'till I'm discharged?"

I answered, "I'm avoiding what we both dread."

He said, "I know, but I wanna get it over with and get to my candy bars."

"Okay, one more question."

He exclaimed, "Shit Jett. What is it?"

"Are you sure you can make it without me?"

"Get outta here before I run my good foot up your ass!"

"Okay, I'm goin'. I got my rental car this morning when you were at physical therapy. I've decided to go out I-66 and jump on the Skyline Drive, hookup with the Parkway (Blue Ridge) and take it all the way home."

He said, "That's gonna take you forever."

"I know. I'm gonna take two days. It'll give me a chance to think. I called Mom this morning and told her I would spend the night on the road and then get there around three or four tomorrow. She was a little disappointed, but you know Mom, she understood."

He said, "Okay, go on and leave!" Our ritual and a brief hug.

I started the car and turned on the air conditioning. I had a sick feeling in my gut. I started to tear up again. What was wrong with me? I closed my eyes for a minute and all of a sudden, I was reliving that last mine explosion that killed Tim and Migs. I started sweating and shaking and was having trouble breathing. I was aware of tightly gripping the steering wheel.

Suddenly someone was pounding on my drivers' side window. I opened my eyes and it was a Major with medical insignia. I tried to pull myself together and lowered the window. He asked, "What's wrong Son?"

He had a kind voice and looked concerned. "Nothing sir, I think I just had a panic attack and I'm better now."

I was familiar with panic attacks. I had suffered from them on and off for years. They were not debilitating, but I was familiar with the experience. This one seemed a little more intense than the others and this wasn't a good sign.

He asked, "Are you sure you're okay?"

"Yes sir. I'll just take a few more minutes and be fine."

He said, "All right, be sure to wait a little longer. Be careful and be safe."

"Thank you, sir."

3

HEADING HOME

I waited a few more minutes and pulled out and headed for I-66 West. Even though it was only about ninety minutes, it seemed like it took forever to get to the entrance of the Skyline Drive. I loved the mountains and looked forward to pulling over at many of the overlooks and enjoying the terrain and the views.

My undergraduate degree was in psychology with a minor in religion. Ace often called me Professor Freud or PF for short. He had an undergraduate degree in sports psychology with a minor in basket weaving. I knew enough psychology to make me dangerous. I was sure that Ace and I were going to be forced to confront the possibility that we already did or would eventually suffer with Post-Traumatic Stress Disorder (PTSD).

I knew I would be prone to suffering from PTSD since I already had problems with anxiety. Ace had the problem of repressing stuff, keeping things bottled up inside him. Based on what we had just been through, this made him a good candidate for PTSD.

I pulled off at an overlook after about thirty minutes into the drive. I sat on a rock looking into the valley. There was a slight breeze and just a few white clouds. The sun was warm at first, but then I started to feel the heat and moved into the shade. I looked around to make sure I was alone and got out a notebook I bought earlier today in the PX.

I felt lost and alone. I had a professor who said our story is an important part of our lives and that it impacts our everyday lives. I decided to write some things about my family to help me remember my roots and what I learned from them in my earlier years. This was part of my story. Maybe it would help to write and think about my family history. I could try to remember some of the things Dad had told me over the years.

My ancestors migrated to Harvest, North Carolina in the late 1890s. Our town was located about sixty miles as the crow flies northeast of Asheville in the high country of the Blue Ridge Mountains.

Elverton, a few miles northwest of Harvest, was important to its growth and development. In those days the population of Harvest was about 600 people and Elverton was about 5000.

When I was born, my grandfather Pop owned the Mountain Inn, a hotel in Harvest, and a hotel in Elverton. His cousin Harold owned two Hollander General Stores, one in Harvest and another in Elverton. Both of these family businesses were begun by their grandfather.

I thought for awhile trying to remember some of my early memories. It was time to get back on the road. I drove and numerous times pulled over for short hikes. After a couple of hours, I took an exit to get something to eat. I found a diner and took a seat where I could watch the door and get out quickly if I needed to. I thought I was hungry, but when the waitress brought the food, I picked at it and had a difficult time getting it down.

I wasn't surprised because my appetite had sucked for several months. On top of that, I missed Ace. I sat there for what seemed like an hour or so. I bought a newspaper and pretended to be reading it, but I wasn't focusing. I just wanted to sit there and not move. I could casually look around and watch people. There were no orders to follow, no formations to make, no duties to perform, no patrols to lead, no mines or snipers to watch for, no one to kill, nothing to be afraid of, nothing to do but sit there and do nothing.

I wondered who these people were. Had any of them been to war or had any of them lost a relative in the war?

Suddenly from out of nowhere, my heart started pounding; I had trouble getting my breath. I had to escape this place. I put cash on the table and left. As I passed the waitress, she smiled and said, "Have a nice day Honey." I couldn't respond. I went out to the parking lot, jumped in my car, locked the door, started it and pulled out. I was in no shape to drive, but I had to get away and be alone. I stopped the car in a deserted pull-off a few hundred meters from the restaurant.

I closed my eyes and tried to calm down. I kept telling myself, "You're gonna be all right." After what seemed forever, but was probably only a few minutes, I relaxed. After ten minutes, I was okay, but exhausted. It was another panic attack. This was not turning out to be a good day - two panic attacks in the past few hours.

I pulled back onto the highway and realized that I didn't know where I wanted to go. Like Ace, why wasn't I excited to get home? Many of our buddies couldn't wait to get home to see their wives, children, girlfriends, and families and that's all they talked about.

I didn't have any of those except a family and Spot and Journee. One part of me wanted to head down the mountain and drive into the sunset. Another part wanted to go back and see Ace. The part that took over turned back up the mountain and headed southwest down the Skyline Drive toward home.

It was approximately 380 miles from the start of the Skyline Drive to home and I wanted to get almost half-way today. The Skyline Drive ran for nearly 100 miles before it turned into the Parkway. I drove for a couple hours, stopping often to sit or walk a little. Soon I was ten or so miles into the Parkway. I took an exit to get gas and picked up a bag of ice and a six-pack of beer.

Honestly, I didn't need the gas, but I needed the beer. I bought a Styrofoam cooler and some cups at the PX so I put my beers on ice and drove back up the mountain and onto the Parkway.

I stopped at the next overlook and pulled to the far end the parking area to be as far away as I could from the two parked cars. I opened a beer and poured it in the cup. I made sure my doors were locked and leaned back and drank my beer. I immediately felt better.

We weren't allowed any alcohol in Iraq. Ace got a lot of passes to go off-post in Germany. We would go to beer halls and drink German beer. It was great beer.

I was feeling better and ready to start writing in my notebook. I don't know if I could say I really wanted to write, but it gave me something to do, something to focus on and that was important. I stayed in the car so I pushed the seat back and opened another beer, which I drank slowly. I forced down some nabs before starting the second beer. All I needed was to get a DUI.

By the time I was born, the two cousins Pop and Harold owned 3,000 acres of what was wilderness in the early days. Shortly after World War II, they met in their attorney's office and instructed him to draw up the paperwork that would split the purchased land equally between the two families.

The attorney was also instructed to add a "rock solid" provision that the land would never be sold or developed. It would remain in the respective families and any family member would be allowed to build a house with restrictions related to minimum disturbance to the natural beauty of the land. Provisions were set in place that would handle any disputes and disagreements among family members.

Members of both families over the years were involved in the family businesses which were successful, expanded, and flourished. Few relatives actually wanted to build houses in the wilderness. They preferred to build in either Harvest or Elverton.

My mind started to wander and worry how Ace was doing. I remembered that last patrol and I could feel the anxiety. There was something about my surroundings here at this overlook; something that reminded me of Iraq.

I had to get back on the road. I kept telling myself that I was gonna be okay; just keep driving. With my mind focused on driving, I calmed down. I wanted to drive for a couple more hours and with occasional stops, that should put me about half-way. The beer and the driving helped me feel better. I would have a couple more beers as soon as I got to the motel. There were lots of thoughts passing through my mind, but they weren't too bad or uncomfortable.

Later, I grew tired and it was time to stop anyway, so I exited the Parkway somewhere around mile-marker eighty or ninety. I picked-up some fast food at a drive through and found a motel. I checked out the motel grounds and then checked in and went to my room.

I picked-up the phone, got an outside line and dialed Ace's ward number. Busy. It figures since there are twenty guys and only one pay phone. I called Mom and told her I was on schedule and should arrive around 3:00 or 4:00 tomorrow. She asked how I was doing. I answered, "I'm doing fine Mom." I knew she wasn't buying that, but she didn't say anymore about it. We talked for a few more minutes and hung up.

I turned on the television, took a shower, opened another beer, laid on the bed, took a couple bites of my hamburger, muted the television for a moment and listened for any sounds outside. I watched some television and tried Ace again. It was still busy. "Shit!" I watched more television and fell asleep even before I finished my beer.

I woke up several times during the night, once to turn off the television. Another time I thought I heard something outside my door. I got up and checked - false alarm. Soon after that, I heard a couple arguing in the next room. And then there were the usual nightmares, but they weren't as bad as some of the other ones. All in all for me, I slept okay.

I woke up right at 0500, went to pee and called Ace. In two rings, he answered, "Ace's hardware, liquor, porno, and cat house. Ace ain't here, Ace speaking."

"I thought you said Ace ain't here."

"I lied. That was just a wish on my part; unfortunately, I'm right here. Did you get drunk and get laid last night?"

"No, did you?" I said hopefully in a playfully voice.

"Funny you should ask. I had nurses lined up outside my door and there was plenty of cold beer. I stopped counting the nurses at ten and stopped counting the cold beers at fourteen."

I asked, "How did you know it was me?"

"There was no one else out in the hallway waiting for a call and who other than you and me wake up right at 0500 and get up even when they don't have too?"

I said, "I got it Dude."

"Don't call me Dude; you know I hate that fucking name." We kept it light and I felt better after we hung up.

I strapped my Daniel Winkler fixed blade knife inside my shorts where no one could see it, secured my room and went for a run. I was gone about forty-five minutes. I showered again, got my gear together and left. I stopped at a local diner. The coffee was great, the pancakes were pretty good, but the sausage was greasy. I ate it all anyway which was a good sign since yesterday my appetite had been nil. I had them make me a ham and cheese sandwich to go so I wouldn't have to go off the mountain again to eat lunch. The waitress was cute and friendly and I left her a five. No panic attacks. Good sign so far.

I stopped at a gas station, topped off my tank, got another bag of ice, a bag of chips and another six-pack just in case my three remaining from yesterday weren't enough. I headed back up the mountain. It was another beautiful day. The sun was up and the sky was clear. I loved these mountains. You could always count on a breeze and the temperature would be cooler up here than down on the plains.

Actually, I felt pretty good when I started down the Parkway, but after driving a few miles, the thoughts about going home caused me to start feeling anxious again. I had to admit that I was looking forward to seeing Mom. We had written what seemed like hundreds of letters.

She was my link to home and that had helped me a lot over the three years, especially the first few months when I was homesick. I wish I could have some alone time with her before I had to face everyone else. No chance.

I should be excited to see all my family, but there was an undercurrent of dread that I couldn't fully understand or explain. I was close to my grandfather Pop. My grandmother, Nana had died while I was overseas. Pop and Nana's son Uncle Henry and his wife Betty were like second parents to me and I felt a close bond with them. Pop's cousin Harold's son was Jack and his wife Ann were two more of my favorite relatives.

This dread had to be causing my two recent panic attacks. Even though Ace and I hadn't talked much about it until yesterday, I think we sensed in each other the difficulties we faced in going back to the "real world." We envisioned going back home together. Somehow going together would have made it okay for each other.

I decided to drive for three hours and then pull off and write in my notebook one more time. That would put me about two hours from home. I stopped at more overlooks and felt good when I got out and took some deep breaths. Several times I thought about drinking a beer, but it wasn't even mid-morning yet. I told myself that I had to stay strong and there would be no drinking before noon.

For most of that time at the overlooks and while driving, I was trying to organize my thoughts and remember more family history. I tried not to think about the experience that lay ahead in a few short hours. I found a secluded overlook and the parking lot was empty. I checked the area, got my stuff and walked down a trail to a good spot for writing.

The view was fabulous. I felt so fortunate that even though I had grown up and spent the first twenty-two years of my life in this beautiful country, I never took it for granted. Every view was different and unique. Down in the valley were areas where the sun illuminated every detail in a kind of yellow hue. It seemed like there was a bustle of activity. There were areas that were still in the shade and they looked like they were still asleep, quiet, with very little movement.

Remembering Family History

Sometime soon after World War II, my great-grandfather and my great-grandmother built a cabin on a ridge. You could see for miles from the front and the back. The family opened a mill some years earlier and the mill furnished the logs. The cabin was beautifully constructed and it was said that not one tree had been cut down without reason. The natural setting was not disturbed.

The cabin was one story with a large deck across the front and back. Inside the front door, there was a large great room that had a sitting area with a large fireplace, a kitchen area with a small table, a large eating area with a big table, a good sized closet that was for storage and the washer and dryer. That room took up the depth of the cabin with a door leading to the back deck.

There were lots of windows. They wanted a lot of light and wanted the views to be visible from all parts of the room. On both sides of the great room, there were two bedrooms with a bath in between. The rooms could fit a double bed and a dresser and each had a large closet. There was a double window in each bedroom for the view and a single window that faced the area on the side of the cabin. The bathrooms were moderate sized with a small storage cabinet.

So far, I had only made a few notations in my notebook. Maybe it was enough just to think about my family. I looked at my watch and it was 12:27. I was ready for that cold beer. I got out my sandwich and chips even though I wasn't hungry. I knew I better eat because I definitely was not going to be hungry when I got home. I wish I had more time to prepare. Not gonna happen.

I liked remembering our family history. It was a nice diversion and seemed to calm my nerves.

My earliest memories were filled with Pop taking Ace and me on hikes. He knew the area, as they say, "like the back of his hand." He had done the same with Henry and Jack who both loved these mountains. Even today, Henry and Jack spend lots of time hiking together. Ace and I went on countless hikes with both of them.

Pop over the years showed Ace and me all the beautiful overlooks and secret waterfalls and taught us about the beauty of nature and respect for all living things in the forest. Sometimes we camped out for two or three days. He never let us kill anything. He said he had no problem with hunters as long as they ate what they killed. But no hunters were ever allowed on any Hollander property.

I remember when Ace asked Pop about killing snakes and he said snakes have as much right to be here as we have and maybe more since they had been here a lot longer than us. Ace asked. "But what if they're poisonous?" Pop said that didn't change anything. He said if we see a snake, slowly back away and pick another path.

He taught us where snakes were likely to be. He also told us a little secret. He said if you aren't afraid of snakes, you will seldom see one. Ace and I aren't afraid of snakes and it's true that in these mountains, we have rarely seen one.

There were a lot of bugs that would show up in the cabin and we were not even allowed to kill bugs. He would say, "Leave it be or take it outside." Ace and I have often talked about those years as some of the best years of our lives.

Pop was groomed by his dad to become the Innkeeper and manage the two hotels. Soon after Nana and Pop were married, they moved into the cabin. Their two children were my dad Clyde Augustus, and my uncle Henry Douglas.

Uncle Henry got his undergraduate degree at the College of Elverton and went to Duke where he got his Ph.D. in history. He lucked into a job as assistant professor of European history at his alma mater in Elverton. A professor unexpectedly retired which opened up a slot in the history department.

He met Betty at Duke and they were married in Raleigh. She loved the mountains and they built a house down the road from the cabin with spectacular views. They didn't have any children. Betty worked at the Inn and loved organizing outings and organizing excursions for the guests. Dad ended up going to the University of North Carolina where he met my mother, Lynne Herndon. He joined a fraternity and loved to drink and party. He got his degree by the skin of his teeth.

Mom was from Eastern North Carolina and an only child. Her mom and dad were killed in an auto accident when she was five. She was raised by her paternal grandparents who gave her a wonderful home. They were older when they got married and her grandmother died in the summer between her sophomore and junior year in college. Her grandfather died a few months later and she said it was from a broken heart. Mom said he worshiped her grandmother.

Mom had no other family. Her maternal grandparents died even before she went to college and they didn't have children. After Mom's grandparents died, Dad started bringing her home for holidays and to stay during summer vacations. Pop and Nana accepted her with open arms and she became a part of the family. She loved to hear Pop talk about the history of the family.

Mom inherited the house and about 200-acres of valuable land. Their family friend and attorney recommended she sell and invest the money. The attorney recommended a friend of his to be her investment banker.

During that summer before they graduated, she wanted to work so Pop gave her a job working at the Inn as a receptionist. She told Pop and Nana that she wanted her salary to go to them to pay for her room and board. They protested, but she insisted. Without her knowing, Pop put the money into a special savings account.

Dad had the same job during the summers working on the grounds crew. He was not a dependable worker. Even in Harvest, he had his group of friends who liked to party. Mom would go out with them some, but she was a light drinker and things would get a little too rowdy so she spent many of her evenings with Pop and Nana, taking hikes and reading.

Because Pop, Henry, and Jack spent a lot of time hiking trails all over these mountains, people in the area and many staying at the Inn and Hotels relied on them for advice and suggestions on trails and levels of difficulty. Jack owned both of the general stores. His office was at the store in Harvest.

Dad and Mom had three children. I was the oldest and born in 1981. Neither of them was able to tell me from where my first name came except to say that Dad picked it out of thin air. My brother, James Berry (Jimmy) was born in 1983, and my sister Sadie Ann was born in 1986.

Soon after they were married, Mom told Dad that she wanted him to cut back on his drinking and that she didn't approve of him going to bars by himself in the evenings. They negotiated one night out a week with the boys. Mom was never able to hold him to that. I guess at some point, she quit trying to change him.

I really don't want to go through a history of Dad's drinking problems after they were married. I can summarize by saying that he turned into a binge drinker and the pattern was that he would have a drink and couldn't stop and would be drunk for a week or so.

He collected several DUIs over the years, but always seemed to get away with little jail time. He did lose his license many times, but he could walk most anywhere. I don't know how Mom did it, but she never left him. Maybe she saw in him something none of us could see.

I hated Dad at times even though he was never physically abusive to Mom or to us. He was the opposite of a mean drunk; he wanted to love on us. Ugh! When Dad wasn't drinking, he was depressed, on edge, and grumpy. For some reason, none of it seemed to bother Jimmy and Sadie. I guess more than anything I hated it for Mom. She deserved better.

She seemed to take it all in stride and found a lot of happiness in being a mom and she loved Pop and Nana. She was like their daughter and she was always taking us up to the cabin to visit them. Many times Henry and Betty would walk up to cabin and spend the day with us.

Ace often came with me and all the boys would go hiking. At first Sadie was too young, but later she just wasn't interested in long hikes. On some of those earlier hikes, Henry would have to carry Jimmy part of the way.

The girls took shorter hikes, or stayed at the cabin or went shopping in Elverton. Mom and Betty were close. I think Mom was able to talk to her about the problems with Dad. Mom didn't want to burden Pop or Nana with problems to do with their son.

One of the saddest days in my young life was the day Pop and Nana told us they were moving out of the cabin. I was about fifteen. He had a little arthritis in his knee and hip and it was getting more challenging to hike the trails around the cabin.

In one of the additions to the Inn, they built an apartment for their retirement years. He and Nana were now ready to make that move. And there were a lot of trails around the Inn that he could easily maneuver without any difficulty.

I was tempted to drink another beer, but decided against it. What kind of man has to have another beer to face his family? I didn't know how to answer that question, but it bothered me.

4
JETT RETURNS TO HARVEST

I arrived home to the welcome party. When I pulled into the driveway, Mom opened the door and Spot came running and jumped all over me, almost knocking me down. I loved on him for a few minutes and then went inside. No sign of Journee.

All the family was there and everyone seemed happy to see me. Pop was walking with a cane, but seemed as mentally sharp as ever.

Throughout the party, I felt anxiety. People kept asking me, "How was it over there?" I know they meant well, but it was the last thing I wanted to talk about. After awhile, I went outside and sat on the back porch and to my surprise, no one followed me. Later I realized Mom had protected that little bit of space I needed. It was out on the porch I was aware of how much I missed Ace. Because Dad was an alcoholic, Mom did not allow alcohol in the house, but I could have really used a beer.

While I was sitting there, Journee sauntered up the steps and gave me a look that said, "Where the hell have you been?" After a few minutes, I coaxed her up to my lap and she moved around until she found a comfortable position and started purring. She was doing her own welcome home greeting on her own terms. That was Journee. Most everything was on her terms.

I went inside and had a nice talk with Pop. He brought me up to date on what he was doing and a brief overview of how the business was going. Eventually, I said, "Pop, do you mind if I stay at the cabin for awhile?"

He answered, "I'm happy for you to use it Son. Have you told your Mom and Dad yet?"

"Not yet, I'll wait for everyone to leave."

He said, "You stay up there as long as you want. No one uses it anymore. I have housekeeping go up there once a month to dust and check on things. It should be in pretty good shape. I never turned off the water except in the winter and never turned off the electricity. It was our home for so many years; I just couldn't do it." A tear ran down his cheek. He quickly recovered, "If you want to stay up there indefinitely, I'll have the phone cut on."

"Thanks Pop, I would and I really appreciate it."

He said, "I'll tell whosever on duty at the front desk to expect you. The key is in the same place in my desk drawer. I'll probably be in bed before you get around to leaving here, but drop by to see me in a day or two for lunch. I have something I want to talk to you about."

"Thanks Pop. Why don't I plan to be at the Inn at twelve noon day after tomorrow?"

He said, "Sounds good Son. Get your mother for me. I want to say my proper goodbyes."

The second time I went out on the back porch, Uncle Henry came out and sat beside me on the glider. He patted me on the knee and we just sat there for awhile rocking back and forth and looking out over the fields. The silence between us was comfortable and neither one of us spoke. Finally he said, "A cold beer sure would taste good." We chuckled. He sat there for a few more minutes, patted me on the knee again, got up and went back inside.

My brother Jimmy married Fran Hartlow from Elverton. She was pleasant and they had a baby Charles. They stayed a little while after everyone else left and then they left. My sister Sadie left earlier with her boyfriend Tom. They were still in school at the College of Elverton and had exams coming up so they needed to "hit the books."

Dad was in the living room watching television and Mom and I were sitting at the kitchen table. She put her hand on mine and looked into my eyes and said, "How are you really doing Honey?"

I always liked talking to her. I would sit in the kitchen and talk to her while she was cooking and she was a good listener. I had been open with her about my teenage problems growing up and as I said earlier, we wrote a lot during the three years I was away.

"I'm not doing so well Mom. I'm glad to be home and it is good to see everyone, but I feel kind of detached, like I'm here, but somehow don't belong."

"Oh Honey, I hate that for you. We all love you so much and missed you and are so glad you're home safely."

I said, "I know and I'm grateful to have all of you. I think it's going to take some time for me to adjust." We sat there for awhile and she finished catching me up on all the news. While she was talking, I felt restless and anxious, but tried to put on a good front for her.

"Mom, I think I'll stay at the cabin for awhile. I'll come by every day to check in."

Dad walked in having overheard that part of the conversation, "Why the hell you wanna go up to that dingy ole place? There's nothing there but rats and snakes."

"Just need some solitude Dad."

"But you just got home," he said.

"Clyde, leave him be. Jett knows what he needs to do."

He turned and walked out his voice trailing off behind him, "I don't get it; he's been gone three years and he wants to leave again."

"Don't mind him Honey. It's true, he doesn't understand. He does love you and he's so proud of you. He would brag about you in town being an Army Ranger and all."

She smiled and continued, "It was a little embarrassing at times."

"I know he loves me Mom. I'm okay. I can't expect Dad to understand. I don't understand myself."

I looked down and we were silent for a few minutes, but just like with Henry, it wasn't awkward. She was waiting for me.

Finally I looked up and said, "I love you Mom and have missed you so much." I started to tear up and we both got up and put our arms around each other.

"I love you too Jett. You do whatever you have to do."

She continued, "Your Dad had your truck serviced and it's ready to go. Why don't you leave your rental car here and your Dad and I can take it over to Elverton in the morning and turn it in."

I said, "I don't want you all to have to do that."

"Its fine, we have a few things to do over there anyway."

I said, "That's a huge help Mom."

I went into my old room and got a few things. Gave Mom a hug and kiss and thanked her for the party. She had packed a bunch of leftovers and said, "This should last you for a few days."

"Thanks Mom."

I went into the living room and thanked Dad for the party and told him I would see him tomorrow. He didn't look up from the TV and mumbled, "See ya."

Spot had been following me all over the house. I looked at mom and she said, "Spot has missed you and I know he wants to go with you. I'll miss him, but that's fine. Journee is another matter. We'll talk later about him."

It was a good feeling to be driving my old truck. It took me back for a few moments to the time before all hell broke loose in my life.

I went down to the 7- Eleven and bought me a twelve-pack of beer, a large bag of ice, and used the pay phone to call Ace. The line was busy. I went to the Inn to get the key to the cabin. I didn't recognize the girl at the front desk. Pop had told her I was coming so she smiled and said, "Mr. Hollander said to expect you."

I smiled back, "Thanks I'll just be a few minutes." I opened the door into the back offices and got the key and waved at her as I left.

The sun was setting as Spot and I headed up the Parkway for the turn off to the cabin. It was a beautiful evening. Everything was so lush and green and wild flowers were growing in the meadows with a few cows lazily grazing. I wondered if it was an easier life to be a cow. Not much to worry about. They didn't even know their days were numbered. No, I think I'll pass on that. I smiled. Anyway, maybe I was a cow in a previous life.

It took approximately ten minutes to get to the turnoff and the cabin was about a mile off the road. Three quarters of the way, I passed Uncle Henry and Betty's house. I was tempted to stop and have a cold one, but then thought I better get on to the cabin while there is still some light.

When I reached the cabin, there was enough light for Spot and me to walk around the outside and check for any signs of recent activity. I checked all the windows and doors from the outside to see if there were any signs of tampering. Everything appeared to be in order. The house seemed secure.

I touched the side of my leg to feel my knife. It was such a part of me that most of the time, I wasn't aware that I had it with me. We walked out along the ridge and I let him run.

We went inside and there was a musty smell. I turned on some lights and opened the windows to let it air out. When I stayed at the cabin with Ace, I always stayed in the back bedroom on the left and Ace stayed in the front bedroom on the right. I put my stuff away, the beer on ice, and the food in the fridge. I opened a beer and sat down on the sofa to relax. Spot nuzzled up next to me and was asleep in a matter of minutes.

The Cabin

I looked around the room and a lot of wonderful memories flooded back. I could see the family gatherings over the years when the room was filled with talk, laughter, and good food. After Pop and Nana moved out, they let me use the cabin.

It was here that Ace and I talked about our dreams and girls and problems and everything else imaginable. We took hikes using the cabin as our base. On some occasions, we packed our gear and went for an overnight in the woods. I felt comfortable and safe here, but I missed Ace.

I closed my eyes and dozed off. When I woke up, it was 0505. We went for a run. Afterwards, I felt better. I slept okay with no nightmares. I was hungry and it felt good to be back in these mountains.

I got one of the left-over casseroles out of the fridge and dug in. It tasted good. Maybe things were going to get better. Maybe I could find some peace here in these hills. Spot started barking and I jumped. There was a knock on the door. I smiled. I knew it would be Uncle Henry.

I said, "You're up awful early for an old guy."

He smiled and gave me a big hug. "Yeah, I thought I needed to come here and make sure you ate your Wheaties."

I asked, "You want some of this casserole?"

He answered with another smile, "I'll pass, but I bet that tastes pretty good after what you're use to."

"It does. Can you sit for a few minutes and talk?"

He brought me up to date on his life. He asked about Ace and I told him that I was worried about him. I said, "It's hard to admit, but I'm also worried about myself. And thanks for sitting with me on the porch yesterday."

"You're welcome," he said.

I told him about trying to recall and write down some of our family history and he asked me how that was going.

"One of my professors said it's important to get in touch with your story, what makes you tic. I have to admit I enjoyed recalling and writing about our family."

He said, "Did you think it was helpful?"

I answered, "Well, it explains why I love nature, have a respect for all living things, and why I'm thankful for all my blessings. You were one of the important people who taught me all those things."

He said, "You know Jett, it goes all the way back to our ancestors who settled here. They passed it down to all of us. Some were interested and some weren't. I think what you learned from them through Pop, me, and Jack will in part make it more challenging to heal from the trauma you've been through over the past three years."

I responded, "I think so too. Pop would never allow us to kill anything that lived." Tears started down my cheeks as I continued finding it difficult to talk. "Henry, we did terrible things over there."

He put his hand on my shoulder and said, "I know and all you learned over the years will also be a huge help in your healing.

The important thing is you have in the last few days revisited your roots and have remembered some of the things that are important to you. They make up a part of the core of who you are and I believe they can also help you heal."

I smiled through my tears, "Got any ideas where I should start?"

He smiled back and said, "All I can say is I have faith in your ability to find the path that will give you the peace we all long for in this life. And you won't be alone. All of us who love you will be here to help you along the way."

"Thank you Henry."

We sat for awhile longer in silence and then he said, "Well, let me head back to the house and get ready for work. What are you and Spot gonna do today?"

I answered, "Pop said I could stay here as long as I want so I've got to get some supplies and food, go by and see Mom, go over and visit with Marge (Ace's Mom) and then drop by the store and see Jack."

He said, "Sounds like a full day. Would you be up for a hike this afternoon around four?"

I responded, "Sure. That sounds great."

"Betty and I want you to come for supper tomorrow night. She knows your Mom is going to ask you to eat with them tonight. Anyway, if that works for you, we thought we would ask Pop and your Mom and Dad to join us. Not sure your Dad will come, but we'll see."

I said "That'll be good. To be honest with you, this time yesterday I would have hesitated, but I'm starting to feel better and I'm surprised. The day before yesterday I had two panic attacks and I could hardly breathe. Something inside me is starting to settle. Maybe it's a combo of becoming aware again of my roots and being back in these mountains with family."

He smiled, "Well I would suggest that you don't try to figure it out today; just let it happen."

"Okay Uncle, thanks."

"I'll meet you here at four." He gave me a hug, petted Spot's head and left.

I showered and shaved and Spot and I left for town. I stopped by to see Mom. I asked her if I could call Ace. It was busy. I sat down and Journee jumped in my lap and purred.

She said, "We turned in the rental car early this morning."

"Thanks again Mom." We had a nice talk. I told her about my visit with Henry and that I was feeling a little better.

"I'm so glad Honey."

"Me too, Mom. I hope it lasts."

"I know it will take some time but I know you'll be fine." Mom was always a person whose glass was half full and that was another part of my roots. She taught me well, but it had been tested many times over the last three years. I had some work to do on that positive approach to life. Mom asked me to come for supper and I accepted. "It will just be your Dad and me. I thought that might be better."

"Thanks Mom, what time do you want me to come?"

"About 6:30 will be fine. Your Dad has to work till 5:30."

I asked, "Mind if I try Ace again?"

"Honey, you don't have to ask; this is your home."

"Okay Mom."

I dialed and it was finally ringing and someone answered and I asked for Sgt Frost. There was a pause with a hand over the receiver and a muffled sound. Then, "He's not on the ward; he's at PT."

"Would you take a message?"

"I don't have anything to write with."

"Okay, just tell him that Jett called and ask him to call me at my Mom's tonight after 1830."

"I don't know if I can remember all that."

"Okay, try to remember, call Jett after 1830 at his Mom's."

"I'll try, but I can't promise anything." And he hung up.

I gave Mom a hug. "Can I leave Spot here with you and pick him up on my way back to the cabin this afternoon."

"That's fine."

I went by to see Pop and he wasn't there. I talked briefly to a few of the employees that I had known and they all seemed glad to see me. I met a receptionist named Sandra that I didn't know. She was friendly and nice looking with great tits. Shit, I had been in the Army too long. What happened to great boobs? I went into Pop's office and called Marge.

"Hey Ma, how're you doin'?" I'd called her Ma as far back as I can remember and she called me Sweetie.

"Jett, hey Sweetie, I'm okay."

I said, "When did you all get back?"

"Last night around 9:00."

"How was Ace when you left?"

"Jett, you know how he is. He tried to put on a good front, but I know better."

"Ma, I'm over at the Inn. Could I come by now?"

"Let's see. It's 11:00. I need to make a quick trip to Elverton. I'll be back by noon. Come on over then and I'll fix you some lunch."

"Okay, see you at 12:00."

Pop wasn't back so I decided to go over to the store and see Jack. The store was bustling with activity. People came from all over the area to shop at Hollander's General Store. There was always a good smell in the store and they had everything you could possible want.

"Hey, Jett," Billy called out from behind one of the counters. He had worked at the store for longer than I could remember. "Welcome home!" I went over and shook his hand. Other people I knew greeted me. After some small talk I asked Billy, "Is Jack here?"

With a big smile he said, "Yeah, he's upstairs in his office with the door closed counting his money." I was feeling good. I took two stairs at a time and walked into the office area and there was no one there so I went over to his door and knocked.

He yelled, "Go away, I don't want any. Don't you know I own this store. I don't need anything you could possibly have." Jack was the biggest tease in Harvest and he was always saying stuff like that.

I yelled back, "I didn't know ya'll sold ice cold beer!"

He yelled back, "In that case by all means come in!"

I opened the door and his big six-foot-four inch frame met me in the middle of the room in a big bear hug, lifting me about a foot off the floor.

"Jett, my boy, it sure is good to see you. Sorry Ann and I missed your party yesterday; we were on our way back from Wisconsin and didn't get in till late. Henry called this morning to let me know you got in safely." We talked mostly about his side of the family.

He didn't ask me any questions about my life in the Army. He did ask how Ace was doing and I gave him the latest news.

I said, "Speaking of Ace, I better get going. I'm due at Marge's for lunch at noon." We embraced with promises to get in some hiking soon.

I pulled up in front of Ace's house and suddenly felt anxiety. It wasn't like the panic attacks from two days ago, but was this underlying feeling of nervousness and uneasiness. I realized I had been successfully distracted so far today and now I was going to talk to Ma about Ace. Would it all come back in ways I didn't expect and could I handle it?

Ace and I treated each other's home like our own. We never knocked. We walked right in. I did and yelled, "Hey Ma."

"I'm in the kitchen Sweetie" We embraced and she said, "I'm so glad to see you."

"Me too you."

She asked, "Are you hungry?"

"Not really, but I could eat one of your famous bologna sandwiches."

She said, "Comin' right up."

I watched her as she moved around the kitchen. She had on what I would call a casual dress, made of some kind of thin material that clung to her body. She was a little overweight, but had a sexy figure. In high school, when Ace wasn't around, some of us guys would say she was the hottest Mom in Harvest and there were quite a number of hot Moms, but she was at the top of my list. Ace would have killed me if he knew.

When I was at Ace's house, we spent a lot of time with her because she was so cool. She listened to us and we talked about our girl friend problems and she would give us advice and tease me because I was so shy around girls. Ace seemed to be a natural lady's man, but I was terrified of girls.

While she was talking to us, I used to pretend that she was sitting in the kitchen naked. I could get hard just watching her move. During those days, she was the subject of many fantasies I had while "jerking off." Sometimes I would pretend she was Mrs. Robinson in that movie with Dustin Hoffman. We would be on a deserted island and she would teach me every conceivable known sex position.

You would think the trauma of war would curb the sexual appetite, but according to my own experience and that of my buddies, this was not the case. We talked about sex and getting laid all the time and there was a lot of taking matters into our own hands, so to speak. We needed diversions and that was about our only one. There were girls available in some areas where we were stationed and at Fort Benning between tours, but Ace and I were always afraid of disease so we stayed with porno magazines.

On our few brief visits back to Harvest while in the service, Ace got "laid" several times. They were like one night stands with girls we had known in high school. April was not one of those girls. I was still shy even then and all I had was masturbation and I did it often. It was a helpful release.

I thought about all these things while Marge was making my sandwich. As she was finishing up, I thought I would love to have sex with her right now. To have her come up, stand in front of me and start massaging my head as I pulled up her dress and saw that she had on no panties. Then she would say, "Jett, Sweetie, I know you must be horny so why don't we go upstairs and I'll take care of all your sexual needs."

Instead of that, she said, "Would you like some lemonade with your sandwich?"

I must have looked startled or flustered or something as she said, "Jett, are you all right? You look like you're distressed and a 1,000 miles away."

I knew I was blushing, but I was able to somewhat recover and say in a kind of halting voice, "No, I'm okay. I'm sorry, what did you ask?"

"Would you like some lemonade?"

"Yes, thanks Ma."

"I know this war has done terrible things to you and Ace."

Thankful that I was scooted under the kitchen table where she could not see my hard dick, I began to recover and said, "Aren't you going to eat anything?"

"No I'm not hungry."

I asked, "Tell me more about your visit with Ace."

I ate my sandwich while she talked about their visit. He was able to get a pass to go out with them yesterday afternoon and she told me what they saw as they drove around DC. "We ate a late lunch at a wonderful seafood restaurant right by the Potomac."

She paused and continued, "Ace just picked at his food. I tried to kid him about the food, saying it must really be good at Walter Reed. He smiled and joked about it and said he wasn't hungry. Jim and Jeff didn't think anything about it, but I'm his momma, Jett and I could feel it. He didn't feel comfortable around us."

She started to tear up and I put my hand on hers and said, "Ma, this Army experience seemed like a good idea when we joined, but we had no clue what it would be like."

The back of her hand felt so soft and I could feel this connection between us. I wanted to pull her up and take her in my arms and stroke her hair and tell her it was going to be okay. Then I thought that is not a platonic thought you piece of shit. Marge needs you. Snap out of it.

I continued, "We experienced things we'll never forget. We want our families to be patient with us. It's gonna take some time for us to get used to being back in what we called in the Army the 'real world'."

"I know that Sweetie; I've done some reading on what war does to people. It's like you just hope and pray it won't be too bad. And I had this feeling yesterday that for Ace and that maybe for you too, it's going to be bad." She gently pulled her hand out from under mine.

I said with all the determination I could muster, "Ace and I are fortunate to have each other. Lots of our friends have gone home alone with no one around that understands what we've been through. Ace and I have always stuck together and we'll get through this."

She smiled faintly and said, "I know you all can do it."

She paused and then said, "Sometimes I feel responsible. Our family has always been in the military and we have always been so proud of that. I hope Ace didn't feel pressure from any of us and I hope he didn't put too much pressure on you."

I replied, "We were old enough to make our own decision. No one made us do anything. Please remember that."

She said, "Okay, I'll try."

She said, "Ace mentioned you're going back to see him in about a week and you're going to pick him up when he's discharged."

"Yeah, that's the plan. I hope it's okay with you all that I bring him home."

She replied, "Honestly we were disappointed, but we're trying to understand the best we can."

She paused and said reflectively, "I've got to talk more with Jeff. He is so curious and has all these questions to ask Ace and you too."

I said, "I think it's a good idea to talk with all your family. It's too painful for either one of us to talk about it right now."

"Ma, I better be going."

"Jett, I tried to call Ace several times this morning and I kept getting a busy signal."

"Yeah, the number we have is a pay phone on the ward and there are about twenty guys making and receiving calls. The only time I am able to reach him is around five in the morning. We're used to getting up about that time everyday."

She hugged me and said, "Thanks for the tip Sweetie. Come back soon."

"I will Ma. I love you."

"I love you too Jett."

I looked back. She was standing in the doorway and tears were running down her cheeks. We were all going to face some challenging times ahead. I hoped and prayed we would all come through it without too many more scars. I felt guilty about my fantasy, but kept telling myself that it was just a fantasy, lighten up a little.

I went back by the Inn to see Pop. "Sandra, is Pop back yet?"

"Yes, Mr. Hollander, he got back about half an hour ago. He said he was going up to take a nap. He said if you came by again to go up and wake him."

"Please call me Jett."

She smiled, "Okay Jett."

"I won't disturb him. Just tell him I came by again and I'll see him tomorrow for lunch."

"I'll tell him." She had a beautiful smile.

I went back to the store to pick up my supplies. Billy said, "Jack is running some errands and he told me if you came back for your supplies before he got back to give you this country ham."

I smiled, "Tell him thanks and that I owe him big time."

I went by the grocery store to get some food items that Jack didn't carry and then dropped by the house to pick up Spot and head to the cabin. I had about two hours before Henry came for our hike.

Even though it had been a pretty good day, I was feeling emotionally drained. As much as I tried to put it out of my mind, and I guess I didn't try very hard, I was still feeling horny. So I got some lotion, went into my own world with Marge and took care of business. I was exhausted and decided to lie down and try to nap.

The next thing I knew, Spot was barking. I jumped out my skin and must have come off the sofa at least a foot. Over the bark, I could hear Henry yelling, "Jett, it's Henry!!"

I let him in and knew I looked shaken as he said, "Are you okay?"

My heart was beating rapidly and I was short of breath. I said, "Yeah, just give me a minute. I'm not used to Spot's loud barking and I was dosing and it startled me."

He said. "Why don't we sit for a few minutes?"

"Yeah, that would help."

He said, "You take as long as you need."

I said, "Sorry about the locked door. I know we never use to lock it, but I feel safer and more comfortable with it secured."

"Jett, that's no big deal. Betty and I lock our door these days too."

We exchanged small talk for a few more minutes and then I said, "Let me go change into some hiking clothes and I'll be right back."

Spot loved to go with us on hikes. He missed out some over the past three years living with Mom and Dad, but Henry and Jack would often come by the house and pick him up. He never strayed far from us. Ace and I had taught him well.

We took one of our favorite trails along the ridge and were gone for over an hour. We talked of old memories in these woods and all the good times we had with Pop.

I asked, "Is Pop hiking much these days?"

He replied, "He's slowing down some, but he still gets out most days. I think he would probably call them walks in the woods. Usually Jack or I go with him on the longer walks, but he often walks around the reservoir by himself. That's always been one of his favorites."

When we returned to the cabin, he said, “That was great. I better get on down to the house. Say hey to your Mom and Dad for me.”

“I will,” and asked, “Any chance you could do another hike tomorrow afternoon?”

“Sure, you want to go a little further tomorrow?”

I smiled, “Yeah, I’d like that.”

“We can go up to Crow’s Nest. That will take a couple of hours. I can get off work and be here by three.”

“Thanks Henry. See you tomorrow.”

I went inside and took a shower. I sat on the sofa and relaxed with Spot snuggled up against me. My first full day at home had been better than I had anticipated. The party was rough, but I got through it pretty well thanks to Mom and Henry.

5

ACE FREAKING OUT

I was ready and getting a little restless so I decided to go down to the house a little early. Mom was in the kitchen working on supper and Dad was taking a shower. It was like old times sitting in the kitchen talking to Mom. I talked to her about my day. I mentioned my visit with Marge. I said, "She is worried about Ace and was upset by the way things went during their visit with him."

Dad walked in and having heard my last sentence said, "That's funny 'cause Jim mentioned it today at the mill and said he thought the visit went well."

Jim and Dad are co-managers of the mill. Pop had set it up that way in case Dad went through a drinking spell, the mill could still continue to operate without a hitch. Jim and Dad had been friends for years and as far as I know, there had never been any problem between them.

Mom said, "That doesn't surprise me. You and Jim aren't the most observant people. It takes a woman and in this case, a mother to notice things like that."

"Well, Lynne, if you say so. I guess we got more important things to do than try to figure out how people are feelin'."

"Go on into the den and watch TV till supper is ready you ole fart."

"Mommmmm!"

Dad said, "No need to be surprised Jett. Your Mom calls me worsen' that when you ain't around."

He came over and slapped her on the butt, smiled and murmured, "Dessert."

She exclaimed, "Get! Go on now!"

My Dad had a wonderful sense of humor, but it could come and go. Sometimes he was meaner than a snake and grumpy as all get out. I've heard that called a "dry drunk."

Dad was still in a good mood and it was nice talking about old times and memories. For awhile, I forgot about stuff and just got lost in the moment of being home and enjoying time with Mom and Dad. We were almost finished when the phone rang. Mom got up to answer it.

It was Ace and Mom talked to him for a few minutes. Dad and I just sat there and it was an awkward silence. Neither one of us knew what to say. We needed Mom to carry on a conversation. I was relieved when I heard Mom say, "Let me get Jett."

I got up a little quicker than I should have, passed Mom in the hallway and picked up the phone.

"Hey man, how goes it?"

"Oh, I'm having a great time. Those nurses won't leave me alone so I'm not getting much sleep. They did run out of cold beer. Other than that, I love it here in this hospital with all these sick soldiers."

I said, "Well, maybe we ought to leave your ass right there. How will all those horny nurses survive after you're gone?"

Mom yelled, "Jeettttt! We heard that, watch your language."

"Sorry Mom."

Ace laughed, "Sounds like old times at your house."

He shifted to a serious mood, "The MD told me they wanted to keep me here about a fucking month. I couldn't believe it. Can you come up here and break me out of this place? I'm goin' crazy and I've only been here a few days. How am I gonna make it for another four weeks?"

"Ace, Walter Reed is not a regular hospital. You can't just leave AMA (against medical advice) like a civilian hospital. The Army would consider you AWOL (absent without leave) and would come after you."

"Well, start trying to figure something out 'cause I'm not staying here for four more weeks. I'll go fucking crazy."

"I saw your Mom today and she's really worried about you."

He said, "I tried to put on a good show, but I couldn't fake it and even if I could, Mom would know. I'm so restless. I can't sit still and read or watch TV. The Yankees were on last night and I couldn't even watch the game. This afternoon, I went off on one of the orderlies and thank God he didn't report me. I'm afraid to go to sleep. The nightmares are getting worse and I wake up sweating and trembling. I gotta get out of here."

"Okay, I got it. While you were talking I thought about how your uncle (a Colonel in the Army) pulled some strings to get us in Ranger School. Maybe he could help. I'll go over and talk to your Mom in the morning and ask her to call him. If we could somehow convince the Army you could get good care closer to home, they might consider letting you go. In the meantime, in the morning, tell the nurse you want to see a hospital chaplain."

He hissed, "I'm not gonna ask anybody if I can see a chaplain."

"Yes the fuck you are!"

"Jeettttt!"

"Sorry Mom!"

"Listen up Ace. If you want outta there bad enough, you need to be willing to do whatever it takes. Tell the chaplain all those problems you just told me about and tell him we're looking for a place closer to home. They have pull and he may be able to help on that end. We'll need all the help we can get."

"Okay, I'll think about it."

"You think about it and I'll think about it and we can both think some more about it and before we know it, your four weeks will be up."

"All right, god dammit! I'll ask to see a chaplain."

"Good! I'll get the ball rolling here. Pop had the phone cut on at the cabin so you can call me."

He asked, "Same number?"

"Yeah, call me about 1430. Henry and I are going hiking around 1500."

He said with all the sarcasm he could muster, "Well isn't that just wonderful. You're goin' on a hike. Why don't you rub it in and while you're at it, you can tell me that you're having banana pudding for desert."

"Mom are we having banana pudding for dessert?"

Mom yelled back, "Jett Hollander, you ought to be ashamed. You know how Ace loves banana pudding."

"Sorry old man. That's a yes and I'll think about you every bite I take. Stop your belly-achin'. You know Mom will make you a batch as soon as you get home. I need to go. Call me tomorrow around 1430."

There was a pause then, "Jett, I gotta get out of here."

"I know." He hung up.

Mom was in the kitchen and said, "He sounded really down."

"Yeah it's bad. I hope we can get him out of there soon."

She asked, "How will you do that?"

"I don't know. I'll start by seeing if Ace's uncle can help."

She said, "I hope it works out. Are you ready for your banana pudding?"

"Everything was so good, but now I've lost my appetite. Would you put some in a Tupperware for me? Ace and I've been together so long, it's like when he's upset, I'm upset."

"I know Honey."

We changed the subject and talked while I helped her with the dishes.

When we finished, I said, "Mom, do you mind if I head on out?"

"Not at all, you go ahead. We'll see you tomorrow night at Betty and Henry's. Here's your banana pudding."

I gave her a big hug. "It was wonderful. I had a good time. I'll say goodbye to Dad and be on my way. Love you."

"I love you too Jett and I'm so glad you're home."

I wanted to stop by and see Betty and Henry before it got too late and talk to him about my conversation with Ace. Betty answered the door. "Come in Jett. How was your first full day back?"

"It was fine. Thank you Betty."

"Henry is on the deck having a nightcap. Would you like something to drink?"

"A beer if you have one."

She said, "Sure do. He keeps plenty on hand."

I slid open the glass doors and he was seated at the far end of the deck. He turned toward me with a smile on his face. "Jett, what a pleasant surprise! I see you already have a beer. Come over and sit and enjoy the view."

I told him about the evening with Mom and Dad and then went into detail about the conversation I had with Ace. He listened with interest. When you talk to Henry, you always have his undivided attention, which always made me feel important. I've been working on doing that same thing with the people around me. Henry has made that one more important part of my roots. He taught me well.

He said, "I want to help. Let me make a few calls tomorrow. I'll let you know when I see you tomorrow afternoon"

"That would be great. Thanks." Betty brought me another beer and we enjoyed some light talk as darkness slowly set in over the valley and then over us. I thanked them and left.

When I got to the cabin, I had a few bites of the banana pudding and put it in the fridge. I was exhausted and decided to turn in. I had this urge to go outside and walk around the perimeter of the cabin.

Wherever we were, we always secured the perimeter. What was I afraid of? Spot would give me plenty of warning and I had my knife. I can't explain it, but I gave in to the thought, "Corporal Hollander, go secure the perimeter." And that's what I did.

The bedroom seemed safer than the sofa. Safer from what? What the hell. I'm home now. Even though I was exhausted, it took me a long time to fall asleep. I kept thinking about the patrol where one of our best friends Harry was hit in the neck by flying shrapnel and bled to death right in front of our eyes.

We couldn't stop the bleeding. That was the early part of our mission and the LT said we had to keep going. He radioed to have the medics pick up his body. We left his best buddy Clifton with him. We got through that awful day with wet and then dried blood all over us.

I don't know how, but I eventually drifted off to sleep, but was startled by the phone ringing. My body did the same thing it did this afternoon and again, I must have lifted about a foot off the bed. I stumbled into the great room and headed toward the ringing phone.

The clock said 3:36. "Hello."

I heard in a hushed but frantic voice, "You've got to get me outta here. I'm goin' crazy."

"Hold on a minute, give me a chance to clear my head." I went to the kitchen sink and splashed cold water on my face several times, dried it, and picked up the phone and said, "I couldn't get to sleep tonight. I was thinking about Harry."

Ace said, "I had a nightmare about Tim and how the LT told me to go out and pick up as many of his body parts I could find."

I said, "I think this problem gets worse the more time we have away from the unit."

He replied, "I'm even starting to have flashbacks."

"Listen up," I said. Does anybody there know you made this call?"

He responded, "The nurse is at her station down the hall. I don't think she saw me and I know she can't hear me."

"Good. You've got to put on a good show for the staff. I know you've had a couple of bad days, but tomorrow you've got to seem better to them."

"Why?" he asked.

"Because if they think you're turning into a nut case, they'll be less likely to let you leave early. Have you asked to see a chaplain?"

"Yes for god's sakes. I still don't know what good that'll do. He's comin' tomorrow at 1000."

"Ace, pay attention to what I'm telling you. I want you to tell the chaplain that you're having some irritability, difficulty sleeping, difficulty getting some thoughts out of your mind, and the feeling at times like you are in a cage and can't get out. Tell him you're feeling better today, but all you want to do is get home so you can recuperate around your family."

I continued, "Tell him that your mom has a brother who's a colonel and that the family is trying to make arrangements for you to be discharged early. Ask him if there is anything he can do to help. You got it?"

"Yeah, but I still don't see how he can help."

I said, "Stop being so stubborn and trust me. He can help, but you've got to tell him what I just said."

"All right."

"Remember, down play your symptoms and even tell him your leg is better. Try to convince him that your biggest problem is not being with your family. And most of all, try not to be yourself. Then he WILL think you're a nut case."

"Thanks Ass Wipe." Pause. "I feel a little better. But Jett, I'm serious. I'm gonna go crazy if I have to stay here and I will go AWOL and I don't care about the consequences."

"Ace, calm down. We're gonna get it done." We talked a few more minutes and then I said, "What time are you gonna call me tomorrow?"

"You've got a short memory."

"No dude, I ask that question to make sure you remembered."

He hung up. I smiled. He hates that name dude.

6

A PLAN TO FREE ACE

I didn't sleep much but guess I dozed until my inner alarm clock went off at 0500. I sure as hell didn't feel like going for a run, but Spot and I took off about ten minutes later. It was grueling. The trails are hilly and some were a major challenge in my present state. When we returned, I showered and ate a good sized portion of banana pudding. It tasted really good. Spot and I went in and lay down on the bed and drifted off without much problem.

Spot started barking and I jumped again. This was getting old. I got up and he was looking out the window continuing to bark. I looked out and didn't see anyone and the clock read 9:57. My lunch with Pop was at 1230 so I had some time to kill. I had not fully unpacked and had a lot of laundry to do. I also decided to do some cleaning around the cabin.

Around 1045 the phone rang and it was Ace. He said with some excitement in his voice, "The chaplain just left and he's going to help us. He said that this was not an unusual request and that he had seen some requests approved and some denied. He said the ones approved were those where the soldier had reasonable access to a VA Center. In a few cases where there was no reasonable access to a VA Center, the requests were approved when the Army was convinced there was a good treatment plan in place and it was not going to cost Uncle Sam much money."

He continued, "The chaplain looked it up and there is a VA Center in Asheville, but he said the Army might not agree that meets the requirements of 'reasonable access'."

I asked, "What kind of treatment plan is he talking about?"

"It's a plan that would include a proper medical treatment for my leg and a proper PT plan for my rehabilitation. He also said he had talked to the Charge Nurse and I had also been diagnosed with PTSD after my behavior yesterday."

Irritated, I said "What else did you do besides attack the orderly?"

He answered, "Not much."

"Well fuck, Ace, you've got to calm your ass down if you want to get outta there." I continued still irritated, "Now they'll want a fuckin' plan for the PTSD."

He said also irritated, "I think that PTSD stuff is bullshit."

Calming down I said, "Ace, I think we both have it. I'm not sure what all that means yet, but what little I've read suggests it fits us to some degree."

He said, "Well maybe you have it, but all I want is to get outta here and I'll be fine."

This was not a good time to argue with him so I just let it go. I said, "The chaplain was a big help. Let me hang up and get to work on this. Don't call me this afternoon. Call me tonight around 2200."

He sounded dejected, "Okay, call Ma and let her know what we're doing."

"I was gonna call her anyway and ask about your uncle helping us, but you should call her yourself just to check in."

He responded, "I'll call her in the morning."

I called Henry and gave him the run down on my conversation with Ace. He said he had made several calls earlier, but had not been able to reach anyone yet. He also said he was going to make another call based on what I had just told him. Said he would see me at 3 and hopefully have some news.

I called Marge and brought her up to date on my conversations with Ace. I told her that Henry was working on some ideas and that I would call her in the morning or sooner if I had anything important to tell her. I said, "It's a little premature at this point, but when we finalize the details, would you call your brother and see if he can help us?"

"Sure Sweetie. Jeremy will help in any way he can."

"Ma, try not to worry. I think we can get him home in a week or so with everybody working together."

She said, "Be sure to let me know what you find out."

"I will."

I looked at the clock and it was time for me to leave. I dropped Spot off with Mom and went over to the Inn. Lucky for me, Sandra was working. She was easy on the eyes. She smiled, "Hey Jett."

I smiled back, "Hey Sandra."

"Your grandfather said to come to his office when you got here."

"Thanks." Mental note: no wedding band.

His door was open. "Hey Pop."

"Come on in Jett." He came from around the desk and gave me a big hug. "How're you doin' Son?"

"Pretty good, Pop. My biggest worry right now is Ace. He's goin' crazy at Walter Reed." I filled him in on all the latest.

He said, "Let me know if I can do anything to help."

"Thanks Pop, we may need you. I'll keep you up to date on the progress."

He said, "I thought we would eat our lunch in here where we can have a little privacy. Do you want your usual?"

"Yes Pop, that's fine?"

"How about to drink?"

"Beer would be great."

He picked up the phone and dialed Brenda's extension. She had been managing the Inn's restaurant as far back as I could remember. Pop obviously had given her a heads up when he said, "Jett will have his usual with a beer and I'll have my usual vegetable plate with some of that cornbread and just bring me water. Thanks Hon."

"Pop, we talked about business and family stuff the other night at the party, but how are you doin'?"

He answered, "Well Jett, I guess I'm doing pretty well. I'll be seventy-five this year and the docs tell me with the exception of the arthritis, I'm in good physical health. I try to stay busy doing this and that. Jack and Henry get me out walking on a regular basis. Jimmy is managing both the Inn and the hotels and doing such a good job that I'm about ready to turn the whole thing over to him. As you know, it's the only job he ever wanted."

He continued, "I told him he needed a business degree but you may remember he still spent all his time over here working with me and barely graduated. In retrospect, he probably didn't need the degree." He chuckled and continued, "He'll tell you I taught him everything he needed to know about managing these three places."

His expression changed as he said, "You know I miss your Nana. She was the love of my life and there's a big empty space that's been in my heart since she passed. I guess the Good Lord's got her a nice place up there in heaven and one day we'll be together for eternity. That thought keeps me goin' a lot of days."

He shifted his gaze down. I wasn't sure what to say and we were silent for a few minutes as I watched a few tears roll down his cheeks. "Jett, dying is a part of living. No one has to tell you that after the hell you've been through. That's just how it is and we all need to do the best we can to make peace with that."

I was still at a loss for words so more silence and then he said, "I want you to know that you can talk to me anytime you want. I'm not going to ask you any questions about what happened over there. Just know that I'm willing to help in any way I can. Please remember that."

"I will, Pop. That means a lot to me."

Right on cue, a soft knock on the door. "Come in." It was Brenda, followed by a waiter named Jesse carrying a big tray perched on one palm.

"Jett, it is so good to see you," she said. "Welcome home young man"

"Thanks Brenda. It's good to see you too." We talked for a few minutes and she introduced me to Jesse and they were gone.

I started out with a few swigs of beer and it tasted good.

"That beer cold enough for you, Son?"

"Perfect Pop." We ate our lunch slowly and talked about the old days, hiking, family functions and all the fun we had. I said, "We're lucky to have such a close family."

"We sure are."

We finished our meal and Pop asked me if I wanted any desert. I declined and then he said, "I don't like loose ends in business and financial matters so Nana and I have over the years talked quite often about our estate. Since she died, I've made a few minor changes, but most of our original plan is still in place. We've had a number of conversations with your Dad and Henry and everyone is on board with our plan. Anyway, I'm informing you and in time will talk to Jimmy and Sadie about some of the particulars in my will because it involves the three of you. First, the Inn and hotels will be divided in this way. Your mom will receive forty-five percent and Henry will receive fifty-five percent. This will of course give him controlling interest and final say in any business decisions. The profits however will be split equally between them.

"Your dad was not pleased about my decision. I did the best I could to explain to him that he has a disease and that I couldn't trust him not to drink. Of course, it will be marital property and I'll leave it up to your Mom to decide how she wants to handle it. Your dad felt a little better when I told him that I was leaving my half ownership in the mill to him. Jack owns the other half and he and your dad have always gotten along well."

He continued, "Your dad will get 500-acres, Henry will get 500-acres surrounding his house. You will get the cabin and 100-acres up on that ridge, and Jimmy and Sadie will each get 200-acres."

"Pop, I'm speechless. Thank you. That cabin means so much to me."

He said that I could treat the cabin as my own from now on and that he would continue to pay all the utilities and taxes until his death. I thanked him again. We talked a little more and I finished my beer. He said, "It's about time for my afternoon nap. Give me a call in a few days and we can walk a couple of laps around the reservoir."

"I'll be sure to call and will look forward to it."

"Me too, Son." I gave him a hug and thanked him again.

It started raining around 1400 and I laid down for a nap. I was tired and had been kind of anxious after leaving the Inn. I dropped off to sleep within a few minutes and had another nightmare. Ace and I and some other Rangers lined up a bunch of women and children and were executing them in groups. The Sergeant said, "Ready, aim, fire!" The crack of the rifles sat me straight up in bed and I was sweating and having trouble breathing. I kept telling myself over and over again that it's okay, calm down. I was finally able to get up and splash some cold water on my face.

I sat on the front deck, watched the rain, and waited for Henry. It wasn't long before I saw him coming through the woods, a short cut from his house to the cabin. He was wearing a vinyl sweat suit which would keep him from getting too wet. I knew the hike was still on. We loved the different seasons and the changes in the weather. I had on a tee-shirt and cut off Army camouflage pants.

He was a little out of breath. We hugged and he sat down in the rocking chair next to mine. "Tell me about your visit with Pop,"

I asked smiling, "First tell me what you know about the new receptionist at the Inn?"

He smiled, "I don't know much about her except that Betty says she's 'cute as a button' and seems sweet. I think she's been working there about a month. That's all I know. Sorry."

"She is cute. I think it's a good sign I noticed her."

"I agree."

I said, "My time with Pop was as always enjoyable and comforting. I love being around him. We had some good talks and I'm sure you're aware that he told me about his will. That is so generous of Pop. I was of course thrilled. It looks like we're gonna be neighbors."

He said, "Yes it does and Betty and I are both very happy about that."

"Me too."

He said, "I have some good news from my contacts at the college. First, one of my good friends in the College of Medicine is a guy named Phil Collins. He is an orthopedic surgeon and did a four-year tour in the Army. I explained to him the situation with Ace and he said he would be happy to follow up with his treatment. Second, I talked with a guy named John Rodgers Kingston who is a visiting professor at the college in the field of neuro-psychology. I found out when I talked with him that he has been given a grant by the federal government to study PTSD among veterans returning from combat situations. The Defense Department is alarmed at the number of combat veterans who are suffering from PTSD and the number who are committing suicide."

He continued, "I told Dr. Kingston about you and Ace and he is eager to meet both of you. He said he is putting together the group he will be working with over the next three to four months. The next step is to have Ace get together with the chaplain again and find out specifically what we need to do to get him discharged; the sooner the better. Why don't you give him a call now?"

"Thanks Henry. This is starting to seem possible."

He said, "Don't get your hopes up too high yet, but I think we have a good chance and having Ace's uncle to help us might push it through more quickly."

"Let me try to get Ace now." He followed me inside and I dialed the number and it was busy. "It's busy. I'll try again after we get back from the hike and if I can't reach him, he's going to call me tonight at 10:00."

We hiked at times with a light drizzle and at other times with a heavy downpour. The forecast said there should be no thunderstorms with this rain. Lucky for us, it was only rain. We enjoyed getting wet. Pop taught us that the rain can be a cleansing experience. Henry went home and I took a shower.

I tried Ace again and lucked out. He was in a little better spirits. I brought him up to date and as Henry suggested, I told him to get with the chaplain ASAP and see what specifically we needed to do. I told him I hoped he could get us some answers tomorrow so we could get to work on it. I suggested he go ahead and call me tonight at 2200 and let me know if he was able to get an appointment tomorrow morning. He agreed and we hung up. I called Marge and gave her a quick update.

The evening was really nice. Even Dad came, which surprised me. Betty is a great cook, but I wasn't hungry. I tried the best I could to eat some so it wouldn't be noticeable. After our meal we sat around the table and talked. Again just like old times except I started to feel some anxiety and got restless. I stayed as long as I could and then thanked Betty and Henry and apologized for having to leave early. I told everyone I was still tired and having some problems sleeping.

Henry followed me outside. "I know you're struggling. Help is coming. Please remember that."

"Thanks Uncle, I will."

He said, "Call me as soon as you hear from Ace," he said. "I have a class tomorrow at 4:00 so I won't be able to hike but we'll get some hiking in this weekend."

"That's good. I always feel better during and after a hike. I'll look forward to it."

Ace called later and told me he was seeing the chaplain in the morning, but did not have a specific time. He said he would call after the meeting.

I had another restless night. No nightmares, but I couldn't get those traumatic thoughts ought of my mind. I was still up at 0500 and Spot joined me for our morning run. I got a few minutes up the trail and felt for my knife and it wasn't there. I wondered if I was slipping. I always had it with me. I went back and got it. After the run, I finished the banana pudding and went to bed. I slept for awhile and went outside to work around the cabin. I left a few windows open so I could hear the phone ring.

It rang around 1115 and Ace was upbeat. He told me the chaplain had taken him down to the personnel section at the hospital and they confirmed what he had told Ace the day before. They gave Ace a form to fill out stating the reasons for the request. She said she would be happy to fax the documents to be completed to support the early discharge.

The lady in Personnel told him the board met every Wednesday and one of their agenda items was to consider and decide on these requests. She said if all the documents could be on her desk by Tuesday noon, she would make sure he was on the docket for the next day. If approved, he could be discharged by that Friday.

Today was Friday so we had some work to do. The chaplain was going to help Ace get his paperwork completed at the hospital. I told Ace to call me back in ten minutes and I would have Henry's fax number so he could give it to Personnel.

I talked with Henry and filled him in on the plan. He gave me his fax number and told me to tell Ace to request Personnel to fax the documents right away if possible. He said the timing was going to be close so he would do everything he could to get the required documents faxed back to Personnel before close of business on Monday.

7
APRIL

It was 1145. After calling Ace and giving him the fax number, I called Marge and gave her the latest. She was elated and told me to thank Henry and everyone else for their help.

I was exhausted again. I wasn't hungry and didn't feel like doing anything. I still have this lingering anxiety. I just wanted to go to sleep and not wake up for a few days. I wondered about my buddies still over there. Were they out on patrol, between patrols, or sitting around talking? Had anyone else been injured and killed?

I was afraid to close my eyes. Migs kept flooding into my mind. I had told him, "You're not going to die on my watch…." And he was fucking dead. I wondered about his family, his girl friend, his dog. We use to talk about our dogs. His dog was Sammee. None of them would ever see him again. How come I survived? Did God protect me? Why didn't He protect Migs. He wore a cross around his neck. He probably loved God more than I do.

What the fuck! I started pacing the floor. My panic started coming back. My heart was racing. I felt like I was going to have another attack. I felt like I was sinking. I hurriedly walked over to the fridge and grabbed a bottle of beer. I turned it up and drank it as fast as I could, spilling some down my shirt.

I opened another one and started on it and went outside and drank more and spilled more and yelled, "What the fuck? What the fuck?" I got louder and soon was shouting at the top of my lungs, "What the fuck? What the fuck?" I was in a rage and mad as hell and didn't want to live. My mind shouted, "At least Migs is at peace!" And then I yelled, "Hell no, Migs is fucking dead and he will never ever see his…." My voice got lower and lower and I started sobbing and shaking and at the top of my lungs screamed, "Whyyyyyyyyyyyyyy?" I fell to the ground and lay there and sobbed and sobbed.

The next thing I knew, someone was shaking me and saying, "Jett!" I jumped and in the same motion swung my right arm backward and knocked someone back away from me and heard a yelp. I was on my feet and looked down and it was April. She was on her back holding her left shoulder and looking terrified. I dropped to my knees and crawled to her side. "April, oh my god, are you all right? I'm so sorry."

She looked at me not sure whether to believe me or not. "Jett, why did you do that?"

"It's complicated April. Please try to understand that I didn't mean it." She looked at me as if she was still trying to figure out if she could believe me. "Here, let me look at your shoulder."

Her expression softened a little and she asked, "It has to do with the war doesn't it?"

"Yeah, it does."

"Okay, you can look at my shoulder." I felt around to see if there was a fracture to her upper arm. Not any that I could tell.

I went through a series of maneuvers to see if there was any other type of damage and could find nothing. I must be turning into some kind of sex addict since I couldn't help but notice that she still has those beautiful and exquisitely formed tits. Well, yeah, where would they have gone? I said, "The good news is that there appears to be no serious damage, but I'm afraid you're going to have a bad bruise."

She said, "It's all right. I'll live."

I said, "You're a nurse. Is there anything else I should check for?"

"No, they trained you well. You did fine." She continued, "I guess you're wondering why I'm here."

"Not really. I assume you wanna ask me about Ace."

She said, "I went by to see you at your house and your Mom said you were staying up here. She called and didn't get an answer, but said you had been hiking a lot and I could go and wait if I wanted to. I work at the hospital now and this afternoon is my only time off until next Tuesday. I couldn't wait any longer."

I said, "Let's go inside where we can be more comfortable. Would you like something cold to drink?"

"Yes thanks, water would be fine."

I got her a glass of water and me a beer.

April was a beautiful girl, well I mean woman. She was about five-six with dark brown hair and was built like a "brick shit house." She was voted best looking and best all around in high school. It was no wonder she and Ace dated in high school and college. He was the star athlete and she was the beautiful cheer leader and a good athlete in her own right. She was also one of the valedictorians of our high school class. Ace didn't make it in that category even though his grades were decent.

She was wearing a white sleeveless blouse and a pair of light blue shorts that came about halfway down her thighs. She had on a pair of white sandals and her hair was in a pony tail. They broke up during their junior year in college. It was complicated and I don't think either one of them ever got over it, but they never got things resolved. The problem in my view was they were both too stubborn and had too much pride.

She said, "I've been talking a lot to Marge. As you know, we've always been close. She has been telling me about her research on veterans returning from war. I've been doing some research myself on PTSD. It doesn't sound pretty. I guess I got a little taste of that first hand a few minutes ago."

"You did. Sorry again."

There was a note of anxiety in her voice as she looked at me expectantly and asked, "How is he Jett?"

"Both of us will have some challenging times ahead. We've done, seen, and experienced things that no human being should have to go through. There's no doubt both of us suffer from PTSD. The only unknown is the level of severity. It's too early for either one of us to know. Ace's problem is he's in denial. He won't admit it and that will be a problem. But I'll do everything I can to help him see this is something we must get through and we can do it together."

She responded, "I finally was able to reach him at the hospital, but our conversation was strained. I asked him if I could come to see him. He made up some lame excuse, but it was obvious he didn't want to see me."

I shared with her some of our conversations about coming home to help her understand it wasn't about her. It was about us. It was our problem. Then I told her about our tentative plan for me to pick him up next week. She smiled and then the smile turned to a look of anxiety.

She said, "Jett, I have never stopped loving him. I can't even tell you why we broke up. I was devastated when you two decided to go into the Army. I didn't understand how he could leave me even when we weren't dating. It didn't make any sense, but that's how I felt. I've dated some since we broke up and at one point about a year ago I was engaged, but two months before the wedding I broke it off."

She started crying, and continued, "The guy was heartbroken. He loved me and was devoted to making me happy. I promised I would never do that again to anyone. I would always love Ace and there would never be anyone else for me. I will stay single if I can't be with him."

We sat in silence for a few minutes. I didn't know what to say. Tears were running down her cheeks and she was blowing her nose. Through her tears she pleaded, "Please tell me you think he still loves me a little and we may have a chance to get back together."

I replied, "I think he still loves you, but he has some serious shit to work through before he can think about working on the relationship."

She pleaded, "What can I do to help?"

"It'll take patience and acceptance of the slow pace and time needed for healing. Henry already has someone lined up to help us and I'm sure he'll help us figure out what to do."

She asked, "Who is it?"

"His name is Dr. Kingston."

There was a ray of hope in her expression. "I've heard some good things about him. One of my friends told me he was a visiting professor at the college and was doing some kind of research. I can't remember how his name came up."

I answered, "I don't know much either, but Henry believes he can help us."

She said, "I hope he can."

"Me too, I usually take a hike around this time of day. Would you like to come along?"

"Yes, that would be great. I usually run around this time of the day."

"OK, good. How's your shoulder?"

She replied, "It feels better." She moved her arm in different directions and said, "I don't feel much pain."

I said, "That's a relief."

She said, "I was going to leave here and go to the gym for a short work out and then run a couple of laps around the reservoir. I have my gym bag in the car. I'll need to change before we leave."

"OK. That's fine. You can use the bedroom where you and Ace..." I hesitated. She smiled, "Jett, you're blushing. I know which one you mean." She gave me a kiss on the cheek and went to get her gym bag.

I said earlier Pop would not allow me to have anyone spend the night at the cabin except Ace. I was fifteen when he made that rule.

When I started college, he said it was okay for me to take people to the cabin, but no wild parties and no under-aged drinking. He also said that if I wanted to use the cabin to be sure and check with his secretary Molly to make sure no one else in the family was using it. Long story short; Ace and April had used his bedroom more times than I can count.

She came out wearing a pair of loose fitting navy shorts that came down almost to her knees and a loose fitting pink sleeveless tee-shirt. I could tell she had on a sports bra underneath the tee-shirt. Her hair was in a pony tail and she had white tennis shoes. She looked really nice, but it was the kind of outfit that didn't show off her body. This was not a girl looking to be picked up at the local gym.

It must have been about 1600 when we started. I put four bottles of water in my back pack and asked if she was up for a two hour hike and she said that would be fine and we were off.

She smiled, "It feels so good to be at the cabin and in these woods. It's here that I have some of my best memories with Ace."

I smiled to myself. We talked about some of my old girl friends who had spent time at the cabin with the three of us.

She asked, "Whatever happened to Jean?"

I replied, "The last I heard she was married and living in Greensboro and has two kids."

"Jett, can I ask you a personal question?"

I smiled, "Sure."

I remember you had a number of different girlfriends. Ace used to tease you a lot by asking which girl you were bringing with us on this date?" She continued, "So what was the reason you never found someone really special in high school or in college?"

"I've asked myself that same question and I have some ideas, but I have this feeling that in the months ahead I'm going to find the answers to that question."

She said, "I hope for your sake you find those answers."

The weather was perfect for the hike. We spent most of the time talking about old times and the fun the three of us had. Sometimes it would be the four of us if I had a date. In that moment I realized, with almost everyone, that I had steered the conversation into talking about old times. That was the only thing I wanted to talk about these days. It was about the only comfortable subject for me. April was in great shape. This particular trail had some rough terrain and some steep inclines. She never seemed any more winded than me.

When we were five minutes from the cabin, she said, "I have one more personal question."

I smiled again. "Fire away."

"What were you doing asleep on the ground when I got here?"

I answered, "Give me a little while to come up with an answer to that one." We reached the cabin and I said, "Would you like to stay for supper? I have a lot of leftovers from my welcome home party and Jack gave me a country ham. We can eat whatever you want."

She hesitated for a moment. "I would like that."

"Great, would you like to take a shower?"

"Yes, thanks."

I asked, "You know where the towels are?"

"Sure do."

"While you're showering, I'll do a few chores and feed Spot. You may remember that if both showers are running at the same time the water pressure isn't too good. Would you holler when you're out?"

"Yes."

I pictured her naked in the shower. I let that image linger for a few moments and then wondered at that moment what part of her body she was washing. My dick started to get hard. Tomorrow, that will be a masturbation site for sure. Okay big boy, let's get our mind on some other thoughts.

I opened the front door and yelled for Spot. He came running from the woods and I saw Henry's back as he was walking down the hill toward his house. I yelled to him and went out to greet him.

He said, "I could see you have company. I didn't want to intrude."

"You're always welcome."

He said, "I know. Anyway, I wanted to give you an update on the progress we made today on Ace's application. It went well. Why don't you come down in the morning and I'll fill you in with the details. Let me head on back."

"Thanks. See you then Uncle."

As I walked back to the cabin, I thought I could tell by his expression that he was pleased I had company. Spot followed me into the kitchen and gulped down his food in about one minute. April yelled that she was out of the shower.

I took my shower and changed into some shorts and a tee-shirt and went barefooted. April had on what looked like another workout outfit. She must keep two in her gym bag. This one was white shorts with a red top - still conservative. Her hair was wet and again in a pony tail. Her faced looked like it was shinning. It must be some kind of moisturizing cream. She smiled and said, "The shower felt good. That hike was a great workout."

"It's one of my favorites." I continued, "I ran into Henry outside when I called for Spot. He had come up to check on me. He said Ace's paperwork was coming together. He was upbeat and told me he would fill me in tomorrow."

"That's wonderful. He's such a nice man. Will you let me know what he says?"

"Yeah, I will and yes, he's special." I went on, "I found some kind of ointment to put on your shoulder. Pop always keeps a sizeable first aid kit filled with all kinds of stuff."

She looked at the tube and said, "This is good stuff. We use it at the hospital. Would you mind putting it on for me?"

"Sure."

There was a little sleeve on her shirt and she rolled it back. I rested her left arm on my right shoulder and started massaging the ointment into her skin. "I can feel the pain, but I think it's only gonna be a bruise."

I said, "I sure hope it's nothing more serious." I wouldn't let my mind go down the road of how sensuous this felt. I said, "How is your friend Flo?"

She went into a short explanation of Flo's life and I did my best to pay attention. When she was finished, I stopped rubbing and said, "I hope that helps."

"I think it will. Thanks." She continued, "While you were showering, I took the liberty of going through the fridge and picking out some things for us to eat. It was easy since you and Ace will eat anything."

"Thanks. What would you like to drink? Henry gave me a couple bottles of wine - one red and one white."

"A glass of white would be nice. Thanks."

I poured her wine and got a beer. We ate on the back deck. It was a beautiful evening with a nice breeze.

We talked and laughed about more memories in high school and college. Near the end of the meal, I asked her if she wanted another glass of wine and she declined. We talked a little more and did the dishes. I asked, "Is there anyone you need to call to let know where you are?"

She laughed, "Jett, we're not in high school." She teased, "I could call my momma if that would make you feel better."

We laughed and she continued, "Last year after breaking off my engagement, I bought a little house on the outskirts of town and now live alone. No one is going to miss me unless I don't show up for work at seven in the morning."

I asked, "Do you always have to work on Saturday and Sunday?"

"No, we rotate once a month."

After the dishes, she asked, "Do you mind if we take a short walk? I ate too much and feel kind of bloated."

"Sure. That's fine. With the breeze, I don't think we'll need any bug spray."

We walked awhile in what felt like a comfortable silence. I noticed lately that I was getting more comfortable with silence around anyone. The sun had set but there was still some light. I looked over at her and tears were running down her cheeks.

I stopped and took her hand and we turned toward each other and I took her other hand and looked into her eyes and with as much seriousness as I could muster, I said, "Does your shoulder hurt that bad?"

She burst out laughing through her tears and started bawling. She put her arms around my neck and pressed close to me with her head resting on my chest and through her sobbing tried to get out the words, "Jett, I miss him so much!!"

As she continued to cry and I gently rubbed her back. It felt so good to have a woman in my arms even though this woman as the song goes "doesn't belong to me." I kept my composure and was proud of myself.

When she stopped crying, I asked, "Are you ready to go back?"

"Yes, I'm ready."

We walked arm in arm for the short distance. Spot followed close behind. She went to the bathroom and when she came back, she said she felt better. She thanked me for being understanding. She sat on the sofa and I sat in an easy chair next to the sofa. "I'll have that glass of wine now." I got her wine and me a beer.

"Jett, I have always thought of you as a brother and felt like we could talk about anything. I remember the many times I talked to you about Ace and me and the times you would talk to me about your girlfriends. We even talked about sexual problems or worries or questions. I always felt so comfortable with you and today was no different. It feels like we picked-up right where we left off three years ago."

"I feel the same way April."

She continued, "There's only one difference for me and I'm embarrassed to say it and even a little scared but I want to continue being open and honest with you."

I was starting to feel some anxiety but said gently, "What is it?"

"Well, remember the brother/sister part?"

"Yeah."

"Well, when you were holding me and comforting me a few minutes ago, I felt sexual toward you. To be more blunt, I wanted to have sex with you right then."

I got up and said, "Wow!" I walked away a few paces and turned to face her. "I don't know what to say." She started to say something, but then stopped and I said, "Well, I guess I do know what to say. I didn't have the nerve to tell you that I wanted to have sex with you as soon as I helped you off the ground this afternoon and knew you were all right. I have been fantasizing, but doing everything in my power to stay focused on other things."

I continued, "I know you love Ace and I love him too. I think we're both sexually vulnerable right now. How long has it been since you've had sex?"

She answered, "Over a year."

"It's been over three years for me. I've always thought of you as tremendously sexy, and I would be lying if I didn't tell you that I've always wanted to have sex with you and have fantasized about you many times. But I always knew even when you and Ace were separated and dating other people that I would never approach you because I always hoped you guys would get back together."

She replied, "I was thinking while in the bathroom, what if Ace doesn't want me? That seems like a real possibility at this point. So why not go ahead and see if Jett wants to do 'it'?" She hesitated and said, "I wrote a lot of letters to him, but I didn't get many back."

"April, it was a whole different world over there. I didn't write nearly as many letters as I should have. We were just trying to survive day to day."

She went on, "It sounds like you're making excuses for him. You always answered my letters and when I saw your Mom, she would say she had heard from you and would give me an update."

"It might help if you ask Ma how many letters she got from Ace. I found comfort in writing letters and as you know, Ace doesn't like to talk about feelings."

She said, "I don't know why I'm going on about this. We haven't been a couple for four years and why would he write to me when he knew I was dating other people? There is so much unresolved stuff between us. I have to face the reality that he might not wanna work it out or maybe he's not capable of working it out. And here I am thinking about asking you if you wanna have sex. What the hell is wrong with me?" Another pause and she laughed, "Well, do you?"

I sat back down in my chair and continued, "There's an old saying that I learned in one of my psychology classes. It went something like this. 'If you're thinking about doing something maybe you shouldn't do, play the tape forward.' So let's play the tape forward. How are we going to feel after it's over? Which one of us is going to tell Ace? Even if the evening is totally innocent, when I tell him about us spending this time together, what's he gonna ask?"

She replied, "Did you fuck her?"

"Exactly."

She said, "There's no way this would be anything but a disaster for all of us."

We sat in silence for a moment. She made a wise move and decided to change the subject and asked, "Can you tell me about this afternoon?"

I hesitated and then said, "Would you like another glass of wine?"

"Yes."

I came back with her wine and a beer for me. I took a couple of swallows and said, "One of the most difficult things about our healing will be talking about it and it's so hard and yet on the other hand, the thoughts are almost constantly intruding into our minds."

She said, "I don't wanna put any pressure on you, but maybe it would help you to talk and would help me to understand so I can help you all heal."

I sat there for awhile trying to figure out where to start and began to feel the anxiety. I took a couple more swallows of beer and could feel the tears welling up in my eyes. Damn, it was so close to the surface. I didn't mind crying in front of April. She had known me since I was a kid.

She said. "Jett come over here and lie down on the sofa and put your head in my lap."

I hesitated for a moment and then asked, "Face down or face up?"

We both laughed - me through my tears. She slapped me playfully on the side my head and said, "Jett Hollander, I'm trying to change the subject and you're not helping any. Lay your ass down."

I looked up at her. We were still smiling and she playfully slapped my cheek. "Bad boy!" I wanted to turn my head in toward her body and bury my face in her tummy and wrap my arms around her and feel safe and secure and be content to die right here.

She started lightly running her fingers through my hair and said, "Now close your eyes and try to relax."

I was thinking about how I could start this story and in that moment, I thought I could tell her anything and everything. "Do you mind if I start by telling you about Ranger School first?"

"You start anywhere you want."

I don't know if it was the beer or if it was April's soothing presence or some combination of the two, but I felt better in this moment than I had in years.

I told her about some of the experiences in Ranger School and what it was like preparing to go to war. I told her about Ace and me being wrapped in the poncho and our conversation about it at Walter Reed. I opened my eyes just a little and she had this big grin on her face. I was so relaxed. I went on with more stories and realized I was starting to get sleepy. I startled a couple of times when drifting off and she didn't say a word. She kept stroking my hair. I kept going and I must have fallen asleep because the next thing I knew, I was shifting positions on the sofa and realized that April was not there. Spot was at my feet curled up and dozing.

8

THANKFUL FOR HENRY

I sat up and stretched and looked at the clock. It was 1:34. I guessed she had just quietly left. I was aware in that moment that the cabin seemed empty. I missed her and wished I had a chance to say goodbye and to thank her for staying and being such a good friend. I wanted to thank her for wanting to have sex with me even though we both knew it would turn into a disaster. I was thinking I wished I had met her first and we had fallen in love. She was such a wonderful person. Then I realized I would have screwed that relationship up just like all the others.

Spot was wagging his tail and I let him out to pee and was surprised to see April's car still in the yard. I glanced over at Ace's bedroom door and it was closed. She had three glasses of wine and maybe was scared to drive. That was great for me, because I loved knowing she was still here. I felt comfortable again.

I let Spot in, made sure the cabin was secure, and went to bed. As usual, I laid there awhile and couldn't sleep. I thought about the evening and how nice it had been and then I thought about Ace. Would he be upset with us? What would he think about our sexual attraction? Had either one of us betrayed him in any way?

I eventually dropped off and woke up right on schedule at 0500. I thought I would be quiet, go on my run, wake her when I got back, and fix her something to eat.

I made a ssssshhhhh noise to Spot and slowly opened my bedroom door. I looked across the room and the bedroom door was open. I quickly looked around the room to see if she might be in the kitchen or on the sofa. The room was empty. I went to the window and looked and her car was gone. My heart sank for a moment. Then I let Spot outside. I went over to the kitchen to get a bottle of water and saw a note on the table.

"Hey Jett: I hope you don't mind I decided to sleep here. When you fell asleep, I realized I was also tired and a little tipsy from the wine. I woke up around 4:00 to pee and decided I felt clear enough to go home. I'm sorry for not saying goodbye. I had such a good time. You know my heart is with Ace, but I want you to know that I love you. You are precious to me beyond words. Yes, like a brother, best friend, confidant, etc. What happened last night in my view was normal and I'm not going to feel guilty or bad about it. I'm proud of both of us for being able to realize that to act on our desires could have been a disaster. I'm leaving my cell phone number and I still have the number at the cabin from the old days. Can we hang out again real soon? Love, A."

I smiled as I read. I couldn't wait to hang out with her again. I felt like in some kind of strange way when I put my head on her lap last night I was experiencing the beginning of my healing. I was also not going to feel guilty, deny, or repress my sexual desires for her. She would be one of my sexual fantasies and it was just fine. I was convinced that I could control myself around her and at some deeper level hoped I wasn't kidding myself.

I went on my run and felt better than I had since returning home. Spot had a ball. It was a gorgeous morning and I felt invigorated. When I got back to the cabin, I ate a snack and went back to bed and slept until around 9:00. Wow, I didn't think 0900. That was a good sign, but it would probably take some time to get back to "real world" time.

I started to clean the cabin, but there wasn't much to do. April had taken care of it. No empty beer bottles and the wine glass had been washed and put away. I went into Ace's bedroom and it was neat and tidy. I think she slept on top of the bedspread. The bathroom was also clean. The only evidence of her being there was a towel hanging over the shower rod and pee in the commode with some toilet paper. I figured she didn't flush because she was afraid it would wake me up. I was looking at the pee and closed my eyes imagining her naked ass on that toilet seat. My dick started getting hard.

I stripped down and turned on the shower. I closed my eyes and imagined her in the shower with me and I started taking care of business. I imagined she was behind me pressing her body against me and it was her hand jerking me off. And in what seemed like a short period of time, I reached the finish line while hollering, "April you do it so good, April you do it so good…."

I was exhausted with a big shit-eatin' grin on my face. I kneeled on the floor of the tub and let the water run over me until I finally got up and bathed. I used her towel to dry off. I peed in the toilet and didn't flush.

I ate something and then called Henry. I asked him if this was a good time for me to come down. He said that Betty was leaving in about thirty minutes to run some errands and asked if that would work for me. I said that would be fine and set the alarm for twenty-five minutes and passed out on the couch.

Henry was working outside when I reached his house. We greeted with our usual hug. He said, "Do you want some coffee or OJ?"

"No thanks, I'm fine. Is there something here I can do to help you?"

He smiled, "That would be great. Jim had one of the men at the mill deliver some wood for our fireplace. I have them dump it because I like to stack it myself. Good exercise."

"I'll be glad to help."

As we worked, he said, "I got the paperwork from Walter Reed and there were a few simple forms for both Dr. Collins and Dr. Kingston to fill out. Judy (Henry's secretary) took them over to their offices and they agreed to have them to me by noon Monday. Our part is looking good."

"I really appreciate your help," I said.

"You know I'm glad to do it. I'll give you a call on Monday after we've faxed the papers back to Personnel at Walter Reed."

"I'll try to get through to Ace when I get back to the cabin. He's gonna be one happy soldier."

He said, "I was surprised, but happy to see that you had a visitor last night."

I'm not sure what kind of expression I had on my face, but I was aware of feeling a little uncomfortable and wondered if Henry could sense that. "Yeah, do you remember April, Ace's old girlfriend?"

"Yes, I remember her. She's hard to forget."

"Yeah, she's beautiful."

"I saw something in the paper last year about her being engaged," he recalled.

"Yeah, she broke it off a couple of months before the wedding date."

"I would have hated to be the guy," he said.

"She said he was very upset and she felt terrible. She finally admitted to herself she had always loved Ace and was not gonna give up on him until she was sure there was no possible chance of them getting together."

Henry asked, "Do you think he still loves her?"

"I don't know. She wrote him a lot of letters while we were in the service and I think he might have written one or two to her. She wanted to visit him at Walter Reed and he told her not to come. Outwardly, he shows no interest. I can't get him to talk about it. He's good at hiding his feelings. I think he even hides them from himself so maybe he loves her and doesn't even know it."

He asked, "How do you feel about her?"

I was surprised by the question and a little embarrassed.

He noticed and quickly said, "Jett, maybe I shouldn't have asked that question."

"No Henry," I replied. "If I can't talk to you and Mom about these things, then there's no one I can talk to. Pop is older and I don't want to burden him. I haven't had sex in three years and she's about as sexy as they come. When I'm with her, I feel comfortable and safe, but I also feel horny." After a pause I said, "I have an idea you're about to tell me to go slow and be careful."

He smiled, "That's true and try the best you can to be clear about any decisions you make. Also, if you want to talk more about this, I'm always eager to listen and help if I can. I won't ask you about this again. You come to me if you want to talk, fair enough?"

I smiled back and agreed, "Yes. Thanks again for helping Ace and helping me."

"You're welcome," he replied. "I talked briefly to Dr. Kingston yesterday and based on what I told him, he is guessing you guys will have a lot of work to do over the coming months. He also said he wanted to meet with each one of you as soon as Ace returns."

"I'm nervous about getting started," I said. "But I know it's important to face this stuff right away. It's already imbedded deep enough. I worry about Ace. He's going to be in denial and will think he doesn't need any help. He has already told me he thinks all this PTSD stuff is bullshit."

"Jett, we were never able to convince your Dad that he needed help. I hope you will have better luck with Ace."

"Me too."

We finished stacking the wood and he said, "Jack and I are going to do the Glen Oak Falls trail around 2:00. Would you like to join us? It takes us about three hours. In the old days, I think Jack, Ace, you and I used to do it in about two and a half hours."

"Yeah, I remember," I said with a grin. "I'd like to go."

He said, "I told Jack I was going to ask you to join us and that we would meet him at the trail head. Let's hike over there from the cabin."

"Sounds good. See you around 1:30."

I had a message from Ace to call him back ASAP. He talked one of the nurses into letting me call one of the nurse's station numbers. Imagine that. Ace did have a way with women. I dialed the number and asked to speak to Sgt. Frost. I gave him the update on the progress on our end. He told me his primary doctor on the ward was in agreement and would fill out the necessary paperwork, giving his recommendation. Ace was excited and hopeful. I cautioned him to remember how the Army sometimes was unpredictable. He told me to thank Henry and said he was late for PT and had to run.

9
ANOTHER PANIC ATTACK

I was relieved he couldn't talk. I felt I needed to tell him about April's visit. He had not brought her up during any previous conversations since I left Walter Reed, but I did not want to keep this a secret. How much would I tell him? If I withheld certain details, I would be keeping a touchy secret. I have to talk with April. I wasn't going to say anything without her okay. Spot and I were about to close the door and the phone rang. "Hello."

"Hey, Jett."

"Hey, April. How's your shoulder?"

"It's better and you were right, there is a light bruise, but it doesn't hurt. How are you doing?"

"I'm okay. I was hoping you would call."

She said, "I'm on a short break and I want to say I am sorry I didn't get to say goodbye."

"That's fine. I got your note. I must have passed out. I didn't hear a thing."

"I tried to be quiet. I know you need your sleep."

"Thanks and thanks for cleaning up."

"You're welcome."

I filled her in on what Henry told me about Ace's application. She said, "That sounds great."

Then I told her about my conversation with Ace and the news that his MD was going to recommend approval of the request.

"Did you tell him about us?" she asked.

"No. I won't say anything to him without your okay. Also, he was in a hurry to hang up because he was late for PT. I was relieved. That was the first time I have ever felt uneasy while talking to him."

There was silence and this time it was not comfortable. Then we started to speak at the same time and I said, "You go ahead."

"This feels awkward," she said, "but can I come back to the cabin after I get off work?"

I felt a tingling in my groin. That was not a good sign, but I said, "Sure, I would love that."

I told her about my hiking plans and she said, "I get off about 3:30 so I can get in my workout. What time do you want me to come?"

I answered, "Would 6:00 be okay?"

"That's perfect. Do you want me to pick up anything on the way?"

I answered, "I'm not sure how much white wine is left. Other than that, I don't think we need anything unless there is something special you would like."

She continued. "I'll pick up a bottle of wine and some special cheese and bread at HGS (Jack's store). Do you have enough beer?"

"Yeah, that sounds good. I've got plenty of beer."

She said, "Gotta go, see you later."

Spot and I headed down the mountain to see Mom. Dad was still at work. The mill was open till 1:00 on Saturdays and sometimes they worked all day if they had a special job. As soon as I sat down, Journee jumped into my lap, started purring and closed her eyes. Mom and I had an easy mother-son chat. I gave her the latest on Ace. I told her April had come to the cabin as she suggested and I had been there when she arrived.

I didn't tell her about me being asleep on the ground and striking April. She was already worried enough. I wasn't ready to tell her more except it was nice having her there and it had made me feel better. She was happy for that.

Mom asked me if I would go to church with the family tomorrow and I said, "Mom, do you mind if I pass. I promise I'll go next Sunday."

"That's fine Honey," she said. "You start back when you're ready." Our family attended St Francis Episcopal Church in Harvest. Those who went to church usually sat together and then went to the Inn for lunch after church. Pop always picked up the bill.

I went over to the Inn to check on Pop. Sandra was at the front desk and gave me that big smile and said Pop was up in his apartment. He was reading a book of poetry. He could recite quite a few poems and always said poetry gave him a feeling of serenity. We talked for awhile and I bought him up to date on Ace. I mentioned that April had paid me a visit at the cabin.

He teased, "I thought we agreed no members of the opposite sex at the cabin." Then corrected himself and said, "Oh that's right, that was a rule when you were in high school. My, how time flies!"

Smiling, he continued, "April's real pretty. I remember that you and Ace and April spent a lot of time at the cabin during your college days."

"We sure did and those are some wonderful memories."

He asked, "Will I see you in church tomorrow?"

"Pop, I'm gonna pass tomorrow, but I told Mom I would be there next Sunday. Would you like to go on that walk around the reservoir tomorrow?"

"That would be nice," he replied. "As you know most everyone eats downstairs after church and then I come up here to rest for a couple of hours. How about coming by around 4:00?"

"I'll be here and will look forward to it. I want to thank you again for your generosity. I'm still overwhelmed with the idea the cabin will belong to me. It will always be a special place."

He said, "I know it will Son and that's important to me."

I went by to see Marge and she wasn't home. I should have called first. I would try to get her on the phone before going hiking. I picked up Spot and Mom gave me half an apple pie to take with me. Dad had gotten off and we chatted for a few minutes and I was off.

It was 1300 when I got back to the cabin. I called Marge. She answered and I gave her the update on Ace. She seemed pleased and then her voice trailed off. "Ma, what's wrong?"

"Jett, you know I can't wait for him to come home, but I'm still scared about what he'll be like. It was a strained visit with him at Walter Reed. He has changed. I know you warned me, but I'm apprehensive and nervous. I felt so helpless the other day. I didn't know what to say to him."

I responded, "I know. I wish I could make you feel better. I still think it would help if you and Mom talked. I know she's going through the same thing with me. Do you want me to ask her to call you?"

She replied, "No, that's all right. I'll call her. I do need someone to talk to and maybe we can help each other." She paused a moment and continued, "How have these last couple of days been for you?"

"I'm doin' pretty well. Hiking is helping and I'm trying to keep busy, but I still have my moments of anxiety and I get startled easily." I decided not to go into any more of my symptoms. She didn't need too many details.

I added, "April came up yesterday afternoon to see me and talk about Ace."

"Yes, I've had a number of talks with April. She loves him very much. I don't know what to say to her Jett. I have no idea how Ace feels about her. I did ask him during our visit if he had heard from her and he was not responsive. I didn't pursue it."

"He also doesn't talk much to me about her. He said he heard she was dating someone and acted like he didn't care. At times I'll push it and he'll say, 'I don't wanna talk about it'."

She said, "We both know how he keeps things to himself."

"It's always been hard to know what he's thinking or feeling and it's even more difficult now."

"Sweetie, I need to run. Keep me posted and let me know when you find out if the request is approved. Love you."

"You too Ma."

I looked at the clock and remembered Henry would arrive in ten minutes. I grabbed a couple bananas and changed into hiking gear. Not long after that, Spot was barking and wagging his tail. The weather was nice with a gentle breeze and some clouds. There was little humidity and it seemed like a perfect day for hiking. In about thirty minutes, we reached the trail head and Jack was standing there with a big grin on his face. He and Henry had their walking sticks and we each had a small back pack with water and snacks. The trail started with a moderate incline for approximately half a mile. Even though we were in good shape, we were breathing deeper than usual. As the trail leveled off, I felt some pressure in my chest and was short of breath. Was this the start of another panic attack? I was starting to feel dizzy."

Jack looked back at me and said, "Jett, are you all right?"

I was starting to gasp for air and felt faint. They both knew I had a history of panic attacks and helped me to the ground. Jack's brother, Matt had suffered from panic disorder and he was familiar with the symptoms and the treatment. They quickly helped me take off my back pack and had me lay with my head a little lower than the rest of my body. Spot was licking the top of my head and Jack started talking to me in this soothing voice,

"Jett, look at me. I want you to focus your eyes on this spot right between my eyes. That's right just keep staring at it and listen to my voice. Henry and I were on this same trail last year and we came upon a black bear with two little cubs trailing behind her. We must have been upwind from her because she had not yet seen us. Keep focusing right here." He pointed to the spot between his eyes. "And we started slowly moving in a direction away from the bear...."

He kept telling the story of how the bear eventually spotted them as they were moving away. She must have sensed they were no threat to her cubs because she kept moving in the other direction. He went on about how fortunate they were and then I had calmed down and the panic passed. Jack continued the directions, "Now drink some water and eat some crackers. Take your time."

Henry looked at Jack and said, "I'm impressed Dr. Hollander."

"Me too," I said.

"No big deal. Matt's psychologist taught us that technique during a family session. All of us had to use it with Matt over the years so I've had practice."

I asked, "How's Matt doing now?"

"He hasn't had a panic attack in years and he still uses deep breathing techniques and other skills he learned in his therapy."

"I didn't have that many bad attacks, but I sure could have used the therapy to learn those skills," I said. "Does he have to take medication?"

"No, but he keeps these two little pink pills with him everywhere he goes. He calls them his 'safety net.' He took them part of the time during his therapy. He says they help relax his mind and body."

I said, "It's puzzling that these last few attacks have come out of the blue. There's no reason for me to panic. Before the Army, they would have been triggered by public speaking and sometimes girls." That got a laugh.

Jack said, "I know these attacks leave you exhausted. Henry, the Chestnut Trail we intersect ahead leads back toward the cabin, right?"

"It sure does. It takes about forty minutes and then we connect with the Ridge Trail which is about five minutes from the cabin."

Jack looked at me, "Are you up for that?"

"Sure, I feel better now. I can make it." So we waited another fifteen minutes and before long we were walking up the steps of the front deck. They came in and we had a beer and sat on the front deck and chatted for awhile. They asked me what I was doing the rest of the day. I told them I was going to pass out on my bed and April was coming around 6:00 and we were gonna eat supper together.

They smiled and Jack said, "Sounds like fun."

"I'm looking forward to it. It helps to keep my mind off stuff."

They mapped out another trail that would take about two hours. They declined another beer, gave me a hug and left.

10

THE DECISION

I secured the door, went into the bedroom followed by Spot and passed out. The next thing I knew, Spot was bounding off the bed and barking. My startle was not as intense this time. I assumed that was a good sign. I guess I had slept heavily because I felt groggy as I crossed the room to the door.

"Hey, Jett." April smiled and gave me a quick kiss on the cheek and headed toward the kitchen. She was wearing a black pair of pants that came down several inches below her knees. She had on a sleeveless white blouse and a pair of black flip flops with some kind of sequins on the straps.

As I followed her, I couldn't keep my eyes off her ass even though the pants were not tight or invitingly sensual. April's ass looked sensual in anything. As she began unloading the bag and putting something into the fridge, I asked, "How's your shoulder?"

"It's fine. There never was any swelling. You can hardly see the bruise and I have no pain,"

"I'm glad to hear that. I felt bad."

"It's all right Jett."

I asked, "How was your day?"

"Fine. We weren't too busy, but there was plenty to do. How was your day?"

"Not bad."

She frowned a little, "That doesn't sound too good. I want you to tell me all about it, but first, do you want a beer?"

"Yes thanks. How about you?"

"I think I'll have a glass of wine."

I offered, "Would you like me to open the bottle you brought?"

"No, I'll just have another glass of the wine we opened last night. Would you like some cheese and bread now?"

"Would you mind if we waited a while?"

"No, that's fine."

She sat on the sofa, kicked off her flip flops, and put her legs under her. I sat in the chair next to the sofa. It was a comfortable arrangement. I had to turn my head about thirty degrees to look at her. She had to do the same. I'm not sure why that was more comfortable. I guess it had to do with last night. I was never aware in the past of being the least bit uncomfortable around April.

She reached over and gently patted my hand in a kind of motherly gesture and said, "Tell me about your day."

I gave her a quick rundown of my day and told her about the panic attack.

She said, "I can't imagine how scary that must be."

"Yeah, it's like I'm out of control and can't get my breath." I told her what Jack did to help me.

"That's awesome. How did he know what to do?"

"His brother Matt suffered from panic attacks as a child and the therapist taught the family some ways to help him."

"That was really fortunate for you that he was there. What do you do when you're alone?"

I replied, "The only choice is to ride 'em out."

She asked, "How does that work`?"

I answered, "The only thing I know to do is keep telling myself, 'I'm okay, just calm down.' I keep saying that over and over."

"Are panic attacks part of the PTSD?"

"I think panic is a separate diagnosis, but it's related. It's strange. I use to have a milder form of panic when I was in high school and college."

"I never knew that," she said with a surprised look on her face.

"I know. I didn't tell many people. I was too embarrassed. I didn't want people to think I was crazy. The strange thing is that I never had a panic attack while I was in the Army. I had my first one in years as I was leaving Walter Reed on Monday. Then I had another one the next day on my way here while sitting in a restaurant. I've had a couple more since I got home and then today."

"So you think it's related to the PTSD?"

"Yes, I think it has to be. Don't get me wrong, I've had plenty of anxiety both while in the Army and since being discharged last week, but a panic attack is very different."

She said, "I can see that."

"I'm puzzled why these recent attacks are coming out of the blue. All my previous ones before the Army were more situational. I'm hoping Dr. Kingston can help me understand what's going on."

She asked, "What kind of situations?"

I explained about the public speaking and girls.

She smiled, "I would have never suspected you were that nervous around girls. You always seemed shy, but not nervous."

"I was fine around you because you were Ace's girlfriend. I was terrified of the girls I was attracted to and who were available."

She smiled and I continued, "I don't think I've ever told anyone else this, not even Ace, but I used to sit by the phone for hours trying to get up the nerve to call one of those girls."

This time she laughed, "I'm sorry Jett, I shouldn't laugh."

"That's okay. It's funny now, but at the time it was miserable."

"Are you still nervous around those attractive and available girls?"

"Well, I haven't had much practice in the last three years, but I didn't feel that as much while in college so I think I may have grown out of it. In college, I had the problem that you asked me about last night. I never stayed in a relationship for long. I either broke it off or the girl broke it off. I remember always being relieved that it was over."

"I wonder why you were relieved."

"I think I may have been looking for the perfect girl. Of course no one I was dating ever measured up to that standard." I paused, looked at her and smiled, "Maybe I thought the perfect girl was already taken."

I looked at her and she was looking down. I said, "You've set the bar really high. Do you think I'll ever find that perfect woman?"

She answered, not looking at me, "Yes, you will. She may not be perfect, but she will be perfect in your eyes."

We sat in silence for a few minutes and then she asked, "Do you feel nervous around me right now?"

I paused and she interjected, "I'm sorry that wasn't a fair question. I need to tell you first I'm feeling nervous around you."

I said, "I have to confess I was really hoping you would call me. I don't know. Was I afraid to call you? Was the old fear creeping back in? I don't think so. It was like I needed to hear your voice and unless you were the one reaching out, it wouldn't be the same. I don't like the way that sounds, but it's true. It was like if you called I could fantasize that you wanted to hear my voice as much as I wanted to hear yours."

She smiled, "You still didn't answer my question."

I joked, "What was your question? Now I remember. Let me think, am I nervous around you? Yes, I would have to say I'm definitely nervous around you right now. Would you like another glass of wine?"

"No thank you, but I would like a bottle of water." I got her a bottle of water and a beer for me.

"Jett, I've been trying to sort out in my mind what happened last night. The head nurse on our floor caught me in deep thought and said, 'April are you with us or are you somewhere else?' I brushed it off, but she was right. I can't do that at work. There are too many details involved in taking care of our patients, but I can tell you all through my exercise I thought of nothing else."

She smiled and continued, "Yes, I wanted to hear your voice and I wanted to come back here to see you. And I still want to have sex with you, but I don't like that phrase. Then I thought, do I mean I want to make love to you? There is that word, but I love Ace."

She went on, "I wondered if making love to you is the closest I can get to making love to him. After all, you guys are practically 'joined at the hip.' I'm sorry. That wasn't nice. I would be using you and..."

I quickly cut her off. "April, it's okay. This is all new to us and it's complicated

I continued, "I think it's important that we try to figure it out and I don't think we can do it unless we're honest with each other."

She said, "I know but I don't want to hurt you."

I said, "Please, let's be honest."

"All right."

I smiled and said, "Okay, I guess we are 'joined at the hip' and I can understand what you mean by making love to me would be the closest thing to making love to him." I thought for a minute, "I am confused with the word love. I told you yesterday that I'd always considered you to be Ace's girlfriend and would never allow myself to think of you in any other way. I couldn't let myself even think about loving you."

I continued, "So what's up with this intense desire to have sex with you? Is it just physical or is there some kind of strong denial mechanism that won't let me face the reality that I have always loved you? As I said a few minutes ago, is that the reason I could never love anyone else?"

We sat in silence for awhile, each with our own thoughts. Then we both looked at each other about the same time and grinned.

She said, "To be continued, how about some cheese and bread?"

"Sounds good to me. I've got an idea. Let's take it up to the rock and eat it there and then take a short hike to work up an appetite for supper."

"I like that idea. I've gotta' pee."

"Me too."

We packed the picnic basket with the bread, cheese, wine for her and a beer for me. Spot was excited about the walk. He had been asleep on the other end of the couch since we sat down.

It was approximately a five minute walk to the rock. The view as usual was magnificent and the sun was about an hour from setting. We sat with our backs to the sun and enjoyed some light conversation and the food and drink. We gave Spot an occasional morsel.

Our hike lasted almost an hour and was more like one of Pop's walks through the woods. The trail was wide and we were able to walk side by side. There was one place in the trail that narrowed a bit, forcing us to walk for a few yards with our shoulders almost touching.

At some point in those few moments, our hands touched and I don't think either one of us was aware of exactly how it happened, but when we emerged from that narrow place on the trail, we were holding hands. It seemed perfectly natural.

We talked the whole hour and there never seemed to be any silence. My nerves settled and she seemed relaxed. We were comfortable together and whenever we had been alone for whatever reason, we never lacked for something to say.

I couldn't tell you much of what we talked about. There was only the feeling of being peaceful and feeling close to this person I had known for years. I didn't care about anything else right now except enjoying the moment.

We stopped at the rock to watch the sunset and pick up the basket. Somewhere right before the rock, I was aware that she gently slipped her hand out of mine.

We sat close to one another, watching the beauty of what was unfolding on the horizon. This time we sat in silence in our own way paying homage to the miracle in front of us. After awhile she turned to me and asked, "Are you hungry?"

"Yes. How about you?"

"I'm hungry too." We gathered our things and headed to the cabin.

We were in the kitchen putting supper together when the phone rang. It startled me and I jumped. We looked at one another. Both of us were a little flushed thinking it might be Ace.

I hesitated thinking I won't answer it, but then I went over and picked it up. It was Mom and she was checking on me. We chatted for a few minutes and I told her April and I were fixing supper. She was glad April was here and would talk to me tomorrow.

April asked, "You were thinking the same thing. Right?"

"Yeah."

"What if it was him? What would you have said?"

"I don't know. We talk at least a couple of times a day and I've only talked to him once today. The chances of him calling sometime this evening are pretty high."

She asked, "You think?"

"Yeah."

I took another swig of beer and she sipped on her wine and asked, "What do you think about me calling him?"

"It makes me nervous."

"Frankly, I'd like to have it behind us. I don't want us to spend the evening thinking at any moment he could call."

She said, "What if you didn't answer it?"

"That feels like it would be the beginning of lying."

"So how much do you tell him?" she asked.

"Everything except our conversations about sex."

She continued cutting up veggies for our salad and asked, "How much do we actually owe him? I love him, but he has given me no signs over the last four years that he gives a shit. He won't talk to you about it. You said yesterday, probably to make me feel good, you think he still loves me, but you don't know. There's no indication that he does."

She was right, but I shifted the conversation, "What about my relationship with him? He's my best friend. Then I wonder if his problems with you are related to the war. So maybe he's just confused and doesn't realize how much he loves you."

She interjected, "But he showed no interest in me the entire year before you all left for the Army and you didn't go to war for another four or five months after you left here."

I asked, "Are we considering the idea we don't owe him any explanation or have any obligation to tell him about our conversations?"

She replied, "I don't feel like I owe him anything. But you might be able to make the case before being intimate with his old girlfriend, not to say that we're going to be intimate, you would want to ask if it's all right with him."

"Yes, if we were going to be intimate, that would make me feel better."

She grinned and said, "So you could call him and say, 'April and I are thinking about fucking, would you have any objections?'"

I grinned back and asked, "Are we thinking about fucking?"

With great indignation in her voice, she said, "How dare you!" And threw the little bit of wine left in her glass in my face. And it must have been my expression because she burst out laughing and kept on laughing. I recovered quickly and sloshed some beer in her face. Then I burst out laughing and I was attempting to pour the rest of the beer over her head and we were in a shoving match each pushing the other and laughing.

As the laughing started to die down, we looked into each others eyes and I reached over and got a dish towel and started gently patting her face and neck. She then took it from me and did the same.

"Oh Jett," she said with tears welling up in her eyes, "Where is this leading?"

I took her in my arms and held her gently as I had done in the past years when she would start crying over some problem or argument she was having with Ace. We stood there only for a few moments and she said, "I have my gym bag in the car with an extra blouse. I'll go get it and change."

"Okay." I changed my tee-shirt.

I was in the kitchen when she came out of her bedroom. She was smiling. "Sorry I took so long. I had to take a sponge bath. Beer is sticky. I'm just glad you didn't get any in my hair."

She flushed a little and continued, "I didn't have an extra sports bra and I'm telling you because I didn't want you to think I was not wearing a bra on purpose."

It was my turn to flush a little as I glanced at her breasts. I admitted, "I'm not sure what to say. I could say that's fine or not to worry about it or no problem or I like you better without a bra or I promise not to stare or...."

She held up her hand and said, "Stop, stop. It's okay you don't respond at all."

"Thanks. I'm relieved." While buttering the bread and keeping my eyes on what I was doing, I continued, "Does that mean that I can't stare even if I've decided that I would now like to respond by asking, 'Do you mind if I stare?'" She picked up a dish towel and threw it at me.

We finished getting our supper ready, and ate on the front deck. We both had water, commenting that more beer and wine was not a good idea. At this point, neither one of us was particularly hungry as we picked at our food taking small bites and chewing more than necessary and washing it down with water.

I said, "Not that we've decided to make love or have sex. But if we did, what's your thought about condoms?"

"I've had sex with two people since Ace and I broke up. The first person was soon after Ace and I broke up. It happened only one time and I insisted on a condom. The second person was my fiancée. We had sex about a dozen times and in the beginning, I insisted on a condom. But, as it got closer to our wedding date, I relented and we didn't use one. What about you?"

"Well, as I told you I haven't had sex in three years. Before that, I had sex with about a half dozen people and I always wore a condom. I was terrified of the girl getting pregnant and that also reduced the risk of STD's."

She asked, "So if we were to have sex, would you want to wear a condom?"

"I admit that I'd be fearful about you getting pregnant."

"What if I told you I just finished my period two days ago.?"

I replied, "I would vote for no condom. How about you?"

"I would vote the same way."

She continued, "We talked a little while ago about being honest. Are we seriously thinking about having sex? All right. Again, that's not fair. I'm so horny I can hardly stand it, but I'm scared of the consequences."

"I feel the same way."

She said, "We're on dangerous ground and I don't know if it's a done deal or not, but the most pressing issue for me at this moment is the telephone call either to Ace or from Ace. I'm leaning toward you calling him. Are you leaning in any particular direction?

I replied, "Yes, I would rather call him."

"What are you going to say to him?"

"I thought I would tell him that you are here and we just had supper and we wanted to call and check on him."

She asked, "What if he starts asking you questions?"

"We don't have anything to hide except our conversations about sex. If he asks, 'Have you all fucked or are you going to fuck?' I'll say no because neither one of us has said, 'let's fuck.' This is getting fucking complicated and I don't wanna think about it anymore. I want you so badly I can hardly stand it. That's all I can think about right now."

I took a deep breath and went on, "Back to the conversation with Ace. I would also like to say that you would like to say 'Hey.' How do you feel about talking to him?"

She hesitated, "I'm not comfortable. Our last conversation was strained, but I'll do it if he will talk to me."

I asked, "What do you say about making the call now?"

"That's fine. Give me a couple of minutes to get my composure."

We picked at our food a little longer and then she said, "I'm ready."

We went inside and I dialed the number to the nurses' station.

He was on the phone within a minute. I said, "Hey man, what're you doin'?"

He said, "Watchin' a ball game. What are you doin'?"

"I'm at the cabin. April is here and we wanted to call and check in."

"What are you all doin'?"

"Well, we went on a short hike after she got here. We just finished eating and were sitting here trying to figure your ass out. You got any recent insights that might help?"

"No."

"I didn't think so. Well, keep us in the loop if any insights pop up. Everything is looking good for Monday. I'm gonna leave here Thursday so I can be there early Friday morning. If everything goes good with the board, start using some of your irresistible charm and fix it so we can get out of there early AM instead of noon."

He replied, "Good luck on that one."

"I know, but at least try. Also, think about whether you wanna take one or two days comin' back. We can talk about it tomorrow. Ma will wanna know."

He said, "Tell her I don't want a party."

"For god's sake Ace, tell her yourself. It's gonna have to come from you."

"Jett, I just can't handle it."

"I understand, but you have to be the one to explain it to her."

He said, "But it would be better comin' from you."

"We can talk about it tomorrow. April wants to say hey. I'll call you in the morning."

I handed her the phone and gestured that I was going outside. Spot followed me to the front yard. I picked up a stick and threw it for Spot to retrieve. After about five minutes, April came out the front door and put her arm around the support and leaned against it with a far away look in her eyes. I asked, "How'd it go?"

"Same old, same old! It's been the same for four years. Uncomfortable, strained, distant. It would be different if this happened after you guys left, but as I said earlier, it was this way a year before you left. Who am I kidding? He doesn't care about me. I don't know how long it's gonna take me to get it."

She turned, started stacking the dishes and plates and took them inside. I picked up the remainder of the stuff and followed her into the kitchen.

I said, "Just put them in the sink. I can get them later. Would you like wine?"

"Yeah, I think I need it this time. Thanks." I poured her wine and got a beer. I secured the front door and felt safe knowing Spot would perform his usual watch dog duties. We sat down and she asked. "What did he say when you told him I was here?"

"He didn't act surprised or upset. But, you know how he is. You never know. He just wanted to know what we'd been doing."

She said, "I think I've been living some kind of fantasy or maybe a fairy tale. In the back of my mind, I thought we would come to our senses and figure out a way we could be together. He was always my hero. He was so good at everything he did and so handsome. I loved being on his arm everywhere we went."

She changed the subject and told me some about her ex-fiancée, "He was nice looking, had a bright and successful future and he treated me like a princess." She went into more details about how they met and what she liked and disliked about him. "Mostly, he was a real good guy."

I asked, "Do you ever hear from him?"

"Occasionally, he'll call me. He works in Winston-Salem and travels up here on business about once a month. We usually go out to eat, but there is nothing there for me."

She started to tear up again. I said, "Scoot over." I sat sideways next to her on the sofa and said, "It's my turn. Look at me." She turned and I reached up behind her head and undid her pony tail band and fluffed out her hair. It felt soft and came down to her shoulders. "OK, head on my lap."

She smiled through her tears and said, "Face up or face down?"

"You're as much a smart ass as me."

"I'm not that bad," she said and laid back. Spot jumped off the end of the sofa and moved to my vacated chair. I reached over and turned the three-way bulb down to low. She closed her eyes and I gently moved her hair so it was out from under her head. I ran my fingers through her hair and gently massaged her scalp. She gave a little moan and said, "That feels nice."

"Good, just relax." I thought it would be good for both of us to have some time to think and reflect. At least I needed it and maybe she did too. I was looking down at her. She was so beautiful and her body was out of a Playboy magazine. I know it's a cliché, but this woman is even more beautiful on the inside than on the outside.

I was trying not to look at her breasts, but I couldn't help myself. I could almost see her nipples through her blouse and I couldn't tell for sure, but they looked erect. I wanted her more than I could put in words. I wondered to myself if it was true that I have always loved her and that love kept me from finding anyone else.

I lightly touched her face, making little circles. First I touched her forehead, then around her eyes, nose, mouth and cheek bones.

My fingers moved around and under her chin and she whispered, "That feels nice too."

In that moment, I thought maybe I did love her and maybe I had loved her for a long time.

Perhaps I had never been able to face it or admit it. She always belonged to Ace and regardless of what happened between them, she would never be mine. Was it possible she could be mine? Was it possible some day she could love me?

Was it really true that Ace no longer loved her? He sure acted like he didn't, but he was so good at hiding his feelings. But, if he loved her, would he have gone four years without trying to patch things up? Even though he didn't show his feelings, would he have kept that love bottled up all these years? Did I owe it to him to tell him I might love April, and I wanted to have sex with her? No, not have sex. I wanted to make love to her. This is starting to seem like rationalization. Am I talking myself into something that I might regret?

She opened her eyes and lazily whispered, "I've gotta' pee. Don't go anywhere."

I watched her walk to the bedroom door and disappear. I leaned my head back and took a deep breath. I didn't know what was going on with April, but in my mind I had reached the point no return. If she was willing, I was going to make love to her.

11
ECSTASY IN THE MOMENT

I looked around as she came out of the bathroom and she had changed clothes. She was in a large light green tee-shirt with lounging sweat pants. They were a cream color with a pattern of little flowers. They were baggy and made of a thin material like silk. She asked, "May I lay my head in your lap again? That felt so good."

"Sure." I started moving my fingers through her hair and then tracing outlines around her face. She closed her eyes and shifted around getting more comfortable. I couldn't make out her breasts as well with the tee-shirt, but the way she was stretched out pulled the material of her sweat pants close around her skin. The material clung to her skin and I could see the outline of her long legs and the v shape between her legs.

Let's face it. Most of us guys are gross. It's a shame that I can't think of the space above and around her privates as anything other than what I had gotten use to calling it in the Army - pussy. If I was being more respectful, what would I call it? Private parts seemed a little childish, but that was certainly better than the other label. Vaginal triangle seemed kind of cold. Genitalia seemed kind of clinical.

I said softly, "April?"

She groaned a little and whispered, "What?"

"I have a question for you."

Softly she said, "All right, as long as you don't stop what you're doing."

"I won't. I promise. This is not meant to be a personal question, but I guess it's a little personal. I was trying not to stare at your body, but I was not being successful. I was admiring your legs and then my eyes moved up toward you know, that area between your legs."

She opened her eyes and tried to look serious, but still whispered, "Yes, go on."

"Well I didn't know what to call it. Us guys have some names, but they're all disrespectful. So if I were to give you a compliment and say you have a nice, attractive, sensual, you know, what would I call it?"

She smiled and closed her eyes and whispered, "I've never thought about it and I'm enjoying this too much to think about it now. So until I come up with something, you have my permission to call it anything you want."

I said softly, "Okay. Thanks. Until I can think of something more respectful, I will refer to it as 'down there.' Now, I'll keep doing what I'm doing and you just relax."

A little time passed and she whispered, "That feels so good."

"I'm glad."

A little more time and then I asked softly, "April?"

"Uh-huh."

"I just want you to know you have beautiful legs, a sensuous down there, and amazing breasts."

She interjected softly, "You can say boobs."

"Okay, thanks. Let me start over."

She interrupted, "No, just start with boobs again."

"Okay, you have amazing boobs and the face of a Greek goddess."

She whispered, "Thank you. That was sweet." She then raised her left arm over her head and rested it on the sofa arm. With her right hand, she took my right hand and guided it under her tee-shirt and raised her right arm and rested it by her left arm.

I began to trace light circles around her left boob and kept gently touching her face with my left hand. I was careful not to touch her nipple, but was getting closer with every circle.

She whispered, "Would you help me take off my tee-shirt?"

I gently helped her ease it over her head. She put her arms behind her head again as if she were pushing her boobs up toward my circling fingers. I could use both hands now still circling both boobs and occasionally lightly brushing over her nipples which were erect and hard.

She murmured, "That feels so good."

My fingers also wandered all around her chest, under arms, and arms. This morning I had thought about cutting my finger nails and was so glad I hadn't gotten around to it. They protruded just enough to increase the sensation.

My right hand continued to move over her upper body as my left hand wandered to the palm of her left hand. Her fingers were loosely closed and I took my middle finger and gently entered her hand and pulled my finger slowly in and out lightly brushing her palm with my fingernail. She made a little pulsating movement lightly encircling my finger as it moved in and out.

Then I gently withdrew my finger and with all fingernails barely touching her arm, slowly moved my hand down to her boobs. Simultaneously, my right hand journeyed down to make little circles around her belly button and then turning my hand over I moved it lower down her body until I reached the waistline of her pants and panties.

I gently lifted the lining of both and lightly moved the back of my fingers from one side of her body to the other. By this time I was getting some soft moans and her breathing rate picked up. The fingers on my left hand were busy moving with intermittent light tugs on her nipples.

I moved my fingers from underneath the hem of her pants and panties and barely brushed the top of her pubic hair area on the outside of her pants as I moved my hand slowly down her right leg. I thought

I detected a slight tightening of her ass and upward movement as I passed over that area.

After moving my fingers down her right leg, I brought them back onto her left leg. As my hand moved up her thigh, she lifted her ass slightly off the sofa. I took both hands and slide her pants down over her ass and down below her knees being careful to leave her panties in place. Then she lifted her left leg and pushed them the rest of the way off of her legs.

Her panties were white with little pink flowers. Nothing sexy in the shape or material, but on her they radiated sensuality. My dick was hard as a rock and I was glad it was between my legs. Otherwise she would have had a rod sticking into the back of her neck.

As far as I could tell, her eyes were closed. She whispered a little out of breath, "More. It feels so good."

I continued to move my left hand all over her upper body using her boobs as a focal point. That hand seemed to know what to do without me consciously directing it. My right hand was moving up and down her legs, moving from the front of her legs to the outside of her legs and back and forth with light strokes. Then as inconspicuously as possible, I took two fingers and starting as close to her feet as I could reach, I moved them slowly down the crevice where her legs came together and stopped a few inches from her panties.

Then I moved them over and around the front and sides as I worked my way down toward her feet. Then back again along the crevice. The first time, her legs seemed a little tense. This time the skin was softer and a little more relaxed so I lightly brushed her panties. The next time, she started spreading them just a little. I could feel the heat and moisture as my fingers didn't slide as easily.

Each time she spread them a little more until I could see the sofa between her legs and each time I brushed lightly the area where I could feel the slit in her panties. I would start low down toward her ass and move my finger up to her clit and barely touch it.

She pulled her feet a little toward her ass so that her knees were slightly bent and at the same time opened her legs a little more. Now I was moving my fingers on the insides of her legs and when I got to her panties, I traced my finger around the edges and then up the slit. I continued to move along the inside of her thighs.

She was letting me know through her moans and increased breathing rate that she liked what I was doing. It seemed like each time I moved my hand back toward her feet, she would move her feet closer to her ass and spread a little more. I could move my hand easily along her inner thighs and under her leg and each time I reached her panties, I would go through the same teasing drill.

The next time I moved down her legs, she brought her feet up as far as she could move them and put her feet so that the bottoms were pressing against each other. She couldn't spread any wider than that. I focused all the attention of my fingers on her inner thighs and on the outside of her panties circling her clit in the same way I had done with her nipples.

Her breathing was more rapid and I kept moving my fingers around her inner thighs, sometimes slightly slipping underneath the edge of the panties and focusing on her clit with more light brushing strokes. Even though the panties were between my finger and her clit, it must have felt good because she started some slow gyrating moves with more moans.

Without warning, she opened her eyes and grabbed my tee-shirt, roughly pulling it over my head. She threw her arms around my neck and pulled herself up. She pressed her mouth on mine, her tongue wildly thrashing inside my mouth. My tongue and mouth met hers with equal passion. We continued searching with our tongues for more and more intimacy.

She held her legs spread by lifting her left leg straight up in the air. I continued to touch and tease the best I could.

We panted heavily and she ordered, "Take off my panties!" She lowered her leg and I reached around behind her ass and jerked and pulled and she moved and twisted her legs until we got them off.

Our tongues were still thrashing around, and she tightened her left arm around my neck. With her legs, she lifted her ass up. She reached down with her right hand and pulled my shorts down. I had anticipated and arched my back and pushed while she was pulling.

Meantime, my hard dick had popped out of hiding and was turning out to be an obstacle. We were pushing and tugging and my dick wanted those pants off more than any of the rest of us. It was holding on like a steel rod. Finally I gasped, "Lift up a little more!" I was able to get my pants over the protruding obstacle.

We kept kissing as I sat up a little higher and she was on me in an instant. She took my dick in her right hand and raised her ass up so she could lightly rub the tip of my dick on any area between her legs that felt good. I could feel the heat and understood better than ever before the term "hot woman."

She was moist and moved my dick around and then inside her a little and then out again. Our tongues were still engaged and we breathed heavily and moaning. It felt so damn good.

Then I thought, "Don't cum, not yet. It will spoil everything. Quick, think of something else. What the fuck can I think about? Don't say fuck."

My thoughts were interrupted with louder moans and she blurted out, "Jett, I want you to fuck me now, fuck me now Jett!" She lowered herself onto my throbbing dick and I was thrusting upward as far as I could and she was moving back and forth and up and down when she started coming. I let go and we reached the ecstasy of the finish line with moans and muffled screams.

She collapsed on me, resting her head on my shoulder. Still out of breath, she managed to say, "I needed that. Oh how I needed that!!!"

My arms were wrapped around her. I scooted my ass forward on the sofa and whispered in her ear, “See if you can move your legs so you can wrap them around me.”

“All right,” she said softly into my ear and still a little out of breath. I moved forward a little more and I don’t know where I got the strength, but I was able to stand up with my arms still wrapped around her back and I carried her into my bedroom. I sat down on the bed and whispered in her ear, “Lay on top of me.” We shifted and maneuvered until she was comfortably with her head resting on my chest. I wanted to feel all her weight on me.

She whispered, “Jett, did you hear me say I needed that?”

“Yes.”

“Did you hear me say it was wonderful?”

“I don’t think I heard that.”

“Well, it was wonderful.”

I said, “It was for me too.”

12
A NIGHTMARE

We must have passed out shortly after that because the next thing I knew, I was thrashing, kicking, and was having trouble breathing and screaming, "Let me outta here. Let me go. I'm innocent!"

Through the horror, I heard someone yelling, "Jett, wake up. Jett wake up."

I opened my eyes and with the light filtering in through the door, I could make out April standing naked beside my bed.

As soon as she determined I was at least partially awake, she quickly moved beside me and wrapped her arms around me and pressed her body against mine. She started gently rocking me, running a hand through my hair and whispering over and over in my ear, "It's all right, it's all right. You just had a bad dream. You're here with me. It's all right."

I was drenched in sweat and still shaking, but in a matter of minutes was able to calm down. She continued to hold me and run her hand through my hair and then softly said, "Wow that was really bad. Do you remember any details?"

I hesitated and hoarsely said, "There wasn't much to it, but it scared the shit out of me. All I remember is I was captured by some terrorists and they were going to execute me. One of the guards kept spitting on me."

I recovered a little more and said, "I'm okay now. I'm sorry. I've gotten you all wet."

"That's all right. Are you sure you're okay?"

"Yeah, I'm fine."

There was just enough light for me to see that she looked away and seemed to be hesitating, but said, "Could we take a shower together?"

Talk about motivation for a quick recovery, I said, "Sure, I would like that."

I had discovered by now that there was no hair in the area we guys use to describe as "wool." I was not surprised as I had heard from my buddies that more and more women preferred to be shaved. Around the barracks, the guys who preferred shaved outnumbered those that didn't about two to one. I was in the majority group.

As we ran the water, she said, "I've never seen you naked and you've never seen me naked, but I feel so comfortable right now."

"Me too. However, I'd have to say that I've seen you naked several hundred times in my fantasies."

I leaned over to check the temperature of the water and she slapped me crisply on the ass and said, "Bad boy!

I stepped aside to let her in the shower first and slapped her equally hard on her ass and said, "Bad girl!"

The showers doubled as a bathtub and were fairly small. When I stepped in, she was already under the water and pulled me to her and kissed me. We stood there kissing as water ran down over us so that we were at times having to come up for air. As she pushed me away from her, she said, "That's your quota of kisses for the moment." And then handed me the soap and she commanded, "Wash me from head to toe."

"I'm not your slave!"

"All right, I'll..."

I interrupted, "Correction, I am you slave. Do you want a wash cloth?"

She gave me a dreamy, sexy look and whispered in my ear, "No, I want to feel your hands on my body."

I began near her neck and lathered her upper body. I put the soap down and dragged my fingernails around her upper body, spending extra time around her boobs. I knelt down and soaped her legs. She spread them enough for me to get my hands between them and when I got to her feet, I massaged them carefully, working my fingers around and in between her toes. She moaned, "That feels wonderful."

I stood up and handed her the soap. She gave it back to me and draped her hands around my neck and in a sexy voice said, "I remember saying from head to toe."

"Ah, so you did. My bad for sure."

She added, "Go light on the soap down there."

She turned sideways and I assumed that meant to wash from both ends so I rubbed a little soap on my hands and slid them down from her tummy and lower back. As I got closer, she spread her legs and squatted down a little. When I reached my destination, she made little gyrating moves with some intermittent moans. I left my fingers still and let her move them anywhere she wanted with her body movements.

A minute or so later, she turned to me and said dreamily, "You can rinse me now." I took the sprayer off the holder and rinsed her and she did the leg spread and little squat so I could reach every area and crevice.

She smiled and said, "Now it's your turn." She gave me a sensual kiss and then started lathering her hands. She soaped me up in sections and used her finger nails dragging them all over my body. I had chill bumps everywhere. I said softly, "I love your fingernails."

She turned me so that my back was to the water and knelt down in front of me, put a little soap on her hands and washed my dick. She moved it gently and slowly back and forth with one hand. With the other, she washed my balls and moved further back and reached all the way up to my lower back and then drug her fingernails back down through my ass and said, "Spray me some water down here."

I reached around and sprayed the water on her head. She gave me a hard slap on the ass and said, "No dummy, not on me, spray it on your pee wee!" I burst out laughing and followed her directions and put the sprayer back.

She took my pee wee in her mouth and started gently massaging my balls. When she moved her head back from my body, she closed down with tongue and mouth. It was a tight sucking sensation. She opened her mouth a little and moved back toward my body. Her mouth was wet and hot.

She was going back and forth and I was doing some moaning myself. After a couple of minutes, she released my pee wee, stood up and said, "Hand me the sprayer." She moved me to the back of the tub and finished rinsing me off.

"That was incredible," I said. She smiled and gave me a peck on the lips.

She said, "Let me rinse my hair." She got under the water and I just looked at her. I couldn't stop thinking about her beauty. She turned off the water. I got a couple of towels and we dried each other. I couldn't believe this was happening. She wrapped a towel around her body and used mine to wrap around her head. "I'm going to the great room to get my clothes. Do you want me to get yours?"

I replied, "No, I'll get mine." We gathered our scattered clothes and brought them back to my bedroom.

She said, "I was afraid that Henry might show up in the morning."

"He might come up here, but when he sees your car, he'll turn back."

She said, "I still feel more comfortable having my clothes in here."

"I understand."

"Do you still have that hair dryer?"

"I don't know. It would be under the sink if I do. Let me check."

She followed me in the bathroom. "Here it is."

"Good, I'm going to move it around my head. Wherever I point it, take your fingers and fluff my hair."

I loved doing that. For me it was intimate and I felt even closer to her. She said, "I think it's dry enough. I didn't want to get your pillows wet."

"That would have been fine. I don't care."

She smiled, "I know you don't." She took her band and wrapped her hair in a pony tail. She unfastened her towel and took me by the hand and led me back into the bedroom. She reached down and pulled the sheet back and we slid between the sheets in the only area that was dry. We were facing each other and she was running her hand through my hair.

She said, "At what point did you decide you were going to have sex with me? There I go again, asking you a question before I put something out there first. I decided I was going for it when I went in to pee and put the tee-shirt and sweat pants on. How about you?"

I responded, "It was also while you were changing that I thought to myself that if you were willing, I was going to make love to you." She looked away for an instant and then looked back at me.

She said, "Maybe, I was finally able to get it through my head that Ace doesn't love me and that I will never get him back."

I said, "I think the key was you reminding me that a year before we joined the Army, he showed little interest in you and that you didn't hear from him even before we left for the war zone. I could never get him to talk about it. It didn't make any sense to hold back."

I continued, "I think I believe that in my heart, but I have to admit that I'm nervous about telling him. He and I are so fragile right now. It would kill me to hurt him. My first choice would have been to wait and tell him before anything happened, but I obviously didn't do that."

She was silent for a few minutes before saying, "I used the phrase a few minutes ago 'have sex' and you said 'make love'."

I responded, "You remember yesterday when I said the reason I never had a steady girlfriend was maybe I had always loved you? Maybe I couldn't be that interested in anyone else?"

She replied, "Yes, I remember and even though I was flattered, it bothered me and still does. Jett, I am so confused about Ace. You know I love him with all my heart, but I don't believe there is much chance that he feels the same about me."

She continued, "I must, however find out one way or the other. I'm not in a committed relationship with him now and I owe him no explanation for what we are doing."

I replied, "I'm in this experience with you and both eyes are open. I know you love him and I know you have to find out how he feels. I admitted to myself while you were changing that maybe I have been in denial for years and have always loved you, but I'm confused and don't know for sure. I am positive without a doubt I have never felt as close and intimate with a woman as I feel with you right now."

I continued, "Is that love? I don't know, but what I do know is that it's a lot more than having sex. Sex with those other girls never came close to what I'm feeling with you."

She said, "Until I find out how Ace feels, I can't use the phrase, 'making love.' You know that I have also had sex with two other men not counting Ace. The way you make love is different from anyone I have ever been with including Ace. You are slow and patient and take your time and the build-up is phenomenal. Ace and I are more wild and passionate from the very first kiss. We fuck our brains out is a more accurate way to describe it."

I felt a tinge of jealousy and thought I could easily join her in fucking our brains out.

She touched my face and continued, "We don't know what the future holds, but right now in this bed, in this moment, I'm happy we're together. I can't, I guess I mean I won't allow myself to go anywhere else with my thoughts."

She pulled herself toward me and pressed her body against mine. I knew we needed to continue our conversation, but there would be plenty of time this week for us to talk. Right now, I wanted to make love to her and savor every moment.

She took my face in her hands and started lightly kissing my forehead, eyes, cheeks, chin, neck, and nibbled at my ears. The kisses felt so tender and so loving. Maybe it was her way of showing me how much she loved me. Not in the same way she loved Ace, but a love that was defined by a connection and bond that would last a lifetime. In this moment, I was content and happy.

She started some light and gentle kisses around my mouth. She traced my mouth with her tongue and slowly took the tip of her tongue made little circles around the tip of my tongue.

Without warning, she rolled on top of me and planted her mouth on mine and both of us were like two people hungering for the taste of each other. Tongues rolled around down and over and entwined, coming up for air and plunging back into the wet abyss, sucking for the nectar of honey that lay within. She spread her legs, pressed and gyrated and in one quick motion grabbed my shoulders and pulled me over on top of her. She spread her legs and hoarsely whispered, "Stick your dick in me Jett! Fuck me Jett!"

I pulled back, reached down and began rubbing the tip of my dick back and forth over and around her clit and then entered a little. I pulled back out and teased her. She moaned and demanded, "Fuck me now Jett, Now! Now! Now!"

I plunged in her with everything I had. I started with slow long strokes each time pushing as far in her as I could go. She wanted it faster and harder, but I was in control and I pressed all my weight on her and continued the long and slow strokes. On one of my slow withdraws she used her right leg to brace her and shifted her weight in a way as to throw me over and before I knew it, I was on my back and she was in control. My dick was still inside her and her mouth was planted on mine in an instant. She rose up and was riding me with quick back and forth motions. Without missing a beat, she leaned over and demanded, "Pull on my nipples with your teeth!"

I complied and she demanded, "Harder!" I pulled and she was saying like a mantra over and over, "It feels so good. It feels so good. It feels so good!" Then she pushed me down and was on my mouth with her passionate and wet kisses." Between gasps for air, she bellowed out, "I'm a bad girl. I'm a bad girl, Jett, I'm a bad girl. I love to fuck, Jett I'm bad. I love to fuck." She was gyrating wildly, "I'm a bad girl!! Spank me Jett, Spank me Jett, I'm a bad girl." I slapped her ass and she said, "Spank my ass Jett. I slapped her again. She was still wildly gyrating and gasped, "I'm starting to cum Jett. I'm starting to cum. Oh my god, I'm coming." I was with her and we were both screaming and letting the built-up emotion spill into the room.

We lay there panting, out of breath and exhausted. She shifted her weight to the side, draped one leg over my two legs, an arm over my chest, and buried her head in the crook of my neck and mumbled, "My sweet Jett." Her breathing slowed down and she was out.

I reached to the side and pulled a sheet over us. I couldn't believe this evening. She lay in my arms and I could hear her breathing and could feel her body pressed against mine. I wanted to stay awake and savor this moment as long as possible. I looked at the clock and it was 2:34. I listened to her breathe and ran my hand along the middle of her back. April was in my arms. Was that all I ever wanted? I didn't know, but it sure felt like it.

I don't think we moved because we were in the same position when I opened my eyes. I looked at the clock, 5:15. I thought she had to be at work at seven so I decided to wake her. I gently stroked different areas of her face and a voice slightly above a whisper said, "April.., April.., April..." She shifted and snuggled closer to me. She mumbled, "Where am I? What time is it?"

I responded, "You're in paradise and its 8:00."

She raised up, "Oh shit!"

I said, "Just kidding, it's just 5:15."

With a worried look she asked, "A.M. or P.M.?"

"A.M."

She plopped back down and snuggled up again and said in a soft and sexy voice, "Wake me when it's time to go to work."

I asked, "What time would that be?"

"You figure it out. I have to be there at 7:00. How much time will it take you to bathe and dress me, feed me breakfast, and get me in my car allowing me twenty minutes to get there?"

"I've got you covered. Go back to sleep."

With her eyes still closed, she smiled and then opened her eyes and rolled over on top of me and gave me a long and lingering kiss. Then she rose up and asked, "Do I have bad breath?"

"I wasn't gonna say anything but…"

She gave me another kiss, sat up and said, "If I can put up with your bad breath, you can put up with mine."

"That's fair."

She rolled over a little into her snuggling position and said, "How did I end up in bed with you. I must have blacked out. The last thing I remember we were eating supper on the front deck. I hope I didn't do anything that I'll regret or that would be too embarrassing."

"Actually, you're fine. After supper, we did the dishes and we were both tired and neither one of us wanted to sleep by ourselves."

She asked, "How did I end up naked?"

"I don't know. When I went to sleep you had all your clothes on. You must have gotten hot or something. But the good news is that you didn't do anything you might regret."

She asked, "If that's true, what's that sticky stuff on my thighs?"

"I have no idea. Would you like me to get a wash cloth and wipe it off?"

Somewhat indignant she said, "No Jett, I can't show you my privates."

"What if I promise not to look?"

She smiled and said, "I've gotta go pretty soon. Will you just hold me for a few minutes?"

I put my arms around her as we lay facing each other. We were silent for awhile. I said, "Are you okay?"

She replied, "I think so. We sure have given ourselves a lot to think about."

"Yeah."

"I better get going. I'll get dressed in the bathroom."

"Can I fix you something to eat?"

She responded, "That's all right. I'll grab something at the house."

"I'll let Spot out while you're getting ready." I kissed her on the forward, got up and grabbed my shorts and tee-shirt and left the bedroom. I stood out on the front deck. There was a nice breeze and the sun was making its' way toward the horizon. My head was spinning with thoughts about the last twelve hours.

She came out on the porch with her bag. Even though a little disheveled, she looked stunning in the early morning light. I wanted desperately to ask her to call in sick and spend the day with me. I thought, 'please don't leave me.'

She smiled, "I wish I didn't have to work today."

"Me too."

"We're a little short handed and I wouldn't feel right 'calling in'."

I said, "I understand. Can we get together after work?"

"Can I call you when I get a break?"

"Sure."

She gave me a hug and peck on the lips. I watched her car disappear into the woods. I went back inside, secured the door, and fell face forward on my bed and started sobbing.

13
THE DAY AFTER

I woke up and looked at the clock, 10:22. No nightmares. No phone call from April. I wanted out of the cabin. I could smell her and see the evidence that reminded me of being intimate with her. I let Spot out and sat down in one of the rockers on the porch. I felt alone and isolated.

What happened last night? I had to think things through. My mind was filled with random thoughts and wouldn't slow down. I wanted to focus, but my mind jumped back into the past. Suddenly, our patrol was climbing out of a rocky ravine. It was blistering hot and we were drenched with sweat.

We were warned there might be snipers. Nothing yet. Our objective was 100-meters up the hill. Then, the suspected snipers opened up on us. We were trapped and pinned down.

Startled by shortness of breath, I gasped for air and was back in the present. I stood up and headed up the trail saying over and over, "It'll pass. It'll pass. It'll pass...." Spot was looking at me and he knew something was wrong. My breathing finally slowed.

I returned to the cabin and got a beer. I didn't give a shit about my noon rule. I needed a beer. The phone rang, startling me. Was it April? "Hello."

Ace said, "Hey bro."

I tried my best not to sound disappointed. "Hey Ace. How's it goin'?"

"Good, I just got back from chapel."

"Well, it's been awhile since you've been to chapel."

"True," he said. "I thought this was a good time to check in with the Man upstairs." He continued, "I'm looking at my watch and your ass doesn't appear to be at church."

"That's true. I just had a fucking flashback. Remember when we got pinned down by those snipers in that rocky ravine?"

"Yeah, how long did it last?" he asked.

"Hell if I know. It seemed like an hour, but was probably a minute or so."

He shot back, "I had some fucking nightmares last night that..." There was a muffled sound that sounded like, "Yes ma'am."

I asked, "What happened?"

"The nurse told me to watch my language. I'll tell you about the nightmares later. You remember Derrick Hawks?"

"Yeah, he was in First Platoon. Wasn't Watson his patrol leader?"

"Right, that's him. He showed up early this morning. A bullet shattered his right shoulder. He's facing a bunch of surgeries. He's really doin' pretty well, but dreadin' the knife. Anyway, he and I are goin' to the Forest Hills rec area today. They've got a lot of activities and some movies. We're hoping to distract each other by keeping busy."

I responded, "I'm glad you got somebody to hang with. Tell him I said hey."

"I will. Call me tomorrow and let me know if all the paperwork got sent to Personnel."

"Will do."

He hung up.

No mention of April. I just can't read him. Well no joke. Who can you really read anyway? You have enough trouble reading yourself. I got another beer.

Everyone would be at church. I thought yesterday I might go down and join the family for lunch at the Inn, but I didn't want to be around anyone right now except April. Anyway, I had no appetite. I needed to hike, but was afraid I'd miss her call.

I thought about cleaning the cabin, but I wanted everything to stay the way it was. It was like she was still here and any minute might walk out of my bedroom. There was a strange comfort in looking over at her wine glass knowing that her lips had been on that glass a few hours ago.

Was I falling in love? Had I always loved her? Was it just the intimacy? I hadn't been with a woman for such a long time. In that area, my life had been on hold for three years. What the fuck! Ace and I had signed up to defend our country. It seemed like a good idea at the time. What good did we do? Did we waste three years of our lives? The few times we got home on leave, everyone we knew seemed to be having a pretty good time.

Other than a few "old timers," and other families who were military or had men or women in the service, no one really thanked us for defending our country against terrorists. The ones that thanked us were probably just being nice. No one really seemed that scared or threatened. Really, outside the military families, most people acted like we weren't even at war. I had some work to do with this budding resentment.

Maybe I need to write in my notebook. I had no chance unless I got out of the cabin. I took it out on the porch, opened it and read the last few entries. No luck. I couldn't concentrate. I could not get my mind to focus.

I had to hike. If I missed her call, I would call her at home after she got off work. I made myself clean the cabin. I turned on the radio and tuned into a local station that played pop music. I turned it up loud. I was swift and thorough. I didn't allow myself time to ponder and think and remember. I just got the job done.

By the time I finished, it was about 1:00. I knew most everyone would be at the Inn. I called the restaurant number and asked to speak to Mom.

"Hello Honey. How are you doing?"

"I'm not having a good day Mom. I'm okay, just restless and fidgety. I need some time to myself. Would you let Pop know that I not feeling well and I'll call him tomorrow? If he's free I'd like to go on our hike then. Mom, don't worry about me. This is normal."

She sounded worried, "Jett, I'll try not to."

"I'm going on a two or three hour hike and I'll call you as soon as I get back to the cabin."

"Please do."

"I will, I love you Mom and give my love to everybody."

About five minutes passed and the phone rang. It was Henry. "You want any company on your hike? We don't have to talk."

I thanked him and told him about my need to be alone for awhile.

"I understand," he said. "I just wanted to check. Hope you have a good hike."

I got my gear together, checked for my knife, and left the cabin.

I knew the hike would help me mentally. When I'm out in the forest, I'm in another world. It's like an escape. I've spent so much of my life in these woods with wonderful experiences. I feel at home and comfortable and safe.

I like my church and the people that make up our church family, but out here I feel especially close to God. There is some kind of special connection to the earth, the beauty, the sounds, the smells, and the feel of the ground beneath me. Someday, I'm going to try to explain it. Right now, I just need to experience it.

As I made my way back to the cabin, I felt renewed and invigorated. Spot looked exhausted. I went to the answering machine and there were two messages. The first one was from Pop. He said to call him in the morning and we could arrange the time for our walk. The second was from April. She said to call her when I got home.

I called Mom first and told her I felt better. She seemed relieved. She said April had called her and had tried several times to reach me, but there was no answer. She invited me down for supper, but I declined promising I would come down for a visit in the morning.

I called April, "Hey there," trying to sound as cheerful as possible.

"Hey, Jett. I was worried about you."

"I just talked to Mom and she told me. I'm sorry. I waited for you to call, but around 1 I just had to get out in the woods."

She replied, "We were swamped at work. I even had to eat my sandwich on the run."

I said, "Sorry you had such a rough day."

"Thanks. Remember, I told you we were short handed and one of our nurses called in sick. It was not pretty. You sound good. Did the hike make you feel better?"

"Yeah, it really helped."

"I'm glad," she said. "Did you hear from Ace?"

I filled her in on our conversation and told her that he didn't ask any questions and didn't volunteer any information.

There was a short pause. Somewhere inside me there were a thousand things I wanted to say to her, but in that moment, I didn't know what to say.

She broke the silence, "Jett, as you might imagine, I'm exhausted. I would like to eat a bite and then crash. I have to work tomorrow, but I wondered if you would like to come here for supper tomorrow. I want to go to the gym after work and then we could meet up at the lake and jog a couple of laps. What do you think?"

I replied again trying to be as upbeat as possible, "That sounds great. I passed out after you left and slept till 10:15 and unlike you had no pressure the rest of my day. I know you need some rest."

"Thanks for understanding. Why don't we plan to meet at the lake at 5:00?"

"I'll be there."

"All right," she said, "I'll run on and get a bite to eat and get ready for bed."

"I hope you sleep well and feel better tomorrow."

"Me too. I'll see you tomorrow." She hung up.

I don't know what I was expecting when I talked to her but that was not it. I yelled, "Well, what did you expect? What the hell? You don't know what you expected! You don't' know shit about anything! You fucking piece of shit! You fucking piece of shit!"

Spot kind of cowered as if I were talking to him. Tears running down my cheeks, I got down on the floor and took him in my arms and petted him and he licked my face. "It's not you old boy. I'm just fucked up."

I kept petting him and the phone rang. I was fucking startled again. "Hello."

"Jett," she was crying, "Jett, I'm so sorry."

I said softly and earnestly, "April, what do you mean?"

"I'm sorry for everything and would never do anything intentionally to hurt you."

I replied, "I know that. You have nothing to be sorry for."

Still crying, she said, "I had to call you back. I'm so confused. I don't know what to do or what to think. All I want to do right now is come to you and have you hold me in your arms and let me sleep. But I don't trust myself."

I replied, "There's nothing in the world that I want more than to hold you too, but I don't trust myself either. I have an idea. Have you eaten yet?"

"I had a few bites. I'm not hungry."

"How about this?" I asked. "Go on to bed and try to go to sleep. I think you'll pass out, but if you can't sleep, call me back and we'll come up with another plan."

Still crying she said, "All right. Jett, I miss you."

"I miss you too. You go on now and cry yourself to sleep."

"All right and thanks."

I felt better. I had done the right thing.

14
THE REGRET

I got a beer and called Pop. We talked for a few minutes about the day and he said he was glad I was feeling better. I asked him if we could walk tomorrow around three and he said that would be fine. I also asked him if I could come in tomorrow and work with the grounds crew for a few hours. He said Charlie would be glad for the extra help.

I turned on that radio station. I needed some noise. I didn't expect to hear from April. I didn't think she would have any trouble falling asleep and staying asleep. I had noticed a few minor things that needed to be done around the cabin so I got the tool box and kept busy for awhile.

Around 8:00, I heard some steps on the porch and at about the same time Spot started barking. It was Henry with a plate of food. "How're you doin?"

"I feel better, thanks."

"Glad to hear that. Betty made a little extra food when she fixed supper and wanted me to bring it up to you."

I smiled, "Thank her for me. That's mighty nice."

"I'm hoping we'll have Ace's paperwork submitted to Walter Reed by around noon tomorrow. Give me a call after lunch and I'll let you know so you can call Ace. If I'm not there, Judy will let you know. I need to get back. You take care."

"Thanks again to both of you."

I was more tired than I realized. I slept hard and as far as I knew there were no nightmares. I got in my early morning run and went back to bed. I left the cabin around nine to go by and see Mom. We talked for awhile and then I went over to the Inn and checked in with Charlie.

The Original Inn

He was glad to see me and kept me busy until it was time for Pop and me to go on our walk. We enjoyed a couple laps around the lake and had some good talks about various hikes we had taken over the years.

When we got back to the Inn, I used the phone in Pop's office to call Henry. Judy answered and said Henry wasn't there, but the paperwork had been faxed to Walter Reed. She called them and they confirmed they had received it. I thanked her and called Ace. He said Personnel had called him down to the office and let him know everything was ready to go.

He was upbeat. Personnel told him everything looked in order. They thought the request would be approved, but they could not promise anything. They told him he should know something by 1500 tomorrow.

I asked, "Have you called Ma?"

"No, I was hoping you would call her for me."

I was frustrated with him, but not in the mood to pursue it. I replied, "Okay, I'll call her, but I think you should be the one to call her tomorrow."

"I will. Thanks man. I know you and Henry have done some work to get this thing done."

"Henry did a lot more than me. I just hope it all works out."

"Me too. By this time tomorrow, we'll have our answer."

I called Ma and filled her in. I gave Pop a hug and left. Sandra was not on the front desk. It must be her day off. Spot and I headed to the cabin. I needed a shower and some clean clothes. I took some extra clothes in case I wanted to change after our run.

Spot and I got there a little before 5:00 and we pulled in at the same time. She looked as beautiful as ever and was sweating from her workout at the gym. She smiled and gave me a hug and a peck on the lips. I asked, "How did you sleep?"

"I fell asleep right away and didn't move till the alarm rang. I still feel tired, but not exhausted."

"Was work as busy today?"

"No, thank goodness," she replied. We were busy, but not overwhelmed. That was a help." She asked about my day and I gave her a run down and she asked, "Did working at the Inn help?"

"Yeah, it did. There was plenty for me to do and Charlie and I talked while we were working. That kept my mind occupied which was a good thing."

She said, "I know we have a lot to talk about, but could we wait until we get to my house?"

"Sure, that would be fine." We jogged at a medium pace. We talked some and there was some awkward silence. What was she thinking? What were we going to do? I didn't have any answers right then because I hadn't allowed myself to think about it.

I followed her over to her house. It was on the side of a hill. It looked like someone had custom built it for a vacation cottage. There were trees in the front and on the side which provided shade from the afternoon sun. I did a quick visual security screening. I needed to check the back yard area.

We walked into an open room with a kitchen area in the left back corner. She had a little kitchen nook with a picture window that faced out the back. There was a larger table over to the right with a sliding glass door that led out to the deck. There were two stuffed chairs and a sofa that made a U shape surrounding a fireplace which was on the front side of the room.

She had some knick-knacks and pictures on the tables and some nice colorful paintings on the walls. The walls were a light tan with attractive curtains. It was cozy and had a warm and comfortable feel to it.

She took me out on the back deck and it had a nice view of the valley and mountains in the distance. I said, "I really like your home. It reflects the woman who lives here; charming, warm, and cozy."

"I'm glad you like it. I enjoy living here."

She turned to go back in the house and turned to me, "I'll put down some water for Spot. Would you like a beer?"

"Yes, thanks. That would be great."

She got the beer out of the fridge and said, "I need to take a quick shower and change. Make yourself comfortable."

"I think I'll sit out on the deck."

"All right, I won't be long."

Spot and I went down the back steps and looked around. We didn't see anything to worry about. I felt for my knife on the inside of my shorts.

It seemed like it was taking her a long time. She came to the sliding door and said, "Sorry, it took longer than I thought. Would you come in for a minute?"

"Sure." I got up and went in the door and she was in the kitchen pouring a glass of wine.

When I got to the kitchen, she set the bottle down and turned and put her arms around me and I could see that she'd been crying. When I saw her tears, my eyes filled up. We held each other for awhile. It wasn't a sensual hug, but we were pressed close together.

For me right now, it was easier to hug than to talk. I was pretty sure I knew what April needed to say so I wanted to make it as easy as possible for her. I said softly, "Can we sit down?"

"Sure." She went over and poured her wine and said, "Would you like another beer?"

"Yes, thanks."

She took me by the hand and led me over to the chair and she sat on the sofa.

I sat on the edge of the chair. We both still had tears running down our cheeks. There was a box of tissues on the lamp table and I reached over and took a couple, patted her cheeks, wiped mine and took her hands.

I smiled at her and said, "You are so beautiful."

She looked down and said softly, "Thank you."

I continued to smile, "I'm going to look back on Saturday and the wee hours of Sunday morning as two of the most wonderful days of my life." More tears began to flow from her eyes.

I went on, "You awakened feelings in me that I never knew existed, feelings that are hard to put into words. I think you know what I mean." She nodded.

I continued, "I think we can say this was not some spontaneous experience that just happened. We had time to think about it and we discussed what we were going to do and why we decided it was a good idea at the time."

She started to speak. I squeezed her hands and said, "Is it okay if I say a few more things?"

"All right."

"I am going to do the best I can not to look back on those two days and feel guilty. I think our reasons were justified. I think the most dominant feeling right now is discomfort. I regret the timing partly because it detracts from this incredible experience."

Tears welled in my eyes again. She squeezed my hands. I continued. "The uncomfortable feeling, for the most part, seems irrational and that is the thought that I have somehow betrayed Ace. Another part of the regret is that this may in some way jeopardize any possibilities of you and Ace getting back together. I would never want to do anything to hurt your chance for happiness." Tears were now rolling down my cheeks.

She pulled me so that we were both standing up. She guided me so that I sat down on the sofa and she sat up against the arm of the sofa and draped her legs across mine. With her finger, she lightly brushed a little strand of hair that had fallen onto my forehead.

She began, "First, I want you to know that I agree that we went into this experience with both eyes open. We are adults and responsible for our actions." I nodded. "That means that we are left to deal with whatever the consequences may be. I know that we would never want to hurt the other, but if one of the consequences is that one or both of us feels emotional pain, I know we will be able to work through it and be all right."

I nodded again. "I have loved that man for years and I really believe there is little chance that we will ever get back together. But, I have to give it one last try before I give up." Tears were now freely rolling down her cheeks. I started to speak, but she whispered, "Just give me a minute."

She blotted her cheeks and continued, "When we tell Ace what happened, I don't know how he will respond. I think we both understand Ace well enough to know that whatever he feels will not be apparent in that moment. He'll probably brush it off. We'll just have to wait and see what happens."

She went on, "Whatever the future holds for us Jett, our time together over these past few days will be as special for me as you said they have been for you. I will never forget them. You will always have that special place in my heart."

I said, "What's more important to me than anything else is that we continue being close. For the time being and maybe for always, there can never be anything else physical. I hope we can always have an emotional intimacy. I want to be able to talk to you about anything and everything knowing you will be there for me. I will always be there for you in good times and bad times."

She put her arms around my neck and whispered in my ear, "Me too Jett. That's what I want more than anything."

We kept the embrace. I think we were a little hesitant to turn loose. When we finally did, I said softly, "I may need a little space for a few days. Does that make sense?"

"Yes, it does and that would be helpful for me too."

I said, "I'm going to miss you terribly."

She touched my face, "I'm going to miss you too my sweet Jett." Tears rolling down our cheeks one more time, we embraced and she kissed me on the cheek.

I said, "I forgot to mention earlier that all the paperwork is at Walter Reed and it looks like the request will be approved. I'll leave on Thursday to pick him up. I'm hoping we can leave to come home on Friday morning. I'll call you tomorrow afternoon as soon as I get the final word."

She asked, "Do you know if you will come back in one or two days?"

"I'll leave that up to him. My guess is that he'll wanna take two days. I'll make sure he calls Ma to let her know. You could call and ask her. She will know by Friday when you get off work."

She said, "I'll do that. Will Marge have a welcome home party for him?"

I responded, "I don't know. I do know that he doesn't want one."

"Jett, I'm really nervous about him coming home, and I'm terrified about seeing him for the first time."

"I know. We'll figure something out that will hopefully make it less terrifying."

She replied, "I don't know if that's possible, but I thank you for wanting to try."

I said, "I would like to see you one more time before I leave. How would you feel about coming up to the cabin after work on Wednesday? We can do a run and hike and then have some supper. I promise I'll be good."

She smiled, "Who's gonna make sure I'm good?"

I smiled back, "If both of us commit to being good, surely one of us will be able to do it."

We decided she would come at five.

"Spot and I will head on out."

She said, "Don't you want something to eat?"

"Thanks for the offer. I think this is the time when I need a little space. I'm sensing that's also true for you. Am I right?"

With some hesitation, she replied, "I don't know what I want anymore, but you're probably right."

We hugged and she whispered in my ear, "I'll miss you."

"I haven't even left yet and I already miss you."

15

SAYING GOODBYE

I rolled down the windows. I needed air. I headed to the cabin and on the way, decided I needed a night out in the woods. About an hour from the cabin, there is a camp site that Ace and I often used for overnight stays. It was secluded and secure. It was on top of some rocks that jutted out from the mountain and had a bunch of vegetation for cover. There was only one entrance and the only people who knew about the entrance were Pop, Henry, Jack, Ace, and me.

I made a quick call to Mom to let her know I was going and would call her in the morning. I called April. No answer. I left a message about where I would be just in case she called. I didn't want her to worry.

Spot and I gathered the gear and a few supplies, secured the house and headed out with just enough daylight to make it. It was a warm night with a gentle breeze. The sky was clear with a half moon I could see between the trees and branches. I disturbed some birds that had roosted for the night. I apologized and before long, we were making our way up the entrance to the site.

It didn't take long to get settled. It was almost dark and I lay on my back and looked up at the stars. I could breathe out here. The air was fresh. This was like home and I could let go and relax. I thought about April and smiled. I would never be the same again. I didn't know exactly what I meant by that but I did know it was true.

Spot and I got cozy and the next thing I knew it was early morning. I looked at my watch and it was 4:56. I slept the best yet since coming home. We went for a hike, came back and ate a ham sandwich, some chips, and an apple. Spot got a dog biscuit. I gathered the gear and headed back to the cabin.

No messages and I was a little disappointed. I called Mom and by 9:00 was down at the Inn spending more time with Charlie. I had lunch with Pop and Jimmy was able to join us. I got home around 4:00 and had a message from Ace. All had gone well and the request had been approved. I called Ma and surprise, surprise, Ace had already called her. I phoned April, Henry, Mom, and Pop.

Ace said he was to report to Personnel at 0800 in the morning and begin his processing for discharge. He also was told he had to continue his physical therapy sessions through his appointment on Thursday. They told him he could be picked up after 1200 on Friday. He said he would see if we could leave earlier. He told me to call him that evening around 2100.

I showered and went down to eat dinner with Mom and Dad. Sadie dropped by for a few minutes to pick up some article Mom had saved for her. She apologized for not seeing more of me. I said, "I haven't been around much either. It's good to see you now."

"It's good to see you too Jett. I've gotta run." And she was gone.

Mom smiled, "She is one active girl."

Dad said after supper, "There's an old classic movie on at 7:00 with Clint Eastwood. Why don't you stay and watch it with me?"

This was the last thing I wanted to do. I felt so restless, but I had hardly seen dad. "Sure, that would be nice."

He said, "Lynne, why don't you join us?"

Mom said, "I'll pass on this one. I have a few things I need to get done before tomorrow."

Mom and I did the dishes and had a nice talk. I didn't share anything about April."

She whispered, "Thanks for watching the movie with your Dad. It will mean a lot to him."

I smiled and lied, "I'm glad to Mom."

She smiled back with that sweet look that said that she and I both knew I was lying, but thanks anyway. About that time from the family room, Dad yelled, "Jett, it's coming on!"

"I'll be right there Dad."

I got back to the cabin about 9:30 and there were no messages from April. What did I expect? We both said we needed some space and I'll see her tomorrow. Let it go man.

I called Ace. He was upbeat and in a good mood. "Three more nights and I'm outta here. I hope I can wait that long."

"Hang on. I'll be there to bail you out in no time."

"Three more days seems like forever," he said.

"I know, but you can do it. I'll call you as soon as I get there on Thursday."

"Good deal." He hung up.

When I got into bed, I closed my eyes and imagined April was lying next to me. I hadn't changed the sheets and there was still a faint odor of our love making. Maybe that wasn't true, but I didn't care. I pulled a couple of pillows to me and snuggled up to them. I could feel Spot against my back and it didn't take me too long to drift off.

I had a restless night with several nightmares. I woke up around 3:00 and was struggling to breath and was soaking wet. I couldn't remember the content but it was something like being pinned down or trapped and we couldn't escape. That pinned down and trapped feeling was showing up as a theme of my nightmares.

I was able to go back to sleep and had another less intense nightmare. I woke at 4:45 and was glad it was just a nightmare and not real. Spot and I took off for our run. I ate something and gave Spot a dog biscuit and we went back to bed. I got up in time to be down at the Inn by 9:00 working with Charlie.

I had lunch with Mom and then stopped by to check on Ma. She told me Ace made it clear he did not want a welcome home party. She was planning to have his favorite meal of chopped steak, smothered in onions with mashed potatoes and a tossed salad with homemade blue cheese dressing. She told me Mom volunteered to make banana pudding.

It would only be the four of them and me. Ma was still nervous about Ace coming home. I told her we would stay with the plan to take one day at a time. She said she asked Ace about taking one or two days to get home and he had told her he didn't know yet. I told her we would let her know on Friday after we got on the road. She gave me a hug and I went back to the Inn and worked till 4:00.

April arrived a little after 5:00 dressed for our run. We hugged and she gave me a peck on the lips.

"You look beautiful." She blushed and turned to get her bag out of the car. I felt a little anxious and said to her as we walked to the cabin, "I feel nervous."

"I feel the same way and I think it was the same for both of us on Monday night at my house."

"Yes," I said and continued, "I guess it has to do with so much happening so fast."

"Probably so."

We went inside and she set her bag down on the sofa and then turned to me and took my hands, looked into my eyes and said, "Jett, I want this last time before Ace comes home to be comfortable for us. I feel closer to you than anyone else in my life. I have never felt more emotionally intimate with anyone including Ace. I love him, but he is hard to get close to."

I said, "Yes, we both know that better than anyone other than Ma."

I took her in my arms and continued, "And I feel closer to you than anyone else in my life other than Mom and it's a different kind of closeness."

She replied, "I know so let's work hard to relax and be comfortable tonight."

She gave me a squeeze and said, "Are you ready to run?"

"Sure, let's do it." I felt better and I think she did too. We had a good run and then did some hiking. We kept the conversation light and raced back to the house from about a hundred meters out laughing as we flew down the path both out of breath when we got to the cabin. She was a great athlete and fast. I had trouble keeping up with her and it was no surprise to me as our football coach had said, "Hollander, if you only had more speed, you would have made a great cornerback."

We climbed the steps into the cabin and I poured her a glass of wine and got a beer. We went out on the back deck, sat down, and caught our breath. We looked out over the valley and the sun was still warm. I looked over at her and the sun lit up her face and skin making that same sheen.

She looked over at me and smiled and said, "Jett, stop looking at me. I'm blushing again."

"May I sneak a peek when you're not looking?"

She smiled again. She sipped on her wine and I drank my beer as we looked out over the beauty in front of us. After awhile, she asked, "Do you mind if I take a shower?"

"No, that's fine. Again, if you'll holler at me when you get out, I'll jump in."

"Will do."

She of course used the other shower. After we showered, we decided to go with ham sandwiches and chips. She made the sandwiches and I set the table, poured her wine, got a beer and put a bowl of chips on the table.

"What time are you gonna leave tomorrow?" she asked.

"I think probably around 7:00 or 8:00. I figure it'll take about eight hours with stops."

"How will you go?"

"I'll take the Parkway up to I-77; go north to I-81, then I-81 to I-66. I'll check in at Forest Hills and then head over to the hospital."

She inquired, "What's Forest Hills?"

"It's an annex to the hospital and they have among a lot of other things rooms for soldiers and their families."

"I'm really apprehensive Jett. I get butterflies every time I think about Ace coming home."

"Yeah me too. That's a new one for me. I never thought I'd have butterflies about seeing Ace."

She said, "Have you thought about when you will tell him?"

"All the time," I replied and continued, "I feel like it's something you and I should agree on."

She said, "I'm gonna leave that up to you. I don't know when I'll see him. I don't owe him any explanation and the first time I see him, I want him to already know about you and me. It happened and if that keeps us from getting together, that means to me there wasn't much of anything there to get us together anyway."

"Are you sure?"

"Yes."

I said, "I would like to tell him at some point on our way back home. I agree with what you said Monday night. I don't think it will have much impact on him right now. He certainly won't get mad. Ace knows you owe him nothing. Consciously, he will not feel betrayed by me, but there may be some issues later. We'll see. I'm still nervous about seeing him and telling him. That has to do with my own feelings about what happened."

"I think I know what you mean. It's like we didn't do anything wrong, but for some reason I feel like I shouldn't have done it.

Do you think that means that we just rationalized our conclusion that it was all right?"

"I don't know April. Maybe we did. And then there is the thought that we are over analyzing it. There is so much entanglement in these kinds of issues. What I'm trying to do is accept we did it, be honest with Ace, and be willing to face whatever consequences arise."

"All right, I'm going to try to do the same." We kind of half smiled at each other and continued to pick at our food. She smiled, "Can we go for a walk and then I'll head on home."

Trying to hide my disappointment, I replied, "Sure. That will be nice."

Spot was already at the door wagging his tail. She said, "Let me help you clean up."

"No, that's fine. I'll get it later. There's not that much anyway."

"All right, let me get my bag and I'll put it in the car."

We walked out the door and when she put her bag in the car, she turned to me and said, "Jett, do you mind if I go on now?"

"No, that's fine," I lied. Tears were running down her cheeks. She gave me a quick hug and got into her car and left. As I watched her car disappear down the road, it was my time for tears.

I was so confused. What was happening to me? There was a whirlwind of different emotions and right now I didn't want to think about it anymore. I went back in and got another beer. Spot was counting on the walk so we went for a short distance and came back. When we got back, I turned on the radio, got another beer, and cleaned up the dishes. I started packing a bag for the trip and looked at the clock. It was 9:23.

The phone rang. I did my exaggerated startle response and picked up the receiver. "Jett," in a soft voice and I could tell she was crying. "I'm so scared and I miss you and I'm sorry I left so abruptly."

"I miss you too and I wish we could just hold each other tonight and sleep in each others arms."

She blew her nose and whispered, "Me too."

There was a pause. I didn't know what to say. She finally broke the silence. "Can I come back and can we sleep in each others' arms? I promise I'll be strong."

"I want that more than anything. Do you think it's a good idea?"

She replied, "I don't care. I just need to have you hold me."

"I want the same."

She said, "I'm off tomorrow so if you want, we can run in the morning and while you're getting ready, I'll make you breakfast and see you off."

"That sounds great."

"I'll be there in about half an hour."

"Okay, I'll be waiting on you."

She hung up and I started pacing and thinking that I've got to be strong too. Then the phone rang again and I jumped again and it was Ace.

"Hey Jett, are you packed and ready to go?"

"No, I've decided you can find you own ride back home."

"That's no big deal. I've got at least five nurses who have volunteered to drive me as long as we take about five days to get there."

"You obviously don't need me."

He asked, "So what time you leaving?"

"I thought I'd get on the road around 8:00 and I should be there around four. I'll check in and be over at the hospital in time for us to eat supper together. Have you been buggin' 'em about getting out before noon on Friday?"

"Yeah and they keep telling me they'll do the best they can, but no promises." We talked a little longer and he hung up.

Shortly I saw April's headlights out front and Spot and I went out to greet her. She got out and hugged me and reached in and got her bag. When we got inside, I could see that she had already taken off her makeup. Her hair was in the usual pony tail and she had on what could be a pair of pajamas or a loose fitting sweat suit. It was light grey. She looked so beautiful.

She said, "I usually watch the 10:00 news while I'm getting ready for bed. Would you mind if we turned it on now and catch the last fifteen minutes or so?"

"No, that's fine."

We sat close together. She took my hand and we watched the rest of the news.

When it was over, she said, "Thanks for letting me come back."

"I'm glad you're here."

She asked, "Are you ready to go to bed?"

"Anytime is fine with me."

She said, "Let me go pee and I'll be ready."

"I'll let Spot in and go pee myself."

She used the other bathroom. I pulled the bedspread back and got under the sheet. She came to the door and hesitated. I lifted the sheet to let her know I still had my clothes on and as an invitation to join me. She reached under the lamp shade and turned the lamp off and crawled in beside me.

We lay on our backs as close together as we could get and held hands. There were a few moments of silence and then she said, "Are we a couple of nut cases or what?"

"Yeah as nutty as they come."

And we laughed and she continued, "I'm not gonna lie. I wish we both felt free to get naked and have more wild passionate sex."

"Me too." More silence.

This time I broke the silence. "I'm so glad you came back tonight. I needed this time with you. I felt so empty when you left."

"I needed you too." She turned toward me and laid her head on my chest and draped her left leg over my legs the same way she did the other night. It felt so good to have her nestled close against me.

"Jett?"

"Yes."

"When you tell Ace, will you go into the details of what we did?"

I answered, "I don't see any reason to do that."

"I don't mind if he knows in general what we did like oral sex and taking a shower together. I would just rather you not give him a detailed description."

"It never occurred to me to do that and I'm almost certain he won't ask for any details. But, if he is interested or even insistent, I promise you I will never tell him anything more than the general."

She whispered, "I feel so safe and comfortable in your arms."

"I love having you in my arms."

More silence. I was listening to her breathing and soon I could tell she had dosed off. I just savored the moments of having her close to me and after awhile, I too drifted off into that other world.

I don't think we moved until around 4:30 when April shifted positions and rolled over on her left side. I don't think she woke up as she almost immediately went into that sleep breathing. As slowly as I could I shifted position and snuggled up close to her. No more sleep for me. I wanted to be awake and savor these moments as long as possible.

As much as I wanted to stay awake, I dosed on and off. I glanced at the clock, 5:45. April needed the sleep and I needed to go for a run. I slowly moved away from her and got out of the bed. I thought I had been successful and then a little above a whisper, "Jett, are you going for a run?"

"Yeah," I responded softly and continued, "Why don't you sleep a little longer and I'll wake you when I get back."

She said, "I want to go with you."

"I would like that." She got out of bed and kissed me on the cheek and headed over to the other bathroom. I let Spot out and got my running clothes on. We were ready about the same time. The run was nice. We didn't talk much, but I loved having her along. April and the woods was a great combo.

When we got back to the cabin, she said, "You go ahead and shower and finish packing and I'll fix you breakfast."

"Thanks." When I came out of my bedroom, the smell of fried country ham filled the air. Mixed in was the smell of coffee and there was a stack of French toast and orange juice. I didn't realize I was so hungry.

She had put some wild flowers in a little vase and set them on the table. I said, "April, you didn't have to go to this much trouble."

"It was no trouble. Remember how I used to fix breakfast for you and Ace?"

"Yeah, I sure do."

She said, "I know you are not a big coffee drinker, but I thought it might taste good with the French toast and put a little caffeine in your system."

"Yeah, right on both counts."

I sat down. She said, "I usually listen to the early morning show while I'm getting ready for work, do you mind if I turn it on?"

"No, that's fine." I ate a pretty good breakfast, but I wasn't as hungry as I thought. April ate just a little and we both had two cups of coffee. We made a comment or two about the news. I was glad for the TV. I don't think either one of us had much left to say.

"April, thanks for breakfast. It was delicious."

"I'm glad you enjoyed it."

I said, "Let me help you clean up."

"No, I'll take care of it. You go ahead and get ready. If you don't mind, after you leave, I'd like to stay here for awhile. I might be able to go back to sleep."

"You can stay here all day if you like."

"Thanks, I might do that."

I brushed my teeth and took a dump. I hoped she didn't come back in here for awhile. The smell was more rank than usual. I closed the bathroom door as I went out not wanting any of that smell to drift out into the great room. I put my toothbrush in my bag and checked to see if I had everything.

She was waiting on me with a paper bag. "I fixed you a couple of ham sandwiches and put in some chips and an apple."

"Thanks."

She smiled. I put my bag down and took her in my arms and whispered, "We're going to get through this. There will be some rough spots, but in the end it will turn out okay. That's true only because we'll make it happen."

We both had tears in our eyes. She gave me a peck on the lips and said, "Be careful and have a safe trip."

"I will, we will."

I wanted to tell her that I loved her and that I already missed her, but I knew it was important to keep that to myself. "I'm going to drop Spot off at Mom's. She offered me her car. I guess I'll take her up on it. I think the truck would make it, but that will be one less thing to be concerned about."

She walked me out to the truck. I put my stuff in the front seat and turned for one more good-bye. We hugged. I got in, rolled the window down and said, "Ace and I will call Ma tomorrow about when we will get home. I suspect he will want to take a couple of days so don't be surprised if we don't get back until Sunday or even Monday. Call Ma tomorrow night and she'll let you know."

"All right, I will."

She looked so sad and scared. I wanted to tell her to get in the truck and let's just start driving and never look back. Now that's a brilliant idea. "I guess I better get going."

I reached out and took her hand and lightly squeezed it and she put my hand up to her lips and I said, "Take care of yourself my sweet April." More tears. I headed down the road and in the mirror, I could see her waving. I stuck my arm out the window and waved.

16
THE REUNION AND REALITY

The drive to D.C. was uneventful. Mom had given me a book tape and it helped me not dwell too much on recent events. I stopped for gas once and started to call the cabin and see if April was there. I decided against it. Maybe she would be asleep or it wasn't a good idea for a number of other reasons.

After I got back on the road, I realized I wanted her to stay at the cabin all day. It was like as long as she was there, we were still connected. As long as she was there, she was still emotionally in my arms and in my heart. When she left, it was like she was walking out of my life and it was over and would never be the same again.

I needed to turn the book tape back on. I did and it helped. I wandered some but for the most part was able to stay with the story. I arrived at Forest Hills and checked in. I called Ace and he wasn't on the ward.

I headed over to the hospital and thought about the difference in my feelings about seeing Ace. If nothing had happened with April, I would feel the same as always; comfortable, happy to see him, and safe knowing he always had my back. I was accepted and loved without judgment. There was a wonderful freedom being myself.

Now, it was different. Even though April and I had come up with a pretty good rationale for our behavior, I couldn't escape the feeling that I had betrayed my best friend. I just wanted to go in and tell him what happened, but I knew that would be selfish. I would just dump it on him and then I would feel better. No, I would have to wait.

So what was I feeling? Nervous? That summed it up. I parked and went to the ward. The nurse said Ace was in the lounge. He was talking to Derrick and looked up and gave me a big smile, our ritual handshake and a big hug.

He said, "Am I glad to see you!"

"Me too Man!"

"Hey Derrick."

"Hey Jett." I gave him a gentle hug. He had a large bandage wrapped around his right shoulder.

We talked awhile catching up on news of friends and what was happening over there. He told me about the ambush and how he got the bullet in his shoulder. No one else had been hurt on that mission. Several other friends had been wounded on other missions, but no more deaths.

I looked at Derrick and said, "Ace told me you have some surgeries ahead."

"Yeah, the first is scheduled the day after tomorrow. The worst thing is that they can't tell me how much use of the arm I'll have at the end of the surgeries."

"I'm sorry to hear that."

He replied, "As you both know, it could be a lot worse."

Ace said, "Let's get something to eat. We got permission to go to the Hills. The food is better there and Derrick and I like to get away from the hospital as often as possible. We have to sign out."

We had a nice evening. Ace was in a good mood as he was getting "out of jail" in the morning. We talked mostly about old times and had a lot of laughs. None of us brought up the nightmare stuff, the suffering and death of our friends.

It was too painful to talk about it. We were avoiding the inevitable. In the future, we would have to make a choice to face and deal with the trauma. Our unconscious minds were already at work sending us intrusive thoughts, flashbacks, and nightmares to remind us that we had work to do.

I dropped them off at the hospital and went back to the Hills. I had to call April. I had to hear her voice whether it was a good idea or not.

"Hey April."

"Jett, I didn't expect to hear from you."

"I know. I just wanted to hear your voice."

"That's sweet. How is he?" I gave her a summary of our conversations and she asked me a few more questions about Ace.

After we hung up, the reality hit home. Her whole focus was on Ace. What did I expect? It seemed like she had been mine for awhile, but now she belonged to Ace whether he wanted her or not. I turned the television on and sat there feeling sorry for myself. When I turned out the lights, I couldn't go to sleep. I had really fucked things up.

When I finally dozed, my sleep was interrupted with another nightmare. I was sweating and having trouble breathing. After a few minutes I calmed down. Thank God, I was at least getting better at calming down. It was 2:47. I put on some shorts and a tee-shirt and went for a walk around the grounds. It was quiet. I thought of April asleep in her bed and how we had been nestled together last night in a wonderful sleep.

I didn't get much more sleep that night. After my morning run, I got some breakfast and called Ace. He excitedly said it looked like we could leave around 1000. He said that Derrick was going to help him get his stuff on a cart and he would be at the east side entrance.

I had an hour to kill so I went to the book store and looked around. It kept going through my mind that all April cares about is Ace.

That wasn't true. I knew she cared about me too, but not in the same way. I thought to myself, "You made this bed so get comfortable; it's your reality."

They were waiting for me. Ace had a big shit-eatin' grin on his face. We all pitched in to load his stuff in the car.

I turned to Derrick. "So your surgery is tomorrow? I hope it goes well."

"Me too," he replied. "I talked with my surgeon this morning. I told him I wanted to get transferred to another hospital closer to home. He said if this surgery goes well, that's an option. So keep me in your prayers."

I hadn't heard that for awhile. I was more use to, "wish me luck" or something like that. Maybe Derrick was religious or maybe he thought prayer was better than luck. Anyway, I said as I gave him a hug, "I sure will. We'll call you in a few days to check. If you have to stay here, we'll be back to visit you." Ace gave him a hug and we were off.

As we pulled out of the parking area, Ace said, "I'm not coming back here even to visit him. I hate this fucking place. I've been miserable since the day I got here. Most of 'em are a bunch of assholes."

"What the fuck Ace? You had a lot of people helping you get outta there."

"I'm not talking about them. I'm talking about everybody else - a bunch of pricks. I wanted to bash their faces in and I almost did a few times. I couldn't sleep and when I did, those fucking nightmares drove me crazy. Everywhere I looked I saw stuff that reminded me of this fucked up war. I'm not coming back here."

"Okay." Neither one of us spoke for awhile.

He said, "I need a beer."

"We only have a few more miles on the Beltway until we get to I-66 and then I'll pull off once we get headed west."

"Jett, I need a fucking beer and I needed one ten minutes ago. My chest is starting to get tight."

There was an exit up ahead. I got off and pulled into a gas station and said, "I'll be back in a minute."

"No, I'm going in with you." He reached in the back to get his crutch and cursed when he couldn't get it out from under some stuff in the back seat.

"You need some help?"

"No!"

He went to the cooler, picked up a six pack and said to the cashier nodding in my direction, "He'll pay for this." He struggled getting out the door with the crutch and beer. I heard a muffled, "fuckin' shit."

I got a Styrofoam cooler, a bag of ice, and a twelve pack. I put the beer in the cooler, poured the ice over it and loaded it into the back seat.

I asked, "You feel any better?"

"Not yet," as he reached back and got another one. We went on in silence for awhile. Finally, he said, "That feels better. I don't know what happened."

"You did better than me. I had a panic attack before I left the parking lot at Walter Reed."

"No shit?"

"Yeah, an officer saw me and I thought he was gonna make me go back in the hospital. But I convinced him I was okay."

We drove on in silence while Ace downed beers three and four.

"Better now?" I asked.

"Yeah, that's better."

17
THE ROAD HOME

"Have you thought about what you want to do about the drive home?"

"Yeah," and he smiled. "I've thought about it a number of times. Let's just drive to Florida and stay down there about a year and then we can go home."

I didn't respond and decided to let him have some time to think about it. I looked over and he looked like he was getting sleepy so I had to jump in. "Ace, in about thirty minutes, we'll reach the turn off for the Skyline Drive. Do you want me to go that way or do you want me to drive further and pick up I-81?"

"Let's take our time and go Skyline Drive. Would you call Ma and tell her we'll be there tomorrow night?"

"Okay, I'll stop at the next pay phone and give her a call."

By the time we reached the entrance to Skyline Drive, Ace was asleep. I pulled over and called Ma. She asked about him and I said he's doing pretty well. Honestly, I didn't know how he was doing. All I had to go on was how I felt on my way home. Ma said she would call Mom and told me to tell him she loved him and for us to be careful.

I got us some sandwiches, chips, and cookies. I thought we would drive for another hour and then pull over and eat our lunch. When I got in the car, I was tempted to reach back and get a beer. One with lunch wouldn't hurt, but one before lunch was not a good idea. I drove for an hour and pulled off at one of the overlooks. Ace was asleep and I didn't want to wake him, but I was hungry and needed that beer. I parked in a space where I could see the car and still have a nice view.

About ten minutes into my lunch, Ace opened the car door rubbing his eyes. He got his crutch out of the back seat and reached in the cooler for another beer. As he approached, he asked, "Got a sandwich for me?"

"Hell no. Why would I get a sandwich for you," I teased as I reached for his sandwich. "How is your leg?"

"It still hurts like hell when I put too much weight on it, but the physical therapy has helped. The Doc said if I follow through with the PT, I should be able to get around without much trouble. I'm not sure what that means and he wouldn't say more than that."

"You were sleeping pretty hard."

"Probably so, I don't think I got any sleep last night. This sandwich is good. I was too nervous to eat breakfast."

"So those beers were on an empty stomach. Now I know why you passed out so quickly."

He smiled, "Yeah, I felt a lot better after the beers." We talked and for the first time he seemed relaxed and more like his old self.

We looked at the view and talked about old times. We finished our lunch and got on the road. We decided to drive a couple more hours and stop for the night. Ace had another beer and within ten minutes, he was asleep again.

He was probably exhausted for many reasons, but for the first time in awhile, I knew he felt safe. He could count on me to take care of anything that might happen.

I drove a little over two hours and got about thirty miles into the Parkway. I exited and drove down the mountain to find a motel.

There were several along Route 11 and I pulled over and checked in. Ace was stirring when I came back to the car.

"Where the fuck are we?" he said a little above a whisper.

"Hell, I don't know. I just came off the mountain. I didn't pay attention to signs. Let's get our stuff in the room. I'm ready for a beer."

We went inside and opened a couple of beers. We put the cooler between our beds and propped ourselves up in our beds and turned on the TV. Some old western was playing on one of the channels. We each drank more beer and fell asleep. I woke up and it was 7:22.

"Ace, wake up."

He stirred and said, "Where am I?"

I gave him a few minutes to get the fog out of his brain. He continued, "I must have passed out. What time is it?"

I told him and said, "Do you want to order in or go out for something to eat?"

"I wanna find a bar and get something stronger than a beer."

"Okay. I'm gonna get a shower." When I came out of the bathroom, I asked him if wanted to shower.

"No, I'll wait till later."

After driving a few miles down the road, we found a place, Steele's Tavern, and pulled into the parking lot. It was pretty crowded. We ordered a draft beer and a couple of shots.

I said, "You ready to order?"

"I'm ready to eat something, but it's not food."

He ordered another shot, drank it, slid off the stool, got his crutch, and headed for a strawberry blonde who was sitting alone at the other end of the bar. She was wearing a beige thin blouse that showed plenty of cleavage. She was kind of attractive and her hair was curly and short.

Ace started a conversation with her and several minutes later, a dude with black hair hanging down to his shoulders, a medium build, and muscular arms covered with tattoos came out of the restroom and headed toward the same girl. There was a brief exchange and Ace came back and sat down beside me.

I asked, "That her boyfriend?"

"I don't know, but it was obvious they were together. When I looked back, they were looking at me and she winked." He looked around the room.

"Lookin' for another prospect?"

"Yup. I've gotta get laid tonight."

"Not wastin' any time!"

"Nope."

"I'm gonna order. Do you want something?"

"Yeah, I want another beer and a shot. No food."

I ordered my food and Ace got his drinks. He kept looking around the room and eventually went over to the pool table and picked up a game. He was able to balance on one leg. He was a good pool player and seemed to be enjoying himself.

I ate my dinner and talked some to the bartender. After finishing, I went to Ace and told him I was ready to leave. He wanted to stay and said he would find a ride to the motel.

While driving, I thought about how different we were. Ace always liked to party and hang out at bars. I didn't mind going for a drink or two, but I always left and he always stayed. He had gotten laid numerous times while we were in the service and my count was zero.

On several occasions, I asked him what it was like to have slept with so many women. He would never talk much about it other than saying it was great and I ought to try it.

I think people wondered how we could be so different and still be so close. We might be different in some ways, but in a lot of other ways we loved the same things. We shared a love for the outdoors, hiking, having fun with our friends, working out, and being together. There was this incredible bond between us.

The motel area was quiet with only a few cars. I checked the area behind the motel. It was open and appeared secure. I got a beer, turned on the TV, and lay back on the bed. Soon, my eyes were heavy. I turned off the TV and light and passed out.

I got up to pee, 2:45, no Ace. I went right back to sleep. I woke at my usual time. No Ace. I guessed he went to some girl's place. I was glad he wasn't back because I wanted to go for my morning run and didn't want to upset him. Not being able to run was going to be a challenge for him. That was a big part of our life.

During my run, I decided that I was going to tell him about April and me when we got back on the road and took our first break at one of the overlooks. I was nervous just thinking about it. Even though objectively, as April and I had discussed a number of times, we had done nothing wrong. However, I couldn't escape the feeling that I had somehow betrayed him.

When I got back to the motel, a car was pulling away from the parking lot and heading up the road in my direction. The strawberry blonde was driving and gave me a little wave and a faint smile as she passed. I smiled and thought it looked like he had accomplished his mission.

He was sprawled across his bed on his back with a shit-eatin' grin on his face. "Wow!" he said. "Remember that strawberry blonde?"

"Yeah, I just passed her on the road."

"She was one hot chick."

"Good for you," I said. "Did you get any sleep?"

"Not much. You mind if I sleep for a few hours and then we can get on the road."

I responded, "No, that's fine. I'll get some breakfast and come back here and watch TV. I'll wake you before checkout time."

"Thanks old buddy," he mumbled and was snoring within a couple of minutes. I showered, got some breakfast, made a stop at the 7-Eleven for more ice and beer, and got sandwiches and chips for lunch.

18
THE CONFESSION

We were on the road by 11:30. Ace only wanted two cups of black coffee. Soon after he finished his coffee, he was asleep again. The caffeine didn't faze him. I was left alone with my thoughts about how I was going to tell my best friend that I had fucked his old girlfriend.

We had 250 miles before reaching home and I decided to drive until Ace woke up. I was putting off our talk about April and me as long as possible. I wondered what she was doing and thinking. I couldn't remember if she was working this weekend. If I had been her, I would have volunteered to work to keep my mind busy. I missed her.

Ace stirred and said he had to pee. It was 3:05. I said, "There's a visitor's center in about fifteen minutes. Can you wait?"

"Yeah, what time is it?" I told him and he continued, "How far from home?"

"Two and a half to three hours."

"You're driving too fast," he stated.

"Got it set right on the speed limit."

He smiled, "It feels like you're goin' a hundred miles an hour."

"You're real eager to get home!"

"Yeah, can't wait. Think back a few weeks ago. How eager were you to get there?"

"I know. I felt the same way."

He sat up straight and said, "Hey, there's an overlook. Let's stop there. I don't wanna be around all those people at the Visitor's Center."

I replied, "Sounds good to me too. Do you think we'll ever be comfortable around groups of people again?"

"I don't know, but a few beers might make it more tolerable. Speaking of beer, how many we got left from yesterday?"

"I got more beer and ice while you were sleeping before we left the motel."

"You're the man!"

I pulled over and parked at the end of the lot. There was only one other vehicle at the other end. Ace got his crutch and headed for the edge of the woods. I got the cooler and sandwiches and a blanket and walked down a path to a secluded spot. He followed me. I spread out the blanket so we could lean against a rock.

As soon as he sat down, I tossed him a beer, got one for myself and took a big swallow.

"Haven't we been here before?" he asked.

"It looks familiar, but I don't know for sure."

I handed him a sandwich and a bag of chips.

After a couple of bites, he said, "I could sit here all day and be fine. I don't know if it's 'cause I've always loved being in the woods or that it's isolated."

He seemed to be deep in thought so I decided to let him have some time to think about it. He then said, "Maybe it's both. I've never really liked crowds, but I've never been as anxious around people like I am now. That fuckin' war. Hand me another beer."

I got me another beer too and replied, "Yeah, it's the same for me. I've spent more time in the woods since I've gotten home. I spent one night in our secluded spot."

"I'd like to go directly there with enough beer and food to last us for a week and use that as a base and hike all our favorite trails."

He paused and after a minute or so I looked over at him and there were a few tears running down his cheeks. He blurted out, "Don't look at me! For a fuckin' minute, I forgot that my fuckin' leg ain't gonna take me on no fuckin' hikes."

We sat in silence. I finally said, "The Doc all but said you would be able to walk."

He broke in, "My bullshit meter tells me he was fuckin' lying."

This was not the time to give him a pep talk. He was not in the mood and I understood. I didn't want anyone telling me that having a positive attitude would help me get over all this shit from the war.

More silence. Finally he said, "When are you going to tell me?"

"Tell you what?"

"Give me a fucking break Jett. You've been acting strange from the first moment I laid eyes on you Thursday. You can't hide shit like me. I can read you like a book and something is bothering you. I thought about it Thursday night while I was trying to go to sleep. The only thing I could think of is that you porked April. Am I right?"

I looked at him and obviously couldn't read him like a book and couldn't tell by his expression what he was thinking or feeling. I looked him in the eyes and then looked down. "Yeah."

He said, "Well, if you thought I was going to be mad, then you don't know me very well. I've had almost no contact with her for four years. What right would I have?"

"I do know you well enough to know that you wouldn't be mad. But I couldn't shake the thought that I had still betrayed you."

He answered, "Well get that thought out of your mind. I don't feel betrayed. I'm glad you finally got laid after three years. I don't know how you waited that long, but we have different views on getting a piece of ass. You take it more seriously than me. You have to feel something before you pork a woman."

I broke in, "Would you stop using that word, 'pork'?"

"There you go. That's my point. Do you love her?"

I hesitated and then said, "I don't know. Maybe. But that doesn't make any difference because she made it very clear that she doesn't love me."

"Well, I don't know if I would believe her 'cause she's a lot like you. She needs to have feelings before she'll have sex."

I interjected, "I think she has feelings for me, but she's definitely not in love with me. I don't know if I should tell you, but she still loves you."

"I guess I'm not surprised. She's written me a bunch and I thought she might still want us to get together. I may have written once in three years. I can't even remember. Hand me another beer."

He went on, "I had a lot of time at the hospital to think about things. I confess that I thought quite a bit about her. I wondered if you two were getting it on after you told me about her being at the cabin. Honestly, it didn't bother me much, but it bothered me a little and that was surprising. Hell, I don't know what I feel about April."

I looked at him earnestly, "Ace that is the most you've shared with me in years. What's goin' on with you?"

"I don't know. I'm so fucking angry about everything. I've got this feeling I'm gonna explode any minute. I'm miserable and there's this voice in my head screaming, 'Shut the fuck up!' You don't have anything stronger than beer do you?"

"No."

He said, "I don't want to talk about this anymore. I want the old Jett back. Stop feeling like you've betrayed me. I'm fucked up, but not the kind who would say I can fuck my brains out, but my old girlfriend can't fuck anybody especially my best friend. That's bullshit."

I had tears in my eyes and he said, "We're both a bunch of cry babies."

We smiled and I said, "Yeah, I guess we are."

He drank one more beer and was content to sit in silence and look out over the countryside. For the first time since we left the hospital, I noticed the sky and saw a few fluffy white clouds. I felt a gentle breeze and marveled at the beauty of the mountains in the distance.

I was home again with my closest friend. As long as we lived, there would only be a handful of people who understood what we had been through. That was fine. It was enough that this one person had stood with me and was willing to give his life in a heartbeat to save mine. He would always be a part of my life.

We would face many challenges ahead, trying to figure out how to heal and find some peace and happiness in our lives. I would be there for him and he would be there for me. Together we would find the path that would set us free.

He surprised me and said, "I'm ready to go."

While he was getting to his feet, I cleaned up and packed our stuff. When I finished, our eyes met and with tears on my cheeks, I went over and embraced him. "I love you Ace."

"I love you too Cry Baby."

We walked to the car and headed for home.

We'd been on the road for about five minutes when Ace said, "Pull over at the Visitors Center and I'll call Mom and let her know we'll be there about 7:00. See if you can find a pay phone away from all the people."

"Are you sure you wanna go home today? We could spend one more night on the road."

"I'm as ready as I'll ever be."

He made his call and returned to the car. He said, "Mom said she was not having a party and it would just be the four of us and you for dinner."

Ace seemed to be deep in thought as we rode on for awhile in silence. I said, "Would you like to stay with me at the cabin?"

Without hesitation, he replied, "That's strange. I was just thinking about asking you if that would be okay with you."

"Then it's settled. Do you think Ma will be upset?" I asked.

"She'll maybe be disappointed, but not upset or surprised."

"That's a good description of how Mom felt when I brought it up after the party. I've tried to keep in close touch by visiting and calling."

"I'll do the same. Do you mind if I get some sleep?"

"No, go ahead."

He slept part of the time and spent the rest of the time talking and trying to be as upbeat as possible. He had only two more beers on that final leg of the trip.

19

ACE RETURNS TO HARVEST

It was 7:10 when we pulled into Ace's driveway. His Dad and Jeffery came out to meet us. I knew Ma was holding back to keep Ace from being overwhelmed. Ace went in and the rest of us got his stuff.

We took our time to give Ace a few minutes with Ma.

We put the stuff in his room and his Dad said, "You guys want a beer?"

We both said yes and Jeffery asked, "Dad, could I have one too?" Jeff was seventeen and a senior in high school.

His Dad looked at Ma and she nodded. "Okay Son, but only one."

We stood around in the kitchen while Ma put the finishing touches on the dinner. I knew Ace was anxious, but he put on a good show. The conversation was light with a few laughs here and there.

During dinner, Ace talked some about his Walter Reed experience, but mainly steered the conversation around to catching up on what everyone had been doing over the last week. I had used that same tactic. If we could keep other people talking, we didn't have to talk.

When dinner was finished, I excused myself saying I needed to go over and check in with Mom and Dad. We said our goodbyes and Ace followed me to the car. "I'll hang around here for another hour or so and then head up to the cabin."

"Sounds good."

I checked in with Mom and Dad. We talked for a few minutes and then Mom said, "Your dad and I have a welcome home gift of you."

"I didn't expect any gift."

"I know, but it's something Marge and I have been talking about. She and Jim are giving the same gift to Ace. We decided to wait until you were both home."

I took off the wrapping paper and could see by the box, it was a cell phone. "Mom and Dad, thanks. I know April has one, but I've always thought it was more for work."

"The lady said you and Ace have to go to the cell phone company and activate the phones."

I thanked them again for the gift and the use of Mom's car and left. Spot and I went to the store to pick up a few items. I stopped for a few minutes to see Henry and Betty to bring them up to date and to thank Henry one more time for all he had done for Ace and me.

When I got to the cabin, I could tell that April had cleaned and straightened up. She knew where we hid the key so she must have come today as there was a vase of fresh wild flowers on the kitchen table.

I put groceries in the fridge and picked up the phone to call her. She picked up on the second ring.

"Hello."

"Hey April."

"Hey Jett. How are you?"

"I'm fine. How 'bout you?"

"I'm all right. Marge called me after Ace called her to let me know you guys were going to arrive around 7:00."

"Thanks for the pretty flowers and the place looks great."

"You're welcome. I came up last night, spent the night and took my time cleaning. The cabin seems like home to me. There are so many wonderful memories. I didn't leave till around 3:00."

I gave her some brief details about our arrival, dinner, and the plan that Ace would be staying here with me for awhile.

She said, "I assume he's not there now."

"Right."

"How is he?"

"Thanks to about a dozen beers over the day, he's doing okay."

"Did you tell him?"

I gave her every detail of our conversation that I could remember. I left out the part where Ace said he had been thinking about her, but didn't know how he felt about her. "I hope I didn't overstep any boundaries by telling him that you still love him."

There was a pause and then, "No that's all right. It's probably better that he knows. It really makes it simpler when I think about it. It's like my cards are on the table and I don't have to play any games concerning how I feel about him."

I replied, "I think that's better too, but I'm sorry I said that without checking with you first."

"Jett, don't think any more about it. I really do think it's for the best."

I asked, "How are you really doin'?"

"I'm nervous just knowing he's back in town and I don't know what to do next. Do I wait around for him to call me or do I call him?"

I interjected, "Remember, I told you I would help you figure something out."

"I remember and I'm open to any ideas you have."

"Tomorrow is Sunday. How about coming for supper on Monday? That would give him a few days to settle in."

"Do you think he'll agree?"

"I don't know, but I think it's worth a try. I'll talk to him about it so I can give you some notice. How do you feel about it?"

"I'm nervous, but while you were gone I had some time to think. I don't want this to drag out. I want to know soon if there's a chance we can get back together."

"I understand, but I think some patience is going to be important. We both have some work to do to return to some form of mental stability. Any important decisions we make about our life need to be put on hold for awhile."

She responded, "I understand, but I'm not sure how long I can wait."

"Maybe the best approach if you can do it is to take one day at a time."

"I just need something to hold on to. I need some kind of hope there's a chance. I'm not going to spend much time without that hope."

"I understand."

"How are you doing Jett?"

"I'm tired, but relieved he knows about us. I miss you and I have to admit it's going to be hard to help you two get back together. I do know if there is any possibility for us, you have to find out whether you have a future with Ace. I'm committed to doing everything I can to help."

"I don't want you to wait around on me. You have to get on with your life."

"I know. I want to do the very same thing I suggested to you and take one day at a time."

She wanted more details about our trip home and I told her as much as I could remember. I left out the strawberry blonde story.

"What time will Ace get to the cabin?"

"I don't know. He should be here soon. Oh, I forgot to tell you that Mom and Dad and Ma and Jim got us cell phones as a welcome home gift."

"That's nice. I think you'll like having them." I told her we would get ours activated in a few days.

We said our good-byes and hung up. I had to get out of the cabin. Spot was ready to go too. I grabbed my flashlight and we headed up the trail.

20

AN UNLIKELY REUNION

When Spot and I came down the trail, I saw Ace's old SUV parked by my truck. Spot took off for the cabin. Ace was sitting on the porch drinking a beer and Spot leaped up on his lap and licked his face and Ace was rubbing his ears. They had quite a reunion.

Spot loved us, but I think there was a special place in his heart for Ace. He always gave Spot special attention by rough housing and they often played chase and fetch.

"What did Ma and your Dad say when you told them you were going to stay up here with me?"

"Dad of course had to make his comment about me just getting home and why couldn't I stay around for a few days."

"I know that one. Dad said the same to me."

"Mom didn't even act disappointed. I think she expected it. She wanted me to come tomorrow for Sunday dinner. I told her I would. She said to bring you too."

"Tell her thanks for the invite, but I promised Mom I would go to church with them and then eat at the Inn."

"I'll tell her," he said and continued, "Did you get your welcome home gift?"

"Yeah. It'll seem different carrying around a phone."

"It shouldn't take us long to get use to it having carried around those radios for three years. How do we get 'em activated?"

"I'll find out on Monday," I answered.

He said, "Let's go to Stanley's for a drink."

Stanley's was a bar and grill on the outskirts of Harvest. We used to hang there a lot before we went into the Army. I responded, "I'm tired and ready to get some sleep. Why don't we hang out here for awhile? Even though you slept some, you've gotta be tired."

"No, I'm not tired, but I won't stay long. You go on to bed. I'll see you in the morning."

Spot didn't want to get off his lap, but he finally jumped down. Ace got his crutch and headed for his SUV. Spot followed, wanting to go with him. I called him back. I hollered, "Be careful. Don't get a DUI."

He hollered back, "Don't worry, I won't."

I went on to bed and must have passed out because I don't remember anything after my head hit the pillow.

Spot

The next thing I knew, I heard someone calling my name. I startled, sat up and looked at the clock, 2:33. I went into the great room and Sammie Adams was standing at the door with another guy I didn't know. They had Ace between them holding him up. His face was bloody and he was semi- conscious.

"Sammie, what the hell happened?"

"We were coming out of Stanley's and found Ace lying face down in the parking lot. We turned him over and he started wildly throwing punches at us. I yelled at him telling him it was me and to calm down. He didn't seem to understand at first, but we finally got him calmed down.

We told him we were going to take him to the ER and he pleaded with us to bring him here. The bleeding looked like it had stopped so we agreed. Jett, by the way, this is my friend, Cecil."

"Hey Cecil, thank you both for bringing him back. Would you all put him on his bed?"

"Sure."

"Thanks, I'll take it from here. I really appreciate y'all doing this."

Sammie said, "Sure you don't need some help?"

"No thanks, I know a nurse and I'll call her. Y'all can take my truck and I'll pick it up tomorrow."

They left and I went back in to check on Ace. Spot was lying on the mattress next to his feet. He mumbled, "Jett, did we get hit by a sniper?"

"No, you got in a fucking fight." Then he seemed to drift back into a drunken' sleep.

I went to the phone and dialed April. A sleepy voice said, "Hello."

"It's me. Ace got in a fight at Stanley's. Sammie and a friend of his brought him here. He wouldn't let them take him to the ER."

A lot more alert now, she said, "Does he need to go to the ER?"

"I don't think so."

She cut in, "Has the bleeding stopped?"

"Yes."

"I'll be there in twenty minutes."

I put some water on to boil and went back in to check on him. He was mumbling something like, "Keep your head down Jett, that fuckin..." and he drifted out again. I shifted him around trying to make him as comfortable as possible. I took off his shoes and put a light blanket over him. I checked on the water and went over to Pop's closet where he kept all his first aid supplies. I got out the things I thought April would need and put them on the dresser in Ace's room. I took the water off the stove and put it in the freezer to cool. I went back in the room to sit with him. In what seemed like only a few minutes, April came in the bedroom door.

"Hey," she said with a faint smile.

She started assessing his facial injuries and while doing that said, "Tell me what Sammie said."

I told her everything Sammie said to me.

She asked, "So he was laying face down in the parking lot?"

"Yeah."

"That may explain his face being bloody. I brought my first aid bag even though I knew Pop had a closet full of stuff. I wanted to make sure I had everything I needed. Knowing you, the water has already been boiled. Am I right?"

"Yeah, you want me to get it?"

"Yes."

I got it out of the freezer and it had cooled down a little.

She said, "While I'm working on cleaning up his face, I want you to cut off his clothes so we can make sure he doesn't have any other injuries. I also want to make sure the bandage on his leg is still in place."

Spot hadn't moved. I asked, "Should I get Spot off the bed?"

"No, he's fine." She talked as she was cleaning his face, "So far nothing more than minor lacerations. His right eye is swollen. I expect it to be black by later in the morning."

Once April finished cleaning his face, it didn't look too bad except for the swelling around his eye. She started pushing on different places around his rib cage and stomach. "I don't see any signs that they kicked him. He would be groaning if anything hurt."

I was working on cutting off his pants. When I got his left pants leg off, we could see that the bandage had been damaged. She went right to work. Being a surgical nurse helped as she without hesitation methodically worked on replacing the bandage.

At times, she would have me lift his leg, but mostly I just watched her work. Her hair was in a pony tail, but strands of her hair had come loose and were hanging around her face. Her complexion in the light had that slight glow and I remembered pressing my lips lightly to different parts of her face. And her lips were slightly parted and would move and close and open again as she worked on his leg. She is a sensuous woman.

She said, "They did a good job at Walter Reed on the bandage."

I replied, "It's supposed to be one of the Army's best." I could tell where the weight of her breasts were pushing down against her tee-shirt. And her ass in profile was round and sensual. Ace was so lucky and he didn't even know it.

April finished bandaging his leg and checked his body again for any other injuries. She asked, "Jett, could you get me a glass of water?"

"Sure."

When I came in with the water, she was sitting in the rocking chair. She looked up when I came into the room. "Thanks."

"You're welcome. What do you think?"

"It appears there's nothing serious. I'm not sure about internal injuries, but there's no sign. I think I'll stay here until I have to get ready for work. You go back to bed."

"I'll sit up with you."

"No, I'm fine and it appears that Ace will be fine too. He'll be sore when he wakes up from a combination of injuries and a hangover."

I said, "Okay, if you're sure."

She nodded. I crossed the room, leaned over and gave her a kiss on the cheek and said, "Thanks for coming."

She smiled, "Thank you for calling me."

I smiled back. "Come on Spot, I'll let you out." He hesitated and then followed me. I knew April wanted some time alone with Ace. The way she looked at him and the way she touched him made it clearer than ever that Ace would always have her heart. I had to do the best I could to move on and let her go. She would never be mine.

I stood out on the porch while Spot searched for a place to pee. I took some deep breaths. The air smelled fresh and the breeze felt good. It was so different from the war. We were injured several times in minor ways. Whether we were lying out in the desert or in our bed, we were always sweating. The heat was at times suffocating. We had made it home and now the battles were taking a different form.

Spot went back into Ace's room. Did Ace have Spot's heart too? I smiled. I didn't mind sharing Spot. It seemed like I tossed and turned and dosed a little. I did better than I thought because when I opened my eyes, it was light out and 8:42. I got up and went to see if April was still here. She was gone and Ace was snoring. Spot opened his eyes and jumped off the bed.

21

A BEGINNING OF SORTS

I did some stretching on the porch. The fog was beautiful, lying like a blanket in the valley for as far as I could see. The sky was clear and the air still. Ace and I were finally home for good. I didn't know what lay ahead for us, but we would find a way to survive.

Spot and I went for a run and were back in about forty-five minutes. I got his crutch and put it by his bed. He was still passed out. The area around his eye looked more swollen and was getting darker.

I heated water for my tea, put the coffee on, shaved, showered, ate an orange, a bagel and some cream cheese. I picked up the phone to call Mom and before I could dial, Ace called out.

He said almost in a whisper, "What the hell happened to me. My head is throbbing and I can hardly see out of my right eye."

"The best we could tell is that you got drunk and either fell on your face in the parking lot or somebody hit you in the face."

"I gotta pee really badly. Help me to the bathroom." After peeing, he said, "Get me a pair of shorts and a tee-shirt out of my duffle bag. I'll be out in a minute. I need a cup of coffee bad."

It took him longer to get dressed than it should have. "You okay?" I yelled.

He yelled back, "Yeah, I'll be there in a minute."

He sat down at the table and started sipping. "My head is killing me. You got any aspirin?"

"Yeah." I got the bottle out of the cabinet. "How many do you want?"

"I'll take four. How'd I get home last night?"

That question triggered emotions I had been holding inside since Sammie and Clyde brought him in last night. I banged on the table and yelled, "That's a fucking good question since you were so drunk you couldn't even stand up. We've been at war for almost three years and barely made it home and on your first night, you were going to fucking drive your sorry ass home when you couldn't even stand up."

I got up and went out on the back deck. I felt a panic attack coming on. I took some deep breaths and started my self-talk. It's okay. I'm okay. It'll pass. More deep breaths, more self-talk and I started calming down. Ace came out the door and sat down at the table.

He said, "I know I fucked up. My bad."

"What the fuck were you thinking?"

"I wasn't thinking." He paused and then said, "No, I didn't wanna think. All the time I was in the hospital, I couldn't shut out these images and the thoughts of all the shit we did over there. And everywhere I looked were the reminders - guys on the ward trying to recover and others who didn't make it. There was no relief. I thought it would be better when Derrick was admitted. But it got worse. He wanted to talk shit and I didn't. I thought I was goin' crazy."

I didn't know what to say. We sat in silence and finally I said, "Yeah, I got it. On the way from the hospital, I was also drinking to silence the images and thoughts. When I got home, I turned from loading up on beer to escaping into the woods. It seems like the only place I can feel comfortable and safe."

He replied, "That's not going to work for me with this fucking leg."

"Not true," I said. "I've talked to Jack and he's checking with some of his business buddies about where we could get a good deal on a couple of dirt bikes. We couldn't ride on some of the trails over in the

National Forest, but there are miles and miles of trails on our property. And all our favorite spots to hang out are accessible where you would only have to walk a short distance."

He replied, "My head hurts. I can't think that far ahead. We can talk about it later." We sat in silence again and then he said, "You never did tell me how I got home last night."

I told him the story up to where I called April. I paused and he said, "Then you called April, right?"

"Yeah, how did you know?"

He replied, "She wrote me a note." He pulled out a piece of paper and handed it to me. "Read it, will ya?"

"Ace, are you sure. This is between you two."

"Yeah, I'm sure. I found it after you got my stuff outta the duffle bag. I tried to read it, but my vision isn't the best and my head hurt so badly, I couldn't focus on it."

"I'll read it."

"Dear Ace: I didn't expect to see you so soon after your trip from Walter Reed. When you read this, your vision will be blurred and your head will be pounding. The intensity will subside by early afternoon. Ask Jett to give you something for the pain. I checked you out from head to toe and couldn't find any other injuries. If you have any internal pain over the next few days, please go to the doctor. Your bandage was torn so I replaced it. Your leg is healing, but you have already been told it will take time and you will need to continue physical therapy. I'm glad you're back from the war. I can't imagine what it must have been like. Jett told me some things, but I'm sure no one could really understand unless they were there. At some point, I would like to talk with you. Please let me know when would be a good time.

Love, April"

When I looked up, Ace seemed to be in deep thought. His eyes were fixed on the view of the mountains in the distance. The fog was gone and the air was clear. I took more deep breaths to help me settle down. I don't know what I expected in the letter, but I was anxious while reading it. Ace could probably tell; he could read me like a book.

He turned to me and said, "I asked you the other day if you loved her. You said maybe. You saw her last night. Has your answer changed?"

"No. I don't even know what the word love means. Was I starving for intimacy, longing for someone to hold me? It's been over three years since I've had any female contact. I just wish I had fucked that new receptionist at the Inn."

He replied, "I don't believe you. Like I said, you and April are a lot alike. You have to have feelings before you all will have sex."

Ace was talking. Something had changed. I had noticed it on the trip from the hospital. I had always wanted to share more stuff with him, but he was so closed in on himself when it came to these topics. I asked, "But are those feelings the same as love?"

He replied, "How the hell would I know the answer to that."

"I don't know the answer either, but remember what I said yesterday. She has feelings, but they are not love. That was so evident last night when I saw the way she took care of you. It was like she was loving you with her hands. The way she touched you was more like caressing. And the look in her eyes was dreamy and far away. As I watched her, I thought how lucky you are and you probably don't even know it."

He said, "I don't wanna talk about it anymore."

"Why not? Are you afraid to feel?"

He yelled, "Damn it Jett, I don't wanna fuckin' talk about it."

"Ace, you're gonna have to face stuff at some point. You can't keep drowning your fear in booze. It's gonna kill you."

Still yelling, "I'm not afraid of anything. I just don't wanna talk about that shit!"

I didn't reply. After a minute or so, he seemed to calm down and I said, "I told you that I drank a bunch of beers on the way home to help me relax and that the woods are my escape. It's hard for me to talk about shit too, but I believe it's the only way we can heal and move on from this three year nightmare."

"How does talking about what it means to love or do you love April or do I love April; and who does April love and do I really mind that you fucked April; or should you feel you betrayed me by fucking April; and what do I think she wants to talk to me about; and how do I feel about that and on and on and more bullshit and how does talking about that help us heal from the fuckin' war?"

I smiled at him but didn't reply. He smiled back and said, "That was pretty damn insightful on my part."

I said, "I need a beer. You want one?"

"No, I've decided I'm not drinking anymore and particularly not on Sunday before 10:00 in the morning."

I got us both a beer. We just sat and looked at the view and drank our beer.

After finishing my beer, I said, "I need to get ready for church. What time is dinner at your house?"

"I think she said to come around 1:00."

I asked, "How are you feelin'?"

He responded, "Pretty good, a little sore, but not much pain. That aspirin really helped."

"You know where the bottle is if you need more. I should be back here by 3:00. I'm gonna talk to Jack at church about the dirt bikes. Are you on-board with that idea?"

"Yeah, I guess."

"I'd like to get them on Monday or Tuesday if possible."

He replied, "I've got a doctor's appointment at 1:00 on Monday and a physical therapy appointment at 2:00."

"Jack said he had a couple of places in mind. They are both in Elverton. I could meet you after your appointments and we could look."

Without much enthusiasm, he said, "Okay."

We both stood up. I gave him a gentle hug. He seemed very fragile to me. He hugged me back and said, "I'll see you this afternoon. I'm gonna get cleaned up and it takes me awhile so I won't be finished before you leave. Tell your Mom that banana pudding was great."

"Say hey to Ma and everybody and thank her for the invite."

"I will. Later Man."

When I left fifteen minutes later, I could hear the water running in his bathroom.

22

EDEN

I told Mom I would meet them at the church. When I pulled up, it was between Sunday school and church and there were a bunch of people standing outside talking, some smoking cigarettes. Mom and Dad were talking to Jack and Ann. I joined them and we all hugged. They were all glad to see me.

I talked to Jack about the trail bikes. He had contacted two of his friends and they were expecting us to come by. He gave me their phone numbers.

We went into the church and my thoughts drifted. I loved this church and the people. So many good memories. I liked our rector. His name was Matthew Patterson. He was in his mid-sixties and was wise, kind, and gentle. We called him, Father Pat. He always seemed to say something I needed to hear.

At some time in the future, I wanted to talk with him about my problems with God and war. I had a lot of questions. Somewhere in those three years of hell, I felt like I lost my faith. I didn't know what I believed anymore. Whether I believed in God or not, Father Pat would always have some words of wisdom to help me in my life.

Henry, Betty, and Jimmy were talking with Pop and some of his friends. There were more hugs and greetings. Jimmy said that Fran had stayed home with Charles who was running a fever. Sadie didn't come to church anymore, but she and Tom would be joining us for lunch at the Inn.

Jack took me by the arm and said he wanted me to meet someone. He steered me to the other end of the pew where a few other people were talking. As we approached, the group broke up and Jack said, "Jett, you remember Aunt Agnes!"

"Yes, I sure do." I gave her a hug and said, "How are you Aunt Agnes?"

Actually Aunt Agnes was not Jack's aunt. She had been Jack's mother Grace's best friend. His mom died of breast cancer about ten years ago. Both women were widowed five years before Grace got cancer. It was probably one of the reasons they became so close. Anyway, Agnes moved in with Grace during that last year before her death and took care of her until she died.

At his mom's funeral, Jack talked about all that Agnes had done for his mom and the family and that the two women had been like sisters. He announced that Agnes would forever be a member of "our family" and that from this day he would call her Aunt Agnes.

"I'm fine Jett, thank you. I want you to meet my niece, Eden Howell."

I turned and extended my hand and met her eyes. I started to say something, but nothing came out. I felt a slight intake of air, a tightening of my chest, and a rush of blood to my head.

She smiled at me rather shyly, but with a warmth and softness. "Hello Jett, nice to meet you." I mumbled something back like nice to meet you too, but I didn't say her name. I forgot I was still holding her hand kind of shaking it, but more holding it. She slowly withdrew her hand and my hand was left suspended in the air.

Jack saved me more embarrassment by saying, "Aunt Agnes used to attend the Presbyterian Church, but last year we asked her to join us for a service. She loved Father Pat so now we get to see her at least once a week. Aunt Agnes, I hope you and Eden will join us for lunch at the Inn."

Aunt Agnes replied, "Thanks for the invitation Jack, but Eden has to leave for home shortly after church. I want to see her off. Maybe next time."

Jack said, "Of course, we'll count on it."

At that point, Father Pat and the acolytes appeared at the rear of the church. Jack said, "Good to see you both. Eden, have a safe trip home."

She smiled and said, "Thanks Jack. Nice to meet you Jett."

"Me too," I mumbled and said, "Good to see you Aunt Agnes." Dad, Mom, and I sat in the pew with Jimmy, Pop, Henry and Betty. Jack, Ann, Aunt Agnes and Eden sat in front of us. Mom looked at me, gave my hand a little squeeze and smiled. She knew I was a little shaken. I was still having a little trouble with my breathing and still embarrassed. I focused on my breathing. A few minutes later, I was a feeling a little better.

Eden was about two people to my right and I couldn't see her well without turning my head. While we were standing and singing hymns I was able to see her better out of the corner of my eyes. She was petite with kind of blue-green eyes, a cute nose, and a wide mouth for the size of her face with sensuous lips. She was about five-foot four with shoulder length sandy blonde hair. Weight about 110. Moderate size breasts and a nice little round butt. I couldn't tell her age but my guess was early thirties. She was wearing a white blouse with black trousers.

What was it about this woman that had rendered me speechless and almost out of breath when I met her? Yes, she was attractive and I am usually shy around attractive women when meeting them for the first time, but this was different. There was something about her, some kind of aura or energy or presence that to me felt like a magnet.

What was up with me? Was this the part of me that is starved for emotional and physical intimacy? Was this the part of me that responded with heart, soul, and body to April? Several times in the past three years, I thought I was going to die without ever knowing the kind of love I dreamed about. Was there now a kind of desperation to find that love?

April gave me a glimpse of what I longed for, but could never have with her. I had noticed Sandra at the front desk and wondered about her. There was more here. Something I couldn't describe. All I know is it felt like this incredible attraction.

Before I knew it, we were standing and Father Pat was leading the procession down the aisle. Where had the time gone? I didn't want it to be over. It's like I could feel her energy from where I was sitting.

The service was over and Aunt Agnes and Eden moved down the pew away from where I stood. Jimmy was ready to exit to our left and I shuffled in that direction. I watched Aunt Agnes and Eden slip out the side door of the church. My heart sank. I wanted to see her, to watch her from a distance, to see how she walked and see the expressions on her face. I wasn't even close to being ready to talk with her.

People moved like snails to the door. Everyone talked and I wanted to climb over the pews to see if I could see her one more time. By the time I reached the front steps, they were nowhere to be seen.

Now that I'm out of the church, I could think, "What the fuck was that?" I'm fucking going out of my mind. I'm trying to figure out if I love April and this woman comes along and I'm mesmerized and I haven't even said a word to her. Holy shit!

A thousand thoughts were going through my mind. Again, am I desperately trying to find someone else because I know April will never be mine? If that were the case, Sandra would be on my mind. She's hot and attractive and has been giving these flirtatious smiles. No, I refuse to believe that. There is something about this woman.

Mom touched me on the arm, smiled, and asked, "Jett, are you all right?"

"Sorry Mom. Yeah, I'm fine."

"She's very pretty, isn't she?"

"Who's pretty?" Mom gave me that I'm your mom and you can't fool me look. I responded, "Mom, I don't understand, but I had this unbelievable attraction to her. It was like I have been looking for this person all my life and I haven't spoken a word to her."

She smiled and said, "While you were out here straining your neck to get a last glimpse of her, Jack came over and told me that Aunt Agnes had introduced you to Eden and that you were speechless."

"I'm not the greatest talker, but I'm seldom speechless. Mom, what's wrong with me?"

"Nothing's wrong with you Honey." She smiled, "It seems like she made quite an impression on you."

I smiled back, "You think? Can a person be smitten without speaking a word?"

She laughed, "Jett, I don't know, but I love seeing that sparkle in your eyes. I don't care if it's logical or not." She gave me a hug and said, "Everyone has headed over to the Inn. I told your Dad that I would ride over with you."

On the way to the Inn, I said, "Mom, I think she must be older than me."

"Jett, the only thing in the world I want for you is to be happy. I don't care how old she is. If you and Eden should happen to work it out, no one will be any happier than your mom. And I can speak for everyone in this family."

I smiled, "Thanks Mom."

She asked, "Is Ace all right?"

"Do you know about last night?"

"You know how fast news travels in this little town."

I gave her a short synopsis of everything that happened including April coming to the cabin to treat his injuries and my talk with Ace this morning.

"I'm glad there were no serious injuries. I worry about his drinking. He could have been killed or killed someone else."

"I know. I can't make him stop, but I'm gonna do everything I can to help him."

We pulled into the parking lot and Mom said, "I have one more concern. I know you and April spent a lot of time together before you went to pick up Ace. How is it between you two?"

"I wonder sometimes if I have always loved her, but I'm making peace with the idea that she will never love anyone but him. She has been really clear with me about that and it's nothing I didn't already know. The time we spent together before I picked up Ace was wonderful. I will always remember it, but I have to move on and I'm handling that pretty well most of the time."

"If you ever want to talk more about it, you know I'm a good listener. Well, let's go in and get something to eat. I asked Jack and Ann to save you a seat across from them. Something told me you might have a few questions for them."

Sure enough, there was a seat where I could talk with both of them. I hugged Mom and she took a seat next to Dad. I went over and gave Pop a hug around the neck, talked a couple of minutes with Sadie and Tom, and slapped hands with everyone else. Everyone was getting ready to place their orders. I knew what I wanted so I didn't have to look at a menu. I exchanged small talk with Jack and Ann.

Jack broke in with a big grin and his usual kidding way and a little louder than I would have liked said, "Well, Jett, what do you wanna know about Eden?"

Ann smacked him on the side of his head, "Jack Hollander, you shut your big fat mouth." Everyone was laughing and someone said, "Ann, smack him again!" They all loved to joke and poke fun at each other.

I tried to never let Jack get the best of me and I said, "Eden who?"

"Yeah, I can understand why you would say that since you never got a chance to get the word hello out of your mouth." He had that same big grin on his face.

"Okay, you got me this time. I wanna know everything."

Jack smiled, "You'll have to ask Ann. She knows a lot more than me."

People started placing orders so all the attention shifted away from me. "Ann, what can you tell me about her?"

"I don't know a lot Jett, but I'll tell you what I know. Eden's father, Morton is the youngest of Agnes' brothers. He moved his family to somewhere between Raleigh and the coast. Morton apparently was the black sheep of the family and estranged from his other siblings. He was married and had six girls. Eden was the oldest."

She continued, "They were poor and Agnes said Morton wouldn't work and they mostly lived off welfare. Eden was 'smart as a whip' to use Agnes words and had good grades in high school. She didn't have the opportunity to go to college so after she graduated, she worked for an insurance agency for about a year. She met someone during that year and he asked her to marry him. I don't remember his name but they got married.

"His family was from Greensboro and they owned a hardware store. Agnes said they had a lot of money. They were married about fifteen years and last year, they got a divorce. No children."

I was doing the math. That would put her around thirty-seven years old. I asked, "Is there anything else?"

"Yes, soon after they got married, she got a job with the Environmental Protection Agency and has worked for them all these years. Agnes said she started out as a secretary and moved up the ladder and now is the director of the Greensboro Division of the EPA. Agnes said the Agency headquarters in D.C. has been trying to lure her to Washington, but she likes the Greensboro area and turns down the promotions. Agnes says she makes good money and got a sizable settlement in her divorce."

"How often does she visit Aunt Agnes?"

She smiled, "I thought you might ask that question. Ever since her divorce, she has been coming about once a month for a weekend.

She loves these mountains and you know Agnes, she can hike with the best of 'em so they spend a lot of time hiking the trails."

I noticed that the table had gotten really quiet and everyone was eating and listening. Everyone could see my disappointment.

Pop said, "Well Jett, go talk to Agnes and see if Eden can come up in a couple of weeks. Maybe instead of telling her the truth that Jett is smitten with her, we could plan some event which would give Agnes a good reason to ask her."

Several others chimed in, "Good idea Pop."

Jack said, "Do we now have unanimous support for Pop's idea?" Everybody, but me raised their hands.

Jack went on, "We seem to have one dissenting vote."

Everybody went, "Boooooooooooooh."

This was going too fast. It all seemed like some kind of a childhood fantasy. I did want to see her again and didn't want to wait a month. I reluctantly raised my hand and everyone cheered and clapped.

It was settled. Everyone started talking and visiting. I half-whispered to Ann, "Anything else?"

She leaned over and said, "Agnes said her marriage was more of an arrangement than a marriage. Her husband had affairs, but Eden didn't care. She focused most of her attention on her career. Last year, his current girlfriend got pregnant and he asked Eden for a divorce. She agreed and got the hefty settlement. I have one last piece of information that will please you." She paused as Jack's teasing had rubbed off on her.

"Ann," I said earnestly, "What is it?"

With a fake puzzled look, she said, "I can't remember." Then a big smile, "Agnes told me this morning before church that Eden mentioned that she might buy a small house up here."

I couldn't hide a big smile.

Everyone was saying their goodbyes and Sadie came up and gave me a hug and said, "I'm eager to meet Eden."

Tom who had a reputation for saying what was on his mind asked, "How do you feel about her being fifteen or so years older than you?"

"I don't know Tom. I haven't had time to think about it, but right off the top of my head, I don't give a damn."

"Okay man, that's cool."

Mom came over and took me by the arm. "I guess we need to think about what kind of event to plan. It would have to be on a Saturday since Eden works. The timing is perfect for a welcome home party for you and Ace and we could have it here at the Inn. That would be a pretty setting with the lake in the background. We could invite a few of your and Ace's friends and both families." She thought for a moment and then continued, "We could do it a week from this coming Saturday. We would need that much time to plan."

"I'm not all that keen on a party, but I don't have any other ideas."

She said, "I'll call Ann and Betty when I get home and see what they think. I'll call you a little later. What are you going to do this afternoon?"

"Go back to the cabin. Ace was going to eat at his house and I told him I would see him after eating with you all at the Inn."

"All right, I'll talk to you later. Love you."

"Love you Mom."

23
SETTLING IN

Ace was not there when I got back to the cabin. I changed and decided to take Spot and go down to see Henry and Betty. Henry met me at the door. Betty had a headache and had gone to bed. He said he had eaten too much at the Inn and needed a hike to try and work off some calories. I needed some exercise too and Spot was wagging his tail. We were off.

We talked about different things. He told me he saw Dr. Kingston on Friday and he was eager to set-up a time to talk with Ace and me. Henry gave him my number at the cabin and said his assistant would give me a call on Monday. We talked about Eden and I told him what had been going through my mind. He was supportive and advised me to take it slow. I mentioned the welcome home party and he liked the idea.

We arrived back at the cabin and Ace's SUV was there. Ace met us at the door and gave him a hug and said, "Henry, I'll never be able to thank you enough for all you did to get me outta that hospital."

"I'm glad it worked out and we're all glad both of you are finally home." They chatted a few minutes and then talked about Ace's appointment tomorrow with Henry's physician friend. After awhile longer, he said he better get back to check on Betty.

"How're you feeling?" I asked.

"Not too bad. My face aches some, but compared to some of the pain we went through, this is nothing."

"How were things at your house?"

He replied, "Good. I'm just starting to appreciate how much I missed Mom's cooking. I was surprised that I was hungry. I got antsy after we ate. Dad wanted me to stay and watch a baseball game, but I told him I wasn't feeling too good."

"What did you tell them about your face?"

"I told them I had a little too much to drink and fell in the parking lot at Stanley's. Dad gave the lecture on getting a DUI and hurting myself or other people. They acted like they knew it was worse than I was letting on, but they didn't say anything else."

"My whole family knew about it. The Harvest gossip line was alive and well."

He said, "I'm gonna get a beer and go back to bed. You wanna a beer?"

"Yeah, thanks."

He went to his bedroom and shut the door. I drank a couple of beers and watched the baseball game. I fell asleep on the sofa. The phone rang and I jumped. "Shit, when is this gonna stop?"

"Hello."

"Jett."

"Hey April. How're you doin'? You must be exhausted."

"Yeah, I'm pretty tired. I was late getting off work and just got home. I'm getting ready to lie down for a nap. How's Ace?"

"He's actually doin' pretty well. He ate dinner at his house and when he got back, he said he didn't have that much pain. He's asleep right now."

"Did he mention the note I left him?"

"Yeah. He asked me to read it to him this morning when he got up. His head was throbbing and his vision out of that one eye was blurred. I thought it was a nice note."

She was silent. I continued. "I haven't told him that you're coming for dinner tomorrow night. We had a rough morning and had a couple of heated exchanges."

"What about?"

I answered, "Mostly about his drinking and being willing to open up and face his problems."

"Did you get anywhere?"

"I'm not sure. On a couple of occasions since I picked him up at Walter Reed, he's been willing to talk a little more about stuff. Nothing too deep, but it's given me hope. I'm not sure how I can help prevent these drinking sprees."

"You can't 'baby sit' him Jett. He's going to have to make that decision for himself. When do you all start work with Dr. Kingston?"

"His secretary is supposed to call tomorrow to set up an appointment."

"Will that be for just you or for Ace too?"

"I'm gonna make it for both of us."

"Good. I'll see you all tomorrow night. What time do you want me to come?"

"Around 6:00 would give me time to exercise. I've got to be careful. You know how he and I always exercised together. We continued while in the Army when we got the opportunity. He's already depressed enough about his leg. I don't want to constantly remind him he can't join me, but I have to keep exercising or I'll go crazy. How long do you think it'll be before he's a hundred percent?"

"I don't know. But I guess it's possible in four to six months. It appears the fracture is healing. A lot will depend on his mental attitude. The physical therapy will be the key and that's something he'll have to do on his own."

I asked, "Did I tell you about my dirt bike idea?"

"No."

I filled her in on the plan.

She responded, "I think that's a great idea. My cousin Johnny has one and I've ridden it before. If things work out, maybe I can borrow his and join you all."

"Sounds good."

She hesitated a little and then said, "I guess we'll have to see how tomorrow night goes."

Yeah, I guess so."

She said, "Take care of yourself. I think about you a lot and miss you. I won't repeat myself. You know what I have to do."

"I miss you too and yes I understand."

"See you tomorrow night." She hung up.

I put on my running clothes and secured my knife and the cabin and we were off. My thoughts turned to Eden and I went over in my mind all the events of the morning. How was I going to get beyond the embarrassment of our meeting? She had to notice I was dumb struck and hardly able to talk. I wonder if she could tell I could hardly breathe. It made me cringe to think about it.

Then my mind drifted back to April. What if she and Ace didn't make it and what if I fell in love with Eden and what if April wanted us to be together. Oh shit! A lot of "what ifs." I couldn't go there. It was too entangled.

I tried to focus on all the beauty around me. The sun was shining through the trees separating the sunbeams as they touched down on the ground. There was a nice breeze that gave the light a kind of waving motion. I felt a little dizzy so I shifted my gaze off the ground. The sky through the trees was light blue and the air was clear. As I ran along the ridge, I came to one of the places where I could see for miles and stopped for a moment.

This had been a day filled with different experiences from one spectrum to the other. From Ace and me in heated discussions to meeting someone who might be the woman of my dreams. Did I have a woman of my dreams? I don't think I had ever thought about it or maybe I had. Shit. I didn't know. As I stood there, I realized I had to get better. I had to heal and put this war behind me. I would never be good for anyone until I had made some good progress in that phase of my life.

The last few days had seemed better in some ways. With the exception of this morning, I didn't remember any recent panic attacks. I didn't seem quite as hyper-vigilant. I still had that exaggerated startle response. The nightmares hadn't been quite as bad and I'd had less beer this past week.

I smiled. Maybe I did have a chance for happiness.

When I returned to the cabin, Ace was still asleep. I wanted a beer, but given my thoughts about drinking less beer, I decided to get water instead. I told myself that I was going to drink beer, but keep it to a more reasonable amount.

I turned the TV on and the game was in extra innings. Spot curled up beside me. Not long afterward Ace came out of his bedroom. Spot got up to greet him. He looked like hell.

"Jett, would you get me a beer? My head is really hurting."

"Do you want more aspirin?"

"Yeah, bring me three."

"Better to wash them down with water. They will act quicker."

He smiled and then winced at the pain, "My bullshit meter picked-up on that one right away."

"It seemed like a good idea at the time," as I handed him the aspirin and beer.

He asked, "What's the score?"

"The Yankees and Red Sox are tied in the bottom of the tenth."

"Who's pitching for the Yankees?"

"Ace, how the hell am I supposed to know, I don't keep up with that shit like you do."

"I just thought you might have heard his name."

"Nope."

We watched the game for awhile. I got antsy and got up to get a beer.

He asked, "Where you goin'?"

"To get a beer."

"Will you get me another one?"

I brought back our beers and we watched more of the game.

I said, "I asked April to come for dinner tomorrow night."

He sat up. "You did what?"

"You heard me."

A pause and then, "I won't be here. I've got other plans."

"What other plans?"

"I'm meeting Sammie and some friends at Stanley's."

"Like shit you are. You haven't even talked to Sammie."

"I saw him this afternoon."

"You lying turd. You didn't see him."

"Jett, I'm not fucking staying here."

"Yes you fucking are staying here even if I have to steal that crutch. You gotta see her at some point and tomorrow night is as good a time as any."

Some Yankee hit a home run and Ace cheered and then winced, "Every time I move the muscles in my face, it hurts like hell. What were we talkin' about?"

"Nothin'. I'm gonna fix me a couple of ham sandwiches. Do you want any?"

"Yeah. I'm not hungry now, but I'll eat them later."

I fixed the food and put his in the fridge. "It's a beautiful evening. I'm gonna eat out on the back deck. Come out and talk to me."

Reluctantly he said, "OK, let me go pee and I'll be there."

We spent a good hour talking about our memories of high school and all the fun we had during those days. That was the first time in awhile we had laughed together. It felt good. We watched some TV and were in bed by 10:00. Spot followed me into my room. Well I'll be damned. Maybe I am number one with Spot after all. I realized that Spot had stayed with Ace because Ace needed him more than I needed him.

I woke up at my usual time. For the first time, I was glad that Ace liked to sleep. It had been a royal pain in the ass over the years to get him up to exercise. When I came out of the room he was asleep on the sofa. The TV was on, but turned down low.

Spot and I left for our morning exercise. I thought to myself that I spoke too soon yesterday. My nightmares last night were fucking terrible. I woke up at least two times sweating and struggling with my breathing. My sheets were soaked. Oh well, so much for that. Maybe I was still making progress in other areas.

When we got back home, I laid down on the bed in the other bedroom on my side of the cabin. I always thought of those two bedrooms on the other side as Ace's bedrooms and these on this side as mine. After my morning nap, I shaved and showered. When I opened the bathroom door, I smelled coffee. I stuck my head out the bedroom door, "What the fuck? You made coffee?"

"I made your ass coffee almost every day we were in the Army so what's up with that comment?"

"I don't even like coffee that much and you've been pretty useless since you got home."

"Dick Head, I've only been home a day and a half."

"Is that all, it seems to me it's been a couple of months taking care of your sorry ass."

He picked up an orange and threw it at me. I caught it in my left hand. Ace was the star pitcher on our college baseball team and I was his catcher. "Nothin's changed," I said. "You never had any pitch I couldn't catch. You're slider, your curve ball, your fast ball, your knuckle ball. I could catch 'em all."

"Well, is that so, Ass Wipe. How about my curve ball in that game with Davis College? You let that one get by you and I saved your ass by tagging the runner out at the plate."

"Only because I made a perfect throw!"

He said, "You remember that windy day when somebody hit that fly ball to Tommy in right field and the ball went right between his arms and hit him in the nuts?" We started laughing.

I followed up, "And they had to call time-out and take him out on a stretcher because he told the medics that it hit him on his pelvic bone and he couldn't walk." We were howling.

"Stop, this is killin' my face."

"Tommy didn't want the girls to know he'd been hit in the balls." More laughter.

I went back in the bedroom and got my sheets to put in the washer.

Ace asked, "Rough night?"

"Yeah. I woke up at least twice with drenched sheets."

"Me too. I kept thinking there was someone outside the window. I finally came in the great room and turned on the TV. I'm goin' to that gun shop in Elverton today and get me a Heckler and Koch 45 Compact. It's gonna have a ten-round magazine."

"That's gonna cost."

"I know, but I'll feel a lot safer at night. I'm gonna blow somebody's fuckin' head off if they break in the cabin."

"I keep my knife with me all the time."

"You know I'm not good with a knife like you. I'll feel more comfortable with a pistol. Do you know if there's a waiting period?"

"Not sure. I think there might be a waiver for veterans."

We ate our breakfast out on the front deck. Ace was feeling better.

I asked, "What time is your appointment?"

"It's 1:00 with the doctor and 2:00 with physical therapy."

"While you're over there, I'm gonna check on the dirt bikes and then stop by Dr. Kingston's office and get us an appointment hopefully for tomorrow."

"Who the hell is Dr. Kingston?"

"He's one of the two people who got your ass out of Walter Reed. Your doctor at Walter Reed wouldn't let you leave until there was a program in place for your physical and mental health."

He said, "I vaguely remember something Doc said to me about that, but honestly I wasn't listening. All I could think of is that I'll do anything to get outta there."

I said, "Check through all those papers you signed. It'll be in there somewhere."

"How often do I have to see this Dr. Kingston?"

"As I understand it, as often as he requires. We're both part of a research project headed up by Dr. Kingston for the National Institute for Mental Health. He is working on the epidemic within the military called Post-Traumatic Stress Disorder also known as PTSD."

"I know what it is Asshole. I'm not gonna be a guinea pig for any research on PTSD."

"Read your discharge papers Butt Hole. This is not voluntary. It's mandatory."

"I'm discharged. They can't touch me."

"They can recall you in a second. You better read those papers. I'm making the appointment for us and you can decide later whether you'll attend. Let the record state that I'm not going to visit you in that psych hospital in Asheville when they lock your ass up."

24
BUSINESS IN ELVERTON

He went to get ready and I made a call to the cell phone company and they said we could drop by anytime and get our phones activated. We left the cabin around noon and headed for Elverton. I dropped Ace off at the front door of the hospital, parked, and went to Dr. Kingston's office to make the appointments.

His office was located in a building adjacent to the hospital. The receptionist's office was empty and a note on the edge of the desk said, "Out to lunch, be back at 1:00." It was 12:50 so I sat down and leafed through a magazine.

Out of nowhere I started feeling anxious. I thought, "What if I have a panic attack here?" My chest started getting tight and I was having a hard time getting air. What if I pass out? I needed fresh air. I had to get outta there. I went out into the hallway and headed for the exit. I almost ran over a little lady in a wheel chair. I blurted out, "Sorry ma'am." Finally outside, I started talking myself down and getting my breathing under control. I sat on a bench out in the courtyard and closed my eyes.

I was extremely discouraged. I thought I was getting better and now it seemed like I was getting worse. It took what seemed like about fifteen minutes and I was ready to give it another try. This was the guy who was going to help us heal.

When I got to the office, a woman somewhere in her fifties looked up from her desk, smiled, and said, "Hello, I'm Janet, Dr. Kingston's assistant, how can I help you?"

I introduced myself and she said, "I was going to call you this afternoon to set up appointments for you and your friend. His name is Ace. Am I right?"

"Yes, that's right." I explained I had to bring him to the hospital so I decided to drop by and see about making the appointments. I asked, "Is there any possibility that we can get started tomorrow?"

She answered, "I think that will work just fine. Let me double check." She looked at a note on her desk and said, "Yes, that will work."

She wrote it down in a little notebook and continued, "Dr Kingston will be working with ten veterans. He has divided you into pairs and will devote one day a week to each group. The day for the two of you will be Tuesdays. Even though he will not spend the whole day with you, he will start at 9:00 and end at the latest 2:00. Some days will be longer and other days will be shorter."

I said, "Tuesdays will work for us."

"Saturday mornings will be set aside for group meetings when all ten of you will meet together. Will that work for you all?"

"Yes."

"Dr Kingston likes to meet away from the office. The first meeting will be at your house or at Ace's house. He likes to see where you're living and the surroundings."

"We live together."

"That will save some time. Would you write down directions to where you live on this paper?"

"He will be there at 9:00 in the morning. How long will it take for him to get from here to your house?"

I responded, "About twenty minutes that time of day."

She stood up and held out her hand and said, "Nice to meet you Jett. Dr. Kingston will see you and Ace in the morning."

I thanked her and left. I was feeling some anxiety about the sessions with Dr. Kingston so I went by Henry's office to see if he had eaten lunch. Judy smiled when I walked in the door and was her friendly self. After a few exchanges, she said, "Your uncle should have gotten out of class about five minutes ago. I expect him back any minute."

At that moment he walked in the door. He gave me a hug and asked if I had eaten lunch. I told him I was hoping we could grab a sandwich. He said, "Let me make one call and I'll be right back."

We went to Hazel's sandwich shop down the street from his office. Hazel's had great sandwiches and sides. I told Henry about setting up our appointments with Dr. Kingston and continued, "Ace says he is refusing to meet with him."

He said, "I'm not surprised. Ace's total focus was getting out of Walter Reed. He probably has no recollection of the agreement he signed."

"Right on target. We had the discussion last night. I told him it wasn't voluntary. He'll do it. He'll just moan and groan and complain."

We smiled and he said, "How is it going with Ace so far?"

I gave him a synopsis of the events and we had a light conversation about different things happening in the family. I told him I was anxious about our meeting with Dr. Kingston. He understood and thought it was normal. We would of course be talking about things we were trying to forget. He was encouraging and had good insights as usual. I always felt better after talking to Henry. We said our goodbyes and I headed over to Harry's bike shop.

Harry was most helpful. He talked a lot about Jack and how they were friends for years. I explained to him we only needed the bikes for about six months and it would be great if he had some used ones for sale. He said he had plenty of used bikes. After looking them over, I selected two medium-sized bikes. He was going to have his mechanic give them a final check and would have them ready in a couple of days.

"Thanks." I pulled out my wallet and he held up his hand and said, "Jack told me to tell you this was his welcome home gift."

We shook hands and I left. I went over to the main hospital waiting area where Ace and I planned to meet after his physical therapy. It was 2:45. I used the pay phone to call Mom about the welcome home picnic.

"Hey Mom, I didn't hear from you last night about the picnic and Ace and I aren't home so I didn't want to miss your call."

"So the picnic is on your mind, is it? Well, imagine that when just a week or two ago you were so against a welcome home party of any kind. I'm trying to remember what I wanted to tell you." Pause.

"Mom, you're as bad as Jack."

She laughed, "I love teasing you. I tried to call you around noon. I talked with Ann yesterday and she thinks it's a great idea. I couldn't reach Betty. She had a bad headache and stayed in bed the rest of yesterday and didn't get out of bed till this morning. She called me and she also thinks it's a great idea."

She continued, "Ann called a little while ago. Agnes thanked her for inviting them and said she would call Eden this evening after she gets off work. Agnes told Ann that Eden was busy with her work and also active in her church. She said it was possible that Eden would not be able to break away. Agnes said she would call Ann tonight and let her know."

"Mom, do you think she has a boyfriend?"

"I don't know Honey. She was divorced last year, but I don't know what time of the year. It's possible, but Agnes said she was busy so if I were you, I think I would go with the idea that she probably doesn't have time for a boyfriend."

"Thanks Mom. Agnes will call Ann and Ann will call you, right?"

"That's right."

"Call me as soon as you find out. Okay?"

Mom was still teasing me, "Are you sure you want me to interrupt your dinner with April and Ace?"

"Yes Mom, I'm sure."

She asked, "Any other news?"

I filled her in on our activities since yesterday and we hung up.

What if Eden couldn't come or didn't want to come? What the hell are you thinking about that for? So are you gonna go out and shoot yourself if she doesn't come? If you are that pitiful, go ahead and end it now.

Ace was walking down the corridor toward the waiting area. I asked, "How'd it go?"

"The doc was okay. He told me that if I did what they told me to do and did my physical therapy that my leg would be almost one hundred percent in four to six months. The physical therapist was a bitch. She reminded me of that captain who ran the mountain phase of Ranger School. He was a prick from head to toe."

"So she was angry, aggressive, and dumb as a rock?"

"Well, she was smart and she didn't seem angry, but she was aggressive as hell."

I responded, "In other words, she wasn't gonna take any shit and expected you to do what she told you to do if you wanted to get better."

"Yeah, and she was also condescending."

I asked, "In what way?"

"Why the fuck are you grilling me?"

"I'm not grilling you. This person whether you like it or not is one of the important keys to you getting better. Your attitude sounds like you're getting off on the wrong foot with her and this might turn into some kind of resistance to what she tells you to do."

"Well, thank you one more time, Dr. Freud! What the fuck would I do without your therapeutic insight into my screwed up personality."

"I've often wondered that myself. Let me offer one more insight. I think you and I have serious problems with authority figures, especially when that authority is female. Remember that female major we saw in the parking lot at the PX? She reprimanded us when we continued to sit on the curb when she passed in front of us. We knew we were supposed to stand and salute an officer in that situation. And after she finished chewing us out and left us standing there, we were pissed off to the max."

"Let's go home. I don't wanna talk about this anymore. Go get the truck. I don't wanna walk to the parking garage."

"Fuck you. I'm not your fucking valet."

"Okay, would you please go get the truck?"

"We've got two more stops to make. One to get your '.45' and the other to get the cell phones activated."

It took another hour to get those two things done. On the ride back to the cabin, I said, "I was surprised they had your .45 in stock."

"Me too. It's a sweet pistol and feels perfect in my hand. Lieutenant Fox had one and let me take it to the range. The guy at the gun shop said I would have to get a 'permit to carry' unless I left it at home. I'll probably leave it at the cabin."

I said, "I think these cell phones will come in handy once we figure out how to work them."

"Yeah, I guess."

I told him about my visit to Dr. Kingston's office and filled him in with the details. I told him that Dr. Kingston would be at the cabin at 9:00 in the morning. I also told him that the dirt bikes would be delivered on Wednesday.

He responded, "I'll write you a check for my bike."

I told him about Jack paying for them.

He didn't comment and we were silent on the rest of the way home. Spot came to meet us as soon as we pulled up. Immediately, I called Jack and thanked him for the dirt bikes. Ace got on the phone and did the same. He said he was happy to do it and it was the least he could do to thank two of Uncle Sam's finest. We chatted a little more about family and then hung up.

Fuck exercise, I'm too tired. I turned to Ace, "Do you want a beer?"

"Thank you for offering. I am thirsty and I would love a beer if you wouldn't mind getting me one, but if it's too much trouble, I would be glad to get it myself and thanks in advance if you do decide to bring me one and please remember that you are the most wonderful friend a piece of shit like me could have."

We started laughing and from the kitchen, I tossed a beer across the room. It wasn't even close to the strike zone and went flying and hit with a thud in the corner. We laughed even harder. I got another one and threw it and it was wide to the left, but it fell onto the sofa.

He hollered, "Stop! Stop! I'll get the one that landed on the sofa and thank you so very much for that act of kindness!!"

I got me a beer and fell into the sofa beside him. We leaned back and drank our beers.

He said, "That felt good."

"Yeah, it sure did."

25

APRIL'S ENTRANCE

We drank in silence and must have drifted off. There was a knock on the front door. The door opened and April yelled, "Anyone home?"

We were both startled and jumped and said about the same time, "Oh shit."

I stood up and knocked the beer can onto the floor. Ace tried to stand up, but fell back on the sofa. I was moving around the end of the sofa when he finally got to his feet.

"April, I'm sorry. We fell asleep."

She gave me a brief hug and said, "That's all right." She went over to Ace and said, "Hey Ace," and put her arms around crutch and all and gave him also a brief hug.

"Hey April."

She said, "Let's put some lights on." She went around the room turning on lights and said, "What's this beer can doing over here in the corner with a puddle of beer around it?"

I said, "Oh shit, I didn't know it leaked. Let me get a towel and wipe it up."

She looked at me and then looked at Ace and them back at me and said, "What have you boys been up to?"

Ace found his tongue and said, "Well to make a long story short, Jett got pissed off because he thought I was ordering him around and so I went through this list of different ways to say please get me a beer and we got to laughing and he got me a beer and… (both of us started laughing again) threw it across the room and you know how Jett could never throw straight and…" We looked at April and she wasn't laughing and we stopped.

I said, "And that obviously doesn't sound funny to you."

Then she smiled and said, "Well that answers the question about whether you've grown up any in the past three years. That's now a no brainer. I can see as usual that you will need a little adult guidance. Jett, don't stand there like a bump on a log with that towel. Go clean up the mess. Ace, sit back down on the sofa while I take a look at the abrasions on your face."

Ace said, "You don't need to do that. I saw a doctor today."

She responded, "He looked at your leg and probably didn't even notice your face. True?"

"Yeah, now that you mention it, he didn't say anything about my face."

She said, "Sit back. I'll be there in a minute."

She headed for the closet with the medical supplies and said to me, "What are you standing there looking at? Go clean up the beer." I did as I was told and Ace leaned back. She brought the kit over and tilted a lamp to shine on Ace's face."

He said, "Hey, that light's in my eyes."

"Fucking get over it Ranger. Now hold still while I take a look. Jett, you got the beer up yet?"

"Most of it."

She continued, "After you get it cleaned up, get a wet cloth and go over the area to make sure no beer smell is left."

"Yes ma'am."

She took some gauze and peroxide and was cleaning the areas around the abrasions. "How's your eye?"

"Hurts a little, but I can see good."

"It looks fine to me. I'm gonna put a little more antibiotic cream on these cuts. They look good too."

I finished my chore and sat down in the chair adjacent to the sofa. She looked at me and then back at Ace. "Looks like I'm gonna have to move in. You guys can't be trusted when left alone. And neither one of you has the manners to offer me a glass of wine. Am I going to have to get it myself?"

I looked at Ace, "I'm not gonna get her a glass of wine. How 'bout you?"

"She can get her own wine."

She kicked me hard in the calf and said slow and insistent, "Get me a fucking glass of wine!"

I got up and she turned to Ace. "You piece of shit, I wrote you a number of letters over these past three years and all I got was a few short sloppy letters. What's up with that?"

Wow, I thought to myself as I was pouring her wine. This is a great strategy. I glanced over at Ace. He looked like, 'Oh shit, what do I say?'.

"All right, cats got your tongue," she said. "For now, if you feel like a piece of shit, nod you head."

He nodded. She continued, "Now that we have that out of the way, we can enjoy our evening."

I brought April her wine and a beer for Ace and me. She smiled and said, "Hey Ace, hey Jett, nice of you guys to invite me to dinner. What's on the menu?"

I responded, "First, Ace and I want to apologize for being asleep when you got here. That was rude. The menu is spaghetti, tossed salad, and garlic bread with apple pie and ice cream for dessert."

She said, "Your apology is accepted. I will be happy to help you all get it ready."

I replied, "That would be great. I have to pee."

Ace interjected, "Me too."

I continued, "Then we can meet in the kitchen in a few minutes."

"Would you like me to put on some music while you're peeing?"

"Yes, that would be nice," I said.

"How about you Ace? Do you want me to put on some music?"

"Yeah, sounds good."

A few minutes later we gathered in the kitchen. Ace and April sat at the kitchen table. I put the salad ingredients in front of them with a large bowl along with the French bread, butter, garlic powder, and shredded parmesan cheese. They knew what to do. I preheated the oven, put the water on to boil, and poured the spaghetti sauce out of the jar into a sauce pan to heat up.

We ate out on the back deck. The conversation was light and fun. We spent most of our time talking about old times and the fun times we had at the cabin. April and I had reminisced about most of these memories, but it was fun to go back over them with Ace. We drank wine and beer and laughed and it seemed like the old days.

Around 9:00 the phone rang. I went inside to answer. It was Mom. "Hey Honey. How is the evening going?"

"It's goin' fine Mom. April and Ace are out on the back deck and we just finished eating. What did you find out?"

"Ann just talked to Agnes a few minutes ago and Eden can't come to the picnic. It had something to do with a meeting at work. But the news is not all bad. Eden will be coming back here this weekend. She has a meeting with a realtor to look for a house."

I was both disappointed and excited. "What about the picnic?"

"We're going ahead with the plans for a week from this Saturday. Is that okay?"

"Sure, that's fine."

"Honey, you sound like you've had quite a bit to drink. You all don't have any plans to leave the cabin do you?"

"I don't. April will drive home, but she hasn't had that much to drink. I won't let Ace leave because he has had more than me."

I told her about our appointment with Dr Kingston in the morning.

"I hope it goes well."

"Me too."

I was disappointed that Eden wasn't coming to the picnic. She may or may not come to church on Sunday. And even if she comes on Sunday, there might not be an opportunity to talk with her.

I hadn't thought about it, but meeting Eden had made it easier to see April and Ace together. This was crazy. I kept asking myself, what was it about Eden? How after one brief meeting could I be so smitten with her? Was this some defense mechanism which would make it easier losing April? It didn't seem like it, but maybe that was driving the incredible attraction to this woman. I decided not to mention her to April or Ace for awhile longer.

I went back outside and joined them. They seemed to be getting along fine. I told them about the picnic and that they were both invited along with Ma, Jim, and Jeffery. Ace didn't seem to be enthused and I wasn't surprised. I wasn't all that enthused myself after learning that Eden wouldn't be there. April on the other hand thought it was a great idea.

We talked awhile longer and then went inside. Ace got another beer and turned on the TV. April helped me clean up the kitchen and sat down next to him. This seemed like a good time to make my exit. I told them I was tired and going to bed. April got up and gave me another brief hug.

Spot stayed out on the sofa with them. It took me awhile to get to sleep. I could hear the muffled sound of the TV. I wondered if they were kissing or making out. It brought back memories of our time on that same couch. I felt jealous and restless. Then Eden came back into my mind and I imagined what it would be like to put my lips on hers.

I must have fallen asleep shortly after those thoughts. I woke at my usual time. My head hurt and I didn't want to run, but I got up anyway and got ready. I was surprised that April was still here. They were asleep and had their legs propped up on the coffee table. April's head rested on Ace's shoulder and they looked peaceful.

I quietly walked through the great room carrying Spot so we wouldn't wake them. We went for our run and quietly returned to my room and went back to bed. I set the alarm for 8:00 so we would have time to get ready for Dr. Kingston. When the alarm went off, I smelled coffee and bacon.

April was in the kitchen and Ace was still sleeping. "Good morning. I was surprised to see you still here when I got up earlier."

"I heard you and Spot leave and come back. I hadn't intended to stay, but we fell asleep watching TV."

"I'm glad you stayed. I don't like you driving home that late even though you didn't have that much wine."

"I was a little tipsy, but I'm also glad I stayed. Would you wake-up Ace? Breakfast is about ready. After we eat, I'll clean up the kitchen and straighten up and you can get ready for your meeting with Dr. Kingston."

"So Ace told you about it?"

"Yeah. He told me and gave me an ear-full of negative comments about it."

"I bet and I'm sure that's a watered down description. I'll wake him up."

We ate breakfast and Ace didn't say two words. He said his leg was hurting from the workout he got in PT yesterday, plus I know he was pissed about the meeting this morning. I had to remember what I was like when I had only been out for a few days. April and I had talked about the big adjustment so I knew she understood his mood.

April and I started cleaning-up while Ace went to take a shower. I said, "I thought your entrance and dialogue with us last night was a stroke of genius."

"It's funny, but it just happened. I was nervous and didn't know how to break the ice."

"Well, it was great. So whatta ya think? How did it go overall?"

She replied, "I think it went fine. We didn't exchange a serious word and there was no physical contact except me putting my head on his shoulder. We needed something like this. I'm pleased."

"I'm glad."

She said, "If you want to go ahead and get your shower, I'll finish these dishes and straighten up."

I said, "I don't mind helping you."

"Jett, it makes me feel good to do it. I feel like I belong and that I am connected to both of you. Go ahead and take your shower when Ace finishes."

"Okay and thanks."

"No, thank you for inviting me and being so kind and understanding."

I smiled, "You're welcome."

26
HOWARD KINGSTON

After a shave and shower, I came out into the great room and it was empty. I went out to the front porch and Ace was sitting in a rocker. April's car was gone. I sat down in the rocker next to his and said, "So, how you doin'?"

"Pissed off would sum it up."

"What about?"

"Well, first you arranged this thing with April without asking me and second, you scheduled this fucking meeting with the shrink. I just got home three days ago and I haven't had time to breathe yet."

I responded, "My bad on the first one. On the second, your agreement with the Army was that you would immediately schedule with Kingston. The Army scheduled the appointment with the leg doc and the only reason they didn't schedule with Kingston was they couldn't get in touch with him. Maybe it would help to think about still being at Walter Reed."

"Damn it Jett, I don't need any fucking lectures from you." He got up and hobbled back into the cabin.

I felt bad for him. I remembered that first week at home and I wouldn't have been ready for this either. I should have tried to schedule for next week. I was eager to get started. I went into the cabin and he was watching TV. I said, "My bad on the second one too. I could have tried to schedule for next week."

Buddy Session One

I sat down beside him and we both watched some mindless program. Not long after that, I heard a vehicle pull up. I got up and went outside. He was driving what looked like an old mid-size Chevy sedan. It was pretty beat up. It was faded and I couldn't tell the color. He got out, waved and said, "Good morning."

"Good morning Dr. Kingston, welcome!" He was thin with white hair and about average height. He had some wrinkles in his face and neck. His skin was tanned so I thought he must like the outdoors. I guessed he was in his mid-sixties. He was dressed in a pair of dark pants with a rather worn dress shirt and carrying a well-worn black brief case. From the outside, he didn't seem to care much about appearances.

He moved as if he were younger than sixty. He came up the stairs, held out his hand and smiled, "I'm Howard Kingston."

"I'm Jett Hollander, Dr. Kingston, nice to meet you."

"Nice to meet you too, Jett."

He had a warm and friendly smile and blue eyes that seemed to sparkle. I liked him immediately. "Come in." I opened the door for him and Ace was getting to his feet.

He went over to Ace and introduced himself.

Ace without smiling said, "Ace Frost." They shook hands.

I asked, "Would you like something to drink?"

"Nothing now thanks. I might take you up on that later." He was looking around and said. "I like your cabin and the setting is beautiful."

I responded, "Thanks. It's been in the family for years. We love it here."

"I can see why." He looked around the cabin again and continued, "The table over there would be a good place to start." I nodded and he went over and started pulling things out of his brief case, arranging them on the table. Ace and I followed and sat down opposite him.

As he was arranging his papers, he smiled and said, "You men can call me whatever you want. Some people call me Howard, some Dr. K, some just K, others Shit Face." He laughed. "Just kidding, it hasn't gotten that bad yet, at least to my face."

We both liked Doc.

Doc

He responded, "That's fine. A number of veterans have called me Doc."

Doc said, "Should I call you Jett and Ace?" We both nodded.

"I want to start off by saying that it's uncommon for me to meet anyone who is looking forward to this kind of experience. Some are suffering enough from symptoms that they will do anything to get relief and the other end of the spectrum is the group who feel forced to participate by family/friends." And he looked at Ace and added, "And those who feel forced by the Army to participate."

Ace raised his hand.

Doc said, "The Army explained the situation to Janet, my assistant. I was reluctant to agree, but understood that you were miserable at Walter Reed and that this was your only way out. I made a commitment to them to make a place for you in this group. Your involvement is your choice. You have a perfect right to quit at anytime. That's true for all the participants."

Ace responded, "The Army won't let me quit."

"That would be between you and the Army. I do require that all participants in the group be committed to the training and do the required work. That includes a willingness to engage in group discussion and to complete the training exercises. Anyone who in my opinion is disruptive to the training and the progress of the group will no longer be a part of the study."

I asked, "I noticed you used the word training several times. What do you mean?"

He replied, "I think most people call this kind of work psychotherapy and group therapy. I like to call it training. One of my roles is to excite a perception within you that change is possible and that you have the resources inside you to make those changes. Those changes come through learning and practicing the skills you will need to reach your goals. I like to think of that as training. You can be in training to run a marathon, to be a soldier, to be a musician, to be carpenter, to be a kind and good person and so on. We will be training to help heal some of the scars left over from combat."

He paused and then seemed to be somewhere else as he had a faraway look in his eyes and said, "It's sad for me that I encounter so many people that seem to be adrift in this short experience of life on this planet. It's like living life on auto pilot. Perhaps the greatest tragedy is our unwillingness to recognize our potential for inner peace, fulfillment, and happiness."

I didn't know what to say and Ace didn't say anything. Finally, Doc came back to us, "Sorry, I left you guys for a moment. So, do you understand why I call this experience training?"

We nodded.

"I have a copy of the agreement for both of you. Read over it and feel free to ask any questions."

The agreement stated the purpose of the study group, the commitment to take seriously the work and follow directions and assignments, a bunch of stuff about confidentiality on both sides. There were other issues related to legal matters. All of it seemed fine to me. I signed my copy. Ace didn't take any time to sign his. I don't think he read it.

He said, "Ace, either you are an incredibly fast reader or you didn't read the agreement."

"I don't care what it says. I don't feel like I have any choice."

Doc responded, "I hope in a few weeks you will believe you made the right decision."

Ace didn't respond and Doc didn't seem to care. However, he handed the agreement back to Ace and said, "I would appreciate you reading this. I don't want there to be any surprises in relation to our agreement."

Ace took the agreement and I assumed he read it. Doc looked over some papers until he was finished.

He had us fill out a form listing address, phone number, notification in case of emergency, and that type of info.

After we were finished, he told us the purpose of the study was to find effective strategies for treating Post-Traumatic Stress Disorder (PTSD) in combat soldiers returning from a war zone. He then elaborated more on the overall purpose of the study to include that the Defense Department was alarmed at the increase in suicides among veterans returning from war.

His goal was to find ten combat veterans who were discharged within the last three months and who would agree to participate in the program. He said that we were numbers nine and ten. He said he would see two at a time once a week and all ten would meet on Saturday mornings. He emphasized that each session would build on previous sessions and that attendance at all sessions was mandatory.

He said, "I have a notebook for each of you with some sections to be labeled later. This will be a place for storing handouts, your own notes, and anything else you want to use it for during the training. During this experience, when we are not in group, I want you to wear a watch that has features like an hourly chime and a stop watch. It looks like both of you have a watch that fits that description. When you're in either the buddy session or larger group, I want you to remove your watches."

We nodded, removed our watches, and put them in our pockets.

He then told us that today he wanted to meet with us separately for about an hour. After that, he wanted to start what he called the training.

He continued, "I want to give you a short sketch of my work history so you can see that I have done a lot of research in this area. I admit to you that I am amazed at the complexity of the brain and excited about the continuing challenge to understand the nature of the consciousness. The bottom line in my opinion is that it doesn't matter how much anyone has studied these areas, there is so much that remains a mystery. I think about it as an adventure that never ends. On this journey, I hope you will learn from me and I know I will learn from you."

He gave us the sketch to look over while he sorted through some papers. After a short while, he asked if we had any questions. I was impressed with what he had done and where he had been, but I didn't have any questions in that moment. Ace didn't say anything.

He asked who wanted to go first. To my surprise, Ace said, "I'll go first."

Doc said, "Let's go sit on the porch."

I said, "I'm going to take my dog Spot for a walk."

I took Spot out the back door and we disappeared up the trail. It was a beautiful day with our usual breeze.

I liked Doc. I had a good feeling about him. He seemed kind and easy to talk to. It was also obvious that he was a "no nonsense" person.

My thoughts drifted to Eden, wondering what her work place was like and who her co-workers and friends were. Then I thought about April and Ace. It had seemed to go pretty well, but I got a feeling I would catch more grief from Ace later on.

When Spot and I arrived at the cabin, they were still on the front porch. I went in and turned on the TV. Soon, Ace came in, "You're up." His expression suggested he was bored or this was a bunch of shit.

I went out to the porch and sat down. Doc explained that he took a lot of notes and that he was listening while writing. He spent the hour asking me questions about my life up until the time we signed up to join the Army. His questions weren't intrusive even though he didn't seem to miss anything. What was most impressive was his keen interest in what I was saying. He made it easy to talk. It was like he made me want to tell him the story of my life. The hour flew by and before I knew it we were finished. Before we went in the house, he said, "We'll take a lunch break. I have my lunch in the car."

I went in the house and told Ace about the lunch break. "Do you want a sandwich and some chips?"

He growled, "Yes please and thanks so much." I would have thrown something at him if Doc hadn't walked in at that moment.

Doc was interested in the history of the cabin so I gave him the short version. He asked a lot of questions and commented that this was the most beautiful mountain setting for a cabin that he had ever seen. Ace didn't say much, but ate two sandwiches and a bunch of chips. I knew Ace wanted a beer and I did too, but we drank Gatorade instead. Doc had a thermos with something hot. It smelled like some kind of tea.

After lunch, we went to the sitting area. Doc pulled up a rocking chair and sat facing us. He began, "I mentioned this morning that we would start the training this afternoon. Ace, this is what I meant earlier when I talked about training exercises. Training to me means learning new skills and practicing them on a consistent basis."

He went on, "We will begin the training by learning the skill of belly breathing. There are many benefits of belly breathing. During our first group session, I will introduce to all of you some of those benefits. I'm asking you to trust me and accept my opinion that this skill is the gate to the healing process. For now, I want to teach you the mechanics of this skill."

He continued, "We are mostly upper chest breathers. In this breathing technique, you inhale air into your belly or the lower portion of your lungs. Take a couple of deep breaths now." Both us were breathing into the upper chest. That seemed real natural since the military was always telling us to "pop up your chest and suck in that gut." He went on, "Now, place your left or right hand below your rib cage. Take some slow easy deep breaths breathing in and out your nose. On the next inhale see if you can breathe into the lower lobes of your lungs."

He gave us some time to practice. "Ace, you seem to be getting the hang of it. Jett, it looks like it is more difficult for you. Sometimes there is a lot of physical tension in the solar plexus (He pointed to the place where the rib cage meets in the middle) making that area rigid.. To loosen up that area you can push out your abdominal muscles when you inhale. This will allow the lower lobes of the lungs to expand without the restriction of tight muscles. After some practice, you can stop pushing out those muscles."

He went on, "I'm going to close my eyes now and place my left hand below my rib cage and when I inhale, I'm going to lower my right hand and when I exhale, I'm going to raise my right hand. I would like for you both to place either hand below your rib cage and see if you can breathe in and out and mimic my pace."

I don't know how long that lasted, but I wondered how breathing could help heal the scars of war? Then I wondered how much longer we'd have to do this. I tried to keep going back to the breathing, but my mind kept thinking about other things. Then he opened his eyes.

He asked us for feedback. I told him about my experience and he asked Ace how he did. Ace said he felt stupid sitting there practicing breathing when he could be at Stanley's having a beer with his friends.

Doc smiled, "Actually a very common reaction is I'd rather be drinking beer or getting laid."

Ace interrupted, "Me too on the second one."

He said, "As I mentioned a few minutes ago, this breathing skill is the gate to healing. Today we used it to help with the training goal of quieting the mind by being attentive, alert, and focused."

For the next hour or so, we did more breathing exercises. He had us lay on our backs with a heavy book on our stomach. This helped us focus more on getting air down into our belly. He had us sitting, standing, walking both frontwards and backwards, intermittently closing and opening our eyes. He took us for a walk in the woods and had us do belly breathing while staring at different scenes and objects. He had us close our eyes and continue to focus on our breathing. In one exercise, he asked us to count backwards starting at twenty. He had us count a number each time we exhaled. The goal was to reach one without breaking our concentration. I struggled to stay focused.

He brought us back in the cabin, had us close our eyes and continued, "Stay focused on your breathing....You might notice how your mind wants to think about other things. It's okay. Just bring your attention back to your breathing....Even though your mind may be thinking of all kinds of different things like how is this going to help? You simply let those thoughts drift away and come back to your breathing. You may have some moments when the mind is quiet and some deeper part of you finds that kind of nice and peaceful....Continue with your breathing. Take a little more time and then open your eyes."

He asked, "Is it true that you want to know how this skill can help you quiet the nightmares, have home feel like home again, have life matter in the same way it did before, reduce the anxiety, quiet the memories of war, get a good night's sleep, reduce the angry outbursts, enjoy a beer without drinking to feel numb, to feel love again, to be comfortable in social situations, to stop jumping out of your skin every time you hear a noise, and to reduce the flashbacks?"

We both nodded.

He went on, "Soon, I will talk with each one of you about your symptoms and your goals. My job is to teach you the skills you need to reach those goals. Your job until this Saturday is to practice the skill of quieting and focusing your mind through the use of deep breathing. I want you twice a day to close your eyes for fifteen minutes and count backwards from fifty with the goal of reaching one without breaking your concentration. You can set the timer on your watch to let you know when fifteen minutes has passed. If you get to one before the timer goes off, repeat the exercise again."

"In addition, during the day, I want you to do some of the same exercises we did a few minutes ago. When going through the exercises, repeat phrases like, 'I'm focusing on my deep breathing. If I have another thought come to mind, I will let it go and return to my breathing. Focusing on my breathing. Concentrating. I am determined to learn this skill.' Feel free to make up your own phrases. I'll give you a handout that lists these phrases. Memorize a few of the phrases and use them and any others you make up while you're using the breathing to quiet your mind."

"One more thing, I want you to set the chime on your watch to ring on the hour. When you hear the chime, interrupt your normal thought process and focus on taking five deep breaths." He smiled, "Of course you can shut off the chime when you go to bed or in other situations where it might be disruptive."

Ace said, "That's a lot of stuff to remember."

"Think back to the time when you were in basic training or to the time spent in Ranger School. That was intense, right?

We nodded.

"Think of this as basic training in overcoming the trauma of combat so you can get on with being content and happy. This training will be mentally intense and will require determination and commitment. The same kind of determination and commitment you showed during your three years in the Army. Without sounding like a drill sergeant, let me calmly ask if there are any questions?"

Neither one of us had any questions. He gave us several handouts to put in our notebook. One was to record the date and time of our fifteen minute focusing exercises and another was the list of assignments. He said, "The reason I decided to see two of you at once is I want you to encourage each other and hold each other accountable. Kind of like the buddy system in Ranger School." Ace and I looked at each other. "Yes, it's true. I went to Ranger School probably before your Mom and Dad were teenagers."

He went on, "I'm counting on both of you to hold each other accountable to do the work assigned."

He gathered his things together and turned to me, "Our first group meeting will be a week from this Saturday. This will give me a chance to have two meetings with each pair. Jett, I would like to hold our first Saturday group meeting here. Would that be OK?"

"Sure." I liked the idea. It would be more comfortable for me.

He said, "Thank you. The Saturday group will meet from 9:00 to noon. Everyone is instructed to bring their own beverage. We will not need any food or snacks." He shook our hands and left.

27

WORRIED ABOUT ACE

As soon as Doc was off the front porch, Ace headed for the fridge, "I need a beer."

I said, "I'll take one too."

We went out on the back deck and Ace said, "What's all that breathing? Is that some kind of Yoga shit or what?"

"I don't understand it either, but I like him and I'm sure he'll explain it to us. Did you call Ma and let her know about the meeting with Doc?"

"Yeah, she called yesterday to ask about my doctor and PT appointments. I told her then."

I said, "I'm gonna set that chime to ring on the hour. Do you want to set yours too?"

"No. I'll do it later."

I yawned, "I'm really tired. I think I'll go take a nap."

"Okay. I gotta get outta here. I'm feeling closed in and like I'm smothering."

"Mom told me to ask you for supper. You wanna go?"

He replied, "No, I think I'll stop by and see Mom for a minute and then just drive around for awhile."

"Okay, so I'll see you later tonight?"

He said, "Yeah, but don't worry about me if I don't come home. I wanna look up Sammie at some point and see what he's up to. I might spend the night at his house."

I went to my room and turned off the chime. I was hoping Ace would set his. Then I passed out. When I awoke, it was 4:37. I set my chime and took Spot for a hike. It felt good to get out of the trail. My mind was clear out here and I could breathe more freely. I practiced my deep breathing. I wondered what Ace was going to do. Maybe he wasn't ready for this kind of experience. I'm not even sure about myself. Is anyone ever ready?

Spot came up to me with a stick and wanted to play fetch. I was more worried about Ace than I was willing to admit. Maybe I didn't do him any favors by helping him get discharged early. Was he suicidal? He was goin' crazy at Walter Reed. His hospital stay had increased the severity of his emotional problems. I think I would have responded the same way seeing all those wounded guys. I had to help him now. I just wasn't sure how.

I needed someone to talk to outside my family. April would have been perfect, but I didn't want to do anything to get in the way of Ace and her getting back together. There wasn't anyone. I had no friends other than Ace and April. Everyone from high school and college had moved on with their lives. I practiced more deep breathing. I wondered if the breathing might be the answer to my panic problems.

I washed up after the hike and headed down the mountain to Mom's. We had a nice dinner, but I wasn't hungry.

My chime rang during the meal. Dad asked, "What's that for?" I explained and then took my five deep breaths. He looked puzzled, but let it go. This was going to be a challenge.

After dinner, Mom and I talked about the meeting with Doc and some about family. I was still tired from the day. She said while we were doing the dishes, "You haven't mentioned Eden tonight."

"I know. I guess I've come to my senses a little. What are the chances that she would ever be interested in me? She is beautiful and successful and probably has guys hitting on her all the time."

"I don't know Honey. I was watching when you all met at church. I don't think I've ever seen your face light up the way it did when your eyes met. I've only seen Eden a half-dozen times, but I've never seen her smile the way she smiled at you. It was like you were both surprised to immediately see something in each other that you had never seen in another person. I was right about you, but I don't know about Eden. And, you have to remember that I'm a hopeless romantic."

"That makes me feel a little better Mom. I guess I'm trying not to get my hopes up. You know I haven't been lucky in love as they say. I don't know sometimes if there's something wrong with me. Am I looking for someone perfect? I know that's not possible and anyway, would I want to be with someone perfect? Now, after this war I feel like damaged goods. I'm longing for intimacy, but at the same time I'm scared to death of finding it. April was wonderful, but she was safe. I knew she would never belong to me."

"I worried about you and April. I knew you all were both vulnerable and lonely."

"Don't worry Mom. April and I worked it out. She has to focus her attention on getting back with Ace. I understand that and will support her in any way I can. Speaking of worry, I'm very concerned about Ace. He is worse than I have ever seen him. He hasn't been the same since he was wounded. He was an incredible soldier. He had a purpose and no one was braver and no one was a better comrade in arms. There is no doubt he would have thrown his body on a grenade to save me or anyone else in our unit. Now, he seems lost and scared."

She said, "All you can do for him is be the best friend you can be and I know you are already doing that. I'm hopeful that Dr. Kingston can help you both."

"I really believe he can, but we're going to have to work at it and I think I'm up for that, but I'm not sure about Ace." She gave me a hug and we went in to watch some TV with Dad.

I fell asleep almost immediately and Mom woke me around 10:00. I thanked Mom and Dad. Spot and I headed home.

Ace's SUV was not there. I was not surprised. I rode back down the mountain and went to Stanley's. His SUV was there. I waited awhile, not sure what to do. Before I decided, he came out and was obviously drunk. He was leaning on Valarie Dodd, an old high school flame, and they went to her car. She seemed sober enough. She helped him in the front seat, got in and drove off.

I went home. I wasn't tired and started to call April, but then decided against it. I couldn't lie to her and I knew it would hurt her to know about Ace and Valarie. News traveled fast in Harvest. She would know soon enough.

After my early morning run, I went back to bed. Why was I so tired? Before breakfast, I did my focusing exercise. I was finding it difficult to keep my mind focused on the breathing. I decided to go down to the Inn and work with Charlie. I called Harry and told him to hold the dirt bikes for a few more days and I would get back to him. I wrote Ace a note and told him where I was and I would be home around 4:00.

It was a good day. The work was strenuous and kept my mind occupied. I had lunch with Pop, which made me feel better. I saw Sandra at the front desk. She was friendly, but my focus was on Eden. I did have a fleeting thought about how Sandra would be in bed. I wondered what her expression would be like when she was having an orgasm. It was time to go back to work.

It seemed like the chime went off constantly. I had to explain it to Pop and Charlie. Both said they liked the idea and were supportive. Charlie smiled and said he was also going to take five deep breaths every time he heard it. He said his wife would be pleased if it helped him be more relaxed.

As I came up the road to the cabin, I could see Ace's SUV parked in front of the cabin. He was asleep. I practiced my focusing exercise and then turned on the TV. Soon, Ace came out of his bedroom. I asked, "How you doin'?"

"Okay. What you been doin'?"

I gave him a run down on my day. "I was worried when you weren't home after I got back from Mom's. I went over to Stanley's to see if you were there. I saw you and Valarie come out and get in her car."

"I told you not to worry about me. So you were checkin' on me?"

"Yeah, I suppose I was."

"I don't need you to take care of me Jett."

"We've been taking care of each other since we were ten-years-old. So you want me to stop now?"

"I don't know what the hell I want. I don't give a shit about anything except getting drunk and getting laid. I feel as useless as tits on a boor hog and you can tell the shrink that I'm not gonna be a part of his research project. I don't give a shit about the consequences."

I said, "I don't know what to say."

"You fuckin don't get it. I don't want you to say anything."

My chime went off and he said cynically, "Be sure to take your deep breaths Jett. You'll feel so much better."

A horn blew out front. "Valarie is picking me up. She is the only one who doesn't care if I get drunk and she's horny as hell. I won't be back till tomorrow." He left and Spot wanted to go with him, but he didn't even notice. Spot came back to me and I rubbed his head, "That's okay old boy, we'll get him back eventually. We just have to be patient."

I called April and lied even though I had told myself I wasn't gonna lie, "Ace has gone out with some drinking buddies. How would you like to go out with me to eat at Sally's?"

"That's sweet, but some of the girls from work asked me to go out for drinks. We don't do a lot socially so I feel obligated to make an appearance." She shifted topics and continued, "My caller ID shows another number than the one at the cabin. Is this your cell number?"

I answered, "Yeah. It's gonna take me a while to get use to it. I was wondering if we could we meet afterwards?"

"All right, why don't I call you when our little group breaks up?"

"Sounds good." We hung up.

Around 8:00, she called and said, "Thanks for trying to spare me. We went to Stanley's and Valarie was there hanging all over Ace. It was crowded and I don't think he even saw me. I'm bummed and don't feel like going out in public. Why don't you come on over and I'll fix something."

"Why don't I get a carry-out at Sally's."

"Thanks Jett. That sounds good. Would you also pick up a bottle of Chardonnay on the way?"

"Sure, I'll phone the order in and be there in about thirty minutes." She already sounded a little tipsy. I hope this is going to turn out to be a good decision.

When I got there, I could see through the window that she was watching TV. I went in and put the stuff in the kitchen. She got up to greet me and put her arms around me. She started crying and said, "Jett, what am I gonna do? I know he doesn't care about Valarie, but it's really painful to see her draped all over him. It's easier to be mad at her than him. He seems pitiful to me and my heart's breaking. I don't know what to do to help him."

"I don't know what to do either. He told me this afternoon that he's not going to be part of Kingston's group. He said he didn't care about the consequences. We are his best and only friends April. We just have to keep trying."

She wiped her tears and asked me to pour her a glass of wine. "There's plenty of beer in the fridge."

We sat on the sofa and she continued talking. "I'm going to call him tomorrow and ask you both to come down here for dinner tomorrow night."

I said, "I don't know if he'll accept, but again, we just gotta keep trying. In the morning I'm going over to talk with Ma. I hate to worry her, but we need to keep each other in the loop so she knows what we're doing and we know what she's doing."

"I think that's a good idea. Is there anyone else we should talk to?"

I responded, "Driving over here, I thought about talking to Valarie. Whatta you think?"

That phrase or question triggered something in her. She started bawling and pleading with me barely able to get the words out, "Jett, why, why can't he love me? What's wrong with me? What have I done to him? Jett, why can't he love me?"

I moved over to the sofa and put my arm around her. She pushed me away. I could see that she was getting angry and she got louder with tears pouring out of her eyes, "Why did he turn to that bitch? I hate her! I hate her! I hate that fucking bitch!" Pleading again, "I would have given him whatever he wanted. I would've fucked his brains out. I would've gotten drunk with him. I would've done anything he wanted!"

I made another attempt to put my arms around her and she put her head on my chest. The anger seemed to subside, but a softer pleading continued, "Jett, why did he turn to her?" She was silent but still whimpering. Then all of a sudden, she looked at me, "Do you think it was because of what happened between us? I don't think I was able to let that thought in my mind till now."

I admitted, "I haven't even thought about that either." I paused, "I need another beer. Do you want more wine?"

She seemed to be in deep thought, but then softly said, "No thanks."

I returned and said, "I don't think that has anything to do with it."

"Why not?"

"When I told him about us on the way home, he was not angry with either one of us. He was rational in the same way we were when we were able to justify what we were doing. He actually got mad at me for feeling that I had somehow betrayed him."

She asked, "We both know that thoughts and feelings don't always go together. What if he rationally understands, but at a feeling level he is upset and angry with both of us?"

"It's possible because even though rationally I was able to justify what we did, at a feeling level, I still felt like I had betrayed him. Maybe the same thing has happened to him. I don't think he would be conscious of that anger, but it may be coming out in his behavior."

She was crying again and this time she was grieving. "Oh Jett, what have we done?"

"April, we went through some traumatic times in the military. I didn't think I needed anyone, but Ace to help me get through it." I smiled, "Beer was a big help too when we had an opportunity to drink. Ace needed more than me and beer. When we were home on leave those few times, why didn't he turn to you then? He turned to Valarie and Frances and one other one I didn't know. Why didn't he turn to you then?"

"I don't know."

"You wrote him letters so he had to know you still cared."

"Maybe he was afraid he might get emotionally involved with me again. Maybe it was too risky."

"Yeah, maybe." We were silent for awhile. I finally said, "I will never forget what happened between us and it will always be tucked away in a special corner of my heart. I think maybe I've already said that."

She reached over and took my hand. I went on, "All three of us have rationally made peace with what happened. I'm going to work hard not to get caught up in the irrational thoughts and related feelings that each of us may or may not be having. They are understandable, but they are not rational. I have enough problems dealing with my rational thoughts and feeling."

She smiled through her tears, "That seems rational." I smiled back. She hugged me and whispered, "Do you mind if I go on to bed?"

"That's fine. I'll put the barbecue in the fridge and lock up on the way out."

"She said, "Why don't you take some barbeque with you?"

"No thanks, I'm not hungry either."

She leaned over and kissed me on the cheek. "If you think it would help to talk with Valarie, you go ahead and do it. I don't think I can take a rejection on the phone so when you see Ace tomorrow, would you tell him about the invitation to supper?"

"Sure, I'll tell him."

Ace was not at home. I took Spot out for a short walk, practiced some on the skills, and went to bed. I had a restless night. No real nightmares but some unsettling dreams and I didn't even remember the content. I did my usual morning routine adding the focusing exercise and I left around nine, Ace still had not come home.

I went to see Ma and talked about Ace. We agreed that all we could do was to continue to reach out to him. Ma said she was going to ask him to go to church on Sunday and to eat with them after church. She said, "Jim and your Dad talked about Ace coming to work for them. Jim will talk with him about that on Sunday."

I went to the Inn and worked with Charlie, had lunch with Pop, and got home around 4:00. Ace's SUV was there. He was drinking beer and watching TV. Spot was lying on the sofa next to him. He looked terrible. His clothes looked dirty and I could tell by his greasy hair that he hadn't showered.

"You look like shit."

He mumbled, "I'm okay."

"Man, I'm worried about you."

He interrupted, raising his voice, "There you go again. Stop worrying about me. I'll be fine."

"April invited us to supper tonight."

"I can't go. Valarie is picking me up again around 7:00."

"Couldn't you cancel with her and spend the evening with us?"

"Jett, I told you all I want to do is get drunk and get laid. With Valarie, there are no complications and I don't have to talk about anything."

I responded, "We can get drunk together and just watch TV. We don't have to talk."

"Look, I know you're trying to help, but I don't want any help. Tell April, I'm sorry about tonight. Can we please not talk anymore about this shit?"

"Okay." I got a beer, and dialed April's number. I got her voice mail. "Hey April, I just talked with Ace and he can't make it tonight and said he was sorry." We sat and watched some reruns of Bonanza and he drank a couple more beers.

The horn sounded. "I gotta go."

"Okay, be careful. See you tomorrow."

Without looking back, he said, "Later."

He was gone. I got another beer and decided that I would get drunk tonight. April called and asked me to come over and I declined. "I'm gonna stay home and get drunk."

While I was sitting there, something on TV triggered a flashback of that last explosion that killed Holton and Migs. I closed my eyes and put my hands over my ears and then the tightness of my chest and problems breathing. I kept telling myself, "This will pass." I tried using Doc's deep breathing technique. I couldn't get a deep breath. Finally, it passed.

I don't know if I got drunk, but I fell asleep on the sofa and didn't wake up till about 2:11. I let Spot out and peed. I had trouble going back to sleep. I kept wondering how I was gonna help my best friend get out of this rut. Finally I drifted off. I only had one nightmare that was related to my earlier flashback, but the content was hazy. I had drenched my sheets again.

It was Friday morning and today was almost a carbon copy of yesterday. This time, when I got home, Ace's SUV was not in the driveway. I found Valarie's phone number in the book and there was no answer. I called Ma and she had not heard from him. I called April and she had not heard. She asked me to come down and run with her and then get 'carry-out' and take it to her house.

I put on my running stuff and took a change of clothes. I met her at the lake and she asked me if I was up to a four mile run through the maze, a trail through the woods with some inclines which made it extra challenging. She set a fast pace. We knocked it out and it almost knocked us out. We were panting at the finish.

We went back to her house, showered, and changed. While we were eating dinner, she said, "I've been thinking today about how helpless we're feeling. I think we have to let the ball be in Ace's court. He's going to have to be the one that does something."

I agreed with her so we talked about other things like her work and my lunches with Pop. After we finished eating, we watched TV for awhile and both yawned almost at the same time. We smiled and I asked, "Do you have to work tomorrow?"

"Yes, but I'm off Sunday and Monday."

I replied, "Okay. Thanks for the dinner. I'll check in with you tomorrow." We hugged and I left.

28

ACE DOWN

I didn't expect to find Ace at home so I went by Stanley's and Valarie's car was in the parking lot. I hoped that Valarie would look after him. There wasn't anything else I could do. I went home, drank a beer, and went to bed.

I was having some kind of strange dream and I kept hearing a ringing and it got louder and louder and I couldn't find out where it was coming from. Then I sat up in bed and realized that it was my phone ringing. I jumped out of bed and raced for the phone. I was too late. Who could it have been? Was Ace in trouble? Was someone in my family sick?

It rang again. I picked it up, "Hello."

"Jett, is that you?"

"Yeah, who is this?"

"Jett, this is Bernard Chapman."

"Hey Bernard, Mom told me you were a deputy sheriff. Is Ace in trouble?"

"Yeah, we got a call from Stanley's about an hour ago. They said Ace was belligerent and causing a scene. Neil Heffner and I went out to check on the situation and Ace was in the parking lot drunk as a skunk, trying to pick a fight with some guy from out of town. Neil and

I were finally able to calm him down and brought him in. We charged him with public intoxication rather than drunk and disorderly. We put him in the "drunk-tank." Do you want me to call Mr. and Mrs. Frost or do you want to call them?"

"Thanks Bernard, I'll call them right now. Can I come down and get Ace?"

"The Judge we got now likes to leave folks in the tank till noon the next day. We could pull some strings, but it might not look right."

"No, that's fine. Is there anybody back there with him?"

"No, it's been a quiet night. He should be able to sleep it off in peace. I'll take him a blanket and pillow. Jett, I'm real sorry. I know you guys just got back from the war. You know, I spent most of my football career keepin' Ace safe so he could complete all those passes. This don't feel right, but it's my job."

"Bernard, you've already helped a lot by reducing the charge. Ace will be grateful and will blame himself for putting you in this situation to start with. I'll call the Frosts and I'll be there to get him at noon tomorrow. Thanks to you and Neil for your help."

I called Ma and let her know. We both expressed the hope this would help Ace come to his senses and admit that he needs help. We were glad he was safe in jail. I decided to wait and call April in the morning. She needed her rest and there was nothing she could do. I had trouble getting back to sleep, but woke up around 5:00. I was exhausted and went back to sleep and didn't wake up till 9:46. I got up and immediately called April. The head nurse said she was busy and would call me back when she got a break. I told her it was important and to please ask her to call me as soon as possible.

I got something to eat and my cell phone rang. "What's wrong?"

I gave her all the details. She was afraid he had been badly hurt so she was relieved that it wasn't anything serious. I told her to call me when she got off work.

I had time to go for a run so Spot and I took off. I showered and shaved and the phone rang. It was Bernard and he was hysterical. Trying to get his breath, "Jett, I took Ace his breakfast at eight and he appreciated me getting him a nice breakfast at Waffle House. His head hurt, but he was in a good mood. I checked on him at 11:00 and he was lying in a puddle of blood. He had cut his wrists. We bandaged his wrists while the ambulance was on the way. They just left. Jett, what if he dies?"

I couldn't get my breath. I was able to get out a few words, "It's not your fault. I'll call you as soon as I know something." I felt like I was suffocating. I was used to crisis and blood and injuries and all that stuff, but I wasn't in the Army where I knew what to do and how to handle things. We were trained to think fast and respond immediately without thinking. But this was different. It's like I was in a foreign land and I was in a panic.

I had to calm down. I had to pull myself together. I paced for a few minutes, tried to focus on my breathing. I kept telling myself, "Calm down, calm down. You can do it." I tried more breathing. I called Ma. I started crying as soon as I heard her voice. I frantically told her that Ace had cut his wrists and they had taken him to the hospital and that I was leaving now and would meet her at the ER. I called April and, thanks be to God, she answered. I was still crying and told her. She said, "I'm going down there right now. I'll meet you there. You called Marge, right?"

"Yeah." She hung up. I got in the truck and took off. As soon as I got to the main road to Elverton, Bernard was waiting for me in a patrol car and motioned for me to follow him. He put on the siren and lights and we were at the hospital in no time. As I pulled up, Ma and Jim were getting out of their car and we all rushed in together. April was behind the nurse's station talking to the doctor. She motioned us back through the private door. She wasn't crying and I took that to mean he was gonna make it.

As soon as we got through the door, she turned to the three of us and said, "He's gonna be all right. He lost a lot of blood, but his type is common so they had plenty on hand and are giving him blood transfusions.

Marge finally lost it. I think she had been holding this cry in for a long time. She had been terrified since we left for the Army and now all that pent up emotion came flooding to the surface. "I wanna see my baby," she kept saying over and over.

April quickly went into nurse mode and took her into one of the treatment rooms and had her lay down on a bed. Within a minute or so another nurse came in and they gave her what must have been a sedative.

I had pulled myself together on the ride to the hospital. Ace was going to be okay. I gave Jim a hug and said, "Close call." I went out into the waiting area and gave Bernard a hug and said, "He's gonna be okay. Thanks for everything. When things calm down, I want us to get together. And thanks for the escort." He was obviously relieved and smiled.

I needed to call Mom and had left my cell phone at the cabin. I went to the nurse's station and asked to use the phone. "I'm sorry sir. There's a telephone out in the lobby for families."

April came out of the treatment room and over heard the conversation and said to the receptionist, "It's all right Fran, he's with me." She took me by the arm and led me down the hall and pulled me into an empty treatment room, pulled the curtain, put her arms around me and she started sobbing, "Oh Jett, we almost lost him." She could hardly talk, but was able to say, "The ER doc is a friend. He told me if it had been another five minutes, he would have died."

I didn't know what to say so I just held her. It didn't take her long to recover and she went back to check on Ma and Jim. She showed me a phone. I called Mom and told her a brief version of the whole story. She was of course shocked and asked how Ma and Jim were doing. I asked her to spread the word to the rest of the family and ask them not to talk about it with anyone outside the family. "I'm not sure what Ma and Jim want other people to know."

Mom said, "Let us know what we can do. Does Jeffery know yet?"

I replied, "He's doing summer soccer and his team is on a road trip and won't be back till tomorrow night late."

"Okay Honey. Give me a call in a few hours and give me an update."

We hung up and I walked back down the hall to the room where Ma was resting. Ma was still in the bed. Jim was sitting in a chair with his head in his hands. April was not in the room. They must have given Ma something strong as she was drifting in and out of a light sleep. She would wake up and mumble, "Are you sure he's okay?" When she saw me, she motioned for me to come over and she took my hand and squeezed it. I squeezed back. She mumbled, "Jett, sit by my bed." I sat down and kept her hand in mine.

I had a million thoughts going through my mind. Did I miss the signs that he was suicidal? What were they? What could I have done differently? He had been "there" for me in so many ways. Had I done everything possible? What will we do now? How can I make sure this never happens again? Will he come to his senses and get some help? Will he do it again? Should I call Dr. Kingston?

Then I had a flashback of his leaning up against that rock with blood oozing out of his leg and the puddle of blood. I remember how worried I was that he would lose too much blood before we could get him to the hospital. Then the image of him lying on that cell floor in another puddle of his blood came flooding into my mind. I shut my eyes tighter trying to erase the images and could feel some tears running down my cheeks.

I felt a gentle hand on my shoulder. I looked up and it was April. Jim was standing beside her. Ma opened her eyes and said, "April is he okay?"

She replied, "He's doing fine. The transfusions will take a little longer than they thought so they'll keep him in the Intensive Care

Unit until tomorrow morning when he'll be transferred to the psych floor. They said the cuts on the wrist were not too bad. He'll have some scarring, but otherwise there is no damage. The psychiatrist will evaluate him and decide what to do. When anyone attempts suicide, they keep them in the hospital for seventy-two hours. So the earliest he can be discharged will be Tuesday around noon. In three or four hours, they'll allow one person back at a time to visit."

Ma asked, "Did you see him?"

"Yes, his color is of course pale, but his vitals are good. He woke up several times and asked for water, but was out again before I could get the straw to his lips."

Ma again, "Did he know you?"

"I don't think he did. He showed no indication that he recognized me."

"Is that normal?"

"Yes at this stage, it is."

Jim hadn't said anything and finally spoke up, "How the hell did this happen in a jail cell. They're supposed to watch for this type of thing."

I responded, "We can ask Bernard, but I know they have precautionary measures they take to prevent suicides. Bernard not only reduced the charges against Ace, but also made a special effort to bring him breakfast and coffee from Waffle House. I'm sure the utensils were plastic. As Rangers, we're taught and trained to improvise in all different kinds of ways. I'm sure Ace could turn that piece of plastic into something as sharp as a razor."

I couldn't tell whether Jim was satisfied with that answer. He didn't say anything else.

April said, "I've got to go back to work. I'll check back in an hour or so and give you all an update. I get off at 3:30 and am off tomorrow and Monday." She hugged us and left.

Jim went out to smoke a cigarette and Ma drifted back to sleep. I stood up and went out into the hallway. I was leaning against the wall, feeling closed in and anxious. I took some deep breaths and that seemed to help a little. I walked out into the waiting area and Valarie was at the window talking to the receptionist. She saw me and broke off the conversation.

"Jett is he okay?"

I gave her the same brief version I gave Mom. There were tears in her eyes and she said, "I feel so responsible. Ace and I were at Stanley's last night. The plan was for him to spend the night at my apartment. Around 11:00, we got in a big fight about something. I can't even remember what it was. I left him there and he didn't even have a ride. I feel terrible." She started crying and said, "It's all my fault!"

I put my arms around her and then guided her across the room to a place where we could sit and have a little privacy. "Valarie, I want you to look me in the eye and listen very carefully to what I'm about to say. You know that I'm Ace's best friend. He and I have been to hell and back in the Army. We're suffering emotional scars and Ace has the added physical problem with his leg. I can assure you beyond any shadow of a doubt that his suicide attempt had nothing to do with what happened between you all last night."

"But Jett, he was so mad at me. He looked like he wanted to kill me."

"That's normal behavior for war veterans. Valarie, trust me, it's complicated. I don't understand it myself, but I do know that you are not responsible for what happened. I want you to give me your phone number and I promise to keep you updated on Ace's condition."

She rummaged through her purse and couldn't find anything to write with. I got a pen from the receptionist and put her number in my wallet. She said, "I have to get back to work. Please call me."

"I promise."

It was 2:15. I went back in to check on Ma. She was sitting up and said, "The nurse said in about an hour we could go up to the ICU waiting room. We tried to talk about other stuff without much success. Jim said that he was going home to work on some projects he had lined up for today. By 3:00 Ma felt strong enough to walk so we went outside and sat on a bench under a tree.

Around 3:30 April came looking for us. She sat down and said, "I just checked on him and he's doing fine. The transfusions are still taking longer than they predicted and he's still out of it. The nurse said he has been semi-conscious several times and keeps asking Jett if everyone else in Bravo is okay. I talked to the doctor and she agrees with me that Jett needs to be with him in case he wakes up. Marge, let me take you in to sit with him for awhile and then Jett can go in."

We went up to ICU and April pointed out the ICU waiting room. I went in and they continued down the hall. April wasn't gone long. She came in and sat down beside me and took my hand. And the tears came again. "We were so busy on my ward that I didn't have time to think, which was a good thing. Jett, I can't believe how close he came to dying. You all had so many narrow escapes over there and then this. What was he thinking?"

I responded, "Over there we had a reason to live and a cause to fight for. Over here now, we struggle to find a reason for living or for a purpose to go on. It's like being lost with no hope of finding what we need, whatever that is."

"Is it that bad for you too?"

"No, I'm lucky. Ace, on a one to ten scale, is living about a nine and I think I'm about a six. His leg injury is one of the things that drive him higher on the scale. You know he loves the woods and exercising as much as you and me and yet he can't get out there and find the relief I get from being in the woods and exercising.

She said, "So he has no outlet and he turns to drinking to get his relief. But he has me and you. Why can't that help him?"

"I know you've heard this before, but I think it's true. The healing has to come from within us. No one can do it for us or make it happen. We have to do it for ourselves. Ace would say, 'Thank you Dr. Freud'." I smiled, "I think I read that in a text book in one of my psych classes."

She smiled back. We sat there in silence for awhile and then I said, "I would like to let Dr. Kingston know what happened. He has a cell phone and gave us his number. Is there a phone here I could use to call him?"

"Sure, let's go up to my floor." She found an office and gave me her cell phone. He answered and I gave him the same brief sketch of what happened.

He said, "I know the chief of psychiatry at the hospital. I know he will let me take over the psychological part of Ace's treatment. You said he would be transferred in the morning so I will be there when he gets to the ward."

I said, "Thank you. I was hoping you could be involved with him here. He told me yesterday he was not going to be in the program and he would take the consequences."

"This will give me a chance to get to know him better and vice versa. I know this program can help him. I'll do my best to help him make the right decision. I'll see you tomorrow." He hung up.

April was waiting for me at the nurse's station. She introduced me to a couple of her friends. One said, "So this is the Jett April has been talking about." She smiled and continued, "Not bad April. You could do worse." We all smiled. I liked her friends. On our way back downstairs, I told her about my conversation with Doc.

"I'm so glad he'll be working with Ace."

"Me too."

April went to check on Ma and Ace. She and Ma came out in a few minutes and April took me back.

He still looked pale and when I mentioned that to April, she said, "You should have seen him a couple hours ago." She continued, "I talked to Marge and I'm going to take her home and go home myself, clean up and change clothes. I convinced Marge there was nothing else she could do today and that she should stay home and come back in the morning.

I told her you and I would stay with him. I'll pick-up some food for us on the way back. Do you have any preference?"

"You know me. Anything is good. Thanks." I followed her out to the waiting room and gave Ma a hug and told her that we would of course call her if there was any change and that we would take good care of her boy."

She teared up and kissed me on the cheek and said, "Bye Sweetie."

April said, "I'll be back in a couple of hours."

I looked over at him and once more couldn't believe that it had come to this. He had always seemed so strong and courageous and now he looked so vulnerable. Yeah, he was a little wild at times, but in many other ways he was grounded and committed to taking care of business. Maybe that was the key. We both didn't know what our business was anymore. We didn't have any business. We were lost and felt alone. I felt like I was starting to let people back in, but I didn't think Ace was able to do that yet. Maybe he saw I was moving and realized he wasn't or couldn't. Maybe I should have realized that sooner and gone out to drink with him at night to make sure he didn't get in any trouble. He always had my back? I was starting to feel guilty. I would have to live with that for now.

Ace woke up a few times and I had brief conversations with him. I told him no one else was injured and that the guys were waiting for him to get out of here so we could raise some hell. Each time, he smiled and was out again.

At one point, I felt anxious and was afraid it was going to turn into a panic attack. I did the deep breathing that Doc taught us and it didn't help. My self-talk seemed to be more effective. I felt better. I would ask Doc why his deep breathing wasn't helping when things slowed down.

One of the things we learned as Rangers was how to sleep in any situation. That came in handy now because the chair was not conducive to taking a nap, but I was able to sleep between the times when Ace woke up.

Soon, April was back with food. She asked if there was any change and I told her none that I knew of and she said she felt better. "How was Ma on the ride home?"

"She was doing as well as can be expected. She was worried about Jim. You know how Ace and Jim are alike. She said she hopes he doesn't keep it bottled up inside, but predicted he would."

I told her Valarie had come by earlier today and I had talked to her in the ER waiting room. "She was crying and blaming herself. She said they got in a big fight at Stanley's around 11:00 and that she had left him there. I assured her that this had nothing to do with their fight. I don't know if she believed me or not. I got her phone number and told her I would let her know how he's doing."

April said, "I wonder how many people know. It's probably all of Harvest by now."

"Yeah, probably so." It sounded like April didn't want to talk about Valarie and I understood. I continued, "While you were gone, I thought about how I could have gone out with him at night and made sure he didn't get in any trouble."

She said, "I think both of us are going to come up with things we might have done to keep this from happening. That's going to make us feel like a piece of shit and it's not going to help anything. What we need to do now in my opinion is figure out what we do from here on out."

I replied, "I think you're right. It's gonna take too much energy to feel bad or guilty. We need to use that energy to go forward. When do you think he'll wake up so we can have a conversation with him?"

"I think that should happen in the morning."

"As soon as he is awake and alert, he is going to be very anxious, antsy, and possibly agitated. Will the staff give him something for his nerves?"

She answered, "Yes, I think so. I'll talk to the doctor or charge nurse and tell them about his history and emotional situation. I still think they'll transfer him to the psych ward in the morning if his vitals are still good and his wrists are starting to heal."

I said, "I will stay the night with him, but would like to go to church in the morning. If you could come back 9:00, it would give me plenty of time to clean up and I can be back here by 1:00 at the latest."

"I'm going to stay tonight too. I can leave here about 7:00, go home, clean up and be back here by 9:00. I'll call Marge and ask her if she wants to come back with me. I don't think Jim will want to sit around in the hospital."

"That sounds good to me." I was glad she was staying and her tone didn't sound like she could be talked into leaving even if I wanted her to leave. I wasn't ready to talk to her about Eden. I was embarrassed to begin with. It sounded like a high school crush. Maybe that was true. She must be a little puzzled about the importance I was putting on going to church. It caused me to face again the idea I was desperate for a relationship. I figured April and Ma would be with Ace and Doc would want to spend time with him in the morning.

During the night, Ace continued to wake up and mumble something and then go back to sleep. Intermittently, April patted his face with a washcloth and rubbed Vaseline on his lips to keep them from drying out. We talked and slept and took turns going out for a break. She left at 7:00 and I dozed for another hour or so, opened my eyes, and Ace was staring at me.

"Where am I?" he asked.

"You're in ICU at the hospital."

"So I didn't make it to heaven and I'm still in hell."

"Yeah."

"I kept thinking we'd been in a dog fight and that I'd been hurt and was bleeding. I remember I kept asking if anyone else was hurt."

"Yeah, you came in and out of it the whole time."

He asked, "You been here all night?"

"Yeah, me and April. She took care of most of the nursing duties which was a help to the staff. She kept your lips moist with Vaseline, wiped your face a lot with a warm wash cloth, and kept going down the hall to get warm blankets to cover you. She just left about an hour ago. She'll be back at 9:00 and your Mom will probably be with her."

"Shit!" He paused and then said, "I'm hungry and thirsty and cold. You wouldn't have any beer would you?"

"Nope, but I'll ask the nurse if you can have something to eat and find out where they keep the warm blankets." He nodded. I went into the hall and found his nurse and she said in a few minutes she would bring something to eat. She told me where to find the warm blankets.

"How long before I can get outta here?"

"The doctors said it would take a few days to get your strength back. You lost a lot of blood and you almost got your wish."

"It took me awhile to get that piece of plastic sharp enough to do the job. If I hadn't taken so much time, I'd be in heaven with all those virgins the terrorists talk about."

"You scared the shit out of us. Over there, I think we did everything possible to make sure we made it back home. I know we're fucking going through a lot of shit, but I didn't think you thought it was bad enough to whack yourself."

"I did."

We were silent for awhile and then the nurse brought Jell-O® and a ginger ale. Ace asked her if she could get him a Big Mac®.

She smiled, "No Big Macs® for you Mr. Frost." She left and Ace ate the Jell-O®.

I decided not to tell him about going to the psych ward. I'd let the doctor break that piece of news to him. He turned on the TV and we watched some sitcom rerun. It was pretty funny in places, but Ace didn't laugh.

April came in with Ma.

Ma went right to the bed and put her hands under his shoulders and held him and whispered something in his ear. Ace started tearing. April came over to the bed and put some Vaseline® on her finger.

"Your lips are dry. I'm going to moisten them." He didn't resist. She got a wash cloth and wiped his face and the tears. She continued, "Are you cold?"

"No, Jett got me a warm blanket."

She asked, "How do you feel?"

"I feel weak."

She said, "It's no fucking wonder. Sorry for the language Marge. You were almost out of blood when you got to the hospital. I'm going down the hall to check with the doctor."

I said, "I'm heading on." I looked at Ace, "I'll be back around 1:00." I hugged Ma and followed April out into the hallway. I gave April a run down on the last two hours.

She said, "By the time you get back here, he'll probably be transferred to the psych ward. Remember to get your cell phone at the cabin and call me before you get back here. I'll let you know if he's been transferred."

29

EDEN AT CHURCH

I stopped at the hospital entrance and used the phone to call Mom. I filled her in on the details and told her that I would meet her and Dad at the church around 10:30. I called Henry yesterday afternoon and asked him to let Spot out for me. He said he would bring him down to their house and I could pick him up when I got back.

Spot was glad to see me. I gave them a brief summary. I told them I wasn't sure what was going to happen and that I was going to drop Spot off at Mom's on the way to church.

Spot and I went for a short walk. I ate some breakfast and got ready for church. In the summer, everyone dressed more casual in slacks and a sport shirt. I had about fifteen minutes to kill before leaving so I did my deep breathing exercise. It was really hard to focus on the breathing. My head was filled with the memory of the last twenty-four hours and the anticipation of seeing Eden. I also practiced the breathing all the way to Mom's where I dropped off Spot. They already had left so I did more breathing until I pulled into the church parking lot.

It was overcast and sprinkling. Everyone would be in the fellowship hall. I took even more deep breaths as I went in the side door. It looked like most all the family was there. I didn't see Aunt Agnes and Eden.

What if she didn't come? Mom came to me and gave me a hug and asked, "How are you Honey?"

"I'm holding up pretty well."

She said, "Everyone is worried about Ace and about you too. What a terrible shock. I can't imagine what it's like to go through that. I've filled everyone in on the details. They know not to ask a lot of questions."

Mom took me by the arm and we moved to where the family was standing and talking. I exchanged hugs with everyone. They were upset and empathetic. I felt loved and comforted. I was so thankful that I had them to understand and lean on.

Aunt Agnes and Eden came in the side door. Eden looked beautiful in a pair of white pants and a burgundy blouse. Jack went over to greet them and they came over and exchanged greetings with all of us. I know Jack worked it so that Mom and I would be the last for them to greet.

Aunt Agnes gave me a hug and said that she was so sorry to hear about Ace. She stepped back and Eden held out her hand and said, "Hello Jett, Aunt Agnes was telling me about your friend. I am so sorry for him and for you."

All I could get out was, "Hello Eden, thank you."

This time thank God we released hands at the same time. She continued, "I can't imagine what it would be like to be in a war. I've read some articles recently trying to explain how traumatic it is for you all and how that can cause problems when you return home. What is your friend's name?"

While Eden was talking, I was taking subtle deep breaths and noticed that Mom had engaged Aunt Agnes in conversation and that Eden and I were essentially having a one-on-one conversation.

I only had enough air to speak in short phrases, "His name is Ace."

"Would it be too forward to ask you how Ace is doing?"

"No, not at all. Physically he'll be fine. Emotionally we both have some work to do."

She asked, "How long were you all in the service."

"We were in for three years and spent two in the Middle East." I remembered how much I didn't want people to ask questions about my experience. I didn't want to talk about it, but I was praying she would keep asking questions. I wanted her to just ask questions so I could watch her.

She said, "Jett, you are going through so much right now. I'm sure you don't want me asking a lot of questions."

I answered a little too quickly, "No, I don't mind you asking questions."

I couldn't read her expression, but she smiled and said, "Did you and Ace grow up together?"

"Yes, we have been best friends since grade school." I was starting to feel a little less nervous, but wasn't quite ready to engage in a normal conversation.

About that time the bell rang and it was time for the service to begin. Aunt Agnes turned from Mom to Eden and said, "I guess it's time to get to our seats." Eden and I smiled at each other.

We went in and sat in the same seats as last Sunday. I took a lot of deep breaths while the service was going on and looked at her as often as possible without being too obvious. I was aware that the breathing helped me feel more comfortable with the idea of talking to her.

After the service was over, everyone went back to the fellowship hall for refreshments. Aunt Agnes and Eden didn't slip out like they did last week so they joined the rest of us. I couldn't just go back to her and start talking. It would feel awkward. I was talking to Jack and Ann and they inconspicuously moved us over to Eden who was talking to Henry and Betty. Somehow we were quickly involved in their conversation and within a few minutes, Eden and I were facing each other.

She asked, "When will you go back to the hospital?"

"Right after I leave here."

"Do you know when he'll be discharged?"

I replied, "I'm not sure, but it could be Tuesday."

"He lives with you, right?"

"Yes. Speaking of that, I understand you came up this weekend to look at some houses."

"That's right. My Realtor® showed me a lot of different places. It's so beautiful here. I would like to have a house with a nice view, but I didn't see anything in my price range that really stood out. The good news is that I'm not in a hurry and now that she knows what I'm looking for, she can keep an eye out for something she thinks I might like."

I wanted to say that I have a great view and you could come and stay at anytime with me for as long as you like, but instead said, "If you'd like, I'll keep an eye out too especially for something that has a great view."

"Thanks Jett. That would be nice." Aunt Agnes came over and said to Eden, "We better go Eden so you can get on the road."

Eden smiled and said, "I will remember you and Ace in my prayers. Good-bye." And they were gone.

I watched her as they moved to the door. I was hoping she might look back, but she didn't. Why would she look back? Who would be interested in a war veteran who has emotional problems and was at least fifteen years younger?

Mom was beside me. "She seems really nice. Did you have a nice chat?"

"It was fine Mom. I've got to focus my attention on Ace. I probably should have stayed with him rather than coming to see Eden."

She said, "I'm glad you came. You needed a break and Ace had April and Marge. Don't beat yourself up. Now go on back and see if you can help Ace get on a better track."

"Thanks Mom, I love you."

30

ACE ON THE PSYCH WARD

I called April and they had moved Ace to the psych ward and he was not pleased. Too bad. She took a minute to ask Ma and Ace about food and gave me the order to include two Big Macs® for Ace. I went back in the fellowship hall and instead of the usual round of good-bye hugs, I waved to anyone who was looking my way, turned and went out the side door. On the way to the hospital, I thought about how the conversation went with Eden. I could at least talk and felt a little less anxious. She seemed concerned and her smile seemed genuine. Beyond that, there was nothing. I had to let it go. I had more pressing matters at hand.

When I got to the hospital, a nurse pointed me to a room where I would find April and Ma. It was the office of a staff member who wasn't working today. "Hey ladies, I bring food."

They smiled and April took the bag and said, "One of the staff psychiatrists is talking with Ace and he isn't happy about it. Dr Kingston called the ward and they told me he has been held up, but will be here within the hour."

Ma said, "I'm done with walking on egg shells around Ace. I want him to get better and we have tried to be sensitive to how he is feeling and what he must be going through, but enough is enough. What we've done so far hasn't done him any good."

April responded, "I agree Marge. I have been doing the same thing, hoping he would notice me and love me and waiting for any little crumbs that he might throw my way. I'm gonna lay my cards on the table and fight for whatever possible future we might have together. And he better have a damn good reason why he doesn't want us to work on our relationship."

"Well said," said I. "Now let's go in there and kick his ass." We did high fives all around. Then April said in a wimpy voice, "You don't think he'll be upset with us, do you?"

We all laughed as Doc poked his head in the door. "I thought I would follow the laughter and find the party."

We kind of stopped in our tracks. Before I could get composed, April said, "Do I know you?"

He responded and held out his hand, "I don't think we've met. I'm Howard Kingston."

With a slight blush and smile, she said, "I'm April St. Clare. This is Ace's mom Marge and of course you know Jett."

Doc shook Marge's hand, "Nice to meet you Marge."

She smiled, "Likewise Dr. Kingston."

"Please call me Howard."

She responded, "I will."

"Hello Jett." We shook hands.

"Hello Doc."

He smiled and said, "Sometimes when tragedy happens, we need a little humor to survive. Would that be the case here?"

We all nodded. He continued, "I got permission from Dr. Kirkpatrick to work with Ace while he's on the psych ward. As you know, the ward intake psychiatrist is talking with Ace now. It would be a great help to me if each of you would give me your version of what happened."

He went on, "I assume you know that I spent an hour alone with Ace last Tuesday. Because of confidentiality, I cannot disclose any information he shared with me. I will be happy to answer if I can any general questions you might have for me."

April started out by telling Doc about her relationship with Ace. From there on, each one of us contributed to putting together our understanding of what happened and shared with him any insights, concerns, and hopes we had for Ace's recovery. He had numerous questions for us.

One of the ward staff came to tell us that the psychiatrist was finished. Doc thought it would be too stressful on Ace to have back-to-back sessions with clinicians. He said he was going home for the afternoon and would return around 7:00 this evening to visit with Ace.

Before he left, he said, "I have a couple of recommendations. The first is to avoid talking about what happened. Keep the conversation light. The second is that you spend time with Ace until about 5:00 and then go home and don't return until tomorrow around 11:00. I believe he needs time alone. I will also be back to visit with him tomorrow morning. Jett, you have my cell number. Call me around 10:00 in the morning and I'll give you an update. You can call Marge and April. Would you be willing to follow my recommendations?" We all nodded.

After Doc left, April said, "Marge, would you like to go in and visit with Ace by yourself for awhile?" She said that would be nice. April continued, "Here are his Big Macs®. We'll be right here if you need us."

Marge left. April said she liked Doc. We talked on and off, read magazines, and I dozed some.

Marge was gone for an hour or so and when she came back, Jim was with her, having arrived about fifteen minutes earlier. Marge said Ace didn't talk much and slept most of the time, but it made her feel good being in the same room with him. She said she and Jim were going home and she would wait for my call in the morning.

After they left, April said, "We have about an hour. Do you want to go in together?"

I replied, "That's up to you. If you would feel more comfortable with me being there, that'll be fine with me."

She said, "I would like that since we are supposed to keep it light."

We walked down the hall and his door was open. He was asleep. April whispered, "I'm thinking they gave him something to settle his nerves."

I said, "Do you think we should wake him?"

"Yes."

I said, "Let me do it. You know how we get startled easily."

"Yes, I remember it well."

I went over to the foot of his bed and started tickling his feet through the sheet and whispering, "Ace, wake up! Ace, wake up! Ace, wake up!"

He started pulling his feet away and rubbing them together like he was trying to get a bug off. I kept tickling. He opened his eyes and looking dazed said, "What the shit Jett? What the fuck are you doing?"

"Trying to wake your lazy ass up."

He asked, "Where's Mom? She was here when I went to sleep?"

April responded, "Your Dad came later and they've gone home. Your Mom will be back in the morning."

He asked, "What time is it?"

April said, "A little after 4:00. How are you feeling?"

"I don't know. I guess okay. I'm exhausted." He looked at me and said, "Remember that obstacle course at Benning? I feel like I've just finished running it for the third time."

"Yeah, that 'baby' was a bear. I beat your time the last time we ran it."

He was getting drowsy again, but managed to say softly, "Bull shit, you…never beat…my best time."

He was gone again. April said, "I don't think there's any use in staying."

"I agree."

We headed for the door and he mumbled, "Where you goin?" Before either of us could answer, he was out again.

We were also exhausted and decided to go home and get some sleep. I told her I would call her in the morning as soon as I heard from Doc. I went by Mom's to get Spot and headed for the cabin. I went right to bed. I got up a few times to pee and let Spot out, but I was out for almost twelve hours. I went for my run at 5:00 and then got back into bed. I set the alarm for 9:00.

I cleaned up, ate something and called Doc a little after 10:00. He said, "I met with Ace last night and this morning and he seems a little better. He gave me permission to talk with his mom and you about his treatment, but not about the content of our conversations. We have him on two medications and Dr. Kirkpatrick and I have encouraged him to stay until Friday so we can observe him and see how he's responding to the meds. It takes time for one of these medications to get in the system so we won't have any clear indication about that for a few weeks."

I asked, "Did he agree to stay?"

"So far, he has not said otherwise."

"What if he decides he wants to leave?"

"We can only keep him for seventy-two hours. After that, he is free to leave unless we believe he is still a risk to himself."

I asked, "Can we visit him?"

He answered, "Kirkpatrick and I agree that it's best for him not to have any visitors until Wednesday. We'll let you know if that changes. Do you or Ace have any guns at the cabin?"

"Ace just bought a .45 and I have already put it in a safe place where he won't be able to find it."

"Good. Sorry Jett, but I have to get going. I'll see you tomorrow at your cabin around 9:00."

"Sounds good, Doc. I'll see you then."

I called Ma and April and gave them the news. Ma told me that Jeffery had been upset and cried when he heard about Ace's attempted suicide. She said, "You know how Jeffery looks up to Ace. He couldn't believe Ace would do such a thing. We tried to explain the best we could."

I told them I would call if there were any updates. I called Mom and gave her the news and asked her to call the family. She said she had talked with Ann and they wondered if we should cancel the picnic on Saturday. I suggested we go ahead and have the picnic, but not associate it with Ace and me coming home. It's just a family picnic and Ace, Ma, Jim, Jeffery, and April are invited."

Mom said, "We've already invited a few of Ace's cousins."

"That's fine. You know how the family loves to get together and are always looking for a reason to have a party. Let's go ahead as planned. Ace may not make it. We can have another one next month."

April and I met for lunch at a little café on Main Street. She had some errands to run and I went over to the Inn to visit with Pop and spent the rest of the afternoon working with Charlie. April and I met at 5:00 for a run. She was working tomorrow and was going to turn in early. I was invited to Henry and Betty's for supper. I planned to call Bernard and Valarie before going to bed. I was still tired from all the stress.

31
ZACCHAEUS

Buddy Session Two

Doc arrived at 9:00 and said Ace was doing a little better. He visited with him earlier that morning.

I asked, "Can you give me more details?"

"What would you like to know?"

I replied, "I'm not sure what to ask, but I wonder if he's eating and sleeping?"

"His appetite has improved since Sunday and he took a nap yesterday. He slept well last night. I've been talking with him about the program and he has been moderately receptive. I'll take that from any of you guys. This is new and I don't expect you to jump on board until you begin to see some results. Any more questions?"

"Has he mentioned us?"

"Yes, he asked why you all had not been visiting and I told him we had requested you not visit for a few days. He seemed disappointed and when I asked why, he would not elaborate."

I asked, "What's the purpose of us not visiting?"

"This is not an exact science Jett, but when someone attempts suicide it can be helpful to give them some time to reflect on what happened and to explore reasons to keep living. Ace and I have spent some time on those subjects during our sessions. Families and friends can sometimes be a distraction to the process."

"Can we see him tomorrow?"

He replied, "Let's give him one more day and shoot for Thursday."

I changed the subject and said, "Will you see him anymore today?"

He replied, "I will stop by on my way home from the office. How have you been doing with the breathing exercises?"

"At first, I thought that chime was going to drive me crazy, but I've gotten used to it. I didn't practice the other exercises as much as you wanted us to, but I did pretty well considering all that went on with Ace. My mind still wants to wander all over the place, but I feel like I'm getting the hang of it. I'm more aware that I can make the shift from thoughts to the breathing. I had a panic attack a few days ago and tried the deep breathing and it didn't work."

"You did well under the circumstances. That awareness you mentioned is very important. Keep up the good work. Most of the skills will take a lot of training. Just keep practicing on the same schedule we set at our last meeting. Remember the breathing for now is designed to quiet and focus the mind. Our next step with the breathing will be to understand the physiological benefits. Later, we will work on using them when symptoms appear. Right now, I want to see how you're doing with the breathing and make sure you're getting air into your diaphragm.

"Close your eyes and begin the breathing; put a hand below your rib cage and pay attention to how focusing on breathing enables your mind to slow down. Be quiet for a moment or perhaps for a series of moments....Now open your eyes and stand up. Pick a point out in front of you to focus on and take more deep breaths. You want a nice easy flowing deep breath. See if you can breathe a little more air into your belly. That's right. If your mind starts to wander, let the thoughts go and come back to your breathing. Notice how smooth that transition is. I want you to walk around the cabin and practice your breathing. Keep your hand on your belly and make sure you are getting plenty of air into that area....Quiet the mind. Notice that you can be aware of your surroundings and still focus on your breathing....Keep moving. That's right, you're doing really well. Okay, you can sit down. What was that like?"

"I do better when you're guiding the exercise. Overall, I thought I did well and feel relaxed."

"I think you are doing well with the mechanics; you're getting plenty of air down low. It sounds like you're becoming more aware of how the breathing quiets the mind. Is that true?"

"Yes."

"Good. Let's move on. I would like for you to tell me about your time in the Army to include details about your combat experiences. Are you willing to talk about it?"

"I think so. The knee jerk response is I don't want to talk about it, but I know if I'm going to get better, I have to at least talk about it with you and the other vets."

"You might be surprised to know a lot of my time spent with Ace in the hospital was spent listening to his experiences."

"I'm surprised he was willing to talk about it."

Doc said, "It wasn't easy. I think it helped that I'm a Ranger and served in Viet Nam."

"I didn't know you served in 'Nam.'"

"I wasn't assigned there until a year or so before the war ended and even though I was with the 101st Airborne Division in a combat zone, I never saw any combat. The war was winding down. I cannot even come close to identifying with what you guys went through, but it helps me to at least be familiar with some aspects of your military experience."

I started at the beginning and told him my story. At first, I had trouble getting the words out, but he was easy to talk to. At times, he would tell me to slow down and take some deep breaths. It was strange I could talk about some of the most traumatic times without much emotion. If they come to me in a flashback, it's like I'm there and I can feel the fear in my mind and my body. I guess that makes sense, but it's still strange. When I had finished and Doc had asked his questions, I looked at the clock and it was almost one.

He said, "I know talking about it is difficult, but it was helpful to me. How do you feel right now?"

"I think I'm okay. Talking about it was a lot easier than having a flashback."

"I often hear that from other veterans."

He went on, "I'm going to leave with you a list of common PTSD symptoms and some others that can be related to PTSD. Look them over and give each of them a number as outlined on the checklist. Fill it out and bring it to the group session on Saturday. I'll go over them with you next Tuesday. Keep practicing the focusing and deep breathing. You have the same homework assignment as last time. I'll see you at 9:00 here at your cabin on Saturday morning."

I asked, "Do you think Ace will come?"

"I'm not sure, but I hope he will." He left.

I looked over the symptom checklist and filled it out.

<u>LIST OF SYMPTOMS</u>

Jett

1. Always 2. Most of the time 3. Half the time
4. Occasionally 5. Never

4 Difficulty falling or staying asleep
4 Easily pissed off
4 Outbursts of anger
5 Getting in fist fights

2 Difficulty concentrating
2 Always on lookout for danger
1 Easily startled by loud noise or sudden movements
2 Distressing memories, images, and thoughts
2 Recurrent nightmares
3 Flashbacks
2 Don't wanna talk about combat experiences
4 Home is a letdown; feels different
4 Not interested in doing stuff you use to enjoy
4 Hard to get close with family and friends
4 Hopeless about the future
3 Don't have a purpose
3 Don't have a direction
4 Pissed off at just about everything
3 Drinking/drugs ease the pain
3 Can't get my mind to stop racing
3 When thinking about combat, I feel guilt
3 When thinking about combat, I feel shame
3 I can't stop the pain
3 I don't know what love is anymore
3 Don't trust people
3 Lost belief in God
3 Angry with God
3 Proud of my country
1 War is insane
3 Life is unfair
2 My self-esteem sucks
5 Trouble finding a job
4 I feel like whacking myself
2 Avoid crowds
1 People don't have a clue what war is like

3 Feel alone/isolated
4 Nothing matters anymore
4 Fearful about leaving your house
2 Have panic attacks
  2 Heart racing
  3 Sweating
  4 Trembling and shaking
  2 Shortness of breath
  4 Choking sensation
  2 Pain and pressure in chest
  3 Nausea
  4 Feel dizzy or lightheaded
  4 Strange feelings; hard to describe
  2 Fear of losing control
  3 Fear of dying
  4 Numbness or tingling sensations
  4 Chills or hot flushes

I ate lunch and went to the Inn to work with Charlie. As I was driving down the mountain, I started feeling some anxiety. I guessed it was related to talking with Doc and going over all those symptoms. I tried the breathing remembering I just wanted to stop the anxious thoughts, the what-if's. I had a little success, but my self-talk helped me the most. By the time I got to the Inn, I felt a little better.

Pop had gone out to run some errands. Charlie laughed and said his wife was pleased that he was more relaxed. We took our deep breaths every time the chime sounded. Around 4:30, I called April and we went jogging together. I told her about the visit with Doc and that he wanted us to wait until Thursday to see Ace.

I said, "I'm going to sneak in and see Ace tonight and take him a couple of Big Macs®. You wanna come?"

She hesitated, "I think it would be better if you went alone. You two need to get connected again. I don't want to put any pressure on you, but honestly, I think his life depends on it."

"I don't feel any pressure. I feel the same way. There were a number of times over there when my life depended on him and he always came through. I don't intend to let him down. I'm gonna follow what we decided on Sunday. He went to hell and back for me and if he wants to try to make my life hell, then he can go for it. This suicide attempt was a wake-up call for me. I'm not gonna let anything happen to him."

She hugged me and said, "Thank you."

I asked, "Do you want to grab something at Sally's?"

After Sally's, we went our separate ways. I stopped by Mom's to fill her in on my visit with Doc and then left for McDonalds® to get Ace's Big Macs. Afterwards, I stopped by the convenience store and got two cold beers. I figured it would be a "piece of cake" to slip in the hospital and psych ward. Ace wasn't on the locked ward and they had liberal visitation at the hospital. I might run into Doc, but even though I liked him, I didn't care. This was my best friend and even though he didn't seem like he wanted my help, I was going to find a way to see him.

I did a recon of the hospital staircases and figured they were the best way to Ace's room without being seen. Getting to his room and the first few minutes of the visit went by without incident. His face lit up when he saw the Big Macs® and he had an emotional orgasm when he saw the beer. He was disappointed that I was gonna drink one of the beers. He had eaten one Big Mac® and started on the second when we heard some footsteps outside the room. There was a knock. While Ace was saying to hold on and that he was naked, we hid the beers.

A female voice said, "Ace Frost, what are you doing naked?"

"Nothing, Mrs. Henry."

"Cover up, I'm comin' in." She came in and looked like a no-nonsense African American woman about six-feet-tall, 200 pounds and I guessed in her late forties or early fifties. "Ace, I thought you weren't supposed to have any visitors."

He responded, "That's true, but this dummy didn't get the word so I didn't wanna hurt his feelings and turn him away. By the way, I'm sorry I didn't introduce you. Mrs. Henry, this is my friend Zacchaeus."

She smiled and sarcastically said, "Well what a nice name and well straight from the story in the Bible. Ain't that somethin'. Well, Zacchaeus, you've got about five minutes to come down outta that tree and get your ass gone. Do I make myself clear?" She smiled again and left. Something in her tone was friendly, but I could tell she meant business about me leaving.

After the door closed, we both burst out laughing.

"What in hell made you think of that name?"

He smiled and answered, "It just came to me outta the blue. Mrs. Henry is always talkin' to me about Jesus and she knows her Bible. As I remember it, the dude was up in some tree and Jesus told him to come down out of that tree and do something, but I don't remember what it was."

That was the first time I'd seen Ace acting like himself since Migs and Holton died. That seemed like a good sign, but I wasn't gonna get my hopes up, not yet.

He continued, "Mrs. Henry is good people. I know she smelled the beer. You better go on. I don't wanna press my luck. I'll never get outta here if I'm not careful. Would you pour out the water in this cup and pour in what's left of your beer. Here, I'm finished. He handed me his empty bottle. We gotta get these bottles outta here. I'm hoping to get out on Thursday. Come back tomorrow night, will ya?"

"Yeah, I'll be here." We did our traditional handshake and hugged which hadn't happened since Walter Reed.

32

LISTENING

I was elated, but trying not to get too cocky. I drove over to April's and gave her a quick rundown of what had happened. She said, "I'm afraid to expect too much."

"Me too." When I got home, I called Marge and then Mom. Spot and I went for a short walk, watched some TV and went to bed.

The next day, I worked with Charlie, exercised with April, and ate supper with Mom and Dad. Later I sneaked in to see Ace with the beer and Big Macs®. Mrs. Henry was off and no one bothered us. I only stayed about thirty minutes. Ace was not as "up" as he had been the night before, but he was still doing pretty well. He told me that Doc said he would be released tomorrow.

He asked, "Can you pick me up tomorrow around 3:00?"

"Sure." I asked, "How's your leg?"

"I think it's better. The PT people came to get me Monday, yesterday and today."

I interjected, "We got a postcard from Derrick. The Army agreed to ship him to another Army hospital closer to home."

"That's great for him and a relief for me. I don't know if I could have made a trip back to Walter Reed to see him."

"It's better for all of us. I guess I better get going."

I went home, made my calls and went to bed. I had a terrible night with nightmares and sweating. When I got up, the sheets were soaked and my bed looked like a bunch of people had a "free for all." I barely made the run, came back and got in another bed and passed out till around 11:00. I went down to work with Charlie and picked-up Ace.

We drove home mostly in silence. I wondered if Ace was going to go back in his shell. I didn't ask him because I didn't want to push him. I got us a beer and he asked me to turn on the TV. After about fifteen minutes, he got up and headed toward the kitchen. He got another beer and instead of coming back to watch more TV, he went out on the back deck. I waited a few minutes, got me another beer and went out to join him.

"You want some company?"

He was staring out over the mountains, but nodded his head. Neither of us said anything and I was determined to let him take the lead.

After awhile as he continued to gaze at the view, "When you look out over the terrain, do you ever imagine Bravo being on patrol out there and how certain places would provide good cover and other places would be a death trap?"

"Yeah," I responded. "Look at that open space in the trees at about ten o'clock. I've thought about Bravo being ordered to take that hill on the other side. How would we do it? The LT would send you, Migs, and me down that ravine over there (pointing) and up that little hill so we could lay down some fire creating a diversion hopefully giving them time to charge across the open area. That's as far as I got."

Smiling, "Makes me glad you weren't the LT Ranger, that's a truly fucked up plan."

Smiling back, "Yeah, I never was good at tactics."

My watch chimed and a couple of seconds later, his watch chimed. We looked at each other and laughed. Ace said, "He's got me doin' that breathing on the chime."

"Yeah?" We both took a few seconds to do the breathing.

Ace said, "In the hospital, Doc took me through a breathing exercise with my eyes closed and it must have lasted fifteen or twenty minutes. Anyway, when I opened my eyes, I felt more relaxed than I had in years. I noticed it didn't take me long to get tense again, but I was surprised and it made me think maybe there's something to this breathing."

"I haven't had that experience. I've tried to use it to help with my panic attacks and it hasn't helped. I told Doc and he said I needed to keep practicing. So I'm doing the breathing exercises more on faith than anything else."

I could see a breeze moving up the side of the mountain as it swayed the trees and rustled their leaves. When it reached us, it felt nice and refreshing. The sun's rays made their way through the trees seeking a destination and causing shadows to move and dart here and there. I was with my friend. He was opening up and talking. As a few tears welled up, I was hoping that this was the beginning of something that might bring something new, vital, and bright into the darkness that held those memories of the last three years.

Then he cut through my fantasy with a knife and said, "Sometimes I don't know if I can do it." I decided to stay quiet. He continued, "I didn't wanna like Doc, but he's a hard man to dislike. He seems to care and he listens and seems to understand. I thought he was gonna judge me and give me a lecture about cutting my wrists and I was gonna go off on him. But he never did. I actually talked to him about a lot of shit. He never said much. Just took a lot of notes. Do you think he can help us?"

"I don't know. After my nightmares last night, I felt like there was no hope. I lay in a pool of sweat most of the night. I wanted to get up and escape to another bed, but I couldn't. It's like I was trapped and paralyzed. My body ached and couldn't move and all I could do was lay there and be engulfed in the ghosts of Holton, Migs, Joel, Freddy, Monty, and…" My voice trailed off.

He said, "I think that time at Walter Reed was the worst for me. These guys kept coming in from Germany. One guy had no legs. Another one had lost both arms and it went on and on. I ran into two guys in the mess hall who were blind. I had times when I was so fucking mad. It felt like I was in a rage. I think it scared me and I stuffed it and was miserable. I thought I was going crazy and losing my mind. The world was slipping away from me. Then, I got in some kind of survival mode and focused all my energy on gettin' outta there. A couple of days before you picked me up, I had this terrifying thought, 'what if getting away from WR doesn't help'?"

He stopped talking and seemed to go somewhere else. I was familiar with that experience. Ace was talking more than I had heard in a long time and all I needed to do was listen just like Doc. He finally continued, "When we were on the way here, I had moments when I felt pretty good. But, I also had moments when I felt like I was gonna lose it. By the time we reached Harvest, I was starting to panic. I wasn't feeling any better than I did at WR so I did what I do best. I stuffed it again and focused on getting drunk and getting laid. We both know where that led."

He went on, "It killed me to see Mom so upset - a good choice of words. But, when I was in that jail cell, I couldn't focus on anything, but this feeling that my fucking life was over. Then I started thinking I should have been out on that point and Holton should still be alive. He had a wife and kid and had his whole life in front of him. I guess that guilt and feelin' like a piece of shit pushed me over the edge. All I could think about was getting it over with. I wasn't going to let the world slip away from me. I was going to slip away from it. I didn't think about Mom, you, Jeffery, Dad or anybody else. I just wanted it over. That was all I could think about. I'll be honest, I've thought about doing it again, but now I couldn't do it to Mom after having seen the expression on her face when I first saw her in the hospital. I'll never forget that."

He was quiet again and then said, "I'm tired. I'm gonna lay down. Will you be here when I wake up?"

"I'm goin' to town in a few minutes and should be back in a couple of hours. You need anything?"

"No. I just need sleep."

He shut the door and in a moment opened it again and said, "Where's my .45?"

"I put it where you can't find it. Before you say anything, I know you can find a way to whack yourself if you want to, but it helps me to know you can't in a moment reach in the drawer and pull out the gun. With something else, you might at least have to think about it for a few moments."

"I don't have the energy to argue." He shut the door.

I phoned Harry at the bike shop hoping they had not closed. I was in luck. I asked him if he could possibly deliver the bikes tomorrow. He said he could and would be glad to do it. I called April and just caught her. She was headed out the door to exercise. I told her I was going over to Ma's and asked her if she wanted to meet me there. She said she would. I met them and told them about our afternoon without going into too many details. I told them about my success with listening and that we might want to try that tactic for now. They agreed. We were hopeful.

Mom told me yesterday that she wanted to cook supper for Ace and me and that I could pick it up after 5:00. I gave her the latest news on Ace and me and then said, "It sure smells good. I think I know what you cooked, but tell me anyway."

"There's fried chicken, mashed potatoes, gravy, green beans, homemade rolls, and a banana pudding."

"Wow!" I thanked her and asked her if she was okay with me going on. "I want to be there when Ace wakes up."

When I got to the cabin, Ace was still asleep. When he awoke about an hour later, we had a couple of beers, watched some TV and ate our supper. After we were finished, I cleaned up while he called Mom and thanked her for the food.

When I sat down to watch some TV with him, he put it on mute and said, "I don't know if it's your Mom's fried chicken or our talk this afternoon or both, but I feel a little better. I've been so stressed since getting back in town. I don't even know if stressed is the right word. Maybe it's like confused, like I don't know what to do and I don't know where to turn. So getting drunk and laid seemed like my only choices."

He paused and went on, "I know you're dealing with a lot of shit too, but you can do some things we both love like exercise and hiking? Do you know how hard it is to be in these woods and not be able to do those things?"

"No, I can't imagine what it's like."

"I heard you mention working at the Inn with Charlie. I can't even do that."

"That's not true. I've talked to Charlie and he said he could use you on his mowing crew. You could mow and I could do the weed eating. That would keep us busy for awhile."

He replied, "I hadn't thought of that. Maybe we could start Monday. I don't feel like I've got all my strength back yet."

"What are the PT people saying about your leg?"

"They say I've made good progress and there's no reason that I won't be 80 to 90 percent in a couple of months. They're now saying if I stay with the PT I could be 100 percent in four or five months."

"That's great news. I can't wait for us to be able to get back out in the woods. Those dirt bikes I mentioned last week are gonna be delivered tomorrow. We can't walk or run, but we can ride."

"Yeah, that's better than nothin'. My problem is I want to be exhausted, to run the trails, to work up a sweat, to gasp for air and collapse on the ground. All my life, I've expressed myself in physical activity and sports. All this stuff about talking and sharing is not my way. I'm trying Jett, but I don't know how to do it and it feels awkward." He got up and went to the kitchen, "Do you want a beer?"

"Yeah, thanks."

He asked, "Did Doc have you fill out that sheet on symptoms?"

"Yeah, did you fill one out?"

He replied, "Yeah. Could I see yours? Mine's in that folder in my bedroom if you wanna see it."

"OK, I'd like to see yours too."

LIST OF SYMPTOMS

Ace

1. Always 2. Most of the time 3. Half the time
4. Occasionally 5. Never

4 Difficulty falling or staying asleep
1 Easily pissed off
2 Outbursts of anger
4 Getting in fist fights
2 Difficulty concentrating
2 Always on lookout for danger
2 Easily startled by loud noise or sudden movements
2 Distressing memories, images, and thoughts
2 Recurrent nightmares
3 Flashbacks
1 Don't wanna talk about combat experiences
1 Home is a letdown; feels different
1 Not interested in doing stuff you use to enjoy
1 Hard to get close to family and friends
2 Hopeless about the future
1 Don't have a purpose

1 Don't have a direction
2 Pissed off at just about everything
1 Drinking/drugs ease the pain
2 Can't get my mind to stop racing
4 When thinking about combat, I feel guilt
3 When thinking about combat, I feel shame
2 I can't stop the pain
2 I don't know what love is anymore
2 Don't trust people
3 Lost belief in God
3 Angry with God
2 Proud of my country
1 War is insane
3 Life is unfair
2 My self-esteem sucks
3 Trouble finding a job
2 I feel like whacking myself
3 Avoids crowds
1 People don't have a clue what war is like
1 Feel alone/isolated
2 Nothing matters anymore
5 Fearful about leaving your house
4 Have panic attacks
    4 Heart racing
    5 Sweating
    5 Trembling and shaking
    5 Shortness of breath
    5 Choking sensation
    5 Pain and pressure in chest
    5 Nausea
    5 Feel dizzy or lightheaded

3 Strange feelings; hard to describe
1 Fear of losing control
4 Fear of dying
5 Numbness or tingling sensations
5 Chills or hot flushes

He said, "I think I could have filled out yours and been pretty accurate, but I was surprised about the severity of the panic attacks. I knew you had 'em but I didn't know they were that severe. Could you have filled out mine and been pretty accurate?"

I replied, "I think I would have been close. I can see the anger, keeping to yourself, and the hopelessness and how that affects your life. I didn't know much about the guilt or shame you felt about the things we've done. We've talked a little about God so I figured we were pretty close on that subject. You've never mentioned having panic attacks and I've never seen any evidence that you have them so I would have been close there too. I would have missed some of the things if you hadn't talked to me earlier today and a few times since WR."

He said, "It seems like we know each other pretty well."

"Yeah, I think we do. Sometime I would like to talk more about those symptoms."

"I can't promise anything right now, but I'm trying."

I said, "That's good enough for me."

"Let's go to Stanley's and get drunk."

I hesitated.

He laughed, "Just kidding. Don't get me wrong though. I want us to be able to get drunk if we want to. But, I don't want to get drunk because I can't stand to live. That's one of the things I've learned in the past few days."

He added, "I still need some beers to take the edge off."

"Yeah, me too."

He said, “I’m talked out and ready to watch TV. Are you okay with that?”

“Yeah, that’s fine. Did I mention that the family is having a picnic on Saturday at the Inn?”

“I think so. I’m not sure I’m up for that, but we’ll see.”

We each had one more beer and dozed on and off. I went on to bed around 10:00.

33
THE BIKES

When I got up the next morning for my run, Ace's bedroom door was closed. As usual, after my run, I went back to bed. There was a knock on the door. I stumbled out of the bedroom to the front door. It was Harry delivering the bikes. We talked for a few minutes and he left.

Ace came out, "Who was that?"

"It was Harry delivering the bikes."

I asked, "Are you hungry?"

"Yeah, I could eat something."

We got some breakfast together and decided to try out the bikes. While he was taking a shower, I called April and filled her in on the news and asked her to call Ma and let her know. I told her I wasn't sure whether we were going to be at the picnic or not. It all depended on how Ace was feeling. I called Mom and gave her an update.

Mom said, "Do the best you can to make the picnic. Everyone will understand, but they will be disappointed."

"I'll do everything I can to get us there."

We hung up. I got cleaned up and when I came out, I could hear Ace outside playing fetch with Spot. I went out on the porch and said, "Would you look at the bikes and see if they are similar to the ones we used to ride. Harry left a manual. It's here on the front porch. Are you up for riding three or four hours?"

He responded, "I guess. We'll have to stop some. My leg will get stiff in one position. I have to be back here by around 3:00. My PT appointment is at 4:00."

"I'm gonna pack us a lunch."

"Remember to pack some beer. Spot wants to go."

"Got it. Since we won't be going that fast, I think he can keep up."

I brought out two old back packs - one for the food and the other for the beer. "You carry the food and I'll get the beer."

"What if we get separated? I'll be stuck with the food and you'll have the beer."

I said, "I thought the pack might be too heavy with you having to be careful with your leg."

"Not true. I'll carry the beer."

"What did you find out about the bikes?"

"They are used, but in good condition. They have that electronic ignition so we don't have to kick start 'em. Other than that, they seem to be similar to what we've ridden before."

We took off and had a great time. Spot was having the time of his life. I rolled mine once when I ran over a log hidden by some leaves. I was going slowly so I wasn't hurt.

He asked, "You okay?"

"Yeah, I'm fine."

"I'm not taking any chances. All I need is to wind up back in the hospital which is not gonna happen."

We picked one of our favorite spots. We had two beers each and lay back on a rock in the shade, rested and talked for about an hour. We worked on our deep breathing. I was surprised how Ace seemed to be taking the breathing seriously. I don't know what happened between him and Doc in the hospital, but he was at least trying to have a better attitude.

We got back on time and Ace left around 3:30 for his PT appointment. I thought about how much fun we had today. It seemed like old times. I had slept well with no nightmares and no panic attacks today so far. I called April and we decided to meet at 4:30 to go for a run. I cleaned up around the cabin and left, stopping by Mom's to return some dishes and thank her for the food.

I got back to the cabin around 6:30. Ace was not home. Mom sent enough food so we could eat leftovers for supper. By 7:30, he was still not home. I called Marge and she said he had dropped by for a visit around 5:30, but had left without saying where he was going. She just assumed he was headed back up here. She said he was in a good mood and she was hoping his attitude and state of mind the past few days was a good sign. I told her I would call her later.

I figured he had gone to Stanley's so I left. His SUV was in the parking lot. I was relieved. I wasn't going to leave him on his own until I knew he would be okay. I went in and he was at the bar talking to some guy I didn't know. His name was Nate and he had been in the Army and was also recently back from the war. They had apparently been trading war stories. I went to the pay phone and called Ma and told her not to worry and that I wouldn't let him drive. I sat with them for an hour. I had a couple of beers, but they were both on their way to getting drunk.

I said, "Ace, let's head back home and get something to eat."

I was surprised when he replied, "Let me have one for the road and I'll be ready to go."

I turned to Nate, "Do you have anyone with you?"

"Yeah, he's my friend Frank. See the dude in the red tee-shirt playing pool. He don't drink. I'm good."

About fifteen minutes later, we shook hands. Ace and I left. He said slightly slurring his words, "You better drive. I don't wanna to go back to Bernard's jail."

We ate and watched some TV. Ace went to bed about 9:30. I cleaned up and went to bed about 10:00.

I followed my usual morning routine with the exception of going back to bed after my run. I got Ace up around 7:30. We ate breakfast and both took showers and cleaned up. It was about 8:45 and I heard a vehicle pull up out front. It was Doc.

34
GROUP SESSION ONE

I opened the door. He smiled and said, "Good morning Zach." I said good morning to him before it registered that he had called me Zach. He went over to the table and started unpacking his papers. I followed him and said, "How did you find out?"

He answered, "Mrs. Henry and I are buddies. She said she had a hard time getting you out of that tree and that you even climbed the tree the next night."

"Wow, I thought I was being so cautious, especially the second night. Are you upset?"

He continued smiling, "Not in the least. I knew you weren't gonna leave your buddy alone in that hospital for too long. It was a little risky bringing in the beer, but it worked out fine."

Ace came out of his bedroom and said, "Hey Doc."

"Hello Ace, How are you?"

"Doin' pretty good."

Several cars and two motorcycles were pulling up. I went over to the front door and let people in. Spot was greeting everyone and I think it took off a little of the edge. I asked Doc if he wanted me to put Spot up and he said that Spot would be fine and that he would be a nice addition to the group. Doc's cell phone rang.

He answered and apparently the person was pretty close and had made one wrong turn after turning off the main road. In a few minutes they pulled up. Ace let them in and it turned out to be Nate from last night at Stanley's and his friend. I couldn't remember the friend's name. I told everyone to put their drinks on the kitchen table or put them in the fridge if they wanted to.

We were standing around and no one was saying much. Doc then directed us to move chairs into a circle and asked everyone to find a seat.

After we were all seated, Doc began, "Well, here we are. I want to thank Jett for allowing us to use his home for our first meeting. We will meet for about three hours every Saturday morning. Speaking of time, when we meet in the group or in the buddy sessions, always put your watches away. These meetings are mandatory. We will take one break. Jett, would you point out where the bathroom is?" I told them there were two bathrooms and pointed in the direction of both. I also told them that there were additional bathrooms outside behind some trees. I got a chuckle from the group.

Doc continued, "Most of you brought something to drink during break. I would prefer no drinks during our sessions. No smoking during the group, but you can of course smoke outside during the break. Each one of you should have my cell number. I think that covers most of the admin stuff. During the sessions, please ask your questions at any time. Are there any questions now?"

There were no questions.

Doc: "I have seen all of you at least twice and it's good to see you gathered together for our first group session. I want to remind you of our confidentiality agreement. Nothing goes out of this room unless we decide otherwise. I am hopeful this group is going to be helpful to each one of you. We will learn many things from each other. I ask you to be supportive and encouraging to each other. Your experiences have been different and yet they have many similar threads. You have a common theme relative to combat.

Doc: "The brain/mind is complex and complicated. In my view, it is presumptuous of any individual or group to claim they have the truth about anything. With that in mind, I want you to know everything I say to you is my perception, my idea, my belief, my opinion, my thought and so on. Even though at times it may seem like I'm making a statement of fact; that is not the case. It is always my perception. In my view, all ideas are incomplete, impermanent, and vulnerable. Actually, I believe that is quite exciting; there are always new things to learn. That attitude can promote a curiosity and a thirst for something new and different. The only thing I know for sure is this table is solid." He lightly banged his fist on a little table by his chair.

He looked around. A guy said, "Sorry Doc, we learned in physics that if you look at that table with a powerful enough micro-scope, you'll see that it has a lot more air than it has mass."

Doc smiled: "Thank you Frank."

Doc: "This experience is designed to excite within you the perception that healing is possible. That each of you possesses inside of you everything you need to move toward and discover a deep and abiding inner peace. We will explore a path that can lead to that goal. In my view, it's never about finding the path; it's about finding a path that works for you. And in most cases, it will work for you directly proportional to your commitment to make it work."

Doc: "At the conclusion of our work together, I predict you will say you found the skills you learned in this group to be insightful and helpful. I also predict you will say the key and most rewarding aspect of this experience was the interaction with each other and the willingness of each one to be supportive and mutually vulnerable. This can be akin to the camaraderie you felt with your comrades during the war. Over there, your life was in danger and you counted on your fellow soldiers to 'have your back' to help you survive. Now, in this place, I hope you will count on each other to help with emotional survival."

He looked around the room to wait for comments and questions. When there were none, he said, "Let's go to work."

Doc: "I have worked with all of you on the deep breathing skill in our first two person sessions. I want to take you through a short review and exercise with the breathing. Everyone close your eyes. I want you to focus on normal breathing. Stay with normal breathing for a few more moments. Now I want you to place your left or right hand below your rib cage. Now take over your breathing and when you inhale, breathe into the lower lobes of your lungs. If you are not getting much movement in your belly, when you breathe in push your stomach muscles out and make room for the air. Make the breath slow and easy until you have a nice rhythm. I'll give you a few more minutes to practice. Now open your eyes. I watched all of you and it seemed like you were doing fairly well. We'll work on it more as we go."

Doc: "Look around the room and take a good look at each person. When you have looked at everyone, close your eyes again and take some slow easy deep breaths.... Let go of your breathing, open your eyes, and look around again and once you have done that, close your eyes again and begin the deep breathing.... Now let go and open your eyes and look around. How many of you felt more relaxed this last time when you looked around the room?"

Most people raised their hand.

Doc: "The deep breathing is a powerful skill. You will experience many benefits as you continue the training. Let's go around the room and each person introduce themselves. When it's your turn, I want you to place your hand on your belly, take two slow deep breaths and say your first name and tell us what you're feeling in that moment."

Doc gestured to his right.

The guy took two quick breaths and said, "I'm Chad and right now I feel uncomfortable." He had a patch over his left eye. He was African American with a medium build. He looked to be about twenty five.

He was muscular with short hair and had a nice smile. He seemed friendly. He was wearing khaki shorts, a red tee-shirt and a pair of sandals.

Doc: "You may or may not have noticed that Chad did a very normal thing. He hurried his breaths. Take your time."

At that point, the older guy sitting three seats down on Doc's left got up and went out the front door. Doc got up and calmly said to the group, "Everyone close your eyes and practice deep breathing until I return."

I don't know how long they were gone, but it didn't seem that long. Doc came in and told us to slow our breathing and open our eyes. The guy followed him in and took his seat.

Doc: "Doug gave me permission to tell you that he had a panic attack. Would anyone else who has panic attacks be willing to raise their hand?" I raised my hand. The guy sitting next to Doug raised his hand and the girl sitting next to Ace raised her hand. A couple of seconds later, Chad raised his hand.

I raised my hand to speak. Doc nodded, "Doug, I'm sorry you had a panic attack, but when you walked out it gave me time to settle. I was five seconds away from getting up and leaving myself." The others with panic were nodding their heads. Doug was looking at the floor still recovering, but looked up and gave us a slight smile.

The woman next to Chad took her deep breaths more slowly and said in a voice that was a little shaky, "My name is Melinda and thanks to Doug and the extra time to do more breathing, I've moved from terrified to scared." Everyone smiled.

Doug said a little above a whisper to Melinda, "Glad I could help."

She was average height and a little heavy set with a pretty round face. Her hair was blond and it came down to her shoulders. She was wearing black slacks with a light purple blouse, black loafers, and it seemed like she had on some make up. I'm guessing in her mid-twenties. Since arriving, she was somewhat withdrawn and scared.

"I'm Paul and I wish I didn't volunteer for this group, but ya'll seem like nice people. Maybe it'll be cool." He was tall and slender with a light, reddish crew cut. He had a fair complexion with a lot of freckles. He was in jeans with a white tee-shirt that had Hard Rock Café® on the front. He had on an old pair of black boots. I guessed he was one of the ones that rode a motorcycle. He had on a New York Yankee baseball cap that looked like it needed an oil change. I think he was in his mid-twenties. He looked like he didn't want to be here.

"I'm Anna and I'm tired of crying and feeling guilty." She had lost her left arm. She was tall with a nice build. I would say she was big boned. She looked like an athlete. Her sandy brown hair was in a pony tail. Her face looked tired and worn from stress and sleepless nights. There was a subtle twinkle in her brown eyes and I thought this woman is down now, but no one or nothing will be able to keep her down. No make up. She was wearing dark green shorts and a light green tee-shirt and white tennis shoes with no socks. I'm guessing early thirties.

"I'm Ace and I could use a beer right now." "Me too," filled the room. Ace looked at Doc. "We got plenty here Doc, how 'bout a beer for everyone who wants one?"

Doc: "The participants aren't allowed to drink, but I'll have one." Everybody started booing.

Doc held up his hands, "All right. I'll tell you this. Everyone who completes this training can join me at Stanley's and the beers will be on me." A cheer went up and the ice was breaking.

Doc looked at me.

"I'm Jett and thanks to the last few minutes, I've moved from panic to anxious."

"My name is Rob and I'm curious about how all this stuff can help." He was short and stocky with black hair that came down over his ears. He had a mustache and had not shaved for a week or so. He had on a pair of cut off jeans and a black tee-shirt with a white skull and cross bones. He had on a pair of black half-boots with dark socks. I guessed he might be the other one who rode the motorcycle.

He looked to be in his late-twenties.

Doug: "I've already been introduced and you know how I feel." Doug had a scar on his right cheek that ran from under his eye to under his chin. He was average height with a medium beer belly. He had tattoos on both upper arms. He was partially bald with a ruddy complexion and his eyes looked blood shot from a lot of drinking and hard living. He looked like one of those career sergeants who had been in the Army most of his life. He hadn't shaved for a few days. Guessing he is in his mid-forties. He was wearing old jeans with a short sleeved button down brown shirt with a pair of well worn brown loafers. There's something about these old soldiers. I liked him. Maybe it had to do with the fact that a few of these old soldiers had saved my life. We youngsters learned to listen to them.

"I'm Nate and I hate groups. I can't see how this will help." He looked hung over from a night of heavy drinking. He was medium build and average height with a shaved head that needed a shave. He had a black goatee with a few days growth on his face. His head was deeply tanned and his face had wrinkles, but he couldn't have been much over thirty. He wore jeans with a plain black tee-shirt. He had a chain attached to his belt with the other end in his pocket. He wore black boots and had his jeans tucked into the boots. He was in the running for owning one of the motorcycles. For some reason, I felt sorry for him. Maybe it was because he had raised his hand when Doc asked how many of us had panic attacks. Or was it a look of defeat in his expression? I wasn't sure.

"I'm Frank and I'm desperate for this to help. Nothin' else has." I noticed when Frank came in he had a bad limp. Frank was a Latino. He looked to be in his late-twenties. He was clean shaven with a short haircut. He had on jeans with a dark blue collared golf-shirt and a pair of dark loafers. I thought he might be an officer by the way he carried himself. In his expression there was exactly what he described;

a desperation. I gathered he was accustomed to being in charge with a lot of self-discipline and now he was going downhill and out of control.

Doc: "All of you know that I'm working with two of you during the week. Would you please identify to the group your partner or what I sometimes like to call your buddy?

The pairs were Chad and Melinda, Paul and Anna, Rob and Doug, Nate and Frank, and Ace and me.

Doc: "You are aware of how much importance I put on the deep breathing. In many ways it's like basic training. The training is invaluable and critical as we get further into our work together. The major and core benefit of this skill is you learn the art of being attentive, alert, and focused. He wrote those three words in large capital letters on the newsprint.

Doc: "We will be working with the brain throughout our training and most of our work will be designed to change the way we think, remember, behave, feel, and live our lives. These changes in the brain can most efficiently be made when our mind is attentive, alert, and focused. They are like a beam of light into the process of healing and change. I call this, "Attention Training." This training is critical for learning how to heal the trauma of combat. The bottom line is to become an expert in these three areas."

Doc: "I have selected deep breathing to help you with that goal. Many of the benefits of deep breathing training will be closely associated with the overall benefit of being attentive, alert, and focused. The first of those benefits is to help you quiet the mind."

Rob: "What's the point of a quiet mind?"

Anna: "For me, I can't get my mind to shut up so I'm game for anything that might help me silence that endless noise."

Most of the group nodded.

Frank: "What's your name again man?"

"Rob."

Frank: "My mind is racing all the time and I'm having all these thoughts about shit that came down over there and the flashbacks are driving me crazy. You don't have any of that?"

Rob: "No. I just focus on other stuff and keep busy." Pause and it was clear that he wasn't finished and barely above a whisper, he said, "Most of the time, I stay drunk."

There was silence. I lowered my head some and looked around and it seemed like everyone was looking at the floor.

Anna was crying and blurted out, "I don't drink. I stay high on pills." Ace reached over and lightly patted her shoulder.

More silence.

Doug: "Booze and pills for me."

More silence.

Doc: "It's very challenging to make an intentional decision to change old habits and change the way you think and behave. Very little can happen until you have learned to become…" He pointed to the newsprint and indicated he wanted us to repeat….

Group: "ATTENTIVE, ALERT, AND FOCUSED!!"

Doc: "A cousin to those three skills is quieting the chatter of the mind."

Ace: "How do we keep deep breathing from being boring?"

Smiles and laughter and "Yeah" burst from some of the group.

Doc: "Let's look at the idea that deep breathing is boring. Is that true?"

Again some murmurs in the group suggesting that, "Yeah, it's boring."

Doc: "I don't find it boring. Is there anyone else here that doesn't think deep breathing is boring?"

That started a discussion among the group that sometimes it was boring and other times it was peaceful and other times it is frustrating and so on.

Doc: "We have logically proven that deep breathing is not boring. Deep breathing is deep breathing, nothing more, nothing less. How we respond to the deep breathing is another matter and we have decided that we respond in different ways and sometimes we respond in similar ways. Ace's question raises an important point. We are the creator of our experience. Ace and a number of others are creating boredom. Some others are creating frustration. Some others are creating a peaceful feeling. This, in my view, is true about life. We create our experience, our drama, our response to whatever we encounter. That means we can never blame anything or anyone on how we think or feel."

Rob: "Yesterday, I told a friend, 'You piss me off!' He fucking did piss me off. What am I suppose to say?"

Doc: "How about, 'I'm pissed off about what you said or did?' When you say it that way, you are accepting responsibility for creating pissed off."

Rob: "But he made me pissed off. If he hadn't been shining the chrome on my bike without asking me, I wouldn't have been pissed off. Nobody touches my bike without my permission."

Doc: "How about you Nate? Would you have been pissed off if someone was shining your chrome without asking?"

Nate: "I'd been happy if a friend was shining my chrome. I hate cleaning my bike."

The group talked about the phrase "you made me angry" and others related to blaming someone else for the thoughts and feelings we create. In the end, I think we all agreed that we do create our own responses to situations and people.

Doc: "If we acknowledge that we create a particular response in our life, we are free to create something different. Freedom is crucial in life and in our work together. If we blame others, situations, and experiences for how we think, feel, and behave, we are trapped hoping people and situations will change. How often does that happen?"

Ace: "I got it. So I'm responsible for creating boredom. How do I create something different?"

Doc: "Is it true that most of you are asking the same question?"

There were nods all around.

Doc: "Each one of you is facing an even more challenging task. You are suffering from the trauma of combat and powerful memories that can never change. Even if you learn to create something new and different with your present relationships and situations, how can you create something new and different when it comes to flashbacks, panic attacks, and intrusive unwanted thoughts related to the war? A long time ago, an alcoholic friend of mine said, 'If I'm not the problem, then there's no solution.' I don't want to leave this topic until we are all on board with this perspective."

Melinda: "I think I understand the concept, but I have no idea what to do with it."

Doc: "Stay tuned. That is the primary goal of this group; to learn how to create something different in all situations. So how do we get started? Would someone please answer that question?"

Frank: "By practicing the breathing and learning to be attentive, alert, and focused which helps us to be able to quiet our minds."

Doc: "Close your eyes and shift your attention from your breathing or from any other thoughts and focus your attention on my voice. Several years ago, I read the story of a boy who was the favorite target of neighborhood bullies. To pay them back he decided to become an expert in one of the martial arts. He found a master/teacher who agreed to teach him the skills. The master said to the boy, 'See the bookcase in the corner?' The boy nodded. 'I want you to begin your training with me by taking each book off the shelf, dropping it on the floor, picking it up and putting it back on the shelf until you have completed that task with every book in the bookcase. Then you can leave and I'll see you next week.' The boy made protestations saying there were at least a hundred books and he had come for training in the martial arts and not to pick-up books. The master left. For the next eight weeks, the same thing happened every week and the boy would protest and the master would leave. Each week, the boy thought about only picking up a few books and leaving, but he would think about the bullies so he did as he was instructed. On the tenth session, the master instructed him to do the same activity and this time he stayed and watched the boy. Half-way through the bookcase, the master said, 'You have taken an important first step and you are now ready to take the next step.' The boy stayed with the master for many weeks and became a champion in martial arts. And needless to say, he kicked some ass."

Doc: "Shift back now to focusing on your breathing. Place your hand on your belly and make sure you are getting plenty of air into that part of your body…and if you have any thoughts, let them go and be attentive to your breathing.…As you practice your breathing, see if you can find the balance between working really hard on your breathing and just hanging out and doing some deep breathing. Find that middle ground of commitment and determination to become an expert where you are simply attentive to focusing on the breathing. When you do that, the breathing will give you the benefits. All you have to do is the training…"

Instead of focusing on the breathing, I was thinking about the story. Was practice and patience the key? Was it determination and motivation? Was it a willingness to do whatever it takes? Was it the discipline and commitment to master something simple? Was it all of those and more stuff I didn't think of? Hell, I didn't know. I guess the main point is to become an expert in deep breathing. Most people here seem like they're suffering more than me, especially Chad with one eye and Anna with one arm. What did I know? Maybe the emotional scars for some are worse. All I know is that I've got a lot of shit I've got to get worked out. I may not need it as much as others, but if I'm to have a life, I have to keep picking up those books.

Doc: "Now open your eyes."

Doc: "There are a number of other benefits of deep breathing. One is it relaxes the body. When you breathe into the lower lobes, the air comes in contact with receptors which then activate that part of the nervous system designed to relax the body. Some of you have already tried to calm anxiety with the deep breathing and it didn't help. After continued training and patience, you will experience this relaxation benefit from the deep breathing. I will be asking you over and over to be aware of physical symptoms like, 'where do you feel that in your body?'"

Doc: "Close your eyes. Begin deep breathing and pay close attention to how it feels as the air moves into your belly and what it feels like to breathe it out of your body. Put your hand on your belly and make sure you're getting plenty of air deep into your lungs.... Imagine that the air is not only going into your lungs, but it's like you're breathing into your whole body...breathing into all parts of your body...down into your legs and feet, into your mid-section, into your upper body, into your arms and hands and into your head. Some people say they like to imagine that their breath is like a cool white mist and it's soothing and calming as it moves into all parts of the body. Others like to imagine their breath as a warm energy penetrating every cell and every muscle. Perhaps you're surprised that it feels nice. Let your breathing slow down and when you're ready, open your eyes."

Doc: "What was that like?"

Everyone seemed to agree that when they focused on the breathing, it helps the body relax. Most expressed some frustration with being able to stay focused. Doc continued to emphasize the importance of practice and training.

Doc: "Consider for a moment the benefit of relaxing the body. Would most of you agree that a lot of symptoms are physical?"

Group nods.

Doc: "How helpful would it be if you could reach a skill level with the breathing where when you felt anxious, nervous, tension in your chest, and had problems breathing, you could interrupt those symptoms and feel your body relaxing?"

Everyone agreed that would be helpful. Someone asked how long it would take to reach that level and someone else asked if we could ever reach that level.

Doc: "It will take..." And he looked at the group for the answer.

Individuals in the group at random said, "Practice, training, hard work, determination, and commitment."

Doc: "Yes, and a belief in your ability to get the job done. I heard a phrase years ago which has always meant a lot to me. 'Argue for your limitations and you get to keep them.' If you think or say, 'I don't think I can do this,' you won't be able to do it."

Doc: "Close your eyes again. Each of you has been struggling with your symptoms. And I don't know if you are already aware that deep breathing can be one of the answers to feeling better or if you are still wondering if it can help. I'm not sure if you might first notice how it can quiet your mind or if you might first notice how certain muscle groups in your body begin to release tension. Whether you feel it right away or in a few days or weeks, you can know that deep breathing does work and that you can choose to make it work for you. Take some time now to focus on your breathing and begin breathing deeply whenever you are ready....Take your time and feel the air moving in and out slow and easy....Maybe again you are aware of your mind becoming more quiet or perhaps your first awareness is feeling more relaxed in some part or all of your body. Take ten more deep breaths now and then open your eyes."

Doc: "I have a question. What was, is, or will be the most important moment in your life?"

I think we were all a little unsure what he meant. Recently, I thought it was the moment I saw Eden.

Nate: "Anytime I'm riding my bike."

Frank: When I learn to be peaceful again."

Anna: "When I stop doing drugs."

Me: "When I meet the woman of my dreams."

There were several other answers along the same line.

Doc: "Everything I say is my perspective and I disagree with all of you. If you're interested in my perspective, I'll give you a hint. It can't be in the past and it can't be in the future."

Paul: "Before ya'll answer, I think we oughta vote on if we care what Doc's thinks. Everybody's got two choices: 1. You care. 2. You don't and we go to Stanley's for a beer."

Most of the group laughed and said, "To Stanley's!"

Anna in a loud voice over the laughter: "At ease soldiers!" She smiled and looked at Doc. "That only leaves right now."

Doc: "Yes it does. Most of you were thinking about the past or future. Am I right?"

Doc: "A lady once told me that she always wanted children and the most important moment in her life would be giving birth to her first child. So why would now be the most important moment in our lives?"

Me: "Because it's all we have?"

Doc: "Where is the past? Can you see it? Is it in this room? Can you touch it? Where does it exist?"

Frank: "Only in our brain, in our memory."

Doc: "Where is the future?"

Ace: "It doesn't exist yet."

Doc: "So the past is somewhere in our brain and the future doesn't exist yet. How many of you feel you spend way too much time living in the past and anticipating the future?"

We raised our hands.

Doc: "Well, I've got some good news. One more benefit of the deep breathing is that it helps us stay present in the moment."

Doug: "What if we don't wanna stay in the moment?"

Melinda: "Yeah, what if the moment is too painful?"

Frank: "Yeah, the question that keeps rolling over and over in my mind ever since I got back is what the fuck do I do now? If now is all I got and I don't know what to do now?" He hesitated.

Ace broke in: "Me too, I got the same question?"

Several others indicated they were dealing with the same dilemma.

Doc: "One answer to the question, 'what do we do now' is, 'we're sitting here in this group trying to figure out if this stuff is going help us or not.'"

Frank: "What's another answer?"

Doc: "Once we learn to focus on the moment, we'll figure out what to do?"

Frank seemed to be overwhelmed by his desperation: "Doc, what I'm trying to tell you is that I can't figure it out. I've been trying." At this point tears are welling up in his eyes and it's obvious that he's trying to hold them back.

Ace gets up and heads for the door. Anna gets up and follows him. Melinda is crying. I have tears in my eyes. The rest have their heads down.

Doc: "I want everyone to close their eyes and focus on breathing."

Frank: "I can't fucking do this. I'm leavin'." I hear him walking to the door. It opens and closes.

Doc: "Stay focused on your breathing. Remember to let any other thoughts drift away and return to your breathing."

I lost track of time. My tears stopped. At some point, the door opened and I heard some rustling around and I was sure that Ace sat down as someone touched my shoulder and I knew it was him. There was some other movement and I was hoping that Anna and Frank had also come back.

Doc: "Everyone with your eyes closed and focusing on your breathing. Pay attention and listen. Let your mind go quiet and somewhere in whatever moments of quietness you experience, say to yourself, 'I can do this.' Repeat that phrase over and over....You might imagine what your life would be like if you could heal this trauma haunting you from your past. What your future would be like if you were free of these symptoms. Take a few moments to get a clear image in your mind of what that would be like...and even though you are considering the importance of each moment, you can be aware that imaging the freedom from your anguish and despair could help with motivation and determination to reach your goals. Believing that you can do it, say 'I can do this' over and over...and now let your breathing slow down. Open your eyes."

While Doc was going through that exercise, I was struggling to focus on my breathing and trying to repeat the phrase, but I kept thinking about Ace, Anna and Frank and wondering what they talked about on the porch. I was also thinking about the other group members and wondered what they were thinking. I kept telling myself to breathe and repeat the phrase but I didn't have much success.

Me: "So it's okay to imagine the future if it helps with motivation and determination in the moment."

Doc: "Yes. Later, some of the exercises will use that technique. Does everyone see how that is different from anticipating the future or being stressed and worried about the future?"

Doc: "It's time for a break. I want you to do this break in silence. Please no talking. Feel free to stay in here or go outside. If you go outside, stay close enough so you can hear this bell ringing which means the break is over. During this period, spend some time focusing on your breathing."

It was strange doing the break in silence, but it was a big relief to me. I didn't want to engage in any small talk with anyone. I would have felt uncomfortable. I got out some glasses in case someone wanted a glass. Ace got some ice out of the fridge and put it in the ice bucket. Some people met my eyes. Anna smiled at me and said with her expression, "Thanks for the glass." Several others smiled. Some were looking down and didn't choose to make eye contact. We all seemed to be a lot more aware of each other. It was nice. I took Spot out to pee. Several stopped to pet him and say hi with their strokes. Doug let Spot lick him on his face. While walking around outside, I worked on my deep breathing. The bell rang.

Doc: "How many of you want to hear another speech from me about the importance of deep breathing?"

No one raised their hand.

Doc: Smiling said, "Why am I not surprised? One more time, remember the kid picking up the books. Same thing. It's not important that you like to do the deep breathing. What's important is that you're determined and committed to doing what it takes to feel better and release or let go of your symptoms. Stay with the training. Does everyone have their notebooks and something to write with?"

Everyone had their notebooks and everyone except Ace and Nate had something to write with. Doc got some pens out of his briefcase and tossed them in their direction.

Doc: "Deep breathing not only helps us with quieting the mind and relaxing the body, but it also helps us with the important skill of being able to live and focus in the moment. I have a training exercise where I want you to focus on staying in the moment and use your deep breathing to help you with that task. The goal is to focus on the moment by being aware of your senses. Here's a handout that will give you some help and more direction. Let's go over it now."

Training Exercise

Staying in the Moment

Doc: "1. Take your notebooks. Go outside and within five minutes find a comfortable place to sit.

2. Take out your watch and set the timer for one minute.

3. When you start the timer, focus for that one minute on one of your senses. If you wander, take a couple of deep breaths to bring

you back to the moment and focusing on that same sense until the chime sounds.

4. When the chime sounds, write this sentence in your notebook and finish it. "In this moment, I…." Reminder: When you complete the sentence, remember to focus on the moment and avoid any references to the past or the future.

5. When you have finished your sentence, set your timer again and shift to another one of your senses and complete the exercise again. With each new experience, create an attitude of interest or curiosity about whatever is happening in that moment.

6. Listed below are some tips on staying with your senses:

SIGHT: Look around and pick something to focus on. It may be the view, a flower, a stick, a bug. You make the choice. Whatever you pick, focus all your attention on that scene or item. See the colors, shapes, textures, size. Do your best not to have an opinion about what you are seeing or compare it with anything you've seen before. Just stay with what you are seeing in the moment.

SOUNDS: Be still and listen. Sometimes it's helpful to close your eyes to cut out any visual distractions. Listen carefully. You may be surprised what you can hear. Don't search in your mind for something to hear. Just stay present in the moment and listen.

TOUCH: Pick up something or touch something. Be aware of texture and how it feels against your skin. Explore other ways it feels in or to your hand or any other thing that comes to mind as you touch it. Let your mind be free to continue exploring.

SMELL: You can close or open your eyes at different times. You might pick up something from the ground or just notice if there is a particular smell in the air. If you happen to fart, (laughter) you can close your eyes and take in the full smell being careful not to judge it as a good or a bad smell. That might be a challenge for some of you, but see if you can choose to just be aware of it without the judgment.

TASTE: Take a small box of raisins on the table by the door. Close your eyes and put a few raisins in your mouth and savor them for awhile moving them around with your tongue. Be open to any subtle changes in taste as the raisins begin to dissolve. If you try this a second time, be open to discovering something quite different than what you experienced the first time."

Doc: "When I ring the bell, return here. Any questions?"

Paul: "What if I'm rite in the middle of tasting them raisins and I fart. Should I stay on the taste of the raisins or focus on the sound of the fart or take in the smell of the fart?"

By the time he finished, everyone including Doc was busting a gut laughing. When we calmed down, Doc said, "In that moment without any thoughts about what you should or should not do, focus on what comes to you in that moment. For some of you the smell may be the most compelling choice."

(Chuckles.)

Doc: "Remember to get your raisins on the way out."

Group Member

The time passed quickly even though it was not an easy exercise. The bell rang and we gathered in the cabin.

Doc: "What was that like?"

There was silence.

Doc: "How many found it difficult to stay in the moment?"

Everyone raised their hand.

Ace: "I did pretty well the first five minutes. Then I started thinking about other things." Others nodded.

Doc: "Could you tell us what kind of other things you were thinking about?"

Ace: "Not in mixed company."

Everyone laughed.

Melinda: "The easiest of the senses for me was taste and touch. I could focus on an object like the raisins and several things I picked off the ground. I found it difficult to stay focused on the others. Sometimes as I looked at the mountains, it would remind me of something in my past and I would go there. Listening wasn't too bad even though I knew I was supposed to let the sounds come to me, I found myself searching for something to listen too. It was the same for me on the smell." She smiled, "Since I didn't create anything to smell."

Frank: "While I was looking for a place to sit, I was wondering how this focusing stuff is gonna help. Then it just came to me again that I've got all these fucking memories in my brain." He paused, looked at Anna and Melinda and said, "I've been meaning to say this all morning. My mom told me it was disrespectful to cuss in front of ladies and I..."

Anna interrupted, "I can't speak for Melinda, but I learned early in my Army experience that cussing is part of the language and I fell right into step. Some of my friends say I have a foul mouth. So I hope I won't offend anyone."

Melinda: "I was the middle child with two older brothers and two younger brothers. My mother used to get on them about their language, but it never did any good. So I'm used to it. And as Anna said, it's part of the Army culture. I'm not offended. I try not to cuss myself, but at times I'm not successful. Most of the time if I do cuss, I'm by myself."

Chad: "I'm not offended, but I'm a Christian and I don't understand why there's so much cussing. There are plenty of ways to express ourselves without using cuss words."

Paul: "I'm real pissed off Frank by your fuckin' dirty language and you're fuckin' up this group by fuckin' with our minds so shut the fuck up."

Everyone even Chad was laughing.

Frank: "I think we need to fucking respect Paul on this. So I was saying that I've got all these fucking memories. We may have already covered this, but I wondered if the purpose of the breathing is also to teach us how to stop thinking about those memories and think about something different."

Doc: "Yes Frank, that's another benefit of the deep breathing. We'll be working on a number of different ways to shift your thinking."

Frank: "I told you all earlier that I don't know what to do now. At this point it makes sense that a partial answer to that question is to work on my deep breathing."

The remaining time was spent with others talking about their experience during the exercise. In general terms, everyone talked about how challenging it was to stay focused on the moment.

Doc: "We have talked about the challenge of staying present in the moment. I want to remind you again what you just did was a training exercise. Our minds are programmed to be all over the place and now it's important you train your mind with deep breathing to be attentive, alert, and focused, which will help you quiet your mind, relax your body, stay present in the moment, and other skills to be discussed later in the training."

Doc: "In our individual sessions last week, I gave you a symptom checklist. Get those out now and I want us to compile a list of the group's goals. I'm going to write them on the newsprint and I'll put them in different categories. Next week, I'll have it typed and give you a copy. Some of you may be reluctant to share some of your goals. That's fine."

In the beginning, everyone seemed to be reluctant and then a few people shared some real personal things and that seemed to open the flood gates. I don't think many people held much back.

<u>Group Goals</u>

Sleep better
Stop nightmares
Stop the flashbacks
Stop angry outbursts
Stop the emotional pain
Get over the guilt and shame
Reduce suicidal thoughts
Stop panic attacks
Stop feeling betrayed
Stop feeling dead inside
Get out of black hole
Reduce startle response
Stop feeling like a coward
Stop wishing I were dead instead of my friend
Stop feeling like a murderer
Stop the self-loathing
Feel like home is home
Stop feeling numb
Stop self-pity
Stop sleeping in the basement

Stop wanting to punch people who thank me for service to my country

Let go of resentment and hatred for people who sent me to war
Stop being angry that people have no idea what we went through
Find a reason to live
Find a purpose for living
Feel hopeful
Reduce drinking and drugs
Be able to drink socially
Stop fucking people to keep my mind occupied
Understand God's role in war
Figure out the purpose of prayer
Stop being angry with God
Improve concentration
Share thoughts and feelings
Slow down my racing mind
Learn to trust people
Learn to love again
Build self-esteem
Be comfortable again in crowds
Get control of my life
Be able to concentrate
Take control of my life
Get back my sense of humor
Be able to make decisions
Get motivated
Get a job

Doc: "Take a few minutes to look these over and see if there are others you want to add to this list. Throughout this experience, we can of course add more goals."

Frank: "This list is helpful. There's some on here that I didn't think about that I want to add to my list."

Doc: "If others feel the same way, open your notebooks and write them on the page with your other goals."

It looked like everyone got out their notebooks and added goals.

Doc: "Throughout our time together, I'll be working with you in our individual sessions on your goals. We will also be working on the group goals in group sessions.

Doc: "Open your notebooks and write down your assignment for next Saturday.

1. I will give each of you a CD that has the breathing exercises. Use the CD twice a day. It will take about 15 minutes. Record the date and time in your notebook.

2. Use the hourly chime on your watch to remind you to take five deep breaths during the day. Take five deep breaths at other times during the day. Associate it with things you do everyday. For instance, every time you get in and out of your vehicle, take five deep breaths. Every time you go to the bathroom, take five deep breaths. You are in training to become an expert in deep breathing.

3. Once a day, I want you to do the 'Staying in the Moment' exercise we did earlier. Again, record the date and time in your notebook.

4. Use your notebook to:

A. Record instances of flashbacks, nightmares, panic attacks and how you responded to those episodes.

B. Daily entry about how you are doing with the training and what questions you have for me and/or the group.

During the individual sessions, I will be asking you to share with me the entries in your notebook."

Nate: "Doc, that's a lot of homework. I feel like I'm back in high school and the teachers gonna grade my homework."

Doc: "That's one of the reasons I'm referring to our work together as training. Each one of you is struggling with some form of PTSD. This experience can seriously contaminate the quality of your life. In my view, this training you'll be doing could be one of the most important challenges of your life. Remember your military training. When you didn't think you could do it, somebody was on your back telling you that you didn't have a choice and you completed the training. You're older and wiser now. I won't be on your back, but I will hold you accountable. Each of you has a choice. My job is to facilitate this process and stand with you on this journey. You have a lot of books to drop and pick up. Be encouraged; you can do it.

Doc: "I'll see each of you during our individual sessions this week and we will gather next Saturday for our group session at nine. I'll let you know later where we will meet. Jett, if you and Ace will show us where the chairs go, we'll help move them back into place. Be sure to pick up any stuff lying around. Jett, where is your trash can?"

I pointed to the closet next to the kitchen.

Doc turned to me, "Thanks for letting us meet in your home." He turned to the group, "Go in peace and find time to play and laugh in the midst of your training."

Everyone helped straighten up and left while Doc packed up his stuff. He turned to me as he was closing his briefcase and said, "Jett, I don't want to impose, but this setting is perfect for our group work. Would you be willing for us to meet here each week? If you need some time to think about it, you can let me know Tuesday during our individual session."

"No, I don't need any time to think about it. That would be fine."

"Thank you. See you guys on Tuesday."

We said goodbye and Ace headed to the fridge and got a beer. "You want one?"

"No thanks, I'll pass for right now."

I looked out the window. Doc's old Chevy was heading down the driveway. Melinda and Anna were talking. Nate and Rob were looking at each other's motorcycles. At least I guessed two out of three. Chad was standing by a car. I assumed he was riding with either Melinda or Anna. Everyone else had gone.

35
THE PICNIC

Ace had turned on the TV and was sitting on the couch drinking his beer. I went in and got a beer and joined him. We watched TV for awhile and then I said, "Do you mind if I turn off the TV? I'd like to talk about this morning."

He sighed and in a voice that was the opposite of enthused he said, "No, go ahead."

I asked, "How did it go for you?"

"Okay I guess."

(Silence) Finally, I said, "It fucking wore me out. I have so many thoughts running through my mind. I don't know if I hated it or liked it or was frustrated by it or helped by it or hell, I don't know. It seemed like we were all so different and yet we all had this war in common. What was the name of the guy who had only one eye?"

"Jett, I didn't keep track of names - Chet or Chad or something like that."

"Chad, I think. Anyway, I came so close to losing an eye on that last patrol. Several times during the group, I closed one eye to see what it was like. Having half of my peripheral vision sucked. Then there was Anna with one arm and Frank with that bad limp. I felt, compared to them, I had nothing to complain about."

"Yeah, I need to stop complaining about my leg."

I asked, "What happened out on the porch when you and Anna and Frank left the group?"

"I felt like I was going to suffocate. I had to get outta there. I went out and sat in a rocker and started trying to get my breathing under control. Anna followed me and sat down beside me. We just rocked for a minute or so and then the other guy, Frank, are you sure his name is Frank?"

"Yeah, I think that's right."

"I'm really bad with names."

I smiled, "Yeah, but I bet you remember the girls' names."

He responded, "Yeah, the other ones name is Molly." I looked at him with a "I know you're shittin' me" look and he said, "OK, the other one's name is Melinda."

"Anyway, Frank came out and walked down the steps and went for a walk. We rocked for a few minutes in silence and then she told me when I reached over and patted her on the back that it helped her when she was crying and talking about doing drugs. She said that her buddy Paul was okay, but she didn't feel a connection with him. She said she was afraid I was going to leave and she wanted me to stay. Hell, I started tearing up. I get that shit from you Jett. I'm turning into a fucking cry baby. I was embarrassed and she reached over and took my hand and she started tearing up and there we were. She squeezed my hand and let go. We rocked for awhile longer and then Frank came back and said, 'What the fuck, I don't have anywhere else to go.' So Anna and I followed him back in. That's it. And I don't want to talk about this anymore. Please turn the TV back on."

"Sure. I'm gonna get some chips and salsa. You want another beer?"

"Yeah."

We sat there for awhile before I asked, "Are you going to the picnic?"

"No!"

"I don't wanna go either, but I think we outta make an appearance."

"Damn it Jett, there you go being my mother again. Stop putting this fucking pressure on me. I just tried to whack myself and just got outta the hospital. Now I'm supposed to go down there in front of all your family and mine, smile, be sweet, nice, thank people for coming, say how wonderful it is to see them again and how's your Aunt Mattie and when is your baby due and this food is just delicious. Have you tried Susie's deviled eggs and aren't they just the best you ever tasted and how is Wilson's cancer treatment? I sure hope he pulls through to have another ten or fifteen treatments of chemo and you outta throw in a few more radiations to fry that little tumor on his penis and I'm so grateful that you're grateful for Jett's and my service to our country. We were proud to serve and we really did regret having to kill women and children and blow up villages, but it was our job and it had to be done and we're just proud that you're proud of us for doin' it 'cause otherwise we'd be feeling a smidgen of guilt, but now we're just fine and you really do need to try those deviled eggs. Enjoyed talkin' to you, but now I need to find a gun and blow my fucking brains out."

He got up and walked outside.

What a ride. When he first started talking, I felt defensive and then when he kept going I started smiling and laughed when he mentioned the tumor on the penis and then when he got to the war stuff, I began to tear up. I followed him out. He was rocking. I sat beside him and we rocked and somewhere in there our chimes went off. I didn't feel like doin' the breathing. We just sat there and rocked and finally dozed off.

Spot woke me up. I looked at my watch. It was 3:05. The picnic started at 4:00. I went inside and took a shower and changed. When I came out into the great room, Ace's shower was running. He came out about ten minutes later and said, "I've decided to go for a few minutes only because Mom will be disappointed and I've hurt her enough especially lately."

I asked, "Do you wanna ride with me?"

"Hell no. You'll stay a lot longer than me and I'm goin' to Stanley's after I leave the picnic. I do need a ride to Stanley's to get my wheels."

I was relieved to see that no one was there except our families and April and a few cousins. Mom and Ma had briefed everyone and as far as I could tell there was no mention of the war or any questions about our war experience. It was low key and not a lot of laughing and telling jokes which was more normal for our families. There was just a nice feeling about the atmosphere. The Inn catered the food and it was served about thirty minutes after we arrived.

As soon as we arrived, Ace went over to Ma and gave her a hug and was trying hard to smile as different people came up and talked with them. I was still exhausted from the morning, but enjoyed talking to different members of both families. Pop and I had a nice talk and planned to get together this week for another walk around the lake. I saw Charlie come out of the back door of the Inn and I went over and talked to him for a few minutes. I mentioned that Ace might be coming to work with me on Monday and he said there was plenty of mowing to do.

On my way back to the picnic, I looked for April and she must have had the same idea because we were walking toward each other. We smiled and hugged and she said, "I know we talked yesterday, but for some reason I feel like I haven't talked to you for a long time."

"Me too."

She continued, "I know that everything that happens in the group is confidential. The hospital is on us all the time about it. But without giving me any details, would you feel comfortable giving me a general idea about how it went for you and Ace?"

"It went pretty well. I was exhausted after it was over. I thought we both did okay. We talked a little about it after everyone left. Like I told you yesterday, I see glimpses of the old Ace from time to time and then I see glimpses of a new Ace who is on a limited basis willing to talk about stuff. I saw you talking with him and Ma a little while ago. What did you think?"

"He seemed uncomfortable, but was trying to put on a good show for Marge."

As she was talking about their conversation, I was remembering how we were together those few days and how close I felt to her. I would never forget the intimacy and ecstasy of that time with her. I would be lying to myself if I didn't admit that I would love to have another night with this sensuous and sexy woman.

While she was talking, she looked away for a moment and something caught her eye and she said, "There's Aunt Agnes and who is that woman with her?"

My heart missed a beat and I looked around and there was Eden walking with Aunt Agnes. Jack and Ann were moving toward them and they exchanged hugs.

I responded, "Oh that's Eden. She's Aunt Agnes's niece from Greensboro."

"She's beautiful. When did you meet her?"

"She was in church two weeks ago with Aunt Agnes."

She was quiet for a few moments and smiled and said, "Was she in church last Sunday?"

I was starting to blush, "Uh yeah, she was there."

She continued smiling, "I was puzzled last week in the hospital when you seemed to be so fixated on getting to church. You have never been a big church-goer and I couldn't figure out why all of a sudden it was so important that you go to church. What do you have to say for yourself?"

I could feel the blood rushing to my face and I couldn't look at her. I started to say something, but couldn't find the right words.

She let me off the hook and said, "Why Jett, you're blushing. You don't have to say anything. I already know the answer. Just looking at her, I can understand why. I have to admit that I'm a little jealous there might be another woman in your life."

"I've only talked to her twice and I'm not gonna lie, I do like her and she's pretty. I have wondered if I'm unconsciously interested in her to take my mind off you. I don't know. I do know that I'm lonely."

I was watching Eden as I talked and I noticed that she was inconspicuously glancing around and I hoped she was looking for me. I turned back to April and she was still smiling and said, "When I get beyond my jealous feelings, I'm glad you have someone to focus your attention on. It makes me feel a little less guilty about us. Anyway, you go on over and see her. I'll wander back over toward Marge and Ace."

"Okay. I'll call you later."

I was feeling nervous as I walked over toward Eden. She had on a pair of yellow shorts that came to right above her knees and a mint colored sleeveless blouse with white tennis shoes. The outfit was conservative and not designed to show off her figure. Her hair was down with a few curls on the end. It was draped over both shoulders.

Jack saw me approaching and motioned for me to come join them, "Hey Jett, come on over." We all exchanged greetings. I hugged everyone, but Eden. I shook her hand and said, "Glad you could come."

Aunt Agnes chimed in, "She had a meeting today that was cancelled so she decided to come on."

I started to feel awkward. I didn't know what to say. Jack and Ann were big talkers so they carried the conversation without any hesitation. We talked about different things going on in the family and during that time I noticed that Ace and April headed for the parking lot. I didn't know if they were going somewhere together or whether they were leaving separately. Jack and Ann worked another maneuver where they were engaged mostly with Aunt Agnes and that left Eden and me free to have a conversation. I was a little flustered and said again, "I'm glad you could make it."

She said, "Me too. How is your friend?"

"He's better. He got out of the hospital Thursday. Thanks for asking." I decided not to say anything else at this point. I asked,

"Are you hungry? I haven't eaten yet and maybe we could check out the food situation."

"That would be fine."

We walked over to the buffet, got our plates, and found an empty table.

"This looks good," she said.

"Yeah, the kitchen staff at the Inn is great. I've never had a bad meal here."

She asked, "How long has the Inn been in your family?"

"My great-great grandfather Gus bought it from the original owner sometime between 1910 and 1915. You know quite a bit about my family through Aunt Agnes, but I don't know much about yours."

She replied, "I'm closer to Aunt Agnes than anyone else in my family other than my mom. Aunt Agnes is my dad's older sister. There's one other sister between them. My mom and dad live in Greenville, NC. I have five sisters, all younger than me."

"Wow, five sisters! What was it like being the oldest?"

"It was all right, but I have always felt responsible for them and it has caused me a lot of stress. I want them to take better care of themselves and they usually don't listen to my advice." She smiled. "They have a mind of their own."

"What about your mom and dad?"

"My mom's a sweetheart, but my dad is a different story. Let's just say he's not one of my favorite people."

I got the feeling that was all she wanted to say about her family, specifically about her dad. We did exchange a little more general information about each others families and I felt more comfortable as the time passed. It was getting easier to talk to her. Some of the family was leaving and dropped by the table to say goodbye. After we finished, I said, "I know you're thinking about buying a place. Have you had any leads since I last talked with you?"

The chime on my watch went off. I cut it off and acted like it was nothing. I wasn't ready to explain something like that to Eden. Needless to say, I didn't take my deep breaths.

She responded to my question, "My realtor called me this past week with some questions for me. We have an appointment next Saturday to look again."

"Great. I've been roaming these mountains since I was little. When you're ready to leave, would you like me to show you some of my favorite areas? I know you're interested in finding a place with a view so we could look in some areas where the views are awesome."

She said, "That's nice of you to offer. Are you sure you don't mind?"

I thought if she only knew how badly I wanted to show her around, she probably wouldn't go. "It's no trouble at all. I'd really like to show you some of the areas you haven't seen."

"I'd like that. I need to let Aunt Agnes know."

She went to check in with Aunt Agnes and I went over to tell Mom and Ma the plan. I asked, "Did April and Ace leave together?"

Ma responded, "They did. I don't know where they were going, but they were talking before they left."

Aunt Agnes and Eden walked over to where we were standing. Aunt Agnes asked, "Jett, would you mind bringing Eden home when you are done? I'm going over to Jack and Ann's for awhile, but should be home no later than 7:00."

"Be happy to bring her home Aunt Agnes. Eden, I don't think you've met Marge. She's Ace's mom." They smiled and shook hands. We talked for a few minutes and then I said, "Eden, I guess we better go while we still have plenty of light."

We said our goodbyes and headed for the truck.

36
BREAKING THE ICE

Once we got on the road, I said, "Sorry for the mess in the truck."

"It looks fine to me." She reached in her purse and continued, "I think I'll put my hair in a pony tail."

"Do you know much about the history of Harvest?"

"I've read some and Aunt Agnes has told me a little, but I don't know much. I would like to hear more about it if you don't mind."

"I like talking about it. Ace said I used to overdo it when telling our buddies in the Army about the history of this part of North Carolina. So stop me if I give you more information than you want."

She said, "I'm sure that won't happen. Go ahead. I want to hear all about it."

I talked about the early history of Harvest and how our family settled here. She asked me some questions and seemed interested. I went down the Parkway and took her into several different areas where there were houses. She said she had not been in those areas as the real estate agent had showed her houses in town.

I asked, "Where do you and Aunt Agnes usually hike?"

"She likes to walk around the lake in Harvest and sometimes we'll take a trail that branches off the path around the lake."

"That's a popular area for walking and hiking. Pop and I usually walk in that same area."

"It seems like you and Pop are very close."

"We are. I can talk to him about anything."

"You're lucky to have him in your life."

"I think so too." Pause. "I want to go back up the Parkway and take you in the other direction."

"Okay."

I asked, "Are you thirsty?"

"Yes, I could use something cold to drink. I also have to use the bathroom."

"I've told you about the cabin. Let's go there for a rest stop and then I'll drive you around different areas up there and show you some of my favorite views."

On the way to the cabin, I went into more of the history about how the land around the cabin had been purchased by Gus and Walter several years after they took over the Inn and the general store. I pointed out the road leading to Jack and Ann's and then pointed out Henry and Betty's house before turning up the road to the cabin. Ace and April's vehicles were parked in front of the cabin.

"Ace and April are here. I know you haven't met either one of them. April is my other best friend. We grew up together. They dated for most of high school and college, but broke up a year or so before Ace and I joined the Army. At this point, they're trying to figure out how they feel about each other. As you might imagine, it's complicated."

She said, "Maybe we shouldn't disturb them."

"I have an idea that they may be gone. Spot, my dog, isn't barking and the only explanation is that they are gone and have taken Spot. Let me go in and check."

I went inside and checked. I opened the screen door and said, "Come in. They aren't here."

"Jett, this is a beautiful cabin."

"Thank you. My great grandfather and grandmother, Will and Connie, built it around 1925. It was a family retreat until Pop and my grandma Nana moved here in the early 1940's. They stayed here until around 1980 when they decided to move into an apartment at the Inn. Nana died while I was in the Army."

"Were you as close to Nana as you are to Pop?"

"We were close, but I spent so much time with Pop outdoors. Not quite as close, but I miss her." I teared up.

"I shouldn't have asked that question. I'm sorry."

"Oh no, that's fine. I have a tendency to tear up over most anything since I got out of the Army." I smiled, "Ace says I'm a cry baby."

"That's not very nice."

"Oh no, it's fine. We're very open with each other and I couldn't repeat to you some of the names I've called him."

She smiled, "All right, I take that back."

"I'm sorry. I'm standing here talking and you have to go to the bathroom." I pointed to my bathroom because I knew it was relatively clean and I wasn't sure about Ace's. I used his and I'm glad I did. It needed some serious cleaning.

While I was looking in the fridge to see what we had to drink, she appeared and I said, "We don't have a large selection. There is one diet coke, Gatorade, beer, and orange juice."

She said, "Diet coke would be fine, but I hate to take your last one."

"That's okay. Would you like the can or would you like a glass with ice?"

"Glass with ice please."

I got a beer and we went to the back deck. I said, "We have two dirt bikes and we keep them out here in the back. I thought they might have taken them. Ace still has trouble getting around on his leg so he can't walk too far. About four or five more months of PT and the leg should be fine."

"That's good news." She was looking at the view. "You have beautiful views from both front and back."

"Yes, they picked a wonderful place to build the cabin."

We were quiet for a few minutes and I got a little uncomfortable. "Would you like to see more beautiful views?"

She smiled, "Yes, I would like that."

I realized that we had been talking a lot about my life. She had given me some details, but I was dying to know more about her. When we pulled out, I said, "Tell me more about your job."

"There's not much more to tell. Being in management has been more stressful than I thought it would be. I loved the field work before I got my promotion. As I look back, I wish I had turned it down. There's not much more to tell you about the job."

"What did you like about the field work?"

"I loved being outdoors and I had this satisfying belief that I was playing some small part in helping to preserve the beauty of the environment. Now I'm pushing papers and don't get to go outdoors all that much."

"Is there any way to change that?"

"I hope so. There is a position coming open next year that I'm going to apply for. My job would be to supervise all the field-work in Central North Carolina. It would be a step down and my boss in Washington tells me that it would end my chances for more promotions. That's fine with me if I can get back outdoors."

"Do you think you have a good chance of getting it?"

"My boss says it's mine if I want it."

"Where would your office be?"

"Winston-Salem. That's one of the reasons I'm looking for a place here. I would be doing a lot of traveling and seldom be in the office. This would be a good location for my home base."

I tried to hide my excitement about her actually living in Harvest. "Well, we've got to find just the right place for you."

"I'm glad to have your help."

"I'm going to pull off here and park. There's a place I want to show you, but we have to walk."

I took her out to one of my favorite vistas. It would be the perfect place for a house. It was on a small knoll surrounded in the back by large boulders and trees. "If someone were to build a house here, it could sit out on the edge with a wrap-around porch that would have a view in three different directions." What I didn't tell her is that even though it took us about ten minutes to get here by vehicle, it was about a five minute walk from the cabin."

"Jett, this is really beautiful."

"Not to say that you would want to build a house here, but what if you did? How would you design it?"

She got a gleam in her eyes. "Well, I don't need a lot of space since it's just me. Do I have unlimited funds?"

"Yes, unlimited funds for your dream house."

"All right. Well, sorry Jett, but I wouldn't want it to be on the edge like you said. I would want it tucked back here among the rocks and trees so that if someone were looking at it from that valley or that mountain in the distance, they would have a difficult time spotting the house. Nothing in nature would be disturbed. I would of course want to use solar energy as much as possible and since this view faces southeast, south, and southwest, that would work really well."

She was walking around looking in all directions and after awhile she said, "It would be a simple house. On one end of the house would be the kitchen, an eating area, and a sitting area. That would be open with lots of large windows. Then the bedroom with large windows would be on the other side of the sitting room. Behind those rooms would be the bathroom, laundry room, storage room and a car port or garage if there was enough room. And I can see a place for a vegetable garden and a few small terraces surrounded by flowers. I like your idea of a wrap-around porch. It would be about five feet deep. Well, what do you think so far?"

"I like it. Would you want a fireplace?"

"Oh yes. On the back wall of the sitting area and I would like for the house to look as natural to the setting as possible. Do you think log homes are a good idea?"

"I don't know a lot about them, but my Dad works at the mill and he knows all about wood so he could help."

She walked out toward the edge of the knoll and stood for awhile. The sun was setting and it threw amazing shadows over the valleys and hills. The view was one of the more spectacular ones in the area. She spent her life trying to protect the environment. This spot must seem like heaven to her. There were no words adequate for this moment. The beauty was not only beyond description, but also beyond any comment. Time seemed to stand still. I couldn't guess how much time passed before she said, "I hesitate to open my mouth because words can't begin to capture the majesty of this view. It reminds me again of the majesty of our tiny planet floating in this vast universe."

She seemed in a dream state and I wasn't about to interrupt this moment for her. I stood beside her, but a little behind her so as not to obstruct her panorama. I glanced at her without moving my head and the glow from the setting sun bathed her face in this orange hue that reminded me of a fairy princess. Her skin was effervescent and I was mesmerized by her beauty.

Then from out of god only knows where came this little voice in my head, 'What if you have a panic attack and mess up this moment for her? What if you can't get your breath? What will she think of you then? What if…?' There goes my fucking brain and I don't know how to stop it. I needed more skills. My chest started getting tight. I was trying to take real slow deep breaths, but I was having trouble breathing. I had to get out of there. I tried to be as inconspicuous as possible and it was like tip toeing out of a room trying not to wake a child. I tried to move out of her peripheral vision by backing up and slowly moving until I was behind her. I then turned wanting to run but heard….

"Jett?"

With as calm a voice as I could muster, I said, "I'm going to the truck to get something. I'll be back in a minute." I kept walking hoping she had turned back around. When I got to the truck, I was able to settle down. At that point the deep breathing seemed to help some. I was able to quiet my brain from all the "what ifs" and focus on the air going in and out of my body. I was feeling better.

What was I going to get out of the truck? I thought for a moment. I had a pair of binoculars under the seat. That would work. I went back to her and she was still standing there. "Sorry I took so long. I had some binoculars and I had a little trouble finding them."

She said, "Perfect timing. I want to show you something. You see that small clearing at about eleven o'clock. It's about two fingers down from the horizon. Something is grazing in that meadow. At first I thought it was cows, but now I think it might be deer. The binoculars will tell us. It's almost too dark to see. Can you see it?"

"No, I can't see it."

"Stand behind me and put your chin on my right shoulder so that your eyes are about level with mine. I'm gonna extend my arm and I want you to look down my arm to my finger tip and see if you can find it."

My heart was beating and this time it was not panic. It was excitement. I could smell her and a few strands of hair blew into my face and tickled my nose and cheeks. I wanted to turn my head a little and gently kiss her cheek.

"Can you see it?"

I wanted to lie and say no but I said, "Yes, I see it and I think they're deer too." I reluctantly pulled back and gave her the binoculars.

She adjusted them and then exclaimed, "Oh Jett, it is deer and there's a little fawn eating right next to the mother. It's so cute. Here, you take a look." She took the strap from around her neck and gave them to me.

"Wow, that's awesome."

She asked, "Could I take one more look? I can barely see them now. The shadows are starting to get darker. Do you mind if we stand here a little longer?"

"We can stand here as long as you want."

After awhile, she said, "I'm ready."

I asked, "Could you stay for awhile. I'll fix you something to eat."

"I'd really would like to, but I better be going. The children will be wondering where I am."

In a surprised voice, "You have kids?"

"Yes, I have seven ranging from 1 to 8."

I responded, "Well I sure have enjoyed meeting you. If I'm ever in the area again, I'll be sure to look you up."

We both laughed and headed for the truck.

She said, "I always thought about buying a house, but thanks to you, I now think I would like to design and build my own house. I know I'll never find a spot like that one, but the other places you showed me are really nice."

"Would you like me to help you find that perfect place for you?"

"Yes, I would like that very much."

I said, "I would like you to meet April, Ace, and Spot. Seriously, can you come back to the cabin?" She hesitated, "It's getting late." She paused and then said, "Yes, I would like that. I'll need to call Aunt Agnes and let her know."

"Great."

37
COMING TOGETHER

We pulled up in front of the cabin. The lights were on and Spot was standing inside the screen door barking. April came to the door and let him out. He came running up and jumped on me and then turned to Eden wagging his tail as I said, "No jump." Eden reached down and let him smell her hand and then reached under his neck and scratched his neck and head.

We walked up on the front porch and while I was introducing them, April smiled, reached out to shake her hand, and said, "Hi Eden, I'm April. Come on in." Ace was getting up from the couch as we walked in the door.

April did the honors, "Eden this is a distant friend of mine. His name is Sgt. Frost, but he goes by..." Looking at Jett she asked, "Is it Ass or Ace, I can't remember."

I said, "You might want to call him Sgt. Frost till he gets to know you."

Eden looked like she didn't know whether to laugh or not.

Ace said, "Eden, don't listen to those two fuck-ups. I'm Ace, nice to meet you."

Eden held out her hand and said, "Nice to meet you too Ass, I mean Ace. I don't know about these other two. Maybe you and I could hang out together."

We laughed and April said, "Eden you're gonna fit right in, but I'm not sure you're gonna take that as a compliment."

Eden smiled and replied, "But I do."

Ace turned to April. "Woman, I'm thirsty and hungry. Get me a beer and start rustlin' up some grub."

"Fuck you Ass, get your own beer and food. I'm not your slave."

Ace looked at Eden and said, "Run for your life girl. These people are corrupt and foul mouthed."

Eden was laughing and heading for the door and said, "Spot, let's go. They're all crazy."

I ran over to the door and begged, "Please Eden, please Spot, Don't go. I'll make them behave."

Eden looked at Spot, "That takes care of the other two, but who's going to control him?" She pointed at me.

Spot was wagging his tail. Eden said to Spot, "Are you sure you can handle him?" Spot kept wagging his tail. "All right, in that case, I'll stay."

April came over and gave Eden a hug and said, "Welcome, we're glad you're here."

April looked at Eden and me and said, "Jett, your Mom and Marge.... Oh, Eden, Marge is Ace's mom. Did you meet her at the picnic?"

"Yes I did."

April said, "Anyway, they brought all the food left over from the picnic. I just got it put away. So besides Ass over there, who's thirsty and hungry?" We all raised our hands. Just so you know Eden, pointing at Ace, he will milk the hurt leg syndrome for all it's worth. Don't let him hook you into waiting on him."

Ace said immediately, "Eden, please, I got this wound defending our country. Please get me a beer. I'm dying of thirst. That bitch over there refuses to help a poor wounded and traumatized veteran. Eden, please help me!"

Eden turned her nose up, took out her cell phone and said to Jett. "I need to call Aunt Agnes."

Ace raising his voice said, "Jett you brought another "B" into our home. I'm done with all of you. I'll be watching TV if you need me."

I asked Eden, "Can you stay awhile? I'll get you home by 11:00."

April yelling from the kitchen, "Ace, cut down the TV, Eden's not going to be able to hear what Agnes says."

Eden responded, "She goes to bed around 12:00 so I know she won't mind. I hate for you to be out so late. Are you sure you want me to stay that late?"

"On second thought, I can take you home now."

"Sorry, I've decided I want to stay." She dialed Aunt Agnes and I went to pee. By the time I came back, she was just getting off the phone. I asked, "Was Aunt Agnes okay with our plan?"

"She was fine."

I said, "You know where the bathroom is. Please make yourself at home."

"Thanks." She headed toward the bathroom. Ace turned off the TV and he and I headed for the kitchen, got a beer and sat down at the table.

Ace said, "April told me she was pretty. How come April and I are just hearing about her?" About that time Eden came toward the kitchen.

April said, "Eden, what would you like to drink? We have beer, white and red wine, and Lynne and Marge brought us a bunch of different kinds of soda."

"Thanks April, I'll have white wine. I can get it. Just show me where the glasses are."

April started to put some of the food out on the table and Eden helped. I said, "Eden, let me help. You've already had a baptism by fire. Take some time to relax."

She sat down and I helped April get everything set out. We helped ourselves and dug in. The conversation was light and fun. Eden fit right in and seemed to be having a good time. After we ate, April asked us if we wanted to play spades.

It turned out that Eden and some of her friends liked to play cards so we played and had some good laughs. The women had another glass or two of wine and Ace and I downed a few more beers. While playing cards, I was able to look at her more closely. Ace said she was pretty. I thought she was beautiful. Her lips were sensuous and full. Her eyes had a sparkle. I wondered if I was the only one who could see that sparkle.

At some point Ace looked at his watch and said, "Hey people, it's 11:30. Did I hear somebody say they were gonna have Eden home by 11:00?"

I said, "Oh shit." I looked at Eden and she seemed fine.

She said, "Aunt Agnes won't care. But she might be worried so I better call her."

I said, "I have an idea."

Ace interjected, "This could be a problem. When he's had a few beers, some of the lights go out."

"Let me finish. Why don't both of you ladies spend the night? We have four bedrooms and four people and there are locks on all the doors, so everyone would be safe and sound and cozy and comfortable."

April said, "Eden, I think you and I need to talk. Let's go to the bedroom I use so we can have a moment of privacy." Eden followed her in the bedroom.

Ace said, "She fits right in. I like her. How old is she?"

"I don't know. I think she's middle to late-thirties."

Ace responded, "She doesn't seem that much older than us. I don't think she cusses, but if she spends much time with us, that will change."

They came out of the bedroom and April said, "I think we've got this worked out."

Eden said, "I need to call Aunt Agnes and let her know."

Eden got her cell phone and disappeared into April's bedroom. April went out to her car and got her gym bag which always seemed to have extra outfits. We heard Eden talking to Aunt Agnes, but couldn't make out what she was saying.

When she got off the phone, Eden said, "Aunt Agnes and I figured that if I got home in the morning by 9:00 that we could make it to church on time. April has something for me to sleep in so I'm all set."

Ace said, "Let's get back to the game. I've got some ground to make up."

I got us another beer and the girls said they had drunk enough wine.

We played till about 1:00 and Eden was way ahead in score. She smiled, "I have a little advantage. I was playing spades before you folks were out of diapers. Now children, it's time to go to bed."

Ace asked, "How old were you when you started playing Spades?"

April and I interjected about the same time, "Ace, that's none of your business."

Eden said, "It's all right." She looked at Ace, "I think I was about thirteen or fourteen."

Ace smiled really big, "That makes you almost old enough to be my mom. I think I'll call you MJ for Mom Junior."

Eden smiled back, "Ass, you can call me whatever you like."

Everyone laughed.

Eden said, "All right kids, let's get this stuff cleaned up before we go to bed."

Ace responded, "MJ, I'm goin' on to bed. My leg hurts."

Eden said, "Before you go, you can gather up those loose cards and put them away."

"Way to go Eden, you got it!" April gave her a high five.

Eden turned to me and said, "Jett, thanks for showing me around today. I really enjoyed it." She looked at April and Ace and said, "Thanks for making me feel at home. I had a good time tonight."

Everyone said something like, you're welcome and we had a good time too.

April picked up her gym bag and said to Eden, "Come on, I'll show you your room and where everything is." Eden was going to sleep in the front bedroom on my side of the cabin. No one had used that room in years.

Ace said he was going on to bed. April didn't come out of Eden's room for awhile. I guess they were talking. When she came out I was waiting for her at the table in the kitchen. She came over and sat down opposite me. She said in a voice low enough so as not to disturb Eden or Ace, "I really like her Jett."

I said, "I was amazed how she fit right in thanks to you and Ace."

"I enjoyed talking to her. She's an interesting person and she asked me some questions about my life and was a good listener. I told her a little about Ace and me. She told me that she hoped it worked out for us if that is what I wanted. I told her I was still confused and she suggested that I do the best I can to be patient."

I asked, "What did you think about her bringing up the age thing?"

"My guess is it was her way of putting that issue out on the table for everyone to see. I would think it was especially for you. I think if I were in her shoes, I would find it difficult to have a relationship with someone thirteen or fourteen years younger than me."

"Why?"

She smiled, "I'm not sure. I'd have to think about it, but I have a feeling you'll find out her reasons soon."

"Yeah, I guess so."

"You've spent some time with her since the picnic. What do you think?"

I responded, "I really like her."

"Is that all you have to say?"

"I guess it is right now."

"All right."

I asked, "How did it go with Ace?"

"We had a good time and especially being out on the bikes together. He's just a different person when you get him out in the woods. We didn't have any serious moments or conversations, but I enjoyed being with him and he seemed to enjoy being with me."

"I'm glad."

She yawned, "Me too. I'm ready to turn in. How about you?"

"I'm ready."

I was tired, but couldn't get my mind off knowing that Eden was on the other side of the bathroom. I smiled remembering a few minutes ago when peeing, I made sure my stream didn't hit the water. Was I trying to keep from waking her or was I trying to hide the fact I occasionally had to do something as gross as take a pee. If that were true, how was I going to handle farts and taking a shit? While brushing my teeth, I noticed a wet wash cloth hanging on the towel rack. As soon as I finished, I took the washcloth, tilted my head back, and laid it open across my face and breathed in hoping to catch a scent of her.

I woke up at my usual time and the house was quiet. I was really tired and decided not to go for my run. But I couldn't get back to sleep. I was thinking about her and wondering if I could go cuddle and get cozy. No luck on getting back to sleep. Spot and I took off. When I got back, it was still quiet so I went back to bed.

The smell of coffee and bacon cooking brought me out of a deep sleep. It was 7:47. April and Eden were moving around the kitchen like they had been "team working" breakfast for years. Eden had on her clothes from last night and April had on a tee-shirt that came down to about two inches above her knees. They looked at me and were softly laughing.

"What?" I asked.

April said, "Your fly is wide open Dick Head."

I was embarrassed and could feel the blood rushing to my face. Eden also looked embarrassed but they kept laughing. I quickly zipped up.

"Well ladies, I'm glad I was able to provide a little early morning entertainment for you all. It smells great in here. Eden, how did you sleep?"

"I slept wonderfully. I was out as soon as my head hit the pillow. April and I decided last night that we would get up around 7:30 and if she hadn't come in to wake me, I'm sure I would still be sleeping. It must be the mountain air."

The three of us sat around the table and talked over breakfast. Eden told April about the different places we saw yesterday. She said I had convinced her to build a house rather than buy one. We each talked more about our lives, work and interests. It was fun and I could have sat there for hours.

I looked at the clock. "I hate to spoil this party, but its 8:45 and we better be going."

We stood up and April said, "Eden, it's been wonderful having you here. These two men are too much for one woman to put up with. I hope we can get together when you come back next week."

"Thank you, April. I really had a good time." They hugged and we headed for the door.

Spot wanted to go and he sat between us on the front seat. We talked about April and Ace and more about different things we saw on the way. As I was walking her to the door, she said, "Jett, thanks for everything. It was a lot of fun."

I wanted to hug her at least, but chickened out in the end and said, "You're welcome. I enjoyed it too. I guess I'll see you in church."

She smiled. "Yes, I'll see you in a little while." She opened the door and closed it behind her.

38
THE BREAKTHROUGH

When I got back to the cabin, April was sitting at the kitchen table with a cup of coffee and reading a book.

"Hey, girl. How ya' doin'?"

"I'm fine, just taking it easy. Ace got up after you left, ate some breakfast and went back to bed. I don't think he has caught up on sleep from the last few weeks."

"Yeah, I think you're right."

She changed the subject, "I've been thinking about it and I hope the age difference to you will not be important. I think she's a 'keeper' Jett."

"I feel the same way, but I worry that it may make a difference to her."

She agreed, "It might, but you'll have to help her change her mind." She went on in a softer voice, "Even though I really like her, I'm still a little jealous. I wonder if that means I want you and Ace to myself?"

She continued, "I'm so horny right now. I wanted Ace to take me back to bed with him and fuck my brains out. I looked for any little sign that he was interested, but there was none. I promised myself that I would not throw myself at him and that he would have to make the first move."

A little above a whisper, I said, "I think that's a good plan. I really believe that he will come around. It's like you are dating again and getting to know each other and taking your time. I think you have some work to do before getting physically intimate. I really believe that his not making a move on you is a good sign. Ace is an expert at fucking. At some level, I think he wants more from you than a physical relationship. Fucking just keeps you at arms length and nothing changes. You and Ace would be skipping over the important questions that have not been answered."

She responded, "Yes, like what happened to us? Why did we go our separate ways? And why didn't we ever talk about it?"

I added, "Yeah, and what were or are we afraid of?"

She said, "I want him to make the first move on those issues too. I think that's important. I don't wanna push him. I'm glad you brought up those points. It helped me to see that I need to put my sexual needs on the back burner."

"I think that's important. I would be lying if I didn't admit that I would like to take care of your every sexual need, but do you agree that this would be a bad thing?"

She paused and thought for a moment and then with a big smile said, "My hesitation scared you. Right?"

I smiled and nodded.

Prodding me she said, "You thought, 'oh my god, why is she hesitating'? Is she going to say, 'let's fuck anyway.' Am I right?"

"Yeah, you're right."

Now a little more serious, she cocked her head and with a curious expression asked, "What if I had said, 'Let's fuck.' Would you have done it?" She quickly interjected, "I'm sorry, I'm sorry, I withdraw the question. That's not fair. Don't answer, please don't answer. I'm sorry." She got up and kissed me on my forehead and went to her bedroom.

I went into Eden's bedroom hoping she had left her bed unmade. Unfortunately, I couldn't tell anyone had been in the room much less slept in it. I looked around for anything she might have left behind. I don't know what I was looking for; maybe a strand of hair. There was nothing.

I went in, shaved and showered. I had a boner in the shower and took care of business. I felt better and relieved. I knew April regretted asking me the question. The complications surrounding us doing it here in the cabin with Ace asleep in the other room were huge and a fucking nightmare. And what about my feelings for Eden? If April had wanted to do "it," I hope I would have been strong enough to say, "I can't for a several different reasons." I'm so glad nothing happened.

I got to church about ten minutes before it started. Aunt Agnes and Eden had not arrived. I talked with the family and everyone wanted to know how it went and I filled them in on the details. The bell rang and we went in. There was still no Eden and Aunt Agnes. What could possibly be wrong? I couldn't focus on church. Had I said something? I kept going over in my mind and couldn't think of anything that would cause Eden not to come.

After the service, we went to the fellowship hall to socialize. I pulled Ann aside and asked her if she would mind calling Aunt Agnes and see if everything was all right. She said that Aunt Agnes doesn't come every Sunday, but she would be glad to call.

She went in the church office to make the call. When she came back, I couldn't read her expression. It seemed normal. She said, "I talked with Eden and she said that Aunt Agnes had a headache when she woke up. Eden asked if you were here. She said to tell you 'thanks for everything.'"

"Did she say anything else?"

"No, that was it."

"Thanks Ann." Jack came over and asked if everything was okay and Ann filled him in. Shortly after that, everyone headed for the door. Most of us were going to the Inn for lunch. I sat by Pop and Jimmy.

We talked for awhile and I asked Pop if we could take our walk tomorrow around 4:00. He said that would work for him.

I followed Mom and Dad to the house. Dad would take his traditional nap in front of a baseball game. I wanted time to catch up with Mom. While I was there, I decided to call and check on Aunt Agnes. She answered and said she was feeling better. I asked her if Eden had left and she said yes that she had left about an hour ago. "I understand that she has an appointment with a Realtor next Saturday. Did she say what time she would get here?"

"She didn't say Jett, but she usually calls me mid-week and we talk about the weekend. If you want, you can call me on Friday and I should know something by then. On the other hand, I can give you her phone number."

"No, that's okay. I'll just call you on Friday. Thanks Aunt Agnes. I'm glad you're feeling better."

I didn't feel comfortable having her phone number unless she gave it to me. Maybe I would ask her for the number next weekend. I talked to Mom for another hour or so and then left.

When I got to the cabin, April's car was still there. I went inside and all three of them were gone. I looked out back and the bikes were gone. Spot must be having a blast. I was so glad that Ace was out in the woods and hoped he would find there what he needs to help him heal. I went into Eden's room. I liked calling that her room now.

I had an idea. I called Mom. "Mom, would you have time this week to come up here and look at the front bedroom on my side? It looks kind of bland. I wondered if you would mind fixing it up with a new bedspread, some new curtains, and pictures. I don't know; whatever you think. Let me know how much it costs and I'll pay you."

She laughed, "Why Jett, I'm going to guess that's the bedroom Eden slept in last night. Isn't that thoughtful of you, wanting her to feel all welcome and cozy? I'll be glad to Honey. I'll not make it too feminine since at some point, she might start sleeping in your bedroom."

"Mom, that's embarrassing."

"Sorry." I could tell she was having a good time, "On the other hand, if you had a little girl, the feminine touch would come in handy."

"I haven't held hands with her yet and you already have us married with a child."

"I know I'm jumping the gun a little."

I interrupted, "That's a lot more than a little."

"All kidding aside, I'm just happy you're interested in someone."

"Me too, thanks Mom."

"I have a free day Wednesday. Will that work for you and Ace?"

"Yes, we're supposed to be working for Charlie this week. That should be fine. I love you."

"Love you too Honey."

I changed and went outside to work on a few projects I had been putting off. About an hour later, I heard the engines of the bikes and before they pulled up, Spot was already jumping on me and wagging his tail saying he had a bang up time with April and Ace. They were smiling. It was so good to see Ace in a good mood. We talked awhile and they said they really liked Eden. I gave them an update. Ace said, "Mom asked all three of us for supper. Do you want to come?"

"No, I'm gonna pass. I ate too much for lunch today and I need to keep working on this porch swing."

"April and I are going to get cleaned up and head on out." He looked at April and said, "Do you want to shower first?"

"Yes since it will take me longer to get ready."

She went inside and Ace talked to me while I worked. I was having trouble figuring out how to get the swing balanced and he showed me how to do it. He was good with his hands.

He said, "While you were gone the other day, I wandered around inside and outside and made a list of projects we need to get working on when my leg gets a little better. Several of them need to be done before winter."

"Okay. Speaking of projects, I talked to Mom a little while ago and she is going to come up here Wednesday and work on the room Eden slept in. It looks too bland. It needed to be done even if we don't work out."

"That sounds good to me." I continued, "How are things goin' with you and April?"

"I think they're goin' good. I've been thinking a lot lately about my suicide attempt. That's some scary shit. As usual, I want to shove it down like everything else, but I'm determined to face it. I'm going to talk to Doc about it on Tuesday. I feel like I gotta second chance. I could be dead. I'm still really confused about stuff, but now by god, I'm going to find out what makes me tick. I keep asking myself the same question Doc asked me: what am I afraid of? What the fuck Jett? You've seen me in combat. I did my job and I did what needed to be done without hesitation. Sure at times I was scared, but I would have given my life for any of you guys. So after having gone through that, why would I be afraid of fucking feelings and any other fucking thing in my life? Nightmares, flashbacks, crazy fucking intrusive thoughts be dammed. I'm gonna beat this shit."

Tears were rolling down my cheeks and he stood and stumbled toward me and put his arms around me and held me tight and said, "And I'm tired of running away from tears." And we were both sobbing and I was shocked at the intensity and force of what seemed like a wailing of grief and pain coming from deep inside him. Almost like an explosion of bottled up energy. And then another set of arms around us and all three of us were sobbing.

I don't know how long we stood there, but after awhile, Ace said, "That felt real damn good," and then I said, "Yeah, real damn good." Then April said, "Yeah, real damn good," and all three of us started laughing and we looked at each other and Ace said, "Look at us, three little cry babies and we don't give a shit."

I eased back a little and it was so natural and beautiful how they slid into each other's arms and held each other and both started crying again and I walked slowly into the house and I heard softly in the midst of their tears, "I'm sorry."

"No, I'm sorry." And perhaps now they were ready to start answering those questions and discover a new level intimacy never before experienced.

Spot and I took off for a hike and decided that we would give them time to do whatever they needed and wanted to do. I said to Spot, "I want to show you Eden's house. Let's walk up there for a little while."

As we walked around the knoll again, I thought about resting my head on her shoulder and how wonderful if felt. I told Spot all about it and he wagged his tail and he seemed to understand that it made me happy. I stood in a few of the places where she had stood and sat down where she had sat, trying to feel a little of her energy. I explored in all directions the area from the spot where Eden described her house. I made a lot of mental notes. We must have been away for over an hour. Their vehicles were gone. When we got inside, I found a note on the kitchen table.

"Hey man. April and I are going to Mom's to eat and I'm going to stay at her place tonight. I'll meet you at the Inn at 9:00 to work with Charlie. My PT appt is at 4:00. April and I are going to meet at the cabin after she gets off work and take the bikes out. Then, April wants to fix us supper using the left overs from the picnic. Hope this works for you. I have my cell phone so call me if you want to. I can't believe that I'm getting ready to write these words, but here goes, love you man. Ace."

Well, well. I teared-up again. Who would have guessed? I was happy for them, but I missed them. I missed Eden. I felt alone. I got me a beer and Spot and I turned on the TV. Later I got a sandwich and another beer. I fell asleep and woke up at 11:48. I went to Eden's room and slept in her bed. I took long whiffs of her pillow hoping I had the right one and snuggled into the sheets and drifted off.

39

A WALK WITH POP

When I got to the Inn, Ace was talking to Charlie. The three of us talked for a few minutes and then Charlie told us what needed to be done. Ace and I didn't have a chance to talk until we stopped for lunch. We got our lunch and went outside and sat at one of the picnic tables. I asked, "How was dinner at Ma's last night?"

"It went well. I know you're dying to ask me about April so I'll beat you to the punch. After you left the cabin, we had a long talk. I would say it's a start. We still have a lot of work to do. We decided not to have sex, which for me is a huge challenge. After we finished that long hug and had the cabin to ourselves, we wanted it bad. But we decided to sit on the couch and talk and it was a mutual decision to abstain. I still can't believe I agreed."

I asked, "Were you able to stay strong last night?"

"Yeah, we agreed that we could only hug. No kisses which would put us both over the edge. Also, we decided sleeping in the same bed would put us over the edge. To be honest, I don't know if we can do it. Last night was really hard. No pun intended. We decided that we needed to work on ourselves and needed to answer our own questions and each other's questions about the relationship before we could take the next step to making love."

Surprised at his description, I said, "I've never heard you utter the phrase making love."

"I have never said it till last night. April told me some about you all and I have to admit hearing about it now was more difficult than when you first told me up on the Parkway. I'm sure that's because I'm facing stuff now instead of being in denial. I may have to challenge you to a duel."

"What weapons would you choose?"

"The same ones I chose when we were younger. Broom sticks."

"I've been practicing. You may want to rethink this whole thing."

He replied, "Not because I'm afraid of you Butt Wipe. I'm afraid I'll start crying in the middle of the duel and be humiliated."

We laughed.

I said, "Speaking of weapons, I put your .45 back in your night stand drawer."

Smiling, he asked, "So you think I'm over being suicidal?"

"Yeah, I do."

Then more seriously, he looked at me and asked, "Why'd you fuck my girl?"

Just as serious, I looked him in the eyes and said, "You tell me."

"Okay, because she wasn't my girl and you were both horny."

I stood up and walked a few steps away and came back. "That's what I tell myself most of the time. But if that's true, why do I still feel so bad about it."

He replied, "That's when feelings override logic. Doc and I talked about it last week."

"Yeah, I guess so."

"Anyway, April was telling me that you had this discussion about the difference between making love and having sex."

I sat back down and looked off in the distance, "You know I'm not real experienced in the fucking department. I mean in comparison to you. Anyway I've only had a few satisfying sexual experiences.

So with April it seemed different. Like I said before, I wondered if I had secretly loved her."

He said, "I wondered that sometimes. I would catch you looking at her. But when we broke up and you didn't make any moves, I figured it wasn't true."

"I don't know. I think I would never allow myself to think of April in anyway other than she was your girl regardless of the circumstances. It's also true that I never picked up any indication from her that she was interested in me as a boyfriend."

He rubbed his head and said, "This stuff is complicated. It's making my head hurt. This is the reason I don't like to deal with feelings."

"Maybe there's a way not to make it so complicated."

"I'm in, how?"

"Remember Doc was telling us about living in the moment and how we get caught up in the past and worry too much about the future. Could we apply that here?"

He responded, "He'd tell us to start with taking ten deep breaths."

"All right, let's try it." We both took ten deep breaths.

He asked, "What next?"

"Hell, I don't know. Why don't we ask him tomorrow?"

"Okay."

"For what it's worth, I think you and April are making the right decision to take it slow."

"I'm not real confident about how long we can hold off. You ready to get back to work? I'll need to leave here around 3:30 to go to my PT appointment. Are you gonna be home for supper?"

"Yeah, I'll be there. I need to stop about the same time as you. Pop and I are going for a walk around 4:00."

I met Pop in front of the Inn and we headed for the lake. I asked him about his day and he gave me a run down on the business at the Inn and the hotels. "Jimmy is doing a fine job. He brought in some marketing consultants from Chapel Hill and met with them for a few days. He briefed me on it this morning and I was impressed. I think all three places have a solid future."

"I'm glad Jimmy has found his niche." I paused. "Pop, I had a nice time with Eden Saturday. She is looking for a place to live up here." I gave him an overview of her plans. "I took her around and showed her different areas and we ended up at that spot about five minutes walk from the cabin. It's the one with the knoll and with some good size rocks and trees."

"I know the one you're talking about. Nana and I use to take picnic lunches up there. It has a great view."

I continued, "Her initial idea was to purchase a house in town. While we were walking around that knoll, I asked her if she could build a house on that spot and what would it be like. She described a little house set back against the rocks and trees with as much solar energy as possible. No trees would be cut down and the house would be a dark wood that would blend in with the surroundings. She said she would want the house to be as inconspicuous as possible."

Pop said, "Let me make it easy Son. The property along that ridge will belong to you after my death. In my will, I ask all of you who will own the land." He paused. "I think you know. We don't own that land. It belongs to Mother Earth."

I smiled, "You've reminded us of that many times."

He went on, "So shall we say it is entrusted to us for a time. Gus and Walter requested that all of us treat the land with respect. You know what that means. I trust your judgment and your commitment to the spirit of that respect. You are free to make any decisions you choose with your portion of the land even before I pass on."

There came the tears again. I stopped and put my arms around my grandfather. "Pop, you taught me so much about the land and life and love and respect for all living things. It is your greatest gift to me and that gift will live on through all of us."

He had a tear too. "You are a very special young man Jett. I love you more that you will ever know."

We started walking again. This time in silence allowing what passed between us to be more important than any words could express. He pointed out an eagle soaring over us and we both smiled. We walked and looked off into the distance knowing that each of us was marveling at this gift from God - each moment a gift to experience and embrace. Pop said so many times that if we would just stand still and be quiet that after awhile we would not be able to tell where our feet stopped and the earth started. The land would become us and we would become the land. It sounded like that was what Doc meant by living in the moment.

I got back to the cabin around 5:30. The vehicles were there, but the three of them were gone. I changed and walked up to the knoll. I sat on the outer edge and closed my eyes and tried to remember everything we had said and done. It had been two days and it seemed like forever. Saturday would never get here. I missed her. I laid back and looked up at the sky. I practiced my deep breathing and watched the clouds change shape.

Out of nowhere, I was back there in combat, triggered I'm sure by looking at the clouds. I did that a lot when we would stop for a break. Half of us would be securing the area and the other half would be resting. I would look at the clouds and dream about being home and then we would be up and moving again. I started my deep breathing again and for the first time it seemed to be of some help. I made a conscious effort to focus on being right here on this knoll thinking about Eden. I relaxed and soon drifted off to sleep. I was awakened by the sound of the dirt bikes up on the trail heading back to the cabin.

I started back and found Ace outside drinking a beer and throwing sticks for Spot to chase and retrieve. They were having fun. I asked, "Hey Man, how was it on the trail?"

"It was great. You 'member that old shed we found one day when we wandered off the north point of the ridge, about half mile down the mountain side?"

"Yeah, that's where we found those snakes, right?"

"Yeah, I took April there. It was quite an adventure getting the bikes down there and back. April took a little tumble, but she's fine. Sometimes I think she's tougher than either one of us. Would you mind getting me another beer? Spot's not finished yet."

"Sure." I went in and the shower was running. I sat out on the porch and drank my beer and talked to Ace. Soon April appeared with a glass of wine. We small talked for a little longer and then went in to eat. We had a nice evening, watched some TV and around 10:00, April said she had to work tomorrow and needed to get her beauty rest. Ace walked her outside and shortly after that we went to bed.

Buddy Session Three

Doc arrived promptly at 9:00.

After a little small talk, we got right to work. He asked us to report what we had recorded in our notebooks about practicing the exercises and to let him know about any questions we might have for him.

Neither one of us had practiced the breathing to the extent that he had requested. He gave us a pep talk and encouraged us to do better before group on Saturday. We talked to him about our discussion yesterday and how it got so complicated that Ace's head hurt and I wanted to drop it. Ace told him we took ten deep breaths, but didn't know what to do after that.

Doc asked, "Did the breathing help?"

Ace said, "Come to think of it, I don't know. I was so intent on wondering about the next step that I didn't notice whether the breathing helped or not."

I said, "Me too."

Doc responded, "Let me check out an assumption. Is it true that you couldn't believe that something as simple as deep breathing could really help you to let go of the complications you were creating?"

We both smiled and I said, "That's true for me."

"Me too," said Ace.

Doc smiled, "I remember those days well. We will be working on different skills to help let go of stuff, but at this point in the training, if ten deep breaths aren't enough, take ten more and so on."

Neither one of us had any more questions. Doc took us through more deep breathing exercises. We walked around inside and then took a walk outside repeating many of the same exercises we had done before. Intermittently, he would ask us to stop and open our senses and tell him about our experience.

I think Ace and I were getting the point and learning to be more focused in the moment.

The rest of the session, he worked with us individually. We went over my symptom checklist. He had a lot of questions for me and took a lot of notes. From that list, we worked on my individual goals. He asked me to go over what I had written in my notebook since Saturday and we discussed those entries. He did a review of the session with us and encouraged us to continue the training. He left.

Ace left to go spend some time with Ma. I went down to the Inn and had lunch with Pop. The rest of the week went pretty well. Two nights in a row, I had nightmares and soaked my sheets, but I had no panic attacks. Ace told me his flashbacks had gotten worse and the breathing hadn't helped much.

On Wednesday, Mom redecorated Eden's room. It looked really nice. It had a warm look and feel to it. The bedspread was a flowered print with a green background. The valance was made of the same material. There were some new rugs and pictures on the walls. The pictures were beautiful nature scenes of the area. Eden would love them. I called Mom and thanked her.

Ace had PT in the afternoon and April had to work the night shift. It was 9:00 and Ace was not home. I found him at Stanley's playing pool. He was almost drunk. I sat down at the bar and Alex, one of the bartenders brought me a beer.

He said, "Ace gave me his keys and told me under no circumstances to let him have the keys back. That was a good thing. Anyway, here they are."

"Thanks Alex. Is it okay if we leave his SUV in the parking lot till in the morning?"

"Sure."

I waited till he finished the game and he gave me no problem about leaving. He slept till we got to the house and then I had to carry him in like a sack of potatoes. I thought I wasn't going to get him up the front steps. The next morning, he didn't bring it up and I decided to let it go. He was doing better and had been responsible about not driving. He would have to figure this out.

I took him down to get his SUV. He said that his dad and my dad wanted to talk to him about a job. He was optimistic. He headed up to the mill. Ace loved working with his hands and often said that college was a waste of his time except for sports and parties.

He called me from April's that evening and told me he had gotten the job at the mill. He was happy. It was Friday and on my lunch break, I called Aunt Agnes and asked if she had heard from Eden.

"Yes Jett, Eden is driving up here after work this afternoon. We're going to do a little shopping and then go get something to eat."

"I would like to spend some time with her, but I hate to impose on her time with you."

"Jett, as you know, I have a lot of family and friends. I keep busy most of the time. I like it that she can spend time with you and your friends. We should be back around 9:00 this evening. Why don't you give her a call?"

"Thanks Aunt Agnes, I will."

That evening over supper with Ace and April, I asked them how they felt about Eden eating with us tomorrow and spending the night. We agreed it was a good idea.

After eating they left. I cleaned up and watched TV. I was nervous about calling her, but I dialed the number. It rang about five times. Eden answered, "Hello."

"Hey Eden, this is Jett. How are you?"

"Hello Jett, I'm fine. How are you?"

"Fine thanks." I asked her about her trip up and the shopping and dinner and where they ate and tried to make a little more small talk. I then asked, "When are you supposed to meet with the Realtor?"

"At 10:00 in the morning."

My heart started beating more rapidly and I stuttered some, "I was uh, I was wondering if you would have lunch with me tomorrow?"

There was a hesitation. My heart now skipped a beat. "Jett, thank you for asking, but I hate to leave Aunt Agnes by herself." I heard Aunt Agnes in the background, "You go on child. I have plenty to do around here and Jack and Ann invited me for dinner tomorrow night. Go on now. I mean it."

"Well Jett, I don't know if you heard Aunt Agnes in the background, but she is urging me to go. So it seems settled. Yes, I will have lunch with you tomorrow."

Trying to hide my excitement, I said, "Great. Will you be finished with the Realtor® by 1:00?"

"Yes, I'm sure I'll be finished by then."

I asked, "Can I pick you up at that time?"

Sure, that sounds fine. I'll see you then."

I had a beer and watched more TV and went to bed. I would see her tomorrow. I was excited and had trouble getting to sleep. I was vaguely aware of Ace coming home, but I had no idea what time it was.

40
GROUP SESSION TWO

People started pulling in the yard around 8:45. A few were mingling outside and talking. Several walked up the trail and we were seated in the circle by 9:00.

Doc: "Welcome everyone. I appreciate you being on time. How are you doing with the breathing exercises?"

Almost all of us were still struggling to make the breathing a priority in our lives. Some said they were having difficulty understanding how the breathing could help with their symptoms. Doc asked us to be patient and keep training. He talked us through a breathing exercise. Some commented that it was easier to focus when Doc was leading the exercise.

Doc: "Let's shift gears. The Attention Training is going to help in many ways, but we must figure out a way to better understand the complexity of the brain/mind. Let's start by asking the question: Who's in charge of your life? Who's running the show? Who's making decisions?"

Anna: "I've never thought about it. I guess I'm in charge, but who is the I that's in charge? I certainly don't feel in charge now. I feel helpless and depressed and scared."

Frank: "But since Doc taught us that we create our experiences, even though you don't feel in charge, that theory says you're creating that helplessness, depression, and fear."

Doc: "Yes and that is to keep us from blaming someone or something outside ourselves for what we experience or create. Anna is saying I don't want to experience those things so is it possible that Anna is not creating them, but some other part of her is responsible for creating helplessness, depression, and fear?"

Paul: "This is some heavy shit."

Frank: "Are you talking about a split personality?"

Doc: "No. How often do you experience this separation in your life? An easy example is when your mind wants you to do something you have decided is not healthy or good for you. Give me some examples of when that happens."

Melinda: "I have decided I want to lose some weight, but my mind tells me that chocolate pie sure looks good. I'll say it does look good, but we're not going to eat any of it. My mind says, but it looks so yummy. Maybe we could just have one bite. And I might say that's not gonna happen or I might say we can have just one bite. Is that what you mean?"

Doc: "Yes. Would someone else give us an example?"

Chad: "I have made the decision I want to get going again on my exercise program. When it comes time to exercise, my mind says that we're tired now and we'll do it tomorrow and I say no we're going to do it now. Sometimes I win out and sometimes my mind wins out."

Doug: "I face that with booze and pills every day. I know that stuff is killing me, but my mind tells me that we can't survive without them and we can stop later, but right now we have to have a drink or pop a pill or we're gonna go crazy."

Me: "My panic attacks often come out of the blue. As soon as I'm aware of the first symptoms, I try to stop 'em, but my mind keeps saying things like what if you can't stop? Everyone will think you're crazy. What if you have a panic attack in church? What if you have a panic attack in front of your new girl friend? What if you never get over them and the 'what if's' go on and on?"

Doc: "During the breathing exercises, I have asked you to make a conscious choice to focus on your breathing. Then I say something like if your mind stirs up a thought, let it go and come back to focusing on your breathing. Your mind is interfering with the breathing exercise by thinking thoughts like, 'This is a waste of time. We have other things to think about and do. Doc is crazy. This stuff is not gonna help. Remember to stop and get beer on the way home. I'm still pissed off at my brother for blowing me off this morning.' Help me out group. What other thoughts is your mind throwing at you while you're trying to concentrate?"

The group came up with a number of other examples.

Frank: "Are you saying the me working on the breathing is different from my mind who is having all those thoughts?"

Doc: "Yes, close your eyes. I want you to spend a few moments in a new role. I want you to be curious about your mind and how it thinks. I want you to be the observer of your thoughts or the thinking of your mind. So just be still and observe what thoughts come up in your mind. Take your time and just observe. Open your eyes. What was that like?"

Nate: "My mind was saying things like what is this shit and how is this gonna help and we could be doin' better things with our time and some of these people may get this stuff, but we don't get it and tell Doc after the session today that we're done and we ain't comin' back."

Rob: "I had some of the same thoughts, but it was strange that I felt like I was watching these thoughts rather than makin' 'em up. They were just comin' at me."

Anna: "So there is a me who is able to be separate from my thoughts and this me can sit back and observe what my mind is doing. Is that it?"

Doc: "Yes. Let's do another exercise that demonstrates the same point. Close your eyes and go back in your memory and find an incident that upset you. It might be an argument or someone hurt your feelings or some incident where you got angry. Take your time. Raise your hand when you have a memory in mind. Now, I want you to replay the incident. Get inside it and go through it and feel everything you felt. Now make a shift and step out of the incident and replay it from a distance. If you are struggling with the watching part, imagine you are sitting in an empty theatre and watching the incident on the big screen. Open your eyes. What was that like?"

Ace: "I was almost drunk and got in a fight. I couldn't feel the physical pain, but I sure remember the anger and rage. When I watched it on the big screen, I smiled and thought, 'that was a good punch you got in.' I knew I was angry. I could see it, but I didn't feel it like I did when I was in the scene."

Anna: "Mine was an argument with my mother. Like Ace, I could feel it when I was in it, but when I watched it, it was different. The intensity of the anger wasn't there."

Several others shared similar experiences.

Doc: "So each of you made the decision to relive the incident and then step outside and observe the incident. Again, who is this 'you,' this Anna, this Ace, this Rob, this Nate that is able to step outside and observe? Let's call it for now the observer or the watcher of the mind. A again become that observer. Close your eyes and take a few deep breaths and then focus on observing your mind thinking and be aware of the contents. Notice how you can observe the thoughts coming and going. Open your eyes."

Doc: "I don't expect this to come easy, but are you getting the idea?"

Chad: "Are you suggesting we can be separate from our thoughts, memories and experiences?"

Doc: "I'm taking it further than that. I'm saying you are separate from your thoughts, memories and experiences unless you chose to identify with them."

Frank: "But it's a part of us. It's part of what defines us and makes us who we are."

Doc: "And I'm suggesting this is the core of your problems."

Paul: "This really is some heavy shit." (Murmurs of agreement)

Doc smiling: "Everyone do your best to stay open and let's explore the idea. I want you to pretend that I have erased everything in your mind. In other words, your mind is empty and you have no memory. For the purposes of the exercise, I do have my memory. Close your eyes and imagine what that would be like. When I tell you to open your eyes, you have no memory."

A few more moments of silence and then Doc said, "Open your eyes."

It was quiet for awhile and then Frank: "Hey! Who are you people?" After a pause, "Does anyone know who I am?"

Paul: "I don't know who I am and I sure as hell don't know who you are."

Doc turning to Frank: "How are you feeling right now?"

Frank: "Well, I don't know why I'm here, but I don't think I really care. I'm not sure what I'm feeling sitting here. It seems okay. I mean I'm just sitting here. I'm not aware of any particular feelings, but I guess I could say it feels nice and I feel peaceful. I'm not sure what nice and peaceful means. As I look at you two people, (he points to Anna and Melinda) I think I feel more drawn to you than the rest of these people, but I don't know why."

Everyone laughs.

Anna: "I feel good, but I don't really know why. What's the deal with the arms? I seem to be the only person who has only one arm. Does anyone know if that's supposed to be a problem?"

Chad: "Yeah, I can only see out of one eye and everyone else has two eyes. Does that make a difference or mean that I'm special or have a problem?"

Rob: "Does anyone know what a problem is?"

Melinda: "Does anybody know why we're here. Not that I mind. I'm just curious. Also, I noticed that I have two of these, pointing to her breasts, and that one, pointing to Anna, also has two, but nobody else does. I wonder what that means."

Doc: "Well, I know why you're here. You are suffering from PTSD?"

Rob: What the fuck is that?"

Nate: "I'm not sure what suffering is and I feel fine so I'm outta here. Bye." He gets up.

I asked: "Where you going?"

Nate: "Get me a beer."

Ace: "Tilt. No fair. You don't know what a beer is."

Nate: "Ain't nobody gonna erase beer from my brain."

(Laughter)

Anna: "Pretending I didn't have any memory of anything was difficult. It was amazing for a moment that I was able to question whether only having one arm was supposed to be a problem. I was free for a moment."

Chad: "Same experience with only having one eye. For one moment, I felt like Anna, I was free."

Doc: "What are some other responses to the exercise?"

Doug: "It was different. I did feel some fear about not knowing where I lived or who my family was, but I got the point."

Melinda: "Just for a moment, I felt that freedom from my problems."

Doc: "The glimpse of that moment of freedom from problems is critically important. Close your eyes and remember those few moments when you felt free. What if you could train yourself to spend more time in the moment free of the trauma of your past, free of anxiety about the future, and free of your mind's endless chatter? You must start by understanding the 'you' in this experience is the 'you' who can learn how to discover that freedom. My job is to teach you how to do that. Open your eyes."

Frank: "You told us to be separate from our thoughts and memories and then you said go back and remember those few moments of freedom? I'm confused."

Doc: "Memory does have some benefits. Be patient. We will get there in a moment. Let's come up with a model that will help us move forward with our training. I hope all of you are now familiar with that part of you that can be separate from past, future, and thoughts. If anyone is still struggling, we'll talk more in our individual sessions. Where does this you that can separate from past, future, and thoughts live?"

Paul: "Up my ass most of the time."

(Laughter)

Paul: "Anything's better than up my ass."

Doc: "Let's say that you live here." He places his palm over his chest. "How about calling it the Center? So far, we've got this 'you' who lives at Center with no memory. Let's bring the mind/memory back into the picture and divide it up. The first category that is available to you at Center is the part of the mind that is filled with all the objective data you need to live your life. It contains information like your name, where you live, members of your family, the identity of your friends, how to drive a vehicle, how to do your job, how to do your laundry and things of that nature. Are there any questions on that category?"

Frank: "Maybe later."

Doc: "The second category of mind/memory available to you at Center is all the lessons you've learned in your life through different experiences. When at Center, they are available to you in the moment you need them. An example is you are driving and see a red light ahead. You stop. You don't have to think about it." Smiling, he continues, "Another example is to learn that deep breathing can help with anxiety and stress."

Doc: "Now it's time to introduce you to the major player in your mind and in your life. His or her name is Focker. Sometimes, I will refer to Focker in the masculine and sometimes in the feminine.

In many ways, Focker has no gender. In general, he is that part of your mind where things aren't going well. She likes to be in charge and for a sizeable portion of your life, he runs the show. When Focker is in charge, the you at Center is on 'auto pilot.' You are not in charge."

Frank: "I think I'm starting to understand. Can you give some examples of how Focker operates?"

Anna: "We're here because our Focker is in charge and it's not going well. I don't have the skills to keep Focker from doing and creating her stuff. So I just give up and feel helpless. Is that true?"

Doc: "Yes."

Rob: "Focker is doin' some funky shit and I don't know how to stop him."

Doug: "Is Focker responsible for my drinking and pills?"

Doc: "Your Focker is convinced you can't make it without drinking and pills."

Melinda: "Is Focker responsible for my despair and depression?"

Doc: "Those emotions are complicated, but Focker would have a role because it is in her nature to be in despair and depressed."

Me: "Are my flashbacks, nightmares, and panic attacks coming from Focker?"

Doc: "Flashbacks, nightmares, intrusive memories and thoughts most often come from the unconscious mind. But Focker has a role to play because of his pessimism, guilt, anger, rage, despair, stress, worry, depression, anxiety, and different types of fears. Panic attacks out of the blue most often come from the unconscious mind. Focker can create situational panic because of his, 'what ifs' and various other forms of fear. Each of you is here because your Focker is out of control and you haven't found a way to do anything about it. Your Focker lives in your head and you live at Center."

Doc: "I'm suggesting that you are not Focker. You are separate and you can operate and function independently from him. You did that a few minutes ago in the exercise. Everyone hold out your hand.

You could say your mind is the fingers and you are in the Center of the palm of your hand. You are connected, but you are still separate. Your thumb and forefinger contain your objective data, your little finger and ring finger contain the lessons you have learned, and your middle finger is Focker."

Melinda: "Could you say more about the 'me' at Center?"

Doc: "You at Center are the decision maker, the gate keeper, the responder, the creator, the planner, the reflector, the contemplator, the learner, the mediator, the observer, the experiencer, the philosopher, and the evaluator to name a few. You, the Melinda at Center is supposed to be in charge, running the show and making good and healthy decisions about your life. Focker, however, has worn you down and is now quite often running the show. We'll talk more about the 'you' at Center later. For now, I would like to help you work on defining and getting to know your mother Focker."

Doc: "I would like for each of you to choose a first name for your Focker."

Paul: "How about 'Dip Shit?'"

Doc smiling: "Thank you Paul. I want you all to see your Focker like a misguided child who needs your help. So I ask you to dispense with such names as Dip Shit, Asshole, Stupid, Crazy, Bad, and so on. In order to help Focker, you guys need to be able to talk."

Chad smiling: "You mean we're going to be talking to ourselves? That's what crazy people do."

Doc: "People who have more serious mental issues sometimes talk to themselves. The difference is they don't know they're doing it and you will be aware of having these conversations. As was mentioned a few minutes ago, some of you already have dialogue with your Focker about eating right, exercising, and drinking, but we're going to take it to another level."

Paul: "I've already named my Focker, Hank. Let me give it a shot. 'Hank, I getting' fuckin' tired of your shit filled flashbacks and if you don't shut the fuck up, I'm gonna kick your ass.' Hank replies, 'You fuckin' piece of shit. If you hadn't volunteered us for that fuckin' war, I wouldn't be in the fuckin' shape I'm in now. Who's gonna kick whose ass?' I reply, "Prepare to die you son of a bitch. I'm gonna take a fuckin' gun and blow your brain's out." Hank replies, "You're just dumb enough to do it. What the fuck do you think is gonna happen to your ass when you blow our brains out?' I reply, "I can do without my fucking middle finger!!"

Everyone was enjoying the show.

Doc smiling: "I think Paul made the point. We just have to work on the content of the dialogue."

Frank: "Focker stirs up all kinds of stuff and over powers us. You're going to teach the 'me' that lives here at Center to intervene and help with the situation?"

Doc: "Yes. Has everyone thought of a name? You can always change it. The first name for my Focker is Harvey."

Paul: "Doc, part of your brain ain't working either?"

Doc: "That's right!"

Paul: "If you can't get Harvey Focker under control, how am I supposed to get Hank Focker to stop being a dip shit? Sorry Doc."

Ace: "Doc's Focker is a lot smaller than our Fockers. Another way to say that is he has a little Focker and we have big Fockers."

(Laughter)

Paul: "Got it!!"

Doc: "OK. What names did you come up with?"

Paul: "Hank Focker."

Frank: "Huck Focker."

Nate: "Barr Focker."

Doug: "Hill Focker."

Rob: "Mac Focker."

Jett: "Tug Focker."

Ace: "Fark Focker."

Anna: "Pee Wee Focker."

Melinda: "Tilda Focker."

Chad: "Lanco Focker."

Doc: "Close your eyes and adjust your body so you are sitting up straight with both feet flat on the floor." It got quiet and Doc continued, "Some of you may be wondering and curious about where all of this is going to lead. Focker has thoughts of skepticism and cynicism. Notice when you shift your attention from those thoughts to your breathing that those thoughts just vanish for a time...and maybe they come back and you shift again to your breathing. Know that as you continue the training that you will become more skilled in quieting your mind, your Focker. A little while ago you discovered a part of yourself that you didn't know existed; a part that can step outside your problems and take charge and figure out what needs to be done. I don't know if you understand that or whether it will take you a few more days to figure out how helpful this part is going to be, but I do know that if you will trust this path, you will soon experience a freedom from the horrors of this war. Now, embrace this moment in the stillness and quietness of being attentive to your breathing. Let it feel nice and freeing that in this moment, you don't need to do anything except pay attention to the flowing of air in and out of your lungs.... Open your eyes."

Me: "Will you ever talk to Tug Focker or will you always be talking to me?"

Doc: "Tug will hear everything I say, but I will always be talking to you. You will be the one talking to Tug."

Frank: "How do I respond to being told by Huck Focker that he's been running the show and doesn't intend to give up the power?"

Doc: "You can ask, 'Is that so?'"

Frank: "And he will say, 'Yeah, that's so smart ass.'"

Ace: "What if Fark Focker doesn't listen and over powers me?"

Doc: "His days are numbered. He may over power you now, but that won't last much longer."

Ace: "And you're going to teach us the skills we need to do that?"

Doc: "Yes."

Doc: "Close your eyes and begin taking deep breaths, focusing all your attention on your breathing. If your Focker starts chattering or talking, shift the focus back to your breathing....Now let Focker talk for a few moments...and now shift back to your breathing. You can be in charge but Focker still has a lot of power so it will take some time to build your skills. This training is designed to teach you those skills to put Focker in quiet mode. Open your eyes."

Nate: "Barr Focker had the floor most of the time."

Paul: "I didn't wanna make Hank shut up. He kept talkin' about how good a cold beer would taste."

Doc: "Hank has no investment in getting well, because he will lose his power to stay in charge and drink."

Frank: "In this model, where are the good and healthy thoughts?"

Doc: "They live at the Center. More on that later."

Anna: "I think I'm starting to get it. Pee Wee kept interrupting my focus at Center, but I was able to regain my focus. I'm struggling with the idea that Pee Wee is separate from me, but still a part of me."

Doc: "You are making the decision that Pee Wee resides in your head, but you do not identify with her. She has no role in defining who you are. Pee Wee is caught up and totally focused in the past and future. You, Anna are seeking to focus in the moment. You were able to do that in the exercise where you had no memory. When you are focusing on your breathing, time does not exist because there is only the moment. Pee Wee is the one who is caught up in the past and the future."

Frank: "Again, so Focker lives in my head and I live at Center?"

Doc: "Yes. That's the way I like to think about it. Before we explore the 'you' at Center, let's get more information on Focker. There are essentially four components to Focker - thinking, feeling, physical, and behaving."

Doc: "We're focusing on PTSD so let's take each component and see if we can come up with a general idea about Focker and his part in PTSD. Keep in mind that these are general ideas and that you will eventually be working with me on creating your own definition of your Focker. I'm going to use newsprint to list the ideas."

Doc: "I've given you some general ideas about Focker. You give me the ideas and I'll write them on the newsprint.

<u>FOCKER'S PTSD</u>

<u>THOUGHTS:</u>

We should feel guilty that our friend/s died and we made it out alive.

We need to suffer to make up for being alive when some friends are dead.

We killed innocent civilians and we're a piece of shit.

We should have refused to do some of the shit we did. We're a coward.

We'll never recover; our life sucks.

We have no reason to live and no purpose in life.

The only way to survive is to drown our pain in booze and drugs.

Our life is a waste.

We resent/hate the people who sent us to war.

You can't trust people.

We can't get our mind to stop racing.

We no longer know the meaning of love.

Nothing matters anymore.

We lost our faith in God.

<u>FEELINGS:</u>

Scared, depressed, paranoid, lonely, angry, suspicious, terrified, anxious, miserable, uptight, useless, guilty, aggressive, embarrassed, ashamed, desperate, vulnerable, hopeless, stubborn, and cynical.

PHYSICAL:

Muscle tension and tightness, low energy, muscle pain, nausea, shortness of breath, pain/pressure in chest, heart racing, sweating, choking sensation, dizzy or light-headed, numbness, tingling sensation.

BEHAVIOR:

Getting drunk and/or high on pills.
Isolation from family and friends.
Getting into fights.
Sabotage relationships.
Always on lookout for danger.
Hypervigilant.
Difficulty getting and/or staying asleep.
Avoiding crowds.

Frank: "Focker was saying 'we' this and 'we' that. So Huck knows I exist?"

Doc: "Yes, for the most part you guys have been 'big buds.' He has had control and you have gone along with pretty much whatever he wanted. That's why he's not happy about you bringing him to this group. He feels threatened and for good reason."

Doc: "This is a good general description of Focker's PTSD. The common response to all that stuff is to judge it as bad. I'm asking you to suspend judgment on your Focker and simply say all things associated with Focker are not working for you. Until a few minutes ago, you totally identified with your Focker and if he is judged as bad, then you're bad. If you judge Focker and see her as the enemy, you will have a real fight on your hands. Some people end up running from their Focker or deny that he exists."

Ace: "I run away and deny. After a moment he said, "That's what I've done all my life."

Nate: "Tell me one more time. What's wrong with wanting to kick the shit out of Barr Focker?"

Doc: "If you fight Barr, he will dig in and be an incredible opponent. Be patient. I'm going to teach you how to deal with him."

Doc: "There is a similar dynamic in the Bible around the word, 'sin.' I can't speak for any of you, but when I hear the word sin or sinner, I think of something bad. You may or may not know that The New Testament is written in Greek. The meaning of the Greek word for sin is actually translated as a 'wrong turn.' That takes away the sting of the word. So if I sin, I'm not a bad person. I made a wrong turn. So instead of carrying around the guilt and all that goes with that, I can start figuring out how to get Centered and make the right turn."

Paul: "So wrong turns and right turns are neither good nor bad.

Doc: "Yes. Focker's wrong turns are not working for you and the right turns you are making at Center are working well. With the acceptance of this philosophy, you will never have any problems. You will only have situations."

Chad: "I think I understand what you're getting at, but what about the act of killing civilians which could include children. Are you saying that we should look at that as either working for us or not working for us?"

Doc: "I know from talking to each of you that many in this room were put in position where they were ordered to kill civilians and in some cases gave the order to kill civilians. That is the insanity of war. The human race has never figured out a way to live in peace with each other. Killing another human being for whatever reason is a tragedy beyond description."

Doc: "I am proposing that it is not healthy and most often destructive to judge Focker or any behavior in the past as good or bad, but to accept it as something that happened that we can never change. You are left with the choice to let Focker do whatever and live in a state of suffering, agony, shame, and guilt or find a path to the truth that will set you free."

Nate: “I’m ready for some truth that will get me free.”

“Me too,” was murmured throughout the room.

Doc: “Who is this ‘you’ who can have a Focker and yet refuse to allow this Focker to define you? Who is this ‘you’ who can observe and witness Focker thinking? Who is this ‘you’ who can learn the skills needed to discover that freedom? You have agreed for now to say your home is at Center.” He places his palm over his chest.

Doc: “Many years ago there was a group of people sitting around a fire talking to the wise one of the village. They were saying how restless they had been over their lives. One of the group spoke up and said, ‘Wise One, we have looked for peace and contentment many different places and we have everything we want, but we are still restless. Where do we find this precious gift?’ The wise one said, ‘Your seeking has been wasted. What you long for is right here.’ They looked around saying, ‘Where, where is it, tell us where it is.’ The wise one smiled and said, ‘It is inside you.’”

Doc looked at all of us and said, “You are about to embark on a journey that will change your life forever. It is the journey of discovering what many wise ones over the centuries have called, ‘your true self.’ In some ways you have been training and preparing for these experiences all of your life. You just didn’t know it. And over the last three weeks, you have had more training and preparation. Now you are ready to begin the adventure of exploring this home within you which has been there all the time, this home that we will call your Center.”

Doc: “Close your eyes and focus on your breathing. Notice the air moving gently in and out of your body, perhaps already noticing your mind becoming quiet and free of thoughts and thinking. Feel your body letting go and relaxing…and now find yourself in a forest on a path. It is quiet here…with only the sound of some birds and what appears to be the running water of a small brook. A few sunbeams are spreading light in places across the floor of the forest and after awhile, you notice the path begins to wind down deeper into a ravine and a little further you find a small clearing and at the end of the clearing, there is a door draped in vines. Without knowing how or why, you know that on the other side of that door is your new home. After years of wandering and searching, you are about to discover your true self and in the process find the truth that will set you free. Behind that door you will find the setting for your new home. Perhaps it's in a forest such as this, perhaps on a deserted beach, perhaps somewhere you have never been but always wanted to go. Take a moment and when you are ready, reach out for the handle. The door will open easily and you can walk through it and bask in the radiance of your new home. Open it now. Look around and open your senses - listen, see, smell, touch, and feel. See if you can leave everything in your brain behind and focus all your attention on checking out, exploring this place without any memories of any other past experiences. Take some time to walk and be totally present there. Be curious about what you see and how you feel and what observations you make about this new place. Perhaps you will notice how fresh and new this experience can be, totally free of past associations. Be open to the idea that in this place, you will find your true self even if you are not sure at this time what that means. Be curious; embrace this adventure, this experience. I don't know if you will start to feel at home here in this moment or whether you will need more time to feel comfortable and relaxed. Perhaps you can be open to the idea that this new home at Center means you will make changes in who you are and how you live. Take time to be present here. You might want to focus again on your breathing or you may just want to be still and quiet and look around. Take your time. This is your Center. Take a few more minutes and then open your eyes remembering that when you open your eyes, your Center is still within you. Open your eyes."

(Silence)

Nate: "I almost fell asleep."

Doc: "Nate, I believe Barr Focker had a say in that. I think he did everything he could to keep you from focusing on the experience.

Our Fockers think they are our true selves so they're not going to lie around and let you discover some other part that's going to take over their turf."

Anna: "I was in and out of the experience. Pee Wee was trying to distract me with other thoughts, but I was able to stay focused for over half of the time. I felt for awhile that I would be okay without my arm; that I could find happiness and a full life. Then Pee Wee started her shit and I let her suck me into feeling sorry for myself. She does that by thinking about all the people who have two arms and comparing us to them. I didn't judge her, but I wanted to think something different like it doesn't matter."

Doc: "The you at Center simply told Pee Wee it doesn't matter." Looking at us. "What if Anna at Center could reach the state where it really doesn't matter?"

Anna: "That would be part of the truth that sets me free. At this point, Pee Wee is still too strong."

Doc: "I promise you that will change."

Ace: "I think I did real well. Fark wasn't able to get through. Whenever he started with his shit, I focused on my breathing and had some good success staying with the experience. I had moments where I thought if I can do this for five minutes, maybe I could do it for ten minutes and so on."

Doug: "I'm still having some trouble with the visual part. I want to see this place, but most of the time, it's not clear. I think I understand the theory behind it and maybe it will come. Will I be able to get it if I can't see it?"

Doc: "Most definitely. I'll work with you individually on the visualization part and I think it will come easier later, but it is not necessary. The important thing is that you understand the concept and we'll weave other ways into the training to make it work for you. Is anyone else struggling with the visual part?" Several others raised their hands.

Others shared similar stories about their experience.

Me: "I was in and out of the experience and was also having a little trouble with the visualization."

Frank: "It was so quiet there. I didn't have enough time to explore. I could see some benefits of being Centered."

Doc: "Let's brainstorm them now and see what we can come up with."

Frank: "Here's what I came up with. We are leaving our Fockers behind. If we can stay at Center and not be pulled away by those same mother Fockers, we are in this place of stillness and quietness. By definition then, it has to be peaceful."

Doc: "Is everybody getting the idea that at Center, we will not allow our Focker to define who we are? We can separate and create our own reality."

Me: "Is our true self how we come into the world. When I look up at that Focker feeling list, I'm wondering how we as a human race reached this fucked-up state? I'm struggling with the whole concept of God, but if there is a God, surely He or She created us in the Center and we must have wandered out and hooked up with Focker. Maybe the definition of our true self at Center is what God intended us to be."

Melinda: "So why don't we explore what we imagine God wanted us to be?"

Ace: "Yeah, like what if we had not wandered away, what would we be like?"

Paul: "This shit is getting deeper."

Chad: "Paul that sounded like Hank Focker speaking?"

Paul: "I guess."

Chad: "Lanco has been driving me crazy. He just said to me, 'Now these people are playing God and pretending to know the mind of God.'

Doug: "How did you know it was Lanco?" Maybe it was you."

Chad: "Because I think we are onto something that can help us. I've never heard anything like this approach and I'm desperate and I'm determined to find out if this is gonna work. Lanco doesn't say anything that's helpful. He's scared and also desperate, but he doesn't trust any of you, especially Doc. He's had some tough experiences where he trusted people and got burned."

Frank: "So what are some traits at Center that would define our true self?"

There was a lot of discussion and Doc wrote the list on the newsprint:

Peaceful	Calm in the midst of a storm
Loving	Lives in the moment
Accepting	Awake
Compassionate	Open
Non-judging	The observer
Free	Passionate
Grateful	Clarity
Forgiving	Patient
Joyful	Curious
Flexible	Wise
Attentive	Alert

Frank: "If we had said nothing about God, would this list be the same? Is this, in a general way, who we are when we get rid of our Fockers or when we go to Center and just be quiet?"

Ace: "Does it make any difference?"

Frank: "I don't know. I'm like Jett. I have some problems with God. I'm not sure if I'm comfortable bringing God into my experience here."

Ace: "So why don't you just leave God out of it and say this is the list you would come up with if you quieted your mind and go to Center?"

Doc: "Remember, all ideas are vulnerable and open to questioning. What I have come to believe over the years is that these and similar traits represent our true self or our true nature. This is who we are without the contamination of fear and the self-focused mentality of our Fockers. We all live out of our true nature from time to time, but you are in some areas of your life caught up in your Focker and that's why you're here. My goal is to help you awaken with more clarity, power, and vitality the traits you see up here on this newsprint. To use our model, my job is to help you be more Centered in your life."

Melinda: "If that's what it means to be Centered, I want more of that."

Doc: "These are general traits. As time passes you must define your own Center. For the rest of your life, if you follow this model, you will be asking, 'What does it mean to be Centered in this situation?' And you will have the skills in most instances to get Centered."

Rob: "You mean, in most instances, we will never be perfect?"

Doc: "Yes."

Melinda: "I'm ready to keep going."

Doc: "Remember how Focker had four dimensions to his existence. In addition to the traits some of which are feelings, your Center has the same dimensions: thoughts, feelings, physical, and behavioral. When you are Centered, what are you thinking in relation to your PTSD? This question will be valid for all other aspects of your life. When you are Centered, what are you thinking in relation to your family, your work, your friends, your life in general? Our focus is on the PTSD. So looking at those Centered traits and remembering your Focker and your symptoms, what are your Centered thoughts?"

Doc had to help us with this experience. There was lively discussion on many of the points and not everyone was comfortable with the group consensus. Some parts Doc asked us to consider the possibility and we could decide later for ourselves.

YOUR TRUE SELF AT CENTER

THOUGHTS:

I cannot change the past; it is what it is.
My memory of the past is just that; a memory.
I can choose how I respond to my memories.

I regret some choices I made in combat situations.
I accept those choices.
I make restitution where possible.
I will mourn the loss of my friends.
I have a past, but it does not define me.
I can experience peace and love in my life.
I am free from worry about the future.
This moment is all there is.
I am at peace.
I do not judge myself or others.
I accept without judgment flashbacks, nightmares, and panic attacks.

<u>FEELINGS:</u>
See the list of Centered traits. Some are feelings as well as traits.

<u>PHYSICAL:</u>
Energized, flowing, fluid, balance and harmony, relaxed, and loose.

<u>BEHAVIOR:</u>
Practicing Centering skills
Being non-judgmental to self and others
Embracing the moment
Loving relationships
Sensitivity to others
Acts of kindness
Taking care of the body through exercise, nutrition, and sleep

Doc: "These are not going to cover all the goals we've listed. We'll add to this list as we go along."

Doc: "Close your eyes, take some deep breaths and go to your Center. You can use the previous suggestion of walking through the forest or you can imagine walking down some steps or floating down or just taking a few more deep breaths. Over time you will decide how you quiet your mind and go to Center. After more training, you will be able to go in a moment's notice and simply be there in an instant. For now, take a little longer and use a little more of your imagination. As before when you first discovered this place, open all your senses and feel the energy.... You are considering this to be the home of your true self and how does it feel in this moment to be peaceful, loving, compassionate, free, patient, clear, and forgiving....Perhaps now open to the idea that this new home at Center means you will be making some changes in how you live and how you make decisions. Take some time now to be present here. You might want to take more deep breathes or you may want to be still and quiet and look around. Take your time....This is your home....Take a few more minutes and then open your eyes remembering that when you open your eyes, your Center is still with you. Open your eyes."

Frank: "I don't get it. When I opened my eyes, I wasn't there anymore. I was back here."

Doc: "You never went anywhere. You were always right here. In the same way, your Center is always with you. To understand more clearly this concept, I asked you to consider choosing a place that symbolizes your Center. It gives you a kind of command Center from which to live and function. It is located in the middle of your chest at heart level. Your Center has always been here." He placed his hand in the middle of his chest. "You just didn't realize it.

Doc: "You thought you and Focker were the same person. In the beginning, you will go to this place many times to personalize it and make it your home. It is here where you will find the truth that sets you free. It is here that you will rest in the quietness and stillness and discover how to spend more of your life in the moment with an overall feeling of inner peace. If you get caught up into Focker's journey, you can close your eyes, take a couple of deep breaths and go to Center and awaken again to who you are."

Ace: "I sometimes don't know who the fuck I am. You are saying I will find out who I am at Center."

Doc: "Finding all the answers to who we are is quite an undertaking. I can promise when you finish this group that you'll have a lot of answers to that question. It's my hope that each of you will also know there will be many more discoveries to be made on your journey."

Anna: "I think I understand what you're saying about being Centered. I'm also seeing it like a training area and Doc is the trainer. I train at my Center and when I open my eyes, I'm ready to begin taking this training with me into the challenges of PTSD and the living of my life. Remember, that's what we did in the Service. We trained and we took those skills into combat. I believe it's the same thing."

Frank: "That helps. Thanks Anna."

Chad: "We train at Center and at some point, we will be able to bring our Center with us when we open our eyes. Some challenges will be more difficult than others. At some point, being Centered in some areas becomes easier and we don't have to think about it. We just do it."

Doc: "You guys are starting to get it more quickly than I did when I first heard these ideas. I think it means you're highly motivated and perhaps smarter than me."

Paul: "That's true. I think I'll take over teaching this stuff next group session."

Nate: "Now there is some real heavy shit!"

Silence and then Doc: "I'm always eager to know if anyone chose a particular setting for their Center."

Frank: "I chose a deserted beach."

Paul: "Stanley's"

Everyone laughed.

Doc: "If Paul wants it to be Stanley's, it's not worse or better than Frank's beach. It's simply Paul's place where he feels comfortable and at home."

Melinda: "Beach."

Chad: "A special lookout about thirty miles down the Parkway."

Ace: "Woods."

Me: "It's a knoll about five minutes walk from here." I might not have picked that place if it weren't for Eden, but I didn't care. That was my place.

Rob: "I was on my bike the whole time so my place at Center was moving."

Doc: "That's a good point. It's your home, it can be stationary or moving or whatever or wherever you want it to be."

Nate: "I had trouble finding a place, but I like Rob's idea. I'll be on my bike."

Doug: "There's a special place in the woods not far from our farm."

Anna: "I think I'll move mine around to different places. Maybe I'll settle on one place and maybe not."

Melinda: "So the idea is that we stay at Center and train to deal with our life moment by moment. Tilda says we should feel guilty because our best friend died and from Center, I respond by saying that we will miss her and be sad, but we will let the guilt go. And she says, 'How the hell are we going to do that?' Since I'm not sure yet how we do that, I tell her to be patient and that I'll get back with her later."

Doc: "Yes."

Silence and then Doc: "That's quite a bit to digest. Why don't we take a break? I'd like for you to pair up with someone other than your buddy. Get your drink and find a place where you can talk about what we just covered. I want you to come back with questions for the group. I don't want us to move forward until everyone understands the process. I will ring the bell."

We all stood up and kind of hesitated. Anna and Melinda walked toward each other and embraced and cried. I went over to Doug and he nodded and said, "I've got some coffee in the truck. Would you like some?"

I wanted something cold, but said, "Sure, do you want me to get a cup?"

He said, "Yeah, how 'bout I meet you out back. Bring Spot if you want to."

Even though Doc said Spot could stay with the group, I put him in my room. We didn't need any reason not to give our total focus to what Doc was teaching us. I got Spot, made sure everyone who needed ice got it and got me a cup and went out the back door. Doug was waiting for me at the end of the porch, sitting on the steps smoking a cigarette. He rubbed Spot's head and let him lick his face and talked to him. Spot had a friend for life. He poured some black coffee in my cup. He smiled and said, "Almost every time I pour coffee out of this thermos, it reminds me of an old crusty lieutenant colonel who was our battalion commander years ago. When we were out in the field, he would have the mess sergeant fill a gallon tin can half full of coffee grounds, pour in the water, and let it simmer over a fire for five or six hours. It looked like syrup and I don't know how he got it down." He chuckled to himself.

I smiled and said, "I want to thank you."

He looked puzzled, "For what?"

"For the numerous times you saved my life."

He looked more puzzled. "Do I know you?"

"Yes and no. I am all those young soldiers who are alive because of you. And you are all those career soldiers who saved our young asses from doing stupid shit and getting ourselves killed."

He smiled, "That's mighty kind of you to say that. It gives an old soldier like me something to feel good about. I did the best I could although sometimes it didn't work out. We lost some fine young men and women and sometimes I blame myself. I guess Doc is trying to help us get over all the old wounds and scars. Sometimes I wonder if I'm too old to grasp this kind of thinking."

I responded, "I don't think it has anything to do with age. I'm struggling too."

Conversation was easy between us. We talked about our Army experiences and had some laughs. We didn't talk about what Doc was teaching us. It was more important for me to get to know him. I was afraid he would stop coming and I wanted him to know I respected him and cared about him. These old soldiers literally saved our lives. I wanted to give something back. He seemed to enjoy talking about old times. Soon, we heard the bell. I thanked him for the coffee and we went inside.

Doc: "Would anyone like to share questions or comments that came up during the break?"

Chad: "Rob and I were still struggling not to judge our Focker as bad. He causes a lot of problems."

Doc: "It's human nature to see Focker as bad and the Center as good. At Center, we are working on the traits of acceptance and non-judging. When referring to an experience, we sometimes say, 'it is what it is.' That's another way of saying you can't change it so accept it and don't judge it. Tilda says to Melinda, 'Go ahead and eat a piece of that cake.' Instead of Melinda saying, 'Shut up you bitch,' she says from Center, 'Tilda, that's not gonna work. I want us to lose a few pounds and eating a piece of that cake is not gonna work for us right now.' I believe she has a much better chance of walking away from the cake if she stays Centered."

Paul: "So Tilda is not a bitch, she just wants a fucking piece of cake."

Ace: "Fark is thinking right now that tonight we're going to go to Stanley's and get drunk. I'm going to Center and accept and not judge Fark. I'm going to tell him that getting drunk is not working for us. And he may overpower me, but soon I'll have the skills to make that decision not to go get drunk."

Frank: "I'm trying to put this together. Each one of us has been to hell and back. The memories of these experiences are traumatic and sickening and abhorrent. You said earlier that since we can't change our history, there is no point to judging it as good or bad. But what if we go back to that moment, how would we look at those moments in our lives?"

Doc: "Let's talk more about these memories of combat. Let's label these intrusive memories as, 'bad and destructive to life.' We are frightened of them and want to get rid of them, suffocate them, erase them, destroy them, escape them, kill them, push them away, control them and be free. That's what we've been taught and its human nature according to our culture. Slay the enemy! That simply means we have a fight on our hands and as I said earlier, 'fighting always makes things worse.' Our training will show you a more effective path."

Doc: "Most of you have done things you are ashamed of and feel guilty about and you are torturing yourself. Some of you believe that you deserve to suffer as punishment for what you've done. Hopefully, at some point you wake up to the idea that nothing helpful is gained by continuing to punish yourself."

Doc: "I'm going to repeat myself and will continue to do it until you all at least have a clear understanding of what I'm saying. It took me a while too. So if you agree that there is no benefit to punishing yourself, the next step is to accept the fact there is nothing you can do to change your history. You are left with the choice of how you respond to that history, how you think about it, how you understand it, how you feel about it, how you live with it, and how, in the midst of your life, you find the path, the course that offers you the chance to have a life with some measure of happiness and peace."

Frank: "I want to hear myself say this again. So the response to these memories is to stop labeling and experiencing them as something bad and traumatic. They are not good or bad; they are memories. That helps us stop fighting them and running from them and labeling them as anything other than memories. They are what they are and there's nothing that can be done about it."

Doc: "Yes, as you learn how to take that first step of acceptance without judgment, something interesting happens. You notice that they, after awhile, begin to fade and lose their intensity."

Rob: "So how does that work? I can try to stop saying they're bad memories and that they're just memories, but I don't think that by itself will help me stop running from 'em or having this sick feeling inside."

Doc: "Good question and good point Rob. So out of the blue, you have a flashback where you're riding down a road and take hostile fire and find cover and tend to your buddy who got shot in the leg. You're yelling for a medic and can't get the bleeding to stop. You're in panic mode. The flashback fades. While you were having the flashback, you started to sweat, your heart was racing, and your chest was tight. All of this happens in a matter of seconds."

Doc: "At this stage of your training, you're not sure what to do except take deep breaths. I think most of you would say at this point in your training that the deep breaths don't help much. What if you decide to continue practicing the deep breathing and become a master in that skill? Can you imagine that if you have that much control over your body that this would be a huge help? Think about all the physical symptoms related to a flashback. If you relax your body, slow your heart rate, release tension and tightness, get your breathing under control, you will be making huge strides in dealing with flashbacks. It's human to be like Ace and create boredom. The Master said, 'Keep picking up the books and when I think you're ready, we will proceed with the training.'"

Doc: "Later you will discover that at Center there is no fear. That's a challenge to understand right now, but you will experience it later. With the absence of fear, that acceptance gives you back what you lost along the way and that is your ability to do something different other than freaking out. You now have other choices and later you will find out the nature of those choices. Having choices brings a lot of relief to the situation. And you'll find those choices at Center."

Chad: "You said a minute ago that the memories start to lose their intensity and there is no fear at Center. Does that mean if we're Centered we won't be afraid?"

Doc: "Yes."

Melinda: "So when I lock my doors at night and keep my .45 in the drawer next to my bed, I'm not being Centered?"

Doc: "Do you do those things because you're afraid or because you're aware that some people are violent and will harm you if they have the chance?"

Melinda: "I'm more aware than I'm afraid."

Doc: "Remember at Center, one of the traits is clarity."

Frank: "What about being Centered when you're ordered to clear the enemy out of that abandoned house?"

Doc: "How many would be afraid?"

We all raised our hands including Doc who asked, "So how do we look at that fear?"

Anna: "I'm not going to judge that fear as bad or wrong or inappropriate."

Doc: "Yes. So, you are partly Centered by not judging the feeling. Maybe that fear kept you alive. Regardless there is no judgment. We embrace the fear and do our job."

Rob: "What if the fear paralyzes you and you can't do your job?"

Doc: "Would someone else like to respond?"

Doug: "You grab him by the collar and yell at him and tell him you don't give a shit about his fear and get his ass in the truck right fucking now and give him a shove with your boot. Sometimes that works and sometimes it doesn't. One guy just sat down and bawled. Luckily we were in a situation where there was a medic close by and we left him behind. I've had guys tell me later that they were glad I pushed them."

Doc: "So if you're the guy who sat down, what's next?"

Anna: "You've got some major shit to deal with. I think everyone here has witnessed or may have even experienced something similar.

My guess is there will be lots of guilt and shame and self-loathing and God only knows what else. And you just hope he or she has someone like Doc to help. Depending on the situation and if his actions put other soldiers in harm's way, I might be really pissed off and judgmental and critical and so on. I hope after a short period of time, I would be able to get Centered and not judge the soldier and not even judge my reaction. Perhaps I'd be more compassionate. I think that frees me up to see the broader picture. This soldier might be put in the stockade or he might end up in the psych ward at a hospital."

Doc: "Anna's example demonstrates another benefit from not judging Focker as bad. You discover more energy and clarity to make choices that are working or will work for you."

Frank: "What was the other benefit again?"

Doc: "You notice that the intensity of the memory begins to fade over a period of time. Focker loves a good fight. If you stop fighting him, he may start to lose interest."

Me: "In Anna's example, she said at Center she did not judge the soldier. We've been talking about not judging Focker. It sounds like being Centered also means not to judge others. Is that true?"

Doc: "That's part of my personal definition of being Centered and from what Anna said, she implied she feels the same way."

Anna: "I was taught all my life not to judge others. I haven't done really well with that all the time, but it's an on-going goal."

Doc: "You are training to use your Center as a lens or portal through which you see and experience all parts of your life. Focker already has her lens and portal in place and will not allow you to come in and take over just because some older asshole suggests that Focker's present lens and portal might not be working. And because you're choosing to refrain from labeling either Focker or your Center as good or bad, you begin to explore the nature of your Center, your new home, and in the process you will perhaps discover the truth that sets you free from Focker and some of the stuff that's not working."

Frank: "What do you mean by 'perhaps' and 'some of the stuff that's not working'?"

Doc: "Perhaps means it's a challenge and it will require commitment and determination. I hope each one of you will make that choice, but I have no way of knowing if that will happen. 'Some of the stuff that's not working' means that nobody gets it all worked out. I've been at this quite a while and as I said earlier, I still have some stuff left to deal with. Some people who know and love me would say, 'He's a lot better than he used to be.'"

Frank: "As I said before, that's still a little discouraging. If you can't get your stuff worked out, how are we going to get our stuff worked out?"

Doc: "I think it's important not to limit yourself based on what someone else can or can't do. I had my own heavy stuff earlier in life and worked through it and can say overall I am content and peaceful with my life. I sincerely believe all of you can reach that same state if you are willing to commit to the work and training ahead."

Chad: "Could you give us more information on how this Centering works?"

Doc: "There are many facets that we will explore, but I'll give you an idea. Recent research tells us that over a period of time, the Centered thoughts can become more powerful than Focker's old thoughts that aren't working. This research calls thoughts, 'circuits.' Let's take the example of the Centered thoughts or circuits that say, 'I cannot change the past; it is what it is. My memory of the past is just that; a memory. I accept it for what it is. Traumatic memories are bad and you have to fight to get rid of them.' Over a period of time the new Centered thoughts or circuits replace Focker's old thoughts or circuits. Much of our training is teaching you how to empower and strengthen those new Centered thoughts or circuits."

Rob: "Will we ever reach the skill level where we never have flashbacks, nightmares, or panic attacks?"

Doc: "We can never say something like you'll never have another flashback, nightmare, or panic attack. What I can say is that if you complete the training and continue to practice your skills, you'll be pleased with the results. That means the intensity will be greatly reduced and choosing a Centered response will be much easier. I know I have said this before, but as the training continues, you will have more clarity about the process. However, feel free to ask more questions now."

Ace: "So, we create Centered experiences that work for us and Focker creates experiences that are not working for us. Is that correct?

Doc: "We talked earlier about how we live on, 'auto pilot.' Sometimes on auto pilot, we are Centered and working-well-stuff is happening and sometimes we are on auto pilot and Focker is in control and not-working-well-stuff is happening. Even though we are not consciously aware of creating those experiences when on auto pilot, it's important to remember that we are ultimately responsible for creating all our experiences. Remember, if we don't understand that reality, we are trapped and can't change."

Doc: "One of the goals is to be able to live on Centered-auto-pilot. In many ways, it's like developing some Centered habits. Right now you have a lot of Focker habits and you're here to build more Centered habits. That's another way of saying again your goal is to strengthen and empower those Centered circuits."

Doc pointed to the Centered ideas on the newsprint that we came up with a little while ago. "These are a guide to help you decide if you are Centered in relationship to PTSD. The Centered traits we listed will help you decide how you are doing in all aspects of your life. As time passes, you will discover how to decide on your definition of Center as it relates to the specific situations in your life."

Anna: "It seems like being Centered is quite a challenge. If we're saying that is how God created us and intended us to be or that our true self is our natural self, why does it seem so difficult? Or I guess I should ask, 'Do you think it's difficult for most people?'"

Doc: "I think that's true Anna. I've thought myself and heard countless other people say that it's easier to let Focker do his thing than make the choice to be Centered?"

Frank: "Why is that?"

Doc: "Human beings have a tendency to be extremely self-focused. Our Focker is the champion of 'What's in it for me? What am I getting out of it? I'm right and you're wrong.' The list is seemingly endless."

Frank: "That sounds pessimistic."

Doc: "There are some really good things happening in our world, but in my view, the Fockers of the human race run rampant through all walks of life and control most of what happens on our planet. I believe being Centered is a challenge for all of us. Having said that, let's move on. I would be happy to discuss what Frank calls my pessimistic ideas on this topic with any of you during our individual sessions."

Doc: "Let me summarize this last few minutes. If you are ultimately responsible for your Focker, you are not trapped or a prisoner of Focker and his philosophy that your past defines you and the future will kick you in the ass if you're not prepared. At Center, you, your true self comes to the realization that for the most part through no fault of your own, you have created a monster with a lot of power. Because you understand and acknowledge that you have created Focker, you are now free to create something new and different. You have made the decision and commitment to engage in the training to live from your Center where you can embrace this moment and live it to the fullest. For starters, this will free you from the illusion that your past defines you and you better be scared and worried about the future."

Ace: "It's been hard for me to accept responsibility for some of the shit that I've created."

Doc: "I think that's true for all of us. I'm hoping to excite in each of you the perception that you are in charge of your own journey. You are not stuck and you will find the path at Center that will take you in the direction you chose for yourself. I hope each one of you will make that commitment to stay engaged in this training process. I'm eager for you to have an open mind and be curious about how all of this will come together."

Doc: "Focker will throw up many reasons for you to take off and get outta here. My guess is that several of you almost didn't come today. I want you to understand what you're dealing with so this is a good time to talk about Focker's resistance to getting better."

Melinda: "Tilda Focker worked on me this morning and kept saying this stuff is not gonna work. I almost didn't get out of bed. Then I thought it wouldn't be fair to Chad since it was my turn to drive."

Several others said they had similar thoughts and feelings.

Doc: "Focker fears change. She wants to call the shots and doesn't like being told what to do. Focker believes that he can take care of business without interference from you. You know Focker really well because until a week ago, you thought you were Focker so get back in her head and come up with some ideas about the resistance to healing and change. I'll write them down on the newsprint."

The group came up with the following:

Doug: "Fear of the unknown"

Rob: "What if it's uncomfortable."

Rob: "I may have to share my feelings."

Anna: "What if this doesn't work. What am I gonna do?"

Nate: "I may have to trust these people and I'd rather keep my distance."

Frank: "What if I lose control and go crazy."

Frank: "I'll have to interact with people."

Chad: "I'll have to give up feeling sorry for myself."

Chad: "I won't get any sympathy."

Ace: "I won't have an excuse for getting drunk."

Nate: "I won't have an excuse for being angry."

Melinda: "I'll have to stop being a victim."

Me: "I'll have to talk to people."

Melinda: "I'll have to stop suffering and feeling guilty for being alive."

Anna: "I won't be able to feel sorry for myself."

Melinda: "I lost my best friend in a mortar attack. She's dead. What right do I have to feel good? I get to suffer."

Doc: "How many of you lost friends?"

Everyone raised their hand.

Doc: "How many of you feel like Melinda?"

Everyone raised their hands.

Me: "Sometimes I feel like if I get better and have somewhat of a normal life, I'm being disloyal to my friends who got killed. So like Melinda, I get to suffer."

Frank: "Or I'll forget about them and dishonor that memory. So I get to punish myself for being alive."

Nate: "I feel guilty saying this but if I get better I might lose my disability check."

Paul: "Well, how 'bout if it don't work we all kick Doc's ass."

Everyone said, "Yeah!"

Doc smiled: "Okay, I got it. I better make this work. I hope each of you can see that resistance to getting better could be an obstacle to overcome. I'll be addressing this with you on an individual basis. Unless you're motivated to get better, Focker will convince you this group is not going to help and he will also let you know that he is getting very fed up with picking up the books."

Doc: "Close your eyes and focus on your breathing. Notice how when you pay attention to your breathing that all other thoughts fade away and your mind can concentrate on the air going in and out of your lungs. If Focker starts talking, be aware of how simple it is to shift your focus back to the breathing....I don't know if you have the hang of it now or whether it will take a little more time, just continue to practice and you will discover how to be more Centered in your life. Open your eyes.

Doc: "During our individual sessions, I will also be working with you on designing an exercise program and helping you assess your eating habits. How many of you are still struggling with sleep issues?"

Almost everyone raised their hand.

Doc: "I'll address that with you individually. For now, watch your caffeine intake after 6:00. If you have problems getting to sleep and/or wake up and can't get back to sleep, use your deep breathing to help quiet your mind and relax your body. Many people over the years have stated that helps them get to sleep or get back to sleep. Later we'll talk about some ideas related to decreasing the frequency and intensity of nightmares."

Doc: "Some of you are struggling with substance abuse of some kind. I urge you to consider and be thinking about Alcoholics Anonymous and Narcotics Anonymous. This is another topic we will discuss individually."

Doug: "I tried AA several times and I didn't like it and it didn't work."

Nate: "My Commanding Officer ordered me to go to AA and I had the same experience as Doug."

Chad: "My uncle went to AA and said it helped him. He still goes to meetings every week."

Doc: "For now, I'm just suggesting you think about it. We'll talk more about it later."

Paul: "I said last week that you people seemed cool, but you're really not that cool. They're some fucked up dudes in this room. Every time I look at you people, my head starts aching. I'm outta here."

Even though he was a cut-up, sometimes he caught most of us off guard. He was Anna's buddy and she knew him better than us and said in a loud command voice, "Private, on your feet. You will report here next Saturday at 0900 with a clean uniform and those disgusting boots polished so I can see my face in them. Is that understood?"

Paul: "Yes ma'am!" he responded in a loud military voice.

Anna: "At ease and take your seat." He saluted and sat down.

Smiling Anna reached over and popped him on the head and he threw up his arms as if he were being assaulted and yelled, "Soldier abuse. Somebody help me."

Nate in a loud voice said, "This is a fucked up group of people!"

Rob in a louder voice said, "Let's get outta here and go to Stanley's!"

A cheer rose from the group.

Doc smiling: "Hold on. No one's leaving here till you get your assignment for next week."

Group: "Boooooooooooooooooo!"

Doc: "Your homework for next Saturday is about the same as last week. In our individual work, we'll go over what we talked about today. Look over your notes from today and the descriptions of Focker's PTSD and Your True Self at Center and come up with questions. Leave no stone unturned. I want each one of you to be on board before we go forward. Every time I ask you to close your eyes, I call that a Centering Meditation. I don't mean to imply a spiritual meditation. You make it whatever you want. Anyway, I've got another CD for each of you with some Centering Meditations. Each time I give you another CD, the previous meditations will also be on the new CD. I would like you to listen to your CD at least twenty minutes twice a day. Remember, it's all part of your training. Are there any questions?"

There were no questions.

Doc: "Close your eyes and focus on your breathing....Be aware of the air moving in and out of your body and now slowly begin to breathe more deeply. As the air moves deep into your lungs, remember how those receptors activate a relaxation response in your body. Perhaps you can feel it right now....Imagine what it will be like when you reach the skill level of moving your body to that Centered state of flowing, fluid, relaxed, and calm...and remembering how powerful the breathing can be in helping you quiet your mind and be at Center to experience a stillness and peacefulness. Focusing on your breathing also means you are present in this moment, free totally of any memories of the past and any concerns about the future…and it's nice to know that if Focker tries to intrude into your moment, you can release her and let her go and come back to your breathing….There is a wonderful freedom in that you can choose in any particular moment to be focused on the here and now. Free of any intrusion in this moment and without knowing how or why, you entertain the idea that being Centered can prepare you in the days and weeks ahead to discover and/or find your path to healing….Be open to the idea that breathing becomes an important path to your Center...and it is at Center that you will find the truth that sets you free. For now, that can encourage you to keep practicing this skill even when Focker wants to do something different. Now let your breathing slow down and open your eyes."

Doc: "I would like us after group next Saturday to leave here and go to Memorial Park in Harvest and have a picnic lunch and engage in some physical activity. We should be finished around 3:00 or 4:00. I know some of you have a longer drive, but this is important. Is there anyone that can't make it?"

I almost instinctively raised my hand, but caught myself in time. Eden would be here, but she would understand.

Doc: "Dress for physical activity. Bring your own lunch and I'll bring soda, juice, and water. I decided not to bring beer until each one of you is clear about your goals regarding drinking and feels comfortable having beer so readily accessible. Go in peace and find time to play and laugh in the midst of your training."

Ace went over and talked to Doug. I was sure he was following my lead during the break. We had talked many times about how we loved the old soldiers. I knew he was also concerned that Doug would eventually leave us. Generally speaking, the old soldiers weren't a "touchy/feely" group. They were smiling and enjoying the conversation.

Melinda came up to me and said, "Jett, thank you for opening your home to us. It's beautiful here and perfect for this experience."

"You're welcome. I'm glad it's working out."

She said, "See you next week."

Doc packed-up his stuff and left. Everyone else seemed to be hanging around. Ace was talking to Doug. Paul had joined them. They were laughing. Anna, Melinda, and Frank were in a group. I was pretty sure they were officers. Rob and Nate, our two bikers, were engaged and Chad was walking toward me.

Chad asked, "Jett are you getting it?"

I responded, "I think I finally understand the importance of the breathing and I guess I understand the theory, but I'm still working on trying to connect all the dots."

"Yeah, that's about where I am." We talked then about our families and where we had been stationed and traded some Army stories. He was from Asheville. He told me his girlfriend had ditched him while he was on his second tour. He said she was "white" and her parents had never approved of them dating. They had planned to "run away" and get married when he came home. He had about two months left to go on his tour when he got the letter. It had been about five months and he was still devastated.

I asked, "Did you ever see her or get to talk with her?"

"No, I tried, but she would never return my calls. Soon after I got back, I followed her to one of the stores in town. Before I could get a word out, she told me it was over and to stay away from her. I prayed about it, but it still hurts. I think my PTSD is worse than it would have been. Melinda and I are partners or buddies as Doc likes to say and she's helped me."

About that time, Melinda came up to us and said, "Chad, I'm ready to go when you are. Take more time to talk with Jett if you like. I'll be in the car." She left.

He said, "We ride together since it takes us about an hour and a half to get here. I don't want to keep her waiting so I'll head on. Thanks for listening."

"I was glad to get to know you better and I'm sorry about your girlfriend."

"Thanks." He left.

Everyone was leaving. Ace came over and said, "I like Doug. I hope he will stay with us."

"Me, too."

41
A FRIENDSHIP WITH EDEN

"I'm going to meet April for lunch. When do you want us to hook up with you and Eden?"

"I'm picking her up at 1:00. I'm gonna suggest we get some take out, hike up to the overlook and eat up there. Then we'll probably ride around and look at more of the area. Why don't we plan to meet back here around 6:00."

"Do we have enough stuff to fix supper?"

I said, "How about hamburgers?"

"I don't care. We're low on beer and wine. April and I'll stop and get both. You can pick up any food stuff we need. You good?"

"Yeah, I'm good. See you later." He left.

I was feeling a little overwhelmed from the group. I needed to talk with Ace. We would find some time later. Now it was time to shift gears and that was a good thing.

When she came to the door, she looked more beautiful than ever. She had on jeans with a loose pink tee-shirt. She had on a white baseball hat and her hair was in a pony tail.

"Hello Jett. Come in."

We talked with Aunt Agnes for a few minutes and then left. She seemed glad I had brought Spot with me. I told her my idea and she said that would be fine. We stopped at Sally's and picked-up our lunch. We talked about what we had done the past week and soon pulled off the Parkway several miles from the turn off to the cabin. Eden wanted to carry the food and I carried the backpack with water and a couple of apples.

A Blue Ridge Overlook

"How did your appointment go with the Realtor?" I asked.

"It was fine. I have been thinking more this week about your idea that I consider building a house and I've decide that's what I want to do. I let her know and thanked her for helping me get a closer look at the community. She suggested we look at the three houses and we did. They were nice, but it helped me be clearer about building. She said she would be happy to look for a building site. I told her that I had a friend from here and that he had agreed to help me find a site. She asked me who my friend was and I told her. She knew your family and knew of you through a younger sister who had been in school with you."

"I'd like to show you more of the area this afternoon and the three of us are hoping you can join us for supper and play spades again."

"Aunt Agnes is eating with Jack and Ann. She must have known you would ask me to have supper with you. She is always asking me about what I do other than work. I have friends, but they are married. They were mostly friends when I was married so they usually do couple things. I've been invited to join them, but I always feel like a fifth wheel. I've been turning them down lately so I guess I need to make some new friends."

"Would you mind if I give you some advice?"

She looked a little surprised and said, "Sure Jett. What is your advice?"

I tried to look like a therapist giving a client some words of wisdom, whatever that means. "Since you will be moving up here in the not too distant future, I would advise you not to make any new friends down where you live now. You would just have to say goodbye to them and that might be painful. So I advise you to begin making new friends up here where you will eventually live."

"Well Jett, I want to thank you for that advice and especially thank you for being concerned about any pain I might feel in the future. I have met three potential friends here. The woman is nice, but the two men are boring and self-centered."

We laughed and I looked at her as mean as I could and said, "So I'm boring, huh?"

"Yes!!" She took off running up the trail.

I took off after her and was surprised that even with the food she was fast. We had been running for a few minutes when she tripped over an exposed root and fell on her face. The bag of food went flying when she tried to break the fall with her hands. I ran to her, threw off the backpack and knelt down beside her. "Eden, are you all right?"

She was pushing herself up with her hands and said, "Oh, that hurts" and went back down.

"What hurts?"

"Both wrists, I guess when I tried to break my fall, I..."

I interrupted, "Hold on a minute. Let me get the picnic blanket." I spread it out on the other side of her and asked, "Can you roll over on the blanket without using your arms."

"Yes." She rolled over.

"When you rolled over, did you feel any other pain?"

She responded, "I don't think so. Would you just help me up? I'm fine."

"I'm obviously not a doctor, but we had extensive training in the Army in first aide so let me make sure nothing's broken."

"Jett, I'm fine. Please just help me up."

"Are you sure?"

"Yes."

"Okay, let me get behind you and put my hands under your arms and help you up." Being careful not to put my hands anywhere near her breasts, I lifted her. She seemed light as a feather. When she tried to steady herself, she backed into me a little and I could feel her ass for a split second. As soon as she was on her feet, I said, "Hold onto my arm while you steady yourself. Try to take a few steps."

She did and said, "My left knee seems a little sore, but I have no problem putting weight on it." She let go of my arm.

I pointed to a little clearing off the trail and said, "Let's take our stuff over there and have our picnic here."

"I'll get the food bag."

"I'll get it. I'm gonna put the blanket down and then get the other stuff."

She walked around testing her knee and seemed fine.

I asked, "Does the knee still hurt?"

"Just a little."

"How 'bout your wrists?"

She was moving them in different directions and said, "My left one seems better, but my right one is sore."

"Let me look at it." I took her wrists one at a time and moved them around gently and felt for any sign that it might be broken. She told me that it was not that painful. Her wrist was tiny and her hand was small. Her hand was lightly calloused which was no surprise since she loved the outdoors. There seemed to be nothing more serious than a slight sprain. She gently pulled her hand away and said, "Thank you. I'm fine now and lucky that I didn't do more damage. The good news is that I'm hungry."

I wasn't too hungry. I was still recovering from just being able to touch her. But, I got the food and told her since she was at least a semi-invalid that I would get it ready. We ate without saying much. I didn't know what she had felt. I did remember that when I put my hands under her arms that she seemed to tense up. I guessed that was natural since that was really the first time I remember touching her except to shake hands.

After we finished, she lay on her back and said, "I love to look at the clouds."

I lay down beside her, making sure that we weren't touching and I wasn't too close to her and said, "I do too." Without knowing why, I continued, "I did it the other day when I was at the knoll I showed you last week. I used to do it when I was overseas and the other day, it brought back bad memories and I thought I was going to have a panic attack."

She turned over on her side and looked at me and said, "Oh Jett, I'm sorry. That sounds terrible. How would you describe a panic attack, if you don't mind me asking?"

"I don't mind at all. I went through all the symptoms and told her about the ones I usually experience."

She asked, "So what did you do?"

I explained our work with Doc and that he was teaching a group of us combat veterans about how to deal with Post-Traumatic Stress Disorder. "It's called PTSD."

She said, "I think I told you that I had read some articles about the traumatic experiences of soldiers and how that affected some of them when they returned home. Is that PTSD? I'm sorry Jett for asking so many questions. If you don't want to talk about it, I understand."

"No that's okay. The article was right. Many of us went through traumatic experiences like killing people and seeing our friends die. And now the memories come back to haunt us in the form of flashbacks, nightmares, and I also have panic attacks. We have a hard time living with those memories so to survive, we do stuff like drink too much, get hooked on pills, withdraw from family and friends, get in fights, and some commit or attempt suicide."

"So that was the reason that Ace attempted suicide."

"Yes."

She asked, "Do you ever think about suicide?"

"From time to time, I've thought about it, but never seriously considered it. I was initially nervous about coming home, but being home has really helped me. I feel so connected to this place and my family. I had some wonderful people guide me through my younger years. Just being back here gives me hope. Many soldiers have the opposite experience when they go home. I think that was true for Ace in the beginning, but he's doing better now."

"Can people other than soldiers have PTSD?"

I answered, "Yes, people who have been sexually abused and/or raped can have it. People in automobile accidents can also have it. Anyone who has had a traumatic experience or experiences can suffer from it."

She was quiet and seemed far away.

I waited awhile and then said, "Now it's my turn to ask a question. Would you tell me what you're thinking?"

She paused a minute, "I was thinking it must be terrible to go through both the experiences and the memories."

"It can be pretty rough at times." More silence and then I said, "Do you see anything interesting in the clouds?"

"I wasn't really looking. I guess I was deep in thought."

We laid there looking up at the clouds for what seemed like a long time. I decided to let her have some time and then she said, "Jett, I've had a good time with you today and last weekend with you, April, and Ace. I could see us becoming good friends. Last Saturday night, I reminded you that I am at least thirteen years or older more than all three of you."

I responded, "Yeah, I remember." I decided to let her finish before protesting.

"This is presumptuous of me, but if you have any thoughts about us becoming romantically involved, I'm asking you to stop those thoughts now."

"I could lie and say no I just want us to be friends, but I wanna be honest with you. Yes, I want us to become friends first, but I hope you might be open to whatever happens."

She took her time answering. "I would like for us to be friends too, but I'm not open to anything else."

"I think I know what you'll say, but would you mind telling me why?"

She responded, "I guess there is the usual thing like relationships are challenging enough without the additional challenge of the age difference. When you get in your forties, which some say is the prime of life, I will be in mid-fifties to sixties. You'll still be in great shape and I'll be getting or already have a bunch of wrinkles and everything will be drooping and who knows when I'll go through menopause. I won't be able to keep up with you exercising and hiking. When I look around, it appears that men generally like younger women, particularly when they get in their forties. I had a personal experience with that recently. I've been around for more years than you and am more mature and it would be like raising a kid." She laughed and said, "All right, that wasn't fair. You seem kind of mature." She laughed again. "OK, maybe you are mature."

I interrupted, "Can I say something?"

"Do you mind if I finish?"

"No, that's fine."

She continued, "You've just come back from the war and I'll guess that you're lonely and in need of affection, comfort, and security. And you might be desperate enough to be attracted to the first woman that comes along. And I've heard that younger men who marry older women are often looking for a mother figure. Not saying that's true, but I've heard that. And I'm recently divorced and the marriage was a big mistake from the beginning. But when we got married, I thought I loved him. I realized later that I never did. So I don't trust my judgment. He was the one that wanted the divorce and even though I didn't love him, it was emotionally painful to be rejected after all those years. Am I now the one who is lonely and in need of affection, comfort, and security? Am I desperate for the intimacy and closeness that I've never had? And I know I'm vulnerable to the attentions of a handsome young man who seems to enjoy my company. And then there's the issue of children. I don't even know if you want children, but time is running out for me. I do enjoy spending time with you, but I want to be honest about the age barrier."

I asked, "You said the possibility that I might be interested. Were you thinking that there was a possibility that you might also be interested?"

She looked at me and said, "I haven't let myself go down that path because of the age difference."

I rolled over onto my stomach being careful not to get too close to her, but I wanted to look at her and she turned her head and looked at me. I smiled, "That's a long list. I think I'll stay a bachelor."

She smiled back, "I'm considering that for myself."

"Doc says we spend too much of our time dwelling in the past and future. He wants us to work on staying in the moment. He wants us to see painful memories as illusions that don't exist. He says the future, of course, is not real because it hasn't happened yet. He wants us to let go of the past and the future and focus in the moment."

She responded, "I like the ideas, but I have no idea how to live like that?"

"The training is designed to identify the skills we'll need and then practice those skills until we get good at using them."

She said, "Almost everything I said has to do with past and future. I'm nowhere near being able to do what Doc is talking about."

"Me neither. I've got a long way to go. So what do we do now?"

She responded, "I guess we're here having a picnic and looking at the clouds."

"Wow. That's a 'Doc answer' if I ever heard one. Could we just be friends?"

She answered, "If we do that, are you possibly setting yourself up to get hurt?"

"Maybe, I'm willing to take that risk. Is there a risk for you?"

"Jett, I'm not going to let it get that far."

I asked, "Are you willing for us to be friends?"

"Yes, as long as it seems like a good idea to both of us."

"You've got a deal." I was not hearing what I wanted to hear, but it was better than nothing.

"Do you plan on coming up here most weekends?"

"My job change has come through and they want me to start right away so I have already talked to Aunt Agnes. I'll be giving my thirty day notice on the house as soon as I go back. I'm so glad I just rented. Otherwise, I would have to go through the process of selling. I'm hoping to move in with her in a few weeks. She said I could stay until my house is built."

Surprised, I said, "I thought your job was going to be based in Winston-Salem."

"I thought I told you the base was changed to Harvest. It's more centrally located in my area of responsibility."

I responded, "I started to lie and tell you maybe you did tell me and I forgot, but that's not possible. If you had told me, believe me, that was not something I would have forgotten."

She looked at me and smiled, "I did mean to tell you."

Trying not to look or act excited I said, "Okay, so in building just a friendship, my first suggestion is to limit the amount of time we spend together. I would say we can see each other every day and night except on Sundays."

She smiled and slapped me on the back and said, "On Sunday, we'll see each other at church."

"Be careful with that wrist." Smiling, "Sorry, I forgot church. Do you want to ride around and look at some other building sites?"

She answered, "Yes that would be fine. Would you mind if we stay here a little while longer and look at clouds?"

"That's fine. Let me know when you're ready."

A minute of so passed and she commented, "You're still on your stomach. You're not looking at the clouds."

"Yes I am. The Army taught us to use eyes in the back of our head."

"I'd hit you again if my wrist didn't hurt."

I rolled over onto my back and looked at clouds, but my mind was in another place. She had so many reasons to keep us from becoming involved. But, it seemed she was still interested in the friendship. What was I going to do? Now more than ever I wanted to be with her in every way I could imagine. It seemed dishonest to continue with my intentions being so clear to me. Should I tell her I would never be able to pull off the friendship scenario? I'm sure that would scare her off and I didn't want to live without her even if it meant we could only be friends. But maybe it was okay to continue even if I knew what I wanted. She could make her own choices and decisions as time passed. Chances are I would be the only one who suffered the loss and the rejection. She could choose not to let it go that far for her and so any emotional pain for her would be minimal. Was I just bull shitting myself?

She said, "Jett, I'm ready if you are."

"Sounds good, how is your wrist?"

"It's a little sore, but it's nothing serious."

"Let me help you stand up and you can see how your knee is holding up."

"That's all right. I can push up with my left hand. Stand close though just in case my knee gives out again."

"Be careful. As soon as you get to your feet, take my arm and let me walk you around a little to make sure your knee will support you."

She took my arm and walked around and her knee seemed to be fine. "It doesn't hurt at all."

I said, "Why don't you sit on that rock and let me gather things up."

"I'm fine, but I do have to pee."

"Okay, I've got some toilet paper. Hold on. Let me find it."

"Thanks. I'll be back in a few minutes."

"Be careful."

We walked down the trail to the truck and spent the rest of the afternoon looking at other possible building sites. She would have to make a decision soon and I was ready to offer to sell her that small plot around the knoll. I figured I'd sell her about an acre. Based on our earlier conversation, I wasn't sure she would accept my offer. It was getting close to 6:00. I asked her if she was ready to go to the cabin and she was ready.

42

AUNT AGNES

April and Ace were there and we picked up right where we left off last weekend. Everyone seemed comfortable. Ace said, "Eden, there was a message on the answering machine for you from Jack. He said to call him when you got here. He left a number."

She said, "I hope nothing is wrong. Hello Ann, this is Eden. I had a message to call you guys."

(Pause) She turned white. "Oh no! When did it happen? Is she all right? Which hospital? I'll be right there." She hung up. "Aunt Agnes had a heart attack. She's in ICU. Ann said they're considering surgery, but they want to talk with me. She said Jack is already there and that she is on the way."

She started crying and April came over and hugged her. I said, "We better go."

April said, "Ace and I will be right behind you."

When we got to the hospital, Jack and Ann were standing at the door to the main entrance. I let her off and went to park the truck. April and Ace pulled into the parking lot about the same time. We went to the ICU waiting room. April left us and went back to see what was happening.

She came back in about fifteen minutes. "The surgeons are recommending a triple by-pass. Ordinarily, the surgery would be an easy decision, but there is a substantial risk to have the surgery at her age. The decision is up to Eden as the next of kin. Jack and Ann are with her and they will make the decision together. They are talking now and I'll go back and keep you all posted." She left.

She came back and said, "They decided that the surgery was the best option. She is being prepped now so it won't be long before they get started. I made arrangements for them to wait in a vacant office near the surgical unit. I'll go back and check on them later. For now, all we can do is wait."

Ace said to April, "This place is freaking me out. I've gotta get out of here." And to me, "Could you make sure April gets back to the cabin?"

"Sure."

He gave April a hug and left.

She said, "I think it brings back too many bad memories."

"Yeah, how is Eden doing?"

"Not well. She is saying she should have never left her this afternoon. That's not rational, but we human beings seem to find ways to make things more painful for ourselves than they already are. I'll do the best I can to comfort her. I'll be back in a little while."

"Thank you, April. Would you tell her I'm out here and if there is anything she needs just let me know."

At that moment, Father Pat came into the waiting room and greeted us. April said, "Father Pat, why don't you come back with me." They left.

After they left, Mom, Henry and Betty came into the waiting room. I filled them in on the latest. Mom said that Pop sent his love and would be praying for her. About an hour later, April came out and said there was no news. She was still in surgery.

In another hour, April came out and I could tell by her expression that the news was not good. "They did everything they could, but her heart was too weak to withstand the stress. She died."

I asked, "How's Eden?"

"Not good. She's having a very difficult time. Jack is taking care of the paperwork. She wanted you to come back."

She took me back and when we reached the door to the room, Father Pat was standing beside Eden who was crying. Ann had her arm around her shoulder and said, "We'll leave you two alone."

I went in and got down on my knees in front of her and took her hands and said, "I'm so sorry."

Sobbing, "Oh Jett, I should have stayed with her. I should have stayed with her."

"I'm so sorry Eden. Is there anything I can do?"

"No." Wiping her tears and blowing her nose. "I'm going to stay with Jack and Ann for the next few days and they'll help me make the arrangements."

Jack walked in and said, "Hey Jett." Looking at Eden, he said, "Eden, all the paperwork has been taken care of so we can leave now. Jett, you can follow us over to the house."

Eden said, "Jack, I'll ride with Jett and get my things and then I'll drive my car over to your house."

Jack responded, "Are you sure you feel okay to drive?"

She answered, "I'll see when I get there. I won't take any chances."

Everyone walked out to the waiting room area. After everyone had spoken to Eden, I nodded to her and took her left arm and put it inside mine. I looked at mom. "Mom, would you take April back to the cabin?" She nodded.

We walked out to the truck. I thought the fresh air would be good for her and a little exercise wouldn't hurt either. She was a little unsteady and I asked her about the knee and she said it was fine.

We rode in silence. I knew she was still crying because she kept wiping her eyes. When we got to the house, I asked her if I could go inside first and check everything out. She nodded and gave me the key.

I turned on a few lights. There was a broken cookie jar in the kitchen. I assumed Aunt Agnes had grabbed for something when she started to fall. The phone was on the floor and it was dead. The paramedics had left some wrappings on the floor. I put the phone back on the hook and cleaned up the other stuff.

I was heading for the front door when it opened and Eden came in and said, "I figured that you were finished with whatever you had to do. Would you mind if I have a little time to myself?"

"No. That's fine. I'll wait in the truck?"

"If you don't mind."

I patted her shoulder and left. I waited in the truck for what seemed like a half an hour or so. I could see the lights going out. She came out the front door with her overnight bag. She was still crying. She said, "I'm not in any shape to drive."

"If you'll leave your keys, I'll get your car over to you tomorrow."

"Thanks Jett." We rode in silence. When we got to Jack and Ann's house, she said, "Would you mind if I go in alone. I'm hoping it will be all right with Jack and Ann if I go to bed."

"That's fine. I'll walk you to the door. Would it be okay if I call you in the morning?"

"Yes."

When she opened the screen door, I said, "Eden, my heart aches for you."

A faint smile and she said, "Goodnight Jett."

April and Ace were watching TV when I got home. "April, thanks for all you did tonight for all of us."

"You're welcome."

Looking at Ace, "How you doin' partner?"

"Better now that I'm away from that hospital."

He asked, "You holding up okay?"

"Yeah, I'm turning in. See you guys in the morning."

I had another nightmare, but in this one I was trying to rescue Eden and I couldn't get to her. She was holding out a hand and I couldn't quite reach it. She was falling into enemy hands and there was nothing I could do about it. I woke up and my bed was soaked again. I took off my tee-shirt and drawers, dried off and got into Eden's bed and wondered if she was having trouble sleeping. I wished she were in this bed with me so I could hold her and comfort her. I finally drifted off to sleep.

Spot and I went for a run at 5:00, came back and went back to bed. I woke up around 9:00 and April had breakfast ready. She called Ace and he came stumbling out looking like he had a worse night than me. April had fixed bacon and pancakes. I didn't realize I was so hungry. Then I remembered I didn't eat any supper last night. I thanked April and went to call Eden.

I dialed Jack's number and he picked-up. "Hey Jack, how are things going this morning?"

"As well as can be expected. Eden didn't sleep much last night and has been real weepy this morning. Ann just convinced her to go back to bed. Why don't you give us a call in a couple of hours."

"Okay. Is there anything I can do right now?"

"Can't think of anything. This afternoon, I think it would be good if Eden got out. I don't know if she will agree, but check in and we'll see what's happening."

April asked, "How are things going?"

I filled them in on the conversation with Jack. I fixed myself another cup of tea and sat down at the table. "How are things going with you all?"

April looked at Ace. He said, "We're doin' good. We decided we needed some help understanding what happened to us over the years. I know it's mostly my shit, but April wants us to work on it together. Yesterday, I asked Doc if he would be willing to see us. We have an appointment at 5:00 tomorrow."

April said, "I've got my own issues. It's not all you Ace."

"Good for you guys. I think it's a great idea."

April asked, "How was it going for you and Eden before Aunt Agnes had her heart attack?"

"The good news is that she will be moving up here in a few weeks due to a job change. She was going to live with Aunt Agnes. While we were on our picnic, she brought up the age thing again. She had been thinking about it this past week and had a list of reasons that a relationship between us wouldn't work."

"I've been thinking about it myself," April said. "You men have a history of liking younger women so when there is that age difference, we wonder how it's going to work based on the usual circumstance."

I responded, "Yeah, that was one of the things she brought up and her 'ex' dumped her for a younger woman so that issue is on her mind."

"What were her other reasons?" April asked.

I went over them the best I could remember and April was in agreement with Eden on most of them.

"We talked about working on a friendship. I'm going to have to wait to see how Aunt Agnes' death affects her." I looked at Ace and continued, "I guess I'll do what Doc suggests and focus on the moment and stop worrying about what may or may not happen. There's some relief in that if I can pull it off. Even if I can only do it half of the time, it'll help."

Ace said, "The stuff Doc talks about makes sense, but it's so different from the usual way we live. I want April to understand it so we can use it in our relationship. I think we have to help and support each other."

We all agreed. I asked, "What are you guys gonna do today?"

Ace responded, "We're gonna take the bikes and take a picnic lunch and spend the afternoon out in the woods. Do you want us to take Spot?"

"Yeah, that would be great. I've got some laundry to do and then get cleaned up. I'll call Jack and will eat with the family after church if Eden's not up for having company."

We chatted a while longer and then each went about getting some stuff done. I called Jack and Eden was still struggling and in bed. Jack said that he and Ann were worried about her and wanted me to come for supper. I ate at the Inn with the family and then hiked up to yesterday's picnic spot. I lay down and looked at the clouds and wished I could find a way to ease her pain. I got to Jack and Ann's about 6:00. Eden was in the kitchen helping Ann with supper. She looked better even though her eyes were still red. They both greeted me and I asked Eden how she was doing.

"I'm feeling a little better and thanks to Jack and Ann, I've been able to sleep. That always helps me."

Ann said, "Eden, we've done about all we can. The oven will take care of the rest. I'm wondering if it might be good for you to get some fresh air. You and Jett could go for a walk. Supper won't be ready till about 7:00."

Eden replied, "That would be nice."

After we got outside, I asked, "How is your knee and wrist?"

"There is a little swelling in both. I can feel some pain, but I can still walk without any trouble. I've had to use my left hand more and it's a little awkward, but manageable."

She continued, "Jett, I imagine everyone is wondering why I'm having such a difficult time. I was very close to Aunt Agnes. She did not get along well with my dad or their sister. She would come down and visit me at least once a month and I have been coming up here at least once a month for as long as I can remember. We enjoyed many of the same things and never had a cross word. We would talk on the phone at least two or three times every week."

"I had no idea you all were that close."

She told me about the many different things they did together and some humorous things that happened to them over the years.

I asked, "Were any of your sisters close to Aunt Agnes?"

"No. My sisters don't travel far from home. One visits me occasionally. Aunt Agnes used to visit us when we were children, but she would never stay long because she didn't like my dad and they argued a lot. When we got older, she stopped coming. Then I moved to Greensboro and we became close. My 'ex' sometimes resented the amount of time I spent with her. I was always puzzled by that since he never seemed that interested in spending time with me."

She continued, "She never liked any of my boyfriends before I married Chase, not that there were that many. She didn't like Chase either. She didn't think he treated me right. I thought he treated me pretty good. I'm sure I didn't treat him any better than he treated me. We didn't want or expect much from each other. Since the divorce, I've had dinner several times with a friend and Aunt Agnes went with us once and she didn't like him either. She said he was arrogant and 'full of himself.' I think she was protective and maybe no one would have ever been good enough. She loved me like a daughter and I loved her very much."

She started crying again and I put my arm around her. She tensed a little, but then seemed to relax. We walked on in silence and then she said, "I think it helped me to talk about it."

"I'm glad."

The meal went better than I had anticipated. Jack and Ann are never at a loss for words. We talked some about Aunt Agnes and other topics related to family and friends. I stayed till about 9:00. Eden seemed to be doing better. They planned to take care of the funeral arrangements tomorrow morning and were tentatively looking at Tuesday evening for visitation and Wednesday for the funeral service. They invited me to supper tomorrow night at the Inn.

I worked with Charlie all day Monday. It was Ace's first day at the mill. The supper at the Inn went fine. The tentative arrangements had become final. Eden was doing better. I made no attempts to talk with her alone. I just wanted to be helpful and supportive. I did ask her if she wanted to go for a drive or walk around the lake tomorrow afternoon. We agreed for me to pick her up around two.

Buddy Session Four

Doc arrived for the fourth session with Ace and me. He asked us how we had been doing with our training.

Ace responded, "I've been doing good. As you know from our session yesterday with April, I've taught her how to do it and we've been practicing it together. That helps a lot since we spend a lot of time together."

I said, "I've had a lot going on this past week, but I've also been practicing."

Doc said, "Some in our group are practicing more than others. You guys are doing well. What's the reason for that?"

I answered, "I think I'm starting to believe that it can really help. I don't think I had any panic attacks this week, but I had a bunch of nightmares. When I woke up, I used the deep breathing and I got back to sleep faster than usual."

Ace said, "The example we used in the group last Saturday about me wanting to get drunk actually happened and I was able to take some breaths and get to Center where I was able to get clear enough to stop myself from going. I've had a few flashbacks this week and they were bad ones. Jett, two of them were that last patrol. I kept seeing Tim's body spread out all over the ground. And I didn't even actually see it. It was like the body was really Logan's." He looked at Doc, "He was a friend who got blown up when his vehicle ran over an IED. Anyway, I tried to do the breathing and it didn't help."

Doc said, "We have more training to do. You guys are starting to get it. I'm very pleased. Let's do another breathing exercise. I want you to focus on normal breathing. Don't take any deep breaths. This is designed to be only about attention. I'm going to let you do this for awhile and I'll tell you when to open your eyes. Remember just normal breathing and if you wander, as always, bring your attention back to the breathing. Open your eyes."

Doc asked, "What was that like?"

I responded, "It seemed easier to me because sometimes I think I focus too much on the mechanics of the deep breathing. When we opened our eyes, I was curious about how long it had lasted. I cheated and looked at the clock and was surprised to find out it was about twenty minutes. It seemed more like about five minutes."

Doc said, "How about you Ace?"

"I think just the opposite of Jett. I like the deep breathing more just because it gives me something else to focus on. It helps to keep me from wandering. I could tell I'm getting better at focusing because like Jett, I thought it was much shorter than twenty minutes."

Doc commented, "As we have discussed before, being attentive, alert, and focused is a timeless state. It's a good sign that you are experiencing that to some degree. It facilitates the journey to Center and the breathing is the core skill that helps you get Centered. Keep picking-up the books."

Doc asked, "Did you all have any questions about the resistance to healing we talked about last Saturday?"

Ace said, "The drinking thing is the biggest for me although I have a few more to add. The next is having sex with just about anybody and as long as I have the excuse of the war, I don't have to share my feelings with anyone."

I said, "I have to give up my guilt about being alive when my friends are dead or my guilt about not having any physical disability like Anna and Chad. Ace and I drank heavily while in the Army when we weren't over there. Since coming home, I've continued to drink more than I did before I left for the Army. It doesn't seem like a problem."

Ace said, "You don't drink half as much as I do."

Doc said we would be talking more about these resistances in the group and individually as needed. He talked about the use of our notebooks and how we would be doing more work in the notebooks starting today. He then said it was time for our individual session. Ace wanted me to go first.

Doc told me he would address the issue of guilt in the group. He asked me to talk about exercise, nutrition, and sleep. After I finished, we came up with some personal goals in those areas. He said that my exercise is good and he had no recommendations except to keep it up. He said to use my notebook and record the following over the next week:

1. A food diary for a week which involves writing down everything I eat and drink.
2. A record of my sleep to include time to bed and time out of bed.
3. Record the time and content of any nightmares. He suggested that I keep my notebook by my bed so I could write down the content as soon as I woke up.
4. Record the time, duration, and symptoms of any panic attacks.
5. Record the amount of alcohol consumed.

He said that having this record would help with refining the goals in these areas.

While he worked with Ace, I went into my room, practiced my breathing and made some charts in the different sections of my notebook. Doc had given us dividers and I labeled them to keep different topics separated. I never imagined that I would be this interested in doing this stuff, but I was beginning to see how this could make a big difference in my life and could help with my healing.

Ace called, saying he and Doc were finished.

Doc said, "Here are the sheets on the Focker PTSD and the Your True Self at Center to put in your notebooks. Study these before group on Saturday. We'll spend more time on them then. Remember, that in the end you will be defining those states as they relate to your life and your experiences. Do you have any questions right now on anything to do with the states?

Ace said, "I have questions, but not on the basic idea of the states. I know you'll be getting to how we can use them and what skills we will need."

Doc responded, "Yes, that true. Do either one of you have any questions on the sheets I just gave you?"

We shook our heads no.

Doc said, "Ace was telling me about your friends' aunt dying. I think one of the most challenging things for a friend in that situation is to know what to say to help ease the pain of suffering."

"Yeah, that's for sure. We had a lot of practice with each other in the war and I never figured what to say to my friends or what to even say to myself."

Doc replied, "By the end of our training, you will have some ideas. I know you will be supportive in whatever way you can, but I suggest that if you are trying to say something helpful that you let it go. One of the things you will learn or perhaps are already learning is that silence is not only okay, but is often helpful and relaxing. A touch, a gentle smile, a thoughtful act such as a single flower picked from a meadow can be comforting. Being with her as a peaceful and compassionate energy goes a long way. Finally, follow your heart, your Center and if you're not sure what to do, take a few breaths, go to Center and it will come to you."

"See you guys Saturday." And he was gone.

43

THE FUNERAL, LANCE AND PANIC

I said, "It's one. I'm picking Eden up at two. Do you want some lunch?"

He did. We fixed our lunch in silence and when we sat down, Ace said, "Jett, I don't know what's happening with me. For the last few weeks, I feel like I've gone through some kind of, I don't know what to call it, maybe some kind of transformation. April and I have been talking about it. For years, I've kept stuff bottled up inside me. I've always tried to be the super athlete, the super soldier, the super whatever. When I tried to whack myself two weeks or so ago, something inside me burst. Remember when we were on the back deck and we started bawling and then April came up and...."

"Yeah, I remember,"

He went on, "I've heard the expression that so and so is a 'time bomb' ready to go off and that was me for sure. But I always had to keep up this image of being able to handle anything, no problem, I'll take care of business. And, inside I was locked tighter than a drum and angry as hell at God-only-knows-what. The only way I could let go was to get drunk." He smiled, "Am I telling you anything you didn't know?"

I smiled, but didn't know what to say so I said nothing.

Ace continued, "Doc and I talked quite a bit about my drinking during my session and he asked me about Alcoholics Anonymous and I told him I didn't want to do that unless it was my only option. I told him I'll keep track of every drink this week with the idea that I want to be able to drink socially. I don't think my issue is craving alcohol for any other reason than I'll explode if I can't find a way to relax. I'm worried Jett. What am I gonna do with all that anger and tension? I have to change the way I look at life, the way I handle stress and all that shit. It's my only hope and I'm starting to believe that Doc is showing me a path to get me there. I'm seein' how effective the deep breathing can be and it's giving me hope. For the past few days, April and I've been practicing it a lot."

I responded, "How can I help?"

"I'm gonna try to limit myself to two beers a day on weekdays and three beers on Saturday and Sunday. Since I have a beer now, that means one to go today. Wow, I can still count. I don't want you to say anything or do anything. It helps that you already seem to have cut back, but this is not your issue. I have to do this on my own. April and I talked about it last night and she's happy that I've made the decision. I'm gonna keep forcing myself to talk about shit. I know you're always ready to listen."

"I am and know you will listen to me too."

"You got it." We stood and did our traditional shake and then hugged.

Ace was going up to the mill and asked me about supper. I told him after spending time with Eden, I was going to eat with Mom and Dad and change down at their house. Ace said he and April would see me at the 'visitation.'

When I got to Jack and Ann's, Eden was ready to go. She was wearing slacks and tennis shoes so I figured we'd be walking. When we got in the truck, I asked her how she was doing and she said she was dreading the visitation and was glad to have the chance to get outside and exercise. I asked if she had heard from any of her family and she said she had talked with her aunt and mom and most of her sisters. No one was coming to the visitation or the funeral.

She said, "Thank you for agreeing to be a pallbearer."

"Glad to do it. Would you like to go to the lake?"

"Aunt Agnes and I loved the walk around the lake and the trails that linked up with the lake. There is another one that we also especially liked. I'd like to take that one if it's all right with you."

"Which one is it?"

"I don't know the name, but I can tell you how to get there."

She gave me directions and it turned out to be the "Hollow Creek Trail."

We walked in silence. It was a beautiful day and I hoped the exercise was helping her feel better. At one point, she reached over and took my hand. I was surprised. After a little while she let my hand go and wiped her tears. "Thank you for agreeing to hike on this trail. It helps me remember what it was like to be with Aunt Agnes."

All I could think to say was, "Your welcome."

Several times, she would see something and point to it and we would exchange a smile. It reminded me of the many times Pop and I did that when we were hiking. We didn't say another word until we got back to the truck.

"Thank you Jett. That was nice."

"I'm glad."

I took her to Jack and Ann's, walked her to the door and she said, "Thanks again and I'll see you tonight."

The visitation was at the funeral home. Eden was occupied most of the time and I noticed she would wipe a tear away from time-to-time. When we got a chance to talk, I was at a loss for words. I mainly just asked how she was holding up and she said she was doing alright. When almost everyone had left, I asked her if she wanted to go out for coffee or a drink and she said she was tired and was going to bed. She thanked me again for taking her on the walk.

The funeral was at 2:00 so I went to work with Charlie until noon. The pallbearers were to be at the funeral home by 1:30. Father Pat did his usual good job and Eden gave a beautiful eulogy. She had difficulty talking a few times, but was able to finish without too much trouble.

The service at the graveside was short. After the service, everyone was invited to the Inn. Eden, Jack, and Ann stood close to the door and everyone was paying their last respects. I positioned myself so I could see Eden most of the time. I loved looking at her without being too obvious. I was talking with April and Ace when I looked over at Eden and a man I had seen at the service, but didn't know was next in line to greet Eden. He said something to her and she gave him a big smile and a hug and they talked for a few minutes. I turned to April and Ace, "Who is he?" They of course had no clue.

When everyone was through the line, Eden went over to him and they started talking. Whoever he was, she seemed glad to see him. After they talked awhile, Henry and Betty went over and joined in the conversation. Henry seemed to know this guy and they were having an animated conversation. Who was he? I was starting to feel some concern. Should I feel jealous? He was attractive with sandy hair, a nice build and about my height. He had a nice smile.

It seemed like they talked forever, but it was probably no more than fifteen minutes. Henry and Betty said goodbye to him and he talked with Eden a few more minutes. He then gave her what looked like his card and they hugged again and he left.

I couldn't wait so I went over to Eden right away and asked her if she would like something to eat. She smiled at me and said she would love something to drink. She walked over to the bar with me and asked for a glass of white wine. I got a beer. I said, "I was impressed with your eulogy; it was beautiful or I guess I should say beautifully done."

"Thanks. I was really nervous and a few times was afraid I wasn't going to be able to finish."

"Well, you did great!"

"The strangest thing happened a little while ago. A high school friend of mine showed up. I hadn't seen him for almost twenty years. It turns out he is a law professor over at Elverton. Your Uncle Henry knows him. He said he had been at the college for about ten years. He was reading the obituaries in the newspaper and ran across my name as one of the relatives of Aunt Agnes. He thought it would have to be me so he came to the funeral."

As she was talking, my heart started beating faster and I thought, "Oh shit, I can't have a panic attack now." I started real subtle deep breaths and kept telling myself to relax, let go, it's okay, you can do it.

It wasn't working. No, I was getting short of breath despite the deep breathing. I took a sip of beer and acted like some beer went down the wrong way. I started coughing and acted like I couldn't stop. I excused myself. Everyone was looking. I went to the men's room and kept coughing to cover the panic attack. I threw some cold water on my face and kept telling myself to calm down and after a minute or so I felt a little better.

Ace came in and said, "You okay?"

In a lowered voice, but through gritted teeth I hissed, "The fucking breathing was fucking useless. Fuck! I made a fucking fool out of myself."

"You had a coughing fit. Whatta ya mean?"

I replied, "That was just a cover for a panic attack I started when Eden was telling me about that guy."

"Well, everyone thinks some beer just went down the wrong way. You okay now?"

"Yeah."

"Well, let's go back there. Focus on your breathing and…

I interrupted, "Damn it, I told you the fucking breathing didn't work."

He put his arm around me and said, "OK. Just keep pretending it was a coughing fit. April went over to talk to Eden so let's go out there and talk to them. We'll talk later."

We went back out and everyone seemed to be looking at me, but most everyone except family had left so it wasn't a big deal. I was more worried what Eden was thinking. We walked up to Eden and April.

Ace said, "When water goes down the wrong way, it's one thing, but when beer goes down the wrong way, it's a nightmare."

Eden looked concerned and said, "Jett, are you all right?"

"Thanks. I'm fine."

The four of us got plates of food and sat down at a table. I was definitely not hungry, but I forced myself to eat and had another beer. April asked Eden, "I know it's too soon to have thought much about it, but what are your plans for the next few days?"

"I'm going to stay with Jack and Ann tonight. In the morning, I'm going back home. I've got some loose ends at work to attend to and then after work on Friday, I'm coming back here. I've decided to stay at Aunt Agnes' house even though I know it will be difficult. I've got to face the fact that she's gone. Jack and I have an appointment on Saturday morning at 10:00 with the estate attorney. Jack is her executor."

April said, "Why don't you come up to the cabin on Friday and have supper with us and spend the night?"

Ace said, "Yeah. I think it would be hard to spend the night there this soon."

Eden hesitated and looked at me. "Are you sure you want me to come?"

I smiled, "Yes, we're sure."

"All right, I will."

Jack came over and chatted for a minute and then looked at Eden. "Ann and I are gonna head on. Do you want to ride with us or do you want Jett to bring you?"

Eden replied, "I think I'll ride with you Jack. I'm really tired and would like to relax a little and then go to bed."

Jack said okay and Eden turned to us, "So I'll be at the cabin around 6:00 on Friday. Will that work for you all?"

We nodded and said, "Yeah, that's fine."

Eden turned to me and asked, "Jett, can I talk with you for a few minutes?"

"Sure."

We walked over toward the door she smiled, "I want to give you my phone number in case you want to call me."

"Thanks and I will call you."

"I don't know how I could have gotten through this without you. Thank you for everything." She smiled, leaned over and gave me a peck on the cheek and said, "See you Friday."

I smiled a shit-eatin' grin and said, "See you Friday."

I stopped to see Henry and Betty on my way back to the cabin. Henry answered the door and smiled, "I thought you might be dropping by. You want a beer?"

"No thanks."

"Betty is resting in the bedroom. Funeral's are tiring for her."

I smiled, "OK, you know why I'm here. Who is he?"

"His name is Lance Foley. He's a professor at the Law School. He's been there about ten years. I have seen him a number of times at faculty functions and we've played tennis half a dozen times. He seems like a nice guy. I know he got a divorce about five years ago and he has two children. They live with their mother in Asheville. I think they stay with him every other weekend. That's about all I know. I was of course surprised to see him at the funeral and had no idea he knew Eden."

"Do you know if he's dating anyone?"

"I know he dates. I don't know if he has a special girl friend."

"I'm thinking about 'taking him out'. I can't handle any competition."

"I'll help you. I'll arrange for a tennis game and you can set your assault rifle up on the roof of the clubhouse and you can pick him off. Wait till we finish though. He usually beats me and I want one last crack at him."

We laughed and spent a few more minutes talking and then I left.

44
TRYING TO GET CENTERED

April and Ace were sitting at the kitchen table talking. I was glad because I needed to talk. They both got up and gave me a hug. Ace had a beer in front of him and smiled, "This is number two.""Good for you my man. I just left Henry and got the low down on the guy." I told them what Henry said. "I haven't even hugged Eden yet and that guy got two hugs. I'm jealous."

April said, "I'm guessing, but that guy is safe and you're not safe."

"She's made it clear that she's not going to ever be anything more than my friend so I should be safe."

April replied, "What she says and what she feels may be different."

"Maybe," I conceded. "I've barely held her hand and yet I am obsessed with the idea that I want to spend the rest of my life with her. In fact, I can't imagine my life without her. That is so immature and childish. How can anybody know that kind of thing after three weeks with only a little time together?"

Ace said, "You know Doc would say don't judge the moment. Let it be what it is and bring that thought to the Center where there's clarity. If you were to do that, what would your Center say?"

I smiled at Ace, "You're really getting this stuff aren't you?"

He didn't smile back and said, "Jett, I either get this stuff or my life is over."

"I got it." I thought for a moment about the Center, "At Center, I would say that I cannot control Eden and what she does. What I can do in this moment is just love her. That's all I can think of."

April said, "That seems like enough for now."

Ace said, "I agree."

"Now, I have to work on the skills that will help me stay at Center. That seems like quite a challenge and I don't even know what skills I'll need."

April said, "Ace has been going over his notes with me. So, when we saw Doc night before last, he gave me more information about the benefits of the breathing. Let's brainstorm this together. One of the benefits of the breathing is that it quiets the mind."

I said, "I was so mad today that the breathing didn't rescue me from that panic attack. I know I have to keep working on it, but I want it to work now."

"Yeah, me too," said Ace. "Doc keeps telling us to be patient and practice."

April said, "Ace told me the coughing was to cover up the panic attack. You sure fooled me so I'm sure Eden didn't know either."

"I've told her about the panic attacks, but I couldn't admit to her that I was panicking over her friend. That would have been too embarrassing."

Ace said, "If Tug is getting all jealous and worried over Lance baby, you don't yet have the skills to quiet Tug."

With a puzzled look, April asked, "Who's Tug?"

Ace explained and when she said Doc's name for that state is 'Focker,' she laughed.

She smiled, "I won't forget Focker." She looked at Ace. "What's your name for your Focker?"

"Fark."

She laughed again, "Ace, you should have gone on and named him 'Fart.'"

I said, "Okay, help me out here. Let's do this by the numbers. First, I don't judge the thought that I want to spend the rest of my life with a person who I barely know as bad or stupid or immature or irrational. That means I don't have to defeat it, fight it, or slay it. What do I do then?"

Ace responded, "I'll be Doc. Close your eyes, take a few deep breaths and go to Center and get some clarity. Open your eyes when you're done."

I opened my eyes. "April, how much did Ace tell you about Centering?"

"A little."

"Well, my place is that knoll where Eden and I have spent some time. I went there in my mind and couldn't come up with anything other than what I said earlier. 'I can't control her so just love her.' There was one other thing I got. 'If it doesn't work out, you'll be okay.' I didn't really wanna hear that one."

Ace said, "I've got a feeling that we're gonna be hearing quite a bit of stuff at Center that we don't wanna hear. But I think we'll have some skills to help us face some of that stuff."

"Yeah, I think you're right. The breathing sure didn't help me yesterday."

Ace said, "Well, if you're focusing on the breathing, you've let the thought go for the moment. Next, with more training, the breathing is going to help you relax your body which has to help. I just thought of something. If we had never had the training, I would have said to you, 'Jett, don't get your panties in a wad, just relax.' You would have had nothing other than the suggestion to stop doing that and relax. Now, we're learning the skills to focus and relax."

I said, "The breathing also puts us in the moment so that gets us out of fretting about the future like will Eden ever love me. Do you think we'll ever be able to do this?"

Ace replied, "I think it's a good start that we're talking about it and taking it seriously. I don't think we'll ever be perfect at going or living at Center, but every little bit counts and why can't we keep getting better and better at it? Like on a scale of one to ten with ten being freaking out worried. Let's say you are a nine now, what would it be like if you could move it down to a four or five?"

I said, "I'd take it!"

April offered, "So if we have quieted the mind, relaxed the body, and are in the moment, it would seem we are able to stay at Center and find out what to do next."

Ace said, "Yes, so the breathing helps us shift into Center and then it helps us to stay Centered."

April commented, "The goal to stay Centered is quite a challenge."

Doc tells us to be patient and we'll be working on that in future group sessions."

I said, "I have to tell you that I do feel better right now. I don't know how long it will last." After a short pause, "I'm going to try to stay Centered as we discuss this stuff that's on my mind. Do you think she will go out with him?"

Ace said, "Yeah. He's an old friend. It would be natural to have lunch or go out to dinner." He looked at me and said, "Breathe Jett, it's all right if she goes out with him."

April said, "Wow, this is hard. If Ace were going out to dinner with an old high school female friend, I would be struggling."

Ace said, "Yeah, I have to take a lot of breaths when I think about you two having sex together. When I'm at Center, I rationally understand, but the thought sometimes takes my breath away."

We were all silent. Ace finally said, "Bottom line is this stuff is tough, but I still believe it can help us. Jett, we really want to put this war behind us and I really do want to put you two having sex behind me. I do want to put a lot of shit in my history behind me. It's baggage I wanna release and I think I'm getting the tools to make it happen. I'm sure it doesn't mean I'll never think about those things, but they won't bother me like they do now."

What a change. Ace was getting' his stuff out in the open and April and I were speechless. Ace broke the silence one more time. "April, are you up for a bike ride?"

"Yes, that would be great."

I said, "Your leg seems to be doing better."

"Yeah, the PT said I could begin walking a little without the crutches. She just said to take it easy."

April asked, "Is your PT pretty?"

"Yeah, she's pretty and hot and gives me great massages on my leg."

"I guess I deserved that answer, but on the other hand..." She slapped him on the side of the head and said, "You better watch yourself dude. I'll kick your ass."

"Well, you don't have to do that Dudette. I've only got eyes for you babe!"

She smiled and said, "It's about time."

He leaned over and pulled her head toward him and gave her a kiss.

I said, "Spot and I'll go for a run. See you when you get back. I'll rustle up something light for supper."

We went our separate ways. The run helped me feel better. When they returned, they also felt better. We agreed to do a twenty minute breathing exercise before we ate supper.

45
EDEN IN HARVEST

After work the next day, Pop and I went for a walk around the lake. Pop was older than Aunt Agnes and it scared me to think we might lose him unexpectedly.

When I got home, Ace was asleep. I called Eden to ask her about the trip back. The line was busy. Was she talking to him? I took some deep breaths and told myself to get Centered. It didn't help.

Ace didn't come out of his room so I ate supper and called Eden again. This time she answered. She said the trip back was difficult because she had too much time to think about how much she was already missing Aunt Agnes. She talked a little about her afternoon at work and that she had another busy day tomorrow. It was a little awkward talking to her. I couldn't think of anything to say. She said she had a lot to do at the house since she was gone for longer than expected and she looked forward to seeing us tomorrow night. We hung up.

I felt empty. I didn't know what I had expected, but I knew that I wasn't Centered. I watched some TV and went to bed.

Eden arrived a little after 6:00. I asked her if she wanted to put her "things" in the bedroom. She walked over to the bedroom door and

I was close behind. After she got in the room, she turned around and said, "Jett, the bedroom looks so nice. I love the décor. Who did this?"

I answered, "Mom."

She smiled, "Well, it's beautiful. I really like it."

April and Ace pulled in and April gave Eden a hug and Ace said that they were going out on the bikes and would be back in a couple of hours.

I asked, "How is your knee?"

She answered, "Almost like new."

"Are you up for a walk to the knoll?"

"Sure, I would like that."

We headed up to the knoll with Spot. I said, "Now I can ask how you're really doing."

"I really am better. The ride up was not too bad. I just focused on looking forward to spending time with you guys. I am glad that I'm not spending the night at Aunt Agnes' house." She was petting Spot and rubbing his head and it looked like Spot had another fan. "I haven't told you that I have a dog and three cats."

"What kind of dog do you have?"

"It's a Cavalier King Charles Spaniel. Her name is Cher."

"I have a cat, Journee, but he lives with mom and dad. We were really tight before I left for the Army, but while I was gone he got real attached to mom. When I got out of the Army, he decided that even though he thought I was a great person, he was going to stay with mom and I could come and visit whenever I wanted."

She smiled. "All my cats are from the Humane Society. Weedee is partially blind, Tambeau has no tail, and Chester only has three legs."

"Who takes care of them when you're up here?"

"I have two teenagers, Christina and Stephanie, who live next door. They are a life saver. When I move here, I'll have to find someone else to help me." She looked out over the mountains. "This is just so beautiful. I don't think I have ever seen a more beautiful view."

I asked, “You were planning to move up here in a few weeks before Aunt Agnes died. What will you do now?”

She answered, “I’m not sure. I assume that the heirs to Aunt Agnes’ estate would be her sister and my dad. They will want to sell the house right away. They might let me stay there until it’s sold. If I buy a piece of property and have a builder and the plans ready to go in say a month, how long do you think it will take before I could move in?”

“I’m guessing about six months. I think I told you that my dad and Ace’s dad, Jim, operate the mill. By the way, I don’t think I told you that Ace is working there now. Anyway, they know most of the builders in the area and they could recommend someone based on your plans and location.”

That’s wonderful,” she said. “I’ve got to find the property first because the design of the house will be partially dictated by the nature of the site.”

“I think that’s a great idea.”

She asked, “You want to look at more clouds? We might see some interesting formations this time of day.”

“Sure.”

We lay there awhile and then she asked, “Do you believe in heaven?”

“Yeah, I think so. Do you?”

“Yes, but I haven’t thought much about it until the last few days. I wonder if Aunt Agnes is looking down on us or if she’s in another place, another part of the universe.”

“We were in a number of situations over there where we could have been killed. I always thought if I died I’d go to heaven, but I never thought much about what it would be like. I felt some comfort in knowing that I would see relatives and pets, but that’s about as far as it got.”

She said, “Sometimes, I wonder if we humans just made all this up about God and heaven to make ourselves feel better.”

“I used to be sure it was all true, but over the last few years, I’ve had a lot of questions. I’ve answered a bunch of ‘em, but I’m still working on others. I'm gonna ask Doc to help me. It's important for me to keep working on the spiritual stuff."

"When you're ready, I would like to know what you find out, because I have a lot of questions myself."

I responded, "I'll remember that. See anything extra special?"

"I love the different colors at this time of day and the reflection of those colors off the clouds."

"Me too, twilight is my favorite time of the day."

She said, "I thought you would be a morning person."

"I like morning too, especially around sunrise. How 'bout you?"

"I like twilight too, but I'm not a big fan of mornings. I'm more of a night person."

I rolled over being careful not to get too close, "What's your favorite food?"

"I like dark chocolate."

"Hey, that's not real food."

She laughed, "It certainly is real food. What's your favorite food?"

"Hot dogs."

Laughing, she said, "Talking about real food, hot dogs are terrible. How can you eat them?"

"I don't. I can't stand hot dogs."

"All right, what's your favorite food?"

I was looking at her, but she was only glancing at me. I really like a lot of foods, but mom's banana pudding is my favorite."

She smiled again, "Well, we're two health nuts when it comes to food. Sweets and deserts."

She looked at me a little longer and I think she was looking more closely at the features of my face. Maybe my imagination. I could hear the sound of the bikes up on the trail.

She said, "I've never ridden one of those disgusting bikes. They add too much pollution to the air." Then she smiled and asked, "Would you teach me to ride?"

I smiled and said, "Sure."

She interrupted, "But you can't tell anyone except April and Ace. I'm an environmentalist and that wouldn't look good."

I smiled again and said, "OK, I'm not real good at keeping secrets, but I'll do the best I can."

"Listen kid, you tell anyone and I'll turn you over my knee and spank you."

I cupped my hands to my mouth and yelled as loud as I could, "Eden wants to learn to ride a dirt bike! Eden wants to pollute the environment by riding a dirt bike!"

She smacked me up-side the head twice and said in a mean voice, "I told you not to tell anyone you brat."

Whining, I said, "I want my spanking and I want it now."

"You should be so lucky Jett Hollander. Now get your butt up. We're going back to the cabin. I never was a mom. I'm beginning to like how that works. I get to tell you what to do."

"Does that mean you'll be my mother figure and some other things?"

She responded, "No, but you are making friends with a 'control freak.' And I'm always right too. You'd do well to remember that little dude."

I said, "You've got some grass and stuff on the back of your slacks. Let me brush that off for you."

"Keep your hands off my slacks kid."

"So I got it now. You can tell me to get my butt off the ground, but I can't brush off your butt. That doesn't seem fair."

"Life is not fair child. That's one important lessen to learn."

We smiled at each other and held a brief gaze. She said, "You make me laugh. That feels good."

I took her hand and said, "Come over here a minute and let's look at the view one more time." When we reached the edge, she gently squeezed my hand and then eased her hand out of mine. "I want to teach you our famous breathing technique." I gave her a quick lessen and said, "Now, look out over the mountains and take some nice and slow deep breaths." We stood there about five minutes. "How was that?"

"I feel very relaxed. That was nice."

We headed back to the cabin and when we were about a hundred meters away, she surprised me and took off running and said, "Race you to the cabin."

She and Spot were flying down the trail and I caught Eden, but not Spot. She said, "Wait till I'm a hundred percent, I'll whip your butt in a race."

As we were walking up the steps to the porch, I said, "There you go again talking about my butt."

She smiled and Ace yelled from the kitchen, "What's this I hear about someone's butt?"

I told them the story and Ace said, "Eden, you should have let Jett brush off your butt. He's really good at that and it's where he got his nickname - Butt Wipe."

We laughed. April moved around in the kitchen and I said, "You women rustle us up some grub." April turned and took Eden by the hand and led her over to the couch and called out, "Let us know when it's ready. And bring us a glass of wine 'Butt Wipes'."

"What color?"

April, "White."

Eden, "White."

"Comin' up."

Ace and I were busy in the kitchen. He pointed to his beer and said, "Number one." I gave him a high-five.

I said, "What do you wanna fix?"

"I don't know. Whatta we got?" I looked in the fridge and the cabinets.

A minute later the girls came over and April said, "Sit down at the table boys. We want something we can eat."

A little before supper was ready, Ace got another beer and said, "Number two."

April exclaimed, "Ace Frost, would you please stop referring to your beers as number one and number two. That's nasty."

Eden chimed in and said, "Right, and especially before we're sitting down to eat."

Ace and I expressed shock at that interpretation of number one and number two and said that we knew where their minds were and they ought to clean up their thinking. Eden was cutting up stalks of celery and tossed one to April and said one, two, three and on three, they both threw the celery at us.

Ace asked me, "Should we let this go or should we retaliate?"

I responded, "We could respond, but if they respond back or get mad at us, they might stop fixing supper and we'd go hungry."

Ace said, "Maybe we should just bide our time and look for opportunities after supper is over."

We high-fived each other.

We had a good time all evening. After supper and after Ace and I finished the dishes at their insistence, we played Spades. We laughed and joked a lot. Again, Eden fit in like it had been the four of us having fun together for years.

Midway through Spades, Ace and I worked out a way for each of us to get a piece of ice. When Ace said, "I need a soda," and got up to get it, I got up and said, "No I'll get it for you." At that point we put the ice down their backs. We howled at their initial shocked response. Then Eden said calmly, "April, let me help you get that ice out and then you can help me get mine out." They acted like it wasn't a big deal and we continued playing cards. I knew April well enough to know she would down play it now, but later there would be consequences.

Several times during the evening, Eden caught me looking at her and one time I caught her looking at me. I knew what I was thinking, but I had no idea what she was thinking. I hoped she was thinking that maybe I wasn't too young after all.

Around 11:00, Ace wanted to watch a rerun of Mash. We sat on the couch with the girls in the middle. The sofa had been around for awhile and had a tendency to sag in the middle. I started out sitting about six inches from Eden, but after awhile as we laughed at Mash, we shifted and near the end, the side of my thigh was touching hers and I could feel the heat. I didn't want it to end.

It did end and April asked if anyone else was ready to go to bed. There was a group consensus and we said, "Good night." April asked Eden if she needed anything and she said she didn't need a thing.

I had a restless night, but I had no nightmares. We ate breakfast and then got showers. April was off today and had a bunch of errands to run and some housework to do.

Eden knew that we had our group meeting this morning and I told her that our group leader wanted us to eat lunch and play some volleyball and that I would call her around 3:00 or 4:00. She said she had a lot of work to do at Aunt Agnes' house and said she might need me to give her a hand after group. I said, "Do you just want me to come over after group is over."

She answered, "Yes that would be great."

We agreed to gather back at the cabin around 6:30. I said I would call April and Ace from Eden's to see about plans for supper. As I walked her to the car, we talked a little about the upcoming meeting with Jack, Ann, and the estate attorney. I watched her pull away and waved to her as she headed down the hill.

I had a wonderful time. I hope she did too.

46

GROUP SESSION THREE

Doc arrived a few minutes early to set up a portable sound box with CD player.

Doc: "Good Morning. I'm glad to see everyone. How many of you had to deal this morning with Focker's resistance to coming here?"

It seemed like everyone raised their hand.

Doc: "So how come everyone is present?"

Doug smiling: "My wife said if I didn't come I could pack my duffle bag and go live at the Salvation Army."

Paul: "I told my Focker he could 'fock off.' I was gonna give Doc one more chance to say something helpful."

Frank: "I still have a few more questions."

A few more answers, some humorous and some more serious.

Doc: "Over the past week, what did you discover about you and your Focker?"

Rob: "I kept telling Mac Focker that getting drunk was not going to help, but he won over all but one time."

Doc: "Avoid language like Focker won and I lost. Why?"

Rob: "Makes it sound like a battle and a fight."

Doc: "Right on and fighting always makes things worse. Also, it's never about winning and losing. It's about getting Centered where things are flowing and working well. Rob, give it another try."

Rob: "Mac just talks me into shit and I don't have skills to talk him out of it."

Doc smiling: "Okay. Anyone else?"

Melinda: "I was amazed at how much of my life was lived on 'auto pilot.' When I reflected on some parts of the week, I was aware that I had been Centered some of the time. I went to church, fixed a meal for my aunt who is sick, played with my nephew for a few hours, had a good talk with my mom and dad, and there were other things too. In each of those things they just happened. I don't remember making any decisions about those activities. I just did them automatically. Tilda created some PTSD moments and from Center, I stepped in and tried to help. I said, 'Let's take deep breaths and be confident that it will help us.' It helped some, but not much. Tilda is still strong and powerful."

Chad: "Like Melinda, I found many positive things about my week when I was Centered and didn't realize it until the reflection. However, Lanco started going on about how I must not be worth much if I couldn't keep my girlfriend from leaving me. Loser and failure were surfacing a lot during that period. I tried to intervene and make us feel better by saying positive things and that God would help us get through this tough time. It was reassuring, but we didn't feel much better."

Ace: "I had an experience where I used the data stored in my brain. I helped Jett fix the balance on the porch swing."

Doc: "Fixing the balance on the porch swing came out of that portion of the brain that stores that kind of information. You could call it a Centered activity unless Ace had struggled and he was having trouble fixing it and Fark said something like, 'You think you're so good at stuff, but you suck at it.'"

Anna: "Pee Wee started feeling sorry for us. She was comparing our life with some of our friends who seem to have everything going for them. I reminded her that for a few moments last week I didn't know there was anything wrong with losing an arm. In spite of that she had me so discouraged that we didn't feel any better. Then I said we're going to do the deep breathing for about ten minutes and I was surprised that it helped. I'm starting to experience the idea that we can only handle one thought at a time. It was a relief to let go of her negative thoughts and I felt at times that I was more in control and Pee Wee was not able to override me."

Frank: "Huck really worked on me about this group. He kept telling me that this stuff isn't going to work and that I'm wasting my time. I kept telling him that it's going to take time and we need to be patient. I'm here so I made the decision over his objections."

Doc: "I'm glad that everyone made it in spite of Focker's objections. Close your eyes and focus on taking some nice and easy deep breaths. That's right....Let all thinking subside as you continue to focus on your breathing....Perhaps you already feel your body relaxing and letting go....Maybe some areas are more relaxed than others. Relax the flow of air in and out of your lungs, drifting into the stillness and quietness, letting your breathing slow down as you journey to Center. Remember last week how you walked in the forest and down a hill to a ravine and through the door into your Center. Now, I'm asking you to experience another way to get to Center, spending a little more time on your breathing. I'll be counting from ten to one and when I say the number one you will be at your Center. Focus your attention on the numbers. You can visualize each number or you can just listen to the number or you can do both. You make the choice, focusing on the number ten and now number nine, now number eight, now number seven... With each number your focus becomes a little sharper and your attention more clear and now number six - attentive, alert, and focused - now on the number five and now number four - your focus even sharper - and now number three - very alert - and now number two and now number one and you are at your Center. Look around and notice what you see while opening all your senses to this experience. You might marvel at the beauty surrounding you in your Center. Be open to a flowing and peaceful energy, looking around for something you might be seeing for the first time, something you missed on previous trips to your Center. Take some time to bask in the radiance of your creation....Take a few more minutes to look around one more time, content in the knowledge that your Center is with you each moment of your life and now that you're learning how to come to your Center, you can come here anytime you choose. Now take a few deep breaths and open your eyes."

Melinda: "I feel like I'm able to get Centered and experience some of the benefits, but when I open my eyes, I sometimes feel this despair. It does feel like a bad habit."

Frank: "Melinda, if I can use your example to see if I'm anywhere close to getting this. Despair is neither good nor bad. It is what it is. Doc, would this mean that Huck is creating despair and I accept the despair? It is what it is and I stay there with Huck for as many moments as I chose. So, we're despairing and despairing and despairing some more and then I reach a moment where I decide to feel something different. While Huck is still despairing, I choose to shift to Center to create a new experience. So I might ask myself at Center, 'What was the despair about anyway?' Then I think it was about losing my friend Freddy on our last mission. So at Center, I'm thinking that this despair is okay, but I'm now ready to create something different. I think I've done enough despair for awhile. It's at this point that I don't know what to do. Am I getting the point Doc?"

Rob: "All that talking to myself would drive me crazy."

Doc: "Rob, if you choose to be open to the experience, you might be surprised that it turns out to be helpful. I just want all of you to be open to exploring these ideas. What did the rest of you think about what Frank said?"

Melinda: "I liked it because when I feel that kind of sadness or despair, it doesn't feel like a choice. I feel stuck in it and my habit is to label it is as depressing and sad and I don't like it. I judge it as bad. And until this training, I didn't realize that Tilda out of habit was doing the despair and I was labeling it as bad. I didn't realize that I could feel the despair with her and then decide that we now need to do something different. I tried to shift to Center several times this weekend, but I struggled to make the shift. I used walking in the forest and down the hill to the ravine, but I still struggled. I liked the counting this morning. I think it helped me get more focused. I think I just need more practice."

Doc: "One path to Center is a quiet mind. The numbers can be a very helpful in shutting down Focker's chatter."

Doug: "I'm an old soldier Doc and I'm really struggling with all this new stuff. Do you think I have a chance to get it?"

Doc: "Absolutely Doug. Most of this is new to everyone and I will help all of you during our individual sessions to better understand it and practice using it. It's a matter of training and believing you can do it. How many others are wondering if they will ever get it and find it helpful?"

Everyone raised their hand.

Doc: "The complexity of the brain/mind never ceases to amaze me. All of what we are about here is an attempt to take something complex and make it into something that we can understand and use for managing these PTSD symptoms. The model will not stand the test of the neuro-scientists, psychologists, and psychotherapists who make their life's work studying the nature of the brain. Some of you will see inconsistencies in the model that I will not be able to explain to your satisfaction. I urge you to keep in mind that our goal here is not to find out if the model will stand the test of any discipline or logical thinking. The sole purpose of the model is to find a system that works and that will help you find peace and happiness in your life. I need your help to refine the model and make sure it's helpful."

Ace: "Doug, you're not alone here. I hope you can see we're all struggling. It's soldiers like you who saved my life on many occasions and you're important to me and important to what we do here. All of you are important to me. I want all of us to get better. I tried to kill myself a few weeks ago and if the jailer who had been a friend of mine in high school, hadn't happened to come back and check on me, I'd be taking a dirt-nap right now."

Nate: "My mom found me passed out on an overdose of pills and booze and she wasn't supposed to be home for another five hours."

Paul: "I took a pistol out in the woods about a month ago and dug my own grave and laid down and was ready to pull the trigger and some bug crawled on me and I thought, 'I don't want a bunch of maggots eating my flesh.' So I postponed whacking myself till I could find a better way."

Most everyone in the group had thought about suicide. Some, like me, were not as serious about it as others. Some said they were too chicken to do it. Chad said he was told that he would go to hell if he killed himself. Anna said she couldn't do it to her family. Rob and Nate said that many times they had thought about running their bikes into a concrete bridge support.

Doc: "This is why the government hired me to explore different types of treatment for PTSD. It is taking its' toll on you combat veterans. If this system turns out to be helpful to you, other soldiers could benefit from what we do here."

Ace: "Let's hang together. We can do this. We have all faced hell on earth and danger that most other people will never face. I'm tired of running from these fucking flashbacks, nightmares, and especially my own feelings. I say, 'Focker bring 'em on.' I know Doc, I'm not supposed to judge that mother Focker, but Fart, I mean Fark is strong and I've got to find the energy and determination to get Centered and find some happiness."

Doc: "One of the wonderful things about meeting in a group is the group energy can excite a more powerful personal energy. That may be already evident or may become more evident later. Ace is right on target. Thank you for urging everyone to stay engaged in what we are doing. Any comments?"

(Silence)

Doc: "Frank and Melinda were talking about their despair. I would like to continue working on the system using less intense topics or feelings. Believe me. We'll get to those later. If I'm you're coach and I'm helping you train to run a marathon, we start slow and build up stamina and strength – the same with our work. I want us to start with some areas that are not as challenging as others. First, it's important to become more comfortable and at home in your Center. This means more meditations and what I call 'interior training' so stay with me."

Doc: "Close your eyes and focus your attention on normal breathing. Now shift your attention to your right foot. Now shift your attention to your nose. Now shift your attention to the thumb on your right hand. Now shift your attention to your left ear. Now shift your attention to the toes on your left foot. Now shift to paying attention to your Focker and be curious about what she will think next. You might be surprised or it might be something he keeps thinking, whatever it is, let her thoughts come and go, remembering to let Focker's thoughts come without any conscious direction from you. That is the you who was shifting to different parts of your body and you may have some nice Centered thoughts about how peaceful you feel right now. Perhaps more pleasant thoughts are coming and going and you may want to stay with those thoughts, but for right now, in this moment, let them drift away and shift your attention back to your breathing. That's right, taking a few nice and easy deep breaths into the quietness and now shifting your attention from your breathing to focusing on your right knee. Now shift your attention to your left knee and now to your mouth and your eyes. Now take a few moments to shift to any other part of your body you choose, where you want to direct your attention. Open your eyes. What was that like?"

Ace: "I think I was getting the idea about shifting. There was a 'me' in charge and that part could choose to guide my attention and could also choose to let Fark Focker emerge in anyway he wanted with no guidance from me. I'm surprised you suggested we also let go of those nice peaceful thoughts. That must be a part of the attention training. We practice shifting our attention and later we'll be more skilled in being able to make those shifts. Is that it?"

Doc: "Yes. Think about this for a moment. When you have experienced your symptoms in the past, you may have wanted to fight them, destroy them, run from them, battle them, slay them, deny them, push them away and on and on. Now you're learning the skill of being in command and being able to shift your attention from one thing to another. This is designed to give you the confidence that you can shift your attention from your symptoms to your breathing and to your Center. And as you get to know your Center, you will discover when you make that shift everything changes and is transformed into something different. Another way to describe that process is you make the shift from focusing your attention on Focker and your symptoms to inviting Focker and these same symptoms into your Center."

Paul: "I'll invite Hank Focker to my Center and offer him a beer."

Laughter.

Doc: "That sounds funny, but think about it for a moment, can you be Centered and have a beer?"

Ace: "I sure hope so."

"Me too," came from some others.

Doc: "We talked about it before. In my opinion, if drinking is working well for you, then you are Centered when having a beer or two."

Nate: "How 'bout three?"

Smiling, Doc answered, "I know I suggested a beer or two, but there is no number. The criteria again is whether or not it's working for you. I believe when you're Centered, you'll discover the wisdom you need to figure it out."

Doc: "So if Nate decides getting drunk is not working, he invites Barr Focker to Center to work out a different plan. At Center, the transformation process begins."

Ace: "So if I invite Fark Focker to my Center in the forest for a picnic and a beer or two, my intention is to have a friendly chat and begin the transformation process. Is that it?"

Doc: "Yes."

Ace: "What are we going to talk about?

Doc: "Would anyone like to take a stab?"

Me: "I take Tug to my knoll in the forest."

Tug says, "What are we doing here?"

I say, "This is my training area to learn how we can stop doing panic attacks."

Tug says, "Good luck on that one. That deep breathing you've been doin' is worthless."

I say, "I'm still learning that skill along with some others.

Tug asks, "Whatta you want from me?"

I answer, "I want you to know that I'm gonna be able to stop this panic and I want you to stop fighting me and freaking out."

Tug responds, "These fuckin' things scare the shit outta me and you want me to just relax?"

I responded, "I want you to come here when the symptoms start and believe we can get the job done."

Tug blurts out, "Are we finished? This is bullshit. What's wrong with you? We used to be in this together and now you're trying to change us and I hate change. I'm leaving. I'm not comfortable here and I'm having trouble breathing in this place."

Me: "He leaves and I start my breathing, look around and notice the beauty here and I feel calm and serene. Is it something like that?"

Doc: "Yes, 'something like that' is a good way to put it, because there is no right way to do this. There is only what works for each one of you. Jett, that seemed to be a good start for you. Is that true?"

Me: "It seems kind of silly and simple, but the funny thing about it is that during the conversation, I didn't feel helpless and I felt in charge. And I wasn't afraid of Tug and I didn't see Tug as the enemy or the advisory. I felt kind of sorry for him. He seemed desperate and afraid. By listening to myself talk to him, I realized I was taking charge and I was in training to learn the skills to overcome the panic attacks."

Ace: "As you were going through that Jett, Fark was saying what a farce. Then I thought about being a squad leader and how I was in charge of making sure our squad accomplished the mission. On some of those missions, I didn't know how we were gonna get it done. The odds seemed so overwhelming, but I was in charge and my attitude was 'comin' fuckin' hell or high water, my guys are gonna take care of business. So when you said a minute ago that you felt in charge, I thought this is no different. In fact, I only have one soldier to deal with and I can sure as hell whip his ass into shape."

Anna: "So it isn't really what Jett said to Tug. It is the fact that Jett is in charge and has a structure and a plan and that gives him motivation and power. There's no more helplessness. Let the training continue."

Frank: "Why couldn't we do this without the model? Why do we need Focker and Centering?"

Melinda: "It gives me a better understanding about how the brain works. It helps me to be able to separate myself from Tilda. I can both experience and observe what she's doing. When there was no separation, I was part of the guilt. Now, even though I'm ultimately responsible for the guilt she creates, I'm separate from that guilt. I am not the guilt. I don't know exactly where this is going, but I do feel like I'm in charge too. I'm now running the show."

Doc: "Please go ahead with other responses."

Chad: "I've already told you all that I'm a Christian so this separate part of me at Center is like my soul - that part of me that goes to heaven. My preacher used to remind us that Jesus said the Kingdom of Heaven is within you and now I know what that means. The Kingdom is right here." He places his palm over his heart.

Me: "Our priest used to begin our service by reminding us that God said, 'Be still and know that I am your God.' And one of our main goals is to quiet the mind or be still. I'm not sure how all of this is going to work for me spiritually since I've got some hang ups about religion in general. I have to say this stuff sure seems to fit with some things I've been taught."

Rob: "I never cared much for religion. We grew up poor and most of the people in the church down the road from our shack treated us like poor worthless white trash. One lady used to bring us food at Thanksgiving and Christmas, but I never knew if she was part of that church. I like the model. It helps me understand what Doc is gettin' at."

Paul: "This is still some heavy shit, but I'm trying to get it."

Doug: "I'm a structured person and the structure helps. Before now, I wouldn't have had no interest in figurin' how the brain works. But I'm desperate and that's hard for me to say, but it has forced me to pay attention and try to learn this stuff. I'm still struggling with seeing things when I close my eyes, but I feel like I'm gettin' the point. I've had a lot of conversations with myself about using pills and alcohol to ease the pain, but now I feel like I have more to work with than, 'you better quit them pills and boozing. It's gonna kill you.'"

Anna starts crying and says, "I'm trying so hard, but sometimes I just want to give up like I don't have any energy left. Pee Wee keeps telling me that except for Chad, everyone else here has two arms and two eyes. She says you all don't get it." Continuing to cry and having difficulty getting out the words, "I get in this deep rut and at times don't see any way out of it."

Melinda comes over and takes her hand and pulls her gently to her feet and with tears rolling down her own cheeks takes her in her arms. Chad gets up with tears dripping from his eye and puts his arms around them. Ace gets up and before long everyone in the room is in this group hug and as best I could tell there were no dry eyes. And Doc on the outside of the circle gently and quietly says: "It is in this moment that you can be reminded that you not only stand together as soldiers sharing a common experience, but also stand together as a group willing to care about and support each other on this healing journey." We all stayed for a few more minutes and then everyone slowly took their seats.

(Silence)

Chad: "I now realize how close my tears are to the surface. I was doing pretty good holding 'em back, but when Anna started crying, I couldn't hold 'em any longer. When I put my arms around Melinda and Anna and then Ace came up and all the rest followed, I think it was the first time since I've been back that I didn't feel alone. I can't explain it beyond that."

Ace: "Until a few weeks ago, I thought crying was a sign of weakness and proved you were a wimp. I have to give Jett credit for helping me get over that, but then he's always been a sissy."

(Smiles around the room)

Paul: "My Daddy when I was little always said I was a cry baby. I've always tried to prove to him that I'm a man. I thought being in the Army would help, but he never said much about it. Then when he found out I was comin' here he said how come I couldn't be a man and get over it without runnin' off to see a shrink and sittin' around in a group to moan and groan and complain. If he could see us, he would say we're all a bunch of snot nosed cry babies."

Doc: "And yet Paul, you came anyway. What happened?"

Paul: "My momma told me not to listen to that ole fart. She said, 'I seen him cry on many occasions.' She told me to go get some help and here I am."

Nate: "I done the same thing with my old man. He never said a kind word to me. I just wanted him to say I was brave or something for goin' off to war and he never did. He died about half way through my second tour." He teared-up and had a tough time getting through that last sentence. And then through the tears and a smile he said, "Don't nobody come over and put their arms around me. I ain't use to that."

Paul: "How 'bout if Anna and Melinda came over and give you a big hug?"

He forced a smile, "Now that'd be another story."

Anna looked at Melinda and said, "Let's go give him that big hug!"

Nate held up his hands and exclaimed, "No, no that's alright. I'm good now."

Rob: "I'll take that big hug if Nate don't want it."

Most all the men, "I'll take a big hug!!"

Smiling, Doc: "Okay, there will be plenty of time for hugs, but let's move along. Is it true that you have just talked through an issue where you decided to stop judging crying as something bad and perhaps now can also refrain from labeling it as good."

Doug interrupted, "Let me say it. Crying is not good or bad, it just is what it is." There were high fives from Rob and Nate sitting next to Doug.

Doc: "As you become more aware of the issue of judging, you might be surprised to find out how we do that all the time. So now that we have decided that crying is neither good nor bad, we are free to choose either response and let it be what it is."

Doc: "Frank, a few minutes ago, you asked about why the model, the Center, and the Fockers. Does it make more sense to you now?"

Frank: "It made sense before. I just wanted to know if it was necessary. I think I can see the benefit more clearly now."

Doc: "Any other questions?" There were no questions. "I want us to do another Centering Meditation, more on getting to know your Center."

"Sit up straight with both feet flat on the floor and look straight ahead and find a point out in front of you. Fix your attention on that point and stare at it and do the best you can to let go of any thoughts about the point or what you see or how you would describe it and simply focus your attention on the point...and now, begin taking some deep breaths continuing to focus on the point....Now your attention is on the point and then on your breathing. Take a few more minutes.... Now close your eyes and journey to your Center and take a few more deep breaths....Look around and open all your senses to the beauty of this very special place, even though you have been here before, be open to seeing things you haven't seen on previous visits to your new home. Notice that any sounds you might hear are part of a deeper silence and silence by definition translates into a peace, a stillness, and a quietness. Noticing in the silence that there can be awareness of the moment as you look around and feel the serenity of this space inside...embracing and celebrating the freedom to be present here and now where there is no past and no future...where everything can be fresh and new. If you're not seeing or visualizing your place, remember it's most important that you focus on the breathing and experience the silence and quietness. The visual may or may not come later. It makes no difference. You know where your Center is and you along with everyone else are learning and discovering what it's like to be here....Be open to the clarity that exists when your mind is quiet...and perhaps along the way you will discover the wisdom of your true self, a wisdom you may not have been aware of in the past, but can now understand has always been there. As time passes you will find new and interesting ways to use your wisdom to make decisions about letting go and healing. It may not be real clear exactly how that will happen, but you can choose to be open, receptive, and listening....While your Focker is quiet, you are free to explore your true self with a curiosity and openness to what might unfold in each moment....I invite you now to be aware of your physical experience at Center. Notice what it feels like to be physically relaxed and calm. Here your muscles are loose and fluid, your blood is flowing smoothly through your body and that turns into a nice and warm energy making its' way into every cell, fiber, and muscle. Being aware that being Centered can bring many physical benefits that promote healing and wholeness, look around again and take a few more minutes. When you are ready, open your eyes."

Doc: "Are you starting to be more familiar with your Center?"

Some said they were doing pretty well and others were struggling.

Frank: "I'm beginning to understand why you're focusing so much on us getting to know our Center and being able to go there and stay there and live there. If I am Centered, Huck takes a nap or I could say Huck doesn't exist in that moment."

Doc: "The central focus and goal of all our training is to help you be more Centered in your life. When you are Centered, Focker has no power. One aspect of the training is to get Focker on board with the Centering. She has in many ways been running the show for a long time and he will fight you to the end for control of your life. Remember, everything we do, every exercise, every meditation, every topic we discuss is designed to assist you in being more Centered in your life. At Center, you are free."

Doc: "With that in mind, I would like for each of you to take a walk outside with the goal of experiencing your walk from your Center. This is a cousin of the exercise we did in the first group session on focusing in the moment. Before leaving, open your notebooks and look over the page on the nature of Center. Be particularly aware of any notes you made that further define your Center. As part of being Centered, see if you can through your senses experience the walk as if you were seeing everything for the first time. It might help to imagine that you have no memory of where you choose to go. I'll ring the bell when I want you to return."

When we returned, everyone talked about the challenge of staying in the moment and experiencing things as fresh and new. Most used deep breathing to help quiet the mind. Some felt peaceful and others felt some frustration with Focker's chatter. Most everyone thought it was helpful to work on staying Centered with eyes open since most of the time we practice being Centered with our eyes closed.

Doc: "You all have made good progress, but I want you to remember that it is critical that you keep practicing the skills. Okay, let's take a break. Spend some time with someone you haven't gotten to know."

I turned to Rob and we got our drinks and went for a short walk. He had described himself as shy and it was true. He was friendly, but I had to keep the conversation going. We talked about each other's families and a little about our military assignments.

Doc: "I want to talk more about the body. We have spent lots of time talking about how the deep breathing helps the body to relax and how your body can feel peaceful and serene when you are Centered. When you have a thought and feeling, your body always responds to that experience. In the early years of human development, if the mind was peaceful, the body would be peaceful. If the mind was creating stress, the body would be in stress mode. Later in our development, we discovered over time that the human race spends so much time in stress mode that the body physically holds on to that stress like a bad habit. Everyone does it to differing degrees. That means when you're peaceful in thought and feeling, your body is not necessarily peaceful depending on how stressed you have been in your life. Now, for complicated reasons, your body doesn't always wait on your thoughts and feelings to have a response. It creates a response on its' own. We have, for instance, referred to it as anxiety or panic coming out of the blue. You say, 'I was doing fine and all of a sudden out of blue, I started feeling nervous or anxious or had trouble breathing. My point is that what's going on in your body can also be complicated. All this is for your information. Questions?"

Chad: "Why is this important?"

Doc: "Because I want you to become more aware of how your body responds to what you're thinking and feeling. I also want you to know that it's not black or white. All of us are already holding some stress in our body so even when you feel peaceful, your body is still holding on to some tension."

Anna: "I know the deep breathing is supposed to relax our body. Does it also have any impact on that tension that we hold on to as a habit?"

Doc: "Yes. It can have a big impact over a period of time which is another benefit of the deep breathing. Remember back to some of our meditations where I have talked about feeling your body relaxed. Close your eyes now and go to Center. Take about ten deep breaths…feel the relaxation and recall what it felt like in previous meditations. Check your body from head to toe. Take a few more deep breaths. Open your eyes. Did everyone feel that physical relaxation?"

Seemed like everyone nodded.

Doc: "How many of you have had anger issues over the last two or three months?" (Pause) "It looks like everyone. I want you to close your eyes and go back in time and pull up a situation where you were angry. I'll give you a few moments. Okay, get into the experience and feel the anger and go through the story or encounter. Feel the anger. Now ask what it feels like in your body. Take some time to explore how your body feels and where you feel it. Open your eyes. What was that like?"

Frank: "I don't know how much I felt it in that moment, but I thought back when I have been angry and I clinch my teeth and my whole body gets tense and a few times when I have been real mad, my body also shakes."

Melinda: "I realized that most of the time I hold my anger inside and my stomach starts to churn and I start to sweat. If I'm really angry, my body tenses up and I start to feel weak in the legs."

Nate: "My body gets real tense and I ball up my fists and I think I might also clinch my teeth."

Ace: "I feel a rush of adrenalin. It's like a funny sensation that feels like all this energy comes into my body and I'm ready to explode. I think I have unusual physical strength when that happens. I can also tell you when the situation is over, I feel totally drained and can hardly move. That's also true when I get in a fight and get my ass whipped."

Paul: "When I get pissed off, my body gets tight and then my head starts hurtin' bad

Doug: "I get tense all over and people tell me I turn red."

Anna: "People tell me too that my face gets real red. I feel it all over my body."

Rob: "My heart starts racing and I ball up my fists."

Me: "I feel tension everywhere in my body and I raise my voice. I thought some about fear and how that causes my whole body to feel weak."

The group took off on fear and all the different ways we feel it in our body. We are becoming more aware of how our bodies respond to our thoughts, feelings, and experiences.

Doc: "One more time. Why are we emphasizing what different experiences feel like in the body?"

Chad: "You have said all along that one of the benefits of breathing is it relaxes the body. We have talked about shifting the way we think about stuff. You're trying to help us realize how helpful the deep breathing can be for reducing our physical symptoms and shifting to Center."

Melinda: "And how can we use the breathing to do that if we're not aware or paying attention to those physical symptoms?"

Frank: "If we focus on the physical symptoms and reduce their intensity, we can more easily make that shift to Center?"

Silence and then Paul: "I don't got as many kernels on my cob as most of ya'll, but if I'm scared about somethin' and feelin' that in my body, I could use the breathin' to work on my body and I think that would help me not to be so scared."

Frank: "When Paul said it would help him not to be so scared, that would mean sometimes I can have one foot in Center and the other foot in Huck Focker's world."

Doc: "Excellent point. The goal is to have more of you at Center and less of you in Focker's world. At times the reverse will be true. And at other times you may feel one hundred percent Centered and at other times totally on board with Focker. Are there any other comments on the importance of being attentive to the physical symptoms?"

Me: "Now that I'm more aware, that's what I've been doing when Tug freaks out about the panic attacks. I've been trying to calm down my body with the deep breathing and never thought much about the logic behind it. If I can get those physical symptoms under control, I'll have a better chance of shifting to Center. I'm not having a lot of success, but with more awareness and attention to my body and more practice on the breathing, I think that will help."

Doc: "This underscores the importance of the deep breathing. Close your eyes and go back to the anger situation and feel it in your body. Do your best to recreate it. Imagine what it would be like if you could use the breathing to effectively interrupt those physical symptoms. Take some deep breaths now and feel the release of those symptoms. Be aware of moving into your Center. Let your breathing slow down and open your eyes. From here on, I'll be asking you to pay more attention to your body. Keep picking up the books."

Doc: "Let's talk more about anger. In my view anger is almost never an emotion that is working well."

Frank interrupted, "Isn't that a judgment against anger?"

Doc: "In one sense of the word, it is a judgment. At some point however, a judgment can become an opinion. In this case, my opinion is that anger is neither good nor bad nor right or wrong. It almost never works for me."

Frank: "You said 'almost never.' Under what circumstances would you say anger is working well?"

Doc: "If someone were physically attacking my loved ones and the anger gave me extra adrenalin to whip their ass. That would fit under the 'working well' category. I'm sure there are other exceptions."

Doc: "Can we agree for the most part that anger is created by Focker?"

Everyone nodded.

Doc: "So, if you respond to someone or something by creating anger, you know that Focker is on the scene. If you're caught off guard, you may give someone the 'bird' or get in an argument before you can get Centered. Remember 'Attention Training.' The goal is to pay attention and interrupt Focker's old patterns."

Frank: "I've got to pay attention and always be watching Huck to make sure he's not gonna go off or start some shit."

Doc: "In the beginning, that's true. Later on, Huck will not be able to stir up anger, because you will be Centered in those situations."

Frank: "I'm eager for more on how to get Centered."

Doc: "I want to go back to the anger exercise you did a few minutes ago. Close your eyes and go back to that experience where you created anger. Experience it and feel it. While you are doing that, listen to what Focker is saying and also pay attention to what that anger feels like in your body. Now I want you to step outside and observe or witness this experience from your Center and now open your eyes."

Ace: "I think I'm getting better at the observing and feeling less intense during the observing. When you suggested that I observe it from Center, it felt even more helpful."

Doc: "I asked you to step outside the experience and observe it from your Center so you could remember this can a helpful technique to use when you reflect on the experience. We did it during the first group. You didn't know about Centering at that point, but most of you said when observing the experience, the anger or stress was less. Now that you observe it from Center, it can be even more helpful."

Doc: "Would someone share their angry experience?"

Rob: "Between tours, I was stationed at Fort Benning and had a two week leave to go home. I was at a bar in town and met up with some high school buddies and they kept calling me, 'soldier boy.' We were laughing and having fun and all of a sudden I realized that I would be back in hell in a few months and they would continue on with their lives enjoying the freedoms I was supposed to be fighting for. Mac really got pissed off and about that time my sister came to pick me up to go to a family outing."

Doc: "Thanks Rob. In this situation, Rob is saved by his sister. I want each of you to imagine that last night you went through the same experience and that you plan to go to the same bar tonight and the same group will probably be there. Your goal is to stay Centered and Focker's goal is to kick some ass."

Doc: "How will you handle the situation? I'm going to give you a step-by-step process. It will probably seem a little long. When you become skilled at doing it, it can take only seconds or a minute or so, sometimes a little longer depending on the situation. Remember again, you are in training to run a marathon and it's going to take some time. I've written out this process on a handout which I'll give you in a few minutes."

Doc: "So after breakfast the next morning, you do the following exercise step by step. I'm going to use Rob since he volunteered."

Doc: "1. <u>Getting Centered</u>. Rob goes to Center on his motorcycle and spends time opening his senses, quieting his mind, and relaxing his body. Later in your training, you will all be able to go to Center and your mind will be automatically quiet and your body will automatically be relaxed. Some situations will be more challenging than others.

2. <u>A Converation with Focker.</u> Rob leaves his Center to talk with Mac about last night. Mac recounts the events and how he got so pissed off.

3. <u>The Physical Symptoms</u>. Rob says, 'It's helpful to be aware of how anger acts out in our body. I've noticed that our heart starts

beating faster and we ball up our fists. Did you feel that last night when you got angry?' Mac says, 'I guess. I'm not sure.'

4. The 'Not Working Well' Thoughts. Rob asks, 'What were you thinking last night?' Mac says, 'That those old friends were a bunch of ungrateful pricks and I wanted to beat the shit out of 'em.' Rob asks, 'Were you also thinking that I'm risking my life for this country and who cares. Everyone is just going on with their lives and I'm over there living in hell to defend their sorry asses. Right?' Mac answers, 'Yeah something like that. What's wrong with that?' Rob says, 'There's nothing wrong with that, but it doesn't work for us. Anger and fights don't lead anywhere. I want to go again tonight and I'm working on being Centered which means I will be creating some different ways to respond to situations like last night.' Mac says, 'I don't know how to make other choices.' Rob says, 'You don't need to make any choices. I'll show you how it works. Just don't fight me.'

5. Invite Focker to Center. Mac asks, 'What the hell are we doing on the motorcycle?' Rob goes into detail about Centering and takes him through the experience of getting to know the place and working on the deep breathing. He tells him it's going to take a little while to feel it, just be patient.

6. The Physical Release. Rob asks, 'How does it feel?' He says, 'I don't know how it feels. I'm too busy wondering what you want.' Rob says, 'Close your eyes again and see if you can just quiet your mind and feel what that's like in our body.' Mac says, 'Don't close your eyes. I don't wanna wreck.' Rob says, 'I've got it. Go on and close your eyes.' Reluctantly, Mac says, 'It feels good. I notice I don't feel tense.' Rob says, 'Good. I want you to spend more time here with me so you can see how good it feels to let go of all that tension and stress in our body. Open your eyes.'

7. The Centered Thoughts. Rob says, 'Our next step is to change the way we think.' Mac asks, 'How do we do that?' Rob answers, 'We remember that the breathing helps relax the body and quiet the mind

which helps us think more clearly. When our mind is quiet and still, we can access a deeper wisdom here at Center. So, we go over the situation and look at what you were thinking and then decide on some different possibilities remembering that on this peaceful ride our mind is clear. Help me out. How could we have thought about that situation differently?' Mac answers, 'I don't have a clue.' Rob says, 'Let me give you some examples. While I'm doing that, let's feel the deep relaxation in our bodies and be aware of the quietness and stillness of our mind. And for now, you pretend that you believe everything I'm saying.' I'm going to list nine possible phrases to give you some ideas. In your actual work, you would probably only pick one or two.

We can stay calm regardless of what they say or do.

We prefer peace over anger, stress, and getting in fights.

We give them no power over our response to their comments.

We can create whatever response we choose in this moment.

They have no clue about war and what it's like and that's okay.

We choose not to blame them for not knowing what we go through in combat.

We do not judge them.

We have the power to create our own response.

We are free to continue talking with them or free to leave.'

8. Practicing the Skills to stay Centered. Mac says, 'You've got me on the bike and it feels pretty good, but what happens when we get out in the real world and go to that bar tonight and they start mouthing off again?' Rob responds, 'I decide before we go in there we're going to stay Centered.'

He says, 'I can't close my eyes and come here 'cause I'll be at the bar.' Rob says, 'Our Center is always with us. It goes wherever we go. It is both our training ground to learn how to go to bars and not get angry and in fights and the place we seek peace and wisdom to help us live our lives.' He says, 'Those are some fancy words.' Rob responds, 'We come here to practice our skills at being Centered and remind ourselves that we have made the decision to do the best we can to stay Centered and live our life in peace and tranquility with ourselves and with others.' Mac asks, 'What does that involve?'

Rob says, 'It means getting on the bike and coming here every day to spend time feeling the energy, practicing the breathing, and training in other ways to help us stay Centered.' Mac asks, 'What other ways?' Rob responds, 'There are a lot of other ways. I want to teach you one of them now.'

9. Mental Rehearsal. 'Let's look around, feel the energy, and take some deep breaths. Stay Centered now with that peaceful mind and relaxed body and remember the scene last night.' Mac says, 'You got a point. It's hard to stir up anger.' Rob says, 'Okay, more deep breaths as we look around and experience the peace and serenity of this place. Let's look at a couple of our Centered statements and make a commitment to embrace those statements and make them true in our life. Remembering those statements and the spirit behind them and feeling the peace and serenity in our body, let's close our eyes and staying Centered go through the scene from last night. In what way is it different for you?' Mac answers, 'Well, it was different. Again, it was hard to stir up the anger. We just stood there and talked to them and they started mouthing off and I thought to myself. What a bunch of pricks. They don't have a clue. But it didn't bother me and you got up and said we'd see them later. But this is us just sitting here. I'm so use to doing things differently. How will I change?' Rob says: 'You don't need to change. Just stop fighting me.'

10. Transformation. Rob says, 'Two things are the key. The first is that you believe those statements I listed a few minutes ago and the second is that we behave as if we do actually believe them. So we do a lot of Centering exercises and mental rehearsing. Then we actually go to the bar tonight and they start the same stuff as last night. We repeat to ourselves some of our statements, take a few deep breaths, remain calm and get Centered. Then we finish our beer and tell them

we'll talk to them later. When we take those two steps, we are on the way to creating a new response to those types of situations. With more practice, we no longer have to think about it when we go into a bar. That's just how we respond to those types of people. It's a new habit and the old habit just fades away.'

11. Commitment and Training. Rob says, "This is not an easy path but with commitment, determination, and training, we can make it happen.' Mac asks, 'What if I'm not interested?' Rob responds, 'I have to keep working on you.'"

Doc: "Okay, that's the long form. I've got this on the newsprint in an abbreviated form. Once you get the hang of it, it's simple." He posts it in front.

Transforming our Symptoms: The Eleven Stepper

1. Getting Centered.
2. A Conversation with Focker.
3. The Physical Symptoms.
4. The "Not Working Well" Thoughts.
5. Invite Focker to Center.
6. The Physical Release.
7. The Centered Thoughts.
8. Practicing the Skills to Stay Centered.
9. Mental Rehearsal.
10. Transformation.
11. Commitment and Training.

Doc: "I have mentioned several times that Focker will resist because she is afraid of change. Again, he is not a bad person. He is just doing the best he can. Jett said he felt sorry for him. In many ways, she's like a little kid."

Frank: "One more time, what is Focker's role in flashbacks and panic attacks?"

Doc: "He doesn't consciously decide to do a flashback or a panic attack. They just come for different reasons. Sometimes something triggers them and sometimes they come out suddenly for seemingly no good reason. It has to do with how the brain works. If you have a traumatic experience, it becomes an imprint on the brain and imprints in many cases will show up later as a memory pop up. They were traumatic at the time when they were experienced and they can be traumatic when they are flashbacks. Most of you know what I mean."

Doc: "So here's where Focker comes in. Remember, before you started this training, you and Focker were the same. You were Focker and Focker was you. That is no longer the case. You occupy the same body and you are connected, but you are also separate. Remember the example of the hand." He holds up his hand. "You are in the middle of the palm and Focker is your middle finger."

Doc: "You remember me saying so often that the brain is complicated and complex. Okay, let's say we have twenty soldiers who go into combat and have similar experiences. After coming home, fifteen have flashbacks and nightmares and the other five never have a flashback or nightmare or any symptoms of PTSD. The reason for that is also complicated and complex and beyond the scope of our work. Sometimes they have problems of a different sort. So until now you and Focker didn't consciously cause these flashbacks and nightmares, but after they popped up, you all became a fertile environment for them to continue popping up. First they were scary as hell and so your first instinct was to be afraid of them. Then you wanted to slay them, conquer them, run from them, get rid of them, blow them up and so on. So for most of you, they have gotten worse."

Doc: "At some point a couple of weeks ago, you discovered that you are not Focker. You were the same as her, because you didn't know it could be any different. So, you have separated and left Focker out in the cold holding the bag. Focker is still scared and doesn't know anyway to handle this stuff other than the way he did it in the past.

He is fearful and the only thing he knows is to slay those fuckin' flashbacks and nightmares and any other PTSD symptoms. He's really scared and suspect of you and all your talk about healing. You've got to convince her there is another way. She will resist, but she can be won over, but you've got your work cut out for you. Frank, does that help?"

Frank: "Yes, for now."

Paul: "This is some heavy shit."

Some nods from others.

Doc: "I know, but in a few weeks, I'm certain you will be saying something different. We are still in basic training."

Doug: "Will I ever get out of basic?"

Smiles and Chad said: "Yeah, basic was a bear!"

Doc: "Any other questions?"

Anna: "On the first step, you have us going to Center. Why can't we just go straight to Focker and have that conversation?"

Doc: "The purpose of that is to get grounded at Center before the conversation. Focker will try to throw you off and it's important to be clear and ready to engage his rationalizations and special pleading for his behavior. As you become more automatically Centered, you can skip that first step."

Doc: "Please continue to be patient. Getting out of basic will happen soon. Let's keep going. I have a handout that lists those abbreviated eleven steps. Beneath those steps, I picked an example of anger and wrote out in long form going through those eleven steps in much the same way I did with you a few minutes ago. I want you now to take your example of anger and write out the narrative of the eleven steps in the same way I have written them out. In step one, I wrote, 'Go to Center and spend a minute or so quieting the mind and relaxing the body.' I want you to actually do that. Close your eyes, look around your Center and then begin the deep breathing. Every time you exhale count a number. Start at thirty and count backwards to one. Be especially aware of how you feel in your body after doing the breathing. Then look around your Center again and open all your senses to experience fully what it's like there. The next step is to invite Focker to your Center. Rob, I used your example. Could you think of another episode of anger?"

Rob: "That will be easy."

Paul: "You've been going back and forth callin' Focker he or she so everyone listen up. The name of my Focker has changed from Hank Focker to Fanny Focker. And my Center ain't Stanley's anymore. It's a room at the Inn in town."

Everyone is splitting a gut.

Nate: "Whatta ya gonna do with Fanny when you get her to Center?"

More laughter.

Paul: "First, we're gonna take a bunch of deep breaths and after we get cozy, we're gonna get connected and I'm gonna tell her not to be scared and she's gonna say, 'Paul I've always wanted you to fuck me. Would you mind doin' me before we get started on the exercise?'"

All the guys were talking about changing their Focker's names. Melinda chimed in and said she wanted to change and Anna said she couldn't change until she asked her husband. We were having fun with that idea.

Doc: "Well, what an interesting idea. Thank you, Paul. Let's think about that for a minute. Would that change the way you see your Focker? I wonder if it would be helpful to have a member of the opposite sex. I like the idea. I think it would be important to pick someone you didn't know. Otherwise, there would probably be additional baggage and challenges. As you go through the exercise, if you men are inclined to pick a woman and you women a man, see if you can figure out what the difference would be and then make your choice."

Paul: "Is fucking allowed?"

Smiling Doc said, "Only if you decide it would help with the healing."

Paul: "That's a 'no brainer.'"

Doc: "Okay, let's get started. I want you all to spread out in here and out on the decks so you'll have plenty of room. Extra pens are on the table. I will be walking around checking on each one to answer any questions you might have."

When trying to think of an angry episode, I realized that I don't have a lot of anger so I had to dig to find something. Then I remembered that I had been angry with Ace a number of times for resisting my suggestions about getting help. I decided because of Eden that my Focker would still be Tug. I went out on the back deck and Anna was already at the table and Doug was at the other end sitting on the stairs smoking and writing. I went to the other end and sat on the steps. I had already taken Tug to Center earlier in this group session, but I knew this was going to be an ongoing process and would happen many times over the next months.

1. Getting Centered. I went to the knoll and did the Centering exercise Doc instructed us to use.

2. A Conversation with Tug. I went to see Tug to talk with him about our conversations with Ace.

3. The Physical Symptoms. I asked him what it felt like in our body when he got angry. He didn't know so I said we tense up and raise our voice. He nodded. I jogged his memory about the incidents with Ace and then asked him to remember what it felt like physically. He said he remembered being tense.

4. The "Not Working Well" Thoughts. I explained anger is not working for us. "You were angry with Ace on a number of occasions. What were you thinking?" We worked together on it and came up with, "He should get some help before he ends up hurting himself or someone else. Why are you so bull-headed? Why can't you see you are hurting the people you are suppose to love? Why can't you talk to me; we've been buddies for almost twenty years? I've got to get you some help or

I'm a sorry ass friend. I'll never recover if something happens to you. Why did you put me in such a vulnerable position with April and now I feel guilty." Tug asked, "What's wrong with those thoughts?"

"Nothing, but again, those thoughts are not working. I want to help you experience what it's like to make another choice." He said, "Why would we wanna do that?" I responded, "Unless we learn to make other choices, we're not going to be able to do anything about the panic attacks, flashbacks, and nightmares."

5. Invite Tug to Center. I took him through about a five minute experience of Centering. "How do you feel now?" He answered, "I feel pretty relaxed."

6. The Physical Release. "Now doing your best to stay Centered in this relaxed feeling, go back and remember what it was like physically when we were arguing with Ace and see if you can stay with your relaxed body." He said, "It was easy because it wasn't real. I'm not there. I'm here." "I know. Doc is having us practice being Centered using our imagination. It is one of the steps to learning how to be more Centered in real life. Away from the actual experience, we hopefully can glimpse the possibility that being Centered while we are talking to Ace means we don't get angry. At this moment we are focusing on releasing the physical part of anger. Do you understand?" "I don't know, maybe.

How do I do that?" I said, "It's more like how do we do that?"

7. The Centered Thoughts. "Our next step is to change the way we think." I explain that being Centered opens us to accessing a greater wisdom inside us and it helps us choose Centered thoughts. I asked him to pretend that he believed these thoughts. I said, "Ace has the freedom to refuse treatment and we are not responsible for that choice. We can want Ace to talk with us, but he has the right to keep things to himself. Ace did not put us in a vulnerable position. We did that on our own. What do you think? Did you have any difficulty believing them?" Tug responded, "They seem true, but it's hard for me to get away from the thought that I ought to be able to make him do what's

right and get some help. It's different from the way I think, but I can see the logic behind it."

8. Practicing the Skills to Stay Centered. "To get good at Centering, we have to come here every day and train. I'm going to take more deep breaths to make sure we're grounded both mentally and physically at Center. As I'm taking the breaths, let's look around and experience the peace and serenity of this place. Now let's look at each statement and make a commitment to embrace those statements and make them true for us.

9. Mental Rehearsal. "And now remembering those statements and the spirit behind them and feeling the peace and serenity in our body, let's close our eyes and play the scenes over as if we were Centered during those experiences....In what way was it different for you?" He responds, "Well, it was different. It was hard to stir up the anger. And I just told him he was free to do whatever he felt was best for him and that I wanted to help any way I could. I told him again that we were sorry about what went down with April?" Smiling, I said, "You didn't actually use the phrase, 'what went down with April,' did you?" With a faint smile, he answered, "No, not in those exact words."

10. Transformation. "The goal of this training in Centering is transformation. It is the skill of taking the parts in our life that are not working well and creating something new and different at Center. We have to become highly skilled and trained in Centering. As that happens we learn how to put our body in a state of calmness and serenity and then we embrace with determination and commitment our Centered thoughts and live them moment-by-moment. When we take those two steps, we are on the way to creating a new response to those situations with Ace. With more practice, we no longer have to think about it when we are confronted by someone who doesn't want to take our advice. That's just how we respond to those types of situations. It's a new habit and the old habit just fades away. In many ways it's very freeing."

11. <u>Commitment and Training</u>. He asked what happens if he loses it and gets angry. I told him that we would just have to keep practicing with a lot of Centering and mental rehearsing.

Doc had been making the rounds and looked over my shoulder a couple of times, but I didn't ask him for any help. I felt like I had a pretty good grasp on the concept. I closed my eyes and leaned up against the side of the house and thought about seeing Eden this afternoon after our group outing.

Doc had us gather back in the cabin and we had some good discussion about the experience. He told us several times that the eleven step process might seem burdensome to begin with, but later it would become a few very simple steps.

Frank: "Yeah, once Focker knows all about Center, we don't have to go through that part of the process."

Paul: "Yeah, like Focker get your lazy ass down here to Center and shut the fuck up while we get Centered. You fucked up again so close your eyes and fucking get Centered. Let go of that fucking tension in your body and get out of your fucked up mind. Somethin' like that?"

Somebody yelled out, "That 'ill preach Brother Paul." Paul is a 'hoot.

Paul: "Don't get me wrong. That's not what I would say to my Fanny Focker. I was just given y'all some ideas for your fucked-up Fockers."

Nate joined Paul in having a woman Focker. He named her Cherry Focker. Everyone else thought it might be too distracting.

Chad said Lanco Focker wanted to know what would eventually come of him. Doc asked for someone to take a stab at an answer.

Ace: "Eventually, he'll come and live with Chad at Center, but he will never take up full-time residence, because nobody's perfect. Lanco would wander out from time to time and Chad would say something like try not to get us into any trouble."

Melinda: "I like it."

It looked like everyone agreed it was a good idea.

Doug: "I'm trying to wrap myself around this model. So Hill Focker and I have the same body, but we have different minds. I can go outside our body, but Hill is stuck in our body. Is that it?"

Doc: "Yes."

Everyone seemed to understand and agree.

Doc asked Paul, "How did Fanny do with the eleven step process?"

Paul: "We had a few beers and I got 'laid.' Just as we were finishing up, there was a knock at the door and she said it might be her boyfriend and I told her that was okay. It's not good or bad. It is what it is. She said that he might have a gun and I said that's also okay, I'll just need to get Centered so I took some deep breaths. She cracked the door and he shoved it open and screamed that I had fucked his girlfriend and I told him that I live in the moment and have no recollection of what took place in the past. He told me he was gonna whack me and I told him that was not right or wrong, good or bad and that I would not judge his decision and accept whatever he decided and he melted and came over and gave me a hug. He left and Fanny asked me if I would like to fuck again and get more of the same? I said that I would like to fuck, but I never try to repeat experiences 'cause I see every moment as fresh and new and then about that time Doc you called us to gather."

Everyone was laughing or smiling and Doc said, "You might not have done the assignment, but you did get some work done. I hope all of you are starting to understand more clearly why I have been talking so much about the importance of practicing these skills. It's very simple. If you don't become an expert in these skills, you are not going to get the results you say you want. You're still in the stage of continuing to pick up the books and you're still in basic training."

Doc: "Open your notebooks and write down your assignment for next Saturday.

1. Do the eyes closed exercise once a day and record in your journal the date and time.

2. Continue to use your hourly chime on your watch to remind you to take your breaths.

3. At least once this week, I want you to do the 'Staying in the Moment' exercise we did in the first group session. Record the date and time in your journal.

4. I've got another CD. There are two different Centering Meditations on that CD. Listen to both of those once a day and record date and time in your journal.

5. Several times listen to the meditations on the first CD and record date and time.

6. In the next few days, I want you to pick a specific fear you have experienced since coming back home and go through the eleven step process with your Focker. Before next Saturday, go over it several times and tweak it or make it more clear. I'll help you with that during our individual meetings.

7. Use your notebook in the same way you did the past two weeks.

During the individual sessions, I will be asking you to share with me the entries in your notebook and we will continue talking about nutrition, exercise, sleep patterns, and follow up on previous individual sessions. Any questions?"

Doc: "Close your eyes and focus on your breathing. Perhaps you notice that it now takes less time for your mind to slow down and be quiet and less time for your body to respond...with each breath now more deeply into the stillness...and now go to Center using the counting or just go there with a few more breaths and find yourself in that very special place. Beginning to understand that your Center can be the place of transformation and healing and that here you have everything you need to reach the goals you have set for yourself...realizing that this process takes time and commitment and attention to doing the necessary work and training...aware that your Focker will for reasons known and unknown put blocks in your mind and discourage this journey...and you can accept the resistance and be empathetic, but also know that Focker will later understand the importance of what you are doing and be able to experience the freedom... Looking around and knowing your Center is like a light always shinning, always there to offer peace and clarity along the way...and I don't know if you can grasp that in this moment or if it will take a few more days but you can be open now to the experience of basking in the radiance of this light...to feeling the release of old worn out patterns of thought and behavior...and to embracing the beauty of this moment...to feel the freedom...to experience the peace and tranquility...taking one more look around...and now open your eyes."

Doc: "Any questions or comments before we adjourn?"

There were none.

Doc: "OK, let's head out for the park. Anyone who doesn't know how to get there can follow me."

We had a good time playing volleyball and pitching horse shoes. Everyone participated and there was a lot of kidding around and joking and teasing and general "grab ass" stuff. Anna did great. I said earlier that I could tell she was an athlete. She did better at volleyball with one arm than several of us did with two arms. We did a lot of rotating so that everyone was on everyone else's team over the afternoon. There was good competitive spirit, but no one took it too seriously. Paul continued to cut up and be the group comedian. I think he has real talent. Doc participated in all the events and held his own even though he is thirty-five to forty years older than most of us. Paul got on Doc several times about how hard he was making us work. I think everyone had a good time. We were done by around 3:30. Everyone left in a good spirits. I think it brought us closer together.

47
EDEN AND LANCE

I was dirty and sweaty after the outing and was tempted to go back to the cabin and clean up before meeting Eden at Aunt Agnes' house. She wanted me for physical labor so I decided to go on with dirt, sweat and all. When I pulled in the driveway, she was carrying a bag of stuff to her car.

She smiled, "How was the group and picnic?"

"Fine, it went well. How did your meeting go at the attorney's office?"

"It went smoothly. Jack handled most of the details. Aunt Agnes left her house to my dad and her sister and she left to me all the contents of the house which will be a big help. When the divorce was final, a lot of the furniture was given to us by Chase's parents and I didn't want any of it. That left me a little short on furniture."

She continued, "It was also sweet of her to leave all of us nieces and nephews $10,000 each. The attorney said he would work on getting the will probated. I asked him if I could live in the house until it was sold. He said he would have to write my dad and aunt to get their permission. Jack told him about my plans to build and he said the house probably wouldn't go on the market anytime soon. I felt relieved I would have a place to stay."

I said, "You always have a place to stay."

"Thank you Jett. That's sweet."

I asked, "How can I help?"

"Aunt Agnes did spring cleaning about three months ago and had a yard sale. She got rid of a lot of things. I've been going through all her personal belongings and boxing up things to give to the Salvation Army. I've got a bunch of boxes packed and I wondered if we could use your truck to haul them.

"I'll start carrying them out."

She said, "I've got them spread throughout the house."

I loaded up the boxes and went back in to find what to do next. She had the closets emptied with the clothes on the bed. She asked me to help her pack the rest of the clothes, shoes and linens that she didn't want to keep. We worked side-by-side.

It was quiet for awhile and then she said, "I called my old school friend this afternoon and he asked me to have lunch with him tomorrow. I was reluctant because I had planned to leave right after church to go home. I have so much to do to get ready for the movers. Did I tell you they're coming to pick up my things a week from this Monday?"

My heart was racing and I wondered if Tug was going to do another panic attack. Hell no, mother Focker. You're not doing that to me again - subtle deep breaths. I can do this; get Centered. She just asked me a question and something about movers coming and I asked somewhat winded, "When are they coming?"

Luckily, she was busy packing boxes and didn't look up to see me flustered. She answered, "A week from this Monday. And now I think I was too optimistic. I don't know how I'm going to get it done because I have to be up here next weekend to get this house ready so I can make room for my things."

Subtle deep breaths and get Centered! Feel the peace! Why wasn't I feeling more peace? Breathe easy, nice and easy. That's a little better. She was saying something about optimistic and moving and making room. Feeling a little better, I said, "I'm sorry. I'm a little confused."

"Jett Hollander, have you been listening to what I said?"

I decided to be honest and responded, "I didn't hear a lot after the phrase, 'old school friend.'"

She looked at me and seemed surprised, "Jett, what are you thinking?"

I responded trying to keep it light, "You and Lance getting married."

She looked at me and I don't think she knew whether to smile and be upset or what. She said, "Jett, we have talked about this."

I chickened out and interrupted, "No no, I didn't mean it to sound like that. I meant you are becoming a really good friend and I don't think Lance would like you hanging around me and Ace and April. I really enjoy the time we spend together. I would miss you."

She looked at me with a curious expression, "All right, I apologize for assuming you were thinking something else. How did you know his name? I don't remember telling you?"

"Uncle Henry told me."

"Right, Henry knows him."

I said, "It came up in a casual conversation." I felt like I was getting deeper in shit.

"Jett, I won't allow anyone to break up our friendship and besides, Lance is an old friend. I have no interest in a relationship with him, but I would like to catch up on the latest about mutual friends. So I am having lunch with him tomorrow after church, but it won't last long because I have to get home. Are you listening now?"

"Yeah, let me come down and help you at your house. I could come down on Wednesday and we could caravan back on Friday. We could move some of your stuff in my truck."

Thoughtfully, "Well, I sure could use your help. Let me think about it and I really appreciate your offer."

We worked on with some light conversation and got quite a bit accomplished. During that time, Tug was working overtime telling me things like "everybody says they're not interested in a relationship and then when they get to know the person that starts to change and he's not married and who wouldn't be interested in a relationship with Eden and he is a lawyer and a professor and well established and what do we have to offer her? We don't even have a career or a real job and she has already made it perfectly clear that she is too old for us so you need to fucking face the music and stop living in a dream world so let's get on with our life and our flashbacks and nightmares and panic attacks. At least we have Spot, our family and the cabin and Ace and April."

Eden asked me if I would mind cutting the grass while she finished boxing up some things in the house. Tug said, "That's right up our alley. We're good at cutting grass." Actually, I was relieved to get out of the house and have some time to think. It was hard to silence Tug. Everything he had just said was in some way true. Doc says in every situation when what is happening is not working, we need to go to Center and figure out what it means to be Centered in the situation.

I need to follow Paul's example with Fanny. Here goes. Eden is going to see Lance for lunch so I need to get Centered and take some deep breaths and relax my body. I will remember I live in the moment and I love her and that I'm enjoying seeing her right now. I have no idea what the future will be. If Eden falls in love with him, that is neither good nor bad, it is what it is and I'll accept it in that moment. I may decide to shoot him or shoot myself or I may decide to be okay and move on with my life. Whatever I decide, I will accept it without judgment. Paul's was funny. Mine isn't funny.

Hell, I don't know. This Centering stuff sounds good, but it sure is hard to put in practice. I finished cutting the grass and went back inside and she was on the phone. When I came into the kitchen, she was saying, "All right, that will be fine. I'll leave right after church and meet you." And then she said, "Thanks for the invitation, but I already have plans. That will be fine. See you tomorrow."

She turned to me and said, "Thanks for cutting the grass. That was Lance. He called to let me know where we were going to eat. He said he wasn't sure he could get reservations at the Elverton Inn because it was really busy after church on Sunday."

Trying to stay as Centered as possible, I asked, "Was he able to get them?"

"Yes, he was."

"It sounds like he asked you out tonight."

She said, "Yes, he wanted to know if I could meet him for a drink. As you heard, I told him I had plans." She looked at me curiously and said, "I can tell you're upset with this whole Lance thing. I'm telling you Jett that I have no interest in him. And I know you said earlier that we are just friends, but your reaction suggests that me seeing him bothers you."

"How can you tell?"

"I guess it's the look on your face."

"Honestly, I'm not happy about it, but I'm trying to get over it." I lied and instead of saying, "I'm terrified that you might fall in love with him and then I won't have a chance to make you fall in love with me," I said, "What if you do fall for him, I'm sure he's not going to be okay with you spending time with me."

"Jett, I was not attracted to him when we were in high school and I'm not attracted to him now. Falling for him is not going to happen." She came over and gave me a little hug, patted me on the back and said, "You have nothing to worry about. You, April, and Ace are becoming very dear friends and I won't let anything get in the way of spending time with you all."

I lied, "That makes me feel better."

She smiled, "Thanks so much for helping me today. I feel better about getting so much accomplished. Are you ready to go?"

"Sure."

"Let me get a few things together. Do you want to call April and Ace and see about dinner?"

"Yeah, thanks for reminding me." I asked, "Do you want me to go on and take the stuff to the Salvation Army and meet you back at the cabin?"

"If you don't mind, I would like to follow you there and help unload the truck. Then I can follow you up to the cabin."

"I don't mind unloading it by myself."

"I know, but I would rather help."

I called April and she said we were going to grill pork chops and that all we needed to do was pick-up some white wine and barbecue sauce."

We left and unloaded the stuff at the SA, went to the store, and headed up to the cabin. On the drive, I was trying to sort and sift everything. I took some deep breaths and went to Center where Doc said there was clarity and I needed some clarity real badly. I kept thinking, "It is what it is." That's real clear. That's reality in every situation. So I can choose to let Tug make a big deal out of it and waste a bunch of energy fretting about it or I can accept it which Doc says gives us the freedom to move forward without the baggage of worry, fear, and stress. Right now, Tug has us carrying all that baggage. I'm just going to deep breathe the rest of the way and see if I can quiet my mind and relax my body. I did and when I got to the cabin and Eden got out of her car, I thought, "She is so beautiful. I can't let Tug waste our time when we're together." I felt better for now.

48
THE RIDE

Spot came out to greet us. April and Ace were sitting on the front porch with wine and a beer. They got up and came out to meet us. April and Eden hugged and then Ace gave Eden a hug. That was a surprise. I couldn't believe the strides he had made in the last few weeks. He was like a different person. Eden and I went inside and she showered in my bathroom and I showered in Ace's bathroom.

When I finished and went to my room to get dressed, I could still hear the shower running. I got a beer, gave Mom a quick call to check in and joined April and Ace on the porch.

April asked, "How's it going?"

I gave them a rundown of the afternoon and told them I had been working on being Centered and I was feeling better. About that time, Eden came out and said, "I hope it was all right that I helped myself to a glass of wine."

In the midst of protestations from Ace and me, she gave us "the finger" and sat down.

I said to April and Ace, "Eden asked me yesterday to teach her to ride a dirt bike." I turned to Eden, "After you finish your wine, I'll take you for a ride so you can get the feel and maybe next weekend you can ride on your own. Would you like to do that?" She looked a little apprehensive, but nodded. I asked, "April, do we have enough time to do that before supper?"

"Sure, Ace can put the chops on when you all get back. I'll put the potatoes in the oven in about a half hour. That would give you all about an hour and a half to ride. Will that be enough time?"

"Yes, that'll be plenty of time. I thought we could ride in the woods for awhile and then go up the Parkway. I'll take her up to Cypress Lookout."

April said, "Johnny's not gonna like it you taking the bike up on the Parkway."

Eden asked, "Whose Johnny?"

April responded, "He's a friend of ours and is the Park Ranger who patrols that section of the Parkway."

Eden said, "Jett, maybe we shouldn't go up there."

I said to April, "I don't think he would be that upset."

Ace said, "April and I were up on the Parkway last week and he caught us and was in a bad mood. I don't know what was going on with him. He said the next time he was going to give us a ticket."

April said, "I forgot to tell you Ace that I found out yesterday Susie, his wife, has been having an affair. They say Johnny found out and was heartbroken and has filed for a divorce and full custody of their two kids."

Ace said, "No wonder he was upset."

I said, "We'll stay off the Parkway. I'll just take the back roads up to the Lookout. I guess you all should keep Spot. It might be a little long for him."

April said, "Yes, I'll put him inside. You all be careful. I took a spill last week."

After Eden finished her wine, we went out back and I explained the workings of the bike. I got on and showed her how to start it and then she climbed on the back. She put her hands around my waist and we took off. I went real slow to start with and asked her how she was doing. She said she was doing fine.

I gradually picked up the speed and soon her arms were around my waist and then before long, she was pressed up against me and holding on pretty tight. I turned my head and asked, "You doin' okay? Am I goin' too fast?"

She replied, "I'm better. No, you're not going too fast. But I know I'm holding on for dear life. Sorry."

I said, "You're fine." And I loved every minute of it. I could feel her body and her breasts pressed tightly against me. It was warm and felt wonderful. We had to lean some on the next curve and I felt her hold a little tighter and she moved her head closer to mine and so that her lips were just an inch or two from my ear. I turned my head and I felt her lips on my ear and asked, "You still doin' okay?"

I turned my head back and she said, "This is exhilarating. I love it. When we get on a straight stretch, you can go faster."

I was in "hog heaven."

In a little while, she said, "I see a lot of beautiful places in my work, but this area is incredible. Every scene has a unique beauty of its' own. And soon this area will be my home."

I thought, "Not soon enough for me." I wish we could have kept going. I didn't want her to stop clinging to me. But we eventually would end up at the Lookout. When we got there, we parked the bike and walked to the Lookout and spent a little time there. Then I took her to another special place. We walked about a half mile and behind some trees and boulder, there was a hidden ledge where two could sit comfortably in solitude and look out over the miles. The drop must be a couple thousand feet. There was no evidence that anyone knew about this place except the three of us and now Eden.

She exclaimed, "Oh my god, this is fantastic!"

We sat there for awhile and just enjoyed the view.

When we got back, Ace and April were watching TV. Ace went out to check on the grill. April and Eden started working in the kitchen and were engaged in girl talk. I went out back to talk with Ace.

I said, "I don't feel like I've seen much of you lately except in the group."

"Yeah with working at the mill and spending time with April, there hasn't been much time to talk."

"Sometimes, I think you're doing better than I am with the group."

He asked, "Whatta ya mean?"

"I don't know. You seem to be grasping the material better. It's like you're getting it and are more committed to practicing the skills."

He responded, "I can't describe what it was like a few weeks ago and during that time at Walter Reed. I thought at times my life was over and then when I tried to whack myself, I felt there would never be any hope for me. I've never felt so out of control and helpless. I don't know if anyone, even you, can understand what that was like. I know I've told you this several times, but the words never do it justice. The point I'm making is that I have come to see this group as a way to take back some control. I now have hope and I love April more now than I ever did in the past. Before, I was too focused on myself and lost and caught up in nothing and everything." He had a far-away look and then looked at me, "It's strange because you have been so worried about me and now I'm worried about you."

A little surprised I asked, "For what reason?"

"I think you're struggling some in the group, because you're having trouble focusing. I think you spend more time thinking about Eden. This stuff is not easy to grasp. Or maybe I should say it is not all that difficult to grasp, but very challenging to put into practice. Am I right?"

I replied, "Maybe."

He went on, "And what scares me the most is that she's saying she's too old for you and now this other guy is around. I don't want you to get hurt. You don't need anything else to distract you while you're trying to figure out how to manage and let go of this PTSD stuff."

"I'm trying to use the skills to help me get through this. I am scared about this other guy. She says there's no attraction, but she only saw him for that brief time at the funeral. I know we don't know the future, but that doesn't help much right now."

April called out, "Ace, how much longer on the pork chops?" He cut into one of them and said, "About ten minutes."

I asked, "What do you think I should do?"

"I don't know. All I know is that this group is the most important thing we got going in our lives right now. This may be the only chance we have to survive the trauma of all the shit that went down over there."

I said, "The only thing I know to do is take one day at a time and try to enjoy the time I have with Eden."

We talked about the group picnic earlier today and how we were feeling closer to the members of the group. We both liked Doug and had taken more time to talk with him. We were both concerned he would drop out.

April again, "Ace, it's been more than ten minutes."

"Got it. There're ready. We'll be right there."

The table was set especially nice with wild flowers and candles. They told us to sit down and they put the food on the table. Then April said she had a surprise and took out of the fridge four goblets with shrimp and cocktail sauce. She set them on the table and both girls speared one and dipped it in cocktail sauce and told us to open wide. We did and Ace started coughing and choking first and then I did the same and we spit it out in the sink. The girls were laughing and high fiving each other and through their tears said we should have seen the look on our faces.

We were good sports, but told them they better be on guard. I asked what they did to make them taste so bad. April said she 'lifted' a used syringe from the hospital that she had used on an HIV patient a few days ago and had filled it with vinegar."

Ace yelled, "An HIV patient!?" And they were busting a gut again. He looked at me. "They got us again."

We had a great time at dinner. We took our time and laughed and talked about all kinds of different topics. Eden had made some chocolate chip cookies with dark chocolate and pecans. They were delicious. We all pitched in and did the dishes. It was about 9:30 when we finished.

April said, "Ace and I have had a long day and I know you all have too. We're gonna spend the night at my house tonight. I have to work tomorrow and get up early. Our things are in the truck so we'll head on." Everyone hugged and they left.

49
THE NIGHTMARE

I asked, "What would you like to do?"

"Could we sit out on the front deck for awhile? Then I would like to turn in pretty early myself if that's all right."

"That's fine. I know you must be exhausted with all you've done today."

She said, "And you must be exhausted too."

"I'm pretty tired."

I tried to get her to talk some about her childhood. She told me some funny stories about things she and her sisters used to do.

"What was it like at school?"

She replied, "Socially we were under the blacks who had many challenging times themselves. Some have used the term, 'poor white trash.' I guess that was us. I was a proud little girl even though we were dirt poor. We got free lunches because we didn't have any money. I was always so embarrassed about that and most of the teachers were good about not calling attention to us. I had a teacher one time in front of the entire class say, 'Well I guess a free lunch has to go to Eden.' I was devastated."

I replied, "That fucking piece of shit. How could someone be so cruel to a child?"

"I know. It was a terrible thing to do. I learned later that several years after that, she died of cancer."

I said, "I guess Satan was calling that bitch home."

"Anyway, I want you to know that I do have some good memories. Aunt Agnes and other relatives tried to help us, but Daddy would take the money and buy booze and things for himself. I had a wonderful granddaddy. We spent a lot of time together and he taught me a lot about life and many of those things I remember to this day. I thank God every day for him."

She smiled, "It seems like you had a very good childhood."

"Yeah. I was fortunate. My only issue was Dad drank a lot and that was a bummer at times, but when I hear your stories, I feel like I had the perfect childhood."

She asked, "Do you mind if I go to bed?"

"No that's fine. Do you know where everything is and do you need anything?"

"Yes and no," she smiled.

"I'll use Ace's bathroom. Do you want me to get you up at any particular time?"

"Are you going to church?"

"I replied, "Yes."

"Would you sit with me? I know Jack and Ann will be there, but I feel more comfortable sitting with you."

"Of course I will. I would like that very much. Have you thought any more about me coming down to help you on Wednesday?"

"Yes, I have. I would like that if you still want to do it."

"I would. Okay. Good." Smiling, I continued, "I'll be exercising in the morning - either a brisk hike or running. Would you like to join me? Is your knee better?"

She said, "It held me back a little on Friday when we raced to the cabin. But otherwise, it's fine. I'm good to go for a run and hike combo.

I can run for about thirty minutes at a medium pace and then maybe we could hike."

"That sounds good to me. I can go any time that suits you." "If we go at 8:00, would that give us enough time to eat, get cleaned up and be there by 10:45?"

I smiled and asked, "How long does it take you to get ready?"

"I'm pretty fast, but I'll have to dry my hair so probably about ten minutes longer than it takes you."

"Eight o'clock it is and I'll wake you up so don't worry about the time. I'll set my alarm."

"I appreciate all the work you did for me today. It was a huge help. I also enjoyed my bike ride. Thanks for taking me." She gave me a brief hug and went to her room and shut the door.

I had quite a bit of trouble getting to sleep. I used the deep breathing and I think it finally helped me to doze off. The next thing I remember is that Ace and I were pinned down by sniper fire and the chopper had left without us. April and Eden were behind us hiding in a room that had no door. We were holding the snipers off but running low on ammo and neither one of us had another clip. The girls were screaming and we were now out of ammo and they were storming the house and I was yelling, run, run, run... and I could hear a faint voice yelling Jett, Jett, Jett, wake up...and I was yelling run, run, run...Jett, Jett, wake up and suddenly something cold was on me and I opened my eyes and Eden had this worried look on her face and I was shaking and dripping in sweat.

She jerked the cold towel off me and started drying my head with another towel. She pulled me to a sitting position and pulled off my tee-shirt. She got on her knees by my side and wiped my chest and back with a dry towel at the same time. I was still trembling and only half conscious. I was still in a daze. I asked, "Are we safe?"

"Yes, we're safe. You're here with us. It's Eden and Spot." I was starting to come around and she was continuing to wipe the sweat off my body and I said, “I’m sorry I woke you up. This was one of the worst ones I’ve had in awhile.”

“I’m just glad I was here. I was afraid to get too close to you because you were jerking and your arms were moving like you were trying to fight off someone. All I could think to do was get a wet towel and throw it on you.”

“That was a perfect idea.”

She said, “Those nightmares must be terrifying. Now go in the bathroom and finish wiping down. Where do you keep your underwear and tee-shirts?”

“Eden, that’s OK, I’m fine now. You go back to bed.”

“Dude, I asked you a question.”

I pointed to the dresser and said, “Top drawer.”

She got me a pair of undershorts and a tee-shirt and said, “Dry off and put these on. I’ll meet you in Ace’s bedroom. Your bed is soaked.”

As I went into my bathroom, she was taking the sheets off my bed and hauling them off to the washer. I went in the bathroom and finished drying off, put on the dry underwear and went into Ace’s bedroom. She had on sweat pants and tee-shirt. She pulled the sheet back and told me to get between the sheets. I did as I was told. She pulled it over me and sat on the edge of the bed. Spot jumped up on the other side. She started rubbing my head and said, “I didn’t realize the nightmares got that bad.”

“Sometimes they do.”

“Can you tell me what it was about?”

I told her as much as I could remember.

So you and Ace were trying to protect April and me. Have I ever been in one of your nightmares before?”

“Last week I was trying to save you from something and I couldn’t get to you. Those are the only two so far.”

She asked, “How are you feeling now?”

“Much better thanks to you and Spot.”

"All right, I'll go on back to my bed. Are you sure you're all right?"

"Yeah, I'm fine. I'm sorry I woke you up. You have so much on your plate. You need your rest."

"I'll be fine. See you in the morning."

I laid there with Spot. I knew I would probably have trouble getting back to sleep. She looked so beautiful in her sweat pants and tee-shirt with her hair pulled back. It felt so good when she was drying me off. I was almost naked in front of her. It was intimate when she was talking about my underwear and tee-shirt. I heard a soft knock on the door which was half way open.

Softly she whispered, "Jett, are you asleep?"

I whispered back, "No, I'm still awake."

"I'm having a little trouble getting back to sleep. I brought a blanket and pillow from my room. Do you mind if I lay down on top of the bedspread?"

"Please get under the sheets. I know you have on clothes and I'll put Spot between us. I would feel bad if you slept on the bedspread."

"All right."

We got settled and Spot obediently stretched out between us and I said, "Do you have enough room?"

"Yes, I have plenty of room. How about you?"

"I'm fine."

She said, "Goodnight. I'll see you in the morning."

"I hope you sleep well."

"You too."

I started my breathing again and I think she drifted off soon after I had taken ten or so breaths. I couldn't believe we were in the same bed. Would I ever get to sleep? I looked at the clock. It was 1:34. I kept breathing and soon I was out. True to form, I woke up early.

"Oh shit!" Spot must not be on the bed. I was on my right side and Eden was cupped up against my back and her left arm was drooped over me and my left arm was over her arm. Her head was close to the back of my neck. I could feel her breath. "Oh shit" again. I was terrified to move so I stayed as still as possible. I just savored the closeness for awhile and then drifted into a light sleep.

I don't know how long we stayed in that position but I heard her whisper, "Holy shit." I smiled. The room was full of sunlight. Then with very subtle moves she started inching back away and then I pressed down lightly with my left arm making it more difficult for her to pull her arm away. I heard another whispered, "Shit."

She stopped pulling on her arm and then pretending to be asleep, I rolled away from her onto my stomach so her arm was free. I could feel the mattress slightly moving and then I heard her move into the great room and she was greeting Spot and she let him out. I called sleepily, "Eden!"

She peeked into the room smiling and said, "Good Morning, how do you feel?"

"I feel like I was hit by a freight train, thanks. How are you doing? Did you sleep okay?"

"Yes, I slept fine. We both must have slept pretty well. It's 8:43. Are you still up for the exercise?"

I responded, "Yes, that 'ill help me clear the cobwebs."

"All right, let me pee and get my running clothes on."

It was a beautiful morning, clear as a bell with a nice breeze. We ran and hiked and took some time to enjoy the scenery. I pointed out some landmarks in the distance. We stopped briefly at the knoll and then headed on back.

I asked, "Are you hungry?"

"I'm starved."

Eden made pancakes and sausage while I cut up some fruit and made the coffee. She explained to me that her grandma had a special recipe for pancakes, but we didn't have any buttermilk. She said milk would do fine. We chit chatted and I had a great time helping her get it all ready. We both ate a hearty breakfast.

She insisted that we do the dishes. After we finished, there were some grapes left in the bowl and I asked her if I could score two points by tossing a grape in her mouth. She agreed only if each of us could have five tries. I was zero for five and she was one for five.

She said, "I kicked your butt on that one."

"Not fair," I said. "My mouth is a lot bigger than yours."

"Spoiled sport, you just can't take losing." She looked at the clock, "Shit, it's 10:15. Are we gonna make it?"

"If we leave here by 10:45, we can be there easy right before the service starts. I'll use Ace's bathroom. As you know, the water pressure is not that great when two people are taking showers. You know where everything is, right?"

While showering, I thought about how neither one of us mentioned the bed and how we slept snuggled up together. She of course didn't know that I knew what happened. I wanted so badly to say something, but it didn't seem like a good time. I thought it might embarrass her and if I have a chance with her, I have to take it slowly. On the other hand, if she had brought it up, I would have seen that as a positive sign. Something like she was breaking the ice. Someday I hoped we could talk about it.

We left a few minutes after 10:45 and got there right at 11. They were singing the opening hymn. We slipped in the side door and scooted in the pew with Mom and Dad. Everyone in the family looked at us and smiled.

I didn't hear any of the sermon. I spent most of my time taking deep breaths trying to get Centered. I was preparing myself for the time when Eden was going to be with Lance. After the service, we chatted with all the family for a few minutes. Eden then told everyone she had to leave and I told them I was going over to the Inn to see Pop. Mom told me while Eden was talking to Ann and Jack that Pop was not feeling well.

I told her about Pop as we were walking to her car. She told me to tell him hello and that she hoped he was feeling better. Somehow, she seemed different when we walked out of the church. She was quiet and somewhat distant. She gave me a little hug and thanked me for helping her yesterday and I thanked her for helping me last night. She smiled and said she had a good time. She asked me to call her tonight and let me know how Pop was doing. She got in the car and left.

50

EDEN PULLS AWAY

I headed over the see Pop, remembering to take a lot of deep breaths on the way. I was feeling peaceful and knew that I was moving to my Center. Then came the truth that in the coming days and weeks would help to set me free. Out of my Center came the insight that whatever she decides, ultimately all that matters is that Eden finds peace and happiness. Tears were rolling down my cheeks and I couldn't figure out why it had taken me so long to come to that awareness. I realized the answer was I had not until now completely been at Center. Tug had been calling the shots by being self-focused. I had dipped a toe or foot into Center and gotten some insight but most of those insights had been about me. They were important and helpful but they did not set me free. My challenge was to stay Centered. God help me!

Pop was still in his pajamas and robe.

"Hey Pop. Sorry to hear you're not feeling well."

"Thanks Son. I don't know what's wrong. I feel real tired. It may be a virus of some kind. I'm glad you came by because I was starting to get a little hungry."

I asked, "Do you want to order something from downstairs or I could go out and get us some lunch?"

"Sally's barbecue sounds good to me for some reason."

"I'll go now and get it. Do you want your usual potato salad and no sauce?"

He answered, "That's perfect Jett. Go get my wallet on the dresser and get the money."

"Since many meals in my life have been on you, how 'bout me paying today."

He smiled, "Okay Son."

As I was walking toward the front door, I looked over and saw Sandra. "Hey Sandra, how're you doin'? I didn't see you when I came in a few minutes ago."

Flashing a big smile she replied, "Why hey Jett. I haven't seen you in a long time."

"Y'all been pretty busy?"

"It's been a little slow this morning, but we have a lot of check-ins this afternoon." The phone rang. "Sorry." She answered it.

I waved and left. So how come I'm just now noticing Sandra again. Tug answered, "We're just coverin' our bases in case it doesn't work out with Eden." Was that true? Probably so. I'd spoken to her a few times, but hadn't really paid much attention. I noticed her boobs again and wondered how friendly she was willing to be. I told Tug to give it a rest.

Pop and I had a nice lunch together in his condo. Almost everyone in the family came by to see how Pop was feeling. They were eating downstairs in the dinning room. With Pop not feeling well, I decided not to bring up the walks after work. I would just check on him everyday and let it be a day to day thing.

I kept wondering how long Eden would be with Lance and then thought, "All that matters is Eden's happiness." That helped some. I watched four or five innings of a baseball game with Pop and then left. I waved at Sandra. She was busy checking people in.

I headed over to see Mom. I told her how much Eden loved the new décor in what I called "her bedroom." I brought her up to date on everything and even told her about the nightmare and us sleeping in the same bed. She gave me some words of encouragement and I sat with Dad a few minutes watching the same game Pop and I had been watching. Then I left for the cabin.

I stopped by to see Henry and Betty and brought them up to date, but left out a few details. I told them they could pass on the information to anyone in the family. I was glad to see that Ace was home. I didn't want to be by myself.

He and April were doing great. He said they had their second session with Doc tomorrow night. He confessed that he had not stayed with his two beer limit over this past week. "I've really been craving the booze and got drunk once and had a six pack at Aprils after we left here last night. I called in sick Thursday and April had to work and I stayed at Stanley's most of the day and almost got in another fight. Jett, why am I so angry? I drove home drunk and was just lucky I didn't get picked up."

"I remember you were in bed when I got home, but I just thought you were tired."

"I told April I didn't feel good, but when she got here on Friday, she said it sounded like I'd been drinking. So I 'fessed up. I had a bad nightmare last Wednesday and I think maybe that triggered my craving. I drank the six-pack after April went to bed last night. I don't think she suspected. I hid the beer cans. But I'm gonna tell her when she gets here. I've done better today so far."

"How can I help?"

"I'm not sure at this point. I'm going to mention it to Doc tomorrow night when April and I meet with him and ask him to help me figure out a plan when we meet on Tuesday. What's goin' on with you?"

I briefed him and said I was trying to get Centered. "I decided on the way home I was going to work on getting and staying Centered by doing a mental exercise. I'm going to take three deep breaths and check my body to make sure I'm physically relaxed and take a few more if I need to and then repeat five times the phrase, 'All that matters is Eden's happiness'" And I want to really mean it, not just say it. Then take three more deep breaths. Whatta' ya think?"

"I like it. Maybe I could come up with something similar on the alcohol craving." He thought for a few minutes and then said, "Staying sober is the key to freedom. How 'bout that?"

"I think that's great. Both phrases are positive which Doc said is important. Do you remember when he talked about making Center more like a habit?"

"Yeah, he said once we select our thought or phrase, we then have to 'live it.' Over a period of time, the thought and behavior will become a new habit or a new pattern."

"You at least have a clear idea about your behavior. You live your phrase by keeping to two beers a day."

He interjected, "I might have to totally stop drinking."

"Yeah, I got it. So you have to figure that out. In my case, I don't know exactly how to live my phrase. I guess I can keep an upbeat attitude and not worry or get jealous or angry or frustrated or feel rejected or hurt or devastated or feel sorry for myself. That will be a huge challenge in itself, but what about some specific behavior?"

He answered, "What about not doing something like spying or checking on her?"

"Yeah, that's good. I just thought about something else. When I was down at the Inn a little while ago, Tug and I were eyeing that cute little hot and sexy number Sandra behind the desk. So if Eden is seeing this new guy, don't go and try to fuck Sandra."

"Well not if you think there's still a chance with you and Eden."

"Yeah, that makes sense. If you can think of any other behaviors for me, let me know. You and I haven't been on a bike ride yet. Are you up for one now?"

"Let's see. It's 4:36. April will be here around 6:00. Yeah, that sounds good."

I asked, "Have you noticed lately neither one of us is using military time?"

"Yeah. I think that's a good thing."

The ride really helped. We took some of our old trails which required attention and some precision. That kept my mind occupied. When we were in the open, I took my breaths and repeated what I decided to call my mantra. I learned that word in one of my psychology classes and I never thought I would ever need one of them. Surprise! You need one.

When we got back to the cabin, April was already home and fixing supper. She didn't want any help so Ace and I sat at the table while I briefed her on my time with Eden. We brought her up to date on what we had talked about earlier. I asked her if she had any ideas on other behaviors related to my mantra."

She answered, "Be kind and understanding toward her if she decides to have dates with this Lance guy. Be supportive and encouraging and don't express anger or frustration toward her. And I agree with you. Don't go for revenge or 'I'll show you and fuck this little hot number at the Inn.'" With an inquisitive smile, she turned to Ace, "Have you ever seen this little hot number?"

"No, but I need to go see Pop tomorrow and check on him. I won't even look in the direction of the front desk. Promise."

"You're lucky I can't find anything to throw at you right now."

I said, "I'm going to call Eden before you find something."

I called and she picked up. "Hey, I'm just checking to make sure you got home safely."

"Thanks, yes I made it fine. How is Pop doing?"

I recounted my visit with him and said, "Thanks for asking."

She volunteered, "I left Elverton around 2:00 so I've had some time to get things done. How has the rest of your day been?"

I gave her a recap and said that Ace and April said to say, "Hey." I went on, "So how was your lunch?"

"It went well. We had a nice time talking about old friends and catching up on any recent news. He hasn't changed much. We talked some about each other's jobs and then I left."

"I'm glad it went well. I'm looking forward to coming down Wednesday to help you with your packing."

There was a brief pause. "Jett, I've been thinking about that. When I got home and looked around, I decided that there wouldn't be any need for you to come. I can do it myself, but I do appreciate you offering."

Trying not to sound disappointed, I said, "Are you sure. I would be happy to help."

She replied, "Yes, I'm sure but thank you just the same."

After a pause, I said, "Okay, so will I see you Friday?"

"Yes, I may be a little later than I was this week. I'll let you know. I guess I better get back to work."

"Okay, if you change your mind, call me."

"I will. Goodbye."

What the fuck was that? Why did she change her mind? Is she already thinking about seeing this guy? Why is she acting distant? What happened in church? I didn't have any answers. I sat there for a few minutes and took a bunch of deep breaths and started repeating my mantra. After about a dozen repetitions, I went into the kitchen and said, "All that matters is Eden's happiness. All that matters is Eden's happiness. All that matters is Eden's happiness." Then they joined in and all of us started repeating it and it got louder and louder and louder. We started laughing and then I started crying and they hugged me and I said through my tears, "I feel like I've lost her and I never even had her."

We stood there a little longer and then April said, "Jett, your happiness matters too."

"I know. I guess another mantra I have to work on is, 'My happiness does not depend on Eden.'"

Ace said, “Yeah, that’s important?”

I asked, “April, how much time before supper?”

“About fifteen minutes.”

“I think I’ll take Spot for a walk. We’ll be back in fifteen. Thanks.”

The walk helped some. We ate and I told them what had happened on the phone with Eden. We watched some TV and I went to bed. I realized when I walked in my room that my sheets were still in the dryer. I went to Eden’s room and crawled in between the sheets and started my breathing and my mantra. I don’t know how many times I repeated it, but I finally got to sleep.

51
ACE GETTING CENTERED

Monday was okay. I worked with Charlie and had lunch with Pop. He was feeling some better and hoped to be back to normal in a few days. I worked late just to keep busy. When I got home, I took Spot for a run. It was almost dark by the time we got back to the cabin. April and Ace had their appointment with Doc and were spending the night at April's. I fixed a sandwich, resisted the urge to call Eden, watched TV and again slept in Eden's bed. I had worked on my mantra all day and had resisted Tug's idea that we go talk to Sandra. I said my mantra till I fell asleep.

Buddy Session Five

We started our session with a Centering Meditation which took about twenty minutes.

Doc explained that from this point on, the buddy sessions were going to be mostly individual work with him. This would give him time to help us with our individual issues.

Ace wanted me to go first as he had some work to do in his notebook.

Doc went over with me my entries in the notebook. I had done most of what he had asked us to do. I was missing a few entries on the Centering exercises, but over all I was pleased with my progress on the skills.

I said, "I've been thinking a lot lately about my issues with God. Would you have time today for me to tell you about my struggles and some things I've been working on?"

Doc said, "Sure. What are you doing for lunch?"

"I'm free."

"I've got a 12:00 appointment in Harvest and another at 2:30. I'm free around 1:00. We could have lunch and talk."

I said, "Great."

He told me where to meet him and then said, "I'm curious about what fear you and Tug picked to use with the eleven step process."

I smiled, "We picked the fear that all this is not going to work and that we'll have to live with the panic, flashbacks, and nightmares for the rest of our lives. I have to tell you that I'm being polite because Tug guaranteed me that to use his words, 'this fucking shit has a snowball's chance in hell of working.'"

Doc smiled back, "Well, how did it go? Take me through it."

"Okay."

"1. I got Centered.

2. I talked with Tug about what happened. He talked about how he freaks out in all three areas and why wouldn't we be scared that we would have to live with them the rest of our life. He said he didn't know if he could survive. He was pessimistic about our chances of getting better. I didn't judge his comments. I told him I would like to focus this exercise on the panic attack we had at the reception following Aunt Agnes' funeral. I explained the situation and the experience to Doc.

3. We talked about the physical symptoms of that attack which were intense and scary. Tug said he mostly remembered the not being able to breath and the trembling and shaking.

4. He went over the 'not working thoughts' which revolved around thinking that Eden was going to get involved with this old friend and in a few days they would be making love and then married in a few weeks and we would never be able to survive if that happened.

5. I led Tug through some Centering Meditations and deep breathing. He was getting to know the drill and was more responsive and cooperative.

6. I told him to stay Centered and let's replay that scene in our minds while we continue to do the deep breathing. He agreed with me if we could just have been Centered before Eden's old friend arrived on the scene, we would have had a better chance of keeping our body relaxed and calm. I said that's the reason we need to practice Centering because if the panic gets going, it's a much bigger challenge to interrupt.

7. We came up with three Centered thoughts that would help us in this situation: All that ultimately matters is Eden's happiness. My happiness does not depend on Eden. We will be able to get Centered regardless of what happens.

8. We repeated them over and over looking out over the mountains and taking deep breaths. At one point we were yelling them at the top of our lungs and then kept saying, "We can do this! We can do this! We can do this!" We repeated the statements several more times.

9. We played the scene again determined to stay at Center. We talked with Eden and asked her to tell us more about her friend. It felt really good for both of us. Tug said he thought he was starting to get the point, but reminded me that he had bigger fish to fry like other panic attacks, flashbacks, and nightmares that come out of the blue.

10. Transformation takes place when we feel physically calm and relaxed as we live and breathe those statements when we are with Eden in real life.

11. Commitment and training are the keys to success."

Doc said, "Well done. Do you have any questions?"

I replied, "I'm eager to get to work on those out of the blue panic attacks and flashbacks."

Doc said, "Sounds good."

He worked with Ace for about an hour and then the three of us talked about nutrition, exercise, and sleep patterns. We did another Centering Meditation and he left.

We started fixing lunch and I asked, "How did it go?"

"Pretty well today, but not so good yesterday. April and I got into some pretty heavy shit with Doc last night and I slept on the couch and she was gone by the time I woke up. Fark wanted to leave after she went in the bedroom and slammed the door, but I'm trying to break old patterns of running away. I was tossing and turning the whole night, but must have really passed out when I finally got to sleep 'cause I didn't hear a thing when she left this morning."

"Good for you on staying."

"Yeah, I know. It's not easy. Fark is already talking to me about going to Stanley's after work and getting drunk."

"What are you gonna do?"

"I keep telling myself to get Centered and asking myself what does it mean to get Centered with April right now? Fark has always been on the run from just about everything except soldiering and sports. He runs from feelings, talking about shit, facing shit, and his fears about getting close to people." He looked at me and said, "Sometimes I wonder if Paul's comment, 'this is some crazy shit' is on target. Do you ever feel like what the fuck am I doing talking to Fark like he's another person. It feels so fucking weird at times and then at other times it makes so much sense."

I said, "I feel the same way and I think everyone else in the group feels that way too. It's different, but it's helping me slowly put some handles on dealing with my shit."

Silence as we ate.

He asked, "What do you think I should do?"

"Sometimes in church, Father Pat will say, 'Follow your heart.' I'm not sure what that means, but I think being Centered is the same thing."

"Doc is always saying that in situations where we're struggling to ask what it means to be Centered. Listening to my heart may be part of the answer. I don't think I've ever listened to my heart whatever that means."

I replied, "I think you listened to your heart when you said that you would not ever do the suicide thing again because you couldn't do that again to Ma."

He was thoughtful and finally said, "Yeah, maybe."

"Doc tells us that Center is a place of peace and tranquility and it is there we find clarity. Does that help?"

He answered, "You up for me trying this out loud?"

"Sure."

"I kind of like the idea about the heart because I know now more than ever how much I love her. So if I'm clear about that, I can tell Fark to shut the fuck up about getting drunk and maybe getting laid or come to Center and help me figure this out. Fark's not gonna like that. He's very resistant to this whole Centering gig as he calls it. So if I'm not afraid and stay with how I feel about April, I think I should pick up her favorite flowers after work and go to her house and tell her I want us to talk it out and get this resolved."

I smiled. "You're really getting this stuff."

"Jett, I'm sorry I keep repeating this, but I need to keep reminding myself. My wake-up call came when I opened my eyes in that hospital bed realizing that I almost ended my life never to see my family or April or you again. I have to get this stuff to survive. I've noticed that my flashbacks have been less intense lately. I get over them without much difficulty. I hope that keeps up." He looked at his watch. "Holy shit, I've got to get to work. I'll call you tonight from April's."

I met Doc at the restaurant and we had a good talk. He had a number of suggestions and things for me to think about. He reminded me of an Army Chaplain I talked to "over there" while all this was going on.

After my time with Doc, I went to the Inn to say hey to Pop and then work the afternoon with Charlie. Pop wasn't up for a walk so I ran three laps around the lake and went home to get cleaned up. Mom had asked me to come for supper so I headed down there and had a nice time. I got home around 7:30 and Ace was sitting on the front porch with a flower in his lap drinking a beer. I asked, "What happened?"

"I was a little late getting off, got my flowers and went to her house and this note was on the door." He handed it to me.

"Ace, I'm still upset about last night. I need some time to think. I'm not blaming you. It's not your fault or my fault. It just hurts. I have gone to a friend's house. Please don't try to find me. I'll be in touch in a few days. Love, April."

"Wow."

He said, "I left all the flowers, but this one by her front door. Fark wanted me to throw 'em in the garbage and leave the note on the door and write 'fuck you' on the note. I vetoed that idea. I don't blame her either, but I do blame myself. Sometimes I feel like a piece of shit." He took another big swig of beer and continued, "I'm two beers over my limit and the good news is that I'm exhausted with getting little sleep last night and we had a rough afternoon at the mill. I'm going to bed."

"I'm sorry it didn't turn out the way you wanted. For what it's worth, I think you made the right decision. I hope somehow you'll feel good about that decision."

"Maybe I will in the morning." He went inside and went to bed.

I resisted the urge to call Eden, watched some TV and slept in Eden's bed again.

I was up at the usual time and on my way back from my run, Ace was coming toward me walking without his cane but with a noticeable limp. He said, "I sure am looking forward to the time when I can run and hike again."

"I'm looking forward to it too. I've missed having you along. How did you sleep?"

"Pretty good until about 5:00. I heard you leave and decided to get out and at least walk a couple miles."

I asked, "So how're you doin'?"

"It's so funny that I knew you were going to ask me and I remember over the years my pat answer to that question was..."

I interrupted, "I don't fucking want to talk about it."

We both laughed. He said, "Right on. I have to pay close attention or Fark will blurt out that same old response. I know Doc keeps saying if we keep working on changing the thoughts and behavior that it will eventually become a habit. I've got a ways to go. I have to admit also that Fark has thrown out 'fuck you April' several times, but I'm not listening to him."

"Good for you."

He continued, "At Center, I feel good about what I did. I'm glad I left the flowers on the porch and I'm going to give her the space she needs. When she contacts me, we're gonna work it out."

"Jett, why is that always so hard for me? It seems like that is a lot easier than being pissed off and pouting and giving her the silent treatment. Doc refuses to spend much time trying to figure it out. He says understanding why we are the way we are satisfies a curiosity, but is not much help in the process of making changes. He wants to focus on the skills we need to make those changes. I guess he's right, but sometimes I'm curious. How you doin' staying Centered with Eden?"

"I'm in and out of Center. I keep saying my phrases and they help me at times and then Tug starts all his shit about her falling in love with Lance. I'd like to wring that Focker's neck even though I know I'm supposed to accept how he feels. So I'm still working on getting him to Center."

He offered, "We both have a lot of work to do."

"Yeah, we do."

After work, Pop was up for going on the walk. I noticed how he was walking slower and seemed a little out of breath at times. He said,

"I never tire of seeing the scenery and every walk brings some new awareness of the unique beauty all around us."

"You've taught me well Pop."

He asked, "How are you and that young lady doing?"

I filled him in on all the latest, including my worry about our age difference and her hooking up with her old college friend.

He said, "Love is a wonderful thing and it brings to us so many varied feelings and experiences. You have the bliss of love and at the same time the pain of worry and rejection. You have the highs and the lows and in my experience, the highs make every low manageable. The moments of intimacy where we glimpse the meaning of the words, 'and the two shall become one.' Perhaps in that experience we know God at the deepest possible level." He continued walking and was looking in the distance and I could see tears running down his cheeks. "Jett, I miss her so much."

And I reached out and slowed him down and stood in front of him and put my arms around him and embraced this grandfather who had loved me dearly and given me so many gifts of insight about nature and life. "Now I know more clearly that I must give my heart to the possibility of this experience and that it will be worth any pain or sadness I might endure along the way. Thank you." And I hugged him tighter and tears rolled down my cheeks.

He said, "Son, do you mind if we head back. I'm getting a little tired."

He put his arm in mine and we walked back to the Inn. On the way back home, I stopped by to see Henry and Betty. Even though I knew Pop hadn't been feeling well, I had been so caught up in my stuff that I had not asked anybody what the doctors were saying.

Henry told me that Pop had congestive heart failure and that the doctors felt like it was under control, but at his age there were possible complications that could flare up and cause problems. Henry said there is no way to know how much longer he had left. I asked him to call me if he heard anything. He told me that Pop had told him how much he enjoyed our walks. I thanked him and left.

52
JETT GETTING CENTERED

When I pulled in, Ace and April's vehicles were there. I thought about turning around so they could have some privacy. Then I thought I would just take Spot and go up to the knoll and hang out. They weren't there and Spot was gone. I looked out back and the bikes were there so they must have walked.

I went over my mantras about Eden and then called her and there was no answer. It was 6:23. I wondered where she was. I went over the mantras and added some deep breathing. I looked around the kitchen to see what we had to eat. I decided to cook for April and Ace and if they weren't hungry, there would be plenty of leftovers. The menu was spaghetti with angel hair pasta, tossed salad, and garlic bread. I opened a beer, turned on some music and went to work.

April, Ace, and Spot came in about an hour or so later. They were smiling and I took that as a good sign. I said, "Welcome home my long lost friends. A culinary delight awaits you in about fifteen minutes."

Ace asked, "Does that mean a big plate with a little piece of salmon, some grass, and raw string beans?"

While he was talking April came over and gave me a hug and said, "Glad to see you stranger."

I gave her a peck on the cheek and said, "Me too glad to see you."

In my best Italian accent, I announced the menu for tonight to high fives around. They went to wash up. Ace came in first and I said, "It must have gone well."

I didn't see that April was almost right behind him and smiling she said, "I would like to hear your reply to that comment Sgt. Frost."

Ace said, "Actually we decided to call it quits and forget the whole thing and just be 'fuck buddies.'"

April jumped on his back and got a choke hold on him and he pretended to be gasping for air and she exclaimed, "Take it back Frost or prepare to take a 'dirt nap.' He stumbled over to the sofa and got on his knees and rolled her over onto the sofa and twisted away and started tickling her. After they settled down, we talked and had something to drink while I finished fixing supper.

Over the course of dinner, they gave me some of the details about their time of discontent. Ace said on their walk they figured out when talking about unresolved and painful memories they both reverted to old patterns and habits.

April asked, "Ace, did you tell Jett I met with Doc by myself last week?"

"No, I forgot to mention it."

She looked at me, "Doc gave me a short course on the model and told me that he would talk to Ace about helping me understand how it works. He said he is also exploring the use of this model for relationships. Anyway, my Focker is named, Foxy. We decided that we would only bring up the past in the sessions with Doc. So we were fine till we got there and some of the old stuff came out. We did fair while we were in his office, but when we were fixing dinner, some stuff came up and Fark and Foxy went at it big time. Foxy finally said, 'Fuck you Fark' and slammed the bedroom door."

She continued, "When I got home from work this afternoon, I found the flowers on the porch, started crying and came here and waited on Ace to get off work."

Ace added, "So while on our walk, we figured out some of the triggers for Foxy and Fark. Our goal is to stay Centered with each other and pay attention to those triggers that arouse those guys."

April smiled, "So when I'm Centered and Fark gets pissed off about something, I say, 'I'm not talking to you Fark. You're not a bad person, but I wanna talk to Ace.' I really think this can help us get some resolution and heal some of the old wounds."

Ace said, "April brought up the idea that we can visit each other's Center and get a tour. April's Center is the beach and I don't know if you remember, but mine is the woods. I can give her a real life tour everyday because mine is everywhere around here."

April asked, "Jett, where is your Center?"

I answered, "The knoll."

She wondered, "Is that the place you and Eden have been going?"

"Yeah, speaking of Eden, I called her earlier and she wasn't home. I think I'll call her now."

April said, "Ace and I'll go sit on the back deck and then we'll do the dishes."

She answered on about the third ring. I said, "Hey Eden, I called earlier and missed you. Just wanted to check in and see how the packing was going."

"It's going fine. I was going to call you later and tell you something."

"What did you want to tell me?"

She put her hand over the receiver and I couldn't hear what she said and then in a somewhat lowered voice, "Lance was in the area on business and his meeting was over around noon and he called and asked if he could come by and see me. I told him that I was really busy and he said he wouldn't stay long. So he came over and saw me packing and insisted that he help me since he had nothing else to do."

Deep breaths and over and over and 'all that matters is Eden's happiness.'

She went on, "He has another meeting in the morning and wants to help me load up the U-Haul tomorrow afternoon. I told him that I appreciated his offer, but that I could manage by myself. But he insisted."

Trying to stay as calm as possible, I said, "It makes me feel like when you told me not to come that I should have insisted or maybe just come on and surprised you."

"No, I thank you for respecting my wishes."

"Eden, I don't know what to say? I wanna ask is he going to spend the night at your house even though I have no right to ask that question."

"Heavens no, he is staying at a motel in town."

Trying to continue to stay as calm as possible, "Okay, well I better let you got back to work."

"Jett, I'm sorry it worked out this way."

"Me too, I'll talk to you later." We hung up.

I went out on the back porch and told them the story. Nobody said anything. We sat there in silence for awhile while I continued to take deep breaths and repeat my mantra.

Finally, April asked me, "What are you thinking?"

"Tug's having a field day. In between my breathing and mantra he is saying, 'I told you so. She is going to end up with what's his face. You're too young for her. He won't let her be friends with you. It's over. Forget her. Let's go pick up Sandra and see if we can get laid.' I'm trying to stay Centered but not having much success."

April asked, "Last Saturday night, did anything happen?"

I gave them a blow-by-blow of everything I could remember. I said, "Something seemed to happen in church because after the service she seemed distant. And of course she was headed to Elverton to meet him for lunch. That didn't help. And when she told me on the phone not to come down to help her, I knew something was up. I just didn't know what it was."

April said, "I caught Eden looking at you a few times last Saturday night. With the bike ride and cuddling in bed, the physical intimacy was something new. I know you also felt an emotional intimacy and I'm not sure about Eden, but my guess is that she did feel something. In church, she had time to think and revisited her opinion that you're too young for her and all the reasons it won't work came flooding into her mind. That explains her being distant after church and not wanting you to come down and help her pack. This guy Lance is obviously interested and she may be open to a relationship with him to get you out of her mind."

"Shit." That was about all I could think of to say.

Ace said, "I'm new to thinking that deeply about anything, but what April said sure makes sense."

I said, "I'm not going to give up on her. If you're right April, she really does have feelings for me. I have to find a way to convince her that we can do this; that we can make it work. Ace, I feel determined like you did not long ago when you said something like, 'what the fuck. I'm tired of being scared of my feelings.' I feel the same way. I'm not going to have a 'pity party' and feel sorry for myself. I'm going to suck it up, get Centered and go to work and 'fuck you Tug.'"

April replied, "I don't envy you. My take on Eden is that she is pretty stubborn."

"I will find a way. I'm counting on you all to help me."

We did the dishes, watched some TV and they left. I felt some sadness as I watched them drive down the hill. They were making a life for themselves and needed a place of their own. It probably wouldn't be long before Ace started moving some of his stuff to April's house. I wanted us all to live together in this cabin and get married and have our children. I'm a dreamer. I went to bed and lay there doing my breathing and working on my mantra. Tug got in there some and when he talked, I felt depressed and hopeless. He wasn't going to keep quiet about this and I had a lot of work to do to get him Centered about Eden.

The next day I had lunch with Mom and brought her up to date on the latest with Eden. I told her everything. After work, Pop didn't feel up for our walk. April called around 6:00 and said she and Ace were bringing Sally's barbecue for supper and that they would be there around 7:00. They left around 9:00, and I had decided earlier while cutting grass at the Inn that I was going to get Centered and call Eden.

"Hey Eden, how's the packing going."

"It's going fine. The U-Haul® is loaded…"

I interrupted, "Sorry, I meant to ask you last night about the U-Haul®. I thought the movers were coming on Monday."

"They are. I wanted to pack-up all the smaller things like kitchen things, linens, knick knacks, clothes, some of my work things, and a bunch of boxes in the garage. It's their smallest trailer. Unfortunately, I have a long day tomorrow at work since I have missed a lot this week. I'm probably not going to get away from here until about 6:00. I had hoped to get there by 6:00 so I don't want you all to hold supper."

"We are going to hold supper. We all want to see you. When you get here, call me and I'll come and help you unhitch the trailer and you can follow me back here."

"Jett, Thanks for offering but I'm not a helpless female. I can unhitch the trailer. I'll call you all when I get there so you'll know when to expect me."

"Sounds good Miss 'I can take care of myself.' Be careful on the way. It gets windy up here and trailers have a tendency to sway and…"

She interrupted, "It can be a little challenging to keep the car from swerving."

"Getting the point, you and April are a lot alike. Independent as can be."

"I'll take that as a compliment."

I replied, "I'm not as independent as you all so any suggestions or advice for me in any area will for the most part be welcome."

"All right, let me run. I've still got a bunch of things to do."

"Okay, see you tomorrow."

That went pretty well. I'm proud of myself. I stayed Centered most of the conversation. Tug raised his head and started to say something and I started focusing on my breathing and there was no space for him to comment. He must have gone back into his cave, because when I stopped focusing on my breathing, there was silence.

I called Ace and April and she picked up. I told her about the conversation and that Eden would be late tomorrow. She wondered if it would be better if she and Ace made some kind of excuse not to be there. We discussed it and both decided that it might be better for all of us to be together and keep it light.

I slept in Eden's bed and had a good night. Friday was normal. Pop felt a little better and we walked. I was home by 6:00. April and Ace were bringing the groceries. I took a chance and made a quick call to Eden. She answered saying she was just getting ready to walk out the door. I told her to be careful. Someone said there might be a shower and the road could be a slippery. She thanked me without saying I was being over protective and said she would call when she got to the house.

April and Ace got here about 7:00 and they took Spot and went on a walk. I cleaned Eden's room and changed the sheets. I didn't know if she would spend the night with all the work that needed to be done at the house. They returned around 8:00 and Eden had called and was on the way.

April and Ace started on supper and I watched for her car to pull up. As it came up the hill, I went out to meet her. I opened the door and said, "I don't mean this in a bad way, but you look tired. You've had a big week."

"I have and I am tired. But I'm glad to be here and see you guys." She gave me a friendly hug.

She only had her purse so I assumed that meant she wasn't spending the night. April and Ace came from the kitchen to greet and hug her. April said, "Jett has a wine glass in the freezer with your name on it.

I got it out to use and he almost bit my head off." April reached over to slap my head, but I ducked away.

Ace said, "Why don't you guys get your drinks and sit out on the back deck. It's going to be a beautiful sunset. I'll get April to finish up supper while I watch some TV."

"Ace Frost, get your Ace ass in the kitchen. I've got multiple tasks for you."

Eden said, "April, I would be glad to help."

"You and Jett go on. We'll call you when it's ready."

I got her wine and a beer for me and we went outside. It was a beautiful evening. She asked, "How was your week?"

"It was fine. We had a good session with Doc on Tuesday morning and the rest of the week I worked at the Inn."

"How is Pop?"

"Henry told me he has congestive heart failure and it's hard to predict how long he'll live. I guess he could live another five or ten years or he could go at any moment. We walked twice this week which I thought was a good sign. You had a rough week. I wish you had let me come down to help you. But since you wouldn't, it was good that your friend happened to be in the area."

"Yes, he was a big help. Yesterday, he came over after his meeting to help me load the U-Haul® and he left for home around 4:00."

I said, "Your movers come on Monday. Will you be going back down there after Monday?"

"After they get the van packed up, I'll finish cleaning the house and turn my key into the land lord. Then I'll drive up here that night and that will be my last trip. As soon as I can, I have to look for an office here. A lot of my work will be in the field, but they want me to have an office with a secretary."

"Have you thought anymore about building?"

"Not much. I still want to, but I've been so busy. After I get moved in, I can continue the search for a piece of property."

"I would like to come over after group tomorrow and help you in any way I can. Would that be okay?"

"Sure, I can use the help." There was a pause. She turned to me. "Jett, I want you to know that I had no idea that Lance was coming to town. If he had asked me if he could come, I would have refused his offer."

"Say no more. I understand what happened and thank you for reassuring me even though you owe me no explanation."

"I believe I do owe you an explanation, but if it's all right with you, I won't mention it again."

"That's fine."

She said, "Ace was right. That's a beautiful sunset. It's so pretty up here. You're so fortunate to live here."

"I know. I never take it for granted. Over the years as we hiked these mountains, Pop taught me to treasure every inch of this land."

"I can imagine how much you'll miss him when he passes. I think I'm still in the denial phase. It has helped me that I've been so busy. I think when things settle down, I'll begin the real grieving phase. I'm not sure what to expect, but I know it's going to be difficult."

We talked a little more about the family and then Ace stuck his head out the door and said, "Come and get it!"

We had our usual good time with joking back and forth and enjoying good food. They had fixed a pork roast with mashed potatoes, green beans, apple sauce, and rolls.

Soon after we all did the dishes, Eden said, "Guys, I'm sorry to be a party pooper but I am exhausted. I need to head on and try to get a good night's sleep. Thanks for a wonderful meal and a great time."

I walked her to the car and gave her a friendly hug and kiss on the check and said, "I hope you sleep well. I should be at the house around one. Why don't I stop at Sally's and pick up some barbecue for lunch?"

She answered, "I would like that. I won't have to think about food. Thanks Jett."

April and Ace were eager to know how I thought it went. I told them I thought it went fine. I felt pretty good for most of the evening. I gave them a synopsis of our conversation out on the back deck and told them that I would be going over to help her tomorrow after group. They stayed the night and April fixed us breakfast and then left to get some housework and errands done.

53
GROUP SESSION FOUR

People started pulling up about 8:45. Several were in a group talking. Ace and I went out to join in the conversation. There was a new feeling of camaraderie. I think some of it had to do with last week's group session and the gathering at the park. I think we were starting to feel more like a unit. It was like we were starting to get invested in everyone finding a way to deal with our problems and find some happiness.

Doc pulled up a little before 9:00 and we followed him inside. He started unpacking his gear and said, "Everyone close your eyes and go to your Center and hang out while I'm getting set up." It seemed like he was purposely making a lot of noise. At one point, he picked up the phone and I could hear him dialing a number and then he started talking to Janet, his secretary. He said, "Why I didn't know that. The group should be interested in that piece of news. I'll be sure to tell them. Okay, thanks." Then he went over to the TV and turned it on and then I realized he was trying to distract us. After a few minutes, he turned it off and there was complete silence for a few minutes. Then he said, "Open your eyes."

Doc: "It's not always going to be quiet and still when you're getting Centered. It's important to practice sometimes with noise in the background. Do that at home this week and after a while you will notice that you are becoming more skilled at getting into Center with or without distractions."

Nate: "What did Janet tell you we would wanna know?"

Doc: "The group will no longer be funded by the federal government and from here on it will cost each of you $200 a session."

Almost on key, we stood up and started saying good-bye to each other.

Doc: "I got it! Everybody sit back down. Why am I having you do so many Centering Meditations?

Paul: "To drive us fuckin' crazy?"

"Yeah!" came from everyone.

Doc: "What's the second reason?"

Doug: "If you don't learn to take apart, clean and reassemble your weapon, after awhile, it won't do what you want it to do."

Doc: "More."

Chad: "When you go out on a mission, you better remember to take everything you need or you might not make it back."

Melinda: "Chances are we aren't gonna get better if we don't learn how to get Centered."

Doc: "But it's so boring and repetitive and you don't even really know if it's gonna work!"

Anna: "Who said this training was going to be fun and entertaining? If we can't trust Doc, who can we trust?"

Rob: "When I think about basic training, I don't remember anything about it being fun and entertaining, but what I learned saved my life on a number of occasions."

Doc: "Break down in pairs, spread out, and designate yourselves one and two."

My eyes met Doug's and we found a space.

Doc: "In a moment, I'm going to give the command, 'Everyone, go to Center.' Close your eyes and I'll give you a couple of minutes to go to Center and spend some time there and I'll tell you when to open your eyes. Got any questions?"

Paul: "Nate and I can't get to who's gonna be one and who's gonna be two and I'm gettin' pissed."

Ace: "I've got five bucks says Nate can whip his ass."

Rob: "I got ten bucks says Paul can whip Nate's ass."

Anna: "Somebody give me a 'night stick' and I got twenty bucks says I can take both of 'em with one arm."

Doc smiling: "Is anybody ready to go to work?"

Frank: "Let's go down to the park and play volleyball."

Paul raising his voice: "Hold on. As the rankin' soldier in this room, I'm orderin' you assholes to settle down and give Doc a chance to resign so we can all go to Stanley's."

Everyone: "Hip hip hooray!!!! Hip hip hooray!!!!"

Doc: "You people have a lot of energy. Let's see if we can shift that energy and start our training."

Everyone: "Boooooooooooooooo!!!!!"

Doug: "All right. That's enough grab-ass. Let's get to work!"

Doc smiling: "Thank you Doug."

Doc: "Everyone, go to Center."

I lost track of time which is a good thing. Maybe it was five minutes or so and then Doc said, "Open your eyes. I want the ones to talk to the twos about how they got to Center, what it was like at Center from both a physical and mental perspective, and how they see Centering as a path to healing. Then twos talk to ones about their experience."

Doug: "I take about ten deep breaths to relax my body and slow down my mind and I'm in this grove of apple trees not far from the farm. Most of the time, I walk through the grove and I like early mornins' just as the sun is comin' up. I can hear a rooster or two and it's real peaceful. Sometimes, I can't see the grove, but I feel relaxed. Most of my thoughts are kinda like I can do this. This is gonna help me move on and get rid of this boozin' and druggin'. One of my big problems is feelin' guilt and shame and I keep workin' on ideas like, 'The past is gone. It's not real. God forgives me. I can forgive myself. Focus on family and gettin' better so I can take care of 'em.' Things like that."

Me: "Does it feel like it's helping?"

Doug: "Sometimes it does and other times, I think I'm takin' two steps backwards. That feelin' comes most of the time when I'm drinkin' and poppin' pills."

Me: "Anything else?"

Doug: "That's 'bout it."

Me: "I use the breathing too, but lately after about five deep breathes, I count backwards from ten to one and when I get to one, I'm walking in the woods. The counting helps me get my mind quite and concentrate. I've been thinking about continuing to do deep breathing while I'm counting like counting a number when I exhale. My favorite time is around twilight. I love sunsets so I usually find a place where I can watch one. It gives me a feeling of peace. My body feels peaceful too. My problems mostly are my panic attacks, flashbacks, and nightmares." Smiling, I continue, "Actually, I have quite a few others like girl friend problems, jumping out of my skin if I hear a noise, drinking too much beer, and I'm with you on the guilt and shame."

Doug: "Is it helpin' you?"

Me: "I'm like you. Sometimes I feel like it's helping and other times I wonder if it's helping at all. I keep telling myself if I just keep training, I'm gonna get better. When I start to have the panic and flashbacks, I'm trying to interrupt them before they get started with the deep breathing and saying they will pass and I'll be fine. I'm also trying not to freak out and fight them. I've noticed that when I can do that, they lose some steam. When I'm thinking about being Centered and have done some deep breathing, and I hear a loud noise, I don't startle as much so that's a good thing."

Doc interrupted: "Let's gather back in the circle."

Me: "I'm working on some of the same phrases you are about the guilt and shame.'

He patted me on the back, "You're a good man, Jett."

Me: "You know how I feel about you."

Doug smiling: "Yeah, I remember."

Doc: "Would some of you share your experience?"

Most people had similar experiences to the ones Doug and I shared.

Doc: "I will continue to emphasize the importance of the deep breathing. Throughout the remainder of our training in the group, I will from time-to-time out of the blue say, 'Go to Center!' Immediately start your deep breathing and first and most important, you should feel your body relaxing."

Frank: "What if we don't feel our body relaxing?"

Doc: "Anybody?"

Chad: "Step up your training 'till you do feel it."

Doc: "Exactly. The deep breathing will eventually help you relax your body. It is also a tangible key to Centering. It opens the gate to the Center."

Frank: "I thought you said quieting the mind is the most important step in getting Centered."

Melinda: "I heard differently. I understood the deep breathing first relaxes the body and then quiets the mind and both help us get Centered."

Doc: "I might have said or implied what you said Frank. I'm splitting hairs here because relaxing the body and quieting the mind hopefully happen simultaneously. What I'm emphasizing now is that I want you to always do the deep breathing and be aware at first of your body relaxing and then you can notice that your mind is becoming quiet. As your mind becomes quiet, that means you are attentive and focused on being Centered and Focker is quiet."

Doc: "Everyone. Go to Center, take a walk and take no memory with you."

I don't know how long he gave us, but I enjoyed not having anything to do except look around and experience the peaceful energy of being in the woods.

Doc: "What was that like?"

Some said their Focker was acting up, but most said they found it easier to do than work on the eleven stepper.

Doc: "Think about the implications. If you can close your eyes and go to Center for five minutes and experience the moments without memory, is it be possible to do it for ten minutes? And if you can do it for ten, minutes, can you do it for longer?"

Frank: "Why don't we just practice Centering without memory and keep it that simple?"

Doc: "In my experience, when Focker is silent and you have access to objective data, wisdom learned from mistakes, and pleasant memories, you need more structure and strategy to handle Focker who has a lot of power. In my view, until you've done the 'grunt work' and spent time in the trenches working with Focker, your goal of healing Focker or silencing Focker will be like climbing a high mountain without snap links and rope."

Ace: "So the eleven-stepper is an example of the 'grunt work?'"

Doc nodded.

Frank: "Then why did you take us through that Centering exercise with no memory if that's not gonna get us where we wanna go?"

Doc: "Good question Frank. I did it to excite a perception that it is possible to quiet the mind with no memory. So you glimpse the possibility and then before you have time to discover how nice it feels, Focker is back telling you this is a bunch of shit. Hopefully, you realize you still have some serious training to do."

Frank: "Got it!"

Doc: "I worked with each of you during your Buddy Session on the eleven-stepper. Did you remember that the eleven-stepper is a by-the-numbers exercise that over a period of time can be condensed to a much shorter form of the same process? Focker will get to know the drill and you won't have to go through much explanation. We'll practice this later. Right now, it's time to get back in the trenches and do more 'grunt work.'"

Doc: "What causes intrusive thoughts, flashbacks, nightmares, and associated panic attacks?"

Paul: "You said last week that Fanny don't cause that stuff, but I forgot what you said."

Doc: "I believe the major cause is the intensity and power of the traumatic imprint or the traumatic memories. I may have been somewhat unfair to Fanny if I implied that she is the culprit who creates those experiences. As I said last week, it's more accurate to say that she is the one who freaks out about them, fights them, judges them, hates them and gets scared and sometimes terrified that they will come back to haunt her. Her gut reaction is to fight which makes them worse. In that way, she contributes to keeping them alive."

Paul: "Fanny says you is blaming her and it ain't fair."

Doc: "Give her my apologies. Now, our training shifts to reducing the intensity and power of those imprints or memories. Fanny is still fixated on the trauma of her combat experience simply because she doesn't know how to do anything else. It's understandable that she would be struggling. Again, the trauma becomes the imprint. Logically speaking then, if we can reduce the power and intensity of the traumatic experiences, we reduce the frequency of intrusive thoughts, flashbacks, nightmares, and associated panic attacks."

Frank: "So how do we do that?"

Ace: "I don't know, but I bet it has something to do with breathing and Centering."

Doc: "I want you to go back in your past and think of the time 'over there' when you were first aware of being scared."

Paul: "How 'bout when I learned I was goin'?"

There are smiles and a "yeah" from most of the group.

Doug: "I've had three tours. I was also afraid when I first got orders, but I didn't really understand what it was going to be like when I got there on my first tour. I had been in transportation almost from the beginning of my service. I was a heavy truck driver. The day I got to my unit, we had two casualties from an IED. That's when the real fear first struck me. The next morning, all of us new arrivals got a briefing about our job. Our unit was stationed at a large supply depot and our job was to move supplies to the different units in our area of operation."

Anna: "I was also in transportation. My first job was in operations and my responsibility was to be out on the road making sure we complied with our mission description. When I first learned that, I was really scared, but no one knew it. Being a woman and believing that we can do most of the jobs you men can do, I was determined to do my part to show we could carry the load. And I did it."

Doug: "When you said you were also in transportation, it came to me that I heard about your accident. You were the operations officer of the unit stationed about fifty miles south of where I was on my third tour. We heard about your bravery and all felt terrible that you lost an arm." Smiling and maybe a little embarrassed, he continued, "Our operations officer was an asshole who never left his office. You were an inspiration to us and we all wished we could have served under you."

Tears were running down her cheeks and she got up and went over to Doug and he didn't hesitate and got up and met her and they embraced. Wow! Here was this crusty Sergeant with tears also running down his cheeks hugging this attractive young officer. More wet eyes and soon we were all surrounding them. Doc was in the background encouraging us to breathe and again feel the depth of this experience. And then we were all back in our seats.

With all this hugging going on, I wondered if an "on-looker" would have been surprised how easily we drifted toward this ritual. I think it's true that we don't come back from combat and become "huggers," but there is an intimacy shared that breaks down the walls many of us had constructed earlier in life. This is not true for all combat soldiers, but there is a bond for most of us that supercedes certain emotional and physical barriers we had before the war.

Ace: "When Jett and I got orders to go, my SOP (Standard Operating Procedure) at the time was to deny any feelings I didn't want to have so I didn't feel much of anything. And it was a good thing because Jett was crying all the time saying he didn't wanna go and would I promise to keep him safe. He kept saying he was gonna miss his momma so much. I had my hands full with him."

Everyone was jumping on the band wagon, "Poor Jett, poor baby," and on and on. I got up and said in a loud voice, "I've had it with you mother fockers, I'm outta here!" At the door, I turned and faked some tears and said, "But, I'm gonna miss Anna and Melinda. I can't leave."

The women got up and came toward me as I walked back in and gave me a big hug. They said, "Poor Jett. You come on back. We won't let these bullies bother you."

Paul got up and said, "I'm also tired of you mother fockers pickin' on me, but I ain't gonna leave 'cause I'll miss Anna and Melinda too."

They gave him his hug and then others got in line for their hugs and Doc said, "Okay, let's break it up. You guys can try to get hugs from Anna and Melinda on your own time." Boos from the group.

Ace: "So in the beginning, I convinced myself I wasn't scared. We had a few days to get settled. Jett and I were in a long range patrol unit and nothing could block my fear when we got our briefing for that first patrol. It was a recon (reconnaissance) mission into a known hostile location. That was the first time I felt the fear. I was scared."

Me: "Well Ace let the cat outta' the bag. I was scared when we got our deployment orders, but it is true that the fear actually became more real when we got our first briefing."

Others shared pretty much the same story. When they first realized they were going to be operating or driving in hostile territory, the fear became more pronounced.

Doc: "I want everyone to close your eyes and go back in time and put yourself in that first situation where you felt the fear....Remember what was going on in your mind and what kind of physical symptoms were present. Was it a nervous stomach, tightness in your chest, trouble breathing, shaking and trembling, something else? Relive it as much as possible....You learned earlier in your training that one way to reduce the intensity of the memory is to step outside the experience and observe it. I want you to take Focker and go to your Center and take a few moments to get settled....As your breathing releases the tension in your body, feel the physical symptoms melting away. Take your time.... You and Focker from here at Center observe that first experience when you realized just how scared you were. Take time right now to select a still image of that experience, a picture that represents the emotions and experience of that event....Have that picture move away from you. It is moving further and further away getting more and more difficult to see. It's getting smaller and smaller until it is like a dot in the distance and then is gone. Now, aware in this moment that you can observe that experience and then let it fade into the distance and disappear, you're free to know that the past simply no longer exists except somewhere deep in the recesses of the mind, in the darkness where there is no light. Over time these memories will begin to fade until they are lost in the no space of timelessness. Basking in the radiance of the Light at Center, feel the freedom to move forward and experience the transformation of the past into the peacefulness of this moment in this place at your Center. Take a few more deep breaths, look around and when you're ready, open your eyes."

Doc: "Okay, what was that like for you?"

Frank: "We were focusing on the eleven step process and now we are doing something different."

Doc: "That's correct. This is an extension of the earlier exercise where we got into an experience and then stepped back to observe the same experience. You noticed that when you stepped back, the intensity of the mental and physical response diminished. We took that a step further a few minutes ago by observing the experience from Center, creating a still frame to represent the experience, and then having it move further and further away until it vanishes."

Frank: "I'm assuming that observing the experience from Center is supposed to be more effective than just observing it like we did earlier."

Doc: "Would someone else answer that."

Melinda: "Observing it from Center seems like we are more focused, more alert, more like I don't know if this is the right word, but more grounded."

Doc: "Yes, exactly. Focused and alert means the brain is more receptive to change and shifting. Being Centered also means you are observing the experience from a base philosophy that states, 'I do not identify with my past. It does not define me. I do not judge it. The memories exist only in my mind. I can let them go. They only have power if I give them that power.' Does any of that sound familiar?"

Paul: "I ain't never heard none of that stuff."

Others chimed in, "Me neither."

Doc: "I would leave now, but I would miss Anna and Melinda."

Chad: "Anna and Melinda have a lot of power." They reached across Paul and gave each other a high five.

Doc: "None of this works without the intense training. That's why we're going to Center over and over again and going over the same phrases over and over and going over the same points over and over. Somewhere along the way, you recognize and experience that going to Center is starting to mean something profound and significant. As we continue our training, you will become more and more aware that most everything comes down to being grounded in your Center. Your Center truly does become that portal and lens through which you see and experience your life."

Nate: "Sometimes all this stuff seems complicated. Then when you talk more, it seems simple and then we do something and it seems complicated again."

Doc: "The more you train, the more simple it becomes. I've got this process on newsprint. This process is nine steps." He turns to the sheet.

<u>Reducing the Intensity of Past Imprints: The Nine-Stepper</u>

1. Pick a Memory Imprint.
2. Be in the experience with Focker (Mind and Body).
3. Take Focker to Center.
4. Observe the Experience from Center.
5. Feel the Emotional and Physical Release.
6. Pick a Still Frame.
7. Repeat Phrases to the Imprint:
   I do not judge you.
   I accept you as part of my history.
   You do not define me.
   Rest-in-peace.
   I am letting you go.
8. Move it Further Away until it Disappears.
9. Feel the Freedom.

Doc: "I've got the long form of the nine-stepper on a handout for your notebook." He passes them around. "Look them over and let me have your comments or questions."

Rob: "Would you go over the difference between this stuff and the eleven step thing we did last week?"

Doc: "Would someone answer that question?"

Anna: "It's funny Rob. I was just asking myself the same question. I think the eleven-stepper is to help us deal with experiences right now." Looking at Doc, "You are always saying at Center we can create something new and different. I've got to figure out how to do that with this missing arm. The eleven-stepper will help me with that. The nine-stepper is to help us with the traumatic memories that cause the flashbacks and nightmares and sometimes cause the panic attacks."

Rob smiled, "I'm a little slow, but I think I got it. The bad memories cause flashbacks and nightmares. We gotta try to put them memories to rest and get rid of 'em so we can cut down on them flashbacks and nightmares."

Ace: "If you're slow, then I'm slow too. I'm glad you asked the question."

Frank: "With the eleven-stepper, we'll know pretty much right away if it's working. But with the nine-stepper, we're not going to get proof that it works. The only gauge we'll have is noticing that we're having less intrusive thoughts, panic attacks, flashbacks, and nightmares."

Me: "And even that will not be real clear because I'm already doing better with my panic attacks, flashbacks, and nightmares. I'm still having 'em but not as frequent."

Some others were also having less of those experiences, but with others, there had been no change and with a couple, it had gotten worse.

Doc: "In our work together, it is important that you always continue to do the training, but you will not always know exactly what part of that training is causing you to get better. You'll have some ideas, but it will be difficult to know for sure. Is it true that as long as you get better, knowing exactly why will not be critically important?"

There were nods all around.

Doc: "In a few minutes, I want you to get in pairs and coach each other through this last exercise. I will demonstrate how I want you to do this. I need a volunteer."

Nate: "I'll do it."

Doc: "Thanks Nate. Let's pull our chairs into the middle. I'm going to be the coach. The coach will have the handout on the nine steps.

I'll ask Nate in a minute to close his eyes and we can begin. I'll tell him each step and when you have completed the step Nate, you will slightly raise a finger to let me know that you have completed that step. Then I will tell you the next step. Each of you will select a memory and for this exercise, please select something not too traumatic. Later we will get to the worst of those experiences. As we're going through this, follow the handout I just gave you and if you want to, make some notes as we go along. Any questions?"

Ace: "On step number 7, are those phrases set in stone?"

Doc: "Thanks Ace. I forgot to mention they are not set in stone and you can select your own phrases. If you do select one or more other phrases or take out a phrase or two, I would like to know what they are because I'm looking for better ones to use. Any other questions?"

Doc: 1. "Okay. Nate, close your eyes and pick an experience."

Nate raises his middle finger and the group bursts out laughing and Doc patiently waits for us to settle down.

Doc: 2. "Relive the experience with Focker. What are you thinking and feeling and what does it feel like in your body?" …Finger up.

Doc: 3. "Take Focker to Center and take some time to get Centered." …Finger up.

Doc: 4. "Observe the experience from Center." …Finger up.

Doc: 5. "Feel the emotional and physical release." …Finger up.

Doc: 6. "Pick a still frame." …Finger up.

Doc: 7. "Repeat these phrases:

I do not judge you.

I accept you as part of my history.

You do not define me.

Rest-in-peace.

I am letting you go." …Finger up.

Doc: 8. "Move it further and further away until it disappears." … Finger up.

Doc: 9: "Feel the freedom." …Finger up. "Open your eyes."

Doc: "At this point, I want you to talk about what it was like. Compare notes and come up with questions. Nate, what was that like for you?"

Nate: "Doug, hand me my sheet. Right thar on top of my notebook. Thanks. It'd help to go down this list.

1. I picked a time when our squad was pinned down in a house and several of my friends got wounded. Nothing too serious, but it was scary.

2. It was easy to get in it. It was my first time in a 'fire fight.' I 'bout shit my pants. All I remember thinking was oh shit, is this whar I'm gonna die?"

3. Cherrie and I hopped on my bike and started ridden'. The wind was blowin' in our face and it was a great day and not too hot. It was just right and we felt free and alive.

4. Then I thought, 'How am I gonna look at a screen and drive at the same time.' Then I was thinkin' that I could put it on auto pilot. Then we looked at it and it was more like a movie. It was hard to feel scared while we was ridin' on the bike.

5. So I felt better and didn't feel much fear. My mind was good. Being Centered was nice, but what helped me most was to think them memories ain't real. They're like a movie.

6. I picked a still frame of us being pinned down.

7. I repeated the phrases like Doc said, but I added my own. 'you ain't real.' That one helped me the most. I ain't gonna use them others.

8. Me and Cherrie pushed it away and made it disappear. I'm done with that memory.

9. We kept ridin' and it felt good."

Doc: "Thanks Nate. Well done. You may or may not have noticed that sometimes Nate used 'we' meaning he and Cherrie and at other times used 'I'. It doesn't make any difference. I just want you to make sure you take Focker with you. Remember, she or he is the one who needs the healing. Nate picking his own phrase points out a critical aspect of the training. And that is, I will offer you a number of suggestions, but the most important thing is that you pick what works for you."

Ace: "Nate said he was done with that memory. Is it possible to be done with a memory like that?"

Doc: "I don't know, but Nate made that statement with confidence. Maybe he is done with it. Maybe it will surprise him and surface again, but it will not have as much or maybe any power over him. He has made a big step toward letting it go."

Nate: "Hell no Doc. It's not a step. I'm fuckin' done with it!!"

Doc: "Sounds good to me."

Melinda: "I really like what Nate discovered about memories not being real. I have struggled when you (looking at Doc) say or imply that they are only in our minds. Now, I think I get it."

Doc: "Remember that Focker's role in these traumatic memories is his reaction to them. He contributes to their frequency by freaking out, but in the first two steps, the goal is to remember the experience and what it felt like. At that point Focker is taken to Center to deal with the memory."

Frank: "Sometimes there is a grey area to me about Fockers role."

Doc: "That's fine. Sometimes the model gets a little murky. I don't want that to get in the way of the overall intention of the exercise. Let me know if it does and we can talk about it during the buddy session or after group."

Frank: "Got it."

Doc: "The key is to keep doing the training, believe that you can do it, and be determined to make it work for you. Are there any more comments or questions?" No questions. "Count off by fives. Start with you Chad. Pair up with your like number. Spread out in the room and on the porches. Take turns being a coach. I'll be around to check on each pair. Really get into it and make sure it's as real as possible.

I'll let you know when to shift roles. Be sure to discuss any questions and comments. Then we'll gather and share insights and experiences."

I was paired with Chad. We went out on the back deck. Paul and Doug were at one end and we took the other. He picked the first time he took enemy fire and I did the same thing. It wasn't nearly as bad as some of the other things that happened, but it was bad enough. I was starting to feel more and more at home in my Center. We were about half-way through me coaching Chad when we heard commotion inside. We both got up and went to the door and Frank was having a flashback. He was sweating and having trouble breathing and started yelling and repeating, "I can't take this anymore. I'm dying."

Doc was coming in the front door and waving for all of us to go back outside and finish the exercise. Ace was Frank's partner and he and Doc stayed in the cabin with Frank. Not long after we resumed the exercise, it got quiet in the cabin. Doc stuck his head out the back door and told us we would gather together in a few minutes.

Chad and I didn't do too well with the exercise. Perhaps in a few days it would come to us as it had come to Nate. I liked Nate's conclusion that memories aren't real. Doc called us inside.

Doc: "What happened to Frank is not unusual. Generally flashbacks come out of the blue when they are least expected, but sometimes, you can trigger one by recalling a memory. Frank, would you mind saying what happened?"

Frank: "I picked a memory that wasn't too intense and when I got to the step where you get into the experience, it's like my mind shifted to my worst and scariest experience of the war. I was there going through it again and as always, it was so real. I didn't hear a thing Ace and Doc were saying. I could see their lips moving, but I couldn't hear the words. Then it started to fade and I was trying to focus on what Doc was saying and eventually was able to calm down."

Doc: "Did anyone else have any variation of a flashback?"

Anna: "We've touched on this idea before, but I wanted to mention it again. Most all the time, the panic attacks, flashbacks, and nightmares have come out of the blue and I felt helpless. I think most of us when we started this group were saying, 'I don't know what to do.' This training is giving me a confidence that I'm eventually going to be able to manage Pee Wee Focker's reaction to these experiences. I do believe that will be part of what helps reduce their intensity and frequency. Again, I like the idea that we're training. And I like the way we're learning how to stop running and turn around and face our Fockers." She raised her voice and loudly with determination said, "Pee Wee Focker, I love you, but this shit is gonna stop."

Nate: "Let's hear it for Anna." The group shouted, "Hip, hip, HOORAY! Hip, hip, HOORAY!"

Ace: Looked at Anna. "You said exactly what I've been feelin' and thinkin'. I'm taking back control of my life. I'm no longer willing to let Fark be the leader and just go along with whatever he wants to do whether it's getting drunk, getting laid, being pissed off, getting in fights, isolating, and having flashbacks. I now have some skills and I'm not the best at 'em yet, but I'm gonna train till I can do it. And as I look around the room, I'm hopin' everyone is startin' to feel this way. Thanks Anna for putting it in words that make my goals even clearer to me."

Paul: "That shit 'ill preach."

Frank: "I know I was one of the most verbal about not knowing what to do, but I have a plan and a direction. Also, I'm likin' the idea all this is training. It gives me hope."

There was silence and then Doc said, "Let's huddle up in the Center of the room." As we huddled putting our arms on each other's shoulders, Doc stayed on the outside of the circle and said, "Close your eyes, take a few deep breaths and go to your Center. Take everyone in the group with you, opening yourself to feel the energy of the group. Everyone is ready to move on with life…free to guide your own ship and take control of your life…in some mysterious way draw on the energy and strength of each other. Feel the support and encouragement. Know that at Center you have everything you need to experience healing and freedom and with continuing determination and commitment; you will find your way to inner peace and happiness. Take a few more deep breaths, perhaps becoming aware that as you open yourself to this experience, you feel so connected to each other that you no longer can tell where your arm and hand ends and the touch of arms, hands, shoulders of the others begin. It's like you can merge together and experience oneness that binds you together in harmony. A few more deep breaths and open your eyes. Let's take a break."

After the break, we spent the rest of the session pairing up with different partners and coaching each other through the nine-stepper and the eleven-stepper. He cautioned us to stay with medium intensity examples in both exercises. It was helpful to hear the experience and ideas of other members of the group.

Doc gave us our assignment for the week which was almost the same as the last group. The only difference was he wanted us to practice both the nine step exercise and eleven-step exercise once each day again with medium intensity examples. He said for us to plan to stay for another 'outing' next week after our group meeting.

Doc left and everyone stayed a little while longer talking in groups.

54
CENTERED RELATIONSHIPS

After the last person left, Ace grabbed a sandwich and took off for the mill. He had promised our dads that he would get to the mill as close to noon as possible. They had a big order to fill this afternoon.

After he left, I realized we hadn't mentioned tonight. I called April and she said they had not talked about it, but she assumed the four of us would do something together. She said the forecast was for clear skies for the next couple of days. She suggested that we go hiking and take a picnic supper with us. She said Ace would be fine with the idea and I could ask Eden and if she wanted to do something different. I could call her and let her know. Otherwise if there is no call, we would stick with that plan. That sounded good to me so we made arrangements about the food and hung up. We would meet around 6:00.

It was a little after noon. I told Eden 1:00 and if I left now and picked up the food I would be about twenty minutes early. I decided to go on.

When I arrived there was a car in her driveway that I didn't recognize. My first thought was that it belonged to Lance. I parked on the road and knocked on the front door. Immediately I heard barking and this cute little brown and white spaniel came running to the door.

She was barking up a storm. Shortly, Eden came to the door and sure enough it was Lance following behind her. I took a deep breath and was determined to stay Centered.

I said, "Hey Eden. This must be Cher."

She answered, "Yes it is. Come on in."

Inside the door, I knelt down and let Cher smell me and then she let me rub her ears and we were immediate friends.

I stood up and Eden said, "Jett Hollander, this is my friend Lance Foley."

He said, "Nice to meet you Jett. Are you any kin to Henry Hollander?"

"Yeah, he's my uncle."

He said, "We teach over at the college. He's a fine man. I like him and respect him."

I said, "Thanks. He's a very special person. Lance, what do you teach?"

"I teach corporate law," and he smiled real big and continued, "And I want to say, but I'm not an attorney because attorney's don't generally have a very good reputation," and he laughed again.

And I was already starting to like him which was contrary to thoughts I had about him previous to now. I smiled back, "Attorneys are not all bad. I know a few nice ones."

He laughed again. "Thanks Jett. I hope I can be counted in that group." He turned to Eden, "I better be off and let you two get to work." He turned to me, "Jett, nice to meet you."

"It's nice to meet you too."

Eden said, "Thanks for coming by."

He gave her a friendly hug and was gone.

I said, "He's very nice."

"Yes, he was always known for having a great personality."

I asked, "Where are Weedee, Tambeau, and Chester?"

"They are all huddled in the back bedroom under the bed. They have only come out a few times for food and water and to use the litter box. After you have been here awhile, I suspect they will wander out."

"Well Ms. Eden, welcome to Harvest!" I gave her a big hug.

She was a little tense, but then relaxed and pulled back and smiled, "Thank you Mr. Jett. I'm glad to be here and thank you for coming to help me. I've spent all morning clearing more things out and making room for my things from the U-Haul. I have more trash bags of stuff and more boxes of dishes and kitchen things for the Salvation Army. Would you mind carrying them out to your truck and then I'll get you to help me move a few heavier things. Did I tell you that I'm going to put most of my furniture in storage? There is no use moving it in and then having to move it out again in six months or so. After that, we can eat our lunch."

"Sounds like a plan."

During lunch I said, "I can see why you like Lance."

"Yes, it seemed like in college everybody liked Lance. He dated the same girl all through college and I heard they had a beautiful wedding, a nice home, and two lovely children. I assumed it was a story book romance and they would live happily ever after. But they are divorced and split time with the children." She looked at me. "Do you think there are any story book romances with 'happily ever after' endings?"

"Wow. I'm a dreamer so I like to think that such a thing is possible. I think there are a lot of story book romances, but it appears something happens over time that interrupts the happily ever after plan. I heard someone say the other day that the divorce rate for first marriages is over fifty percent. I sometimes wonder if a good portion of those who are still married are not happy and are staying together for reasons like children, finances, religion, fear of change or being alone. You told me a little about your situation. What do you think happens?"

She responded, "Mine was not a story book romance. I thought I loved him, but now I'm sure I never did. So we don't count in this discussion. I don't have much experience in relationships so I don't know what happens. Unfortunately, I've never met anyone who in the later years of a relationship still had that spark. Surely there are some people who still feel it after years together."

"Maybe it's the nature of the spark that changes. I think Pop and Nana kept that spark alive. From the outside looking in, they seemed happy together. They were always affectionate and had a great sense of humor. They would tease each other and laugh. I never saw them have an argument although I know they did 'cause they both could be stubborn. They seemed to have a mutual respect for each other. Pop was always going on about Nana this and Nana that." I smiled. "But they also valued their space. They had mutual interests, but also had different interests. He really misses her. I think he is ready to die and join her in the afterlife." I looked at Eden. "I think they had it; that story book relationship."

She thoughtfully said, "I guess then it is possible."

Silence and then I said, "We didn't talk about tonight. April suggested we hike and take a picnic supper. Would you come with us?"

"Would you mind if I take a rain check? I'm so tired from this week. I would just like to crawl in bed early and pass out."

Trying not to sound too disappointed, I answered, "I understand. You've had a couple of tough weeks. It looks like we have a full afternoon of work ahead of us. After I take the stuff to the Salvation Army, how 'bout me stopping at the store and picking up the stuff for a nice light supper. I will fix it while you relax with a glass of wine. Then we can eat and I'll clean up and go home. Whatta ya say?"

She smiled, "All right. That sounds nice."

"Let me call April and tell her that we'll pass for tonight."

She said, "Do you mind if I call her? I want to thank her for the invitation and say, 'Hey.'"

She was on the phone with April for at least thirty minutes. As I came in and out of the house, I heard her laughing several times.

It seemed they were becoming good friends. The rest of the afternoon I unloaded the U-Haul® and she was busy arranging things and putting things away. During the middle of the afternoon, she got a call and I only heard bits and pieces, but I guessed it was Lance. Was she really talking in a lower voice or was I just imaging it? They talked for about five minutes. Before I knew it, the clock on the wall struck 6:00 and we were at a good stopping place.

I said, "I'll take the stuff to the Salvation Army and pick up some groceries. Would it be bold for me to suggest that you relax and soak in the tub with a glass of wine?"

She looked at me and smiled, "It is a little bold, but I have to admit it's an inviting idea. I've used a lot of muscles these last days I don't ordinarily use and I can feel it."

"Okay. It's settled. I'm gonna drop the things off at the SA, make a quick trip to the cabin to shower and clean up, get the groceries, pick up a box of condoms, and I should be back in about an hour. Do you need anything at the store?"

It took a minute for her to catch what I said and she started laughing and said, "You're gonna pick up what?"

"The groceries?"

"No, you said something else." Trying to keep a straight face, "Oh, you mean the condoms. Oh, I'm sorry. I didn't mean anything by that. I just like to keep a box of condoms in the truck and I've run out and it always makes me a little nervous. I go through 'em pretty fast and I just like to keep a good supply on hand. Do you need anything?"

Also with a straight face she answered, "Yes thank you. Could you pick me up a large tube of scented lubricant and a box of tampons?"

"How large a tube and what brand of tampons?"

That was as far as we could get. We both burst out laughing.

She slapped me on the head and exclaimed, "Get outta here." She pushed me out through the screen door and slammed the front door behind me.

I smiled as I walked toward the truck and thought to myself that I'm never giving up on this woman. If there is such a thing as a soul mate, she is mine.

I was back in about an hour and the front door was open. I knocked. "Come on in Butt Wipe." She was arranging some dishes in the cabinet and looked stunning in yellow shorts, a white blouse, with a pony tail and white flip flops.

"How was your bath?"

"That was a great idea. I feel much better."

"I'm glad. Now, I wanna fix supper for you. All I need is a cutting board and two large bowls and a beer."

She showed me where everything was and asked, "Do you want to eat in the kitchen or do you want to eat on the patio in the back?"

"You choose."

"All right, let's eat in here. Can I help?"

"No, just sit and talk to me."

"All right, this is nice."

I asked, "Have you thought any more about the story book relationships?"

"Some while I was soaking in the tub."

"Do you have any new insights?"

"I was thinking more about my friends who are married and I still couldn't think of one who has one of those close relationships like Pop and Nana. Some do better than others, but I sometimes wonder how happy they are. The spark seems to fade after awhile and then they seem to settle into a kind of routine. Maybe people can be happy in that routine. If someone were to have that spark, I guess the question is, 'how do you keep it alive?'"

"Doc keeps talking to us about what he calls, 'Attention Training.' I think I might have mentioned it. Anyway, he is teaching us to pay attention to our lives, how we think and feel, and how we make decisions and how we choose to behave and how we can change all those things. I thought more about this while I was running my errands and stocking up on condoms." She threw a peanut at me. I continued, "Anyway, what if a couple was trained to pay attention and they loved the spark between them and decided they would be determined to find ways in one form or another to keep that spark going? Do you think they could do it?"

She said, "Let's talk about the spark. What is it?"

"You tell me first what you think it is?"

She thought for a moment and then said, "For me, I think it would come gradually after getting to know a person. It seems much more emotional than it does physical. I can think a man is attractive, but I've never had these firework sexual urges go off by just being around a good looking man. And while I was married, I never allowed myself to stray. I didn't love him, but I wasn't going to cheat."

"Tell me more about the emotional side."

She responded, "I guess I need to confess that I would first have to find a man I thought was physically attractive. Not necessarily in a sexual way. I'm not sure I can explain." She smiled and said, "I was out with one of my friends some years ago and she turned to me and nodded toward a guy and used a phrase I had never heard. She said, 'That guy is hot.' I responded by saying, 'He doesn't seem hot; he's not sweating.' I took a lot of teasing about that over the years. I've never been turned on by just looking at a man, but I do have an opinion about what I consider physically attractive."

"Makes sense to me."

"All right, so here goes for the emotional side. First, I have to feel safe. That comes from my background. While growing up, with the exception of my granddaddy, I never felt safe around any males." She seemed to drift off in thought.

That was important information that I needed to always remember with her. I wanted to ask her to tell me more, but I knew that was something that she would have to tell me on her own. I looked over at her and there were a few tears. I spotted a box of tissues and handed her one and touched her on the shoulder and went over to resume cutting up vegetables. I wish I could have taken her in my arms and kissed away those tears, but that was out of the question.

More silence and then she said, "So first, I have to feel safe. That's somewhat of a challenge since how do you know anyone's safe until you get to know them and even then, you can't be sure. I guess that's the reason I haven't been on many dates since my divorce. Since I've never really had a close relationship with any man, I've spent a lot of time thinking about what it would be like and what I would be looking for in a man. So Jett Hollander, here are some of my traits. Hey!" And I looked over at her and she smiled and said, "Don't get your hopes up young man because even though you may have some of these traits, you are way too young for an older woman like me."

"Okay Mom, I'm waiting for that list."

She began: "Kind, compassionate, gentle, a good listener, confident but not cocky, assertive but not aggressive, spiritual, has a job and is self-supportive, observant, giving, loves the outdoors, environmentalist, and sense of humor."

"Wow, what a list. I'm good to go on every trait and since you didn't list, 'around same age,' I meet all criteria. Will you marry me?"

She smiled. You're a 'hoot' Jett Hollander, but you're still too young and you're not safe. After you had been with me for awhile, you'd find some nice young 'thing' and leave me."

I didn't smile and said with my best look of devotion and commitment, "That would never ever happen!" She seemed a little embarrassed and I smiled and said, "Well, you've turned me down so now I have to win your heart with my cooking. The menu is fresh salmon salad with homemade croutons and my special homemade vinaigrette dressing and my special garlic bread."

"Well, well, isn't that interesting since I saw you get most everything from a bag or bottle."

"There may be a few minor consistencies in my statement, but let's eat and see if it's any good."

She took a bite of the salad and said, "This is good."

"Glad you like it. You never did get to the part of defining the spark."

"I guess it's something I would feel once I got to know the person. Honestly, I don't know what the spark would feel like. I've never had it for anyone. I said earlier that it would be more emotional for me, but there would also be the physical attraction. Sex with Chase was always more of a duty. I'm not gonna lie. Sometimes it felt physically good, but there was never any emotional intimacy. Now you can tell me what you think."

"Like you, I must find the woman physically attractive. For me and I think for most men the sexual surfaces right away. I think it's just how we're wired. I've dated some girls where I felt that sexual attraction, but I've never felt the emotional intimacy. I've thought quite a bit about that lately. Why is there no emotional intimacy?"

She asked, "Do you have any answers to that question?"

"Sometimes I think I just haven't met the right person. Then I wonder if that's just an excuse. I need more time to try and figure it out. I have to admit that I'm wondering if I'm afraid of that kind of intimacy." This was definitely not the time to tell her I may have always loved April. "I've got more work to do on that issue."

I hesitated and then said, "There are any number of women I can be physically attracted to, but at this point in my life, I don't want just the physical. I want that emotional intimacy. And I think the emotional gives the physical that spark. So to me, keeping the emotional intimacy alive and well keeps the spark going."

She asked, "So how do you think two people can keep that emotional intimacy going?"

"In most relationships, I think both people have to consistently be awake and pay attention to that goal. They have to be committed to keeping the spark alive. I don't know if Pop and Nana ever consciously made that commitment. They just seemed to love each other and that was enough. Maybe that same thing happens with other couples too."

She responded, "I'm not sure there are that many, but I could be wrong."

I said, "Maybe it happens more than we realize."

"Yes maybe so."

Silence and then I said, "Cher is so well mannered. She doesn't beg at all."

She smiled, "She's a sweetheart. The spark between me and Cher has always been there."

"Yeah, I could say the same about Spot. Well, I know you're tired. Let me do these dishes and I'll head on home."

She said, "I'll help you."

I asked, "Will I see you in church tomorrow?"

She hesitated and answered, "Lance invited me to go with him to his church. After he invited me, I thought it would be a good time for me to take him out to lunch to repay him for helping me pack. And then he offered to drive me around after lunch and look for property to build on. You've showed me some beautiful places, but I felt awkward refusing him."

Breathing and staying Centered was all I could think of and it helped some, but my heart was beating faster and Tug kept saying you're losing her. I kept focusing on my breathing. I turned to her and said, "Okay. Could I call you tomorrow evening and check in?"

"Sure."

We finished up the dishes and she said, "Thanks for helping me today and fixing supper. I enjoyed it."

"My pleasure. I'll miss seeing you at church. Have a good time tomorrow."

She gave me a hug that lasted a little longer than usual and said, "Call me tomorrow."

On the way home, I held onto that longer hug for dear life choosing to see it as a sign she cares about me and knows it's hard for me that she's going to spend time with him. When I got to the cabin, there were no vehicles so I figured April and Ace had decided to stay at her house. I wished they were here so I could talk about Eden. I took Spot for a short walk, got a beer, and plopped down in front of the TV.

I couldn't focus on the TV. I kept working on Centering and saying over and over, "Eden's happiness is of ultimate importance." I felt some peace, but then Tug started his shit and I imagined them sleeping together and him giving her oral sex. I was getting the first symptoms of a panic attack. I yelled, "No fucking way you Focker!!" Then I was determined to get Centered and started the breathing again and could feel my body responding and said, "Tug, go ahead and give me your best shot. I accept the symptoms. Go ahead. Let's do some rapid heart rate and have trouble breathing. Go ahead. I embrace it. I accept it. Let's do it. I'm open arms." I took all that shit back a minute or so later when I had the worst panic attack ever. I thought I was dying. Soon the symptoms passed and I lay exhausted on the floor.

I woke up sometime later still on the floor. I went to my bed and slept till 8:23. I couldn't remember the last time I had slept that late. Spot and I went for our run and I was surprised that I felt pretty good. When I got back to the cabin, Ace's SUV was there. He was in the shower so I fixed pancakes and sausage.

When he appeared, he said, "Hey there. April had to go to work early and I was too lazy to fix myself anything to eat. Have you got enough for me?"

"Yeah, I figured April had to work and that you might be hungry." I brought him up to date on my situation with Eden.

He asked, "So, how're you doin'?"

I told him about last night and the panic. "I told Tug to bring on his best shot and all that stuff about acceptance and non-judgment and Tug fuckin' kicked my ass with the worst panic attack I ever had."

By that time we were both laughing. I got up and played the scene over saying bring it on and on.

"I thought I was fuckin' dying."

After we settled down, I said, "You know, even though Tug kicked my ass, I had this feeling of power that enabled me to take that shot. I didn't fight it. I embraced it. In some kind of strange way I didn't feel helpless and a victim. To quote Paul, 'That's some crazy shit.' And another strange thing is I feel good this morning. It's like I vomited all this emotional and physical shit and trauma out my system. It's like I purged and I feel better. I don't know how I'll feel later, but I'm livin' in the moment so we'll see what happens."

He said, "I think what Doc is teaching us is going to help in a lot of areas. We may not understand exactly how it works, but the important thing is we know what to do and we start feeling better."

"Yeah, that makes sense."

He continued, "I haven't done so well. April and I got in another fight last night and instead of trying to get Centered, Fark convinced me to go to Stanley's and get drunk. I called April at work while you were out with Spot. She wasn't in a good mood. She told me that Chip called her around 2:00 this morning and asked her to come and pick me up. She told him she had to work this morning and she wasn't going to come and pick up my sorry ass. She told him to call a cab and have the cab driver leave me on the front porch. That's where I was when I woke up this morning. I had to get a cab to get back to Stanley's."

I smiled, "Have some more pancakes and sausage."

"I will. How come I'm hungry and feelin' better?"

I responded, "Do you think it's starting to sink in that even though some heavy shit went down last night, it only existed when you were living it and today, it's no longer real and doesn't exist. The only thing that's real is you and me sittin' here eatin' pancakes and sausage."

He answered, "I should be in a deep fucking depression with a bunch of guilt and remorse, but I don't feel that way. I accept it and

I'm not judging it. In fact, I'm looking forward to talking with April and apologizing and making a commitment to do better. I'm lookin' forward to the next time Fark wants to get drunk so I can tell him it's not gonna happen. And right now I'm sittin' here enjoying you and me hangin' out."

I added, "Some would say you need to feel like a piece of shit or that apology is empty. They would say you didn't even suffer for all those bad reactions and decisions. You're gettin' off pretty easy. They would say all you do is just say I'm sorry and you're off the fucking hook. No problem."

He said, "I heard Doc say once that guilt is a waste of time and is a form of self-indulgence. He would say to let it go and take all the energy you would use to feel like a piece of shit and channel it into the determination and commitment to stay Centered. That's what I'm gonna do."

"Sometimes when I think about this experience with Doc, I'm amazed that all ten of us combat veterans are working our butts off doing all this breathing and Centering."

He replied, "I don't think some veterans would do this type of stuff. I think Doc picked us because we were desperate. I bet he rejected some because he thought they wouldn't be motivated to do the work. Frankly, I don't think I would have stayed if I hadn't tried to 'whack' myself." He had a far away look for a few moments and then turned and asked, "Okay, so what are you thinking about Eden?"

"I believe I have a legitimate concern that she will end up with Lance, but since I don't know the future, I'm going to do everything in my power to let that go and take one day at a time or maybe one moment at a time. I'm going to try my best to win her heart. And right now, I'm sittin' here talkin' with my best friend."

He said, "Good for you. Why don't we take the bikes out and head up to Jackson Ridge? We can park them there and I think I can make that two mile round trip hike to the peak. We can take a sandwich and some chips and eat up there. If we go the back way, we should be back here by around 4:00. Whatta ya think?"

"Let's do it."

I called Mom to update her on what was happening with Eden and to let her know I wouldn't be in church.

It was another beautiful day and we had a great time. I thought some about Eden and Lance, but it wasn't painful. I knew even though she might decide to be with him, I would find a way to survive. I was determined not to be jealous or angry and to do everything I could to stay Centered. If I could do that, I would find my path to that freedom Doc talks about.

55

GOD AND WAR

When we returned to the cabin, Ace called April and she was going to exercise and then come over and join us for supper. When she arrived, I took Spot for a walk and we stayed gone about an hour. When we got back, they were fixing our meal. We brought April up to date on our conversations earlier and they told me about their talk while I was gone. After we finished eating, they went for walk. I took some deep breaths, got Centered, and called Eden.

"Hey, how're ya' doin'?"

"Hey, Jett. I'm fine. How are you?"

I told her about my day and asked her how things went with Lance.

"We had a nice time. He showed me some beautiful building sites. I have to admit they all seem beautiful to me. I love this part of the country and I think I could be happy with any of them."

I didn't want to ask her for any more details. "Well, I'm glad it went well. So what's your schedule for this week?"

"Did I tell that my friend from work will meet the movers at my apartment and when they're finished, she and another friend are going to clean the place, lock up and turn in the keys?"

"No, that's great. I'm glad you won't have to go back down there."

"I'm taking tomorrow off to finish getting things settled here at the house. Tuesday, I have to look for office space and put an advertisement in the paper for an assistant. Lance's secretary has a sister who is looking for a job so that may be a possibility. I'm responsible for operations in ten counties and I have a meeting with the people working in those counties on Thursday morning. Does the Inn have a small meeting room I might rent for a day?"

"Yes, they have several. Call Connie at the Inn. She's in charge of setting up business meetings." I gave her the telephone number and continued, "I wondered if you might be interested in taking a break for a couple of hours around noon tomorrow. I'll pack some food and I have a special place I'd like to show you."

There was silence and then, "Thanks Jett. I have so much left to do. It sounds like fun, but I better take a rain check."

"Come on. You have to take a break and eat at some point. I won't keep you more than a couple of hours. And I'll offer my services the rest of the afternoon to help make up for the time you weren't working. Come on. You'll love this spot."

More silence. "You are persistent. All right, do you want to pick me up around noon?"

"Sounds good. Do you like Subway?" She said that would be fine. I got her order and told her I would see her tomorrow.

April and Ace left around nine. I watched a little TV and went to bed. I slept well. I got to the Inn around 7:00 and continued on a project Charlie had given me last week. I wanted to make good progress since I wasn't going to work this afternoon. I checked on Pop around 10:00 and he wasn't doing great, but had his usual positive attitude. I told him I'd check on him later this afternoon or tomorrow after work to see if he was up for a walk around the lake.

I knocked on her door a little after 12:00. She looked beautiful in khaki shorts and a green top and a khaki baseball cap with her pony tail sticking out the back. She had on her hiking shoes with white socks. Her legs were kind of slender, but full and muscular from her years of hiking and her life in the outdoors.

She smiled and gave me a brief hug and said, "Hey Jett, I can't believe I let you talk me into taking this break. I still have so much to do. But honestly, I need the break. Lance brought me home around 4:00 and I worked until about 9:00 when I collapsed into bed."

I was thankful she told me she didn't spend all day and the evening with him. I said, "This place is a good hike from the cabin, but I'm going to drive us so that it won't take us but about ten minutes to walk there."

She asked about Pop and we exchanged small talk. I asked her if she liked Lance's church and she said it was fine. She said they were a little too conservative for her. The preacher was a little too loud and all he talked about was being saved and accepting Jesus.

She said, "There wasn't anything wrong with it. I just don't enjoy that type of service. Frankly, it reminds me too much of the church we went to when I was growing up. We were poor and granddaddy used to make us all get in the truck and he would give each one of us a penny to put in the offering. We didn't have any Sunday clothes so we stood out, but I remember being proud that we had money to put in the offering. As we got older, a few men in the church, one who was an elder, tried to convince us to have sex with them."

Silence and then she continued, "We were poor and they thought they could take advantage of us. I'm not sure, but I think one of my sisters gave in. She would never talk about it. You think it would turn me off to church, but I realized later it wasn't the church, it was people. Anyway, when I go to church, I want to hear less about being saved and more about what it means to live a Christian life and the forgiveness of God when we don't do too well. That's what I like about Father Pat." She smiled, "That was a long answer to your question."

"I like hearing about your life. It didn't seem long to me." I pulled off the road and we got our food and headed down the trail. When we got to the entrance, I said, "If you were walking in this area, would you think there was anything beyond that boulder?"

"No, I wouldn't."

I showed her a way that everyone would think goes nowhere. We squeezed and twisted and then had to use a tree coming out of the rocks to hold onto and then we were in the space on the other side of the boulder. She was surprised saying, "I would have never thought in a million years this place would be here. The view seems very similar to the view from our knoll." She smiled and a little embarrassed said, "I mean the knoll."

I acted like I didn't catch it or "paid it no mind" as we use to say. I replied, "Yeah, the knoll, as the crow flies, is about a mile from here towards the cabin. The view is similar."

She said, "It is breath taking. And on this ledge, there's open space to be in the sun and space to be in the shade if it's too hot."

"Soon after I returned home, I came up here and spent the night. If you think it's beautiful in the daytime, you should see it on a clear night. It's magnificent. Are you hungry?"

"Yes, I didn't eat much breakfast."

I spread out the blanket and told her to lay back and rest while I get the food out. There was a light breeze with a few scattered clouds. Rain was forecast for later in the afternoon. I glanced at her and her eyes were closed and she looked peaceful and content. My eyes strayed down to her legs and I imagined what she would look like naked in the sun. I shifted my thoughts back to getting the food out before something started getting hard. That's all I needed was for her to see a "boner" through my shorts.

"It's ready." She sat up. While eating, we looked at the view and I pointed out different landmarks on the horizon and down in the valley. It was light conversation. We laughed and had a good time. After we finished, she suggested we look at clouds again. We talked about different formations and laughed at some of them.

We were partially shaded by the trees and there were some sunbeams coming down through the trees directing light in and out of our eyes as the breeze shifted the branches of the trees. She rolled over and rested on her elbows. She looked at me and asked, "Do you believe God is in control of things?"

I answered, "No."

She went on, "That would sound blasphemous to a lot of people."

"I know. Doc taught us about the complexity of the brain/mind and said he believed it was presumptuous of any person or group to claim they had the Truth about anything. So I don't claim to have the Truth. Doc has taught us that all we have is our perception which he suggested would change quite often as we learn and discover new things and ideas. I respect other people's perceptions and would ask the same from them. Do you want me to go on?"

She smiled, "Yes, go ahead. It sounds like you've given this a lot of thought."

"Somewhere between my first and second tour, I started questioning why God would allow war. I talked to different people and I always got the same answer. They essentially said that God does not cause war, but He allows it. Then I started getting angry with God. My question was if you can do something about it, why don't you stop this insanity? Some would tell me it's God's will not to stop it and that pissed me off even more. I had been a Christian all my life and I was about to lose my faith."

She said, "You must have gotten it worked out since you still go to church. Did you find the answer to your question?"

"Since I talked with you last about God, Doc and I had lunch and we spent the whole time talking about God and religion. That conversation helped me a lot, but I owe my spiritual life to a special Army Chaplain. His name was John Rodgers. I'll never forget him. He recommended different books and since we had a lot of down time between missions, I read everything I could get my hands on.

I spent a lot of time on that second tour having long conversations with Chaplain Rodgers. Do you want me to go on?"

She smiled, "Do I have to worry about being struck by lightning? It's getting kind of cloudy."

I looked at her and smiled back, "So far, I've survived, but proceed at your own risk."

"All right, go on."

"I believe God created this planet and gave us everything we need to make it a paradise. God said my Spirit which permeates the universe will be inside you and dwell there as long as you live. I've other business in the Universe. Go in peace and love and create happiness. And then in the Garden of Eden, your garden," I smiled, "we learned that humans had a better idea and here we are."

"So you believe we're in control and not God?"

I responded, "Look around, whatta you think?"

"It's pretty messed up. As you said a few minutes ago, some will say God allows pain and evil in the world, but does not cause it."

I said, "I accepted that earlier, but there came a time when that idea didn't work for me anymore. In my view, God's intervention was to create us and our world and give us His Spirit within. So after the metaphor of the seven days, God's intervention ended. God left to take care of other business in the universe and left us with His Spirit which means we have everything we need to live in love and peace and create happiness. There was nothing else left for God to do. God then is not involved in any way in the events of our world. God lives in the world through His Spirit within us." I hesitated.

She said, "I think that's a scary thought for a lot of people."

"I understand that. If you look around, you see God everywhere in many of the different aspects of the creation, both in our world and in us humans. It's everywhere in nature and in the many ways the Spirit of God is manifested in the world through the peace and love of people everywhere." I smiled and said, "I believe that's why God came back after being gone awhile and checked in and said, 'stop asking me for special favors. Heed the words of the Psalmist who said that I am your Shepherd through my Spirit and you have everything you need to live in peace and love and be happy. Go inside and discover the miracle. Let me remind you again that if you want to know me through the Spirit within, be still and you will find me. So there's nothing to be afraid of since perfect love casts out fear.'"

She said, "In church yesterday, I heard phrases like, we ask you to be present in our service today, we ask a special blessing on so and so, we just ask you to heal the pain, we ask you to be especially with these folks as they go through this ordeal, and we ask your healing touch on our sister, and be with all those who have special needs. What do you think about those prayers?"

"Many people find great comfort in those prayers and I would never suggest they change what works for them. They do not fit my theology which says that God is always within us so we never have to ask for God's presence for any reason or ask for any special blessings. My prayer in that area is to ask that each of us be aware that the Spirit is within us and that's where the miracle is. That's where the Light is always shining guiding our path and showing us the way. The Light doesn't go anywhere or get any brighter or need any special nudging from us. Once again, the Psalmist reminds us, 'The Lord is my Shepherd, I have everything I need.' Everything we need and long for is already inside us. We are responsible for finding our way to the Spirit within."

She asked, "How do you find the way?"

"God says if you want to know me, be still, be quiet, stop talking, be silent." I smiled, "In other words, shut up. Jesus also told us if we want to know the way, the truth, and the life we should follow him and remember to love God and love your neighbor."

She asked, "How do we be still? Our minds are so active. My mind never shuts up. There is a constant stream of chatter."

"I've been trying to answer that question myself and Doc has given me the first glimpse of how to quiet the mind and be still. And as you might imagine, it's a huge challenge."

I had already taught her the deep breathing skill and I explained in more detail the benefits of the breathing and then gave her a quick overview of the meaning of being Centered.

She said, "I want to hear more about that later, but I'm more interested right now in what you're saying about prayer. So we don't need to ask God for help so what is the purpose of prayer?"

"I don't mean I don't ask God for help. My prayer all the time is to help me know that You are inside me at my Center and that from You I will find courage, strength, guidance, hope, inner peace, clarity, wisdom, grace, mercy, and forgiveness. Help me to know that you walk with me every step along the way. Notice that I never mentioned asking God to intervene in the outside events of life. Hopefully each of us will have an impact on what happens in our world and in that way God will intervene."

"What else about prayer?"

I answered, "I also focus on thanksgiving and confession. And I don't believe I ever have to ask for forgiveness. I believe we are forgiven in the moment we recognize we have made a wrong turn. Doc told us the Greek word for sin is 'wrong turn.' So I may go over my sins, but at the end I say, 'Thank you for loving me even in the midst of my most unlovable moments.'" I smiled, "I have to admit that I've been asking God for things all my life and it's not easy to break that habit. So I'll slip and ask God to keep Pop alive 'cause I need him and don't want him to die. I'll ask God to protect my loved ones or keep us safe on a trip."

"But you don't believe God will keep Pop alive a little longer or that He will protect your loved ones or keep you safe on a trip, right?"

"No, I believe Pop will die when a whole lot of physical and emotional things come together. God is not in the business of protecting loved ones or keeping families safe on trips. In my view, God has nothing to do with those things. But, I've been in the habit of asking God for help all my life and it's very difficult to stop and it makes me feel better."

She looked puzzled and said, "So even though you don't believe God intervenes in that way, you still ask?"

Smiling, I said, "Yeah, I feel better thinking God is in control and will protect us. Then when I look at the fact that some of the most spiritual people have experienced the worst kinds of tragedies, I have to shift to God didn't protect us, but it was God's will and I won't question God's will. That way, He is still in control. Or I could approach it like God's will was not for that family of five to be killed by a drunken truck driver, but He allowed it to happen. Now I'm back to my problem that God allows war. So then I say to God, 'So You could have kept that family from being killed, but you didn't choose to or you could have stopped wars, but you didn't want to? I could no longer believe that."

She said, "When it comes to death, I've heard all my life that God will take you in His own good time or God called him/her home or it was his/her time or it was God's plan for your aunt to die." A tear appeared in the corner of her eye.

I took a napkin and blotted her tears.

She continued, "Do you believe that God has a plan for us?"

"Yes."

She asked, "What is His plan for you?"

"He wants me to live in peace and love and to be happy."

"Is that it?"

I answered, "Yes."

She smiled, "I guess His plan for me would be the same?"

"I believe that is God's only plan for all of us."

"Why aren't we better at doing that?"

I replied, "Because we decided we had a better plan than that one."

She said, "You have some strange views."

"I know. They are new and sometimes even feel strange to me."

We were silent for awhile. Then she asked, "What about Jesus?"

"What specifically do you mean?"

"Well, I don't know. Do you believe he died for our sins?"

"No."

She looked at me and said, "Holy shit!"

I said, "I don't believe he died for our sins. I believe he died because of our sins."

"Whatta you mean?"

"In my view, Jesus was the embodiment of perfect love. He modeled God's plan for us. He lived in peace and love. At a deeper unconscious level, we couldn't stand to be reminded that we were living in sin so we crucified him."

She said, "I've heard all my life that Jesus died for my sins so God could forgive me. That's the only way to salvation. That's the only way to be saved."

"When I talked with Chaplain Rodgers about that same issue, he said I needed to start with the question, 'Who is God?'"

She asked, "Well, what did you find out?"

"I'll try to summarize in a couple of minutes the conclusion to months of prayer and study." Smiling I said, "Someday, if you want the long answer, I'll take you through the painstaking search."

I hesitated.

She said, "Go on."

"Remember, I'm not claiming that I have the truth. I only know what is true for me. And I am in no way trying to convince you that you should believe my truth."

She replied, "Give me a little respect Dude. I'll make up my own mind about what I believe."

A little embarrassed, I said, "Thanks for reminding me. Okay. The Bible says we were made in God's image. I don't believe that.

I believe we made God in our image and we did it for a good reason. How were we going to understand the Creator of the universe, the Life Force in all things, the Source of all Being if we didn't attach to this Being a description that we could understand? The problem however came when there was no awareness of that concept. There was no deeper understanding that we had to be careful not to project onto God our own personality. So instead of saying, 'We've got to figure out how we can describe the Creator so we can connect and have a relationship, we took the events of our experience which we caused as a result of Adam and Eve and created a God that closely resembled our personality."

I continued, "So we ended up with a God who loved some and didn't love others, who blessed some and punished others, who commanded us to spare some and kill others, who has the power to stop human suffering, but allows it to go on as if he is up there saying, 'I told you so,' or 'you made your bed, you have to lay in it.' I guess that's okay for people like you and me, but when it comes to little children suffering and dying from starvation and millions of innocents being killed in war, I couldn't handle that anymore." I looked at her and hesitated again.

She said again, "Go on."

"So in the Old Testament, we have an angry God who requires sacrifice in order to forgive. It made sense then when Jesus came that He could be the ultimate sacrifice to a God who would only forgive us if Jesus paid the price and died for our sins. Obviously, I have a lot of problems with this view of God. As I read and studied Scripture, I began to get a different picture of God. From the teachings of Jesus and many of the writers of the Old and New Testaments, I got a picture of God who loves unconditionally. He tells us that what's most important is to live in peace and love and the Spirit will always be with us as our ultimate source of everything we need to follow His plan for us."

She said, "My head is swimming. Give me a few minutes." She put her head down on the blanket. After awhile, she lifted her head up and said, "People will say you must not believe in the Bible. Is that true?"

"I don't believe that God dictated the Bible. I do believe that a lot in the Bible is inspired by God. I also believe that a lot in the Bible is inspired by human beings who were much more interested in their own agenda than in spiritual truth. And when I studied how the Bible was put together and who actually decided what would go into it and what was left out, that only reinforced the idea that parts of it were man inspired and not God inspired."

She asked, "But how do you know the difference?"

"Be still and know that I am your God is the first step. In the quietness, the Spirit will guide our discernment and help us find the truth that will set us free to live in peace and love and be happy. As I said earlier, we talk too much. We're always talking and it's very difficult to be still."

"Keep going."

"My mind wants to throw in all kinds of stuff which takes me off the path." I gave her a brief overview of Focker. She got a big kick out of the name. "My Focker's name is Tug."

She laughed, "Your Focker has a first name?"

"Yes. He is always tugging at me because he's afraid and very self-focused. Among a lot of other things, he's angry with you because you think I'm too young for you and he's jealous of Lance and wants to whip his butt. The Spirit of God lives at my Center, here in my heart, and here life is about peace and love. When I'm Centered, nothing else matters except you finding love and happiness."

She smiled, "Jett that is so sweet." And then added, "But you're still too young for me. So the idea is pretty simple, but it's not all that easy to find peace and love and be happy."

"I think we make it harder than it is and I'm trying to figure out how to make it easier. Even though that is not Doc's purpose for working with us, I'm finding that what he is teaching us to help with PTSD is also helping me with my spiritual journey."

She said, "I want to hear more about that later, but for now, give me a couple of minutes to try and sort out some of what you've said." Silence for awhile. "See if I've got this right. Your first problem was related to why God was allowing war to happen and why He didn't stop it if He had the power to do it? Right?"

"Yeah."

"And your answer to that question is that God has nothing to do with the war or any pain and evil in the world. There is no involvement. His intervention and personal involvement ended with the creation of our world and human life. He gave us this beautiful planet and His Spirit within us and said, 'Have a great life. Go in peace and love and be happy. Always remember that I leave my Spirit with you which is all you will ever need.' Is that it?"

I responded, "When I said God's intervention and involvement ended after creation, I meant that God is not outwardly changing the natural order and order of events in our world. The human race and the planet were set in motion to evolve moment by moment day after day and its' been going on for millions of years."

She asked, "Do you mean He doesn't stop natural disasters or tragedies or heal cancer or grant special favors?"

"Yes. That's what I mean. I believe that the only intervention of God after creation is the Spirit within us. That is by far the most intimate and powerful intervention possible. And when we live out of that Spirit, we become God's intervention in the world. If you want a miracle, you don't have to pray for it. Just pray that you will find the miracle within you. It is that miracle that gives us the potential to follow Jesus when he said, '...Be in the world but not of it.' And in addition, look at God's creation and you will see miracles everywhere, in all living things, and in many people as they live the miracle."

She said, “I see it every day in my work. Sometimes I forget to see it as a miracle. What about when I read how someone was miraculously cured of cancer?”

“That kind of miracle happens often and in many different forms. The potential for healing lies within us and sometimes that takes the form of physical healing, but more often it takes the form of acceptance and peace about impending death. I wonder if I would be able to experience this acceptance and peace. And my answer is, ‘Not without God’s help at my Center.’ Bottom line again, it has nothing to do with God’s special intervention and everything to do with God’s miracle within us.”

I continued, “A few years ago, I was watching a movie where someone asked God, ‘Why don’t you stop pain and evil?’ And God said, ‘This is why I gave you each other.’ I guess that sums up what I’m trying to say.”

“So God is totally off the hook? His only intervention is through His Spirit within us.”

“Yes. And that is an incredibly powerful intervention.”

She looked at me in a quizzical way and I continued, “And everything that I’ve said today is my evolving belief system and it’s important to me. Beyond all the words and beliefs, I think there is something much more critically important and it is summarized by a Bible school song we sung when we were kids. ‘They will know we are Christians by our love, by our love. They will know we are Christians by our love.’ I substitute the word ‘spiritual’ for ‘Christians.’”

“Yes, I remember it.” She paused and then asked, “Is it true that when referring to God, you never use the pronouns He or Him? Is that your way of getting away from humanizing God?”

“I slip sometimes, but I’m trying to get out of that habit because it doesn’t line up with my understanding of God.”

She said, “Is it true that you don’t believe in a personal God?”

"Yes and no. I don't believe in a God like us humans with all the wide range of feelings. But how can God get any more personal than to live inside us through the Spirit?"

She asked, "Who else have you shared this with?"

"I've discussed it with Doc, some with Chaplain Rodgers, and now with you."

"You've got to be kidding me."

"No. And this is the first time I've expressed all of this out loud. The talk with Doc helped me to put more things in place. And it's amazing how much talking to you has helped me become clearer about what I believe."

She asked, "Is there more?"

"Yeah, do you want the long version right now?"

She laughed, "I don't even know if I wanted the short version. Why haven't you told anyone else and why did you choose to tell me?"

I answered, "I think about these things every morning on my run. As I said a minute ago, I'm just starting to put some of it together. Parts of it still seem disjointed. I've got a lot more praying, thinking, and studying to do and I hope to do that at my Center where the Spirit can continue to guide me. I'm not ready to share it with anyone else right now."

"But again, why me?" she interrupted.

"Because I want you to know who I am and what I believe."

"I don't know whether to thank you or be mad at you."

I responded, "How about just seeing it as getting to know Jett and seeing how screwed up he is?"

She laughed, "I don't see you as screwed up. You've given me a lot to think about. Well, I guess I better get on back. I've still got some work to do."

56
THE STORM

We had been so focused on the conversation that we had not noticed that clouds had moved in and it looked like the rain could start falling at any moment.

I said, "It might be better for us to stay here till these clouds pass. We have some shelter here, but there's not much shelter on the way back to the truck."

At that point the rain started falling and the wind picked up. I said, "The way the wind is blowing we can be partly protected over here on this side of the rock. The other side of the blanket is waterproof. It will help some."

I quickly cleared off the blanket and put it around my shoulders and sat down and spread my legs and motioned for her to come and sit between my legs. She hesitated, but then sat and I wrapped the blanket around both of us so that only our heads were showing. She seemed kind of stiff at first, but then started to relax and let her back rest up against my chest and then leaned her head into the crook of my neck. I was careful to keep my legs spread enough so our legs wouldn't touch.

She said, "Rain has its own special beauty. My mentor during the early days of my work with the EPA taught me that there is no bad weather. All weather has its own special beauty if we are willing to look for it. I think you would have liked him. I think you all would have had a lot in common."

I asked, "Where is he now?"

"He died suddenly several years ago. He was our assistant director in Washington. Everyone seemed to love him. He was a gentle spirit. His wife and children were devastated. There were over a thousand people at his funeral."

As she was talking, I was having a hard time concentrating. I was busy taking long breaths smelling her hair and being intensely aware of her body resting against mine. I hoped it would rain all afternoon. Then to my surprise, she let her legs move so they rested against mine. Since we had on shorts, the feeling of skin against skin was sensuous and I felt a wave of chills in my body.

I said, "I'm happy you had the chance to know him and learn from him."

"Me too, I'll always remember him."

We sat in silence for awhile and the rain kept coming down. I would have given anything to know what she was thinking. She seemed comfortable and it was like we were snuggled together like two lovers.

Then she said, "Jett?"

"Yeah?"

"I want to be honest with you. It feels so comfortable sitting like this. I feel so safe with you. I keep telling myself that you are just a friend and we are two friends sitting here in the rain. But in my heart, I know you want more and I get scared of my own feelings. I owe it to you to tell you I had a friend who was married to a guy twelve years younger than her. When she turned fifty, he divorced her and married a girl in her mid-twenties. I really liked him. He was sweet and kind and good to her and I was shocked when she told me he wanted a divorce. I was her closest friend and I sat with her through the nightmare of her pain. It took her two years to get over him to the point where she could be herself again. Does that help you understand why I am so reluctant to even consider someone that much younger than me?"

"Yeah, that helps me understand. I remember looking you in the eyes recently and telling you something like I would never ever leave you. That was Tug talking. I feel Centered in this moment and know that I could never make a promise like that. I could say that I'm predicting that I'll never ever leave you. We are vulnerable in so many ways when we commit to a relationship. Your friend died leaving his wife a widow. Your friend's husband left. There are so many unknowns."

She said, "I think I know where you're going with this. When I was around six, I had a little dog. Her name was Shibee. We always had cats and dogs hanging around and each of us sisters had our special pet. Shibee followed me everywhere. She was my shadow. We would go on long walks together. I loved her more than anything. When I was sixteen, she was run over by a tractor and I was devastated. I grieved for months and swore I would never have another dog. I had cats but I never allowed myself to get too close. At some point I realized that I was missing something really important in my life and got Cher. I had to tell myself that the love and joy I will get from her will outweigh the pain of someday losing her."

I didn't know what to say. She reached up under the blanket to wipe a few tears. My arms held her just a little bit tighter. I was glad she came to that conclusion about her dog, but we knew it's different with dogs. You're going to get, most of the time, unconditional love from them. They won't lie, cheat, pout, hold onto anger, or be possessive. It wasn't the same. She could do it with Cher, but could she do it with me or with anyone else? That's something she would have to figure out for herself. I was not going to give up.

It started to rain harder. I pulled the blanket a little tighter. We had some protection from the big rock and some over hanging trees with thick foliage, but the rain was dripping on our heads. I felt so good and without realizing it, I must have sighed and she turned her head and asked a little above a whisper, "Did you say something?" At that moment, the way her face was positioned, my lips were resting on her cheek and I leaned up a little and she leaned back a little and we kissed.

It was not a passionate kiss. It was soft and warm as we both slightly opened our mouth and gently moved around the tip of our tongues. The water was dripping down our faces and the drops made their way into the kiss. It didn't last long as she slowly turned her head away. I didn't move my head and my lips traced her cheeks until they rested on her ear and I whispered, "I'm sorry."

We sat there for awhile in silence. Her body still seemed relaxed and I wondered what she was thinking. Finally she said, "The rain seems to be letting up."

"It does."

She asked, "Do you mind if we leave?"

"No. That's fine." She stood up and reached down to give me a hand. When I stood up, she put her arms around me and rested her head on my chest. After a few moments, she said, "I'm the one who should say, 'I'm sorry.'"

On the way to her house, we didn't talk much. It seemed like she was pulling away again. I remember this happened after we went on the bike ride and ended up sleeping in the same bed, and now after snuggling under the blanket and the kiss. Maybe after a little physical intimacy, she is afraid of what she felt. I hoped that was true.

When we got to the house, she thanked me and said she had a good time. She asked me to call her sometime. I walked her to the door and we exchanged a friendly hug and she went inside. I guess she had decided she didn't want my help this afternoon.

I went back to the Inn and finished up some work. Pop wasn't up for a walk so we talked awhile and then I left. I called Henry from the

Inn to see if he wanted to go hiking. He had plans so I went home. I took Spot for a hike/run and came back by the knoll and stayed there for a little while. I went home, fixed my supper, read for awhile, watched some TV and went to bed. I decided against calling Eden. I think she needed some space.

Buddy Session Six

Ace pulled in about 8:30 and said their session with Doc last night went pretty good. They worked specifically on how to stay Centered when either one brought up a subject that had traditionally caused arguments. After the session, they had gone out to eat and had a nice evening.

Doc pulled up a little before nine.

He took us through a Centering Meditation and had us keep our eyes open. We stayed inside for about ten minutes and he told us to focus on one point for a time and then look around and notice and see things and feel connected to everything. Then we walked outside for about ten minutes and did the same thing. Then he asked us about exercise, nutrition, and sleep. I told him my nightmares were not as intense and not as frequent as they had been. Ace reported the same thing.

Ace went first today. I looked over my notebook and reviewed what I had done this past week. I had not practiced my breathing with the same consistency as I had in past weeks. I knew this required more attention because it was the easiest to practice. I didn't have to close my eyes or stop what I was doing. All I had to do was remember to do it while I was driving or working or any other time. There was no excuse for not finding more time to practice a skill that required nothing but remembering to do it. From Center, I let it go with a commitment to be more diligent in my training.

During my time with Doc, I shared that my eleven step exercise revolved around my issues with Eden. I was proud of how I had handled the challenges most of the time. My nine step exercises were going well. I had graduated to more intense and frightening imprints of the past. It must be helping some because I had fewer flashbacks and nightmares. I told Doc about my recent panic attack and he smiled and wasn't surprised when I told him I felt better the next day.

57
JETT TAKES A FALL

Ace left for work after his session with Doc. After Doc left, I went to work. Pop was still not feeling well so I stayed and talked with him for about an hour. Mom had asked me for dinner so I didn't get home till about 9:00. Ace was not home. I figured he was staying at April's.

I called Eden, but there was no answer. I left her a message and said I was just checking on her day. Of course I wondered if she was out with Lance. About fifteen minutes later, she called me back and said she had been in the shower. She said she had no luck finding an office, but had a few leads. She had called Lance's secretary's sister and initial impressions were good. They were meeting tomorrow. She said Connie had reserved a meeting room for Thursday so she was all set. Soon after that we hung up. She seemed a little friendlier tonight. Tug said she just felt sorry for me. I read some and got sleepy and went to bed. I lay awake for awhile and thought about the kiss and soon drifted off to sleep.

After work on Wednesday, Pop was up for a short walk. He seemed to be feeling a little better. April and Ace had invited me to come over and eat supper with them. I left April's about 9:00 and decided to drive by Eden's house. I wasn't going inside. I just wanted to be able to look at the house and get a rush out of knowing she was in there probably continuing to work on getting settled. I smiled. As I pulled onto the street my heart started beating faster. Lance's car was parked in the driveway. I stopped and decided not to drive by the house. I backed up and pulled onto the other street and headed for home.

I had this ache in my heart. I was on the verge of tears. Tug said he told me so and she was too old for us anyway and let's go fuck Sandra. I told him to shut the fuck up. I focused on my breathing. I had to get Centered and experience this moment from there. The moment was full of sadness and tears. I missed her and loved her and was probably losing her. This was my moment. This was me being in the now. I accepted and embraced my grieving. And soon I was exhausted and settled into some kind of peace. I pictured her smiling and happy. Tug wanted to punch Lance in the face. At Center, I managed to believe I would survive this and maybe it was best for Eden. Maybe I was too young for her.

Understandably, I had a restless night. I was ready to get up and run before my usual time. I went to work and found it difficult to focus on what I was doing. Around 9:00, I asked Connie what room Eden would be using for her meeting and I managed to find some work near the entrance to that part of the Inn. I wanted to see her. She arrived about fifteen minutes before 10:00 and had a briefcase on wheels. I met her as she was walking up the sidewalk and asked her if I could help her carry anything. She smiled and said she didn't have that much but thanked me. She said she was sorry that she couldn't talk. She had to get set up before the others arrived.

She seemed friendly. I knew they were going to stay for lunch and I decided it would be best if I wasn't anywhere near that exit from the Inn around the time they would be leaving. I went to see Pop after work and he was not feeling well again. I was starting to worry more about him. He had lost some of his zest for life. Maybe what I told Eden was true. Maybe he was ready to join Nana.

I headed home and couldn't hold back the tears. I was losing Pop. He didn't seem to have the will to live. I took Spot on a hike. I was doing fair until on the way back we stopped at the knoll. It was another beautiful evening and I wondered if I'm losing Eden too. I didn't want to give up, but she was spending time with Lance and they were a good pair together. It was almost a natural. Maybe she wasn't attracted right now, but it could come later. We got back to the house around 8:00. I forced down an apple and orange and tried to read, but couldn't focus. I finally watched some TV. About 10:00, I was ready to go to bed and Tug said, "Why don't we drive down and see if Dick Head Lance is at Eden's?" I told him no and that I was going to bed.

I looked at the clock at 11:08 and Tug said, "We can't sleep. Let's take a ride into town." I gave in. I needed to be close to her. I imagined her snuggled in bed with Cher. I decided I would pull in her driveway and try to get some sleep knowing that I would wake before her and be gone. We pulled onto her street and his car was in the driveway and the house was dark. It literally took my breath away. I drove on feeling like a panic attack was imminent. Tug said, "Let's go break the fuckin' door down and catch them doing a 'sixty-nine'." I couldn't breathe and I was crying and my heart was beating out of my chest. I had to pull over. I just sat there and didn't give a shit whether I was in panic mode or not. Shortly after that, I realized my breathing was okay and my heart had slowed down. I was just crying. That was it.

After awhile, my tears subsided. I drove to the Parkway and headed south. What was it about this woman? I had to go over it one more time. Had I convinced myself that she was my soul mate? Was it because I had never allowed myself to get close to a woman? Was it because I had glimpsed the ecstasy of emotional and physical intimacy with April and now longed for it myself and desperately needed to have it and feel it? Did I just pick the first attractive woman that came along or was it something about Eden that made her that special person? I had so many questions and was too grief stricken to think about any answers.

I don't remember much else about the drive. I had all the windows down and the next thing I knew I was about 200 miles down the Parkway and on the outskirts of Asheville. I got off at an exit and drove around and found a diner open. I got a cup of coffee to jolt me. I felt like I had been hit by a Mack truck.

I must have stayed in the diner for an hour or so. I don't remember much. When I left, the first light of day was dawning. I headed home and when I got about two hours up the Parkway, I called Charlie to let him know I probably wouldn't get to work until around 11:00 or so. I cried some more and I guess eventually was cried out. When I got home, I had a message from April. She said that she and Eden wanted to cook supper for me and Ace tonight at her house. She said to come around 6:00.

I had trouble focusing at work, but frankly my work didn't require much focusing. The whole time I was trying to answer my questions from last night. I wasn't having much luck. I felt like I was pretty Centered. When I wasn't thinking about anything, Tug would take over. He was busy checking out other girls coming and going at the Inn. He was especially friendly with Sandra when we went in to eat lunch with Pop. Tug had always been in charge when it came to women. He was both fascinated and intimidated around women. Maybe that was the reason we had never had a close relationship. At least I had come to the conclusion the experience with April had been the catalyst that woke me up and helped me realize I longed for intimacy with a woman. That was the only one of my questions I had been able to answer.

Pop could see that I was struggling. He wanted to know what was bothering me and I told him it was just woman problems. He smiled and said, "Do you want to talk about it?"

"Thanks for the offer Pop, but I'll be fine. I just need a little time to sort it out." Actually, I think he was too tired to get involved.

"If you change your mind, I'll be glad to help in any way I can."

During the afternoon, I was trying to figure out why Eden would want to be with the four of us. She was already sleeping with Lance. It was a Friday night and it seemed like they would be going out together. Maybe Lance had his children this weekend.

I was determined to pull it together and try to stay Centered. Tug wanted sympathy and he was also angry. He wanted to cause a scene. That was not going to happen. I picked up a couple bottles of wine and arrived a little after 6:00. The three of them were standing in the kitchen laughing about something. They took one look at me and almost in unison said, "Jett, what's wrong?"

They all gave me a hug and Eden asked, "Is Pop alright?"

"He's not doing well, but he's fine for now. I just had a bad night and didn't get much sleep." I forced a smile and said, "I'm just exhausted."

Ace asked, "Was it nightmares?"

I answered, "Yeah, you could say that."

Ace brought me a beer and I took a couple of swallows and realized I couldn't do this. We had gravitated to the kitchen, but they were all still looking at me. I looked at Eden and asked, "Would you mind taking a walk with me?"

She looked a little surprised and answered, "Not at all."

When we got outside, she asked, "Jett, what's wrong?"

I took some deep breaths determined again to stay Centered. "I assume you know that I care about you or maybe you know that I think I love you even though since I've never been in love before, I'm not sure I know what love is."

She said, "You have not made it a secret that you care for me. I don't think I ever allowed myself to think that you might love me until the other day when we kissed."

I asked, "Is that because you think I'm too young for you?"

"I guess. I wanted to be your friend and I didn't want you loving me to make it difficult for the four of us to spend time together."

I said, "Last weekend, we went on the bike ride and then ended up in the same bed. Remember when you woke up cuddled up against me. I was awake and heard you say in a low voice, 'Oh shit!' Then you slowly scooted back. We had a nice breakfast and you seemed fine. Then we went to church and after church it seemed like you were distant. Then Monday under the blanket, I felt so close to you and then we kissed. When we got in the truck, it felt like you were distant again."

She hesitated and then responded, "All three of those experiences were more enjoyable than I wanted them to be. In church, I had time to reflect and I got scared. I felt too close to you for comfort and yet I wanted to continue to see you. I was too nervous to let you come down to help me pack and that's why I told you not to come. I promised myself that I would not get in any situation where there was any kind of physical intimacy. Then on Monday when it rained, I couldn't say that I wasn't going to get under the blanket with you. When I got under, I felt close to you and then I wanted you to kiss me even after I had told you about my friend getting jilted. Knowing how you feel about me I felt terrible about the kiss. When we got to the truck, I pulled away again which was not fair and I apologize for doing that to you twice."

"I forgive you."

"Jett, what happened between us has not changed my mind about you being too young for me."

I said, "I told myself that I would never give up and that one day you would come to love me. Now I know that it will never happen and I have to give up."

She said, "Even though I think it's a good decision for you and I know it's none of my business, but I'm curious why you're giving up."

"I found out that you love Lance."

She questioned rather loudly, "You found out I loved Lance? I'm eagerly waiting for you to tell me how you found out that I love Lance since I didn't know it myself."

"I had supper with Mom and Dad on Wednesday night and when I left there, I had this longing to be close to you and I knew I couldn't see you so I decided to drive by your house and get the thrill of just being a few yards away. His car was parked at your house. I had a restless night and the next day, I made a point to be close to the entrance you would be using for your meeting. You seemed friendly but a little distant. That afternoon, I went to see Pop and he wasn't doing well which upset me even more. Last night I felt like I was losing two of the most important people in my life. I went to bed but couldn't sleep. After tossing and turning, I had this longing again just to be near you. I thought I would go down and park in your driveway and sleep there. I knew I would wake up before you so you wouldn't see me."

She interrupted and said, "And you drove down and saw Lance's car parked in the driveway and the lights were out?"

"Yes."

"I'm not going to lie to you. Lance has been very attentive and he has shown up several times at the house without being invited or calling. I have to admit that I'm somewhat flattered. Last night, he came around supper time so I invited him to stay. He brought a bottle of wine and I didn't care for it so he ended up drinking most of the bottle. He was not steady on his feet so I would not let him drive home. I took him home myself and he made arrangements to pick up his car early this morning."

"Oh." I forced a little smile, "I don't think I've ever been in so much pain."

We walked on in silence for awhile. Finally she said, "I feel terrible that you went through that for no reason. I was hoping that we could be friends, but maybe that's not possible for either one of us. You probably think I'm being stubborn about the age thing. When my close friend went through that terrible divorce I literally felt her pain. It was like I went through the divorce myself."

She wiped away a few tears and continued, "You and I have already talked about how vulnerable we are in a relationship. The age difference in my view makes me more vulnerable and it scares me. You are handsome and a wonderful person. Young women will flock to you. I know you would probably be faithful to me, but I would always be worried that someone was going to catch your eye. People today don't seem to care whether a person is in a committed relationship or not. I've seen it happen time and again with men and women in my work situation. While I was married, I had a number of men make advances knowing that I was married. I have self-esteem problems anyway so I would think I'm not good enough to keep you."

I had been taking a lot of deep breaths and was doing everything I could to stay Centered. While she was talking I wanted to jump in and say, 'It won't be like that. I'll always be faithful. I can offer you a safe and secure future with me. Please let me show you that I can do that.' Instead I said, "I wish I could offer you a safe and secure future with me. At Center, I know that I can't offer that to you and it's unfair to pretend I can."

She responded, "No one can offer that to me and maybe I'll stay single."

"Before Lance came into the picture, I felt like I had time and a chance to win your heart. He is obviously interested in you and is pursuing you. He is nice looking, has a great personality, has a good job, and would appear to be a great catch. Because of the way you feel about the age difference, I can't compete with him. I'm not saying he's right for you or that you'll fall in love with him, but after last night, I can't take the chance. I think I felt the kind of pain your friend felt when her husband left her. I don't expect you to believe that since I've only known you for a month or so, but you don't know how deeply I feel about you."

We walked on in silence. She said, "It sounds like you're saying that you can't see me anymore."

"I hate the word 'can't' but in this situation, it seems right. I want to see you and spend time with you, but if I don't have you then I can't lose you. I have to find a way to survive this PTSD and the loss of Pop. Losing you during this time in my life seems more than I can bear." I paused and then continued, "I hope you will be great friends with April and Ace. They really like you and I know they will understand how we both feel."

She stopped and took my hands and looked into my eyes, "I can see that you're hurting and in a lot of pain. I would never hurt you intentionally. This is difficult for me too, but I believe it's the best decision for both of us."

We hugged and walked back to April's house in silence. When we got there, I said to everyone, "I'm going to go home. I'm sorry to break up the party."

Ace said, "I'm going to. I'll be along in a few minutes."

I responded, "No, you stay here. I'm okay."

"Like hell you are. Go on. I'll catch up with you at the cabin. Don't go anywhere." April gave me a hug and then Eden with her head lowered came and gave me a hug. I could see that she was crying. I left.

I wanted to go to Stanley's and get drunk, but I knew that was only going to make it worse and Ace would find me anyway and drag me outta there. After letting Spot out, I got a beer and plopped onto the sofa. I was exhausted. I felt like I had nothing to live for. I loved my family, but Pop was dying and so much of my time over the past month had been focused on Eden. With her out of my mind, what was I going to think about and do? I had made her the center of my thoughts and had done everything I could to make her the center of my life. Ace came in the door and put some food down on the kitchen table and got himself a beer.

He sat down on the sofa and said, "I'd recommend that we get drunk, but I know better than you will ever know that getting drunk, (and he put emphasis on each word) does not fucking help!"

"Did Eden leave after I left?"

He answered, "No, she was crying and April told me to take some food for us and then they disappeared into her bedroom. You may or may not know it, but they have become good friends. They talk on the phone everyday and met twice for lunch this week."

"No, I didn't know they had gotten that close. In a way, that makes me feel better."

He asked, "In what way?"

"Well, you and April are my best friends. If she's close to April, it's like I still have a little connection with her. That may seem crazy."

He interrupted, "No, I got it. So what happened to you all?"

I gave him a quick summary.

"So last night, you thought she and Butt Wipe Lance were getting it on?"

"Yeah, and it 'bout killed me."

He said, "Yeah, it seems like you got a little off Center."

"How 'bout way off Center?"

He replied, "Yeah. I bet Tug had a field day giving you a bunch of shit."

"Yeah, he went on and on how he had told me so and that I had no business getting hooked up with a 'mom figure' and that we needed to look for younger chicks with big tits and have some fun. He kept trying to get me to go after Sandra and fuck her."

He smiled, "She's pretty hot. He may be on to something."

"That's all I need."

He said, "You know my history. That road leads nowhere." Then he said, "I know you're not hungry, but would you sit with me in the kitchen. I haven't had anything to eat since 11:00 and I'm starving?"

He made me a small plate and I picked at the food and downed another beer. I said, "I don't know how I'm gonna get through group tomorrow."

He said, "As difficult as it seems, the timing may be helpful. You can focus on ways that the training can help you deal with your issues. It's becoming clear that the training applies to everything in life. April and I are using the skills and it's really helping us. I know your stuff is more challenging, but you may come out of group tomorrow with a little better handle on things. The group fun and games may also help. That will happen on one condition."

"What's that?"

He replied, "You have to be open and want to discover ways to get a better handle on things."

"You're starting to sound like Doc."

He said, "Hell, I should. I see him three days a week."

After we finished supper, Ace said, "I wanna call April and check in."

I asked, "You want some privacy?"

"No." He dialed. "Hey Babe, how's it goin'?"

"We're doin' pretty well."

"No, he barely touched his food. Okay, I'll try to get him to eat something later. Is Eden still there? Yeah, that'll work out fine. I'm gonna stay here with Jett."

I said, "You don't have to. I'll be fine."

He said, "Hold on Babe, Jett's talking." He put his hand over the receiver and said to me, "I'm stayin.'"

"I'm back. I forgot to tell you I'm off all day tomorrow. We have another outing at the park with the group after our meeting so I won't be finished until about 4:00. I'll come after we finish.

"Yeah, that'll work. If you're not back, I'll just get cleaned up and wait on you.

"Yeah, I don't want him to be alone tomorrow night either. The three of us can do something.

"Yeah, that'll work. Tell Eden Jett and I said 'hey.' I love you." He hung up.

I asked, "What's goin' on over there?"

"Eden is having a hard time too. She's gonna spend the night with April. Tomorrow, they're gonna have a 'girls' day,' whatever that means. April wasn't sure if she would be back by 4:00."

I said, "I'm so glad Eden has April. She doesn't know a lot of people. Tug says he doesn't want her turning to Lance for emotional support. 'Tug, shut the fuck up.' I just want her to be okay. If Lance is the one to help her then I'll just have to deal with it. 'Tug, shut the fuck up I said!'"

He asked, "What did Tug say?"

"He said that you and I need to get drunk and get laid."

"Fark, don't start you mother Focker, that's not gonna happen."

We both burst out laughing. It felt good to laugh. Ace asked, "Are we fucking crazy or not?"

I said, "To quote a wise man." And we said loudly in unison, "This is some crazy shit!"

We watched some TV and the next thing I knew, it was dark and I was stretched out on the sofa with a blanket over me and I could hear the snoring coming from Ace's room. I got in my bed and slept solid till Ace woke me about 8:00. We had breakfast and got cleaned up.

58
GROUP SESSION FIVE

The first vehicle pulled up about 8:40. It was Anna. We exchanged hugs and she sat down at the kitchen table and had a cup of coffee. She had been crying. She found out two days ago that her husband cheated on her while she was deployed. She called Doc and he met with her yesterday and she felt some better, but was still struggling.

I said, "The woman I love thinks I'm too young for her. Pee Wee and Tug could have a 'field day' with that information." We all smiled and other vehicles were pulling up.

Doc came in and asked everyone to be seated and asked us to close our eyes. "Go to Center and begin deep breathing. Until I let you know, focus only on your breathing and what it feels like to move the air in and out of your body. If you have another thought or Focker wants to talk, shift and focus on your breathing....Let your breathing slow down and open your eyes."

Silence and then Frank: "We keep doing the same things over and over again. There is some new stuff, but will we ever move beyond the deep breathing?"

Doug: "I've had the same question, but I got my answer a few minutes ago. I had trouble focusing on my breathing because Hill Focker wanted to be pissed off and focus on something my wife said before I left home this morning. It was hard to make that shift. I need more training."

Doc: "Sometimes, former clients will come back to therapy. I'll ask them if they are still doing Attention Training with the breathing and Centering and every time, they say, 'No.' My advice to you is to continue training for the rest of your life. You will perhaps discover some new training techniques. For instance, Melinda might say she found by listening to classical music while she did her breathing it was easier for her to focus. Frank may say he listens to the sound of waves while training at his Center."

Doc: "When you want to create something new and different in your life or silence Focker or let go of the past or stop dreaming or worrying about the future or make changes in your life or accomplish a task or reach a goal, what do you do?"

Rob: "You go to Center."

Doc: "How do you get to Center?"

Chad: "Relax your body and quiet your mind."

Doc: "And what is an effective way to relax your body and quiet your mind?"

Rob: "Deep breathing."

Doc: "What are some other benefits of deep breathing that help with Centering and staying Centered?"

Me: "Focusing and concentrating."

Doc: "What else?"

Paul: "Stop hanging out with Fanny and get to Center."

Doc: "What else?"

Anna: "Helps us be more aware of our body."

Doc: "And why is it important to be aware of your body?"

Frank: "Because most of our symptoms have a physical component and the deep breathing and focusing help release the tension and stress which can help reduce our symptoms."

Me: "Like pain and pressure in my chest and thinking my heart is gonna pound outta my chest."

Ace: "Which helps to reduce and relieve other panic symptoms."

Doc: "So that's why I go on and on and on about closing your eyes and focusing on your breathing? And why are we doing these Centering Meditations over and over again and doing those between sessions and in our sleep and on and on and on?"

Ace: "Because defining our Center and getting to our Center and living from our Center is the skill, or as someone else said contains the truth that sets us free to heal."

Doc: "Yes. There is one other aspect of Centering that's important. What it is?"

Melinda: "Getting to know what it feels like, experiencing the many different facets of our Center. I mean like feeling the peacefulness."

Doc: "Yes. Very important and how do we reach the skill level of being able to be Centered and stay Centered?"

Frank: "Instead of asking a question, I'm going to answer a question. Training."

Doc: "I want to paraphrase what Ace and Melinda said a few minutes ago. Your Center is the place/area/space within you of transformation. It becomes powerful directly proportional to your ability to define it, go there, experience it, and live it. That's why I'm always asking you, 'What was it like? What did you feel? How did your body respond?'"

Frank: "Sometimes it's hard for me to explain how I feel at Center. I feel peace, but how do you explain what it feels like to feel peaceful. Someone earlier said peace felt nice."

Doc: "One of the fascinating things about our Center is that we are not required to manufacture the experience of Center. It already exists without any help from us."

Frank: "Then why did we spend all that time coming up with a definition of Center? We had thoughts, feelings, physical, and behavior."

Doc: "Remember last week when you asked, 'Why don't we just keep it simple and do no memory experiences of Center?' The answer to that is our minds are too active and our Fockers are too powerful. As I said last time, we humans have to do the 'grunt work' to be able to maximize the use of our Center."

Ace: "Go on with what you were saying about everything already exists at Center."

Doc: "Jett told us that his pastor opens his worship services with the Scripture, 'Be still and know that I am your God.' I like to paraphrase that verse by God saying to us, 'If you want to know me, be quiet.'"

Paul: "In other words, shut the f--- up. Sorry God."

Anna: "So if we were able to be quiet and still, we would experience our Center. We would experience peace, love, joy, forgiveness, compassion, tranquility, and acceptance and so on. These already exist at Center?"

Doc: "Yes they do."

Me: "But because it's so difficult to get quiet and still, we have to do the grunt work and the training by the numbers to have a chance to get to Center, experience it, and try to live it."

Chad: "Melinda was telling us how without realizing it, she noticed that at times she was Centered. I can't remember exactly what she said, but it had to do with being kind and considerate of others."

Doc: "Yes. I didn't pick this group because you are never Centered. I picked you because you are struggling with getting Centered in relation to your combat experience. I firmly believe, however, that this training will help you in every aspect of your life to be more Centered. Are there any other comments or questions?" No questions. "Okay. Everyone go to Center."

I was aware as I took my deep breaths and felt my body and walked along a path in the woods I had never seen before that I was starting to get it. It was starting to feel like from here everything really is okay and the panic attacks, nightmares, flashbacks were only momentary experiences and I no longer needed to be afraid of them. And I could smile and marvel at how much I loved Eden and my greatest gift to her would be to let her go. And tears started to run down my cheeks and I was sad and peaceful and I would embrace acceptance with all my strength. And I felt Centered. The training and repetition and commitment were helping me find peace and love.

Anna: "For the first time, I truly felt it was going to be all right that I only had one arm. When I opened my eyes, Pee Wee said to 'Fuck off.' She was tired of all this Centering bullshit. Life sucks and you'll never convince me otherwise.'" Smiling she continued, "It sounds like I've got more work to do."

Others shared and it seemed like the first part of our group this morning had helped all of us to reach a deeper awareness of how Centering could help us heal. Doc had been going over the same material from the beginning and I think for most of us it was finally starting to sink in. We were still picking up books, but I sensed we were getting closer to being ready to go beyond that stage.

Me: "All my life, Tug has convinced me if there was something unpleasant we didn't want to think about, the best solution was to keep the mind busy and occupied. We just crowded the other thoughts out. I'm dealing with some sadness over the loss of someone I love. For the first time, I felt acceptance of the situation and the belief that I would be okay. It was a powerful experience."

Frank: "What happened to Tug? Is he automatically at Center?"

Doc: "When you are Centered, your Focker is transformed in that moment. Transformation means that the darkness becomes the Light. Notice I said in that moment. Your Focker will never be totally transformed. When you are Centered, it will seem like he doesn't exist and she doesn't in that moment. He will raise his head at times. She will return."

Ace: "How often and in what circumstances?"

Doc: "Your ability to stay Centered will depend on your commitment to do whatever it takes and that involves a lot of training. Let's say you have been training to be more Centered when it comes to anger and you notice you're doing better. That of course doesn't mean Focker is totally transformed and won't slip in there on some occasions and stir up anger. But he has much less power. The goal is always to be more Centered in every situation."

Frank: "So Focker is never totally transformed?"

Doc: "Some of you shared that you've had suicidal thoughts. Let's say at some point you say I feel completely Centered when it comes to killing myself. You also say that you don't know the future but you predict that part of Focker that wanted us to kill ourselves is totally transformed."

Frank: "It sounds like it's never black or white. Focker will live on stirring up more challenges in different areas of our lives."

Doc: "I predict if you stay with your training that Focker will have a much smaller role in your life."

Me: "Tug is pulling at me again and I'm starting to feel hopeless about my situation."

Doc: "So what would you advise Jett to do?"

Nate: "Go to Center."

Doc smiling: "Jett, do you know how to go to Center?"

Me: "Yes. I know how to do it. I may do the basics we practiced a few minutes ago or I may do an eleven stepper with Tug if he persists."

Doc: "Sounds like a plan."

Anna: "That sounds so easy and it's not easy, right?"

Doc: "No Anna. It's not easy, but if each of you continues the training, I promise you it will become much easier with most of your issues and in most of your situations. One of my clients recently told me her Focker was almost completely transformed or silent. She has been training for quite some time. What you will discover is your commitment right now to getting Centered and your willingness to train will be well worth your time and effort. You'll find that some issues are easier than others. Some will be very challenging and always remember and know healing is possible. At times you will need patience and perseverance, but it will pay off in the end."

Doc: "The nine-stepper is designed to help with the out of the blue panic attacks, intrusive thoughts, flashbacks, and nightmares. How many of you have noticed these out of the blue experiences are not as frequent as they were six weeks ago?"

Nate interjected, "Mine ain't as often, but I had a doozey of a panic attack the other day. 'Bout blew me a new butt hole."

It seemed like everyone said the experiences were getting less frequent.

I told the group about my big panic attack several days ago and how I said to bring it on. "It was like yours Nate. 'Bout ripped me a new one too. The strange thing was that I felt better after it happened. The only thing I could figure was that I felt more in charge. I wasn't scared or running away. I said give me your best shot and it did. Don't get me wrong. I thought I was dying during the attack but overall it was different."

Doc: "Again, this is a process that takes time. Each of you will have different experiences. The important thing is to stay with the training. Each of you will have your own personal challenges. Some of you may want to discuss some of your issues with the group and others may want to discuss other issues with me during our individual meetings. During those meetings, we will continue to talk about your individual goals."

Doug: "I'm slow with this stuff, but I liked that eleven stepper exercise. My wife and I are having serious problems and Hill Focker is raising hell. I like that exercise because it helps us work with stuff we're dealing with right now. I practiced it all week to help me get Centered and let go of Hill's anger, resentment, and hostility toward my wife. I'm embarrassed to say that Hill almost hit her about ten days ago." He paused and it looked like he started to cry, but regained his composure. "I'm really trying to stay with the program here, but it's awkward as hell talking about Hill almost hitting my wife. Hell, I wanted to hit her too."

Doc: "Doug, in that moment, you got caught up in Hill's experience and for that moment, you identified with him. That makes perfect sense. Keep up the good work however with separating yourself from Hill. Please go on."

Doug: "Doc helped me get better at using that exercise in our individual session last week. Anyway, I've practiced it for the last ten days or so and took Hill to Center a bunch of times. I couldn't believe two nights ago, I was able to sit down and have a good conversation with her." He forced a little smile, "However, Hill got pissed off again this morning before I left when she made that comment I mentioned a while ago."

Anna blurted out: "I found out my husband cheated on me while I was deployed."

Paul said under his breath, "Fuckin' asshole."

Anna: Tears started flowing. Ace put his hand on her shoulder and Melinda motioned to Paul to change chairs with her and she reached over and took her hand. "I can't talk about it right now, but I couldn't hold it in any longer."

Doc: "Take your time Anna." Pause. "Let's all close our eyes. Focus on breathing and going to Center remembering that in the quietness and stillness of the mind is peace and tranquility. Sometimes, it will be more challenging to get to Center, remembering that it's okay for it to take longer. With continued training, you will find it easier to shift into that space that offers freedom from the memories and the problems. Sometimes it takes a little longer to experience that freedom. With acceptance of the time it may take, you can, with a renewed strength and determination, continue on that journey and on that path, knowing that you will find what you need at Center to move on with your life. Take a little more time to focus just on the breathing and now open your eyes."

Doc: After silence, "For this next experience, I have picked how I would like you to pair up. I want you to pick something you are currently working on and take turns taking it through the eleven-step exercise. You might have the exercise memorized and if not, refer to your notebook." He turned the sheet on the board and I was paired with Anna. "As usual, you can find your own spot. Please stay within earshot."

Anna and Melinda were hugging. I waited till they were finished and then asked where she wanted to go. She asked, "Would it be all right if we went on the back deck?"

"Sure."

"Jett, I may not be much good at this today. I'm still in a lot of pain."

"I can tell. I'm so sorry. Would you just like to talk or do you want to try the exercise?"

She responded, "It helps to talk, but I've done a lot of that in the past few days. If you don't mind, I'll try to fit my situation into this exercise and see what happens."

"Would you like for me to talk you through it or do you want to do it on your own?"

She answered, "Talking me through would help."

"Are you ready?"

"Yes."

"Okay. Close your eyes and focus on your breathing and let me know when you get to Center."

After a few minutes, she softly said, "I'm there."

"Would you describe what your Center is like and then how you feel."

"I'm in a beautiful meadow. There is a nice breeze and it is gently blowing my hair and I can smell the fragrance of the many wild flowers. The sun is shining and the temperature is just right. There are a few fluffy white clouds and they have sharp edges so the contrast of the white and blue is quite amazing. There are some mountains in the distance and a few of them have snow at the highest elevations. I'm walking toward a few trees at the edge of the meadow and I hear the sound of a stream that I can't yet see. Now I can see it and I'm going down to the edge and I kneel down and put my hands in the water. It is cold and refreshing and I cup my hands and drink and I can feel it going down."

Pause. She begins to cry. I take her hand and say, "See if you can stay right where you are and remember that tears and sadness are just fine. You can just let then flow as long as you desire."

She slides her hand out of mine and reaches into her pocket for a Kleenex and wipes her tears. I say, "Take your time and when you're ready, tell me how you're feeling."

Pause. "I'm looking around at the beauty of this place and I'm lonely. I feel peaceful, but I also feel empty. I want to share this experience with my husband Brandon. I want us to walk hand in hand and laugh and run and play and make love." She starts to cry again and opens her eyes and sees that I'm crying. She takes my hand and says, "Jett, we are both in a lot of pain."

"Yes. I feel so badly for you, but I guess I'm crying because what you want with Brandon is what I want with the woman I love."

She said, "I feel badly for you too. We're a pair. I guess that's why Doc put us together. Do you want to try again or would you rather just talk?"

"We could try again if you want."

"I would like to try too. I need some help. I have an idea. Would you come with me to my Center? Maybe I won't feel so lonely."

"I would like that. I guess we can close our eyes and go there." I paused and continued, "You have a beautiful place."

"Thank you. It is special. It's my favorite place to get Centered."

"So how are you feeling now?"

"I'm feeling more peaceful now."

I asked, "Are you ready to talk with Pee Wee?"

She laughed, "Do I have too?"

"Not if you don't want to."

"All right, Pee Wee, you little piece of shit, 'What have you got to say for yourself?'"

Pee Wee: "I'm pissed off, angry, hurt, devastated, mad as hell, resentful, and ready to bash his fucking head in."

Anna: "I've been right there with you for the last couple of days, but now I want us to move on."

Pee Wee: "I don't wanna go to Center. You've been draggin' me there everyday. Sometimes it helps with other stuff, but I don't want any help with that bastard."

Anna: "We're going to find a way to move forward. I don't want to be stuck in those feelings you just expressed."

Pee Wee: "I guess you mean I don't have any choice."

Anna: "Yes, but first, let's talk about what it feels like in our body to have these feelings."

Pee Wee: "Tense, tight, stressed to name a few."

Anna: "So what thoughts keep all this stuff goin'?"

Pee Wee: "We spent a year of our life in that hell and he couldn't even keep his pecker in his pants until we got home. That son of a bitch! How dare he treat us like that. He's a cheating, lying bastard. And I wanna tell the world what he did to us. Will that do?"

Anna: "I want you to come over here with me at Center and meet a friend."

Pee Wee: "Fuck." She looks at me. "Dude, what's your name?"

Me: "Jett."

Pee Wee: She looks at Anna. "You already got a new boyfriend? He's cute. Yes!" She pumps her arm and fist. "Let's dump Fart Face."

Anna: "No, Jett's a friend."

Pee Wee: She looks at me seductively. "After we're finished here, handsome, let's ditch Anna. You and I can get it on together."

Anna: "Pee Wee, behave yourself. Come over here and sit on the bank with Jett and me."

Pee Wee: "I get all soupy and sloppy over here. It does something to my head. I can't think straight. Over here it's all about peace and love. All right you win, I'm starting to let go and relax and I'm starting to think that maybe we can give Asshole another chance but maybe not. Maybe we need to listen to what he has to say. Somebody said, 'If you've never done anything horrible, you can throw the first stone.' Maybe we should remember that. We've got some work to do. What the fuck am I saying? I can't believe those words came out of my mouth."

Anna: "For now let's take some more deep breaths and make sure we have let go of all that tension and tightness in our body." We did some breathing. "Now, let's take Jett around and show him more of our Center. Pee Wee, you be the guide and tell him what we see and experience here."

They gave me a tour and by the time we got back to the bank of the creek, Pee Wee said she was even more relaxed.

Anna: "So we've got to work on what we're going to say to Brandon when we get home later today. I think it might be helpful instead of yelling and screaming at him to stay peaceful and let him know how hurt and devastated we are. Let's close our eyes and imagine doing that." They took some time to play that out in their mind.

Anna: "We have to work on believing that we can go forward and find the right path for us. We don't know what the future holds, but we can work on making clear choices that feel right for us. Staying Centered and being committed to that path will help us find our way."

Pee Wee: "Okay, already. Let me outta here. I've got other shit to attend to. I don't have time to hang out here and take deep breaths. Somebody's got to be takin' care of business. I'm gone."

We opened our eyes and smiled.

Doc stuck his head out the door and said, "Five minutes."

Anna: "Jett, I'm sorry. I took most of the time."

Me: "That's fine. I learned some things from you that will help me. I noticed you took your time getting Centered. I've been rushing that part. It makes sense that getting grounded at Center in the beginning will have a positive influence on the outcome. Also, you got Pee Wee more involved. I need to pay more attention to Tug and what got us in trouble in the first place. That's what needs healing; those not working well thoughts and feelings."

Anna: "I remember a short assignment when I was in charge of the firing range that most of the new recruits where eager to get a chance to fire their weapons. I had to remind them several times that we have to do it by the numbers. Anyway, when Doc told us that we had to do these step exercises by the numbers, I might have taken it a little too seriously."

Me: "I don't think so. It reminded me to slow down."

Anna: "I have to admit, I'm looking forward to the time when I can just jerk Pee Wee down to Center and take care of business. Jett, I'm so sorry about your girlfriend breaking things off."

Me: "She wasn't even my girlfriend. I just knew after spending time with her over the period of a few weeks that she was the one for me." I smiled. "Can I put you on the spot?"

Smiling, Anna: "I've been in some extremely hot spots over the past few years. I'm sure this is gonna be a piece of cake. Go ahead."

Me: She is twelve or thirteen years older than me. Do you think she's too old for me?"

Anna: "Absolutely not. But the issue is you may be too young for her. I think when the woman is older than the man there are more challenges for the woman."

Doc stuck his head out the door, "Let's gather."

Anna: "Let's talk more."

Me: "I'd like that. Thanks."

We hugged and went inside.

Doc: "Let's go around the room. Give me some feedback,"

Anna and I didn't share with the group how we slightly modified the exercise. At that point, neither one of us was in much shape to talk about it. In general, the group was still talking about the exercise being too long. Doc reminded us again to stay with by the numbers for a while longer and said he would work us on the shortened version during next week's group. Everyone liked the idea that you could tell soon after the exercise if it was helping in contrast to the nine-stepper, where you had to wait and see if it is going to help.

Doc: "Okay. It's time for a break."

I looked at Anna and she was looking at me. We went for a walk. Anna listened intently to my description of how I felt and seemed to understand what I was going through. Then she asked if I wanted her to tell me what she thought Eden might be going through and I wanted to hear what she had to say. Anna wondered if Eden had experienced problems in her past with rejection. Then what she said was similar to what Eden and April had both told me.

I responded, "I'm working on trying to stay Centered. Do you have any suggestions about what I should do?"

She said, "I would ask that question to the people who know and love you and get as many suggestions as you can and then spend some time at Center figuring out what you think is best."

"I'm interested in what you think."

She said, "The good news is that you don't have to make any decisions today. Take your time and be patient. Give her time to think more about it. I don't want to give you the 'big head,' but I think you're a wonderful person. Some woman is gonna be lucky to get you. I hope at some point she will realize that and be willing to take the risks on being with someone younger."

"Thank you."

We walked back the rest of the way in silence each with our own personal challenges facing us in the days ahead.

Doc: "Did any questions surface during the break?"

Doug: "On the mental rehearsal part, what if you don't know what to rehearse?"

Doc: "Spend more time at Center and believe that you will find some answers. I believe it will come to you in the silence. Remember that your Center is about peace and love. So you might say to yourself, 'If I stay peaceful and loving, what would I do?'"

Paul: "This is…"

Group: "Some heavy shit."

Doc: "Yes. To believe that if you would just be quiet, you might find some clarity and direction is some heavy shit. Keep working on it and keep asking questions related to what it means to be Centered in this situation. You will get there."

Doc: "Since most of you in this group are struggling in one form or another with relationships, I think this may be a good time to talk about communication skills. If you do not know how to communicate, the chances of getting things worked out are not good. I'm going to talk about five basic ideas that I believe will be helpful. In order to use these skills, it's important for you and Focker to be Centered. Focker is not interested in good communication. Focker is interested in being right, blaming, being heard, not listening, making assumptions, and manipulation to name only a few. Here are some guidelines:

1. Stop trying to be right and remember that every thought is a perception, an opinion, or a belief. Begin sentences with phrases like it seems to me, in my view, or my take on it. It is freeing, because you never have to defend a perception.
2. If you don't have to be right or get defensive, you are free to actually listen to what the other person is saying.
3. If you are puzzled by their perception, be curious and gather more information by asking, 'I don't understand, tell me more.'
4. Avoid assumptions. If you do make an assumption, check it out.
5. Be honest and open even if you are anxious about doing so.

If you and Focker are Centered, these will come easily for you. However with Centered living, it takes attention and training. I have a handout on these communication ideas somewhere in my briefcase. I'll give it to you before I leave. If you are struggling in a relationship, I would suggest that you ask your partner if he or she would be interested in reading over these ideas on communication and discussing them. Any questions?"

Doug: "What if I can stay Centered and her Focker is runnin' wild? What if she isn't interested in these commo ideas?"

Doc: "Stay Centered and keep Focker at Center. He will be itching to join the argument. You could say, if you can get a word in, 'I would like to talk, but I'm not going to argue or raise my voice.' Let's say she screams louder and calls you every name in the book. You continue to stay Centered and notice that when you are Centered, she has no power over you. You could say, 'I would like to talk when you calm down. I'm not staying and listening to your verbal abuse. I'll be ready to talk when you're ready.'"

Doug: "What if she follows you and keeps yelling?"

Doc: "If there is no way to get away from her, you take more deep breaths; stay Centered, and let her give you her best shot. After her initial rage that you won't fight, she will eventually run out of energy because there is no fuel to keep the fire going."

Rob: "What if the other person turns to physical abuse?"

Doc: "If the man is getting abused, he may be able to physically restrain the woman. If the woman is getting abused, get away if you can to a safe place. Call the police as soon as you can."

Anna: "Pee Wee and I went off on my husband. We gave him our best shot. He just sat there and took it and I did eventually run out of energy and then I broke down and bawled."

Doc: "I urge all of you who are having relationship difficulties to bring that up when I meet with you individually. There are different circumstances in each relationship."

Doc: "Let's close our eyes and go to Center....If Focker wants to talk and think, focus on some breathing and notice how easily you can move into the stillness...and if Focker is being persistent, continue to focus on your breathing and say, 'Later Focker, we can talk later, Chill!' You are learning day by day and moment by moment that your Center can be like an oasis in the midst of lots of chatter and activities. I don't know if you have fully discovered that by now or whether it will take a little more time, but I do know if you do the training you will soon be aware of how peaceful and serene you can be in this deep place within. As you continue to come here, you will discover what is unique and special for you....Be open to an unfolding, flowing experience where you are free to explore this space and find new and wonderful resources for healing. You will know here is where you have the power to let go of that which keeps you identified with your past, where you can chose freedom from the burdens of historical trauma by simply being present here where they cannot exist. You can continue to be present right here, right now at Center confident in your experience here where you can find all that you need for letting go and surrendering the past...and moving on, you can feel the joy of celebrating the moment without anything to crowd in or intrude into your Center. It's quite amazing to find out that this place has been here all along and now that you are more skilled at coming to Center, you can perhaps think of it as your new home. You can let go of the wandering and searching for something that has always been illusive and difficult to find. This is your home at the level of your heart and nothing can ever change that for it has and always will be the core of your very being. It is the Source of life itself, your Center always and forever. Embrace it and when you are ready, you can open your eyes."

Frank: "When we open our eyes, do we come out of Center or do we stay there?"

Doc: "Somebody help me."

Nate: "That depends on you. If you let Focker start some shit, he'll jerk yer ass right outta Center."

Doc: "The goal is to stay Centered with your eyes open. Remember that you, your true self, are taking back the power and energy to guide your life from Center. This entire experience is designed to teach you the skills you need to do that and to help you with your training."

Doc: "Time to do some practical work with the nine-stepper. Remember, the purpose of this exercise is to reduce the intensity of the imprinted traumatic memories; precisely following the steps of the exercise increases the efficiency of the exercise. We're going to break down three times in pairs. Each person will take turns doing the exercise. You will have three opportunities to do the exercise. I will give you specific instructions about the memories before we began each segment. Either stay in this room or out on one of the decks. I will be going from group to group to observe and answer questions.

Do not fight panic or flashbacks or any other emotional response to the experience. I will be close by to assist where needed. Are there any questions?"

Doc: "Take a few minutes to pick a partner."

I caught Frank's eye and he nodded.

Doc: "Everyone got a partner? In this first of three segments, I want you to work on a combat memory that you would describe as moderately intense. It can be one you have been working on this past week. It doesn't matter. I want each of you to take along your partner and explain the process as you go?"

Paul interrupted: "Say what?"

Anna interjected: "Doc, Jett and I did that a little while ago when we did the eleven-stepper. It worked great for us." She went on to explain to the group in some detail how we did it and I interjected a few comments about how it helped me to go along with Anna and Pee Wee. She turned to Doc. "Was that close to what you had in mind?"

Doc: "Yes it is close, but my idea was a little different. However, I like the one you and Jett did better than mine. Does anyone have any questions for Anna or Jett?"

Frank: "It sounds like Jett was sometimes participating in the experience and at other times, he was observing."

Doc: "Okay. This may be a little confusing. Anna and Jett, would you pull your chairs to the Center and do a short version of what you did earlier?"

We did that and after it was over, everyone seemed to understand.

Chad and I went out on one end of the front deck. I knew he lost his girlfriend while deployed. I gave him a brief summary about Eden and me.

Chad: "I can feel your pain man."

We talked a little and he wanted me to go first.

Me: "Let's close our eyes and I'll do the best I can to describe this experience. We had been sent out on a recon patrol and were climbing up this mountain and had pretty good cover. It was about 0300 and the sky was clear and there was a sliver of moon and the stars were shinning as brightly as I had ever seen them. A beautiful scene but there was too much light for comfort. Without warning, we heard a shot and my friend Edward fell to the ground about two meters in front of me. He had been hit in the neck and blood was spurting out and when I got to him, I'll never forget the look in his eyes. Something like terrified. It only lasted a few moments and he was gone. He lay there in my arms; blood everywhere. Ace came up behind me and saw that he was dead and said he was going to check on the rest of the squad. There's more to the story but that's the worst part of my memory.

Me: "I'm gonna play the scene several times in my mind doing the best I can to relive it. As I do that I am feeling shocked, terrified, sad, and picturing Ace and me having to tell Edward's parents that he died in my arms. Tears are running down my cheeks. One more life snuffed out by this insane war. I'm angry. I'm feeling anxious and lost. Tug says, 'It's gonna be us next and I can't believe you signed up for this fucking nightmare experience.'"

Me: "I'm taking Tug to Center. Chad, come with us and we'll show you around. We are in the woods walking along one of our favorite trails early in the morning. Our dog Spot is with us and we can see through the trees that the sun will be coming up in a matter of minutes. The birds are singing their songs. Through an opening in the trees, we can see a blanket of fog in the valley. Little dew drops are falling off the leaves of the rhododendron along the path. Tug is yawning and wondering why we couldn't have slept a little longer."

I continue: "It is quiet and I am reminding Tug of St Paul's words that the peace of God is the peace that passes all understanding. I believe God is at the core of our Center. Tug is not religious so he struggles with the God part, but he's coming along, aren't you Tug? He answers, 'If you say so.' Chad, we are going to sit on this rock and watch the sun come up. Please join us. We are going to focus on breathing and letting the moment bring a new and fresh experience."

After a few minutes have passed, I continue, "Now we're going back in the woods and we have a small little space that is our amphitheater. And in front of us about ten feet away is one of those large TV's and we're going to watch this memory several times remaining peaceful and calm emotionally and physically. We play it several times and feel the peace and calm. I admit that I've used this situation a number of times and early on it was more difficult that it was today."

"Now, we will pick a still frame of me holding Edward with blood all over us. It is a clear and sharp image. And we are repeating our phrases over and over. 'I do not judge you. You are a part of my history. You do not define me. It's time to say goodbye. I am letting you go.'"

"We are now moving the image further away. It is getting more difficult to make out the image. It is moving further and further away, getting smaller and smaller and now it looks like a speck on the horizon and then it is gone. It is no longer real. It is gone. We are looking around and feeling the peace and freedom. We take a few more minutes to do that and then I say, 'Thank you Spirit of God within me.'"

Me: "We can open our eyes now." We both smile.

Chad: "Thank you. That really helped me get a better idea how to experience this exercise."

Me: "Anna taught me how to slow down and get into the experience. I was rushing through and this feels much more helpful."

Chad: "I want to make God a bigger part of my experience. I liked your ideas. Now I have to work on deciding how to experience God at my Center."

Chad went through the nine steps and then we gathered in the cabin. No one experienced any serious side effects of doing the exercise. I could tell by looking around there were some tears. Each of us found another partner and Doc told us to pick a more intense memory.

During the next round, I was with Paul and he had a bad flashback. Doc was right there to help him through it, but he didn't want his help. He worked through it on his own and also wanted no help from me. Paul was always cutting up. I wondered if he used that as a mask to cover up for some heavy stuff he was holding inside him. I wasn't sure if we would ever know. To his credit, he asked me if he could go through again the part of the exercise where he would identify with the memory. That part had caused the flashback. He was determined to detach from that memory which had been his most intense memory of the war. He went through each step with a thoroughness that surprised me. At the end, he smiled and said, "A few more times and I'll be done with that fuckin' memory."

My next partner was Melinda. She had shared a little about her memory in an earlier group meeting. She had a tough time. Her memory was the mortar hitting their position and crawling on her knees out the tent and seeing her best friend's body in pieces scattered on the ground. During the first part of the exercise where she was identifying with the memory, she became hysterical and bawled and bawled. She kept repeating, "Joan, I'm so sorry." Doc came to help but hesitated. She let me take her in my arms and hold and rock her back and forth. Tears were rolling down my cheeks too. Doc went inside.

Someone who has never been in combat may wonder why I was crying. There is no way for me to express in words the identification many of us have with our comrades. Many of us saw so much pain and suffering that it stirred within us an agony and helplessness of unspeakable intensity. I believe for a long time to come, tears will always be close to the surface. We can handle the tears and sadness if we can just be free of the intensity of the intrusive nature of the memories, panic attacks, flashbacks, and nightmares. Doc repeatedly encouraged us to be patient and continue to train with commitment and determination. I believed this training was my only path to some semblance of a happy life.

Melinda started again and was able to get through the nine steps even though she had to stop several times. She let me coach her some through feeling the emotional and physical release at Center. Her phrases were a little different. She said, "Joan, I have to let you go. My tears can't bring you back. I miss you so much. You will always be with me at my Center. I love you. I'm letting this memory go, but will keep you with me always." She said. "Jett, I'm not ready to do the still frame part of the exercise. It feels so final and I just can't do it yet. Joan and I were lovers."

I was surprised and then felt this incredible emptiness. She would never see Joan again. I took her in my arms again and whispered, "I can't imagine what you have been through." We cried and I just held her.

After awhile, the crying stopped and she said, "Thank you Jett. Now it's my time to be with you."

Me: "One of my worst memories was on a mission to destroy an enemy stronghold. Our mission was to check out the position and depending on what we found to call in an air strike. We confirmed there was enemy activity. We had been told there were no women and children in the compound. Ace and I were positioned on some high ground about fifty meters from the target and we had a good view of the entire area. The LT called in the strike and once it started we saw several women and children coming out of the houses. As we helplessly watched them die in the midst of explosions and flames, we cried out, "Noooooooooooooooooooo!!!! Neither one of us have ever gotten over that."

Melinda helped me through the steps and I felt a little better after we finished. It was going to take a lot of work to let go of that imprint.

Doc called us together and most everyone shared something about their experience over the last hour or so. Melinda shared about her experience and also let everyone else know she was gay and that she and Joan were lovers. It didn't seem to make any difference to anyone. There were some horrifying stories and it was clear we all had a lot of work to do. Doc reminded us that we were getting close to the end of learning the different skills and that our challenge would be to continue the training.

Doc gave us our assignment for next time.

1. Review your goals and we will assess during the next individual meeting.

2. Continue to use hourly chime for deep breathing reminder.

3. On a daily basis, listen to at least two of the Centering meditations.

4. Twice this week, do the eleven step exercise.

5. Each day, do the nine step exercise.

6. Record any panic attacks, flashbacks, or nightmares with associated content in your notebook.

We left for the park and had a great time playing games, eating and snacking. It was light and fun and we joked around and teased each other. By 4:00 we were exhausted. At the end, Doc had us all lay on the ground on our backs with our heads the middle of a circle. Shoulders were touching. Nate and Doug were on either side of me. We were a tight knit group of bodies. And Paul said, "This is… in unison… some crazy shit." We all laughed. Doc lay down with us and when we got comfortable, he began with slight pauses between directions.

"Surprised as you may be, I'm going to suggest that you take some nice easy deep breaths. As you let go of thoughts and focus on your breathing, shift around to get nice and comfortable and feel your body resting on the ground. With a few more breaths, close your eyes and go to Center and take Focker with you. Feel your body connected to the ground, to the earth, and feel your shoulders touching the person next to you. At some point and maybe already, you will not be able to tell where your body ends and the earth begins, or where your shoulders end and the shoulders of the persons next to you begin. Even though our work together has emphasized the importance of being in the moment, it's perfectly fine to reflect on a day like today, remembering some of you have experienced the feelings of sadness, pain, shame, sorrow and regret. A little later you were able to create something different, to have fun, laugh, play and enjoy the moments spent with friends and comrades. Be open to the energy of the group that binds you together on this important path, an energy that enables you to know that you will never be alone. The connection you feel to each one in the group makes it possible for you to feel both the pain and joy of each other and to support, encourage, and understand things that perhaps no one else ever will. It's a bond that helps you see the possibilities for healing both in yourself and in each other. You may or may not be presently aware of the power of this bond, but it builds in strength and energy as each day passes. Be attentive again to your breathing. Let your whole body feel this experience, this connection to each other and to the earth that gives us its resources for healing and wholeness. Open your eyes and simply be still and quiet and attentive to this moment…a few more moments…"

Doc stood up and we gathered around him in a close knit ball and he said, "Go in peace and love." And we did.

59
STILL STRUGGLING

Perhaps for awhile, I could go in peace and love. And maybe if I could do it for awhile, I could do it for awhile longer. The group was not over. It would never be over for any of us. We would always be in training to focus on the moment, to let go of the past, to be free of the trauma and ghosts of the war.

Many people who had not been in combat were dealing with their own demons. Their demons were living in a trance, on auto pilot or sleep walking with no clue about the deeper meaning of life. They had no concept or awareness of what it meant to live in peace and love. Were we better off than most people? At least we had the opportunity to look closely at our demons and figure out that we could sometimes leave them behind if we were willing to train and learn the necessary skills.

Tug was calm after our Centering meditation and he was no longer angry at Eden, but he left Center and said that we couldn't live without Eden and that if she didn't come back to us we were doomed to a life of misery. Even though I was still at Center, I didn't have the energy to argue with him or try to convince him that he was wrong. Hell, I felt like leaving Center myself and having a pity party with him.

Before we left the cabin after our morning group session, Ace talked with April and she and Eden were going over to Elverton to pick up some things Eden needed for her house. Later they were going on a hike and were going to do take out and go back to April's house. Eden was planning to spend the night again and they were thinking about going to church in the morning.

When we got home, we got a beer and decided to catch the end of a ball game. I don't think I got half way through my beer before I fell asleep. It was 6:38 when I woke up. Ace was in the shower and I decided to take one myself. Neither of us was hungry so we decided to take the bikes out and then go for a short hike up on the ridge. Spot was dying to go so he came with us. We parked our bikes and started walking.

I said, "Did you fall asleep watching the game?"

"Yeah, it felt good. I was tired. That emotional work we did this morning was draining."

I responded, "Yeah, for me too."

He asked, "Did you find anything that helped with all you're going through with Eden?"

"Anna helped me and it was good to focus on the exercises. I guess I could say it all helped some. Did you find the group helpful today?"

He answered, "Yeah, I did. Sometimes I wish I could feel the results quicker. I want to be over this shit."

"Me too," I replied.

He asked, "So how are you feelin' right now about Eden?"

"About the same, but I feel a little better that she's spending so much time with April. I can't stand to think about her being with Lance. Tug and I are really struggling with that and I'm having a tough time getting Centered."

He said, "I can relate. I'm still struggling with the images of you and April having sex and that's in the past. If I thought you and April might have sex in the future, it would tear me up."

There was an awkward silence. I didn't know what to say. He continued, "I have never paid much attention to the inner workings of the mind and emotions, but I'm finding it both fascinating and puzzling at the same time. I can intellectually understand exactly what happened between you and April and why it happened and how it happened, but why doesn't that give me relief from these images?"

I responded, "Is it possible that it is giving you some relief and you don't know it. Maybe it would be a lot worse if you hadn't worked it out at Center where you have that understanding. If Fark is anything like Tug and I think they're blood brothers, he's pissed off at me like, 'How could you do that to me? I don't give a shit about your reasons and rationalizations. We are supposed to be best friends. We have had each others' back for years. You fuckin' turned your back on me. How could you do that after all we've been through. You fuckin' piece of shit.' Is that close to what Fark is thinking?"

"Fuck! You nailed it. How did you know?"

I replied, "Because that's exactly what I've said to myself over and over again since it happened. All you have to do is change a few words like, 'How could you do that to Ace etc. and you're off and running.'" I continued, "Tug and I did it together. We were both responsible. If I had been Centered, it would have never happened."

He asked, "Whatta ya mean?"

"The rationalizations were just that and Tug and I put them together. If I had been Centered, I would have said that Ace is my best friend and there may be a remote chance that they will be able to work it out. I will not do anything to jeopardize that possibility. No fucking way. That's why I still think about it much more than you realize. I know at Center that I betrayed you and I can't ever forgive myself for that."

"What if I forgive you?"

"I hope in time you will forgive me, but that will not change how I feel about myself."

He smiled, "Don't worry, I haven't forgiven you yet. You could always do an 'eleven stepper' on it. Maybe that will help."

"I wish or then again, I don't wish because I'm not ready to let myself off the hook."

He said, "I didn't realize that it was still bothering you that much."

"I'm embarrassed to bring it up."

He said, "Okay. Let me do my work on this. Fark is pissed at you and I join him at times. But when I get Centered, I'm clear that I had given April and you no reason to think that there was any future for us. April and I have spent a lot of time trying to figure out what happened to us and why we struggled so much. We've come up with some answers which have helped us understand some of what was going on. I was not capable enough of looking deeply inside to know that I had always loved her and always would. I was terrified of intimacy which would have required me to face my thoughts and emotions. I didn't know that at the time, but it is clear to me now. So when Centered, I'm not angry with you. I understand that neither one of you thought there was any future for April and me."

I said, "At my Center, I say that Ace is your best friend and regardless of what had happened in the past with April, you needed to make sure there was no chance for anything in the future. I don't think if the shoe had been on the other foot that you would have betrayed me. So if you ever change your mind at Center and think that it was a betrayal, I hope you will be able to forgive me."

"As Doc reminds us often, living at Center is about living in the moment and letting go of the past and future. It sure is a challenge, but a worthy one and I will continue to work on letting it go. If I continue to struggle and get pissed, I hope you will forgive me."

I replied, "I do and I will."

He said, "April told me I could share with you anything that would be helpful to me. She let me know that she was not going to apologize to me for the time you were together. She said the only tinge of guilt came from it being you, my best friend. She said if it had been another guy, she would have felt totally justified. And Centered or not, I can't argue with that one bit. Even Fark can't come up with anything. I understood from the start that even though I have been angry at both of you from time to time, those feelings weren't rational."

I asked, "Are you doing better now even though Fark is still pissed?"

"Yeah, I'm doing better."

"Do you think that April would tell Eden about what happened?"

He answered, "I would be shocked if she did tell her."

"Why?"

"I think she understands that Eden and you have at least a fragile relationship right now and she would never do anything to hurt the chances of it working out."

I said, "That's what I thought too, but I needed some reassurance. If Eden found out about that, I think she would see it as a betrayal of our friendship and it would give her further reason not to take a chance with me. I've thought about it a lot and if April agrees, I do owe Eden the truth about what happened. I don't want to start out withholding stuff that she has a right to know. I don't know what the hell I'm talking about. We've agreed that it's best not to see each other anymore."

"Well, I don't know about that, but I know that's the deal on the table right now." He smiled and continued, "Fuck, we've already been through the war. Now we got almost as much stress and shit to deal with at home." He paused and kept smiling, "Well, I guess it ain't quite as bad."

I said, "Yeah, it's different kind of pain, but it sure hurts."

We had about another hundred meters to go till we got to the bikes. We had left them in the trees a few meters off the beaten path at one of the scenic overlooks. When we got there, I turned to him and said, "I'm glad we did this. Maybe what happened will never get totally resolved between us, but talking about it from time to time helps me feel a little better."

He smiled and gave me a big hug and said, "I love you man."

Before I could respond, we heard this guy up in the scenic parking lot say, "Hey Earl, there's a couple queers over here and I think there're about ready to suck each other's dicks. Might be fun to watch."

We looked at each other and smirked. I told Spot to stay and we walked up the path. When we got up to the parking area, we saw four bikes parked and three guys coming toward us to join the fourth. They all had shiny motorcycles and were dressed in black vests, jeans, and bandanas stretched around their head. Each of them had a beard and they all looked about six feet with four identical beer bellies protruding over their big shinny belt buckles.

We watched them closely and determined that Earl was the leader and he said, "Well you queers coming up here in the light to give us a show."

As soon as we got out in the open, their expression changed just ever so slightly. Ace being 6'2" and 210 and me being an inch or so under that and about 190, we presented a formidable challenge. We weren't cut like guys who spend their lives in the gym, but each had a week's growth of black hair on our faces and good builds.

I turned to Ace and said, "Do you smell something?"

Ace looked at them and said, "You 'wanna be a vet' tough guys need to take a bath."

I said, "But not necessarily together."

The vocal one asked, "Is there any reason why we shouldn't kick your faggot asses?"

Ace turned to me and said, "Jett, what's four times two hundred and six?"

"Eight hundred and twenty-four."

Ace said, "Earl, there's eight hundred and twenty-four reasons you should get on your bikes and ride away."

Earl asked, "What the fuck does that mean?"

I said, "That's the collective number of bones in your smelly bodies."

Then they spread out into a half moon.

I looked at Earl and asked, "Is this your plan?"

Earl nodded.

Ace added, "You need to go round up some friends."

Earl a little less confident said, "We don't need anyone else to fucking kick your asses."

Ace said, "This is starting to get boring. Who's your two toughest?"

Earl said, "Me and Jed."

I said, "In the interest of spilling a minimum amount of your blood, we have a plan. Anyone got a coin?"

The one on the right flank eagerly said, "I got one."

Earl said, "Shut the fuck up James. Whatta ya want with a coin?"

I said, "We need to flip to see which one of us is gonna take on you and Jed. I hope for your sake my buddy loses. Last week he accidentally broke some guys back and he died on the way to the hospital."

Ace said, "Well I'd rather be dead than blind."

I said, "I told you that was also an accident and I felt real bad about it. I only meant to take out one eye and my fingers slipped. Come on James give us the coin."

Before Earl could stop him, he pulled it out of his pocket and flipped it to me.

I said, "Call it."

Ace said "Heads."

It was heads. I said, "Heads. That's not fair. You've won the last two times. How about going two out of three?"

"Nope, I'm in. Tie my left arm around my body with your belt."

Earl looking more concerned said, "What the fuck for?"

Ace answered, "It evens the odds and I'd have him tie both arms if I didn't need one arm to keep my balance. My weapons are my feet, not my hands."

At that point, a radio on one of the bikes came on and bellowed, "Earl, come in, this is Hank."

Earl looked at us and said, "You faggots ain't worth it." They moved to their bikes and rode off.

Ace said, "You know the old saying, 'The best fights are the ones you don't get involved in.'"

60

CHICKEN N' DUMPLINS

We got home about 8:30 and April's car was there. I said, "I thought April and Eden were gonna hang at her house."

"Me too, I wonder what she's doing here?"

Tug said to me, "Eden probably got a date with Dick Head Lance."

I said, "Shut the fuck up Tug!"

Ace asked, "What did he say this time."

"Never mind," I snapped. We walked into the cabin and found April busy in the kitchen. Maybe Tug was right. I had hoped Eden would be here." Tug said he knew I wasn't ready to give her up.

Ace trying to keep it light said, "I don't know what you're fixing, but it sure smells good."

"It's a surprise so you'll just have to wait and find out."

We exchanged hugs and as I was about to ask April about Eden, I heard the commode in my bathroom flush and a moment or so later, Eden stood in the door of her bedroom with a faint smile. She looked a little embarrassed. I didn't have a clue about my expression, but I was of course surprised to see her. She looked beautiful in a white dress with large yellow flowered prints. Her hair was down and she had on white flats.

I walked toward her and she hesitated and then walked toward me. I took her in my arms and picked her off the floor. It was the most intimate hug of my life. Neither of us squeezed. We just gently wrapped our arms around each other and let our bodies come together. She whispered in my ear, "I missed you."

I responded, "And I missed you."

We just stood there and held each other.

Finally Ace said, "I'm gettin' hungry."

April said, "Tonight, we're in for a treat. This is Eden's grandmother's recipe for chicken'n dumplings. I watched her make it and I can't wait to taste it." She turned to Ace and said, "I've got chips and salsa to tide us over while Eden and Jett have a chance to talk."

Ace said, "Don't take too long, chips and salsa ain't gonna do it."

Eden got her wine and I got a beer and she took my hand and led me out onto the back deck. The sun was close to going down and it was a perfect setting. I turned the chairs so we were sitting close and could easily see each other and the sunset.

We sat there for a few minutes in silence and then she said, "Twenty-four hours ago, I told you I couldn't do this anymore and I was sincere."

I asked, "What changed your mind?"

"I was miserable thinking I wouldn't see you again. I cried myself to sleep last night. I don't know what I would have done if it hadn't been for April. Most of the time she just listened to me about how scared I was over falling in love with you and then losing you to some younger woman. Then we did the old pros and cons list." She smiled, "I have to admit at first the cons list was a lot longer than the pros list."

I smiled and said, "I think I know most of the cons list. You said 'at first' so the pros list started to pick up a few entries?"

Very seriously she said, "Well, the pros list was pretty skimpy for the longest time and for awhile I thought I would never come up with anything." She laughed.

I smiled, "And at some point you thought of a couple of things?"

She gazed into my eyes and said, "Oh Jett." She scooted onto the edge of the chair and with one hand outlined with her finger the features of my face and as she was gently running her hand through my hair, her eyes filled with tears and she said, "I've never allowed myself to fall in love. It was too dangerous and I couldn't take the risk. With you, there was some part of me that I couldn't control and it was almost like she was saying she didn't care about our fears. And then when we parted yesterday and I was so miserable, I started thinking that being without you and never having a chance to love you might be worse than loving you and losing you."

With both hands, she pulled my head toward her and started lightly kissing my forehead, cheeks, and brushing my lips several times.

Ace stuck his head out the door, "I think you guys got a lot of time ahead of you to talk so you don't have to get everything said now. I'm starving. Can we eat?"

I was speechless and couldn't wipe this shit-eatin' grin off my face and Eden smiled, "Ass Frost, go eat more chips."

"Come on guys! I want some chicken'n dumplings."

Eden said, "Give us two more minutes." I heard the screen door close and she kissed me and gently outlined my lips with her tongue and then opened her mouth a little wider and softly, we explored each other's tongues. My body was full of sensations craving to hold her and make love to her and never let her go.

We went into the cabin arm in arm. April gave us a big smile and said, "You two look mighty happy. All right, the cornbread is almost ready to come out so everybody get something to drink and Eden can serve our plates."

I went over to April and with tears in both of our eyes, we hugged and I whispered in her ear, "I'll always remember that you saved my life. Thank you."

She whispered, "I'm so happy for you."

We had light conversation during our meal. Soon after we sat down, I found her feet with my feet and she slipped off her flats and I was already bare-footed so we had fun exploring each other's feet and toes. I asked them to tell us about what they did over the past twenty-four hours.

April said, "We had a lot to talk about and I think it was about 4:00 in the morning when Eden decided that Butt Wipe just might be worth the risk."

Eden interrupted, "Was it that I thought he was worth the risk or wasn't worth the risk? Anyway, I was up for an adventure and what the heck if he didn't work out I could go find me some other young dude."

April looked reflective, "You know that might have been it. We were both really tired. Anyway, once we got that worked out, we passed out and slept till noon and then had a great time this afternoon. We had lunch at the Tavern in Elverton, went for a walk, planned tonight, went shopping to get a new dress for Eden, picked up our groceries, and came here. We knew you guys would be gone so it worked out perfectly. Eden why don't you tell them about all those dress shops and all the different dresses you tried on."

Ace interjected, "Uh, I would really like to hear about that, but Eden could I get more chicken and dumplings?"

Eden replied, "Sure Ace, but first, let me tell you about this one real pretty little outfit that would be great for church. It had lace around the cuffs of the sleeves." She smiled, "Well you may not be interested in that particular one. Do you think he would want to hear about the purple dress with the orange stripes?"

April replied, "Oh yes, his favorite color is purple?"

Ace turned to me, "Is this what it's gonna be like for the rest of our lives?"

I replied, "Did you all by any chance shop for underwear or little skimpy negligees?"

Ace said, "Yeah, did you?"

Eden kicked me under the table.

"Ouch! That hurt."

April said, "I think I can speak for Eden and say that we feel disrespected and are not inclined to discuss with either one of you those intimate details of our shopping day." She turned to Eden and said, "We may need those dildos we bought today for tonight."

We all laughed. Eden took Ace's plate and got him more chicken and dumplings. Then she turned to me and in her sweetest little southern accent with eye lashes fluttering, "Jeeeeeeett would you like more of my chicken'n dumplings?"

With the continuation of my shit-eatin' grin expression, I replied, "I'd love to eat some of your dumplings."

She whacked me up-side the head and said, "You wish."

We smiled and April said, "It's like we haven't missed a beat since that first night we were together."

Ace held up his tea glass and made a toast, "To many more of the same!" We clicked glasses. I looked at Eden. She winked at me. I think this has to be the happiest day of my life.

The four of us did the dishes and teased and laughed.

After we finished, Eden said, "Well, I better be going. It's getting late."

Trying not to look too disappointed, I asked, "Do you really have to go?"

She responded, "Well, no one has asked me to stay and I don't like to impose on people."

Before I could respond, April said, "Well, why don't you come down and spend another night with me?"

Ace and I answered at the same time, "Wait a minute, hold on?"

Ace asked, "Could you give me and Jett a chance to put a plan together?"

April replied, "Well, don't take all night. Eden and I don't have time to just stand here while you all have a meeting."

We huddled up and talked for a few minutes and then I said, "Okay, here's our plan. April, you and Ace are going to your house and Eden and I will stay here."

Eden said, "Is that it?"

"Yes."

Eden said, "Well, I feel disrespected again. You expect me to stay here without a chaperone?"

I interrupted, "But the other night you stayed…"

She interrupted, "That was an entirely different situation and don't confuse the two."

I looked at Ace, "But I'm not confused."

April waved us off and said to Eden, "Let's you and me talk." They went into the great room and whispered some and came back.

April said, "All right. Here's the deal. Ace, I am reasonably comfortable with you sleeping at my house."

She turned to Eden who said, "I am not comfortable without a chaperone so if you agree to take me home and pick-up Cher, I will consider staying the night."

Ace and I did a high five and said, "We have a plan!"

We agreed to gather here in the morning around 11:00, have breakfast and plan our day. They were off.

I took Eden in my arms, "You have made me the happiest man in the world."

She said, "Jett, we've got a lot of things to work on and I ask you to please take it slow. I have to tell you that I'm still scared, but also that I am determined not to let that fear get in the way of our relationship."

"I understand and we will take it slow."

She said, "Thanks. I knew you would understand. Oh, about Cher. I didn't want to leave her by herself. The cats are fine, but I always leave her with a friend when I'm out of town over night."

"That's perfectly fine. Spot gets along with everyone. I hope Cher will like him."

She said, "I've never had any problem before. She loves to eat so I see that as the only potential issue. She always growls at the cats if they come near her food."

"We'll just feed them in separate rooms."

"That sounds good."

The introduction of Spot and Cher went smoothly. They smelled each other several times and Cher checked out the cabin and Spot followed her around. Cher eventually ended up on Eden's bed where she had put her gym bag.

61
EMOTIONAL INTIMACY

A storm was moving in and there was a chill in the air and we decided to build a fire. I got it started and Eden changed into something more comfortable. She had on a lime green tee-shirt and a pair of white sweat pants cut off right above the knees. I watched her walk toward the kitchen and it looked as if she didn't have on any underwear as the material outlined the crack in her buttocks. Wow. Crack in her buttocks? What happened to crack in her ass? Did I feel it was disrespectful to refer to her buttocks as an ass? Hell, I don't know, but I needed to get my mind wrapped around going slowly. I guess in this situation that meant getting Centered. Tug was ready to fuck her buns now. Anyway, she got a glass of wine and brought me a beer and we settled in on the sofa facing the fire.

We put our feet on the large ottoman and sat as close together as we could get. She sipped her wine and I took some swigs of beer. The fingers of her right hand were entangled with the fingers of my left hand and they rested on the crevice between our thighs. Finally I said, "This is like a dream come true. This time last night, I was trying to figure out how to live my life without you."

She asked, "Did you get it figured out?"

I answered, "Yeah. It took about five minutes."

"Well, that spoiled it for me. I was just getting ready to ask if I could kiss you and now I'm outta the mood."

I said, "I take it back. Please get back in the mood. I've been dying to kiss you, but was afraid that I would be moving too fast."

"All right, I guess you can kiss me." She leaned her head on the back of the sofa and it was my turn to lightly kiss her face and then I moved to both sides of her neck and then in turn took each hand and arm and kissed up to her elbow. Then she pulled my head to her so that our lips and tongue were moving and active. It was clear that she wanted those kisses to be soft and sensuous. It was like there was time to savor the taste of her. There was no hurry and it was incredibly passionate.

Then I realized she was crying. I pulled back a little and kissed her tears. I said in a low voice, "Do you wanna talk about it?"

"This is like a dream for me too. I am feeling stirrings in my body that I've never felt before. I've never allowed myself to let go like this. Part of me wants to pull back and say that I'm really tired and ready for bed and I'll see you in the morning. Another part of me wants you to make love to me all night long."

I didn't know what to say. She put her arms around my neck and buried her head in the crook of my shoulder. And then she whispered, "Jett, I think I've been looking for you all my life and now that you're here, I'm afraid that I'll wake up and discover that it was all a dream and you won't be real. I don't know if I could bear it."

I said, "Why don't you pinch both of us so we'll know it's not a dream."

She said, "All right." I could tell by her voice that she was smiling through her tears. "I pinched myself and you're still here. Now I'll pinch you."

I said, "You're still here so it must not be that kind of a dream."

She said, "I have to pee."

"Me too, I'll use Ace's bathroom."

As usual, I locked and secured the house. When I finished, she was sitting on the sofa and asked, "Can we stretch out?"

"Sure. I can move the ottoman and put down a soft pad. How does that sound?"

"That's fine."

I got the pad and a couple of pillows and a light blanket. I lay on my back and she cuddled up to me on her side and draped one leg over me and laid her head on my shoulder and my arm rested on her back.

"Jett?"

"Yeah?"

"Are you sure we're not dreaming?"

"No, but I'm glad we passed the pinching test."

"Me too."

We lay there in silence and before long I could tell she was drifting off into a light sleep. Her breathing changed a little and there were little subtle jerks in her body. I was so happy. The skin of her leg against mine was sensuous and I could feel her breast through our tee-shirts. I was a little disappointed that we didn't kiss more, but I knew she cried herself to sleep last night and I had slept terribly myself. It had been a long day for both of us. This was taking it slowly and it was going to be a challenge at times, but I was determined to be patient and let her guide the physical part at her own pace. Soon after that, I lost consciousness.

I was aware that we shifted around during the night and it was still dark when she shook me gently and said in a low voice, "Jett, Jett."

"Yeah?"

"Let's get in my bed."

We got up and she took me by the hand and led me in her bedroom, moved Cher over, pulled back the covers, and got in with her clothes on. I followed behind her and cuddled up against her back. She turned her head back toward me and whispered, "I love being cozy with you."

"And me too with you." She turned back and we shifted a little and she was asleep soon after that. I smiled and thought how special it is to go slow and savor these intimate moments. The anticipation of making love to her was almost more than I could bear, but I was learning the art of savoring the moment and letting it unfold gradually one moment at a time. That was the very thing Doc was trying to teach us about all aspects of life. And with Eden, it would be a piece of cake to live each moment to the fullest and celebrate it as unique and fascinating. And then I was out.

I was awakened by soft gentle kisses on my face and when I opened my eyes, the sun beams were flowing in the window from behind her making their way through her hair and giving her the glow of an angel. She smiled and said, "Good morning."

"Good morning to you. Will you promise to never stop kissing my face like that? It feels so good."

She answered, "Yes, I promise."

Then she snuggled up to me and put her arms around my neck and we shifted around so we were in a hugging position on our sides. She pressed her body against mine and said, "Will you promise to never stop holding me close?"

"Yes, I promise."

I moved my hand slowly under the back of her tee-shirt and when I touched her skin, she tensed and I withdrew it and said, "Oh, I'm sorry."

"No," she said. "I'm the one who's sorry. It's just a knee jerk reaction and something I need to work on. I want you to touch me. It's just that if I'm caught off guard, I tense up. It's just a bad habit. Listen to me saying that if I'm caught off guard. Jett, I don't want to be on guard all the time.

That's a terrible way to live. Put your hand back there again and let me take a few of those deep breaths you taught me a few weeks ago."

I did as she told me and I could feel her releasing the tension. I gently rubbed her back and she seemed to relax.

She tentatively asked, "Can you reach under my shirt with your other hand and unfasten my bra?"

"Are you sure?"

She answered, "Yes."

I had a little trouble even with two hands and we laughed as she tried to explain the combination. Once it was done, I traced all around her back with the tips of my fingers. Still just a little tense and in a few moments, she seemed to totally relax. She pressed tighter against me and said, "That feels heavenly." I wanted to trace around on her sides and under her arms, but decided that was going too far too fast. She said, "Oh Jett, that feels so good. Please don't ever stop doing that either." She reached with her free arm and lifted my tee - shirt and started doing the same to my back except she was using a light touch with her fingernails.

I said, "I hate to steal your expression, but that also feels heavenly." About that time, my whole body did a shriving jerk."

"Are you all right?"

"Yeah, what you're doing just sent a shiver all through my body."

So we lay there in a kind of blissful state exploring each other's back and then with a reluctant tone she said, "I've gotta pee and waiting much longer could pose a problem."

I took Spot and Cher out front and let them pee and poop. When I turned around to come back, she was standing on the front porch watching us. When I came up the steps, she stopped me with one step to go and put her arms around my neck and said, "That's better. Now we're almost level." And we kissed and we opened our mouths wider and I was getting hard and there was no hiding that.

We came up for air and using all the clarity and strength I could muster, I said, "I saw the time was about 8:30. Are you up for a run and a visit to our knoll?"

I couldn't read her expression, but I think I detected a little relief and disappointment at the same time. She said, "Sure, but I want two more kisses first."

I smiled, "I could possibly spare one, but if I spare two, all offers for a run and visit to our knoll are off."

She laughed, "All right, how about one and a half?"

"You got it."

I didn't think the first kiss was going to end and when it did, she said, "We better pass on the half-kiss because if we don't, I'll be the one calling off the run."

While we were changing, the phone rang. It was April. She asked, "How are you guys doing?"

I said, "We're fine. So what's happenin'?"

"Let me speak to my girl."

"Sure."

Eden was coming out of her room. "April wants to speak to you."

In a cheerful voice she said, "Hey April." Smiling and looking at me, "Yes, it's all wonderful! How are you all doing? We couldn't be better. What time? Hold on let me double check with Jett." She covered the receiver. "April and Ace have a few errands to run and want to spend the afternoon just relaxing at her house. They thought maybe we could meet at Sally's around 6:00. That sounds good to me, how about you?" I said, "Sounds great." She said to April, "That's fine with us. You guys have a nice day and we'll see you tonight. Thanks."

She asked, "Are you up for a cup of tea before we go on our run?"

"Sure."

While the water was brewing, she said, "Since April and Ace aren't coming, how would you feel about going to church and maybe having lunch with your family at the Inn?"

"Yeah, I guess that would be okay."

She smiled, "I want everyone to know that we're together. I think about walking in on your arm and everyone seeing us and smiling and being happy for us. And then we could visit more at lunch and go up and see Pop if he's not able to make it."

I smiled back, "I think that's a wonderful idea and that will save me some phone calls. I know everybody is wondering and I especially want to see Mom and to tell her and Pop too. When I talked to Mom on the phone Friday and saw him the same day, they both knew something was wrong."

I looked at the clock. "It's 8:45. I think we have time to do the run, get a bite of breakfast and be there by 10:45. Whatta you think?"

She said, "If we can be back here by 9:30, I think I can make it. I only want a bowl of cereal and piece of toast for breakfast. I'm going to wear that same dress I had on last night."

"I'll be glad to wash your back for you if that'll help."

"I'm sure you would Jett Hollander." She grinned, "I'll pass for right now."

We went on our run and spent about five minutes at the knoll and headed home. We were in the truck by 10:35.

When we got there, as usual, everyone was standing outside talking. No one noticed us at first. Eden had her arm enfolded into mine and as soon as we got out of the parking lot and on the sidewalk, they saw us and there was a kind of group gasp and then they started clapping and everybody including us had big smiles. Mom came out to greet us and took us both in her arms and tears were rolling down her cheeks and said, "Well children, I'm speechless, but so happy for both of you."

We sat between Mom and Dad and it was the best church service I had attended in a long time. I'm not particularly proud of that, but it's true. Pop was not able to come to the service, but he was going to try and join everyone for lunch. Eden and I left a little early after church to go see Pop. Henry would always go up and get him when the family arrived so we told Henry we would bring him down.

He was glad to see us and relieved that I was no longer in so much emotional pain. We gave him a summary update on our relationship. He seemed a little better today, so I was encouraged. We enjoyed the lunch and spent time talking with everyone. Mom and Eden spent a lot of time talking and you could tell they liked each other and that was no surprise. They were both wonderful human beings.

62

AN INTERLUDE

From there, we went to Eden's house so she could pick up some things to take to the cabin. When we got in the house, she went to the kitchen to do some things and looked over at her answering machine. She had six messages. She said, "I forgot to look at this last night when we picked up Cher. I don't think I've gotten but one or two messages since I changed the greeting. I hope it wasn't anything important. My cell phone is dead and it won't recharge. I've got to get another one this week."

I asked her if she wanted me to go in the other room and she said there was nothing here that she wouldn't want me to hear. There were two messages from Lance just wanting to get together for dinner or lunch. The other four were from her boss's boss Don Kelly in Raleigh. The summary was that he had been trying to get hold of her since Friday evening. The Director of the EPA in Washington had called a meeting of all the regional directors to discuss some special projects that had been assigned about six months ago. Even though The White House had originally said they wanted the report in about eight months, they had called and said they needed it this coming Friday. It had to do with budget problems and Congress was pushing them for some answers. Since Eden was the project officer, she needed to be prepared to brief

Don on Monday at noon in Washington and work on the project with him so he could report to the Director later in the week. He told her to be prepared to stay in DC until noon on Friday. They had booked a room for her at the Key Bridge Marriott and had made arrangements for an early check-in so she could make the noon meeting tomorrow. They would leave a message at the desk on where to meet and it would be somewhere in the hotel.

She said, "Oh shit, oh shit, oh shit! I'm not prepared to brief anyone on this project. I've got a bunch of work left to do."

My military mind went to work on a quick contingency plan. I asked her, "Do you have all the information on the project here?"

"Yes. It's in the back bedroom with all my work stuff."

"Okay. You need to trust me. I want you to go pack a bag and get all your project materials together and by the time you finish, I'll have a plan."

"Jett, this is not your problem. I'll figure out how to get this done."

I smiled, "As of some moment yesterday, you decided to be with me for now and the way I see it that means your problems are my problems and my problems are your problems. We're a team from this point on unless at some point, one of us decides differently. Whatta ya think?"

Hesitantly, "Okay."

"Do you wanna call your boss now and let him know you'll be there?"

"Yes."

"After you talk to him, please get your things together and leave the rest to me."

I called Ace at April's and luckily they were back from shopping. "I need your help." I gave him a quick rundown of the situation. "I've got to get her on the road right away. I need you to call the Key Bridge Marriott in Washington and tell them Eden Howell has a reservation starting tomorrow and that she wants to check in late tonight and would they have a room available. If they don't, find us a room as closes possible to that Marriott. In either case, get us directions from I-66. Check the map and find the quickest route to DC. I'll head up the Parkway and call you in about an hour. I'm gonna ask Mom if I can take her car. I'll probably be back tomorrow or Tuesday. Call Charlie in the morning and let him know my situation. I've got to stop at the cabin and pick out a few things and we'll be on our way. I'll get Mom to pick-up Spot and Cher. Thanks my man. I'll talk to you in a little while."

He said "Got you covered. Bye."

I called Mom and she said the car would be ready and she'd take care of the dogs.

Eden walked in the room with her suitcase and two briefcases. I said, "I want you to close your eyes and take a couple of deep breaths and do the best you can to quiet your mind." After about fifteen seconds, I said, "Now with a clear mind decide if there is anything you're going to need that is not in the suitcase or briefcases. Take your time and let me know when you are as certain as you can be that you have everything you need."

She opened her eyes and said, "I forgot my dildo."

We burst out laughing. I said, "I can help you with that one."

We secured her house and I briefed her on the plan. "Mom's front seat is wide so there should be plenty of room for you to work while I drive. You can sleep when it gets dark and when we get checked in, you will still have the rest of the night and in the morning before you meet with your boss at noon."

We were on the Parkway headed north by 3:00. She leaned over and kissed me and said, "Thanks to you, I think I can get this knocked out before noon tomorrow."

After an hour or so, I called Ace and we were good to go at the Marriott. He gave me directions from I-66 to the hotel and then gave me the quickest route to DC. It didn't get dark until about 8:30.

About half-way into the trip, she closed up her paperwork and stretched out across the seat on her back and put her head in my lap. She was looking up at me and reached up and touched my face and said, "Thank you for helping me."

"You're welcome." I asked, "You hungry?"

"Not really. Those snacks you brought will tide me over." She slept for an hour or so and was back to work.

I said, 'We should be there by 10:00."

Check in was easy. She got her work area set up at the desk and we went over the hotel restaurant menu. Then we ordered room service.

While eating she said, "I think I can finish this up in about three hours. After we finish, I think I'll take a shower and we can sleep till about 7:00. That will give me plenty of time to be ready by noon. The bad news is that there is still a lot of work to be done before reporting to the director. The good news is there will be four of us working on it. We should have until about Thursday according to the message and we'll need every minute of it."

I said, "You're gonna be busy so I think I'll head back home in the morning."

"Oh Jett, I want you to stay, but I'm afraid we'll be working around the clock and I would be worried about you having nothing to do."

"I could find plenty to do here, but I think it would be best to focus all your attention on your work."

She came around the table, sat on my lap, put her arms around my neck and said, "But I will miss you so much. After these weeks of looking forward to spending any small amount of time with you, I don't want to be apart whenever I'm not at work."

I smiled, "You really wanted to be with me that much even after we just met?"

She blushed a little, "Yes. Even though I couldn't admit it to myself, I treasured every moment we were together. I'll tell you more about that later." She passionately kissed me. Then we held each other for awhile and she whispered in my ear, "I want our first time to be special and not hurried and in a hotel room. Do you agree?"

"No. I mean yes. I mean it will be hard. No, I mean it will be difficult." We laughed.

She gave me another passionate kiss and said, "I'm gonna take my shower. It won't take me long."

I called Ace and Mom and gave them an update.

When she came out of the shower, she was in a pair of pajamas that were pretty conservative. They were dark green with buttons in the front and the bottoms came down to her knees. She said, "Given what I said a few minutes ago, I was careful not to wear anything too revealing." She smiled, "I figure if I can help you stay strong, I'm helping me stay strong."

I responded, "I'm sorry, but you in anything or nothing is not going to help me stay strong. I'm gonna do it because it's what we both want. But thanks for trying."

She walked over and gave me a hug and said, "I'm so happy Jett. I can hardly stand it." We kissed passionately and when we came up for air, she said, "You better go take your shower. I'm starting to feel weak."

I headed for the bathroom door and then stopped. "Oh, I forgot to tell you that I called the front desk for a wake-up at 7:00. Also, before I leave in the morning, I can call and get you a reservation to fly from Reagan International on Friday morning to Greensboro and I can pick you up there. How does that sound?"

"You think of everything. I'm not used to it, but it sure is nice. That will be fine. While I'm thinking about it, I'll lay out my credit card on the desk. I get reimbursed for any expenses."

I took my shower and all I had to wear was underwear and a pair of shorts. I went back into the room and it was almost dark. There was a little light coming in through the drapes and I could make out the furniture and Eden was already under the covers. I took off the shorts and she lifted the sheet and I could see that she had taken her top off.

She held out her arms and as I slid under the sheet she rolled on top of me and we kissed and I could feel her breasts on my chest. They were the perfect size for her body, but any size would have been perfect. After a few moments, we were both panting and she hugged me tight and whispered in my ear, "I'm getting weaker and weaker. I want you inside me in the worst way. Please help me be strong."

I said, "Let's remember this moment all week long and if you agree that this coming Friday can be our night, then the anticipation will be unbelievable. Whatta ya think?"

"All right, I'm gonna turn over and you cuddle and maybe because we're so tired we'll be able to fall asleep. I'm gonna be strong. I'm gonna be strong. I'm getting sleepy. I know I'm getting sleepy."

I cuddled up against her and my right arm was draped over her side and she took my hand and moved it slowly up to her breasts and said, "Good night my Jett."

"Good night Eden."

My dick was hard as a rock and it was a little embarrassing, but she pushed up against it and said in a lazy voice, "I'm glad you're hard. Otherwise I'd be worried that I didn't turn you on."

It seemed like she got to sleep right away. I was awake for awhile but soon drifted off. I woke up and there was a little daylight coming in through the drapes. We both must have been exhausted because we were in the same position as we had been before falling asleep. I moved back as gently and slowly as I could, but she woke up and turned over and grabbed on to me and in a sleepy voice said, "Jett, where are you going?"

"It's 6:00 and I'm going for a run."

She interrupted and said, "I wanna go with you."

"Sweetheart, why don't you go back to sleep and get another hour."

She said, "Maybe I will. I'm so tired. Give me a kiss." And she plopped onto the pillow and pulled the sheet over her.

The run was wonderful. I followed the Potomac down to Memorial Bridge and ran up one side of the Reflection Pool to the Washington Monument and back on the other side and then back to the Hotel. Eden was up and dressed and in some casual clothes working at the desk. She got up and gave me a hug and asked about my run. Then she said, "You called me 'sweetheart' this morning. Am I your sweetheart?"

"Yes you are and a lot more my darling."

"Oh, so now I'm also your darling. I love this."

We talked for a few minutes and I showered and we ordered room service. After we finished eating, I went downstairs to make arrangements for her flight to Greensboro. She would arrive around 1:00 in the afternoon.

It was 9:12 when I got back to the room. She was hard at work at the desk. She looked up and smiled, "Can you stay a little longer?"

"I got a newspaper. I'll read it and then leave. How about that?"

"That sounds better than leaving now."

I asked, "How are you comin' with your work?"

"Thanks to you, I'll be ready to help us get a good start on getting everything put together."

"I'm glad I could help." I read a lot more in the paper than I usually do. I wanted to be with her as long as possible. When I folded it up she came over and sat in my lap.

"Jett, this is going to be so hard." She smiled, "I mean difficult. Please be careful and will you call me every night? I think we'll be working late, but you can leave me a message and I'll call you when I get to the room. Already, I can't wait to see you again. Call me when you get home and if I'm not here, leave me a message so I'll know you made it safely back. Say 'hey' to April and Ace and thank Ace and your Mom for helping us and tell your Mom I really appreciate her taking care of Cher. I'll call April this afternoon after our initial meeting."

One more passionate kiss and I left. I got down to the lobby and turned around and went back up to the room and knocked on the door and she said, "Who is it?"

"It's me." She opened the door and pulled me in and we threw our arms around each other and held on for dear life."

She whispered, "I wanna quit my job and us just disappear and spend the rest of our lives making love and traveling and hiking and being together. I don't want to let you out of my sight." She had tears in her eyes.

"That's what I want too. Okay. Let me get outta here before we decide to take off and go."

"One more kiss," she said.

As I pulled out of the parking lot, I glanced up to about where I figured the room was and wondered how I was going to get through these next five days. Yesterday, she was with me and now each minute would put more distance between us. I decided to go back the way we came so I could get home as soon as possible. On the one hand, I wanted time to think and savor the memories of our time together and on the other hand, I wanted to get home so I could get into the routine and hopefully the time would pass faster.

63
THE WAITING

About 100 miles from home, I called Eden's room and left a message. I called Ace and asked if I could meet him and April for supper at Sally's. He said they talked about it this morning and they wanted me to come to April's house for supper. They had their session with Doc at 5:00 and I was to meet them at her house at 6:30. Then I called Mom and said I would pick up the dogs on my way to the cabin. Mom asked me to eat with them tomorrow night and said she had also invited Jimmy and family and Sadie and Tom.

I called Eden's room and left a message that I had gotten home safely and told her of my plans for the evening. While I was walking Spot and Cher, she called and she was jealous that I was eating supper with April and Ace and that she was stuck with a working supper in a conference room.

In the morning, I called her about 7:30 and she was just about to walk out the door for a working breakfast. She said, "I miss you so much, but I'm glad you didn't stay. There have been no breaks so far except to sleep. And I'm sorry but I'm already a little late so I'll talk to you later. I miss you."

Buddy Session Seven

Ace came up about 8:30 and we had a nice talk. The focus of our conversations of late had been on Eden and me and I was eager to know in more detail how he and April were doing. Last night they seemed like they were doing really well. He said they had one argument over the last four or five days. He said it wasn't as intense and they got it resolved. I was glad to hear things were going well.

Doc arrived a little before nine. He reminded us that this would be the next to last buddy session and that there were three group sessions left. I think both of us had forgotten there would only be eight sessions.

Ace asked, "What do we do after the sessions are over?"

Doc responded, "I will summarize a list of all the training that will keep you plenty busy. I'm also exploring the idea of setting up the structure for a 'peer group.' That means if some of you or maybe all of you wanted to keep meeting, there could be a format for you to follow something along the lines of Alcoholics Anonymous."

I said, "I really like that idea and I know I would be interested in continuing maybe twice a month."

Ace said, "Same for me. I hope you will help us set that up."

Doc responded, "Let's check with the group and see the level of interest."

We did a Centering Meditation and Ace wanted to go first so he could go to work after his session with Doc.

I filled Doc in on my latest news about Eden. He asked me to take him through a nine stepper using an intense memory of a combat situation. After it was over, he said that I had a good handle on how to effectively use the exercise. I told him I had some major panic attacks last week around my issues with Eden, but I had no flashbacks and only one nightmare of medium intensity. We went down my list of goals and talked about each one and how I was doing. He encouraged me to consistently continue the training and not to get cocky when things seemed to be going well. I remembered he had told us last Saturday that many of his repeat clients had been those who had stopped training.

It seemed like Friday was never going to get here. We talked on the phone several times each night and once early each morning. She would call me during a break and when she got back to the room. We left each other messages during the day. She had been working almost non-stop and she said they would be ready for their portion of the briefing late Thursday. She said she had already reserved a seat on the shuttle to Reagan International on Friday morning and couldn't wait to see me.

I've never been so happy and so lonely at the same time. Ace was staying at April's and I wanted them to be staying at the cabin. But I kept busy and worked longer hours at the Inn, visited Pop every day and was encouraged he seemed to be feeling better. I continued to run in the mornings and sometimes after work. Henry and Betty invited me to dinner on Wednesday at Mom's urging I'm sure. I always enjoyed talking to them. It was a nice evening.

I cleaned the cabin on Thursday evening and changed sheets. I wanted everything to be ready for Eden. April had given me some ideas on how to make things romantic. I had gotten Eden's favorite wine and dark chocolate candy and was going to pick some fresh wild flowers before leaving for the airport. I had candles and had planned to grill some steaks with baked potato and tossed salad with rolls. I was getting more excited by the minute.

I called her around 9:00 P.M. and she had just gotten back to her room. She said the presentation had gone well and that her boss was pleased. He had taken everyone out to eat. She sounded exhausted. I said, "How would it be if I hung up and let you get some sleep?"

"I don't want you to hang up, but I'm so tired. Would you call me in the morning around 8:00 to make sure I'm up?"

"Sure. I hope you sleep well. I can't wait to see you."

"Jett, I'm so excited. I can't wait to see you too." We hung up.

Around 11:00, the phone rang. "Hey Jett, did I wake you up?"

"No, I had just gotten in bed."

"I had to pee and then I didn't remember if I told you how much I missed you and how excited I am to be seeing you tomorrow."

I responded, "Yes, but I love hearing it again."

"All right, I'm still tired. Call me at 8:00."

I slept pretty well and since I had everything ready, I went to work at 7:00 to pass the time. I called Eden at 8:00 and she was too excited to sleep so she had been up for an hour or so. She also said she was getting an earlier shuttle to the airport to be sure she had plenty of time to catch her flight. I told her I was going to leave around 10:00 and I would meet her at the baggage claim.

I arrived at the airport early and decided to get a sandwich. The message board said the flight was on time so I had about an hour.

I knew which direction she would be coming from when she landed so I hid behind a wall and when she passed me I was careful not to startle her so I stayed about six feet behind her and said, "May I help you Madame?"

She whirled around dropped her briefcase and flung herself into my arms. "Yes, you may help me. Kiss me!" And we kissed and we held on as if it had been years since we had last seen each other.

And then a voice from behind us said, "Wow, I wish someone missed me that much."

We both looked around and Eden said, "Right, Sean, I'm really lucky."

And I said, "And I'm really lucky."

We let go and Eden put her arm around my waist and said, "Sean Farley, this is my boyfriend Jett Hollander."

We shook hands and Eden turned to me and said, "Sean has been a colleague for some time now. He's a good friend." We exchanged small talk for a few minutes and he left.

We got her a sandwich and drink to go and hit the road. It was an overcast day and it looked like rain. As she slid up close to me, I was glad my truck didn't have bucket seats. She nibbled on her sandwich and told me about her week. She said one of the guys from the Raleigh office had tried to pick her up. "He was flirting with me in the bar while I was with several of my friends and I told him politely that I had a boyfriend and I wasn't interested. He had too much to drink and was persistent and Sean told him to leave me alone. He drifted off and soon after I got to the room, there was a knock and I asked who it was and it was him. I told him to go away or I would call the front desk. I didn't hear any more from him." Then she softly elbowed me in the ribs and said, "And he was kind of cute too."

Looking as guilty as I could, I said, "Thanks for telling me that. It makes it a little easier for me to tell you that I got really lonely on Tuesday night and had sex with one of the waitresses at Sally's, but I didn't enjoy it that much."

We laughed and she leaned up and kissed me on the cheek. It started raining about half way home and she snuggled closer to me and I started to put my arm around her and then said, "I better keep both hands on the wheel." Shortly after that, she put her head in my lap and went to sleep. When we got on the outskirts of Harvest, I woke her and asked if she would like to go by her house before going to the cabin. Sleepily, she replied, "Yes, thanks."

It took her about fifteen minutes to get her things together. I volunteered to do the liter box and put out fresh food and water. She checked her answering machine and said, "I have five messages from Lance plus the two before I left. As I told you before, he has been kind of persistent and I don't know his intentions or even if he has any or whether he just wants to be friends, but I don't want him to have any expectations. I'd like to call him."

"Would you like for me to wait outside?"

"No, I'd rather you be here. Just give me a minute to figure out how to put this in words." After a minute or two, she looked at a sheet of paper and dialed, "Hello Lance. How are you? I know. I got your messages a few minutes ago. I had to go out of town unexpectedly on business. No, I wouldn't want you to think that I ignored your calls. That would have been rude. Well, thank you for the invitations. This feels a little awkward, but I need to share something with you. I introduced you to Jett Hollander last week. Yes, he liked you too and thought you were very nice. Anyway, Jett and I are now in a committed relationship and I hope you and I can still be friends and have an occasional lunch together. Lance, are you there? Yes, it was rather sudden, but both of us have been thinking seriously about it for some time now. We just hadn't found the right time to let each other know it. Well thank you Lance. That's sweet. I'll tell him. All right, goodbye."

She smiled and said, "Lance said to tell Jett he's a lucky man and that I wish you both well."

I walked over and took her in my arms and said, "Yes, I sure am a lucky man. I thought you handled that perfectly. I was impressed."

"You don't mind if we have an occasional lunch?"

"Absolutely not, but if I did, I would consider that my problem and not yours and would under no circumstances try to stand in your way."

She kissed me and said, "Let's go home."

64
BLISS

We got to the cabin around 4:30 and I carried her across the threshold and we held on to each other and talked about how happy we were. She got her things unpacked while I took care of a few things in the kitchen. When she came out, she said, "This is our special night and I want it just to be us, but how would you feel if I call April and invite she and Ace for supper tomorrow night?"

I came over and hugged her and said, "You will never know how much it means to me that you feel so close to both of them. They are so much a part of my life and I want them to always be a part of our lives. A part of me wants to have you all to myself for the next year, but the other part wants those that we love and care about to be with us and share our lives together. I was also moved last Sunday when you wanted to go to church and lunch with our family. That means so much to me. Thank you my sweetheart."

She kissed me and called April. While they were talking, I got the wild flowers I had picked this morning out of Ace's room and put them on the table in the kitchen. She smiled and blew me a kiss. I turned the oven on to preheat for the baked potatoes and went outside to make sure the grill was ready to go. When I came in, she was saying goodbye to April. "I'm a little nervous, but it's the good kind. I love you too. See you guys tomorrow."

Spot and Cher were on the front deck and Spot was barking. I said, "Spot wants to go on a walk. Are you up for that?"

"Yes, that would be nice. Let me change into more comfortable shoes. I love those flowers. They are beautiful.

"I'm glad you like them. They're pretty, but not as pretty as you."

She said, "I'm blushing. Be back in a minute."

The dogs had a blast. They took turns chasing each other. We couldn't believe how well they were getting along. Spot finally had a playmate. We walked hand in hand and stopped at the knoll and after we got the dogs to calm down, we had fun remembering other times we had been there.

I asked, "Do you remember the first time when you saw the deer out in the distance and had me look down your arm to your finger so I could see where they were?"

"Yes, I remember it well."

I said, "I was taking deep breaths trying to take in all of you and my lips were so close to your neck and I was dying to kiss your neck. Let me show you. Let's get in the same position. I wanted to smell the fragrance of your skin and wanted to kiss your neck like this and nibble on your ear."

She interrupted, "You're giving me chill bumps. Oh, that feels so good and do you know what I wanted to do?"

"No."

"I wanted to turn around slowly and kiss you gently on the lips like this over and over again, bury my head in your chest and have you hold me close like you're doing now."

I questioned, "But you barely knew me."

"And you barely knew me. What was going on with us? We seemed to know so early that we wanted to be together. You were more up front about it and I was hiding behind the age thing, scared to let myself feel what my heart was telling me."

As I continued to hold her, I said, "Remember all that time we were looking for property. I didn't know how long it would take to win your heart, but I was desperate to have you close by. All this property belongs to Pop so I went and talked to him about you having a plot here to build your house. He said he trusted my judgment and that I could do whatever I wanted to with the hundred acres along this ridge which, along with the cabin, would belong to me when he passes on."

She squeezed tighter and said, "I had no idea. All I know is that I was only interested in being as close to you as I could be. So the closer a piece of property was to you, the better I liked it."

She turned around and I wrapped my arms around her and she pressed her body back against mine and we looked out over the miles and we swayed back and forth and then she looked to her left, pulled away from me a little and yelled, "Cher! No! Cher! Come!"

I broke away and walked quickly ten meters and knelt down and held my hand out and said, "Cher, come, come on Cher, come." And Eden was behind me saying, "Cher, come." Cher wandered over to us and Eden came from behind me and picked her up and hugged her."

I said, "That's my fault. Spot is used to these drop offs and cliffs and doesn't get too close anymore. We'll have to teach Cher to be careful."

"When I saw her over there standing on the edge, my heart took a leap."

I said, "That's real scary. We'll work on her."

We changed into comfortable lounging clothes. She put on a pair of yellow loose shorts that came down to her knees and a white sleeveless blouse that was made of a soft material that you could almost see through and her hair was down. She didn't have on a bra. I said, "You look beautiful in that outfit."

"April helped me pick these out last weekend."

"I like your taste."

She asked, "Thank you. What can I do?"

"There's your favorite white wine in the fridge. Would you like to choose some music? There are some cassettes and CD's over in that drawer. There's probably a wide range and some may be pretty old. Different people have contributed to the collection over the years. I'll go out and see how the grill is coming."

When I came back in, Barbara Streisand was singing. Eden said, "She's one of my favorites."

"I like her too."

We had a romantic dinner. We traded bites of food and she wanted me to try her wine which even though it was white went amazingly well with the red meat. I liked it. She liked her steak medium well and I liked mine medium and we tasted each others. She teased me about liking catsup with my steak and I teased her about liking steak sauce. Neither one of us ate very much. When we were finished and putting the dishes in the sink, one of her favorite Streisand songs came on and she wanted to dance.

I said, "I'm just an average to below average dancer."

"Me too," she said.

It was slow and nice. We started out in the traditional dancing position and before long had our arms around each other and our bodies were swaying together and we exchanged a few light and moist kisses from time to time. I gently rubbed her back and she kissed my neck. When I moved my hand up under her blouse, she gave a subtle groan as I moved my finger tips over her skin. Another nice song came on and we continued. She stopped for a moment and unbuttoned her blouse and we continued not dancing as close which gave me room to move my fingers up and down her sides and lightly under her arms and then lightly over her nipples and she gave a little shiver.

She took me by the hand and led me into her bedroom and when we got beside her bed, she started pulling off my tee - shirt and I helped her remove her blouse and she gently pushed me onto the bed so I lay on my back. She straddled me and said, "Please do that again with your fingers."

I moved my fingertips all around her upper body and lightly brushing her nipples and circling her breasts and on her back and sides and underarms and arms and fingers and palms and face and neck. She was slowly moving her hips back a forth and spread her legs a little wider so as to open her body to me. Her eyes were closed and she leaned over and kissed me and pushed her legs down so that she was lying on top of me.

As we continued kissing, I moved my hands down her back and slid my fingers under the loose elastic in her shorts and then brought them out and each time I would go a little further into her shorts and found out soon there were no panties. I lightly massaged her buttocks and she made subtle gyrating moves. She said, "Take 'em off." She lifted up to give me room and she started working on the button on my shorts.

I said, "Let me help you with that." And we were naked and she lay on top of me and spread her legs and we kissed more passionately and she reached down and guided me in about an inch and then started slow rhythmic movements and gradually was moving down and taking a little more of me into her each time and we were panting and I was afraid I was going to cum first. I tried to think about something else and the kisses were wilder and more passionate and finally I was all the way in and it didn't take either one of us long after that.

We lay in an exhausted heap on the bed and she reached around and pulled the sheet over us and continued to lie on top of me. We were still out of breath and just held each other. I was sweating and she took part of the sheet and wiped my face.

Still a little out of breath, I said, "That was incredible." Tears were welling up in my eyes and I took her face in my hands and kissed her gently and then looked in her eyes and softly said, "Eden Howell, I too have been looking for you all my life and with all my heart, I love you."

She lay on my chest with her arms into her sides and I wrapped her in my arms and she said, "I can't describe what it was like when we were finally naked and our skin was touching. It was so amazingly intimate and sensuous. That was my first time making love. I'll remember it for the rest of my life."

She shifted around so that she was lying beside me with her leg draped over me and her head in the crook of my shoulder. We lay there for awhile and then I said, "Now I know what they mean by afterglow. It's hard for me to put it in words, but I feel so close to you. It may sound corny, but for the first time in my life, I know what it means to become one body and one spirit."

"I think that would only sound corny to someone who has never experienced it. I have the same feeling and it is all so new and exciting and wonderful."

We must have drifted off into a light sleep because my next awareness was Eden softly kissing my face and it was almost dark. I asked, "How long did we sleep?"

"I'm not sure. I was out myself for a little while. I woke up about ten minutes ago and had the best time just looking at you. Do you remember us talking, I think it was last weekend, when I told you I thought I loved Chase, but now I know I never did?"

"Yeah, I remember."

She continued, "You probably didn't understand what I meant by that statement. I have been infatuated before and I felt affection for Chase at times, but I wondered if that was as good as it got. When I met you and got to know you, I realized that I had never before experienced love. That's what I meant by 'now I know that I never did love Chase.'"

Smiling, "I wish I had understood that. I would have felt more confident."

She said, "It scares me to think that I might have been so stubborn about the age thing that we would have never had a chance to be together." She kissed me gently and lovingly and whispered in my ear, "My sweet Jett, I love you so very much."

We kissed and held each for awhile and then she whispered, "Make love to me again."

I rolled over on top and with every passionate kiss, the desire to connect, to be inside her grew more intense and she took my dick in her hand and was massaging her clit and then moving it all around the opening and back to her clit and then said, "Fill me up Jett. I want all of you inside me. Please, now. I want you now."

I slid into that hot and moist part of her body and moved slowly back and forth and I said, "I love you my Eden, I love you my sweetheart," and we were panting and she wrapped her legs around me and started moving faster and almost gasping for air saying, "I love you Jett. Make love to me. I love you Jett." And then we reached that moment of ecstasy and joy and release and....

We snuggled and passed out from exhaustion and from all that had happened in the last days of anticipation and excitement and the culmination of the celebration of our love for each other.

I woke up at 6:50 and tried to ease out of bed to let Eden sleep, but she stirred and barely opened her eyes and said, "Where am I?" She looked around and said to me, "And who are you?" She smiled and said, "Come here you hunk of a man. What's your name handsome?"

I answered, "Some call me Butt Wipe, but you can call me Asshole."

"Well give me a good morning kiss Asshole. Come, don't be shy. I won't bite you," Giving me a sexy look, "But I might bite you, but not right now."

We laughed and hugged and kissed and she said, "Jett, I am so happy. Can we make love six times before your group gets here?"

"Maybe seven if we hurry."

We hugged again. She said, "All right, after all you did to help me get through this past week, it's my turn to help us get organized. What time will Ace get here?"

"He usually gets here about 8:30."

"Here's my suggestion. It's almost 7:00. We take the dogs for a walk, come back and take a shower."

I interrupted, "Together?"

"If you promise to be a good boy and only wash my back," she ordered. "There will be no time for extra-curricular activities. Then we'll straighten up the cabin and have a light breakfast. I think we can pull that off by 8:30."

"I like it."

She continued, "When I talked to April last night, we made plans to spend the morning together. What time will the group be over?"

"We usually finish around twelve."

She said, "Why don't I plan to be back here around 12:30. This morning, April and I will decide on the menu for tonight and I'll go by the store and pick up what we need. I'll also pick up a few things for us to take on a picnic lunch today if the weather holds. How does that sound?"

"It sounds great. Thanks for taking care of all the details."

We executed the plan intermingled with hugs and kisses. The shower was wonderful and Eden made sure we stuck to the plan. She did let me dry her off except for her "privates" which she insisted drying herself. I said you can dry my "privates" anytime.

She winked and said, "Maybe later." We laughed and had fun and then Ace arrived and they hugged hello. Eden and I hugged with a peck goodbye and she headed for the door.

Ace said, "Eden, I almost forgot, April said she would meet you at Josie's coffee shop on Main Street." She waved and was gone.

65
GROUP SESSION SIX

Ace had pulled in at 8:30 and everyone arrived shortly after Eden left. That was so different from the beginning when I think everyone was reluctant to be here. Now we wanted to be with the people who understood us and could relate to our stuff.

When Anna came through the door, I went over to her and gave her a hug and asked, "How are things going with Brandon?"

She answered, "A little better. He wants us to work it out and has been doing everything he can to prove he loves me. I'm still struggling, but I think the marriage is worth saving. I don't know, but maybe I'm more focused on saving it for the children. If we didn't have any children, I'm not sure if I would have the motivation to stay and work on it. How about you? Are there any new developments in your life?"

I smiled slightly and gave her an update.

"Jett, I'm so happy for you." She gave me another hug. "It sounds like you have a great chance at having a wonderful relationship. I hope for you the very best."

"Thanks Anna. I hope things will get better for you and Brandon."

With a sigh she replied, "Me too."

Doc walked in the door and asked us to take our seats.

Doc: "While I'm getting my things unpacked, please close your eyes and begin focusing on your breathing and going to Center. Look around and see if you can discover something you have never seen before at your Center. Continuing to focus on your breathing and being Centered.... Now open your eyes."

Doc: "What is the purpose of the eleven-stepper exercise?"

Doug: "To work on issues in our present life that may or may not be related to the war. I remember that because I'm still using it to help me with the issues between my wife and myself. I'm using it and even though it seems like I'm just doing much of the same thing over and over, I can tell it's helping me get Centered with her."

Chad: "It's an exercise we can use in about any situation where we're trying to get Centered."

Doc: "If that's true, why would we need the nine-stepper?"

Nate: "It helps us let go of them damn memories we can't get outta our heads."

Doc: "Good. Is everyone clear on the difference? Are there any questions?"

Doc: "I mentioned last week that we would be working on shorter exercises for the eleven and nine stepper. I will keep reminding you to avoid using the shortened form of both exercises for the more challenging issues in your life and for those memories that are continuing to be intense and intrusive in your life. In my view, shortcuts usually don't work as well."

Doc: "We'll start with the shortened version of the eleven-stepper. Once again, if you have used the longer form of the eleven-stepper and have been successful to some degree, now would be the time to use the shorter exercise with the same issue. Close your eyes and feel the physical discomfort and remember one or two not working well thoughts. Invite Focker to Center. Begin to feel the release of the physical discomfort. Think a couple of Centered thoughts. Now rehearse the situation from

Center. Then think or say, 'I can do this' and be confident that you can do it. Open your eyes."

Ace: "I can see why you would have to use the longer form of the exercise before you could effectively use the shorter form. To use the shorter form, you need a lot of information at your finger tips. Am I getting this right?"

Doc: "Yes. I have the shorter form of the exercise on the newsprint."

1. Remember not working well thoughts.
2. Feel the physical discomfort.
3. Invite Focker to Center.
4. Feel the release of physical discomfort.
5. Think a couple of Centered thoughts.
6. Rehearse the situation.
7. Believe you can do it.

Doc: "By now, all of you are familiar with the eleven step process. However, get out your notebooks and turn to that page that lists the eleven steps. Okay. Now someone answer Ace's question. 'Am I getting this right?'"

Melinda: "When you look at the shortened form on paper, it doesn't look a lot shorter than the longer form. All of us are getting more accustomed to being Centered so we can just get Centered as opposed to going to Center and hanging out there and feeling what it's like. The steps on the longer form take more time because when you first begin working with a situation, you're trying to figure out what is the physical discomfort and what's the content of Focker's 'not working well' thoughts. Then you are taking time to feel what it's like to release the physical discomfort and on and on. In a way, once you have all that information and you can quickly recall it, the long process can be made into a much shorter process. So Ace, is that what you were referring to?"

Ace: "Yeah."

Doc: "Questions or comments?"

Doc: "When doing the shorter form, please pay particular attention to the physical discomfort. At Center with the aid of the deep breathing, there can be such a profound release of the physical symptoms and it's important to experience that release."

Doc: "I want you to break down in pairs and do the following. One person will pick a situation to work on. Go through the eleven step process and take your partner with you explaining out loud what you are doing. Remember, we did that last week. Once you have finished the eleven-stepper, go through the shortened process with the same situation again, talking out loud so your partner can follow you. Repeat the short process two more times using the same situation. Then switch over. Are there any questions?"

Doc walked around and checked on us. It seemed like everyone was starting to be more comfortable with the exercises. Paul and I had been a pair and we breezed though it without a hitch.

Doc called us back together and everyone seemed to be getting it. It was time for a break.

Rob, Doug, and I ended taking Spot and Cher for a walk. Doug and Rob loved dogs and the dogs really took to them. I enjoyed listening to Doug talk about his two dogs and how they went everywhere together. He said his wife told him, "You love them dogs better than your own kids." He smiled and said, "There're a lot easier to deal with." We laughed.

Me: "Rob, I was curious about where you got your Focker name."

Rob: "Mac was a friend of my Dad's and he was mean as a snake and none of us kids liked him."

Me: "How 'bout you Doug?"

Doug: "I had a one star General on my third tour that I didn't like. His last name was Hill."

It was time to gather.

Doc: "With the nine step exercise, we have been working on reducing the intensity of traumatic memories. Again, one more time, I am encouraging each of you to stay with the exercise by the numbers. Once you believe you have become proficient in using the nine-stepper and are having fewer issues with those memories, you can also do a shorter exercise to further help you let go."

Doc: "In the eleven-stepper, the shortened form was very similar to the long form with a few less steps. With the nine-stepper, this is not the case. This one will be something a little different because in this exercise, we know that memories cannot exist at Center. There is no past or future at Center. There is only the now."

Frank: "If they can't exist at Center, how can we in the nine-stepper actually work with those memories from Center?"

Doc: "Remember, when you take a memory to Center, you discover through a longer process that the memory can't exist there. The very act of observing the memory from Center begins the work of not identifying with it. Remember in the earlier groups all the work we did with observing situations and noticing how by observing them, we could begin to separate ourselves from that situation?"

There were nods all around.

Doc: "So by the act of observing, we begin separating from the memory. Continuing with the nine-stepper, we experience the physical and emotional release from the memory at Center which helps us to further separate from the memory. Then we pick the still frame and move it further and further away and think, 'I'm letting you go,' or some phrase to support the separation from the memory. All of that supports the idea that memories can't exist at Center.

Doc: "To more directly answer Frank's question, you can define your work with your Center in any way you choose whether it seems logical or not. The key is to pick what works in helping you to stay

Centered. For the purpose of this shorter exercise, it is helpful to remember that memories can't exist there so you take a different approach. I'll tell you about this approach in a minute. Are you all with me on this? Frank, did that answer your question?"

Frank: "I can do 'whatever' with my Center as long as it works."

Doc: "Here is an example of the shorter version. Close your eyes and take Focker to Center. Experience being Centered....Now bring in a memory and repeat statements like, 'It dissolves and vanishes, memories can't survive at Center, the memory is weaker and weaker, the memory diminishes more and more, and I am not my memory. The next step is to say or think, 'I'm letting it go.' Repeat the part of the exercise where you bring in the memory and finish by saying 'I'm letting it go.' With your eyes still closed, I'll take you through a few repetitions. Now bring in the memory and repeat statements like, 'It dissolves and vanishes, memories can't survive at Center, the memory is weaker and weaker, the memory diminishes more and more, and I am not my memory. Then say or think, 'I'm letting it go.' Now bring in the memory and repeat statements like, 'It dissolves and vanishes, memories can't survive at Center, the memory is weaker and weaker, the memory diminishes more and more, and I am not my memory. Then say or think, 'I'm letting it go.' Now bring in the memory and repeat statements like, 'It dissolves and vanishes, memories can't survive at Center, the memory is weaker and weaker, the memory diminishes more and more, and I am not my memory. Then say or think, 'I'm letting it go.' Open your eyes."

Doc: "I have on the newsprint the quick and easy steps of the nine-stepper. Use this exercise with one memory at a time. I'm passing out now for your notebooks a copy of what's on the newsprint."

1. Take Focker to Center.
2. Experience being Centered.
3. Bring in a memory.

4. Repeat statements such as, it dissolves and vanishes, memories can't survive at Center, the memory is weaker and weaker, the memory diminishes more and more, I am not my memory.

5. Say or think, "I'm letting it go."

6. Repeat steps 3-5 about ten times.

Doc: "One more time. Remember to use the longer version of the nine stepper for the more serious and intrusive memories. When you're making some progress, you can switch to the shorter version of the nine-stepper with those same memories. At some point, you will notice that those memories and related symptoms of combat are diminishing."

Ace: "You mean the time when we no longer have symptoms related to the war?"

Doc: "Yes or those symptoms are negligible."

Frank: "How can a memory vanish and then get weaker and then diminish?"

Doc: "It vanishes in that experience at Center. But it may still be alive in your memory bank. So the suggestion is that when it vanishes in your momentary experience, it diminishes in your memory bank. Does that make sense to everyone?"

Me: "Yeah, I have this one memory not related to the war that I keep playing over and over and it would vanish in that moment but it wasn't gone in my memory bank 'cause Tug kept bringing it up. I was surprised later after more training the memory started to lose some of its power."

Ace: "Is it true that memories can exist at Center if we want them too?"

Doc: "Yes. This was a training exercise to show you at Center, you have the power to choose to dissolve and make those memories vanish and diminish over a period of time. So, you want to keep some memories at Center, as we discussed in an earlier group, about the identity of your family and friends, your profession, where you live, etc.

Be careful, however, with the memories you choose. At Center, you have this wonderful opportunity to see each moment with a fresh and new perspective without the impact of memories."

Chad: "So that means even though at Center you have practical memories about relationships and job, it's still important to experience each one in the moment with a new and fresh experience."

Doc: "Yes. Regardless of the context of the experience or the situation, you have the ability in each moment to see it in a different way."

Chad: "So if Lanco is experiencing my job as boring, the goal is to get Centered where boring can't exist and look for ways to see it in a different way?"

Doc: "Yes. Remember, at Center there's no data, no thoughts, no nothing that can create boredom. Focker is the only one who can create boredom."

Rob: "What if I'm on my motorcycle and it's the most beautiful and perfect day for riding. I might think to myself that it don't get much better than this. Are you saying I need to remember that it can get better?"

Doc: "Yes, in a way. But it's helpful not to compare experiences. Then you let go of one being better than another. The experiences are just different. That way you're not trying to recreate the same great experience. You're open to creating something different. That keeps you from saying that this ride wasn't as good as that one yesterday. Instead, you might say this one was different from yesterday. Not better or worse or even about the same. It was just different."

Rob: "Is that really important?"

Doc: "That concept is part of the training. If you can do it in that kind of situation, it might help you do it in some situation you believe is more important. The idea is to live in the moment where ideally you don't remember yesterday's ride. You are totally focused on the ride today, right now, in this moment. And if someone were to ask you, 'How was your ride today?' You might say, 'Nice, the sun felt good and the fresh air was wonderful.' Then they might say, "You said your ride yesterday was nice too. How do they compare?' You could say, 'I don't know. I don't remember my ride yesterday.' Or you could say, 'All I remember is that it was nice too.'"

Doc: "What if someone came up to you and said, 'What was it like over there?' And you answered, 'Over where?'" We all smiled. "Why sure, Rob remembers that ride and sure, you remember what it was like over there, but the goal is to let it go, release it, diminish it, and let it fade away. For now, for the most part it has no relevance in your life. It is part of the past and as one wise person once said about his past, and I quote, 'it ain't real and I'm fuckin' done with it.'"

Frank: "What do you mean for the most part it has no relevance?"

Doc: "I was referring to the bond you felt with comrades and to life lessons learned. Other than those, in my view, there is no relevance."

Chad: "I've been in the habit of totally identifying with my past so in the last couple of weeks, one of my goals has been to go to Center and focus on how I feel in the moment. Sometimes, Lanco Focker will stir up feelings of insecurity and worthlessness related to the break up with my ex-girlfriend and I get caught up in them. I'm working on the nine-stepper with those feelings by going to Center where they dissolve and vanish and I let them go. I like those words in describing what happens to feelings at Center."

Frank: "But sometimes, it's okay to identify with our past."

Ace: "I know I've said this before, but I don't mind identifying with those things in my past that I'm proud of or those personality traits that are working well for me. But to live in the moment, I don't need to identify with anything in my past other than lessons learned through different experiences. I might like to reminisce about some things. I might smile in that moment and say to myself. 'You did pretty well.' But I don't think they add any value to my life at Center. I really like the idea that in each moment I can create, to use the phrase one more time, something new and different."

Doc: "That's a good example of Ace defining his own Center. He may agree with a lot of my suggestions, but he may also continue to tweak his own view of Center as he searches for different ways to effectively use the skill of Centering.

Doc: "We talked in an earlier group about self-esteem which is a concept caught is self-identification with the past. Remember that Focker is the one who is concerned about self-esteem. Whether she thinks she has good or bad self-esteem doesn't ultimately matter to her. The subject of self-esteem keeps her in charge of your life. When you discover at Center that self-esteem is irrelevant and unimportant, Focker loses control of that aspect of your life. Ace, is that what you were suggesting a few minutes ago?"

Ace: "Yes, but I didn't make the direct connection of self-esteem to Fark Focker. That was helpful."

Doc: "Anything else on self-esteem?" Silence.

Doc: "Let's work on the nine-stepper. We'll do these exercises with three different partners. Pick out partners that you haven't gotten to know very well. One partner will be designated A and the other partner will be B. A will do a nine-stepper on a traumatic memory and like earlier, take your partner with you. After doing the nine-stepper, A will take the handout I gave you a few minutes ago and do a shortened form of the nine-stepper with a different memory of less intensity."

Nate: "Do we have to repeat those steps in the short form ten times?"

Doc: "Yes. The repetition is an important part of the training. When A has finished, then B will do the same exercises. Any questions?"

Doug: "On the short form, the memory is like a 'still frame' of the experience. Is that right?"

Doc: "Yes, it can be. In that moment, do the best you can to see it and feel it in that second or so and then it dissolves and vanishes. Pick your own way to dissolve it. I use the Star Trek image they showed when putting people in what I call the transport capsule. Use whatever works."

Nate: "I like the idea that the picture moves away from me like a shot out of a rocket and it's gone."

Doc: "Whatever works."

Doug: "I'm getting better, but I still struggle some with seeing the image or picture."

Doc: "Keep working on it. Remember the movie screen or one of those big TV's directly in front of you. For any of you who may be struggling with the images, do the best you can. Remember to also try to feel what the experience was like and then that feeling also dissolves and vanishes and you feel peace. Even though we are saying this is a shorter way to practice letting go of memories, take your time and don't hurry it. In the end however, do what works best for you."

Ace: "And we will know if it's working by paying attention to the frequency of reoccurrence?"

Doc: "Yes. I've had you write in your notebooks each week the number of occurrences of intrusive thoughts, panic attacks, flashbacks, and nightmares. Continue to do that so you will be able to chart your progress."

Doc: "Anymore questions or comments?"

After we finished doing the exercises in three different pairs, we had our group discussion and everyone seemed to be getting it.

Doc: "Any questions on what we did today? Okay. Get out your notebooks and write down the assignment for next week.

1. Continue to use hourly chime for deep breathing reminder.
2. Each day, listen to at least one of the Centering Meditation CDs.
3. Each day, practice one nine-stepper and one shortened form of the nine-stepper. You decide on which memories you want to use. I'll ask you about it in our individual session.
4. Write in your notebook a summary of any progress you have made since we started working together.
5. Record any panic attacks, flashbacks, nightmares, or intrusive thought episodes in your notebook.

Doc: "We have two more group sessions. At the end of the last session, I want us to have another picnic outing at the Park. Please invite your families and any close friends. Next Saturday, I need a count which does not have to be precise, but gives me a ball park figure. The food will be catered. Go in love and peace."

Soon afterward, Doc was gone. Everyone stayed for another fifteen or twenty minutes.

66
THE KNOLL

Ace told me they were busy at the mill and he was expected to work this afternoon. He said he and April would see us around 6:00.

I asked Anna if she had time to stay a few minutes and talk. She said, "I do. That would be nice."

I said, "Last week, you helped me more than you will ever realize. At times, I didn't know if I could go on. You gave me hope I could survive regardless of the outcome. You told me to be patient and understanding with Eden. I knew you understood what I was going through and could identify with my pain. I think that helped the most. I wasn't betrayed and I have no long history with Eden and no children so I can only have a partial understanding of what you're going through. I hope that helps some."

"That's sweet Jett. I'm glad I was able to help. Maybe you're right, maybe the most important gift is the empathy."

"Do you want to talk about what is going on now with you and Brandon?"

She answered, "I had a session with Doc yesterday and it helped to get it all out. But I'll bring you up to date." She told me about several conversations she had with Brandon and told me he was trying and was sorry and wanted it to work. She continued, "We had sex a couple of times and it was nice. But this week, I have been more hurt than angry. I have cried a lot and wondered as I told you earlier if I really do still love him or if I'm going to try for the sake of the children. Brandon is going with me next week for a session with Doc. I guess we'll see what happens."

At that point, Eden pulled up in the truck.

Anna asked, "Is that Eden?"

"Yes."

"I'm glad to have a chance to meet her."

Eden got out of the truck and came toward us and said, "Would you guys like for me to take the dogs for a walk?"

As she came up the steps, Anna said, "No that's fine. Hello Eden, I'm Anna." She reached out and with her one arm gave Eden a hug and continued, "It's so nice to meet you. I've heard a lot about you and I want you to know how happy I am for you and Jett."

"Thank you Anna. I've never been happier in my life."

Anna said, "I have to go. Eden, Doc told us before he left that we will have a picnic at the end of our last session and our families and loved ones will be invited. I look forward to getting to know you better. I need to get going." She hugged me and said, "Thanks for your kind words." And as she was walking down the steps she turned and said, "I don't mind if you want to share my situation with Eden."

We watched her pull away. Eden said, "She seems nice."

"You will like her. I'm happy that you all will have a chance to get to know each other at the picnic." Smiling, "That is if you accept my invitation."

She smiled and took my hand and led me down to the truck to help bring in groceries and a shopping bag, "I'll have to give your invitation serious consideration."

Before I opened the truck door, I took her in my arms and said, "I missed you."

She teased, "You did not. You were busy with your group living in the moment."

I teased back, "Okay, but I did think about you once."

"In what context were you thinking about me?"

I replied, "Well, I'll give you a hint. You didn't have any clothes on."

"I should have known."

I kissed her and said, "It feels so wonderful to hold you and kiss you."

She teased again, "Yes, it's not bad. All right, time to get these groceries in the cabin and put away." When we walked in the cabin, she said, "The cabin looks just like it did when I left."

"Yeah, everybody pitches in to straighten up before they leave." We put stuff away and I asked, "So what would you like to do now?"

She cuddled up to me and put her head on my chest and I put my arms around her and she said, "My first choice is to make love all afternoon, but I have a small problem. I'm pretty sore down there right now. The way I see that for you is it's good news and bad news. The good news is it means since I'm sore after two times that I'm not use to sexual activity and you already know the bad news."

"That's not bad news. That's just news."

"All right Dr. Hollander, I get it. That's a cousin of there's no good weather or bad weather, right?"

I responded, "You got it!"

"Since we planned on taking the children to the knoll for a picnic, are you still up for that?"

"I sure am. That sounds great."

"I have to be back here by 4:00 so I'll have time to make a blueberry cobbler for supper. April and I have already planned our menu."

We got everything together and headed out the door. Spot and Cher were excited. We took our time getting there and it was a little overcast but pleasant. Eden had brought some wine, French bread, and Jarlsberg cheese. She also brought a couple of treats for Spot and Cher. We spent some time working with Cher about not getting too close to the edge. She did well.

We took turns feeding each other with kisses in between and after eating did our traditional activity of watching clouds.

She asked, "You remember when we watched clouds the last time?"

"Sure do."

She continued, "When it started to rain and we were under that blanket together and I was leaning against you and your arms were around me, I felt like I had died and gone to heaven. The man I was falling in love with, the man who was becoming the most important person in my life had me safely enfolded in his arms and all I wanted was for that moment to never end. And then somehow we ended up kissing and I melted and I longed for more of those gentle kisses. I love soft and gentle kisses."

"You've made that clear and I'm glad, because to me they're much more passionate."

She continued, "Bunny Focker spoke up on the walk to the truck and said, 'You idiot, I told you he's too young for you. Sure he would love to get in your pants, but trust me, it wouldn't take him long to find some young thing.' That's when I went back into my shell."

"So Bunny Focker was the problem all the time; sounds like you and April have been figuring out the Focker figures. I love the name Bunny."

"You might love the name, but she can cause problems. Anyway, April explained to me more about our Fockers. Understanding what was happening helped me figure out what I really wanted. April and I talked a lot about Bunny and her Focker, Foxy, over that twenty-four hour period."

I said, "Well, I'll always be glad you had that time together."

"Me to," she answered and then continued, "I still wanna pinch myself. This moment really is my dream. The last time we were watching clouds, I wanted to do this." She rolled over on top of me and nestled her head in the crook of my neck and shifted her body around getting comfortable and said, "And I wanted to tell you to watch clouds and describe them to me."

"Okay, its overcast as you well know, but let me look and see if I can see anything interesting. It's getting really dark and I can't see anything."

She said, "It's dark for me too. Let me guess. Your eyes are closed too."

"You got it. I want no visual input. I just want to savor this moment and be open to experience the woman of my dreams in my arms. And I wanted to do something I couldn't do so I'll do it now." I reached down and lightly stroked the curves of her buttocks. I thought for god's sake Jett, you could at least say butt instead of buttocks.

She softly said, "That feels good."

I chuckled and she said, "What?"

"When I was growing up, Mom always called them buttocks. But since being a teenager, all my friends called the buttocks an ass. So that's what I've gotten used to and yet with you, I don't think of touching your ass. I think of touching your buttocks."

She laughed, "I think I like 'ass' better than 'buttocks' although I think of that as a compliment to my southern belle image. Why Jeeeeeeeett, I can't beeeeelieve you would ever call my buttocks an ass. How crude and un-lady like and if you're upset by that you can just kiss my ass."

"I'm extremely upset. Can I kiss your ass now or do I have to wait till later?"

In her most lady-like accent, "Why Jett, I'm so embarrassed you would take me literally on that, but since you did, later would be fine."

We spent the rest of our time at the knoll looking at clouds and kissing and holding each other. We were back at the cabin a little after 4:00. Eden started on the blueberry cobbler and I went outside and did some chores. It was strange. Now that we were free to be together, we were free to be separated for a short while. Until this time, I would have never left her side if I had a choice.

67
APRIL AND ACE

April arrived a little before 6:00 and said Ace was still at work, but would be here around 7:00. I had plenty to do outside and I could hear them in the kitchen laughing and having a good time. I had worked up a sweat so I took a shower before joining the girls in the kitchen.

Ace arrived, took a shower and joined us. We sat at the kitchen table, had a drink and talked about our weeks. April left for a minute and when she came back said, "Ace and I have a surprise for you. I'll let you tell them Ace."

"Last night, I asked April to marry me and she shocked me by saying yes."

Ace and April

April said, "We wanted you two to be the first people to know so I took off the ring before I left the house this morning so we could surprise you. I have to admit Eden that I was dying to tell you this morning on the phone, but Ace made me promise to wait till tonight."

We all hugged and I made a couple of toasts and it was a wonderful celebration. After dinner, Ace said, "Jett, I bought a couple of cigars. Would you girls mind if Jett and I went for a walk and smoked our cigars? We'll help with the dishes when we get back."

April replied, "You guys go ahead and have your boy time. That will give us a chance to have some girl time."

I said, "We'll take the dogs and Eden, I'll keep a watchful eye on Cher."

As soon as we got outside, we lit up and I said, "Let's walk up this other trail. Okay with you?"

He said, "Sure. Well are you surprised I asked her?"

"No, I'm not surprised. You've made a lot of changes in the last two months. You've discovered your real self and without Fark to contaminate your life, you're free to feel what's been there for years. In my view you two were always meant for each other. I just didn't know if you would figure out how to make it happen."

He said, "I wanted April to know that I was ready to commit my life to her. Doc has really helped us get clear, find and learn the skills that will help us interrupt all those old patterns that got in our way. We have a ways to go and I guess couples always have challenges, but we are completely committed to do whatever it takes to finding happiness together."

I smiled, "And I'm so happy for both of you. You can see it written all over your faces when you look at each other."

"For the same reason, it looks like you and Eden are doing great. You look like you've just discovered the secret for a happy life."

I said, "So far, it's been incredible."

"The war gave us the gift of a lot of lessons learned. It forced me to grow up and face who I was and who I was becoming. I'm just lucky as hell I lived to make the discovery. I wish I could tell you I'm totally over this alcohol problem, but I've got a ways to go. Most nights I can stick with my two beer limit, but it seems that about one or two nights a week, I end up getting drunk. Sometimes I go to Stanley's and at other times, I'm with April at her house."

I asked, "How is April doing with that?"

"She's been to several Al Anon meetings and told me she would be supportive of my recovery, but she was not going to nag me and try to get me to stop drinking. She said I had to make that decision on my own. I think she is overall pleased with my progress, but I'm not going to kid myself and pretend I don't have a problem. This engagement is part of my commitment to me and to her that I will take care of business when it comes to alcohol."

I said, "I will help too. Just let me know what you need from me."

"I will. Thanks."

We walked a little further up the path and came to a partial clearing on the ridge. This was a little higher than the cabin and the view was magnificent. I said, "This is one of my favorite spots on the property."

He agreed, "We've spent a lot of time with our legs dangling over that rock over there talking about our dreams for the future. I think that happened mostly when we were in high school. I don't remember us talking about becoming Army Rangers."

"I think it was more about us traveling the world as a couple of bachelors and getting laid with different girls in different countries."

He replied, "Yeah that seems more like it."

"I've had this idea for a long time and now I want to share it with you. I would like to give you and April for your wedding gift five acres of land on this spot, hoping that you will want to build your house here. The property would be about two hundred feet or so along this ridge and two acres on both sides of the mountain. Whatta ya say?"

There was a short pause and he had a look of shocked surprise. "I'm stunned. I'm speechless. Oh my God! April is going to go ape shit over this." He gave me a hug and said, "I thought all this land belonged to Pop."

"It does, but he told me I will inherit the cabin and one hundred acres along this ridge and that if I want to do something with it before he dies, its fine with him."

He said, "I still don't know what to say. You know how much I love this land. This is like my home. This is where I feel I belong. What a wonderful gift Jett. Thank you." He gave me another hug.

"You know I'll always want you and April close to me and hopefully to Eden and me. I want to spend my life with you guys and I hope we can grow old together. We're family in every important aspect of the word. You are my brother and always will be."

We started our walk to the cabin and I continued, "I would rather you tell April about the wedding gift when you're alone. I haven't told Eden and I'll wait till you all leave."

By the time we got to the cabin, our cigars had become stumps in the side of our mouth. We tossed them before walking in the cabin. April said, "You all stink. I hate those nasty old cigars."

Ace said, "April, if you would just try one, I'm fairly certain you would change your mind."

She said, "Well Eden, I guess we ought to get us a couple of big stogies and light up next time the boys wanna have sex with us."

Ace and I did some quick back peddling with that image.

We played spades till about 10:30 and it was the men against the women. We had a great time teasing and laughing. About halfway into the game, we had the blueberry cobbler with some vanilla ice cream. It was delicious.

Before they left, we planned a hike and picnic for tomorrow afternoon around one. We stood on the front deck and watched them disappear around the curve.

I asked, "Would you like to sit out here on the deck for a few minutes?"

Sure, "If you'll let me sit on your lap."

"My pleasure, I'm sure." We kissed for awhile and it all felt so comfortable, sensuous and right. I was home. I was Centered with the love of my life living completely in the moment. I was at peace and content. We sat there for awhile in a comfortable and soothing silence. I told her about offering Ace the land up on the ridge as a wedding gift and I didn't want to say anything to April. "I wanted Ace to be the one to tell her."

She said, "That's so exciting. So, if by some chance we figure out a way to make our relationship work, April and Ace will be our neighbors."

"Are you saying that if we do work out you would agree to live with me in the cabin?"

She replied, "I guess I am because it doesn't make any sense for me to build a house on our knoll. Bunny says for me to go ahead and build because you could turn out to be a real butt hole or asshole."

"Bunny and I are going to need to have a talk."

"She wants to say something to you. Go ahead Bunny."

Bunny said, "I have no reason to talk to you about anything and if you end up hurting us, I will find a way to make you pay. She may be all loving and sweet, but I can be a bitch if I need to. Don't forget it Jett Hollander!"

I smiled, "Okay, I got it. She doesn't pull any punches. She and Tug need to hook up. I take that back. She and Tug do not need to hook up."

She smiled, "I'm putting her to bed. Speaking of bed, are you about ready?"

"I am." I asked, "How do you feel about skipping church tomorrow?"

"That's fine. What did you have in mind to replace church?"

"Lying around, taking it easy. I'm already hoping Monday will be a long time coming. I hate to think of being away from you during the day."

She said, "I know. I dread that too. And I've got a super busy week. I've got to get moved into my office, finalize the hiring of an assistant, and get a new cell phone. Being gone last week has put me behind. I've been hesitating to tell you that I have to go to Greensboro on Thursday morning and won't be back until Friday evening."

"At least it's only one day. I was without you four nights last week so it helps to remember that. I can help you move your stuff to the new office. I think you said it was furnished so at least you won't have to deal with office furniture."

"Yes, I'm glad about that. Let me straighten up and put up some dishes that have been draining."

I took Spot and Cher for a short walk and then checked around the outside of the house. When I came in, I could hear her in the bathroom. I secured the cabin.

I sat on the edge of her bed and waited for her. She came out in this little skimpy outfit and seemed a little embarrassed. She came over and lifted my shirt and then unbuckled my belt and unzipped my pants and pulled them off. She wanted me to leave on my drawers.

She pushed me onto my back and laid on top of me and said, "I love laying on top of you like this."

We kissed and I put my arms around her. I wanted to feel every part of her pressing down on me. She rested her head on my chest and I ran my finger through her hair and asked, "How do you feel about spending most of your nights here?"

She answered, "I've been thinking about it and wondering what to do. I need to check on my kitties once a day."

I interrupted, "They can live here. My cat Journee would be here if he and Mom weren't so attached. Being gone three years didn't help. I was afraid that Spot wouldn't want to leave Mom and Dad, but he was ready to be with me. He loves the outdoors and they don't do much hiking."

"Let's take our time figuring out what would be best. I know I'll have to stay at Aunt Agnes' house." She paused. "I guess I just need to call it my house for now. Anyway, I'll need to stay at my house on Wednesday night before I leave."

"Would you mind if I stayed with you? I've been sleeping alone all my life and I want you near me every night if that's okay with you."

She smiled and said, "I'll think about it."

I rolled over and was on top of her and kissed her face and neck and brushed her lips with my tongue. I slid down some so I could circle her breast and nipples with my tongue and then lightly pulling the nipples with my lips.

She whispered, "That feels good. Pull just a little harder. That's it. That's it."

I continued with my tongue and with my fingers, I began lightly messaging and moving my finger tips over that area with her skimpy panties still on. She was responding by moving her ass in a circular motion. Shortly after that, I moved down her body with my tongue.

I gently shifted her body position so that her ass was on the edge of the bed and I positioned myself facing her with my knees on the floor. Leaving her panties on, she spread her legs as wide as they would go and with my tongue, I moved up and down her inner thighs. With my fingers, I continued with a kind of tickling motion on the outside of her panties and then lifting them slightly with my fingers, I lightly brushed up and down her pubic hairs with the backs of my fingers being careful to make brushing contact with her clit.

She was softly moaning and saying over and over, "That feels good." Then she said, "Take 'em off Jett. Take 'em off." I obliged and then took the tips of my fingers and started moving them in little circular motions on her inner thighs and began to tease between her legs with my tongue. I moved it in and out and again only lightly brushing her clit from time to time. With a quiet kind of desperation she pleaded, "More on the clit Jett, more of the clit."

I lifted her ass with a cheek in each hand and let her moans guide the movement of my tongue. I was in and out of her and using my tongue and lips to gently massage around and on her clit. Her legs were moving back and forth and she continued to guide my movements with her groans. And then she was coming with muffled screams emerging from somewhere deep inside. When the screams subsided, she reached down and putting hands on each side of my head said, "Come and kiss me and hold me." After that first deep kiss, she said, "I want you inside me now." And I said, "But you're sore and I don't want to hurt you."

She kissed me again and took one of her hands and reached down and guided me inside her. She thrust her body toward me so that I would go in all the way. It took my breath away as she kissed me again and again. I stayed most all the way in and our bodies came together in short mutual thrusts. In very little time, it felt like I exploded inside her and out of me came a deep guttural almost primitive groan as tears ran down my cheeks. It was in the ecstasy of that moment that I experienced again two becoming one flesh. Then we were simultaneously saying I love you over and over again and tears were running and then we started laughing. I felt like another release of some kind like we were having an emotional orgasm.

Neither one of us wanted to let go as we clung to each other and kissed the tears away. She asked, "Have you ever heard the phrase that the music exists between the notes?"

"No I don't think so."

"Well, I just experienced that love exists beyond the flesh. I guess I knew that, but I had never actually known what that would feel like."

I said, "The guttural groan of mine was almost embarrassing, but it came out of me spontaneously and it felt like my soul had longed for that moment all my life, like I had finally found the ultimate gift of God. You are the core of that gift and I love you with all my heart and soul."

"And you too my darling Jett with all my heart and soul. I am forever yours."

We held onto each other and when one of us jerked, we opened our eyes and giggled, then got up to use the bathroom and get some water. I had never been so happy. Soon after that we were asleep in each other's arms.

68
LIFE UNFOLDING

We woke up the next morning around 8:00. We snuggled and kissed for awhile and couldn't stop smiling. We went for a run and hike with the dogs and spent a few minutes at the knoll. It looked like rain so we headed back to the cabin. A few minutes from the cabin, the rain poured. It was a warm morning and the water felt good to us so we just stood still, embraced, and enjoyed it.

She said, "This is so refreshing and I love mixing rain with our kisses."

"Me too," I agreed. She had on a tee - shirt and it was soaked. Her nipples were hard and I was getting hard and I said, "Someday, let's make love in a down pour."

She said, "We could go to that secret place where we had our picnic last week."

"That would be the perfect place."

She asked, "Are you ready to go inside?"

"Whenever you are."

We got some old towels and wiped off the dogs, even though they weren't as wet as we were. They had gone to the front deck. Then Eden took me by the hand and led me into the bathroom and turned on the shower and started taking my clothes off. She took hers off and we got in the shower.

We took turns bathing each other. She let me wash her hair. It was so sensuous to touch her and run my hands over her body. While washing my hair, she was stretching her arms to reach my head and her breasts stood out and I wanted to take one in my mouth and massage it with my tongue.

We dried each other and I carried her into my bedroom. When I put her on the bed, she pulled me down and positioned me on my back and sat on top of me."

"I love being on top so I can dominate you and be in charge. I never had that before and I'm enjoying it."

I said, "Whatever we do, let's be gentle. I don't want you to be sore."

She smiled, leaned down and kissed me. I kissed her breasts and then she sat on me and guided me inside her. We locked our fingers together with palms facing and she moved her arms and I was resisting and it seemed to turn her on. She was moving slowly and looking at me and saying, "I can't believe how good this feels. I love you and I love the way you fill me up. I feel so close to you."

Then she leaned over and kissed me and slid her legs down. I held her close and pressed her upper body against mine so the only thing she could move was her hips and legs. We kissed long and deep and only took a quick break to come up for air. She was moving in a rhythm and I was matching her rhythm with my body. She was moving a little faster and while continuing to kiss me, she started cuming. She came up for air to let out a groan and then planted her mouth on mine. Her tongue lashed around inside my mouth. She groaned in a humming sound and I started cuming and we were both groaning with an occasional gasp for air. And then she buried her head in my neck and held on tight and we lay there panting and trying to catch our breath.

"Oh, Jett, where have you been all my life?"

"I love you my sweetheart. My life will never be the same again."

She said, "I love you. I love you. I love you."

It felt like there was nothing else to say or do except lay in each other arms, be still and quiet and in our own way celebrate and enjoy the discovery of our love. We did and we slept and the next thing I knew it was 11:43.

I ran my fingers through her hair and whispered, "Hey there my little darling."

She opened her eyes, smiled, and said, "Hey Jett."

The phone rang. I asked, "Do you think I should get it?"

"You probably should, but hurry back."

It was Ace telling us they would be about an hour late and would see us at 2:00. We cuddled for awhile longer and then got up. Eden took another shower and I got the sheets off the bed and started some laundry. I dressed and took Spot and Cher for a walk. When we got back, Eden was in the kitchen fixing us a light breakfast.

April and Ace arrived a little after 2:00. She came in first and came right to me and gave me a big hug and said, "Jett, thank you so much for the incredible wedding gift. We are so excited." She hugged Eden and they were like a couple of school girls talking about being neighbors.

Ace said, "So much for thinking that April might want to build a house somewhere else."

I smiled, "You guys may feel like I have made you happy, but I can't imagine living my life without you all being a stone's throw from where we are. So you have made us happy by accepting the gift.

While the girls got the picnic together, Ace and I sat in the kitchen and the four of us talked. Eden said, "Get off your butt or ass if you prefer and put those sheets in the dryer."

I looked at Ace and dejectedly said, "I had hoped the honeymoon would last a little longer." I looked at Eden, "Yes dear, right away dear, whatever you say dear."

April gave Eden a high five and said, “We're getting' these guys whipped right into shape and since we'll be living so close to each other, we can do a tag team if needed.”

Ace said, “We'll be at Stanley's if you need us.”

April said, “No. First, we don't ever need you. Second, sometimes we will want you around if it suits us. Third, today we want you to join us so make yourselves useful and get all the stuff together. The food is ready to put in the basket.”

Ace and I replied in unison, “Yes dear, right away dear, whatever you say dear.”

Ace said to me under his breath, “We're fucked!”

April said, “What was that Ace Frost?”

Ace paused for a couple of seconds and replied, “I said, we suck.”

April said, “Well, I think Eden and I appreciate some humility in you guys from time to time.”

We decided to have our picnic on the building site. Eden and April spent a lot of time walking around talking about designs and where to put the house.

Ace said, “When I told April last night about your gift, she got really excited and had a hard time getting to sleep. I was wondering how we would qualify for a loan. Your dad and mine talked to me a couple of weeks ago, asking about plans for some day building a house. They said there were lots of ways to keep the cost of lumber reasonable.”

I said, “Being a veteran will be a huge help. I heard someone talking about VA loans. I also think there are a number of ways to keep the costs down. Isn't Matt Hendricks' dad a contractor? Matt was one of your favorite receivers in high school. With all the people we know, I think you'll be able to make your house affordable.

Ace said, “I saved up some money while in the Army and April has a savings so I think we'll be okay.”

We spent another hour on the site and then went back to the cabin. The girls wanted to go to the bookstore in Elverton and look at house plans. I called Mom and checked in. Ace and I took the bikes and went for a ride and then a short hike.

It was a good day. April and Ace left about 9:00. We were both exhausted. We sat on the sofa and talked about the coming week. I asked, "Will you spend the night here this week except for Wednesday?"

She smiled, "I guess so since you can't seem to be without me."

"You're right on that, but I've been thinking that I would stay here on Wednesday. That way we can keep the dogs here and also it will give you a little space."

She said, "What if I don't want any space?"

"Then, I'll stay with you."

She said, "Why don't we see how the week is going."

"It sounds good to me."

We talked over things each of us had to do this week. If the office was ready, I would help her move in on Tuesday after the session with Doc. She predicted this was going to be a long week for her and that she might be getting to the cabin late each night. I told her I would have supper ready and we could focus on getting enough rest. I said, "I love making love to you, but I also love just being with you and having you close is more important than anything else."

She reached up and touched my face and kissed me gently and said, "Thank you."

We kissed again and got ready for bed. We were too tired to put the clean sheets on her bed so we slept in mine. We kissed and cuddled and were asleep in no time.

I took her to her house around 7:00 in the morning. I helped get her things into the house, kissed her and left. As I was about to pull out of the driveway, she came running out of the house and exclaimed, "I want one more of those soft, gentle, lingering kisses to think about during the day."

I went over to the Inn and checked on Pop. He was having breakfast. I filled him in on the events of the past few days and gave him a "heads up" on giving April and Ace five acres up from the cabin. He was fine with that. We agreed to walk around the lake this afternoon if he was up for it. I went by the house to see Mom and then went to the Inn and got my orders from Charlie. It was a good day and I had a lot of wonderful memories floating around in my head.

Eden got her new cell phone first thing this morning and we talked several times during the day. In our second conversation, at the end she said, "I should be home around 7:00." Her using the word "home" was of course music to my ears. After work, Pop and I went for our walk and I stopped by to see Mom for a few minutes. When I got home, I took the dogs for a walk and then went for a run.

I had supper ready when she pulled up. The dogs and I went out to greet her. We kissed and she said, "I missed that today. I can't wait till the weekend when we don't have to leave each other." She said there was a large suitcase filled with clothes and stuff in the car. I had already made the bed and I sat on it and watched her unpack and put clothes away in the drawers and personalize her room with pictures and little knick-knacks.

We ate supper and went for a walk and talked about our day. She was pleased that the office would be ready in the morning and that her new assistant would start on Tuesday. She wanted me to help her move into the new office in the morning. I told her that Doc would be here at 9:00 and that I would go first and should be able to meet her at the house at 10:30. Everything she had would fit into my truck so we decided to move her and then have lunch together.

I said, "I was thinking today how you have totally occupied my mind ever since I saw you at church on that Sunday. I thought about how your career is already set and established and that I didn't have a real job yet. I have been talking to Doc about going to graduate school at Elverton for a Masters in psychology. He has been very supportive and thinks I could complete my course work in two years and be able with clinical experience to get my license in three years."

She said, “So your undergraduate work was in psychology?”

“Yeah.”

“What’s your next step?”

I responded, “I called Doc today and he said I had no time to waste if I wanted to get started this fall. He called me back later in the day to tell me he had arranged an appointment with the Chair of the department tomorrow at 3:00. Following that appointment, I am to meet with an advisor who will help me get my schedule set up for the fall.”

She said, “You’re moving quickly. Does that mean I’ll hardly ever get to see you?”

“No, if that were the case I’d keep working for Charlie until he retired and take his job. I’m so fortunate that Charlie can always use me so I’ll have a lot of flexibility with my work schedule and plan to spend time studying when I’m not with you.”

She said, “You’ve been giving this some thought.”

“Yeah, I’ve been thinking about the career path for awhile, but I hadn’t done anything about it till today. It feels good to have those meetings set for tomorrow. It’s time and I want to be able to contribute more to our finances and I want you to be proud of me. The GI Bill will help me with tuition and books and I have some money saved so I shouldn’t need to borrow any money.”

She turned and pulled me into her arms and said, “I’m already proud to be with you. You remember Sunday before yesterday how I wanted to go to church and have everyone see me on your arm.” Then she kissed me and whispered in my ear, “I love you.”

I said, “And I love you sweetheart.”

We finished our walk content to be silent arm in arm walking down the path to our “home.”

Eden called April and they talked for awhile. I got a beer and watched a little baseball. I could tell by their conversation that things were not going too well at their house. Eden got off the phone and said they had gotten into a fight after they left their appointment with Doc and Ace slammed the door and left. April wanted me to go down to Stanley's and check on him and take him to the cabin since we have the buddy session with Doc in the morning.

I told Eden not to wait up for me and I would bring him back as soon as I could.

When I got to Stanley's, Ace was sitting at the end of the bar by himself. This was a different scenario for Ace when he was in a bar. Usually, he was the life of the party, talking to people, laughing and occasionally getting angry and into fights. As I got closer to him, I could see he was not intoxicated and he looked depressed. Someone from the area of the pool table hollered, "Ace, I've been practicing and I'm ready to whip your ass."

Ace hollered back, "Another time Roscoe!"

I looked at Chip, "Could I get a beer?"

Ace said, "Did April call you?"

"No. She and Eden are on the phone a lot and Eden called her to check in and I guess got the word that you'd left mad. April wanted me to come down here and get you and take you back to the cabin to make sure you'd make the meeting in the morning with Doc."

Ace said, "It seems like we're doin' good 'til we go see Doc. Then stuff gets brought up and we either leave there mad or get in an argument on the way home about something that was said during the session."

"I think that's normal for couples having problems. It's a cousin of holding stuff inside to avoid conflict or facing 'whatever.' Remember, that's your biggest goal to stop doing that shit."

He responded, "I know."

"You and April talked several times about how you're trying to stay Centered when stuff comes up. Hell, that's true for all of us. And I get it now why Doc is always telling us we have to train to reach the point where we can be more Centered. You seem to be doin' better gettin' stuff out, but you're still struggling with the rest of us to stay Centered in other areas. Am I right?"

"Yeah, I just forget and go off. Then I run away and come here and wanna do what I've always done - punch out and forget." He gets Chip's attention and motions for another beer.

I said, "Doc has always said it will be a life-long challenge."

"I know. Sometimes I worry about myself. I still have this craving for alcohol and I wonder if Fark stirs up the pot so we'll have an excuse to drink. I wanna talk with Doc about that in the morning. I gotta get it figured out. I don't wanna take this problem into our marriage" He looked over at the pool tables and said, "There's a table open. Let's shoot a couple games."

We stayed till about 11:00 and headed home. Ace had three beers and I had two and he wanted to drive so I followed him. There was a lamp on in the great room, but otherwise the house was dark.

I crawled in and snuggled up to Eden. She turned over and pulled me close to her and asked, "Is Ace all right?"

I gave her a quick run-down and she kissed me and rolled over so I could cuddle from behind. It took her no time to get back to sleep and it didn't take me long. We got up early. I went for a run and she got ready for work. We ate a light breakfast and she was gone by 7:30. Ace got up around 8:30.

<u>Final Buddy Session</u>

Doc started off with a Centering Meditation and then met with us individually. Ace had agreed to let me go first.

We spent a lot of my session going over the symptom checklist I filled out in the beginning. Doc wanted me to go down the list and rate each symptom. He was interested in the areas of improvement and my explanation about what had helped. He also wanted to know any areas where the symptoms had gotten worse. None of mine were worse.

I said, "I'm still struggling with the 'exaggerated startle response.'"

Doc said, "Generally that one takes more time and patience. However, this is a good time to review the general process of healing that we've been working on over the last weeks. In most issues related to the challenges in your life, the first question to ask yourself is the same. 'What does it mean to be Centered in this situation?' So how would you answer that question?"

I responded, "I don't want to jump out of my skin every time I hear a noise. So the answer is to be calm and relaxed when I hear loud noises."

Doc said, "That covers the physical and behavioral aspect of being Centered. The next question is, 'What would be the content of your thinking?'"

I said, "My thinking would be along the lines of, 'I can be peaceful and safe even when I hear loud noises.' And something like 'As time passes, I will feel more confident about being Centered with loud noises.'"

Doc said, "Very good. Now the question is, 'What kind of training do I need to get Centered with those loud noises?'"

I answered, "Continued work on the deep breathing and Centering Meditations. The eleven-stepper would also help. I think all the training I've done to help with the panic attacks would contribute to helping me with this issue."

He said, "I agree, the more Centered you become in other areas of your life, the more Centered you will be with the startle response. As time passes, you can get more creative with your training ideas. You could ask Eden and Ace to help you. Figure out a plan with them so they can create some sudden noises that might startle you. Have them use more low key noises in the beginning. When you have made good progress with those, you can then graduate to the more intense noises and sounds."

I asked, "Could you give me more specifics on that?"

"Sure. Let's say you are walking in the woods and Eden says, 'In the next twenty minutes or so, I'm going to make some noises.' You and Eden then are walking in the woods talking and you want to stay Centered. Then Eden makes a noise of some kind twice during the twenty minutes. When you reach the point where you can stay Centered during that exercise with Eden or Ace, you are ready to move on to the next step. That step could be Eden making those low key noises without any warning. When you stay Centered with those noises, you're ready to move to the next level."

"What's the next level?"

Doc answered, "Once you get the idea of that training exercise, I think you'll be able to create the next steps. There are many variables. For instance, the next step could be the one I suggested about making louder noises with the twenty minute warning and then making louder noises with no warning. Once you decide what to do, all you have to remember is not to move on to the next level until you have made good progress on the present level. This training exercise is sometimes known as 'systematic desensitization.' You can also use some mental rehearsing like in the eleven-stepper with this technique."

The last part of our individual session, Doc had me lead him through a twenty minute Centering Meditation.

He said, "Jett, you have made great strides in your training. I'm especially impressed with the way you have learned to interrupt your panic attacks. Lots of people end up taking some form of an anti-anxiety medication, but you have been determined to do it without the medication. Good for you. I hope you will follow your plan to become a psychotherapist. I'll be glad to help you in any way I can. Let me know how your appointments go later today."

"Thanks Doc. I will. I'll always remember what you've done for me and all the soldiers in our group."

We embraced and Doc called for Ace. I left to go to Eden's.

69

JETT AND ACE MAKE IMPORTANT DECISIONS

We moved her into her new office and she introduced me to her new assistant, Charlotte. We went to lunch at a new sandwich shop on Main Street and tasted each other's food and shared some laughs and leaned across the table several times and kissed.

She said, "I talked with April this morning and she invited us to supper. I can't get there before 7:00 and she said that was fine."

"That sounds good. I have those two appointments this afternoon and then Pop and I are supposed to walk around 5:00. That will give me time to go for a run, take the dogs for a walk, and get a shower. Do you want me to meet you there?"

As we walked outside, she answered, "Yes. I will run by the house and check on the cats. I hope your appointments go well."

"Thanks." She tensed up when I put my arms around her and I quickly let go. She said, "It's all right Jett. I'm not used to this kind of affection in public. It's just a knee jerk reaction so put your arms around me again. I want to stop doing that."

I did, then smiled and asked, "How are you going to make it without seeing me until 7:00?"

"I can't do it. Take me to the cabin now. I'm tingling somewhere in my body. I just can't figure out where it is."

I replied, "Should I feel around and see if I can find it?"

She laughed, "I think I'll pass on that one. But you better let me go so I can stop thinking about making love and start thinking about doing my job."

"I love you sweetheart." We kissed and walked in opposite directions. I stopped after ten feet or so, turned around and watched her and then in a few seconds she turned around and blew me a kiss."

The meetings at the college went well. The Chair already had my transcript and suggested I go to the admissions office after seeing my advisor. The admissions office told me the GI Bill would be a substantial help with expenses. It seemed like everything was falling into place.

I got to April's about 6:45 and Ace was in the shower. I asked, "How are things going?"

She answered, "He just got here about ten minutes ago and said he was sorry about last night. He said his session with Doc this morning went well and he was eager to tell me about it."

"That sounds positive. He didn't have that much to drink at Stanley's. He's different April. He's not like the old Ace, but as you well know, he is struggling with the alcohol."

"I know he's going to make it. And our fighting is not all his fault. I'm still dealing with a lot of shit. We're moving. We just have to stay engaged with our goals to stay Centered. Will you ever tell Eden about you and me?"

"I've wanted to talk with you about that. I feel like it's confidential between you and me and Ace and I would never share it without getting the okay from you. I would like to tell her at some point. How do you feel about it?"

She replied, "Foxy Focker doesn't want you to say anything and I'm a little embarrassed, but I want you to tell her if you want to."

I asked, "How do you think she'll respond?"

"Well I don't think she'll respond like they do in the movies and get all pissed off, but I think it will take her a little time to adjust. If you don't mind, I would appreciate it if you would tell me when you tell her so I'll know. I have to admit that I'll be relieved when we have that conversation. Eden and I are getting really close and I think she feels exactly like me and doesn't want secrets between us."

I responded, "I'll definitely let you know when I tell her. I just have to wait for the right moment."

She observed, "It sounds like you might be nervous about telling her."

I paused and then responded, "Yeah, and maybe a little scared. I guess those two feelings are cousins. I've just found her and I can't imagine losing her."

"Like I said a minute ago, I think she'll be fine."

Ace walked in and asked, "What are you two talking about?"

I looked at April and asked, "Should we tell him?"

"I don't care. Go ahead."

I said, "We're having you committed to the Elverton Alcohol, Drug and Sexual Abuse Treatment Program for two years. Go pack your bags."

Ace asked, "Can I have one more beer before I leave?"

Eden rang the bell and opened the front door and said in her most cheerful voice, "Hey Everyone. How you guys doin'?"

I took her in my arms and gave her a big bear hug, "Hey Sweetheart. I missed you."

She gave me a kiss and said, "I bet I missed you more than you missed me."

Ace turned to April and said, "Maybe we oughta go ahead and eat while they figure out who missed each other the most."

Eden said, "Hold on Ass, I mean Ace. We'll figure that out later."

Things were a little subdued while we ate. April and Ace hadn't had time to talk. It was pleasant, but there wasn't the usual bantering back and forth between us. Everyone helped with the dishes and when we finished, Ace said, "Can we all sit down? I have something I wanna talk about."

He continued, "You all know I have been dealing with this alcohol problem. I keep thinking I'm doing better and then I'll get this craving to have a drink. I'm gonna say that Fark is the one with the psychological craving, but the physical craving comes from our body. So Fark is telling me right now, 'Shut the fuck up. This is nobody's business but ours.' I'm Centered right now and I'm not gonna pay any attention to him at the moment. Jett and I were talking last night and sometimes I think Fark starts fights with you April so he can suck me up into his world and we can go drink."

I said, "You didn't drink that much last night so Fark didn't get his way."

"Yeah, but I got into an argument with April and ended up at Stanley's."

April interjected, "It wasn't all you Ace. I was just as much at fault."

Ace responded, "April, that may be true, but Doc shared with me a saying that he thinks originated in AA. It was, 'I'm responsible for cleaning my side of the street.' So that's how I feel."

April said, "And I'm responsible for cleaning my side of the street. I like it."

Ace went on, "So Doc and I spent most of my individual session this morning talking about my abuse of alcohol and we agreed that there's a possibility that I'm an alcoholic. If that's not true, I definitely have a drinking problem. He was strongly encouraging me to start going to AA meetings. Fark was freaking out while he was talking and he adamantly says he will not go with me to any fucking AA meetings."

Eden asked, "How do you handle it when Fark won't go, but you have decided to go?"

April said, "Ace, let me try to answer that question. Eden, I'm still learning about this Focker model myself. So Jett and Ace, tell me if I'm wrong, but I think Ace will say to Fark that he doesn't have a choice. So Ace goes anyway and Fark sleeps through the AA meeting. I have some ideas about what's next, but it's still kind of hazy."

Ace reached over and took her hand and said, "Good work Peaches."

I interrupted, "Peaches. I like that."

April looking a little embarrassed said, "Ace loves peaches so he started calling me that."

I looked adoringly at Eden and said, "That's really neat. Eden calls me her banana."

She slapped me on the side of the head and exclaimed, "I do not call you my banana."

Ace looked at April and said, "Peaches, you can call me your banana anytime you want."

I said, "I guess we're not too far off the subject. Wine is made from grapes and each of you girls had a cherry at one time." I got boos from the girls and a high five from Ace.

April looking at Ace said, "All right honey. Go ahead and finish answering Eden's question."

Ace said, "April was right. Fark has to go to the meeting, but I can't make him listen. First, I have to figure out what it means to be Centered when it comes to alcohol. I'm assuming AA will have a lot to teach me and will help me with figuring that out. I'm not looking forward to going, but I have to do something. I trust Doc and he thinks AA will help me."

He continued, "Doc also said that he will make some calls and find out about the make-up of different groups and based on that will recommend several of the groups."

April asked, "What do you mean by make-up?"

Ace replied, "He thinks it would be helpful to start in a group made up of men close to my age. He wasn't sure he could find that group, but said he would do his best and at the least have a couple of recommendations."

Eden asked, "Once you know what it means to be Centered, how do you get Fark on board?"

Ace answered, "I don't know for sure yet. Doc has taught us a number of ways to work with our Fockers. I'll just have to figure out which of those ways will be most helpful. I'll be glad to let you folks know what works. I do know as I get stronger at Center with the alcohol issue, Fark will have trouble having as much influence on me."

We talked a little more and then Eden and I left.

After we got in bed, we talked about April and Ace and his decision to go to AA. Neither of us knew much about it, but were hopeful it would help him. We talked about her day and how she felt about her job in the new location. She was enthused and thought it was professionally going to be a good fit. Smiling and winking, she said it might also be a nice fit for her personally, but she needed a little more time to think about it. She gave me a warm and sexy kiss.

She said, "I had a visit this afternoon from Lance."

"What did he want?"

She answered, "He said that I must have known that he was interested in more than a friendship and that he wanted to make sure I was certain about you. On his way to my office, he saw us walk into the café and decided to wait. He sat on a park bench across the street from the café. He saw us come out and watched our interaction and it seemed to him that I had no reservations about you. He followed me to my office and decided to make sure his assumption was right."

Smiling and confident I asked, "And what did you tell him?"

"Do you want me to tease you or do you want it straight?"

"All I want is you."

We made love and went to sleep.

The plan for Wednesday was to meet at Sally's for supper. Eden had to get up early on Thursday morning so she could be in Greensboro by 9:00. We decided I would sleep at the cabin and she would sleep at her house. That evening we talked for an hour on the phone.

Near the end of the conversation, she asked, "What was our reason for sleeping apart?"

"Something about you having to get up early and get on the road."

She said, "Right now, that seems like a big mistake. I'm starting to tingle in a certain area and I'm willing to take care of business, but I would love to have some help."

Excitedly I said, "Hold that thought or hold that position or don't move your hand or...Hell, I'll be there in a minute."

The house looked dark. I used my key and went straight to her bedroom. The bedside lamp was on, but was covered with some red garment that gave a sensuous glow to the room. She was standing across the room in a full length bathrobe and as I approached her, she opened the bathrobe to reveal a black bra with an opening the size of a quarter so the nipples were protruding and a black lacey garter belt with black hose and no panties.

She said in a sexy voice, "I was saving this for a special occasion, but as someone said, 'there is no time like the present.'"

My clothes were off and the bathrobe fell to the floor and she jumped into my arms and wrapped her legs around me. We kissed and kissed each hungry for the taste of the other. Then she sat me on the edge of her bed and knelt between my legs and was tugging on my nipples with her teeth and I was running my hands through her hair. Then she slowly started moving down my body with her kisses and I leaned back resting on my arms.

When she got to the area between my legs, she teased me with kisses to my inner thighs while lightly caressing my balls and wrapping her hand around my dick with slow movements back and forth. Then she put it in her mouth and continued massaging my balls with her hands. I don't know how I kept from cuming, but after a few minutes I said, "I wanna cum inside you, I wanna cum inside you."

She gasped, "Take off my bra," as she continued making these incredible sucking motions.

Then she got up and grabbed some pillows and quickly stacked and straddled the pillows so her ass was up in the air and said, "I want you to fuck me from behind. Put it in now. Put it in now."

Instead I took my hands and spread her ass cheeks and buried my face into her and there was a muffled scream and then, "Jett, please fuck me, fuck me with your tongue, fuck me with your tongue." Soon after that, "Now, fuck me with your dick, now, please, now, Jett now!"

I moved in behind her and she yelled, "Pinch my nipples and fuck me. Pinch 'em harder." In a few minutes, we both exploded in ecstasy and passion. Exhausted, we rolled over and she turned to face me and we just lay there panting.

I said, "Incredible. Never in my life have I felt like this. I've died and gone to heaven."

She still a little out of breath said, "Me too."

Shortly after that, she said, "I'll miss you tomorrow night, but my body down there will probably need a little time to regroup." Then she started tickling me and continued, "So I'll be all ready for Friday night."

With a shit eatin' grin, I replied, "Sounds good to me."

We settled in and lay in silence for awhile and then I said, "I'm speechless. I tell you I love you and I do, but words simply can never express what I feel in my heart."

She said, "I feel the same way. I got a little carried away with the 'F' word."

I said, "I thought it was sexy and a 'turn on.' For me there is this incredible emotional and spiritual intimacy to our love making and then there's the dirty and raunchy side of having sex. For me they sometimes go together and sometimes are separate. Tonight for me, they both merged together."

She replied, "I'm not sure until I met you that I experienced any of the emotional and spiritual intimacy, but I did experience the other side. I think that's the only way I could get through it. I fantasized about other people because I was never that attracted to the men I was with."

I said, "Did you feel both sides of it tonight?"

"Yes, I did. Since we had never talked about it, I wasn't sure how you would feel."

Smiling, "Well, I'm glad we got that worked out. You wanna fuck again before we go to sleep?"

She laughed, "All right, don't take it too far." She hugged me and whispered in my ear, "Do you mind if we go to sleep?"

We awoke around 6:00. I fixed her breakfast while she finished packing. She was gone by 7:00 and I headed back to the cabin to check on Spot and Cher. After work, I went by to visit with Pop and then over to see April and Ace. He had been to his first AA meeting and said it wasn't too bad. It was mostly a younger group with a few old timers. Ace said they talked about him finding a sponsor and he already had someone in mind, but he was going to wait a little longer before asking him.

I asked, "What's a sponsor do?"

"I think he is like a mentor and someone you can call at anytime when you're struggling. Someone in the group said that a sponsor is someone who will not 'cosign your bullshit.' I think I'm gonna like these AA phrases."

I inquired, "Are you gonna have to give up drinking?"

"Yes, the goal is to stay clean and sober. That also means staying away from pills and shit like that."

I said, "Well, I'm not gonna drink around you."

"That's not necessary. April and I have already talked about it and she will still have an occasional glass of wine. I hope Eden will do the same. I don't like wine anyway so that's no temptation."

I replied, "That's fine and I know I don't have to, but I wanna do it. After all, neither of us had anything to drink for our two years over there. I don't even know if I missed it that much."

He said, "I did. Sometimes I felt like I would've killed for a cold beer."

April said, "I'm so proud of you for going to AA. It makes me feel even more special that you refuse to bring a drinking problem into our marriage."

Ace responded, "That's really important, but when I shared that with the group, they told me it was critically important for me to stay clean and sober because that's what I wanted for me. They emphasized I must first of all do it for myself. Benefits for loved ones would be icing on the cake."

I looked at both of them and said, "I wanted to give both of you a 'heads up.' I'm going to tell Eden tomorrow night about what happened between you and me April."

April looked at Ace, "While you were in the shower Tuesday, Jett talked to me about telling Eden." She gave Ace a summary of our conversation.

Ace said to me, "Not that it matters much, but I'm fine with you telling Eden."

I said, "It matters to me what both of you feel and think about it."

April said, "Ace and I have talked on and on about not having secrets from each other. I'm glad you're going to tell her. I'm just not looking forward to Saturday morning when she comes to pick me up for our girls' day out."

I left around 7:00 and ate supper with Mom and Dad.

When I got home, I called Eden.

She said, "Well, you're lucky I answered. I've had a lot of invitations for drinks and I'm getting that tingling feeling again and you're too far away to take care of my needs. What should a girl do? I probably shouldn't go to someone's room for a drink."

"I can be there in ninety minutes. Wait up for me."

She interrupted, "All right Jett. I'll be a good girl. I don't want you to drive all the way down here. But what am I gonna do about this tingling feeling?"

We ended up having phone sex which was a first for both of us. After things cooled down, we discussed plans for the weekend. We were going to have supper here tomorrow night. Ace and I were both going back to work after our group meeting. Eden and April would spend their Saturday together. The four of us would hike around 6:00 and either eat at the knoll or come back to the house.

70
EDEN'S PTSD

Eden pulled in around 7:30. We walked up to the knoll with the dogs. I told her about Ace and AA and she told me about her meeting in Greensboro. I had prepared supper and we ate out on the back deck. There were two beers in the fridge and I was going to polish them off so there would be no beer in the cabin when Ace arrived in the morning. Actually, I also had a glass of wine while we did the dishes, because I planned to tell Eden about me and April after we were finished with the dishes.

We decided to sit out on the front deck. It was a beautiful evening and Cher jumped up on Eden's lap. We were quiet for a few minutes and then she said, "All right. What's going on? You've been fidgety ever since I got here and I've never seen you chase beer with wine. My mind is going wild with guessing and it's scaring me a little."

I said, "Okay. I'm sorry. I'm not a good actor. I've been hesitating to tell you something that I want you to know." I started from the beginning and gave her all the details. She was quiet during the entire time and it was starting to get dark so it was hard to read her face.

After I was finished, she said, "I'd like to go inside. I have to pee and then we'll talk. Would you pour me another glass of wine?" She closed her bedroom door.

It must have been about fifteen or twenty minutes before she came back into the room. By that time, I was scared. When she opened the door, I could tell she had been crying.

I went and put my arms around her and kissed her forehead and held her close to me. I said, "Oh Eden, I'm so sorry. I never want to make you cry."

She kissed me on the cheek, looked into my eyes and said, "I'm not even sure why I'm crying. I don't cry very often and there are a number of times in my life when I should have cried, but didn't. Maybe I'm using this as an excuse to cry. After a brief moment, I think at some level I knew you and April must have been together. It's the way she looks at you sometimes. I've thought she must be in love with both of you guys, but had to choose one."

I responded, "She was clear with me the whole time that she loved Ace, but wanted the physical intimacy with me. As I said, I was confused and wondered if I had always loved her. The clarity for me came the first day I laid eyes on you in church. That sounds crazy, but I felt a kind of energy or connection with you that I've never felt before in my life."

We cuddled on the sofa and she said, "Sounds like you and Ace have spent considerable time trying to work it out between you. That must have been tough for both of you."

"Yes it has been tough. Even though I think Ace has made progress in forgiving me, I'll never forgive myself. From a rational point of view, Ace understands how it happened so there is no blame or pointing fingers. It's just difficult for us to get beyond the emotional pain. I don't care how much rationalization there might be, I will always see it as inexcusable on my part. I think it's different for April. I'm sure she'll tell you about it tomorrow."

She said, "I'm so disappointed in myself because I'm stirring up all these insecure thoughts like is she better in bed than me or do you think she's prettier than me or do you think she has a sexier body than me or would you still like to have sex with her or does she give better oral sex than me or is she more fun to be with than me or is she a better cook than me?"

I held onto her and kissed her tears and hated myself for putting her through this ordeal. She cried for a few more minutes and then the tears subsided and she clung to me and said, "These tears are a lot more complicated than this situation with you and April. It seems like it just opened the floodgates. Does April know you're telling me tonight?"

"Yes, and she's a little nervous about seeing you tomorrow."

She said, "Let me call her now. I don't want her to be nervous about seeing me."

I asked, "Are you sure?"

"Yes." She went to the phone and dialed. "Hey April, it's me. I'm all right. Jett just told me about you and him. No, no, I'm all right. I just started crying and I told Jett that these tears are related to much more than what happened between you all. I'm going to tell Jett tonight and I'll tell you tomorrow. No. I'm fine. Could we meet at your house in the morning instead of Josie's? Thanks. I'll see you in the morning."

She turned to me and said, "Let me go in and wash my face. I'll be right back."

"That's fine. I'll take the dogs out for a few minutes."

When I got back inside, she was sitting on the sofa. She said, "Jett, I love you. I have some problems with insecurity and I'm going to need you to be patient with me and try to understand. I'll get over this and I'm not going to let this get in the way of my relationship with you or with April. I will not allow it to happen."

I hugged her and kissed her softly on the lips. She clung to me again and we held each other.

She said, "At first, what really shocked me was my reaction to what you told me. I broke down and sobbed in the bathroom when the logical reaction would be to be surprised and maybe a little jealous.

I hadn't cried in years before Aunt Agnes died. I think her death was the first step in me facing the reality of my past. I didn't know it at the time, but after the funeral, I was able to push the trauma back into my mind."

"What trauma are you talking about?" Now it was my turn to wonder what she was going to say. "I still don't understand. What happened to you?"

"I am the oldest of six girls and our father sexually, physically, and emotionally abused us until we left home. It was a living nightmare. I told you we were poor white trash of Eastern North Carolina and my momma was for physical and mental reasons unable to stop him. Each of us perhaps with the exception of the youngest is mentally scarred. We have kept it a secret from everyone else including ourselves. A few of us have talked about it a little, but never in any depth. Jett, I was ashamed to tell you and afraid to say anything for fear you might have the same reaction as my ex-husband. In an intimate moment soon after we were married, I told him just a little about it and he said he never wanted to hear another word about it and I was devastated."

I scooted over to her and took her in my arms and she started crying and I said, "We will find a way to help you heal and I will stand with you and listen and encourage and comfort and love you with all my heart."

We went in and took a shower together and Eden said, "Let's allow the water to cleanse us and give us hope for the future." We washed each other and held each other and just stood under the water letting it work it's healing power. We got in bed without clothes, cuddled and thanked God for each other and for the love that we shared. I don't remember anything after that.

When I woke up, it was 6:05. I turned over and Eden wasn't in the bed. Maybe she was in the bathroom, but the door was open. Then I noticed a piece of paper on the night stand. It was a note. "Jett, don't worry. I had trouble sleeping. I'm at the knoll. I know you'll be up at

6:00 so go ahead with your run and on your way back, come by the knoll and we'll walk back together."

I flew out the front door and sprinted to the knoll. I found her sitting on the edge of a drop off looking into the distance. I didn't want to startle her so I yelled from the path and went to her. I put my arms around her and she was cold. She had been crying. "Sweetheart, when you're upset and can't sleep, please always wake me. I can't imagine what it was like in the hell you grew up in and from what you said, you've been carrying this trauma alone inside for all these years. I can't erase the trauma, but I can tell you that you'll never be alone again. I will be there every step of the way and we will get through this together."

She started sobbing and shifted around until she was sitting in my lap and put her arms around my neck wanting me to cradle her like a small child. I put one arm under her bent legs and the other around her back and under her arm and rocked her back and forth whispering, "My sweetheart, it's okay, I'm here. It's gonna be okay. I love you. Just cry and cry. It's gonna be fine. We will get through this. Everything will be fine." I kept rocking her and she couldn't stop crying or maybe she didn't wanna stop. The flood gates had opened and I was glad she had made the first step even though it was painful.

I don't know how long we stayed there, but I eventually stood up with her in my arms and carried her to the cabin. I set her on the sofa and told her not to move. I put on some coffee and went in the bathroom and turned on the tub water. She shuffled into the bathroom and said she had to pee and that she would call me when she got in the tub. I went to the kitchen and toasted a piece of bread and put butter and preserves on it like I had seen her do. I poured her a cup of coffee with cream and sweetener. I knocked on the door and she said to come in. She was soaking in the water and I sat down on the edge of the tub. She whispered, "This feels really good. Thank you for taking such good care of me."

"For the rest of your life, you'll have me."

She leaned over and said, "Kiss me." I did and she said, "I've got a lot of work to do. Before you got to the knoll, I remembered things Daddy did to me that I had not allowed myself to think about for years. I don't know what to do with those memories. Do you think Doc would help me?"

"I know he will help you. He told me in confidence the other day that he and his wife had decided to settle here. He wanted me to knowhe would mentor me through my graduate work."

I reached into the tub to check the temperature and said, "It's not as warm as it was. Can I add some hot water?"

"Thanks. Not too much. What time is it?"

"I looked at the clock while I was in the kitchen and it was 7:56."

She said, "Let me soak in here a few more minutes and then I'll get ready. It won't take me long and I'm not going to wear any make-up. Do you mind if I have a little time to myself?"

"No, not at all," I agreed. "Do you need more coffee or another piece of toast?"

"Thanks. I would like another cup of coffee, but no more toast." She looked at me and reached up with a wet hand and caressed my face and said, "Jett, I love you."

I said, "You have my heart always and forever." I didn't care what I had said earlier about it not being realistic to make a promise like that. That's the way I felt and I would never leave this woman. Not ever.

"I'll take the dogs for a walk and I'll check on you when I get back. Are you sure you're all right?"

A faint smile, "Yes, I'm sure."

On my way to the front door, I decided to let the dogs play out in the front and I was going to check on her every few minutes. I almost lost Ace and I wasn't going to lose Eden. I called April and Ace and asked April if she could come and pick up Eden. I didn't think she was in any shape to drive. I told her I couldn't talk right now. I quietly checked on her a dozen or so times and I could hear her moving around. The last time I checked, she opened the door and I was standing there listening.

She smiled and I said, "Oops, caught in the act." I explained about almost losing Ace and I wasn't going to lose her.

She put her arms around me and rested her head on my chest. "Please be patient with me. I'm scared. I now know I have been scared for a very long time. Thank you for not running away or rejecting me. With your help, maybe I'll finally be able to knock down these walls I have around myself."

I held her close to me and told her I would be with her every step of the way and I would never let anything happen to her.

She kissed me on the cheek. I asked, "Would you like some privacy to get dressed?"

"Would you mind?"

"No, not at all, I hope you don't mind, but I called April and asked her to pick you up. I'm afraid for you to drive right now."

"That wasn't necessary, but thanks."

About 8:30, April and Ace pulled up. Eden had not come out of her room yet and April knocked on the door and went in. I gave Ace a quick summary and they came out and Ace hugged Eden. I walked them to the car and Eden put her arms around my neck and said, "I want you to focus on your group. We'll get through this and I don't want you to worry. She gave me a kiss and got in the car. I watched them pull away. It wasn't until that moment that I allowed myself to think that she had a very serious case of PTSD.

71
GROUP SESSION SEVEN

As soon as they disappeared around the turn, people started to arrive. Anna was the first and I gave her a quick summary. She hugged me and gave me some words of encouragement. As others arrived, I asked Ace to go out on the back deck with me.

Ace asked, "You gonna be able to get through group?"

"Yeah, I've got to get Centered. I need to get as much out of these last two sessions as possible. I think I'm gonna need all the skills I can muster to keep going with my own healing and to 'be there' for Eden."

Ace looked off into the distance and said, "We've come a long way Jett. It's a whole new way of life for me and I'm still scared. The four of us have a lot of work to do, but we're gonna make it. We'll all help Eden and keep supporting and encouraging each other." We hugged and went back inside.

Doc arrived, looked around and asked Frank if he knew why Nate hadn't arrived.

Frank: "I haven't seen him since our buddy session on Wednesday."

Doc: "Has anyone else seen or heard from Nate?"

Rob: "We went for a bike ride on Sunday and I didn't notice anything different."

Doc: "I'll give him a call in a moment. Let's get started. Do a Centering Meditation and I'll let you know when to open your eyes."

It was hard to get my mind off Eden and now I was worried about Nate. Had he been in an accident? Did he get drunk last night? Did he hurt himself? I kept trying to get Centered, but was not able to quiet my mind. Tug said that he knew this was going to happen with someone in the group and it proved this shit was not going to work.

Doc: "Open your eyes. I called Nate and got his voice mail. How many are having trouble getting Centered?"

Everyone raised a hand. We discussed how we were all worried about him. Rob wanted to know if he should go down to Stanley's to see if he was there.

Ace: "Stanley's doesn't open till 11:00."

Doc: "Let's keep going for now. I'll try again during the break. I want you to do another Centering meditation. How many of you were trying to get to Center without the use of deep breathing to help?"

It seemed like everyone raised their hand.

Melinda: "We have practiced going to Center everyday for the past weeks. I have gotten good at just being able to close my eyes and go there. I haven't needed the breathing to help get Centered."

Others said the same thing.

Doc: "What am I getting ready to say?"

Anna: "Sometimes it will be more challenging to get to Center. In those cases use the deep breathing."

Doc: "Yes. Close your eyes and go to Center."

I used the breathing and it helped more with my frustration than anything. When I couldn't get my thoughts off Eden and Nate, I had something tangible to focus on. At least I knew that Eden was safe with April. When I got to Center, I brought Nate down with me and showed him around and asked him to feel accepted, cared for and to feel the peace. We sat there awhile in silence. Then I said to him, "Wherever you are, I hope you can feel this." I decided this was my prayer for him.

Doc: "Open your eyes."

Everyone said the breathing helped, but it was still a challenge.

Doug smiling: "I wanna tell y'all I've been sleepin' in the basement since I got back. That was the only place I felt safe. Last night, I came upstairs and slept with my wife." Hoots and Hollers (HH) from the group!

Doug: "I ain't gonna lie. I didn't sleep too well, but it's a start."

Me: "I'm still carrying my knife with me everywhere I go, but this past week before I went to bed, I didn't check the perimeter but one time." HH

Ace: "I went to two AA meetings last week and I asked my girlfriend to marry me." HH.

Chad: "I had a date last night. It didn't work out, but at least I tried. That was a big step for me. Melinda helped me on the drive up today. I'm going to selectively remember that I took the risk and forget that it didn't work out." HH.

Doc: "That's a good example of tweaking your Center in whatever way it works."

Anna: "My husband and I are going to see Doc for counseling and I think we have a chance of working it out. Wednesday night, we made love." Tears rolled down her cheeks and she struggled to get it out. "I let him see me naked for the first time since I lost my arm. He said all the right things and I was even able to have an orgasm." HH.

Rob: "I finally let my mom and dad have a welcome home party for me and I did pretty well. I only drank three beers. Several of my family and friends thanked me for my service and instead of wanting to punch them in the nose, I said, 'No problem.'" HH.

Frank: "I can't think of one specific thing to tell you. Remember when we first started the group and I was desperate for help saying that I didn't know what to do. The desperation is gone and I do know what to do. I feel like I've got a long way to go, but I'm gonna be okay." HH.

Paul: "I've stopped fuckin' Fanny Focker. I told her we ain't gonna hang out no more." HH.

Doc: "You guys are getting it done - one step at a time, one moment at a time."

Ace: "Let's hear it for Doc!" HH.

Doc: "Thanks. Back to work. What is your most important goal when you are struggling or wanting to make changes in your life?"

Frank: "Since I'm the expert in asking questions, one more time I'm going to try and answer a question."

Paul: "Yeah. That'd be good 'cause none of the rest of us knows the answer."

Frank: "I've forgotten my answer so I have to ask another question. Doc, what was your question again?"

Doc: "I'll buy a six pack of beer for the person who answers the question."

Group: Various ways of saying, "GET CENTERED AND STAY CENTERED!!"

Paul yells out, "I get Ace's six pack!!"

Doc: "Nobody gets a six pack. I lied. Anything to bring you soldiers back to the moment."

"Boooooooooooooooooooooooo!"

Doc: "Open your notebooks and find the handouts on Group Goals; Traits of the Centered State; Your True Self at Center; Focker's PTSD; and your Symptom Checklist."

Chad: "I left my notebook at home."

Melinda: "You can look on mine."

Doc: "Take a few minutes to look over those handouts and I want you to find situations that may be especially challenging for you."

Frank: "I noticed that you used the word 'situation' rather than 'problem.' Instead of asking why you did that, I'm going to again attempt to offer an answer. Since acceptance is one of the traits of being Centered, there is no such thing as a problem. There are only situations."

Doc: "What response do you have to Frank's answer?"

Anna: "Pee Wee thinks it's a fucked up answer. She says that's ridiculous; everyone has problems. I like Frank's answer. That's the way I want to understand losing my arm. It's not a problem. It's a situation and I might add there will be some challenges ahead. Pee Wee is not ready to give up on making the lost arm a major problem."

Chad: "My situation has to do with trusting people. It goes back further than my girlfriend dumping me. I've struggled with that for quite some time. Lanco says, 'No wonder you got a problem with that. You really can't trust anybody.'"

Doc: "Let's address Lanco's comment. I want you to break down into groups of three. Remember the goal is always to get Centered and stay Centered. Remember again, this is a process. You begin by being curious and conducting an inquiry. What is Focker's position on this situation? What does it mean to get Centered in this situation? In both instances that includes thoughts, feelings, physical experience, and behavior. Then the question, 'What skills are needed to get Centered and stay Centered?'"

We came back to the group and shared insights.

Fockers Thoughts: I don't trust people. People will fuck me over. I can't handle rejection.

Fockers Feelings: Vulnerable, hopeless, paranoid, lonely, suspicious, fearful, and anxious.

Fockers Physical Response: Muscle tension and nervous stomach.

Fockers Behavior: Isolates and sabotages relationships.

Centered Thoughts: I accept that some people will not accept me or like me. I accept that some people may choose to terminate our relationship. I accept that some people will not be truthful and honest. I am grateful for the experience of this relationship. I wish this person well. I am free to grieve the loss of someone special in my life without judgment. It is in the stillness that I experience the peace that sets me free to let go and move on to new experiences in each moment. I am open to exploring new relationships and fresh experiences in each moment. I can do this. In the final analysis, I will seek to be Centered with acceptance and the awareness that I have everything I need to get on with my life.

Centered Feelings: Peace, sadness, grief, free, grateful, forgiving, attentive, compassionate and open.

Centered Physical Response: Relaxed, calm and flowing.

Centered Behavior: Reaches out for new and fresh relationships; embraces the moment.

Needed Skills: Deep breathing, attention training, Centering Meditation, nine and eleven steppers, positive attitude.

Doc: "We've explored some ideas that can be used to help with getting Centered with Lanco Focker's trust issues. Chad, what are your comments?"

Chad: "If Lanco wasn't around, I wouldn't have trust issues with people."

Anna: "At Center, trust is an irrelevant concept. What is trust? It is me trusting you to be like me, to do what I want you to do, to meet my expectations, to be someone you're not. I'm not expressing that very well, but as I think we all know trust issues don't exist at Center. My husband, Brandon had an affair while I was gone. At Center, I am free to grieve and be sad without judgment. I am also free to leave Center and hook up with Pee Wee and let her kick some ass also without judgment. Not long after I check in with her, maybe an hour, maybe a few days, I will know this is not working and I will invite Pee Wee to Center where she will soon be transformed. The darkness cannot live in the light. I am now free to begin letting go and getting clear about this moment and my intentions for right now. In the future, I may stay with him or I may leave him without any judgment either way. For now in this moment, I am committed to working on the relationship."

Paul: "Wow."

Anna: "Now I have the challenge to live that commitment. It takes a lot of energy. Would someone else answer how I'm going to pull that off?"

Doc: "Let me summarize and then someone can help Anna with ideas about pulling off the challenge. As a group we answered in some general ways what it means to be Centered on this trust issue. Anna took it a step further and defined her Center in relationship to her situation. Then she asked the second question. Now that I know where I'm headed, how do I get Centered and stay Centered?"

Rob: "I enjoy carpenter work and it just came to me that Doc has helped us put together a toolbox of skills. When I ask how do I get Centered and stay Centered, I reach into my toolbox and go to work."

Anna: "I've had a moment to get my breath. Let me reach in my tool box and see what I can find. I'm looking in my toolbox and I'm amazed my toolbox is very small and light weight. It's becoming clearer that there aren't many tools to choose from and the skills are pretty simple. It's not about the number of tools. It's about the training to use those tools effectively. So the answer to the second question on how to get Centered and stay Centered is about the training required to master the skills."

Me: "Anna, so what will your training be like?"

Anna thought for a moment: "Earlier, I didn't fully understand why Doc had us over and over and over doing Centered Meditations. Now, I think I'm finally starting to get it. He talked about the transformation of Pee Wee at Center. It's like we have to train ourselves to experience our Center. I can tell you for me that it has not come easily."

Rob: "I'm still struggling with that experience."

Anna: "Something simple was what helped me more than anything. Doc, you were always talking about that quality of peace at Center. You implied or maybe even said that the peace was the foundation or cornerstone of our Center or something like that. And I was trying to go there and be in my beautiful place and feel the peace. And sometimes I could and sometimes I couldn't, but most of the time that peace was illusive. I was trying so hard to find it and feel it. Would anybody like to guess what I found for me was the answer?"

Paul: "How 'bout me takin' a wild hairy ass guess - the fucking deep breathing."

Anna: "YES!! The fucking deep breathing! The very first skill Doc taught us which in the beginning bored most of us to tears. So now would everyone close your eyes? Go to your Center and get comfortable in that place. Look around and see the beauty. Now, in that place, focus attention on your breathing and begin some deep breaths. Stay with your breathing and I'll let you know when to open your eyes. Open your eyes. What was that like?"

I looked around and tears were rolling down Doc's cheeks.

Doug: "Doc. What's wrong?"

Doc: "Nothing. Please answer Anna's question."

Everyone said they experienced peace as long as they could focus on the breathing. Various Fockers in the group were at times distracting the experience at Center.

Anna: "It is in quieting the mind, our Fockers, that we discover the meaning and experience of inner peace. So what we need is more..."

Group: "Training!"

Doug: "Okay Doc, what about the tears?"

Doc: "It is a beautiful thing for me to observe that your Center is moving from something you perhaps believe in to something you know and experience within yourself. And it is also moving to watch you all at times take over the process and direction of this group."

Anna: "So the deep breathing becomes the core skill to help with the Centering Meditations, the nine and eleven steppers, and the ongoing discovery about the power of the moment. Chad, I'm sorry. I took over the issue and monopolized the discussion."

Chad: "That worked out good for me. All the things you said helped me with my issue of trust. I know the training is the key and I've got some good ideas from you guys to help with defining my Center when it comes to trust. For me right now, the Centered thoughts are the key. I can use those thoughts to help me with the nine-stepper on getting beyond and letting go of old painful memories of rejection and the eleven stepper to help me move forward to create some new and different experiences."

Doc: "As each of you continues the training in whatever situation arises, what happens?"

Me: "We strengthen our Centered brain circuits by changing the way we think and by living those thoughts. At some point, we become aware that being Centered in this particular situation is coming easier and we are training less. The Centered circuits are getting stronger and Focker is rarely on the scene in that situation."

Rob: "But she hangs out in the shadow of our minds to kick our ass in other situations."

Doc: "Yes. Are we ready to move on to another situation?" After a pause, "Take out your handout on Focker's PTSD. Would anyone like to address any of those issues?"

Frank: "I know we have talked about the guilt and shame, but could we go over that again?"

Doc: "How many of you are still struggling with that situation?" It seemed like everyone raised their hand. "Who wants to start?"

Doug: "I think the first place to start is not with Focker, but with what actually happened over there."

Doc: "I agree. That shouldn't be too difficult because we have been working on these memories for the nine-stepper. The goal there was to reduce the intensity of the imprint. Now we're looking at them for another reason. They hold the story that stirs up guilt and shame or related feelings. Everyone break down into groups of two. With Nate missing, there will be one group of three."

Ace and Doug and I got together.

About that time, we all heard a motorcycle pull into the yard. Thank God Nate had made it. We heard him come up the steps and I guessed he sat down in one of the rockers. He would wait until the break to join us.

Doc: "Take a few minutes and share with each other two memories that stir up guilt and shame."

Ace and I talked about the one when we gave the LT the all clear about no civilians and he called in the air strike that killed the women and children. My other one was Migs dying after I promised him he wouldn't die on my watch. Ace's was when he lost two of his squad on an ambush during our first tour. He blamed himself for not insuring the approach to the enemy position was secure. Doug had lost numerous drivers in his platoon during his tours in Iraq. Some he had held in his arms while they bleed to death or died for other reasons.

Doc: "Now that you have identified the memories, what is your Focker telling you? Refer to your handout on Fockers PTSD. You came up with that list in the second group and many of them may be applicable to what you are thinking right now. Also, identify feelings, physical responses, and behavior. I wonder how many of you will see a change in your previous experience of those memories six weeks ago."

All three of us were doing better and had seen improvement. In fact we were all surprised we had made that much progress.

Doc: "Now look at both of your handouts on the Centered state. Make sure at Center you have addressed every one of Focker's thoughts. Take some time to get those down on paper."

Ace had difficulty coming up with a Centered phrase on his perceived failure to secure the approach to the enemy position. I was in his squad and I felt like he did all that was possible to make sure it was secure. He disagreed. In addition to some of the thoughts already written on the handout, he came up with, "I will ask God to forgive me and do the best I can to live with the reality that those soldiers may still be alive if I had done a better job. I cannot change it. It is what it is."

Doc: "You now have all the information you need to go forward with your training plan. It may include using every tool in your toolbox. You have everything you need to get to Center and stay Centered."

Ace: "I just shared with Jett and Doug that I consciously will not let go of my sadness and remorse over the loss of three soldiers, because I did not properly do my job. In fact, as I just said that, it occurred to me I feel those same feelings about many of my experiences during those two tours. That doesn't mean I have to kill myself, be an alcoholic, or have a miserable life. I will commit myself to being as Centered as possible in my life and I am already discovering ways to find peace and happiness along the way. But I choose to carry a remembrance of that situation at Center as a reminder to be humble and committed to being a good person. I agree with Doc that guilt and shame are a form of self-indulgence and my goal is to let them go."

Doc: "For what it's worth, I accept your decision without judgment and respect your right to choose for yourself what it means to be Centered. This is one more example that each of you must define your own Center and make peace with that ongoing part of your life's journey."

Doug: "Sadness and remorse are so much better than guilt and shame. I like that."

Frank: "But are we letting ourselves off the hook? Many of us did some horrible shit. Why shouldn't we feel guilt and shame?"

Doug: "I would say we're free to feel as much guilt and shame as we want to. And I believe there's some truth to the idea that we should feel some guilt and shame for what we've done. But at what point does it become a 'pity party' and feeling 'poor me ain't it awful.' Everybody see what a piece of shit I am. I don't know how anybody draws that line in the sand for someone else. I like Ace's idea. I'm ready to stop feeling sorry for myself and shift into sadness and remorse."

It seemed like everyone had those types of situations not only in combat, but at other times in their life when they had done something that caused terrible pain to someone else. We all agreed that we would find a way to be as Centered as possible in relation to those situations. I had more challenging combat situations to deal with, but this was also related to how I felt about betraying Ace. I would live with that wrong turn for the rest of my life.

Frank: "So it's not all fun and warm and cozy at Center?"

Doc: "You combat soldiers have major challenges to face. There is no magic, no wand to wave and make it all go away. But if you continue your training, you will see results. What I've suggested are guidelines to consider. You make your own decision about the nature of your Center. I encourage you to continue asking the question, 'Is my definition of Center working well for me?'"

Doc: "I know we're all relieved that Nate's here. It's time for a break. Give me a moment to go outside and ask Nate to take a walk with me."

By the time Doc and Nate walked in, we were back in our seats being entertained by an interaction between Paul and Doug.

Nate: "I apologize to everybody for not gettin' here till now. I got smashed last night and passed out on the way home. Lucky I didn't kill someone else or myself. Doc wants me to start AA, but I don't know if I can give it up."

Ace: "I don't know if anyone in this room besides me understands what you mean, (several in the group raised their hand), but I know and everyone in my AA group knows what you're goin' through. I'd like to talk to you when we're finished today if you're up for it."

Nate: "I will Ace, but this stuff has got me by the tail."

Ace: "I'd like to talk to you anyway."

Nate: "You got it."

Doc: "Everyone do a Centering Meditation."

Even though Eden was still on my mind, it was easier to focus now that Nate was back. I think it reminded all of us when we were over there how we might see a friend one day and the next he or she wouldn't come back. Sometimes they just got held up, sometimes they were in the hospital, and at other times they were dead. I wondered earlier if I would ever see Nate again and he was obviously lucky to be alive - close call. How many of those had all of us had? I started the breathing and went to Center hiking upon the ridge. Up here, I was free as a breeze. If I could be that here in the forest, could I eventually learn to do it in other settings? That was my hope and Doc had convinced me that it was my call and my decision.

Doc: "Look again at the group goals and your personal goals and let's pick another situation."

We spent the rest of the group time in different pairs leading each other through breathing exercises, Centering meditations, and walking through both the long form and short form of the nine and eleven steppers. I found it helpful to lead someone else through the exercises. It gave me more personal confidence that I could do it for myself. Doc told us there was not much new to learn and from here on out, it was all about the training.

Doc: "It's about time to wrap it up for today. Have you given more thought to continuing this group on a regular basis?"

Everyone was in agreement that we would like to meet every other Saturday here at the cabin from 9:00 to 10:30. Melinda and Chad were the only ones who had a long drive, but they were committed to making it work. Doc said he would provide us with a recommended format to use. He also suggested we rotate the person who would be in charge of getting here a little early and making sure the group had any materials needed and would keep an eye on the clock for break time and the ending time. He said we would talk more about it next week at our last group meeting.

Doc: "When we finish today, everyone let me know how many family and friends will be coming to the picnic next Saturday after our final group meeting. I asked Rob earlier if he would lead us in a closing Centering Meditation."

Rob: "Okay I've been practicin' this so y'all take it easy on me."

Paul: "You go for it bro. Just glad Doc didn't ask me."

Doc: "That's one of the nice things about the peer group. All of you will have a chance to lead different exercises. You'll be surprised after a period of time that it will get easier. Rob, just stay Centered yourself. You'll do fine."

Rob's voice with a little quiver: "All right, okay. Close your eyes and start breathin'. I mean start focusin' on breathing. Take some deep breaths now. Make sure y'all 'er doin' belly breathin.' If your Focker gives you any problem, tell him I'll whip his or her ass after we're finished. Go on to Center now. Don't think 'bout nothin' else 'cept where you are right now, right here. You can do it. Stay in the moment. See what's around ya. Be still and listen, you might hear somethin' real nice. I'm gonna let you be on your own for 'while. If you need to, tell Focker to shut the fuck up. Just be peaceful. You can do it. I'll be quiet for a bit. Okay, open 'em up."

There was a round of applause and cheer for Rob. He seemed a little embarrassed, but had this big smile on his face.

I followed Doc outside and told him about Eden. I asked if he would be willing to work with her and he said he would be glad to work with her. "Have her call Janet and make an appointment. Tell her I'll look forward to seeing her."

Everyone stayed around for awhile and talked and then with the exception of Nate and Ace, everyone was gone. They were on the back deck talking. All of a sudden, I felt empty and alone. Eden was with April and everyone but Ace and Nate had left. I felt like I was in some sort of a vacuum.

72
MUTUAL REASSURANCE

I called Eden and they were still at April's. I asked, "Are you feeling any better?"

"I'm about the same. Well, maybe a little worse. I've been giving details to April about what happened to me. It brings back all the pain and suffering. You know about that, right?"

"I sure do. Would you like me to come down now?"

"No, that's all right. April and I are going to eat lunch and then we're going to the lake. We'll take a blanket to sit on and do some walking. I think getting out and the exercise will do me some good. If I'm up for it, we'll do some hiking. We'll meet you all at the cabin around 5:00. Will that be okay?"

"Yes, that's fine."

She asked, "Would you mind planning supper?"

"No, I'll be glad to. If you need me, call. I'll probably be mowing this afternoon so I won't be able to hear the phone, but I'll keep checking my messages."

"I will. I love you Jett."

"I hurt for you and I love you too sweetheart."

We hung up.

Ace was out front saying goodbye to Nate. He came inside and said, "Nate is resisting AA. I remember that well. I don't know if I can convince him to keep going to meetings long enough for him to see the benefits they offer. They teach us right off the bat that no one can do it for us. We have to be committed to working the program. So I'll do the best I can and the rest is up to him. How're you holdin' up?"

"I'm in a state of shock. When the group left, I felt alone and empty. I don't know what the hell that's about."

He responded, "The group's about over and even though we'll keep going, I think we'll all miss Doc. You were on a honeymoon with Eden and now she's going through even more hell than we went through. Shocked, alone, and empty all seem to fit. Do you want me to call Dad and take off the afternoon?"

"No thanks. I'll go down and do some mowing. Charlie's behind and needs my help. The girls said they would meet us here at 5:00. Is that good for you?"

"Yeah, Dad said yesterday that today might be kind of slow. So I should be back here easy by 5:00. Remember to take a lot of deep breaths and get Centered. We'll work on what that means later. I'm gonna grab a sandwich and try to make a 1:00 AA meeting and then head to work."

"I'm gonna stop at Mom's and get a sandwich. I'll see you around 5:00."

Mom teared-up while I was telling her about Eden.

She said, "I can't imagine how horrible that would be to live like that for all those years. Bless her heart and she's been holding it in all this time. What a terrible burden to carry around."

"Doc has agreed to work with her."

"That's good. How are you holding up Honey?"

"I'm not doin' too well, but I'll be all right. I've got a lot of skills that will help me get through this. I can't imagine life without Eden and I'll do everything I can to support and help her. For right now Mom, I would rather keep this between you and me. April and Ace know, but I want Eden to make the decision on who else knows."

I left and reported to Charlie and started mowing. I checked my messages during the afternoon and there was nothing from Eden. At 4:00, I went by to say hey to Pop and put on a good show. I don't think he could tell there was anything wrong. He seemed to be doing pretty good. I left, picked up some groceries, and went home.

Eden's door was closed and there was a note taped on the door. "Hey Jett, I was so tried this afternoon that April brought me home. It's about 2:30 and I hope I can sleep for a couple of hours. April and Ace are coming at seven instead of five so you and I can have a little time together. When you get home, come in and lay with me. I miss you and love you."

I took a shower in Ace's bathroom hoping that I wouldn't wake her. I quietly opened the door and tried to slide in beside her without waking her. She stirred and turned over and put her arms around my neck and whispered, "I'm so glad you're home. Hold me close. I need to feel safe and secure in your arms. I'm so afraid I'll wake up and be back in hell."

"You're right here with me sweetheart and I'll keep you safe and secure."

She clung to me. We laid in silence for awhile. Then she said, "Jett, are we gonna be all right?"

"Yes, my love. We're gonna be better than all right. I promise you."

"You didn't sign on for this and I'm afraid with all you've been through it'll be too much for you to handle."

"We both suffer from PTSD and we'll help and support each other and do our training together and we'll get it done together."

She said, "I don't have much to give you right now."

"You've already given me a lot. It's my turn to give back to you."

"What did you mean by training?"

"I talked with Doc before he left today and he said he would look forward to working with you. He said to call Janet, his secretary, and set up an appointment. Doc calls the work we do to get Centered and stay Centered, 'training.' It would be best for him to explain it to you."

"April told me he has her journaling. It would be scary, but I think that would help me."

"He didn't have us journal, but he had us keep a notebook that in some ways was like a journal."

"Jett?"

"Yes Sweetheart."

"I want to tell you all about what happened, but I'm going to have to take it slowly. I told April some this morning and I think I talked too much about it. I've got to remember that I kept most of this inside for years. I need some time to adjust to bringing it back into my life."

"I understand. You do it at your own pace and tell me when you need to take a break." After a moment I asked, "Can I say something?"

"Yes."

"You said I didn't sign on for this, but I figured something had happened. Most of the time when I first gave you a hug or took your arm and more recently touched your skin, you would tense up. In the past few weeks, we've even talked about it. You said to give you a little time and that you were working on it. Now I know why that happens."

"Yes. That's one of my symptoms. Did you notice anything else?"

"Not at the time, but I was thinking today about your earlier concern about our age difference. You had what I thought were some logical reasons to be concerned, but now I can see from your history why that would be scary for you. Your dad, some men in the church, and your ex-husband all betrayed you in traumatic ways. Is it true in general that most of the men in your life have hurt you in one way or another?"

"Not all men. Did I tell you about my granddaddy?"

"Yes, some, but tell me again."

"He was the only important man in my life I could count on and I loved him so much. I spent as much time with him as possible. I always felt safe with him and he taught me so much about life. We lived with him and my grandmother Beam for a few years. His only fault as far as I knew was his drinking. It scared me because he and Daddy would get drunk and Daddy was a mean drunk and would try to get Granddaddy to fight him. He would pull a knife and taunt him. I was terrified and would cry and beg Daddy not to hurt him."

She started crying and I held her tight. I whispered, "It's over now my love. You're here with me and you're safe." I was rubbing her back and whispering, "I love you, I'll keep you safe, it's okay, you're safe now."

"You said you were close to one of your sisters."

"Pretty close. We talk about every two weeks or so. I don't intentionally avoid talking about my family. I think it's a part of my cover-up and not wanting to remember. I always dread going home and it's usually not as bad as I think it will be. My childhood wasn't all bad, but it's the bad stuff that overwhelms me. My sisters and I had some good times growing up and playing together. We didn't have any toys or things like that, but we had our cats and dogs and good imaginations. So when I'm home, we spend a lot of time laughing about old memories."

"I'm glad. How is it seeing your daddy?"

"Over the years I've learned for Momma's sake to tolerate seeing him. I can't stand him and it's difficult to be in the same room. When I'm there, we'll often go over and pick up Momma and take her with us."

I said, "I was saying a few minutes ago that I can see why you might have some major trust issues with men. No wonder you had the same issues with me. And then I tell you about this thing with me and April and I'm sure you picked up on my issue of feeling like I betrayed my best friend. Key word, 'betrayed.' And that must have triggered all kinds of traumatic thoughts and feelings. I can't imagine what that is like. Here's another untrustworthy male in my life."

"Yes, that's part of what has been on my mind, but you are so different from all these other males. April and I talked about it last night. So, I'm not going anywhere if you'll still have this damaged female."

"I will never see you as a damaged female and will always be thankful that you came into my life. Since you're not going anywhere, I assume you will have this male who is struggling to survive his own trauma and his own poor judgment and behavior."

"Yes I will. Now, can we take a break?"

"Yes we can."

She asked, "Can you see the clock?"

"Yes. It's 5:55."

"Will you make love to me?"

We started out with gentle kisses on each others face and then nice and soft kisses with our tongues lightly touching and exploring. We gradually removed the rest of our clothes and were content to go slowly, moving into different positions without penetration and feeling the touch of our bodies at different angles and in different places. It was like we wanted every part of us to be connected, but that final intimate connection, which we would savor, would come when we could wait no longer. It seemed like I tasted every part of her body unable to get enough of her. It was like one extended and unending emotional orgasm. She moved on top of me and was wet and moist and she moved her body so I slide into her and she pushed backwards until I could go in no further. There was no motion other than the pulsating of our bodies except my subtle thrusts without movement and her tightening around me. She put her arms around my neck and we kissed deep and long, coming up only briefly for air and a soft, "I love you" and continuing to feel the subtle pulsating moves of our bodies. We could not connect any deeper either physically, emotionally, or spiritually. It was intensely intimate and I hoped it would never end. Then within the midst of a passionate kiss, she began the sound of wanting to scream, but keeping her mouth and tongue firmly planted on mine, began moving wildly back and forth. Then we had to have air to let out the screams of release and ecstasy. There were pledges of love pouring out from deep within us. And then we collapsed and held each other tightly as if we thought the other might escape. We passed out and the next thing we knew the dogs were barking and Eden sleepily asked, "What is it?"

I looked at the clock and it was 7:18. I exclaimed, "Holy shit, we over slept."

April hollered, "Ace and I will take the dogs for a walk. Would thirty minutes be enough time?"

I hollered back, "That would be perfect. Sorry! Thanks!"

Eden said, "Hold me for a minute before we get up." I did and then we started laughing which for us seemed to be another form of release. We got in the shower and let the water do its magic. We dried each other and she let me put lotion on her body. We got dressed and went to the kitchen to get organized for supper.

73
COMMITMENT

Soon after that, April, Ace, and the dogs came in the door. Ace said, "From now on, give us a heads up." We started laughing. He continued, "I mean let us know if you're gonna have a marathon love making session so we don't have to cut ours short. April kept telling me, 'We gotta get out of bed and get ready. We're supposed to be there at 7:00.'"

I said, "Ace, I thought you told me a couple of weeks ago that you decided not to have sex until you were married."

"I did, but April couldn't wait so I reluctantly gave in."

April responded, "Why don't you two get a ginger ale and go out on the back deck and catch up while Eden and I have a glass of water and do the same. Oh Jett, what did you plan for supper?"

I said, "Hamburgers and chips."

"You and Ace get the grill going. Eden and I aren't about to cook those hamburgers in here."

There was a breeze and the sky was overcast. It wasn't chilly, but it reminded me that fall was coming. I got the grill started and asked, "How was your AA meeting today?"

"It went fine. It's not my favorite group. They're mostly older than me and it seems most of them smoke. Doc said he wanted me to try different groups and find the ones I like best. The two he picked out for me are working out real well. I still don't have a sponsor, but I hope to have one by this time next week. It seemed like you all must have done okay this afternoon."

I gave him a summary. "We're gonna be okay, but she's been holding a lot inside for a long time."

He said, "This thing with you and April has been painful for all of us." He held up his hand, "Now, I'm not blaming. I'm wondering if it's been a wake-up call for Eden. She's been holding that shit in for a long time. I know better than most that holding stuff in will come back to bite you on the ass in the long run. I don't know what that would mean for her, but it can't be good."

Looking off in the distance and thinking about what Ace had said, I responded, "Yeah, I think you're right. That stuff doesn't just go away. It hangs around and raises its head in different ways."

"Yeah, and another good thing is Doc is here. He may have told you too, but he assured April and me he would be around to see us in therapy as long as was needed."

I said, "Yeah. He said he and his wife liked the area and planned to live here."

"That's a very comforting thought," he commented.

"It sure is. Why do I feel like tearing up?"

He said, "Talking about holding stuff in, we've got a shit load of grieving that has been pent up inside us. The other day April and I were watching TV and for no reason, I started sobbing and couldn't stop. April held me until it finally ran its course. We talked some about the stuff that had happened over the past four years and there were plenty of reasons to be sobbing."

"I know. It's strange how easy it is for me to lose sight of all those reasons. I hope I can do some sobbing myself, but right now, I have to focus on taking care of Eden."

"Your time will come. I won't let you forget. It's part of getting better and getting on with being Centered in the moment."

April opened the screen door and said, "All right boys, we have bolstered each other's resolve, but we're still not ready to deal with you all so Ace, come get the patties. You can come back in when the burgers are ready. Make sure Eden's and mine are medium well - no medium and no well. Medium well, got it?"

"Yes dear." Looking at me, Ace commented, "Here we go again. For the rest of our lives."

"What was that Ace Frost?"

"I'll be right there Hon."

Under the circumstances, we had a nice evening. Eden was trying her best to enjoy being together. We played spades again and the girls won which was probably a good thing. They left about 11:00 and said they would check in with us in the morning.

In the middle of the night which was no surprise, Eden had a nightmare. She was thrashing around and yelling, "No Daddy, don't do that Daddy. Daddy, no! Please leave me alone, No! No!"

I was trying to wake her and she kicked me in the balls and I went tumbling off the bed and hit my head on her dresser. I stumbled up bent over in pain and yelled as loud as I could, "Eden, Eden, Wake up! Wake up! It's me, Jett! Wake up!" And she was sobbing and yelling, "No! No! No!"

Then I remembered the wet towel she used on me. I rushed to the bathroom, wet the towel, and threw it on top of her and it worked. She came out of it, but was crying and groggy and yelled, "Jett, what are you doing? What happened?"

I pulled the towel off her and wrapped my arms around her and whispered in her ear, "You're okay Sweetheart. You were having a nightmare. You're okay, you're safe. You're here with me. I've got you. You're safe."

She continued crying, "Oh Jett, it was so real. I was there and he was...," And her voice trailed off and she was whimpering like a child.

"I've got you. It's okay. You're safe now." I rocked her back and forth and she clung to me and I kept reassuring her. Soon, the whimpering stopped and she shivered. She was sopping wet from her sweat and the wet towel.

I said, "Let me get a hot shower going. I carried her into the bathroom and sat her on the commode and turned on the shower. We got in together and held each other. There were no words. Just two bodies being momentarily cleansed of horror, pain, and sadness.

She said, "I'm ready to get out." I dried her and led her into my room and put her in my bed. I started to go back in the bathroom to finish drying myself and she said, "Jett, don't leave me."

"I'm right here." I quickly dried and crawled in beside her.

She turned on her side facing away from me and said, "Put your arms around me and hold me and don't let me go." She was asleep within minutes and I don't remember anything soon after that until I woke up at 7:46.

We were in the same position and I could tell by her breathing that she was still asleep. I gently moved, trying not to wake her and she stirred and sleepily said, "What time is it?"

"Almost 8:00."

"Do you mind if I take another shower? I still feel dirty."

"I'll fix us something to eat. Do you want toast and coffee?"

"Yes. That would be fine. Give me a kiss."

After breakfast, we took the dogs for a long walk. April called Eden while we were walking and they decided it would be good for Eden to get out so they were going to shop in Elverton for a couple of hours this afternoon. They would meet Ace and me at Sally's at 6:00 and then we would go the movies. There was some comedy playing they both wanted to see. I had never heard of it.

When we got back to the cabin, we lay on the couch together and watched a rerun of some show Eden liked. We fell asleep and woke at 11:48. We made some sandwiches and walked up to the knoll. There were a few clouds in the sky and the temperature was a little cool with a breeze. We played with the dogs and tried to look at clouds, but Eden got restless and wanted to go back to the cabin.

She left about 3:00 and Ace showed up a while after that and we watched the last quarter of one pre-season NFL game and the first quarter of a second one. Ace said, "We've got an hour before we leave. Let's sit out on the front deck."

I volunteered, "I'm a little nervous about going to the movies. How do you feel about it?"

"Before our work in the group, I would have not agreed to go. It's dark and closed in. Even now, I want to sit on the aisle."

"I want the aisle too and close to an exit. We'll sit in front of you all so we can both have an aisle seat. I may have to do some deep breathing, but I'm pretty sure I can do it."

We rocked for a few minutes and I said, "This thing has hit her hard. It seems like she is starting to show signs of depression. I'm not surprised, but I can feel she is slowly withdrawing. And I'm starting to feel in a funk."

He asked, "What does it mean to get Centered?"

"Tug wants to have a pity party and says all women are fucked up. He says, 'Why do you think for all these years I've kept us from being in a close relationship? It always leads to more fucking trouble than it's worth. One minute they're happy, the next minute they're sad. Then they give you the silent treatment and then they withhold sex.' And Tug kept going saying, 'I haven't said much about Eden because you've seemed bound and determined, come hell or high water, to get serious and make some kind of long term commitment. I was just waitin' for something to happen and here we are.'"

Ace responded, "Tug's on a fucking roll. Don't let him screw this up for you. Fark kept me separated from April for years and now I feel like I wasted a lot of time listening to his bullshit. I think you need to get Centered and talk to Tug. Do an eleven stepper with him and bust his balls."

"I don't have the energy right now for an eleven stepper. I think I'll just get some Centered thoughts together. Give me a moment to think about it." After a few minutes, I said, "Here's what I got so far: 'There is no perfection in the world. Each of us has our challenges and situations. Love is about acceptance of the other person as they are and a willingness to support, encourage, and stand with this person in the midst of their situations. The focus is on giving of oneself with compassion, empathy, forgiveness, and affection. It is in giving the gift in each moment that we receive the joy and happiness that comes with being in love.' I notice there's not a lot of what's in it for me."

Ace responded, "That stuff will preach. Doc talked about the importance of not having expectations. That is such a challenge. What if I'm doing all those things and I'm not getting much in return other than the joy and happiness of giving?"

"I think that's post-graduate work in Centering."

"Yeah, me too, I'm glad that's not my situation with April."

"Same here with Eden," I agreed. "Remember when I was freaking out about Lance?"

Ace smiling answered, "No. I will not define you by your past."

"Thanks. Anyway, I remember it and I'm using it as a way of helping me in the present. Something like a lesson learned."

"In that case, yes, I do remember it."

"I think when she started to pull back yesterday and today, it reminded me of the times she pulled back because she said I was too young. So it hooked Tug and he started freaking out and backing away to keep us from getting hurt. That was the reason for my funk. I've made the shift to Center with the help of those Centered thoughts and I'm aware now this is different. I'll help her get through this and will not let Tug take over again in this situation."

We met the girls for supper and went to the movie. Eden did pretty well. Not her usual self, but smiled some and laughed once or twice. The movie was funny and a nice love story. Ace and I did better than we expected. Thank you Doc.

When we got home, we talked about our coming week. She said, "This is going to be a busy week at work. I think that's a good thing. I'll call Doc's secretary in the morning and make my appointment. I'm going to find a way to take his first available. I'll have to plan work around the appointment."

I offered, "School starts next week. I have my first class a week from this Tuesday. I have an orientation for graduate students this Thursday. I'll get my books while I'm on campus. The rest of the week, I'll work with Charlie."

After we got in bed, she wanted me to cuddle behind her. "Jett, I'm really scared. It's like I wanna run away from it again and shove it all back inside me. Bunny says bringing all that stuff up is not gonna help. I talked with April today about the ways this stuff surfaces in my life."

I said, "We talked about the tensing when I touch you and the trust issues with men. What other ways does it come out?"

"I know Doc will help me more clearly understand what happens, but I feel like a victim in some parts of my life. I have anxiety, feel insecure and inadequate. I'm paranoid about people not liking me, talking about me, and thinking the worst about me. I come across as a strong woman, but that's an act. I'm outspoken and lots of times I have to be right and prove the other person wrong. This is the only way I can survive. I hide my true feelings to cover up my feeling of being vulnerable. I have a difficult time being soft and affectionate and forgiving. I'm stubborn and controlling. I think most of these are related to the helplessness I felt growing up. It's like I'll never allow myself to get in that situation again. My 'ex' said I was cold and one time he said I was, 'frigid.' I think you and I are off to a great start sexually, but I worry that later on that will change. These are just random thoughts and it's all I can think of right now."

"I know you have nightmares. Have you ever had any flashbacks?"

"A year or so after I left home, I had some for a few years. However, they soon subsided. I think that was part of me stuffing everything inside. I had to do that as a child to survive so I'm good at it, but the nightmares have never stopped. The frequency is not as bad over the last five or so years. I average about one a month."

I said, "I had a lot of trauma during those two years over there. I can't imagine how you survived the trauma you lived through for the first eighteen years of your life."

She turned around to face me and her face was wet with tears. "Jett, it's clear that I love you with all my heart. I believe things happen for a reason. Telling me about you and April was exactly what I needed to wake me up. I have a chance for happiness with you. Ace said he didn't want to bring his alcohol problems into his marriage. I feel the same way about my PTSD. We have a chance for a wonderful life together and I have to begin to face and deal with my demons."

We wrapped ourselves in each other's arms and I said, "I will walk with you each step of the way and with Doc's help, we will find the path to peace and happiness."

And she held me a little tighter.

74
FINAL GROUP SESSION

I was worried about Eden, but I was determined to focus my attention on this last group and get as much as possible out of our last meeting with Doc. I wanted to do it for both of us.

Everyone but Paul and Doug arrived around 8:30. We were in our circle talking about our final group session. Everyone was relieved we would meet again in two weeks. Ace wondered how it would be without Doc in the group. Frank said he felt like Doc had been preparing us to go forward on our own. Nate told us he had been to two AA meetings with Ace and didn't like AA, but he was going to keep going for a few more weeks. A little before 9:00, Paul and Doug walked in followed by Doc.

Doc: "Everyone, take some time to get Centered. Wait a minute. I just thought some of you may say you were already Centered when I walked in."

Frank: "I think because I have been training to get Centered with my eyes closed that I sometimes forget the goal is to be Centered in life with our eyes open. So is being Centered with our eyes closed is like a training ground?"

Doc: "Yes, but it's much more than a training ground. It's an experience in itself. Each of you is in the process of creating your own

Center which becomes the core of who you are and a lens, portal, or filter through which you experience your life. It's like everything that enters your life through your senses, your mind, and your Focker filters through your Center to be transformed or transmuted into something new and fresh that unfolds in each moment."

Nate: "What's transmuted?"

Doc: "It's a cousin of transformation. It's like being changed from one state to another. It's like Focker is changed from the state of not working well to the Centered state. Defining the nature of Center is one of our continuing goals. Another important goal is to experience what we define and create at Center. The transformation and transmutation process happens in the moments when we experience our Center.

Me: "And in those moments Focker ceases to exist. Since we've lived most of our life with Focker in charge, he will continue to resist going to Center. He doesn't need it and doesn't want it and sees it as a threat to his existence. Tug says he doesn't need any Centered portal, lens, or filter to take care of business just like he's always done."

Melinda: "So we make progress in the transformation of one of Focker's areas, but she has more areas where she's in charge. It would seem there are no clear cut boundaries. I may make some good progress with Tilda's anger and notice after lots of training I can most of the time stay Centered when those old anger triggers surface. On the other hand, she may be alive and well in the area of jealousy. Does that ring true for you all?"

Doug: "It works for me. The goal is to be as Centered as possible in all phases of life and it'll be a 'tough road to hoe.'"

Doc: "I'll remind you again that before you ever started this group, each of you at times was living from your Center. You just didn't know to call it that."

Ace: "I believe that, but it's sometimes hard for me to remember when it was true."

From others came, "Me too."

Doc: "Focker doesn't want you to remember."

Paul: "Shut up Fanny Focker."

Doc: "Did anyone else detect in Paul's tone a little less anger at Fanny."

Nate: "Yeah. Before he would have said, 'Shut the fuck up Fanny Focker.'"

Doc: "Why is it we don't want to be angry with Focker?"

Paul: "Fightin' always makes it worse."

Chad: "Acceptance of Focker takes away some of his power."

Anna: "Acceptance and non-judging is one of the cornerstones of my Center. When I'm not fighting Pee Wee and I'm Centered, she is silent."

Doc: "Focker is like a misguided child who sees life through a clouded lens of warped perceptions and expectations that create fear, pain, inadequacy, suffering, hopelessness, guilt, cynicism, hatred, and anxiety, to name a few. Focker equals insanity. He builds your identity around your past and seeks to convince you that this is your true self. She has done a good job, but the days of her being in charge of your life can be numbered. You have quite a challenge and one of the initial steps as Anna suggests is acceptance and non-judgment. It's up to you."

Paul smiling: "Now Fanny, you shut your sweet littl' trap."

Doc: "Good work Paul. Focker does however play an important role in your life. Would anyone like to take a stab at that?"

Anna: "Pee Wee serves as a red flag or a wake-up call that I'm not Centered."

Doc: "Yes. You are paying attention and Focker is a reminder to keep training to get Centered and stay Centered. Any comments or questions?"

Doc: "Okay, if we were to start the group again today, I would change my opening statement and say something like, 'Close your eyes and go to Center and if you're already Centered, close your eyes and stay at Center.' So do that now and as always, I'll let you know when to open your eyes."

Doc: "Open your eyes and remember to stay Centered. In silence, go for a short walk outside and when you hear the bell, stay Centered and silent and return to the room."

Doug went to my bedroom door and as he had done on other occasions when we went outside, he took Spot and lately Cher for a walk. They both loved him. Doug had told me that he used his dogs and cats to help him with Centering. I went up the path and sat on top of the rock gazing out over the distance wondering how Eden was doing. I was scared for her and for us. It was so clear in this moment how we never know what will happen in the future. The bell rang.

Doc: "How many of you believe you're getting more skilled in experiencing your Center?"

Doug: "It's always been difficult for me to see myself at Center when I close my eyes. I can see the scene, but it's hard puttin' myself there. But now I'm startin' to feel it more. The peace comes when it's quiet. And now I'm talkin' more to myself reminding me to stay peaceful and Centered. I'm startin' to know what that means and how it feels. Gettin' Centered has saved my marriage and my wife is even doin' the deep breathing."

Doc: "I gonna ask for a few volunteers to lead the group in a Centering Meditation. Remember, this is not about how smooth and easy you do it. It's about getting the practice of saying it out loud which can help you be more skilled at going to Center. It's human nature to wonder how others will do, but remember to focus on the experience. It's not about grading another's performance. It's about going to Center. Who would like to volunteer?"

Anna raised her hand.

I worked hard to focus on my journey to Center. I was determined not to evaluate/judge Anna. It was irrelevant and had no importance in the moment. My biggest concern was related to how I was able to focus on my own journey to Center. Tug said, "Anna's sexy. I bet she would be fun in the rack." I said, "Shut up Tug."

Doc: "Thank you Anna. I want to review again the process for dealing with any situation in your life where you want to make some changes or where Focker is stirring up things. I have this as a handout." He passed it around.

1. Be curious. Conduct an inquiry.
2. Fockers position (Thoughts, feelings, physical experience, behavior).
3. Centered response to situation (Thoughts, feelings, physical experience, behavior).
4. Skills needed to be Centered.
5. Execution of skills to get Centered and stay Centered.

Frank: "And to make that experience more powerful or as you said Doc to create new circuits in our brain, we change the way we think and then change the way we behave. Then it's like we get in the habit of being Centered with that situation."

Doc: "And what makes all this happen?"

Paul: "The fuckin' breathing and the fuckin' training."

Doc: "When will you be finished with the training?"

Ace: "In about an hour and a half and then we can adjourn to Stanley's. Hold it, does Stanley's sell soda?"

Paul: "Ace is my favorite person to share a six pack with."

Melinda: "All right, settle down you wild people. Doc, I was looking through the group goals sheet and we've covered a lot of 'em. I don't remember us talking specifically about the two goals, 'find a reason to live' and 'find a purpose for living.'"

Anna: "I'm looking at that sheet where we listed our ideas on the traits at Center."

Peaceful	Calm in the midst of a storm
Loving	Lives in the moment
Accepting	Awake
Compassionate	Open
Non-judging	The observer
Free	Passionate
Grateful	Clarity
Forgiving	Patient
Joyful	Curious
Flexible	Wise
Attentive	Alert

Anna: "If most of those fit our idea of what it means to be Centered, I think the answer to finding a reason to live and a purpose would be found at Center."

Melinda: "When I look at that list, it seems overwhelming and it feels like it would be impossible to live like that."

Ace: "I think it goes back to being in the moment. Doc has drilled that into us for eight weeks and then I started AA and they're always saying to take one step at a time."

Doug: "If I take one step at a time, I can only be one thing on that sheet at a time."

Nate: "Means I got one situation so I got one answer."

Me: "I think that would mean when we're talking about a purpose for living and a reason to live, we're getting a long way from living in the moment. And yes, Melinda it sure does seem overwhelming to me. It's a cousin of the self-esteem issue."

Frank: "I could ask, 'Do you have meaning and purpose in your life and a reason to live?'"

Paul: "Let me confer with my Fanny." Pausing and smiling he reports, "Fanny said 'Drinkin' and fuckin' was her purpose and reason to live. Shit, I got a lotta work to do on her ass. Anyway, long story short, ummmm, I done forgot your question."

Frank: "Do you have meaning and purpose in your life and a reason to live?"

Paul: "Oh yeah, I got it. You mean 'now?'"

There was applause from the group.

Melinda: "I find it so easy to forget some things about being Centered. Living in the moment is one of the cornerstones at Center. I think remembering that answers a lot of questions and gives us a lot of help in defining our Center. How could I forget that?"

Doc: "Because this is new to each one of you. Some things will be more challenging to remember than others. Personally, some of that will have to do with your Focker's issues. She will work hard to make you forget what you've learned. Remember when we talked about resistance. Go back and review that from time to time and it will help you understand what might be getting in the way of your progress."

Chad: "That moment-to-moment living is starting to make more sense and it really helps me with the meaning and purpose in life issue. It is freeing to know that my meaning and purpose in life is to be Centered in each moment. So if someone in my life is doing something that hurts Lanco or makes him mad, my purpose in that moment is acceptance or to be non-judgmental. In my next moment, my purpose might be to forgive that person, and my next moment after that might be to be patient with that person and on and on."

Me: "Melinda mentioned that living in the moment is one of the cornerstones of Center. When I look at our group goals, another cornerstone would be the acceptance or non-judging that Anna and Chad just mentioned."

Rob: "So first, it's livin' in the moment. Then second, it's acceptance of the moment."

Ace: "Those two cornerstones open a lot of Centered doors. Fark says, 'Bout time pin head. I got that on the first day. That don't mean it's worth a shit.' At ease Fark. Living in the moment releases us from the past and acceptance of right now frees us to find healing. Is it possible that all this is simpler than we imagined and that we're making it more complicated than it is?"

Doc: "There are many aspects of this approach which are simple. The mind however can be complex. If your goal is to understand the inner workings of your Focker's mind, you can get bogged down. It's challenging enough to figure out what he's up to. Understanding how Focker got the way he is can sometimes be useful, but is not necessary for getting Centered. If you want to go that deep, get some professional help to assist you."

Doc: "I agree that living in the moment and acceptance are an important part of the foundation of the Centered state. They are both a challenge for all of us and as you correctly pointed out a few minutes ago, the key to getting to Center and staying at Center is training. I want to ask you again, when will you be finished with the training?"

Melinda: "I think we know that the training continues for the rest of our life."

Paul: "Not me. You mean I gotta do this shit for the rest of my life. Fanny dear, just calm down. We can do it girl."

Melinda: "I gotta be honest. I get caught up with Tilda sometime and think do we really have to do this for the rest of our life? Doc, does it get easier?"

Doc: "It is challenging now and I can promise you that it will be less challenging as time passes. Later on in your life, the overall training goal will be to stay attentive and focused in the moment. That will play a major role in helping you to get Centered and stay Centered. Yes, Melinda. It does get easier and later on, you will find it's something you look forward to as it becomes the reminder and the path to Centered living and the freedom to live those Centered traits."

Frank: "But we will never always be Centered?"

Doc: "I don't believe we humans ever make it that far, but as my family and friends say about me, 'He's a lot more Centered than he use to be.' Remember, Center is not something you believe in. It's an experience, a way of being in the world. Do not seek your Center in training. Just train and you will go there, to that deeper place which has been there all along."

Doc: "Who else would volunteer to lead the Centering Meditation?"

Chad did. I did better focusing on the experience.

Me: "I wonder how many tie a spiritual dimension to being Centered. I think most of you know I do, but you probably weren't aware that didn't happen 'till I got some things worked out with Doc's help. I shared early in the group that I had some issues with God."

Doc: "I believe I have talked with everyone in individual sessions who wanted to talk about the spiritual. Did I leave anyone out?"

No response.

Me: "Does anyone else make that connection?"

Rob: "How do you make that connection?"

I shared some of the same beliefs with them I shared with Eden. From there: "I have tried to figure out how transformation takes place at Center. That's when some of my favorite Bible verses started coming into my mind. I'll just paraphrase since I don't know the exact wording. 'Perfect love casts out fear. If you live in love, you live in God and God lives in you. Jesus is the Light of the world. God's peace is so strong it can't be described. Jesus says that He leaves His peace with us. The Lord is my Shepherd, I have everything I need. Be not anxious about your life. Jesus says the Kingdom is within us.' All of those fit my general idea of being Centered. If Jesus is the Light, then that Light is always shining at Center. God to me is like an Energy that's in all of us and in all parts of the universe."

Ace: "I'll be passing the offering basket. Dig deep into your pockets and don't hold back. Reach way down in there and remember you are contributing to me and Jett's life style. Jett, while I'm passin' the basket, would you lead the group in some rounds of 'Row, row, row your boat, gently down the stream....'"

Nate: "I've gotta song request. In Bible school, we sang this song, 'This littl' light of mine, I'm gonna let it shine....' Jett sure has let his little light shine. I'm so darn proud of 'im." Nate stood up and led us in several verses of the song and then said, "I'm callin' on bro Paul to lead us in a word of prayer and for god's sakes Paul, keep Fanny's mouth shut."

We were all cracking up and Doc finally said, "Okay, the tent revival will continue at the park after we eat."

Doc: "Jett raises an interesting question. What does it take at Center for the transformation to take place? Is it God? Is it the power of quieting the mind and allowing something deeper within us to influence the transformation? Is it the power of a particular way of understanding our Center like a Centered philosophy. Is it in a particular way of meditating? Is it a particular way we create the Center that fuels the transformation? Or is it a combination of all those things or something else we haven't thought of?"

Rob: "I'll take the combo."

Doc: "Is there within us at Center an Ancient Wisdom, a Sacred Presence, the very Source of life, a Unified Consciousness, a Light that never goes out, an Invisible Energy, an Inner Peace, a Spiritual Guide, a Radiant Joy? The list could go on and on."

Doc: "Perhaps there is no one answer to that question. I have simply set up a training plan to help each of you discover your Center and have a role in defining what it means for you to be Centered in your life. How important is it to be able to give a definitive answer to Jett's question? Maybe you are finally left with the path of your choosing and perhaps along the way as your training progresses, you will discover your personal answers to that question."

Doc: "Would someone volunteer now for the Centering Meditation?"

Melinda did. I did even better that time focusing on my Center.

Doc: "Thank you Melinda. Before we take a break, I want to reiterate the importance of paying attention to your body. Everything Focker does plays out in the body in some form of a symptom. The deep breathing, in addition to the numerous other benefits, directly intervenes to lessen the physical symptom. Feel the various forms of stress in the body and then feel the release as your continue the breathing and your journey to Center. Some teachers believe the body is the gateway to the mind. I would mostly agree, but be more inclined to say a gateway to the mind. Are there any comments or questions?"

Doc: "Let's take a break."

None of us left the cabin. We hung out in small groups. I wondered if there was some separation anxiety.

He rang the bell.

Doc: "Would someone else volunteer to lead a Centering Meditation?"

Nate: "I wrote out a bunch of phrases. I might as well do it since I done went to th' trouble."

He did. My focus was getting better and I realized one more time the importance of the training.

Doc: "Does anyone have any questions about what we have covered over the last eight weeks?"

Frank: "I don't have any now, but I'll have a thousand later. I know you're a visiting professor over at the College. Will you be leaving soon and how will we reach you if we have a question?"

Doc: "My wife and I like this area and have decided to settle here. The College has offered me a position which will allow me to continue my research."

Applause.

Doc: "Thank you. My wife and I are pleased about the decision.

Doc: "Over the years, I have read a number of books and had some wonderful teachers/mentors. I have collected a number of definitions of Center and I want to share them with you and ask for your comments and feedback. I believe some of these points go to a deeper core within our Center which is to me quite fascinating. Many of these are particularly challenging for me and from time to time, I will glimpse one or two of them in an experience. Many of them are similar to what we have already discussed."

A Definition of Center, (ADC) Doc: "It is only in the silence at Center that you discover the past doesn't exist."

Chad: "I think I'm starting to get it and in those moments, I feel the freedom."

ADC, Doc: "When you can observe Focker, you are not caught up in his drama."

ADC, Doc: "When you live in the moment, time does not exist. As that happens, life becomes a series of moments and things like age are irrelevant."

Anna smiling, "Does that mean we need to quit celebrating our birthday?"

Doc: "You do whatever you want. At my age, I'm working on not celebrating my birthday any more than I would celebrate any other day." Doc smiling: "I have encouraged my family, however, not to take that literally and stop giving me gifts and taking me out to eat."

Paul: "Got it!"

ADC, Doc: "Transformation is happening. Sometimes there is quick insight and change. At other times, it happens gradually. Be patient and engage the training and it will unfold within you."

ADC, Doc: "At Center, there is no personality present to be hurt, judged, offended, rejected, defensive, suffering, angry, and so on."

Ace: "I get it by our general definition of being Centered, but that one for me is a real challenge."

Doug: "I know I keep bringing up this situation with my wife, but that statement was what made the difference. It was a choice I made not to let anything my wife said upset me. Doc, that phrase turned on a light for me. Hill Focker wasn't around to get upset, angry, and defensive. I was free at Center to stay calm."

Paul: "And Doc is gettin' ready to say, 'If you can do it once, you kin get it done more often.' Am I rite Doc?"

Doc: "Right on target Paul."

Frank: "Ace talked about his sadness and remorse at Center over what happened during the war. Doc, according to what you said about no personality at Center, the person who made that statement wouldn't have anyone at Center to be sad and remorseful."

Doc: "I would caution all of you again not to get caught up in what anyone else says about Centering. Based on the statement, that person would agree with your interpretation Frank. There is no one there to be sad and remorseful. Ace in his personal interpretation of Center has said there is someone at Center who is sad and remorseful and that works well for him. No one is ever right or wrong about Centering. You define your own Center. Ace, did I express your thoughts accurately?"

Ace: "Yeah, that's it Doc."

Melinda: "Tilda is still influencing me by saying that's a scary thing not even to have a personality. She says if you don't have a personality, who the hell are you? I have to remind myself that I am at Center living in this moment and why the hell do I need a personality to define me?"

ADC, Doc: "I am not my past. I am not the future. I simply am."

Me: "Free to create in each moment something fresh and new."

Frank: "Huck Focker is yelling, 'How the hell do you do that?' Huck had the same desperation he had eight weeks ago, desperate to find a way out of the misery, pain and suffering. Right now he's crying and I'm taking him down to Center and telling him, 'don't worry little fellow, I know how to do that. I'll take you with me on this journey of healing. Come with me.'"

ADC, Doc: "Do not seek the Light for when you stop seeking it, you discover you are the Light. Go to Center. Bask in the Radiance of the Light and see what happens."

Chad: "I like that verse Jett said where it is written that God is love and if you live in love you live in God and God lives in you. That means to me we are one with God and we are one with the Light. All we have to do is go to Center and experience the connection, the oneness, the unity. Then we are free to be curious and see what happens."

Several said they were still struggling with the concept of God and couldn't go there with Chad or me. They were choosing to see their Center as the space of peace and love within without any particular religious connection.

Doc: "Each of you is on your own journey and responsible for finding your truth along the way. I ask each of you to be humble and respectful of the right of others to disagree and follow another path. What is of ultimate importance, in my view, is that you discover that everything you need in life is and has always been within you at Center."

Doc: "We're getting close to the end of our group sessions. I understand all of you will be meeting here in two weeks. If it's okay with you and with Anna, I would like to designate her as the person who will lead the first peer group meeting. I will mail to you Anna a suggested format for the first group session. I am asking for feedback from all of you as I plan to develop a format to make this training available for combat veterans and anyone else suffering from PTSD."

Doc: "You combat veterans have experienced unspeakable trauma in your young lives. I have never suggested that this training will wipe away the trauma experienced during your time immersed in the insanity of that war. It is my hope that you will find your path to Center. I believe that having glimpsed the possibility for a life of peace and happiness, you will find the way to your Center. It is there you will discover the truth that sets you free."

Doc: "I said in the beginning I would learn much from you during this experience. That has happened beyond my expectations. It has been a distinct pleasure to work with each one of you and I feel honored to have done so. I thank you for contributing to this study and experience. I hope to see each of you from time to time."

Anna: "I think I can speak on behalf of each one here that from the bottom of our heart at Center, we thank you for everything you have given to us and how for some of us you have literally helped save our lives. We will always remember you with warmth and affection and the greatest of admiration and respect."

Everyone stood and applauded. There was not a dry eye in the group as far as I could tell. We were all embracing and then Doc: "Let's gather in the middle of the room and do our closing meditation. With our eyes closed and a few deep breaths, let us journey to Center. Bring everyone in the group to your Center and tell us all about your special place. While you are talking to us, we suddenly disappear and are gone. And a few moments later, we are back standing there smiling. Then we are gone again. Then we are back again and with some relief, you become aware that we will always be there with you if you invite us. You can feel comfort in knowing that we will always be with you to support you and accept you and embrace you and love you for who you are in each moment. And it is in that awareness that you will always experience us as a source of strength and courage and hope. So come back now to this room with your eyes remaining closed and feel the energy surrounding you knowing that the awareness of this energy right here, right now will be with you forever to guide you and be a lamp unto your feet. So in each moment, open to receiving this gift and being grateful. We can now open our eyes and go in peace and love."

More tears and hugs and as Doc packed up his things, he wiped his eyes with a Kleenex and then smiled on the way out and said, "See you at the park."

Most of us were clear in the beginning that we didn't like groups and where uncomfortable and wondered why we agreed to be a part of this group. Now look at us. All of us wanted to continue meeting even when Doc wasn't physically present. In combat, the situation of survival in the worst of circumstances had drawn us together in an incredible bond and closeness. In this group, the situation was different. It was our willingness after time had passed to open ourselves in a way that none of us had ever done before. We didn't lay our physical lives on the line as we did over there, but we laid our emotional lives on the line which took a different kind of courage. Some of us would not realize the depth of our connection until later and some of us even now were aware that because of this experience and these comrades, we would never be the same again in some fresh and new ways.

AUTHOR'S NOTE

I hope in some important way this novel gives a measure of hope to those of you who suffer from PTSD. We live in a world of quick fixes, pills, booze and drugs. Those quick fixes have in my view no lasting value and will in many cases cause you to be numb to the experience of life. There are other consequences to those approaches which can lead to increased problems and sometimes trauma. Perhaps feeling numb is appealing right now in the midst of your suffering and pain. Even though that is understandable, it keeps you stuck in a rut of misery and suffering with no hope for healing.

I attempted to articulate in the novel the challenge facing those of you who suffer from PTSD. Each member of the group in the novel reached a state of desperation in order to make the commitment to do whatever was required to get some relief. I call it "training" in order to emphasize the dedication and hard work that is required.

If you are suffering from PTSD, there are excellent treatment approaches available. The important thing is to get help from professionals trained in the treatment of PTSD. In addition to the resources listed in Appendix B, there may be in your town or area clinicians trained in the treatment of PTSD. I urge you to take that first step and make the call.

My goal is to expand my present website to include a section that can be used by mental health clinicians in their treatment of clients suffering from PTSD. The same approach used in the novel would be available for therapists to use in whatever way seems appropriate to them.

Sgt. Grey said (see quote in front of the book) those who have not been to war will never understand what we have experienced. In the process of writing the novel, it occurred to me that it might be helpful to design a peer group approach using some of the treatment ideas suggested in the novel. Alcoholics Anonymous (AA) uses a similar peer group model. There is, however, much work to be done to make the peer group model a viable alternative in the treatment of PTSD. Some portions of the information on the website can be used in a peer group approach.

As of the printing of this novel, I am working on the creation of the PTSD portion of my website. To find the latest details on these endeavors and who to contact about further information, go to my website, www.bankshudson.com.

APPENDIX A

SOME PTSD SYMPTOMS AND RELATED THINKING

This is similar to the symptom checklist used in the novel.

Difficulty falling or staying asleep
Outbursts of anger
Getting in fist fights
Difficulty concentrating
Always on the lookout for danger
Easily startled by loud noises or sudden movements
Intrusive and distressing memories, images, and thoughts
Recurrent nightmares
Flashbacks of traumatic experiences
Don't want to talk about combat experiences
Home is a letdown; feels different
Not interested in doing stuff you use to enjoy
Hard to get close with family and friends
Hopeless about the future
Don't have a purpose or direction
Alcohol/drugs ease the pain
Can't get my mind to stop racing
When thinking about my combat experience, I feel guilt and/or shame

Sometimes, I feel numb.
I can't stop the pain
I don't know what love is anymore
Don't trust people
Lost belief in God
Angry with God
Angry at my country
Life is unfair
My self-esteem sucks
I feel like whacking myself
Avoid crowds
People don't have a clue what war is like
Feel alone/isolated
Nothing matters anymore
Fearful about leaving your house
Have panic attacks
    Heart racing
    Sweating
    Trembling and shaking
    Shortness of breath
    Choking sensation
    Pain and pressure in chest
    Nausea
    Feel dizzy or lightheaded
    Strange feelings; hard to describe
    Fear of losing control
    Fear of dying
    Numbness or tingling sensations
    Chills or hot flushes

If one or any of these symptoms is impairing your ability to function in the normal activities of your life, seek professional help.

APPENDIX B

RESOURCES

Coalition of Iraq and Afghanistan Veterans. (www.coalitionforveterans.org).

National Center for PTSD, Department of Veterans Affairs, VA Medical Center, White River Junction, VT. 05009. Phone: 1-802-296-6300.

National suicide-prevention hotline. 1-800-273-8255.

Department of Veterans Affairs suicide-prevention website. (www.mentalhealth.va.gov/suicide prevention).

The Center for Mind Body Medicine. "Doc" in the novel would be a member of this group. (www.cmbm.org). Go to website and click on, "Global Trauma Relief" and then click on, "Healing our Troops" and read. Scroll down and click on, "Find a Practitioner".

Department of Defense Helpline. 1-800-796-9699. Information on where to get help.

Operation Proper Exit. (www.troopsfirstfoundation.org).

Outward Bound for Veterans. (www.outwardbound.org/veteran-adventures/journey).

Defense and Veteran Brain Injury Center. (www.dvbic.org).

Veteran's Crisis Line. (www.veteranscrisisline.net). 1-800-273-8255.

National Military Family Association. (www.nmfa.org). 1-800-260-0218.

The US Department of Veterans Affairs. Washington, D.C. 20420. 1-800-827-1000. (www.va.org).

Military Aid Societies. Help with emergency assistance for personal and family crisis for active and retired military and their families.

Armed Forces Relief Trust. (www.afrtrust.org).
Army Emergency Relief. (www.aerhq.org).
Navy-Marine Corps Relief Society. (www.nmcrs.org).
Air Force Aid Society. (www.afas.org).
Coast Guard Mutual Assistance. (www.cgmahq.org).

National Self-Help Clearinghouse. Refers to self-help and support groups. (www.selfhelpweb.org).

National Clearinghouse for Alcohol and Drug Information. Provides referrals to detoxification and rehabilitation programs as well as alcohol and drug support groups. (www.findtreatment.samhsa.gov). 1-800-662-4357.

Alcoholics Anonymous. See local phone listings to obtain a list of dates and times of meetings.

Recoveringme.com. Recovering(me) is a web based recovery program that offers an easily accessible and private way to start getting answers to the problems posed by addiction.

Veteran's Treatment Court. (www.justiceforvets.org). Visit this website to find how this court helps veterans struggling with legal challenges.

BIBLIOGRAPHY

Bennett-Goleman, T. *Emotional Alchemy: How the Mind Can Heal the Heart.* New York: Three Rivers Press, 2001.

Bohm, D. *Unfolding Meaning.* London and New York: Ark Paperbacks, 1987.

Capra, F. *The Tao of Physics.* Boulder, Colorado: Shambhala, 1975.

Chopra, D. *Quantum Healing: Exploring the Frontiers of Mind/Body Medicine.* New York: Bantam Books, 1989.

Edgette, J. H., and Edgette, J. S. *The Handbook of Hypnotic Phenomena in Psychotherapy.* New York: Brunner/Mazel Publishers, 1995.

Ferrucci, P. *What We May Be: Techniques for Psychological and Spiritual Growth Through Psychosynthesis.* Los Angeles: J. P. Tarcher, Inc., 1982.

Freke, T. *Lucid Living.* New York: Hay House, Inc., 2005.

Friedman, B. *The War I Always Wanted: The Illusion of Glory and the Reality of War.* St. Paul, MN: Zenith Press, 2007.

Harmon, W. and H. Rheingold. *Higher Creativity: Liberating the Unconscious for Breakthrough Insights.* Los Angeles: J. P. Tarcher, Inc., 1984.

Kabat-Zinn, J. *Coming to our Senses.* New York: Hyperion, 2005.

Kabat-Zinn, J. *Wherever you Go There You Are. New York*: Hyperion, 1994.

Millman, D. *Way of the Peaceful Warrior.* Tiburon, CA: H.J. Kramer, Inc., 1984.

Niebuhr, R. *The Nature and Destiny of Man.* Vol 2. New York: Charles Scribner's Sons, 1964.

Powers, K. *The Yellow Birds.* New York: Little, Brown, and Company, 2012.

Robbins, A. *Unlimited Power: The Way to Peak Personal Achievement.* New York: Fawcett Columbine, 1986.

Schiraldi, G. *The Post-Traumatic Stress Disorder Sourcebook: A Guide to Healing, Recovery, and Growth.* 2nd ed. New York: McGraw Hill, 2009.

Schwartz, J. M. and S. Begley. *The Mind and The Brain: Neuroplasticity and the Power of Mental Force.* New York: ReganBooks, 2002.

Siegel, R. *The Mindfulness Solution: Everyday Practices for Everyday Problems.* New York: The Guilford Press, 2010.

Suzuki, S. *Zen Mind, Beginners Mind.* New York and Tokyo: Weatherhill, 1970.

Tillich, P. *The New Being.* New York: Charles Scribner's Sons, 1955.

Tolle, E. *The Power of Now: A Guide to Spiritual Enlightenment.* Novato, CA: New World Library and Vancouver, B.C. Canada: Nameste Publishing, 1999.

Wolinsky, S. *Quantum Consciousness: The Guide to Experiencing Quantum Psychology* Norfolk, Connecticut: Bramble Books, 1993.

Wolinsky, S. *Trances People Live: Healing Approaches in Quantum Psychology.* Connecticut: The Bramble Company, 1991.

www.ingramcontent.com/pod-product-compliance
Lightning Source LLC
Chambersburg PA
CBHW071946270326
41928CB00009B/1367
* 9 7 8 0 6 1 5 9 3 2 4 9 1 *